The Journal of American History®
Published by the Organization of American Historians

Vol. 99   No. 2   September 2012

© 2012 by the Organization of American Historians

The *Journal of American History*, formerly the *Mississippi Valley Historical Review*, is published quarterly by the Organization of American Historians.

Manuscript submissions, books for review, and correspondence concerning those and all other editorial matters should be addressed to the **Editorial Office: *Journal of American History*, 1215 East Atwater Ave., Bloomington, Indiana 47401-3703,** USA (telephone: 812-855-2816; fax: 812-855-9939; e-mail: jah@oah.org).

Guidelines for manuscript submission can be found at the *Journal* Web site: http://www .journalofamericanhistory.org.

Please do not submit a manuscript that has been published or that is currently under consideration for publication elsewhere in either article or book form. The *Journal* will not consider submissions that duplicate other published works in either wording or substance.

The Organization of American Historians disclaims responsibility for statements, whether of fact or of opinion, made by contributors.

Correspondence concerning change of address, membership, dues, and the annual meeting should be addressed to the **Executive Office: Organization of American Historians, 112 North Bryan Ave., Bloomington, Indiana 47408-4141,** USA (telephone: 812-855-7311; fax: 812-855-0696; e-mail: oah@oah.org; Web site: http://www.oah.org).

The Organization of American Historians promotes excellence in the scholarship, teaching, and presentation of American history and encourages wide discussion of historical questions and equitable treatment of all practitioners of history.

Individual members of the Organization of American Historians will receive the *Journal* or the *OAH Magazine of History*. All members receive the *Annual Meeting Program*. To become a member, go to http://www.oah.org.

For information pertaining to OAH membership, please see the masthead.

The *Journal of American History* (ISSN: 0021-8723) is the leading scholarly publication and the journal of record in the field of American history. Published quarterly in March, June, September, and December, the *Journal* continues its nine-decade-long career presenting original articles on American history. Each volume of the *Journal* features a variety of works that deal with a wide range of American history, including state-of-the-field essays, broadly inclusive book reviews, and reviews of films, museum exhibitions, and Web sites.

Subscriptions

A subscription to the *Journal of American History* comprises 4 issues. Prices include postage; for subscribers outside the Americas, issues are sent air freight.
Annual Subscription Rate (Volume 98, issue 4, Volume 99, issues 1-3, 2012)
Corporate—Print and online access: £255/$376/€303; Print edition only: £221/$326/€263; Site-wide online access only: £245/$361/€293
Institutional—Print and online access: £204/$300/€243; Print edition only: £176/$260/€210; Site-wide online access only: £196/$289/€234

There are other subscription rates applicable for academic institutions and public libraries; for a complete listing, please visit www.jahist .oxfordjournals.org/subscriptions. Please note: € rates apply in Europe, $ in the US and Canada, and £ in the UK and elsewhere. Payment for orders to be delivered within Europe should be made in €. There are other subscription rates available; for a complete listing, please visit www.jahist.oxfordjournals.org/subscriptions.

Full prepayment in the correct currency is required for all orders. Payment should be in US dollars for orders being delivered to the USA or Canada; Euros for orders being delivered within Europe (excluding the UK); GBP Sterling for orders being delivered elsewhere (i.e., not being delivered to USA, Canada, or Europe). All orders should be accompanied by full payment and sent to your nearest Oxford Journals office. Subscriptions are accepted for complete volumes only. Orders are regarded as firm, and payments are not refundable. Our prices include dispatch by Standard Air. Claims must be notified within four months of dispatch/order date (whichever is later).

Subscriptions in the EEC may be subject to European VAT. If registered, please supply details to avoid unnecessary charges. For subscriptions that include online versions, a proportion of the subscription price may be subject to UK VAT. Subscribers in Canada, please add GST to the prices quoted.

The current year and two previous years' issues are available from Oxford Journals. Previous volumes can be obtained from the Periodicals Service Company, 11 Main Street, Germantown, NY 12526, USA. E-mail: psc@periodicals.com. Tel: (518) 537-4700. Fax: (518) 537-5899.

Contact information

Journals Customer Service Department, Oxford Journals, Great Clarendon Street, Oxford OX2 6DP, UK. E-mail: jnls.cust.serv@ oxfordjournals.org. Tel: +44 (0)1865 353907. Fax: +44 (0)1865 353485. **In the Americas, please contact:** Journals Customer Service Department, Oxford Journals, 2001 Evans Road, Cary, NC 27513, USA. E-mail: jnlorders@oxfordjournals.org. Tel: (800) 852-7323 (toll-free in USA/Canada) or (919) 677-0977. Fax: (919) 677-1714. **In Japan, please contact:** Journals Customer Service Department, Oxford Journals, 4-5-10-8F Shiba, Minato-ku, Tokyo, 108-8386, Japan. E-mail: custserv.jp@oxfordjournals.org. Tel: (81) 3 5444 5858. Fax: (81) 3 3454 2929.

Methods of payment

Payment should be made: by cheque (to Oxford Journals, Cashiers Office, Great Clarendon Street, Oxford, OX2 6DP, UK); by bank transfer [to Barclays Bank Plc, Oxford Office, Oxford (bank sort code 20-65-18) (UK); overseas only Swift code BARC GB22 (GB£ Sterling Account no. 70299332, IBAN GB89BARC20651870299332; US$ Dollars Account no. 66014600, IBAN GB27BARC2065 1866014600; EU€ EURO Account no. 78923655, IBAN GB16BARC20651878923655]; or by credit card (Mastercard, Visa, Switch or American Express).

Postal information

The *Journal of American History* is published by the Organization of American Historians, 112 North Bryan Ave., Bloomington, Indiana 47408-4141. Periodicals Postage Paid at Bloomington, IN and additional mailing offices. Please send changes of address to *Journal of American History*, Journals Customer Service Department, Oxford University Press, 2001 Evans Road, Cary, NC 27513, USA.

Oxford Journals environmental and ethical policies

Oxford Journals is committed to working with the global community to bring the highest quality research to the widest possible audience. Oxford Journals will protect the environment by implementing environmentally friendly policies and practices wherever possible. Please see http://www.oxfordjournals.org/ethicalpolicies.html for further information on Oxford Journals' environmental and ethical policies.

Digital object identifiers

For information on dois and to resolve them, please visit www.doi.org.

Permissions

For information on how to request permissions to reproduce articles or information from this journal, please visit www.oxfordjournals.org /permissions.

Advertising

Advertising, inserts, and artwork inquiries should be addressed to Advertising and Special Sales, Oxford Journals, Oxford University Press, Great Clarendon Street, Oxford, OX2 6DP, UK. Tel: +44 (0)1865 354767; Fax: +44 (0)1865 353774; E-mail: jnlsadvertising @oxfordjournals.org.

Disclaimer

Statements of fact and opinion in the articles in *Journal of American History* are those of the respective authors and contributors and not of the Organization of American Historians or Oxford University Press. Neither Oxford University Press nor the Organization of American Historians make any representation, express or implied, in respect of the accuracy of the material in this journal and cannot accept any legal responsibility or liability for any errors or omissions that may be made.

Instructions for Authors

Full instructions for manuscript preparation and submission can be found at: http://www.journalofamericanhistory.org or http://www .oxfordjournals.org/our_journals/jahist/for_authors/ms_preparation.html.

Contents

Book Reviews

Web Site Reviews

Editor's Annual Report, 2011–2012

Letters to the Editor

Announcements

Recent Scholarship

Previews

The scholarly consensus on slavery's centrality to the causes of disunion has not mooted debates in the field, which continued to diversify during the first decade of the twenty-first century. **Michael E. Woods** clarifies existing and potential debates by evaluating three trends in the recent literature: the impulse to transcend spatial and temporal boundaries in the study of American sectionalism; attention to northern sectionalism and southern proslavery American nationalism; and a resurgent awareness of the salience of class and class conflict, particularly related to northern critiques of the "slave power," in the escalation of sectional tension. Beneath a veneer of consensus lies considerable interpretive disagreement that should inform scholarly and public debate of the Civil War's origins.

Matthew Pehl adds to a small but growing historiography that links the concerns of the "new labor history" with recent, innovative approaches to the study of religion. Focusing on Detroit, he argues that the cultural politics of World War II were fundamentally shaped by ideas about working-class religion. Religious activists on the left aspired to craft a religious identity that supported industrial unionism and social democracy, but they also feared that religion could be harnessed to support fascism. Ministers on the right, meanwhile, appealed to workers with a very different religious identity and warned that "corrupted" leftist religion would lead to communism.

While the racial themes of Hollywood films have been well documented by scholars, struggles to break down racial barriers in the film labor market are underdocumented. Although self-identifying as liberal, late 1960s Hollywood was in fact resistant to employing and promoting minorities, leading the Justice Department to take the extraordinary step of preparing lawsuits under Title VII of the 1964 Civil Rights Act against practically the entire industry. **Eithne Quinn** examines Hollywood's racial politics during these pivotal early years of affirmative action, looking at black and federal activism as well as the responses of studio management and craft unions. She uncovers Hollywood's role in anti–affirmative action lobbying and in the formulation and propagation of emergent "color-blind" neoconservative discourses that forwarded laissez-faire approaches to achieving racial equality.

Little should be written about postwar American cities without considering the conditions for and consequences of white flight. But what if some of the white people who

doi: 10.1093/jahist/jas301

left cities after World War II believed they could leave the city and still remain invested in it? **Lila Corwin Berman** explains that this was the case for Jews living in Detroit, who left the city rapidly yet created a new remote politics of urban investment. Contradictions, arising from Jews' warring desires to take advantage of the privileges afforded to white suburbanites and to remain embedded in urban life, coursed through their new politics of remote urbanism. Berman concludes that urbanism, more so than whiteness or liberalism, defined the contours of postwar Jewish life and, even, of postwar Jewish white flight.

What Twenty-First-Century Historians Have Said about the Causes of Disunion: A Civil War Sesquicentennial Review of the Recent Literature

Michael E. Woods

Professional historians can be an argumentative lot, but by the dawn of the twenty-first century, a broad consensus regarding Civil War causation clearly reigned. Few mainstream scholars would deny that Abraham Lincoln got it right in his second inaugural address—that slavery was "somehow" the cause of the war. Public statements by preeminent historians reaffirmed that slavery's centrality had been proven beyond a reasonable doubt. Writing for the popular Civil War magazine *North and South* in November 2000, James M. McPherson pointed out that during the war, "few people in either North or South would have dissented" from Lincoln's slavery-oriented account of the war's origins. In ten remarkably efficient pages, McPherson dismantled arguments that the war was fought over tariffs, states' rights, or the abstract principle of secession. That same year, Charles Joyner penned a report on Civil War causation for release at a Columbia, South Carolina, press conference at the peak of the Palmetto State's Confederate flag debate. Endorsed by dozens of scholars and later published in *Callaloo,* it concluded that the "historical record . . . clearly shows that the cause for which the South seceded and fought a devastating war was slavery."[1]

Michael E. Woods received his Ph.D. in May 2012 from the University of South Carolina, where he is now a postdoctoral fellow in the Department of History.

I would like to thank David Dangerfield, Allen Driggers, Tiffany Florvil, Margaret Gillikin, Ramon Jackson, Evan Kutzler, Tyler Parry, David Prior, Tara Strauch, Beth Toyofuku, and Ann Tucker for their comments on an early version of this essay, and to extend special thanks to Mark M. Smith for perceptive criticism of multiple drafts. I would also like to thank Edward Linenthal for his expert criticism and guidance through the publication process and to express my gratitude to the four *JAH* readers, Ann Fabian, James M. McPherson, Randall Miller, and one anonymous reviewer, for their exceptionally thoughtful and helpful comments on the piece.

Readers may contact Woods at woodsme2@mailbox.sc.edu.

[1] The title of this article borrows from Howard K. Beale, "What Historians Have Said about the Causes of the Civil War," *Social Science Research Bulletin,* 54 (1946), 53–102. Abraham Lincoln, "Second Inaugural Address," in *The Collected Works of Abraham Lincoln,* ed. Roy P. Basler (9 vols., New Brunswick, 1953–1955), VIII, 332–33; James M. McPherson, "What Caused the Civil War?," *North and South,* 4 (Nov. 2000), 12–22, esp. 13. This consensus extends into college textbooks, many written by James McPherson, which "contain little debate over war causation since they recognize that slavery was the root cause of the war." See William B. Rogers and Terese Martyn, "A Consensus at Last: American Civil War Texts and the Topics That Dominate the College Classroom," *History Teacher,* 41 (Aug. 2008), 519–30, esp. 530. See also Aaron Charles Sheehan-Dean, "A Book for Every Perspective: Current Civil War and Reconstruction Textbooks," *Civil War History,* 51 (Sept. 2005), 317–24. Charles W. Joyner, "The Flag Controversy and the Causes of the Civil War: A Statement by Historians," *Callaloo: A Journal of African Diaspora Arts and Letters,* 24 (Winter 2001), 196–98, esp. 197. For lengthier exposés of slavery, secession, and postbellum mythmaking from recent years, see Charles B. Dew, *Apostles of Disunion: Southern Secession Commissioners and the Causes of the Civil War* (Charlottesville, 2001); and James W. Loewen and

doi: 10.1093/jahist/jas272

Despite the impulse to close ranks amid the culture wars, however, professional historians have not abandoned the debate over Civil War causation. Rather, they have rightly concluded that there is not much of a consensus on the topic after all. Elizabeth Varon remarks that although "scholars can agree that slavery, more than any other issue, divided North and South, there is still much to be said about why slavery proved so divisive and why sectional compromise ultimately proved elusive." And as Edward Ayers observes: "slavery and freedom remain the keys to understanding the war, but they are the place to begin our questions, not to end them."[2] The continuing flood of scholarship on the sectional conflict suggests that many other historians agree. Recent work on the topic reveals two widely acknowledged truths: that slavery was at the heart of the sectional conflict and that there is more to learn about precisely what this means, not least because slavery was always a multifaceted issue.

This essay analyzes the extensive literature on Civil War causation published since 2000, a body of work that has not been analyzed at length. This survey cannot be comprehensive but seeks instead to clarify current debates in a field long defined by distinct interpretive schools—such as those of the progressives, revisionists, and modernization theorists—whose boundaries are now blurrier. To be sure, echoes still reverberate of the venerable arguments between historians who emphasize abstract economic, social, or political forces and those who stress human agency. The classic interpretive schools still command allegiance, with fundamentalists who accentuate concrete sectional differences dueling against revisionists, for whom contingency, chance, and irrationality are paramount. But recent students of Civil War causation have not merely plowed familiar furrows. They have broken fresh ground, challenged long-standing assumptions, and provided new perspectives on old debates. This essay explores three key issues that vein the recent scholarship: the geographic and temporal parameters of the sectional conflict, the relationship between sectionalism and nationalism, and the relative significance of race and class in sectional politics. All three problems stimulated important research long before 2000, but recent work has taken them in new directions. These themes are particularly helpful for navigating the recent scholarship, and by using them to organize and evaluate the latest literature, this essay underscores fruitful avenues for future study of a subject that remains central in American historiography.[3]

Edward H. Sebesta, eds., *The Confederate and Neo-Confederate Reader: The "Great Truth" about the "Lost Cause"* (Jackson, 2010).

[2] Elizabeth R. Varon, *Disunion! The Coming of the American Civil War, 1789–1859* (Chapel Hill, 2008), 4. Edward L. Ayers, *What Caused the Civil War? Reflections on the South and Southern History* (New York, 2005), 128. For Edward Ayers's call for reinvigorated debate on the causes, conduct, and consequences of the Civil War, see *ibid.*, 131–44.

[3] For analyses of earlier literature, see Beale, "What Historians Have Said about the Causes of the Civil War"; Thomas J. Pressly, *Americans Interpret Their Civil War* (New York, 1962); David M. Potter, "The Literature on the Background of the Civil War," in *The South and the Sectional Conflict*, by David M. Potter (Baton Rouge, 1968), 87–150; and Eric Foner, "The Causes of the American Civil War: Recent Interpretations and New Directions," *Civil War History*, 20 (Sept. 1974), 197–214. For more recent historiographical assessments of specific topics related to the sectional crisis, see Lacy K. Ford, ed., *A Companion to the Civil War and Reconstruction* (Malden, 2005), 25–200. For a reinterpretation of the full century and a half of scholarship on Civil War causation that briefly samples recent literature, see Frank Towers, "Partisans, New History, and Modernization: The Historiography of the Civil War's Causes, 1861–2011," *Journal of the Civil War Era*, 1 (June 2011), 237–64. Several important bodies of literature are underrepresented in my historiography. One is work on the five months between Abraham Lincoln's election and the bombardment of Fort Sumter, which addresses the question of why and how secession sparked a shooting war. This outcome was not inevitable, because the causes of disunion were not

Space, Time, and Sectionalism

Historians of the sectional conflict, like their colleagues in other fields, have consciously expanded the geographic and chronological confines of their research. Crossing the borders of the nation-state and reaching back toward the American Revolution, many recent studies of the war's origins situate the clash over slavery within a broad spatial and temporal context. The ramifications of this work will not be entirely clear until an enterprising scholar incorporates those studies into a new synthesis, but this essay will offer a preliminary evaluation.

Scholarship following the transnational turn in American history has silenced lingering doubts that nineteenth-century Americans of all regions, classes, and colors were deeply

identical to the causes of the Civil War itself. This essay focuses on the former topic. For recent interpretations of the latter, see Dew, *Apostles of Disunion;* David Detzer, *Allegiance: Fort Sumter, Charleston, and the Beginning of the Civil War* (New York, 2001); Larry D. Mansch, *Abraham Lincoln, President-Elect: The Four Critical Months from Election to Inauguration* (Jefferson, 2005); Nelson D. Lankford, *Cry Havoc! The Crooked Road to Civil War, 1861* (New York, 2007); Russell McClintock, *Lincoln and the Decision for War: The Northern Response to Secession* (Chapel Hill, 2008); Harold Holzer, *Lincoln President-Elect: Abraham Lincoln and the Great Secession Winter, 1860–1861* (New York, 2008); Lawrence M. Denton, *William Henry Seward and the Secession Crisis: The Effort to Prevent Civil War* (Jefferson, 2009); William J. Cooper Jr., "The Critical Signpost on the Journey toward Secession," *Journal of Southern History,* 77 (Feb. 2011), 3–16; Emory M. Thomas, *The Dogs of War, 1861* (New York, 2011); and Adam Goodheart, *1861: The Civil War Awakening* (New York, 2011). Biographies are also not explored systematically here. Recent biographies related to the coming of the Civil War include William C. Davis, *Rhett: The Turbulent Life and Times of a Fire-Eater* (Columbia, S.C., 2001); John L. Myers, *Henry Wilson and the Coming of the Civil War* (Lanham, 2005); John M. Belohlavek, *Broken Glass: Caleb Cushing and the Shattering of the Union* (Kent, 2005); Eric H. Walther, *William Lowndes Yancey and the Coming of the Civil War* (Chapel Hill, 2006); and Denton, *William Henry Seward and the Secession Crisis.* Thanks in part to the close proximity of Lincoln's bicentennial birthday and the Civil War sesquicentennial, scholarship on the sixteenth president continues to burgeon. For analyses of this vast literature see James Oakes, "Lincoln and His Commas," *Civil War History,* 54 (June 2008), 176–93; Sean Wilentz, "Who Lincoln Was," *New Republic,* July 15, 2009, pp. 24–47; and Nicole Etcheson, "Abraham Lincoln and the Nation's Greatest Quarrel: A Review Essay," *Journal of Southern History,* 76 (May 2010), 401–16. For an account of Lincoln historiography in the *Journal of American History,* see Allen C. Guelzo, "The Not-So-Grand Review: Abraham Lincoln in the *Journal of American History,*" *Journal of American History,* 96 (Sept. 2009), 400–416. That biography and studies of the secession winter are thriving suggests a possible waning of the long-dominant "irrepressible conflict" interpretation, as both approaches emphasize contingency and individual agency. Collective biography, particularly on Lincoln's relationships with other key figures, has also flourished. On Lincoln and Frederick Douglass, see James Oakes, *The Radical and the Republican: Frederick Douglass, Abraham Lincoln, and the Triumph of Antislavery Politics* (New York, 2007); Paul Kendrick and Stephen Kendrick, *Douglass and Lincoln: How a Revolutionary Black Leader and a Reluctant Liberator Struggled to End Slavery and Save the Union* (New York, 2008); and John Stauffer, *Giants: The Parallel Lives of Frederick Douglass and Abraham Lincoln* (New York, 2008). On Lincoln and Stephen A. Douglas, see Allen C. Guelzo, *Lincoln and Douglas: The Debates That Defined America* (New York, 2008); and Roy Morris, *The Long Pursuit: Abraham Lincoln's Thirty-Year Struggle with Stephen Douglas for the Heart and Soul of America* (New York, 2008). A third body of literature that needs further historiographical analysis relates to gender and the coming of the Civil War. See, for example, Michael D. Pierson, *Free Hearts and Free Homes: Gender and American Antislavery Politics* (Chapel Hill, 2003); Nina Silber, *Gender and the Sectional Conflict* (Chapel Hill, 2008); Kristen Tegtmeier Oertel, *Bleeding Borders: Race, Gender, and Violence in Pre–Civil War Kansas* (Baton Rouge, 2009); and Stephanie McCurry, *Confederate Reckoning: Power and Politics in the Civil War South* (Cambridge, Mass., 2010). For discussions of the classic schools of scholarship, see Kenneth M. Stampp, "The Irrepressible Conflict," in *The Imperiled Union: Essays on the Background of the Civil War,* by Kenneth M. Stampp (New York, 1980), 191–245; Ayers, *What Caused the Civil War?,* 132–33; and Gary J. Kornblith, "Rethinking the Coming of the Civil War: A Counterfactual Exercise," *Journal of American History,* 90 (June 2003), 78–79. For a call for a synthesis of the fundamentalist and revisionist interpretations, see Ayers, *What Caused the Civil War?* On the continued relevance of these camps, see James Huston, "Interpreting the Causation Sequence: The Meaning of the Events Leading to the Civil War," *Reviews in American History,* 34 (Sept. 2006), 329. The coming of the Civil War has long shaped discussions of historical causation, including Lee Benson and Cushing Strout, "Causation and the American Civil War: Two Appraisals," *History and Theory,* 1 (no. 2, 1961), 163–85; and William Dray and Newton Garver, "Some Causal Accounts of the American Civil War," *Daedalus,* 91 (Summer 1962), 578–98.

influenced by people, ideas, and events from abroad. Historians have long known that the causes of the Civil War cannot be understood outside the context of international affairs, particularly the Mexican-American War (1846–1848). Three of the most influential narrative histories of the Civil War era open either on Mexican soil (those written by Allan Nevins and James McPherson) or with the transnational journey from Mexico City to Washington of the 1848 Treaty of Guadalupe Hidalgo (David M. Potter's *The Impending Crisis*). The domestic political influence of the annexation of Texas, Caribbean filibustering, and the Ostend Manifesto, a widely publicized message written to President Franklin Pierce in 1854 that called for the acquisition of Cuba, are similarly well established.[4]

Recent studies by Edward Bartlett Rugemer and Matthew J. Clavin, among others, build on that foundation to show that the international dimensions of the sectional conflict transcended the bitterly contested question of territorial expansion. Rugemer, for instance, demonstrates that Caribbean emancipation informed U.S. debates over slavery from the Haitian Revolution (1791–1804) through Reconstruction. Situating sectional politics within the Atlantic history of slavery and abolition, he illustrates how arguments for and against U.S. slavery drew from competing interpretations of emancipation in the British West Indies. Britain's "mighty experiment" thus provided "useable history for an increasingly divided nation." Proslavery ideologues learned that abolitionism sparked insurrection, that Africans and their descendants would become idlers or murderers or both if released from bondage, and that British radicals sought to undermine the peculiar institution wherever it persisted. To slavery's foes, the same history revealed that antislavery activism worked, that emancipation could be peaceful and profitable, and that servitude, not skin tone, degraded enslaved laborers. Clavin's study of American memory of Toussaint L'Ouverture indicates that the Haitian Revolution cast an equally long shadow over antebellum history. Construed as a catastrophic race war, the revolution haunted slaveholders with the prospect of an alliance between ostensibly savage slaves and fanatical whites. Understood as a hopeful story of the downtrodden overthrowing their oppressors, however, Haitian history furnished abolitionists, white and black, with an inspiring example of heroic self-liberation by the enslaved. By the 1850s it also furnished abolitionists, many of whom were frustrated by the abysmally slow progress of emancipation in the United States, with a precedent for swift, violent revolution and the vindication of black masculinity. The Haitian Revolution thus provided "resonant, polarizing, and

[4] Key works on the transnational turn include "Toward the Internationalization of American History: A Round Table," *Journal of American History*, 79 (Sept. 1992), 432–542; Carl J. Guarneri, "Internationalizing the United States Survey Course: American History for a Global Age," *History Teacher*, 36 (Nov. 2002), 37–64; Thomas Bender, ed., *Rethinking American History in a Global Age* (Berkeley, 2002); Thomas Bender, *A Nation among Nations: America's Place in World History* (New York, 2006); and Ian Tyrrell, *Transnational Nation: United States History in Global Perspective since 1789* (Basingstoke, 2007). Allan Nevins, *Ordeal of the Union* (2 vols., New York, 1947), I, 3–5; James McPherson, *Battle Cry of Freedom: The Civil War Era* (New York, 1988), 3–5; David M. Potter, *The Impending Crisis, 1848–1861*, completed and ed. Don E. Fehrenbacher (New York, 1976), 1–6. On continental expansion and sectional conflict, see Michael A. Morrison, *Slavery and the American West: The Eclipse of Manifest Destiny and the Coming of the Civil War* (Chapel Hill, 1997). On the divisive influence of sectionalized fantasies of tropical conquest, see Robert E. May, *The Southern Dream of a Caribbean Empire, 1854–1861* (Baton Rouge, 1973). For an early work on Haiti's transnational significance, see Alfred N. Hunt, *Haiti's Influence on Antebellum America: Slumbering Volcano in the Caribbean* (Baton Rouge, 1988). On the relationship between the Ostend Manifesto and domestic politics, see Robert E. May, "A 'Southern Strategy' for the 1850s: Northern Democrats, the Tropics, and Expansion of the National Domain," *Louisiana Studies*, 14 (Winter 1975), 333–59, esp. 337–42; and John Ashworth, *Slavery, Capitalism, and Politics in the Antebellum Republic*, vol. II: *The Coming of the Civil War, 1850–1861* (New York, 2007), 395–98.

ultimately subversive symbols" for antislavery and proslavery partisans alike and helped "provoke a violent confrontation and determine the fate of slavery in the United States."[5]

These findings will surprise few students of Civil War causation, but they demonstrate that the international aspects of the sectional conflict did not begin and end with Manifest Destiny. They also encourage Atlantic historians to pay more attention to the nineteenth century, particularly to the period after British emancipation. Rugemer and Clavin point out that deep connections among Atlantic rim societies persisted far into the nineteenth century and that, like other struggles over New World slavery, the American Civil War is an Atlantic story. One of their most stimulating contributions may therefore be to encourage Atlantic historians to widen their temporal perspectives to include the middle third of the nineteenth century. By foregrounding the hotly contested public memory of the Haitian Revolution, Rugemer and Clavin push the story of American sectionalism back into the late eighteenth and early nineteenth centuries, suggesting that crossing geographic boundaries can go hand in hand with stretching the temporal limits of sectionalism.[6]

The internationalizing impulse has also nurtured economic interpretations of the sectional struggle. Brian Schoen, Peter Onuf, and Nicholas Onuf situate antebellum politics within the context of global trade, reinvigorating economic analysis of sectionalism without summoning the ghosts of Charles Beard and Mary Beard. Readers may balk at their emphasis on tariff debates, but these histories are plainly not Confederate apologia. As Schoen points out, chattel slavery expanded in the American South, even as it withered throughout most of the Atlantic world, because southern masters embraced the nineteenth century's most important crop: cotton. Like the oil titans of a later age, southern cotton planters reveled in the economic indispensability of their product. Schoen adopts a cotton-centered perspective from which to examine southern political economy, from the earliest cotton boom to the secession crisis. "Broad regional faith in cotton's global power," he argues, "both informed secessionists' actions and provided them an indispensable tool for mobilizing otherwise reluctant confederates." Planters'

---

[5] Edward Bartlett Rugemer, *The Problem of Emancipation: The Caribbean Roots of the American Civil War* (Baton Rouge, 2008), 7; Matthew J. Clavin, *Toussaint Louverture and the American Civil War: The Promise and Peril of a Second Haitian Revolution* (Philadelphia, 2010), 5. Other recent transnational studies of Civil War causation include Timothy Roberts, "The European Revolutions of 1848 and Antebellum Violence in Kansas," *Journal of the West*, 44 (Fall 2005), 58–68; Gerald Horne, *The Deepest South: The United States, Brazil, and the African Slave Trade* (New York, 2007); McCurry, *Confederate Reckoning*; and Mischa Honeck, *We Are the Revolutionists: German-Speaking Immigrants and American Abolitionists after 1848* (Athens, Ga., 2011). Several recent dissertations explore the equally permeable boundary between North and South. See Joseph T. Rainer, "The Honorable Fraternity of Moving Merchants: Yankee Peddlers in the Old South, 1800–1860" (Ph.D. diss., College of William and Mary, 2000); Wesley Brian Borucki, "Yankees in King Cotton's Court: Northerners in Antebellum and Wartime Alabama" (Ph.D. diss., University of Alabama, 2002); Eric William Plaag, "Strangers in a Strange Land: Northern Travelers and the Coming of the American Civil War" (Ph.D. diss., University of South Carolina, 2006); and Alana K. Bevan, "'We Are the Same People': The Leverich Family of New York and Their Antebellum American Inter-regional Network of Elites" (Ph.D. diss., Johns Hopkins University, 2009). On the "mighty experiment," see Seymour Drescher, *The Mighty Experiment: Free Labor versus Slavery in British Emancipation* (New York, 2002). The compelling scholarship on global antislavery undoubtedly encouraged the internationalization of Civil War causation studies. David Brion Davis's contributions remain indispensable. See David Brion Davis, *The Problem of Slavery in Western Culture* (Ithaca, 1966); David Brion Davis, *The Problem of Slavery in the Age of Revolution, 1770–1823* (Ithaca, 1975); and David Brion Davis, *Inhuman Bondage: The Rise and Fall of Slavery in the New World* (New York, 2006). For a work that places antebellum southern thought, including proslavery ideology, into an international context, see Michael O'Brien, *Conjectures of Order: Intellectual Life in the American South, 1810–1860* (2 vols., Chapel Hill, 2004).

[6] Rugemer, *Problem of Emancipation*, 6–7; Clavin, *Toussaint Louverture and the American Civil War*, 9–10.

commitment to the production and overseas sale of cotton shaped southern politics and business practices. It impelled westward expansion, informed planters' jealous defense of slavery, and wedded them to free trade. An arrogant faith in their commanding economic position gave planters the impetus and the confidence to secede when northern Republicans threatened to block the expansion of slavery and increase the tariff. The Onufs reveal a similar dynamic at work in their complementary study, *Nations, Markets, and War*. Like Schoen, they portray slaveholders as forward-looking businessmen who espoused free-trade liberalism in defense of their economic interests. Entangled in political competition with Yankee protectionists throughout the early national and antebellum years, slaveholders seceded when it became clear that their vision for the nation's political economy—most importantly its trade policy—could no longer prevail.[7]

These authors examine Civil War causation within a global context, though in a way more reminiscent of traditional economic history than similar to other recent transnational scholarship. But perhaps the most significant contribution made by these authors lies beyond internationalizing American history. After all, most historians of the Old South have recognized that the region's economic and political power depended on the Atlantic cotton trade, and scholars of the Confederacy demonstrated long ago that overconfidence in cotton's international leverage led southern elites to pursue a disastrous foreign policy. What these recent studies reveal is that cotton-centered diplomatic and domestic politics long predated southern independence and had roots in the late eighteenth century, when slaveholders' decision to enlarge King Cotton's domain set them on a turbulent political course that led to Appomattox. The Onufs and Schoen, then, like Rugemer and Clavin, expand not only the geographic parameters of the sectional conflict but also its temporal boundaries.[8]

These four important histories reinforce recent work that emphasizes the eruption of the sectional conflict at least a generation before the 1820 Missouri Compromise. If the conflict over Missouri was a "firebell in the night," as Thomas Jefferson called it, it was a rather tardy alarm. This scholarship mirrors a propensity among political historians—most notably scholars of the civil rights movement—to write "long histories." Like their colleagues who dispute the Montgomery-to-Memphis narrative of the civil rights era, political historians of the early republic have questioned conventional periodization by showing that sectionalism did not spring fully grown from the head of James Tallmadge, the New York congressman whose February 1819 proposal to bar the further extension of slavery into Missouri unleashed the political storm that was calmed, for the moment,

[7] Brian Schoen, *The Fragile Fabric of Union: Cotton, Federal Politics, and the Global Origins of the Civil War* (Baltimore, 2009), 10; Nicholas Onuf and Peter Onuf, *Nations, Markets, and War: Modern History and the American Civil War* (Charlottesville, 2006). John Majewski offers a different perspective on slavery and free trade, acknowledging that slaveholders were hardly united in favor of protection and arguing that the moderate Confederate tariff represented a compromise between protectionists and free traders. See John Majewski, *Modernizing a Slave Economy: The Economic Vision of the Confederate Nation* (Chapel Hill, 2009).

[8] On the centrality of cotton exports in the economic history of the South—and the United States—see Douglass C. North, *The Economic Growth of the United States, 1790–1860* (Englewood Cliffs, 1961). On the Old South's place in world economic history and its dependency on the global cotton market, see Elizabeth Fox-Genovese and Eugene D. Genovese, "The Slave Economies in Political Perspective," in *Fruits of Merchant Capital: Slavery and Bourgeois Property in the Rise and Expansion of Capitalism,* by Elizabeth Fox-Genovese and Eugene D. Genovese (New York, 1983), 34–60. On the cotton trade and Confederate diplomacy, see Frank Lawrence Owsley Sr., *King Cotton Diplomacy: Foreign Relations of the Confederate States of America* (Chicago, 1931). On the early history of the cotton kingdom, see Adam Rothman, *Slave Country: American Expansion and the Origins of the Deep South* (Cambridge, Mass., 2005).

by the Missouri Compromise. Matthew Mason, for instance, maintains that "there never was a time between the Revolution and the Civil War in which slavery went unchallenged." Mason shows that political partisans battered their rivals with the club of slavery, with New England Federalists proving especially adept at denouncing their Jeffersonian opponents as minions of southern slaveholders. In a series of encounters, from the closure of the Atlantic slave trade in 1807 to the opening (fire)bell of the Missouri crisis, slavery remained a central question in American politics. Even the outbreak of war in 1812 failed to suppress the issue.[9]

A complementary study by John Craig Hammond confirms that slavery roiled American politics from the late eighteenth century on and that its westward expansion proved especially divisive years before the Missouri fracas. As America's weak national government continued to bring more western acreage under its nominal control, it had to accede to local preferences regarding slavery. Much of the fierce conflict over slavery therefore occurred at the territorial and state levels. Hammond astutely juxtaposes the histories of slave states such as Louisiana and Missouri alongside those of Ohio and Indiana, where proslavery policies were defeated. In every case, local politics proved decisive. Neither the rise nor the extent of the cotton kingdom was a foregone conclusion, and the quarrel over its expansion profoundly influenced territorial and state politics north and south of the Ohio River. Bringing the growing scholarship on both early republic slavery and proslavery ideology into conversation with political history, Hammond demonstrates that the bitterness of the Missouri debate stemmed from that dispute's contentious prehistory, not from its novelty. Just as social, economic, and intellectual historians have traced the "long history" of the antebellum South back to its once relatively neglected early national origins, political historians have uncovered the deep roots of political discord over slavery's expansion.[10]

Scholars have applied the "long history" principle to other aspects of Civil War causation as well. In his study of the slave power thesis, Leonard L. Richards finds that northern anxieties about slaveholders' inordinate political influence germinated during the 1787 Constitutional Convention. Jan Lewis's argument that the concessions made to southern delegates at the convention emboldened them to demand special protection for slavery suggests that those apprehensions were sensible. David L. Lightner demonstrates that northern demands for a congressional ban on the domestic slave trade, designed to strike a powerful and, thanks to the interstate commerce clause, constitutional blow

---

[9] Thomas Jefferson to John Holmes, April 22, 1820, *Library of Congress: Thomas Jefferson,* http://www.loc.gov/exhibits/jefferson/159.html. The foundational text for "long movement" scholarship is Jacquelyn Dowd Hall, "The Long Civil Rights Movement and the Political Uses of the Past," *Journal of American History,* 91 (March 2005), 1233–63. An influential application of this paradigm is Glenda Elizabeth Gilmore, *Defying Dixie: The Radical Roots of Civil Rights, 1919–1950* (New York, 2008). For a sharp critique of the long movement concept, see Sundiata Keita Cha-Jua and Clarence Lang, "The 'Long Movement' as Vampire: Temporal and Spatial Fallacies in Recent Black Freedom Studies," *Journal of African American History,* 92 (Spring 2007), 265–88. Matthew Mason, *Slavery and Politics in the Early American Republic* (Chapel Hill, 2006), 5.

[10] John Craig Hammond, *Slavery, Freedom, and Expansion in the Early American West* (Charlottesville, 2007). For an accessible introduction to the early struggles over slavery, see Gary J. Kornblith, *Slavery and Sectional Strife in the Early American Republic, 1776–1821* (Lanham, 2010). On slavery's post-Revolution expansion, see Rothman, *Slave Country.* For the social and intellectual history of early proslavery thought, see Jeffrey Robert Young, ed., *Proslavery and Sectional Thought in the Early South, 1740–1829: An Anthology* (Columbia, S.C., 2006); Charles F. Irons, *The Origins of Proslavery Christianity: White and Black Evangelicals in Colonial and Antebellum Virginia* (Chapel Hill, 2008); and Lacy K. Ford, *Deliver Us from Evil: The Slavery Question in the Old South* (New York, 2009).

against slavery extension emerged during the first decade of the nineteenth century and informed antislavery strategy for the next fifty years. Richard S. Newman emphasizes that abolitionist politics long predated William Lloyd Garrison's founding of the *Liberator* in 1831. Like William W. Freehling, who followed the "road to disunion" back to the American Revolution, Newman commences his study of American abolitionism with the establishment of the Pennsylvania Abolition Society in 1775. Most recently, Christopher Childers has invited historians to explore the early history of the doctrine of popular sovereignty.[11]

Skeptics might ask where the logic of these studies will lead. Why not push the origins of sectional strife even further back into colonial history? Why not begin, as did a recent overview of Civil War causation, with the initial arrival of African slaves in Virginia in 1619? This critique has a point—hopefully we will never read an article called "Christopher Columbus and the Coming of the American Civil War"—but two virtues of recent work on the long sectional conflict merit emphasis. First, its extended view mirrors the very long, if chronically selective, memories of late antebellum partisans. By the 1850s few sectional provocateurs failed to trace northern belligerence toward the South, and vice versa, back to the eighteenth century. Massachusetts Republican John B. Alley reminded Congress in April 1860 that slavery had been "a disturbing element in our national politics ever since the organization of the Government." "In fact," Alley recalled, "political differences were occasioned by it, and sectional prejudices grew out of it, at a period long anterior to the formation of the Federal compact." Eight tumultuous months later, U.S. senator Robert Toombs recounted to the Georgia legislature a litany of northern aggressions and insisted that protectionism and abolitionism had tainted Yankee politics from "*the very first Congress.*" Tellingly, the study of historical memory, most famously used to analyze remembrance of the Civil War, has moved the study of Civil War causation more firmly into the decades between the nation's founding and the Missouri Compromise. Memories of the Haitian Revolution shaped antebellum expectations for emancipation. Similarly, recollections of southern economic sacrifice during Jefferson's 1807 embargo and the War of 1812 heightened white southerners' outrage over their "exclusion" from conquered Mexican territory more than three decades later. And as Margot Minardi has shown, Massachusetts abolitionists used public memory of the American Revolution to champion emancipation and racial equality. The Missouri-to-Sumter narrative conceals that these distant events haunted the memories of late antebellum Americans. Early national battles over slavery did not make the Civil War inevitable, but in the hands of propagandists they could make the war *seem* inevitable to many contemporaries.[12]

---

[11] Leonard L. Richards, *The Slave Power: The Free North and Southern Domination, 1780–1860* (Baton Rouge, 2000), 28–51; Jan Lewis, "The Three-Fifths Clause and the Origins of Sectionalism," in *Congress and the Emergence of Sectionalism: From the Missouri Compromise to the Age of Jackson,* ed. Paul Finkelman and Donald R. Kennon (Athens, Ohio, 2008), 19–46; David L. Lightner, *Slavery and the Commerce Power: How the Struggle against the Interstate Slave Trade Led to the Civil War* (New Haven, 2006); Richard S. Newman, *The Transformation of American Abolitionism: Fighting Slavery in the Early Republic* (Chapel Hill, 2002); Christopher Childers, "Interpreting Popular Sovereignty: A Historiographical Essay," *Civil War History,* 57 (March 2011), 48–70. For a discussion of the temporal parameters of his own work, see William W. Freehling, *The Road to Disunion,* vol. I: *Secessionists at Bay, 1776–1854* (New York, 1990), vii.

[12] Paul Calore, *The Causes of the Civil War: The Political, Cultural, Economic, and Territorial Disputes between North and South* (Jefferson, 2008). John B. Alley, *Speech of Hon. John B. Alley, of Mass., on the Principles and Purposes of the Republican Party: Delivered in the House of Representatives of the United States, Monday, April 30,*

Second, proponents of the long view of Civil War causation have not made a simplistic argument for continuity. Elizabeth Varon's study of the evolution of disunion as a political concept and rhetorical device from 1789 to 1859 demonstrates that long histories need not obscure change over time. Arguing that "sectional tensions deriving from the diverging interests of the free labor North and the slaveholding South" were "as old as the republic itself," Varon adopts a long perspective on sectional tension. But her nuanced analysis of the diverse and shifting political uses of disunion rhetoric suggests that what historians conveniently call *the* sectional conflict was in fact a series of overlapping clashes, each with its own dynamics and idiom. Quite literally, the terms of sectional debate remained in flux. The language of disunion came in five varieties—"a *prophecy* of national ruin, a *threat* of withdrawal from the federal compact, an *accusation* of treasonous plotting, a *process* of sectional alienation, and a *program* for regional independence"—and the specific meanings of each cannot be interpreted accurately without regard to historical context, for "their uses changed and shifted over time." To cite just one example, the concept of disunion as a process of increasing alienation between North and South gained credibility during the 1850s as proslavery and antislavery elements clashed, often violently, over the Fugitive Slave Act of 1850 and the extension of slavery into Kansas. Republican senator William Henry Seward's famous "irrepressible conflict" speech of 1858 took this interpretation of disunion, one that had long languished on the radical margins of sectional politics, and thrust it into mainstream discourse. Shifting political circumstances reshaped the terms of political debate from the 1830s, when the view of disunion as an irreversible process flourished only among abolitionists and southern extremists, to the late 1850s, when a leading contender for the presidential nomination of a major party could express it openly.[13]

Consistent with Varon's emphasis on the instability of political rhetoric, other recent studies of Civil War causation have spotlighted two well-known and important forks in the road to disunion. Thanks to their fresh perspective on the crisis of 1819–1821, scholars of early national sectionalism have identified the Missouri struggle as the first of these turning points. The battle over slavery in Missouri, Robert Pierce Forbes argues, was "a crack in the master narrative" of American history that fundamentally altered how Americans thought about slavery and the Union. In the South, it nurtured a less crassly

---

1860 (Washington, 1860), 2; Robert Toombs, *Speech of Hon. Robert Toombs, on the Crisis. Delivered before the Georgia Legislature, December 7, 1860* (Washington, 1860), 5. Emphasis in original. Clavin, *Toussaint Louverture and the American Civil War;* Schoen, *Fragile Fabric of Union,* 99; Margot Minardi, *Making Slavery History: Abolitionism and the Politics of Memory in Massachusetts* (New York, 2010). On the memory of the American Revolution in William Lloyd Garrison's proudly anachronistic rhetoric, see Robert Fanuzzi, *Abolition's Public Sphere* (Minneapolis, 2003). On abolitionists' use of public commemorations of British emancipation to recruit new activists, see Julie Roy Jeffrey, "'No Occurrence in Human History Is More Deserving of Commemoration Than This': Abolitionist Celebrations of Freedom," in *Prophets of Protest: Reconsidering the History of American Abolitionism,* ed. Timothy Patrick McCarthy and John Stauffer (New York, 2006), 200–219. On the link between collective memory of the Texas Revolution and the growth of Confederate nationalism in Texas, see Andrew F. Lang, "Memory, the Texas Revolution, and Secession: The Birth of Confederate Nationalism in the Lone Star State," *Southwestern Historical Quarterly,* 114 (July 2010), 21–36. On the memory of the Civil War, see, for example, David W. Blight, *Race and Reunion: The Civil War in American Memory* (Cambridge, Mass., 2001); William Alan Blair, *Cities of the Dead: Contesting the Memory of the Civil War in the South, 1865–1914* (Chapel Hill, 2004); Alice Fahs and Joan Waugh, eds., *The Memory of the Civil War in American Culture* (Chapel Hill, 2004); and Gary W. Gallagher, *Causes Won, Lost, and Forgotten: How Hollywood and Popular Art Shape What We Know about the Civil War* (Chapel Hill, 2008).
[13] Varon, *Disunion!,* 5, 17, 317–22, esp. 17, 5. Emphasis in original.

self-interested defense of servitude. Simultaneously, it tempted northerners to conceptually separate "the South" from "America," thereby sectionalizing the moral problem of
slavery and conflating northern values and interests with those of the nation. The intensity of the crisis demonstrated that the slavery debate threatened the Union, prompting
Jacksonian-era politicians to suppress the topic and stymie sectionalists for a generation.
But even as the Missouri controversy impressed moderates with the need for compromise, it fostered "a new clarity in the sectional politics of the United States and moved
each section toward greater coherence on the slavery issue" by refining arguments for and
against the peculiar institution. The competing ideologies that defined antebellum sectional politics coalesced during the contest over Missouri, now portrayed as a milestone
rather than a starter's pistol.[14]

A diverse body of scholarship identifies a second period of discontinuity stretching
from 1845 to 1850. This literature confirms rather than challenges traditional periodization, for those years have long marked the beginning of the "Civil War era." This time
span has attracted considerable attention because the slavery expansion debate intensified
markedly between the annexation of Texas in 1845 and the Compromise of 1850. Not
surprisingly, recent work on slavery's contested westward extension continues to present
the late 1840s as a key turning point—perhaps a point of no return—in the sectional
conflict. As Michael S. Green puts it, by 1848, "something in American political life
clearly had snapped.... [T]he genies that [James K.] Polk, [David] Wilmot, and their
allies had let out of the bottle would not be put back in."[15]

Scholars not specifically interested in slavery expansion have also identified the late
1840s as a decisive period. In his history of southern race mythology—the notion that
white southerners' "Norman" ancestry elevated them over Saxon-descended
northerners—Ritchie Devon Watson Jr. identifies these years as a transition period
between two theories of sectional difference. White southerners' U.S. nationalism persisted into the 1840s, he argues, and although they recognized cultural differences
between the Yankees and themselves, the dissimilarities were not imagined in racial
terms. After 1850, however, white southerners increasingly argued for innate differences
between the white southern "race" and its ostensibly inferior northern rival. This mythology was a "key element" in the "flowering of southern nationalism before and during the
Civil War." Susan-Mary Grant has shown that northern opinion of the South underwent
a simultaneous shift, with the slave power thesis gaining widespread credibility by the

[14] Robert Pierce Forbes, *The Missouri Compromise and Its Aftermath: Slavery and the Meaning of America*
(Chapel Hill, 2007), 3. Mason, *Slavery and Politics in the Early American Republic*, 211.
[15] Michael S. Green, *Politics and America in Crisis: The Coming of the Civil War* (Santa Barbara, 2010), 17–18.
For recent studies of the slavery expansion issue in the late 1840s and early 1850s, see Joel H. Silbey, *Storm over
Texas: The Annexation Controversy and the Road to Civil War* (New York, 2005); Leonard L. Richards, *The Califor-
nia Gold Rush and the Coming of the Civil War* (New York, 2007); John C. Waugh, *On the Brink of Civil War: The
Compromise of 1850 and How It Changed the Course of American History* (Wilmington, 2003); Robert V. Remini,
At the Edge of the Precipice: Henry Clay and the Compromise That Saved the Union (New York, 2010); and Steven
E. Woodworth, *Manifest Destinies: America's Westward Expansion and the Road to the Civil War* (New York, 2010).
Also in the late 1840s, antislavery activists shifted away from efforts to abolish the interstate slave trade and toward
the restriction of slavery's expansion. See Lightner, *Slavery and the Commerce Power*, 113–39. General histories that
begin in the 1845–1850 period include Arthur Charles Cole, *The Irrepressible Conflict, 1850–1865* (New York,
1934); Nevins, *Ordeal of the Union*; Potter, *Impending Crisis*; Ludwell H. Johnson, *Division and Reunion: America,
1848–1877* (New York, 1978); McPherson, *Battle Cry of Freedom*; Richard H. Sewell, *A House Divided: Sectionalism and Civil War, 1848–1865* (Baltimore, 1988); Robert Cook, *Civil War America: Making a Nation, 1848–1877*
(London, 2003); and Green, *Politics and America in Crisis*.

late 1840s. The year 1850 marked an economic turning point as well. Marc Egnal posits that around that year, a generation of economic integration between North and South gave way to an emerging "Lake Economy," which knit the Northwest and Northeast into an economic and political alliance at odds with the South. Taken together, this scholarship reaffirms what historians have long suspected about the sectional conflict: despite sectionalism's oft-recalled roots in the early national period, the late 1840s represents an important period of discontinuity. It is unsurprising that these years climaxed with a secession scare and a makeshift compromise reached not through bona fide give-and-take but rather through the political dexterity of Senator Stephen A. Douglas.[16]

That Douglas succeeded where the eminent Henry Clay had failed suggests another late 1840s discontinuity that deserves more scholarly attention. Thirty-six years older than the Little Giant, Clay was already Speaker of the House when Douglas was born in 1813. Douglas's shepherding of Clay's smashed omnibus bill through the Senate in 1850 "marked a changing of the guard from an older generation, whose time already might have passed, to a new generation whose time had yet to come." This passing of the torch symbolized a broader shift in political personnel. The Thirty-First Congress, which passed the compromise measures of 1850, was a youthful assembly. The average age for representatives was forty-three, only two were older than sixty-two, and more than half were freshmen. The Senate was similarly youthful, particularly its Democratic members, fewer than half of whom had reached age fifty. Moreover, the deaths of John C. Calhoun, Henry Clay, and Daniel Webster between March 1850 and October 1852 signaled to many observers the end of an era. In 1851 members of the University of Virginia's Southern Rights Association reminded their southern peers that "soon the destinies of the South must be entrusted to our keeping. The present occupants of the arena of action must soon pass away, and we be called upon to fill their places. . . . It becomes therefore our sacred duty to prepare for the contest."[17]

Students of Civil War causation would do well to probe this intergenerational transfer of power. This analysis need not revive the argument, most popular in the 1930s and 1940s, that the "blundering generation" of hot-headed and self-serving politicos who grasped the reins of power around 1850 brought on an unnecessary war. Caricaturing the rising generation as exceptionally inept is not required to profitably contrast the socioeconomic environments, political contexts, and intellectual milieus in which Clay's and Douglas's respective generations matured. These differences, and the generational conflict that they engendered, may have an important bearing on both the origins and the timing of the Civil War. Peter Carmichael's study of Virginia's last antebellum generation explores this subject in detail. Historians have long recognized that disproportionately high numbers of young white southerners supported secession. Carmichael offers a

---

[16] Ritchie Devon Watson Jr., *Normans and Saxons: Southern Race Mythology and the Intellectual History of the American Civil War* (Baton Rouge, 2008), 28. Susan-Mary Grant, *North over South: Northern Nationalism and American Identity in the Antebellum Era* (Lawrence, 2000), 61–80; Marc Egnal, *Clash of Extremes: The Economic Origins of the Civil War* (New York, 2009), 21–122. For accessible accounts of the Compromise of 1850, see Waugh, *On the Brink of Civil War;* and Remini, *At the Edge of the Precipice.*

[17] Green, *Politics and America in Crisis,* 41. On the ages of representatives and senators in 1850, see Holman Hamilton, *Prologue to Conflict: The Crisis and Compromise of 1850* (New York, 1964), 32, 40. On the deaths of John C. Calhoun, Daniel Webster, and Henry Clay, see Merrill D. Peterson, *The Great Triumvirate: Webster, Clay, and Calhoun* (New York, 1987), 494. "Address, 1851, of the Southern Rights Association of the University of Virginia to the Young Men of the South" [Dec. 19, 1850?], folder 1, box 1, William Henry Gist Papers (South Caroliniana Library, University of South Carolina, Columbia).

compelling explanation for why this was so, without portraying his subjects as mediocre statesmen or citing the eternal impetuousness of youth. Deftly blending cultural, social, economic, and political history, Carmichael rejects the notion that young Virginia gentlemen who came of age in the late 1850s were immature, impassioned, and reckless. They were, he argues, idealistic and ambitious men who believed deeply in progress but worried that their elders had squandered Virginia's traditional economic and political preeminence. Confronted with their state's apparent degeneration and their own lack of opportunity for advancement, Carmichael's young Virginians endorsed a pair of solutions that put them at odds with their conservative elders: economic diversification and, after John Brown's 1859 raid on Harpers Ferry, southern independence. Whether this generational dynamic extended beyond Virginia remains to be seen. But other recent works, including Stephen Berry's study of young white men in the Old South and Jon Grinspan's essay on youthful Republicans during the 1860 presidential campaign, indicate that similar concerns about progress, decline, and sectional destiny haunted many young minds on the eve of the Civil War. More work in this area is necessary, especially on how members of the new generation remembered the sectional conflict that had been raging since before they were born. Clearly, though, the generation that ascended to national leadership during the 1850s came of age in a very different world than had its predecessor. Further analysis of this shift promises to link the insights of the long sectional conflict approach (particularly regarding public memory) with the emphasis on late 1840s discontinuity that veins recent scholarship on sectionalism.[18]

The Historian's Use of Sectionalism and Vice Versa

Recent historians have challenged conventional periodization by expanding the chronological scope of the sectional conflict, even as they confirm two key moments of historical discontinuity. This work revises older interpretations of Civil War causation without overturning them. A second trend in the literature, however, is potentially more provocative. A number of powerfully argued studies building on David Potter's classic essay, "The Historian's Use of Nationalism and Vice Versa," have answered his call for closer scrutiny of the "seemingly manifest difference between the loyalties of a nationalistic North and a sectionalistic South." Impatient with historians who read separatism into all aspects of prewar southern politics or Unionism into all things northern, Potter admonished scholars not to project Civil War loyalties back into the antebellum period. A more nuanced approach would reveal "that in the North as well as in the South there were deep sectional impulses, and support or nonsupport of the Union was sometimes a

---

[18] The classic statement of this "revisionist" interpretation is J. G. Randall, "The Blundering Generation," *Mississippi Valley Historical Review*, 27 (June 1940), 3–28. For a different psychological interpretation of generational influences on politics, see George B. Forgie, *Patricide in the House Divided: A Psychological Interpretation of Lincoln and His Age* (New York, 1979). For a generational analysis of the rise of immediate abolitionism around 1830, see James L. Huston, "The Experiential Basis of the Northern Antislavery Impulse," *Journal of Southern History*, 56 (Nov. 1990), 633–35. Peter S. Carmichael, *The Last Generation: Young Virginians in Peace, War, and Reunion* (Chapel Hill, 2005). Earlier works that emphasize secession's popularity among youthful southern whites include William L. Barney, *The Secessionist Impulse: Alabama and Mississippi in 1860* (Princeton, 1974); and Henry James Walker, "Henry Clayton and the Secession Movement in Alabama," *Southern Studies*, 4 (Winter 1993), 341–60. Stephen W. Berry II, *All That Makes a Man: Love and Ambition in the Civil War South* (New York, 2003); Jon Grinspan, "'Young Men for War': The Wide Awakes and Lincoln's 1860 Presidential Campaign," *Journal of American History*, 96 (Sept. 2009), 357–78.

matter of sectional tactics rather than of national loyalty." Recent scholars have accepted Potter's challenge, and their findings contribute to an emerging reinterpretation of the sectional conflict and the timing of secession.[19]

Disentangling northern from national interests and values has been difficult thanks in part to the Civil War itself (in which "the North" and "the Union" overlapped, albeit imperfectly) and because of the northern victory and the temptation to classify the Old South as an un-American aberration. But several recent studies have risen to the task. Challenging the notion that the antebellum North must have been nationalistic because of its opposition to slavery and its role in the Civil War, Susan-Mary Grant argues that by the 1850s a stereotyped view of the South and a sense of moral and economic superiority had created a powerful northern sectional identity. Championed by the Republican party, this identity flowered into an exclusionary nationalism in which the South served as a negative reference point for the articulation of ostensibly national values, goals, and identities based on the North's flattering self-image. This sectionalism-cum-nationalism eventually corroded national ties by convincing northerners that the South represented an internal threat to the nation. Although this vision became genuinely national after the war, in the antebellum period it was sectionally specific and bitterly divisive. "It was not the case," Grant concludes, "that the northern ideology of the antebellum period was American, truly national, and supportive of the Union and the southern ideology was wholly sectional and destructive of the Union." Matthew Mason makes a related point about early national politics, noting that the original sectionalists were antislavery New England Federalists whose flirtation with secession in 1815 crippled their party. Never simply the repository of authentic American values, the nineteenth-century North developed a sectional identity in opposition to an imagined (though not fictitious) South. Only victory in the Civil War allowed for the reconstruction of the rest of the nation in this image.[20]

If victory in the war obscured northern sectionalism, it was the defense of slavery, coupled with defeat, that has distorted our view of American nationalism in the Old South. The United States was founded as a slaveholding nation, and there was unfortunately nothing necessarily un-American about slavery in the early nineteenth century. Slavery existed in tension with, not purely in opposition to, the nation's perennially imperfect political institutions, and its place in the young republic was a hotly contested question with a highly contingent resolution. Moreover, despite their pretensions to being an embattled minority, southern elites long succeeded in harnessing national ideals and federal power to their own interests. Thus, defense of slavery was neither inevitably nor invariably secessionist. This is a key theme of Robert Bonner's expertly crafted history of the rise and fall of proslavery American nationalism. Adopting a long-sectional-conflict perspective, Bonner challenges historians who have "conflate[d] an understandable revulsion at proslavery ideology with a willful disassociation of bondage from prevailing American norms." He details the efforts of proslavery southerners to integrate slavery into national identity and policy and to harmonize slaveholding with American

---

[19] David M. Potter, "The Historian's Use of Nationalism and Vice Versa," in *South and the Sectional Conflict*, by Potter, 34–83, esp. 75, 65.

[20] Grant, *North over South*, 6; Mason, *Slavery and Politics in the Early American Republic*, 42–74. See also Kevin M. Gannon, "Calculating the Value of Union: States' Rights, Nullification, and Secession in the North, 1800–1848" (Ph.D. diss., University of South Carolina, 2002).

expansionism, republicanism, constitutionalism, and evangelicalism. Appropriating the quintessentially American sense of national purpose, proslavery nationalists "invited outsiders to consider [slavery's] compatibility with broadly shared notions of American values and visions of a globally redeeming national mission." This effort ended in defeat, but not because proslavery southerners chronically privileged separatism over nationalism. Rather, it was their failure to bind slavery to American nationalism—signaled by the Republican triumph in 1860—that finally drove slaveholders to secede. Lincoln's victory "effectively ended the prospects for achieving proslavery Americanism within the federal Union," forcing slavery's champions to pin their hopes to a new nation-state. Confederate nationalism was more a response to the demise of proslavery American nationalism than the cause of its death.[21]

Other recent studies of slaveholders' efforts to nationalize their goals and interests complement Bonner's skilled analysis. Matthew J. Karp casts proslavery politicians not as jumpy sectionalists but as confident imperialists who sponsored an ambitious and costly expansion of American naval power to protect slavery against foreign encroachment and to exert national influence overseas. For these slaveholding nationalists, "federal power was not a danger to be feared, but a force to be utilized," right up to the 1860 election. Similarly, Brian Schoen has explored cotton planters' efforts to ensure that national policy on tariff rates and slavery's territorial status remained favorable to their interests. As cotton prices boomed during the 1850s, planters grew richer and the stakes grew higher, especially as their national political power waned with the ascension of the overtly sectional Republican party. The simultaneous increase in planters' economic might and decline in their political dominance made for an explosive mixture that shattered the bonds of the Union. Still, one must not focus solely on cases in which proslavery nationalism was thwarted, for its successes convinced many northerners of the veracity of the slave power thesis, helping further corrode the Union. James L. Huston shows that both southern efforts to nationalize property rights in slaves and the prospect of slavery becoming a national institution—in the sense that a fully integrated national market could bring slave and free labor into competition—fueled northern sectionalism and promoted the rise of the Republican party. Proslavery nationalism and its policy implications thus emboldened the political party whose victory in 1860 convinced proslavery southerners that their goals could not be realized within the Union.[22]

---

[21] Robert E. Bonner, *Mastering America: Southern Slaveholders and the Crisis of American Nationhood* (New York, 2009), xv, 84, 217. On slaveholders' influence over national policy and their use of federal power to advance proslavery interests, see Don E. Fehrenbacher, *The Slaveholding Republic: An Account of the United States Government's Relations to Slavery,* completed and ed. Ward M. McAfee (New York, 2001); Robin L. Einhorn, *American Taxation, American Slavery* (Chicago, 2006); and George William Van Cleve, *A Slaveholders' Union: Slavery, Politics, and the Constitution in the Early Republic* (Chicago, 2010). For a work that argues that the slave power thesis was not mere paranoia and disputes the dismissive interpretation of earlier historians, see Richards, *Slave Power.* Works that Leonard Richards disputes include Chauncey S. Boucher, "*In re* That Aggressive Slavocracy," *Mississippi Valley Historical Review,* 8 (June–Sept. 1921), 13–79; and David Brion Davis, *The Slave Power Conspiracy and the Paranoid Style* (Baton Rouge, 1970). The painful shift from proslavery American nationalism to proslavery southern nationalism can be traced in the career of the Alabama Whig Henry Washington Hilliard. See David I. Durham, *A Southern Moderate in Radical Times: Henry Washington Hilliard, 1808–1892* (Baton Rouge, 2008).

[22] Matthew J. Karp, "Slavery and American Sea Power: The Navalist Impulse in the Antebellum South," *Journal of Southern History,* 77 (May 2011), 283–324, esp. 290; Schoen, *Fragile Fabric of Union,* 197–259; James L. Huston, *Calculating the Value of the Union: Slavery, Property Rights, and the Economic Origins of the Civil War* (Chapel Hill, 2003).

As the standard-bearers of northern and southern interests battled for national power, both sides emphasized that their respective ideologies were consistent with the nation's most cherished principles. Shearer Davis Bowman has argued that "northern and southern partisans of white sectionalism tended to see their respective sections as engaged in the high-minded defense of vested interests, outraged rights and liberties, and imperiled honor, all embedded in a society and way of life they deemed authentically American." In a sense, both sides were right. Recent scholarship in such varied fields as intellectual, religious, political, and literary history suggests that although often incompatible, the values and ideals of the contending sections flowed from a common source. Work by Margaret Abruzzo on proslavery and antislavery humanitarianism, John Patrick Daly and Mark A. Noll on evangelical Protestantism, Sean Wilentz on political democracy, and Diane N. Capitani on domestic sentimental fiction suggests that the highly politicized differences between northern and southern ideologies masked those ideologies' common intellectual roots. Some scholars have argued for more fundamental difference, maintaining that southern thinkers roundly rejected democracy and liberal capitalism, while others have gone too far in the other direction in presenting northern and southern whites as equally committed to liberalism. But the dominant thrust of recent work on sectional ideologies suggests that they represented two hostile sides of a single coin minted at the nation's founding. Since a coin flip cannot end in a tie, both sides struggled for control of the national government to put their incompatible ideals into practice. The nationalization of northern ideals was a hotly contested outcome, made possible only by armed conflict. Conversely, the sectionalization of white southern ideals was not inevitable. Proponents of both sections drew on nationalism and sectionalism alike, embracing the former when they felt powerful and the latter when they felt weak. "As long as the Government is on our side," proslavery Democrat and future South Carolina governor Francis W. Pickens wrote in 1857, "I am for sustaining it and using its power for our benefit.... [if] our opponents reverse the present state of things *then* I am *for war*."[23]

Together, recent studies of northern sectionalism and southern nationalism make a compelling case for why the Civil War broke out when it did. If the South was always a separatist minority and if the North always defended the American way, secession might

---

[23] Shearer Davis Bowman, *At the Precipice: Americans North and South during the Secession Crisis* (Chapel Hill, 2010), 12. Margaret Abruzzo, *Polemical Pain: Slavery, Cruelty, and the Rise of Humanitarianism* (Baltimore, 2011); John Patrick Daly, *When Slavery Was Called Freedom: Evangelicalism, Proslavery, and the Causes of the Civil War* (Lexington, Ky., 2002); Mark A. Noll, *The Civil War as a Theological Crisis* (Chapel Hill, 2006); Sean Wilentz, *The Rise of American Democracy: Jefferson to Lincoln* (New York, 2005), esp. xxii, 576, 791; Diane N. Capitani, *Truthful Pictures: Slavery Ordained by God in the Domestic Sentimental Novel of the Nineteenth-Century South* (Lanham, 2009). On the antidemocratic impulse behind secession in South Carolina and, ostensibly, the rest of the Confederacy, see Manisha Sinha, *The Counterrevolution of Slavery: Politics and Ideology in Antebellum South Carolina* (Chapel Hill, 2000). See also Patricia Roberts-Miller, *Fanatical Schemes: Proslavery Rhetoric and the Tragedy of Consensus* (Tuscaloosa, 2009). On the southern rejection of bourgeois liberalism and capitalism, see Elizabeth Fox-Genovese and Eugene D. Genovese, *The Mind of the Master Class: History and Faith in the Southern Slaveholders' Worldview* (New York, 2005); and Elizabeth Fox-Genovese and Eugene D. Genovese, *Slavery in White and Black: Class and Race in the Southern Slaveholders' New World Order* (New York, 2008). For the argument that both sections were equally dedicated to liberalism, see David F. Ericson, *The Debate over Slavery: Antislavery and Proslavery Liberalism in Antebellum America* (New York, 2000). For a compelling argument that secession stemmed from a fierce reaction against nineteenth-century liberal trends *and* from fealty to the true American republic, see McCurry, *Confederate Reckoning*, 12–13. Francis W. Pickens to Benjamin F. Perry, June 27, 1857, folder 3, box 1, B. F. Perry Papers (Southern Historical Collection, University of North Carolina, Chapel Hill). Emphasis in original.

well have come long before 1861. It is more helpful to view the sectional conflict as one between equally authentic (not morally equivalent) strands of American nationalism grappling for the power to govern the entire country according to sectionally specific values. Southern slaveholders ruled what was in many ways the weaker section, but constitutional privileges such as the infamous three-fifths clause, along with other advantageous provisions such as the rule requiring a two-thirds majority in the nominations of Democratic presidential candidates, allowed them to remain dominant prior to 1860, until their successes aroused a sense of *northern* sectionalism robust enough to lift the Republican party into power. Almost overnight, the proslavery nationalist project collapsed. Only then did decisive numbers of southern whites countenance disunion, a drastic measure whose use had long been resisted within the South. The Civil War erupted when northern sectionalism grew powerful enough to undermine southern nationalism.[24]

. . . With Liberty and Justice for Whom?

In the model of Civil War causation sketched above, northern voters who joined the Republicans fretted over the fate of liberty in a slaveholding republic. But whose liberty was at stake? Recent scholarship powerfully demonstrates that for moderate opponents of slavery the most damnable aspect of the institution was not what it did to slaves but what it allowed slaveholders to do to northern whites. Popular antislavery grew from trepidation about the power of the slaveholding class and its threat to republican liberty, not from uproar against proslavery racism and racial oppression. And since this concern fueled the Republican party's rapid growth and 1860 presidential triumph, white northerners' indignant response to slaveholders' clout contributed significantly to the coming of the war by providing secessionists with a pretext for disunion. According to this interpretation of northern politics, slavery remains at the root of the sectional conflict even though racial egalitarianism did not inspire the most popular brands of antislavery politics and even though many of the debates over slavery, as Eric Foner has pointed out, "were only marginally related to race." At the same time, recent scholarship on southern politics foregrounds slave agency and persuasively demonstrates that conflict between masters and slaves directly affected national affairs. If the fate of the enslaved did not preoccupy most northern whites, the same cannot be said of their southern counterparts, whose politics are intelligible only in the context of slave resistance. In sum, recent work confirms the centrality of slavery in the coming of the war in a very specific and nuanced way, showing that the actions and contested status of enslaved people influenced southern politics directly and northern politics more obliquely. This work reveals an asymmetry in the politics of slavery: in the South it revolved around maintaining control over slaves in the name of white supremacy and planters' interests, while in the North it centered on the problem of the slaveholding class.[25]

---

[24] On the fragility of an antebellum nationalism built on ideals that developed clashing sectional characteristics, see Melinda Lawson, *Patriot Fires: Forging a New American Nationalism in the Civil War North* (Lawrence, 2002), 8–9.

[25] This work expands on a theme advanced in Russel B. Nye, *Fettered Freedom: Civil Liberties and the Slavery Controversy, 1830–1860* (1949; East Lansing, 1964). Eric Foner, *The Fiery Trial: Abraham Lincoln and American Slavery* (New York, 2010), 120.

Some forty years ago, Larry Gara urged historians to make a "crucial distinction" between self-interested opposition to slaveholder power and moral opposition to slavery as an oppressive institution. Gara praised his contemporaries for restoring slavery to narratives of the sectional conflict but worried that "the impact of the new scholarship might prove more misleading than helpful." Recognizing that antiracism and support for African American civil rights informed scholarly interpretations of Civil War causation, Gara warned:

> Moral indignation at racial prejudice in the twentieth century does not necessarily provide the key to an understanding of the dispute between the sections in the nineteenth century. While some abolitionists were indignant at the slave system and what it did to black men, many more northerners became antisouthern and antislavery because of what the slave system did or threatened to do to them. A failure to recognize this can easily lead us into a blind alley of oversimplification, and to view the events of a hundred years ago as a morality play with heroes and villains rather than a plausible presentation of a human dilemma.

Most antislavery politicians and the northern voters who supported them, Gara argued, cared little about the sufferings of slaves. Instead, they "feared the effect of continued national rule by slaveholding interests on northern rights, on civil liberties, on desired economic measures and on the future of free white labor itself." Only by acknowledging this fact, Gara believed, could scholars understand Civil War causation *and* the postwar persistence of racial prejudice.[26]

Many twenty-first century scholars have taken this point to heart while implicitly challenging Gara's stark contrast between moral and self-interested antislavery. They stress the primary importance of white liberty in popular antislavery critiques but show that slavery's "moderate" opponents were no less morally outraged than their "radical" counterparts. Slavery could be condemned on moral grounds for a wide variety of reasons, some of which had much to do with enslaved people and some of which—whether they stressed the degeneracy of southern society, the undemocratic influence of slaveholders' political clout, or the threat that proslavery zealots posed to civil liberties—did not. Thus, recent scholars have made Gara's "crucial distinction" while underlining the moral dimensions of ostensibly moderate, conservative, or racist antislavery arguments. Popular antislavery strove to protect democratic politics from the machinations of a legally privileged and economically potent ruling class. Slaveholders' inordinate political power was itself a moral problem. These findings may prompt historians to reconsider the relative emphasis placed on class and race in the origins and meanings of the Civil War, particularly regarding the political behavior of the nonabolitionist northern majority.[27]

Numerous recent studies emphasize that perceived threats to white freedom pushed northerners to oppose the slave power, support the Republican party, and prosecute the Civil War on behalf of liberty and the Union. Nicole Etcheson's study of the violent struggle between proslavery and antislavery forces over Kansas during the mid-1850s contends that the key issue at stake was freedom for white settlers. During the Civil War many Kansans who had fought for the admission of their state under an antislavery

---

[26] Larry Gara, "Slavery and the Slave Power: A Crucial Distinction," *Civil War History,* 15 (March 1969), 5–18, esp. 9, 6.

[27] On the difficulty of placing antislavery activists on a spectrum of political opinion, see Frederick J. Blue, *No Taint of Compromise: Crusaders in Antislavery Politics* (Baton Rouge, 2005), 265.

constitution applauded emancipation, but Etcheson persuasively argues that "Bleeding Kansas began as a struggle to secure the political liberties of whites." Racist pioneers from both sections battled to ensure that the plains would remain a haven for white freedom, disagreeing primarily over slavery's compatibility with that goal. Similarly, Matthew Mason shows that antislavery politics in the early national period, spearheaded by Federalists, thrived only when northern voters recognized "how slavery impinged on their rights and interests." Russell McClintock's analysis of the 1860 election and northerners' reaction to secession and the bombardment of Fort Sumter indicates that anxiety over slaveholders' power encouraged a decisive, violent northern response. As the antislavery position edged closer to the mainstream of northern politics, critiques of slavery grounded in sympathy for enslaved people faded as less philanthropic assaults on the institution proliferated. Carol Lasser's study of the shifting emphasis of antislavery rhetoric demonstrates that between the 1830s and the 1850s, "self-interest replaced sin as a basis for antislavery organizing," as antislavery appeals increasingly "stressed the self-interest of northern farmers and workers—mainly white and mainly male." Ultimately, popular antislavery cast "free white men, rather than enslaved African American women," as "the victims of 'the peculiar institution.'"[28]

Even histories of fugitive slave cases underscore the preeminence of white liberty as the activating concern for many northerners. As the historian Earl M. Maltz has pointed out, the fugitive slave issue was never isolated from other political controversies. Thanks to the Kansas-Nebraska Act, which seemed to prove the existence of a southern plot to spread slavery onto previously free western soil, fugitive slave cases during and after 1854 aroused increased hostility among white northerners who suspected that slaveholders threatened the liberties of all Americans. Those fears intensified throughout the 1850s in response to cases in which free northerners stood trial for violation of the Fugitive Slave Act. In two of the three cases explored by Steven Lubet the defendants were not runaway slaves but predominantly white northerners accused of abetting fugitives from slavery. The Fugitive Slave Act's criminalization of noncompliance with slave catchers proved especially odious. "For all of its blatant unfairness," Lubet argues, "the Act might have been considered tolerable in the North—at least among non-abolitionists—if it had been directed only at blacks." It was not, of course, and some of the act's most celebrated cases placed white northerners in legal jeopardy for crossing swords with the slave power. Two recent studies of the Joshua Glover case reinforce this point. Formerly a slave in St. Louis, Glover escaped to Wisconsin and, with the help of sympathetic white residents, from there to Canada in 1854. But the dramatic confrontation between free-state citizens and the slaveholder-dominated federal government only began with Glover's successful flight, since the political reverberations of the case echoed for many years after Glover reached Canadian soil. Debates over the rights and duties of citizens, over the boundaries of state and federal sovereignty, and over the constitutionality of the Fugitive Slave Act hinged on the prosecution of the primarily white Wisconsinites who aided

[28] Nicole Etcheson, *Bleeding Kansas: Contested Liberty in the Civil War Era* (Lawrence, 2004), 8; Mason, *Slavery and Politics in the Early American Republic*, 5; McClintock, *Lincoln and the Decision for War*, 26–28. On the importance of "the Union"—antebellum shorthand for an experiment in democratic self-government freighted with world-historical significance—in arousing the northern war effort, see Gary W. Gallagher, *The Union War* (Cambridge, Mass., 2011). Carol Lasser, "Voyeuristic Abolitionism: Sex, Gender, and the Transformation of Antislavery Rhetoric," *Journal of the Early Republic*, 28 (Spring 2008), 113, 112.

Glover's escape. None gained more notoriety than Sherman Booth, the Milwaukee newspaper editor whose case bounced between state and federal courts from 1854 to 1859, and whose attorney, Byron Paine, capitalized on his own resulting popularity to win a seat on the Wisconsin Supreme Court. Long after attention left Glover, who was undoubtedly relieved to be out of the public eye, conflicts over northern state rights and individual rights highlighted the threat to white liberty posed by the slave power and its federal agents.[29]

Of course, the white northerners prosecuted under proslavery law would have remained in obscurity if not for the daring escapes made by enslaved people. As Stanley Harrold has shown, runaway slaves sparked dozens of bloody skirmishes in the antebellum borderland between slavery and freedom. To stress the importance of conflicts over white liberty in the coming of the Civil War is not to ignore the political impact of slave resistance. Quite the reverse: recent studies of Civil War causation have deftly explored the relationship between slave agency and sectional antagonism, revealing that slave resistance provoked conflict between whites, even in situations where racial justice was not the main point of contention. Northern sectionalism was a reaction against proslavery belligerence, which was fueled by internal conflicts in the South. Narratives of Civil War causation that focus on white northerners' fears for their liberties depend on slave agency, for the aggressiveness of the slave power was, essentially, a response to the power of slaves.[30]

Revealingly, recent works by John Ashworth and William W. Freehling both stress this theme. Both scholars published long-awaited second volumes of their accounts of Civil War causation in 2007. Beyond this coincidence, however, it would be difficult to find two historians more dissimilar than Ashworth, a Marxist who privileges labor systems and class relations, and Freehling, a master storyteller who stresses contingency and individual consciousness. For all their methodological and ideological differences, however, Ashworth and Freehling concur on an essential point: the struggle between masters and slaves accelerated the sectional conflict by forcing masters to support undemocratic policies that threatened northern liberties. The resulting hostility of northerners toward slaveholders provoked a fierce response, and the cycle continued. By weaving the day-to-day contest between masters and slaves into their political analyses, both authors fashion a "reintegrated" American history that blends the insights of social and political history.[31]

---

[29] Earl M. Maltz, *Fugitive Slave on Trial: The Anthony Burns Case and Abolitionist Outrage* (Lawrence, 2010), 54. Steven Lubet, *Fugitive Justice: Runaways, Rescuers, and Slavery on Trial* (Cambridge, Mass., 2010), 44. The white defendants Steven Lubet examines are Castner Hanway, charged with treason for his involvement in an 1851 Christiana, Pennsylvania, clash, and Simeon Bushnell, a participant in an 1858 Oberlin, Ohio, slave rescue. The third case Lubet looks at is that of the fugitive slave Anthony Burns. H. Robert Baker, *The Rescue of Joshua Glover: A Fugitive Slave, the Constitution, and the Coming of the Civil War* (Athens, Ohio, 2006); Ruby West Jackson and Walter T. McDonald, *Finding Freedom: The Untold Story of Joshua Glover, Runaway Slave* (Madison, 2007).

[30] Stanley Harrold, *Border War: Fighting over Slavery before the Civil War* (Chapel Hill, 2010). On fugitive slaves and national politics, see R. J. M. Blackett, "Dispossessing Massa: Fugitive Slaves and the Politics of Slavery after 1850," *American Nineteenth Century History,* 10 (June 2009), 119–36.

[31] John Ashworth, *Slavery, Capitalism, and Politics in the Antebellum Republic,* vol. I: *Commerce and Compromise, 1820–1850* (New York, 1995); Ashworth, *Slavery, Capitalism, and Politics in the Antebellum Republic,* II; William W. Freehling, *The Road to Disunion,* vol. II: *Secessionists Triumphant, 1854–1961* (New York, 2007). For an exploration of their differences, see John Ashworth, "William W. Freehling and the Politics of the Old South," *American Nineteenth Century History,* 5 (Spring 2004), 1–29. On the "reintegration" of political and social history, see William W. Freehling, *The Reintegration of American History: Slavery and the Civil War* (New York, 1994).

According to Ashworth, class conflict forced ruling elites in both sections to pursue clashing political and economic policies. Thus, structural divergence in social and economic systems between North and South inflamed the political and ideological strife that resulted in disunion. Class conflict was especially problematic in the South, whose enslaved population did not accept proslavery principles in the same way that, by the 1850s, some northern workers embraced free-labor ideology. Instead, interminable slave resistance compelled southern masters to gag congressional debate over slavery, to demand stringent fugitive slave laws, and to agitate for a territorial slave code—in short, to act the part of an authoritarian slave power. "Behind every event in the history of the sectional controversy," Ashworth argues in his first volume, "lurked the consequences of black resistance to slavery." A dozen years of additional work confirmed this thesis. In his second volume, Ashworth contends that "the opposition of the slaves to their own enslavement is the fundamental, irreplaceable cause of the War." The Civil War did not begin as a massive slave rebellion because southern masters managed to contain the unrest that threatened their rule, but the price of this success was a deteriorating relationship with northerners. By contending for their freedom, slaves obliged their masters to behave in ways that convinced even the most bigoted northern whites that slavery menaced their own liberties.[32]

Freehling tells a similar tale in his own inimitable idiom. At the outset of the second volume of *The Road to Disunion,* he points to the underlying tension between slavery and democracy in antebellum America, referring to the Old South's

> colliding democratic and despotic governing systems. The Old South combined dictatorship over blacks with republicanism for whites, supposedly cleanly severed by an All-Mighty Color Line. But to preserve dictatorial dominion over blacks, the slaveholding minority sometimes trenched on majoritarian government for whites, in the nation as well as in their section. . . . Northerners called the militant slavocracy the Slave Power, meaning that those with autocratic power over blacks also deployed undemocratic power over whites. Most Yankees hardly embraced blacks or abolitionists. Yet racist Northerners would fight the Slave Power to the death to preserve their white men's majoritarian rights.

Like Ashworth, Freehling recognizes that the preservation of "dictatorship over blacks" would have been simple if slaves had been contented and docile—and so it was anything but simple. "The nature of masters' dictatorship over blacks compelled their partial closure of republicanism for whites. Furthermore, the nature of slaves' resistances propelled their uninvited (and important) intrusions into white men's political upheavals." Proslavery southerners insisted that slavery bolstered white democracy, but their response to slave resistance convinced many northerners that slaveholders were aristocratic bullies. In Ashworth's and Freehling's capable hands, the story of the sectional conflict over slavery appears far more complicated than the "morality play" that Gara rightly criticized four decades ago. Without the threat to northern liberties posed by the slave power, most northern whites would not have welcomed the Republican party's moderate strain of antislavery politics. Although slaves themselves did not always figure prominently in the moderate antislavery argument, slave resistance ultimately made the slave power thesis plausible.[33]

[32] Ashworth, *Slavery, Capitalism, and Politics in the Antebellum Republic,* I, 6, II, 1.
[33] Freehling, *Road to Disunion,* II, xii, xiii. On the relationship between slave resistance and politics in antebellum Virginia, see William A. Link, *Roots of Secession: Slavery and Politics in Antebellum Virginia* (Chapel Hill,

Scholars who foreground northern concern for white liberty in a slaveholding republic underline the importance of class conflict between northern voters and southern elites in the coming of the Civil War. Moderate antislavery northerners condemned slaveholders for aristocratic pretensions and tyrannical policies, not for racial bigotry. But for many scholars, race remains the key to understanding antebellum sectional politics. The tendency remains strong to frame the sectional conflict and the Civil War as one campaign in a longer struggle for racial justice. Not surprisingly, studies of radical abolitionism are the most likely works to employ this framework. Radical abolitionists nurtured a strikingly egalitarian conception of race and fought for a social vision that most scholars share but one that the modern world has not yet realized, and therein lies their appeal. Moreover, those who foreground race in the coming of the war do not naïvely suggest that all northern whites were racial egalitarians. Since the 1960s, commitment to an admirable antiracist ideal, not wishful thinking, has given a powerful boost to a primarily racial interpretation of the sectional conflict. But the recent scholarly emphasis on issues of class and the slave power suggests that framing the sectional conflict as a clash over racial injustice is not the most useful approach to understanding Civil War causation.[34]

The slave power was defined not by racism but by slaveholders' capacity to use federal law and muscle to advance their class interests. Proslavery racism was, like all racism, reprehensible, but it is easily, even when subtly, overstated in accounts of Civil War causation. It is, for example, hardly incorrect to refer to the proslavery ideologue James Henry Hammond as "a fiercely racist South Carolina politician," but that characterization emphasizes a trait he shared with most northern voters rather than what alienated Hammond from them and thus hastened the rise of the Republican party and the outbreak of war. What distinguished Hammond from his northern antagonists was his "mudsill" theory of society (which he outlined in an 1858 Senate speech) and its implications for American class relations. Proceeding from the presumption that every functioning society must rest upon the labors of a degraded "mudsill" class, Hammond argued that the southern laboring class, because it was enslaved, was materially better off and politically less threatening than its northern counterpart. Hammond's highly public articulation of this theory outraged proponents of free labor and made him a particularly notorious proslavery propagandist. Illinois Republicans who rallied under a banner declaring "Small-Fisted Farmers, Mud Sills of Society, Greasy Mechanics, for A. Lincoln" recognized the deep-seated class dimensions of their party's conflict with Hammond and his ilk. Moreover, Hammond's comparison of the northern and southern working classes suggests a curious ambiguity in the relative importance of class and race in proslavery ideology. This subject demands further scholarly attention, but important advances have recently been made. On the one hand, Elizabeth Fox-Genovese and Eugene D. Genovese have indicated that the irascible George Fitzhugh, who proclaimed

---

2003). On the political consequences of mass panic over suspected slave revolts in 1860, see Donald E. Reynolds, *Texas Terror: The Slave Insurrection Panic of 1860 and the Secession of the Lower South* (Baton Rouge, 2007).

[34] John Stauffer, *The Black Hearts of Men: Radical Abolitionists and the Transformation of Race* (Cambridge, Mass., 2001); David S. Reynolds, *John Brown, Abolitionist: The Man Who Killed Slavery, Sparked the Civil War, and Seeded Civil Rights* (New York, 2005); Fergus M. Bordewich, *Bound for Canaan: The Epic Story of the Underground Railroad, America's First Civil Rights Movement* (New York, 2006); James Brewer Stewart, *Abolitionist Politics and the Coming of the Civil War* (Amherst, 2008); Ford Risley, *Abolition and the Press: The Moral Struggle against Slavery* (Evanston, 2008).

that working people of all colors would be better off as slaves, was not alone in developing a defense of slavery compatible with racism but ultimately based on class relations.
On the other hand, slaveholders, at least as much as any other antebellum Americans,
benefited from portraying slavery as a fundamentally racial issue. As Frank Towers has
shown, planters feared the day when nonslaveholding southern whites might begin to
think in terms of class and shuddered at the prospect of working-class politics in southern cities. That one of the most strident articulations of the race-based proslavery
argument—which promised that the subjugation of blacks made equals of all white
men—appeared in 1860 was no coincidence, as southern elites sought to ensure regional
white unity on the eve of a possible revolution. In pursuit of their interests, southern
ideologues drew on both class- and race-based arguments, and if the latter stand out to
modern readers, the former did more to alienate individuals in the free states. Slaveholders' conflict with northern voters, the collision that triggered secession and war, grew not
out of clashing racial views but out of competition for political power.[35]

The most broadly appealing brands of antislavery defined this competition as one
between classes. Proponents of popular antislavery presented sectional issues in terms of
class more often than race, and with tremendous effect. Their interpretation of sectional
friction generated mass sympathy for a cause that otherwise would have remained a
fringe movement. This moderate antislavery ideology is easily discounted if we attribute
genuine antislavery sentiments only to those few northerners uncontaminated by racism.
It grew from many sources: Jacksonian antipathy to concentrated economic and political
power; an often-radical producerism that would guarantee to the worker the fruits of his
labor; a demand for land reform that would reserve western soil for white farmers; and a
morally charged concern about the fate of democracy in a nation dominated by slaveholders. Class-based Jacksonian radicalism thus informed the ideology of the Free Soil
party and, crucially, the Republicans. Antislavery politicians such as New Hampshire's
John P. Hale, a Democrat who drifted into the Republican ranks via the Free Soil party,
"defined the controversy over slavery and its continuation as an issue between aristocratic
slave owners and 'sturdy republicans' rather than between innocent slaves and sinful
masters," points out Jonathan H. Earle. It was this contest that aroused a northern
majority to vote Lincoln into office and to enlist in the Union army. The issues of
money, power, class, and democracy that concerned Jacksonian and other moderate antislavery northerners were not less morally charged because they focused on white liberty
and equality in a republic. Nor should we forget that this class-based antislavery critique
contained the seeds of a racial egalitarianism that sprouted, however feebly, during the
Civil War. The experience of war often turned whites-only egalitarianism into a far more

---

[35] Varon, *Disunion!*, 103. Elizabeth Varon mentions the speech but not its impact on northern workers. See
ibid., 308–10. For the class implications of James Henry Hammond's theory, see Samantha Maziarz, "Mudsill
Theory," in *Class in America: An Encyclopedia*, ed. Robert E. Weir (3 vols., Westport, 2007), II, 549–50. On
northerners' response to the speech, see Drew Gilpin Faust, *James Henry Hammond and the Old South: A Design
for Mastery* (Baton Rouge, 1982), 347. On the Republican banner, see McPherson, *Battle Cry of Freedom*, 196–98.
Fox-Genovese and Genovese, *Slavery in White and Black*. Frank Towers, *The Urban South and the Coming of the
Civil War* (Charlottesville, 2004). J. D. B. DeBow, *The Interest in Slavery of the Southern Non-slaveholder: The Right
of Peaceful Secession; Slavery in the Bible* (Charleston, 1860). On elite secessionists' heavy-handed efforts to mobilize
nonslaveholding whites behind secession and the only partial success of racist demagoguery, see McCurry, *Confederate Reckoning*, 38–84.

sweeping notion of human equality. To ignore this transformation is to discount the radicalizing influence that the Civil War had on many northern soldiers and civilians.[36]

When coupled with an analysis of southern politics that emphasizes slave agency, this revival of scholarly interest in popular antislavery ideology offers not only a convincing interpretation of Civil War causation but also a politically and pedagogically important narrative about class and politics in American history. Adam Rothman's 2005 essay on the slave power is a model of this fresh and constructive approach. On one level, he presents an accessible introduction to the history and historiography of nineteenth-century slaveholders. But the chief contribution of the work lies in the context in which the essay was published: an anthology on American elite classes, from early national merchant capitalists to postwar anti–New Dealers, and their relationship with American democracy. Casting the slave power in this light gives the sectional conflict a bold new meaning, one that reveals the Civil War to have been both much more than and much less than a precursor to the civil rights movement. It appears as a struggle between (an imperfect) popular democracy and one of the most powerful and deeply rooted interests in antebellum politics. One might argue that Americans simply replaced one set of masters—southern planters—with another, the rising robber barons. Nevertheless, the Civil War offers one of precious few instances in American history in which a potent, entrenched, incredibly wealthy, and constitutionally privileged elite class was thoroughly ousted from national power. This makes the class-based issues that helped spark the war too important to forget.[37]

That narrative may also aid in the quest for that holy grail of academic history: a receptive public audience. The neo-Confederate outcry against the alleged anti-southern bias of McPherson's 2000 "What Caused the Civil War?" essay and the ongoing controversy over the Confederate flag indicate that much of the public does not share in the scholarly consensus on slavery's central place in Civil War causation. Unfortunately, no quick fix exists for popular misconceptions about the war, but scholarship that frames the conflict over slavery as a struggle in which the liberties of all Americans were at stake may influence minds closed to depictions of the war as an antiracist crusade. This is not to argue that historians should pander to popular prejudice or that race is not a central theme in the history of the Civil War era. Rather, historians can and should capitalize on the political and pedagogical advantages of an important body of scholarship that sharpens our understanding of Civil War causation by explaining why even incorrigible

---

[36] In his vindication of Jacksonian antislavery, Daniel Feller criticizes the "fixation with race" that leads too many scholars "to question the sincerity or good intentions of any but the most outspoken racial egalitarians among the opponents of slavery." Daniel Feller, "A Brother in Arms: Benjamin Tappan and the Antislavery Democracy," *Journal of American History*, 88 (June 2001), 50. Jonathan H. Earle, *Jacksonian Antislavery and the Politics of Free Soil, 1824–1854* (Chapel Hill, 2004), 92; Feller, "Brother in Arms"; Suzanne Cooper Guasco, "'The Deadly Influence of Negro Capitalists': Southern Yeomen and Resistance to the Expansion of Slavery in Illinois," *Civil War History*, 47 (March 2001), 7–29; Sean Wilentz, "Jeffersonian Democracy and the Origins of Political Antislavery in the United States: The Missouri Crisis Revisited," *Journal of the Historical Society*, 4 (Sept. 2004), 375–401. Etcheson, *Bleeding Kansas*, 190–253; Chandra Manning, *What This Cruel War Was Over: Soldiers, Slavery, and the Civil War* (New York, 2007), 12, 221; Mark E. Neely Jr., "Politics Purified: Religion and the Growth of Antislavery Idealism in Republican Ideology during the Civil War," in *The Birth of the Grand Old Party: The Republicans' First Generation*, ed. Robert F. Engs and Randall M. Miller (Philadelphia, 2002), 103–27.

[37] Adam Rothman, "The 'Slave Power' in the United States, 1783–1865," in *Ruling America: A History of Wealth and Power in a Democracy*, ed. Steve Fraser and Gary Gerstle (Cambridge, Mass., 2005), 64–91. On the collapse of planters' national power, despite their continued regional dominance, see Steven Hahn, "Class and State in Postemancipation Societies: Southern Planters in Comparative Perspective," *American Historical Review*, 95 (Feb. 1990), 75–98.

northern racists voted and fought against southern slaveholders, and that reminds us that slavery impacted all antebellum Americans, North and South, black and white. When northerners urged the "necessity" of defending their liberty against the encroaching "tyranny" of a government "under the absolute control of an oligarchy of southern slave holders," as Judge F. C. White of Utica, New York, wrote in 1858, they meant precisely what they said. To gainsay the salience of race in the causes, course, and outcome of the Civil War would be a terrible mistake, but it would be equally misleading to neglect the matters of class, power, and democracy at the heart of the slavery debate; these issues contributed mightily to the origins of the nation's bloodiest conflict and to its modern-day significance.[38]

Whatever its ultimate fate in the classroom and public discourse, recent scholarship on the coming of the Civil War reveals an impatience with old interpretive categories, an eagerness to challenge the basic parameters that have long guided scholarly thinking on the topic, and a healthy skepticism of narratives that explain the war with comforting, simplistic formulae. The broad consensus on slavery's centrality has not stifled rapid growth and diversification in the field. Indeed, the proliferation of works on Civil War causation presents a serious challenge to anyone seeking to synthesize the recent literature into a single tidy interpretation. Rather than suggest an all-encompassing model, this essay has outlined three broad themes that could provide fertile ground for future debate. A reaction against the expanding geographic and temporal breadth of Civil War causation studies, for example, might prompt scholars to return to tightly focused, state-level analyses of antebellum politics. Recent political histories of antebellum Mississippi and Louisiana suggest that this approach has much to contribute to our understanding of how national debates filtered down to state and local levels. Other scholars might take an explicitly comparative approach and analyze the causes, course, and results of the American Civil War alongside those of roughly contemporaneous intrastate conflicts, including the Reform War (1857–1861) in Mexico and China's Taiping Rebellion (1850–1864). Comparative history's vast potential has been amply demonstrated by Enrico Dal Lago's study of agrarian elites and regionalism in the Old South and Italy, and by Don H. Doyle's edited collection on secession movements around the globe. Similarly, scholars undoubtedly will challenge the interpretive emphases on proslavery American nationalism, antislavery northern sectionalism, and the class dimensions of the sectional conflict that pervade much of the recent scholarship and receive close attention in this essay. But others might carry on this work by studying phenomena such as the disunionist thrust of radical abolitionism. The campaign for free-state secession never sank deep roots in northern soil. But by the late 1850s it was a frequent topic of editorials in abolitionist publications such as the *National Anti-Slavery Standard,* and it captured mainstream headlines through events such as the 1857 Worcester Disunion Convention.

[38] F. C. White to John P. Hale, Feb. 16, 1858, folder 8, box 12, John P. Hale Papers (New Hampshire Historical Society, Concord). On the response to McPherson's essay, see John M. Coski, "Historians under Fire: The Public and the Memory of the Civil War," *Cultural Resource Management,* 25 (no. 4, 2002), 13–15. On the Confederate flag controversy, see J. Michael Martinez, William D. Richardson, and Ron McNinch-Su, eds., *Confederate Symbols in the Contemporary South* (Gainesville, 2000); K. Michael Prince, *Rally 'Round the Flag, Boys! South Carolina and the Confederate Flag* (Columbia, S.C., 2004); and John M. Coski, *The Confederate Battle Flag: America's Most Embattled Emblem* (Cambridge, Mass., 2005).

And even if race, southern sectionalism, and northern Unionism dominate future narratives of Civil War causation, further debate will sharpen our analysis of an easily mythologized period of American history.[39]

These debates will be no less meaningful because of scholars' near-universal acknowledgement of the centrality of slavery in the coming of the Civil War. Instead, they illustrate C. Vann Woodward's observation that "most of the important debates over history . . . have not been about absolute but about relative matters, not about the existence but about the degree or extent of the phenomenon in question." Beneath a veneer of consensus lies interpretive nuance and healthy disagreement, which we can hope will inform both academic and popular commemoration of the Civil War sesquicentennial.[40]

[39] Christopher J. Olsen, *Political Culture and Secession in Mississippi: Masculinity, Honor, and the Antiparty Tradition, 1830–1860* (New York, 2000); John M. Sacher, *A Perfect War of Politics: Parties, Politicians, and Democracy in Louisiana, 1824–1861* (Baton Rouge, 2003). Enrico Dal Lago, *Agrarian Elites: American Slaveholders and Southern Italian Landowners, 1815–1861* (Baton Rouge, 2005); Don H. Doyle, ed., *Secession as an International Phenomenon: From America's Civil War to Contemporary Separatist Movements* (Athens, Ga., 2010). On the Worcester Disunion Convention, see Eric Foner, *Free Soil, Free Labor, Free Men: The Ideology of the Republican Party before the Civil War* (New York, 1995), 140–41; and Ericson, *Debate over Slavery*, 74–79.

[40] C. Vann Woodward, *Thinking Back: The Perils of Writing History* (Baton Rouge, 1986), 79.

"Apostles of Fascism," "Communist Clergy," and the UAW: Political Ideology and Working-Class Religion in Detroit, 1919–1945

Matthew Pehl

Zygmund Dobrzynski, the national director of the Ford Motor Company organizing drive for the United Automobile Workers of America (UAW), attended a religious revival in 1938. Leading the service was the pugnacious Southern Baptist preacher J. Frank Norris. Four years earlier Norris had accepted the pastorate at Detroit's Temple Baptist Church, aiming his fundamentalist ministry at the thousands of working-class southern whites who had been drawn north by the lure of industrial jobs. At this particular revival Norris was flanked by the sheriff of the Flint, Michigan, police department and a prominent executive of the Ford Motor Company, and he produced a typically ebullient performance: burning a Soviet flag, denouncing unionism, and promoting a nationalistic Americanism. To a stunned Dobrzynski, Norris seemed to be a "raving minister" using the "pulpit as a mask to promote dictatorship," and in the pages of the UAW organ he countered that the UAW contained "thousands of church-goers who recognize the putrid character of the Norris falsifications." Dobrzynski concluded by turning the rhetorical tables, denouncing Norris as a Judas who "sold out the ONE who had led the oppressed peoples of those days in protest against human bondage."[1]

Dobrzysnki's close encounter with revivalism reveals a great deal about the shifting relationship between religion, politics, and class in the United States during the late 1930s and early 1940s. The event demonstrates that religion remained a potent force within working-class culture—and that the UAW knew it. Dobrzynski's reaction suggests that the UAW was urgently struggling to assert its own moral discourse—grounded in the modernist liberalism of the Social Gospel—against Norris's doctrines of individualism and biblical literalism. Even more, however, the event reveals the cultural interpenetration of religious and political ideas in the context of a world that was sliding toward catastrophic, ideologically driven warfare. Dobrzynski could sense that religion held political consequences: it might promote dictatorship, or, alternatively, believers might reject

Matthew Pehl is an assistant professor of history at Augustana College in Sioux Falls, South Dakota.

My colleagues at Augustana—Michael Mullin, Margaret Preston, Geoffrey Dipple, and Cory Conover—have created an exceptional and enriching work environment. I would also like to acknowledge my graduate advisers, particularly Jacqueline Jones, Michael Willrich, and Robert Orsi. John McGreevy has provided abundant support, encouragement, and resources. Additionally, a portion of this research was made possible by a Mark C. Stevens travel grant from the Bentley Historical Library at the University of Michigan; my thanks to them.

Readers may contact Pehl at mpehl@augie.edu.

[1] Zygmund Dobrzynski, "Raving Minister Uses Pulpit as a Mask to Promote Dictatorship," *United Automobile Worker,* June 11, 1938, p. 3; Barry Hankins, *God's Rascal: J. Frank Norris and the Beginnings of Southern Fundamentalism* (Lexington, Ky., 1996), 90–117, esp. 115. Emphasis in original.

doi: 10.1093/jahist/jas261

Norris's falsifications and embrace a progressive democracy. Critically, he recognized the intended target of Norris's politically charged religion was Detroit's working class.

The subject of working-class religion has long drifted in a curious historiographical no-man's-land. Influenced by materialist theories of history, generations of labor historians have been primed to relegate religion to the peripheries of working-class life. Evelyn Savidge Sterne noted that American labor historians have a tendency "to overlook religion or to dismiss it as a negative influence that distracted workers from more 'radical' or 'political' forms of activism." Historians of religion, meanwhile, have nurtured their own blind spots. Often coming from faith-based backgrounds, many scholars of religion have remained unmoved by Marxist-inspired approaches to the past (even as they scrutinize socially rooted power relations) and thus have eschewed a forthright engagement with religion as a class phenomenon. The typical practice of demarcating religious history by denominations (such as Protestantism, Catholicism, or Judaism) has consistently suggested that boundaries of belief rather than economic structures were most important in shaping communities of religiously oriented workers.[2]

Recent works have provided significant insight on working-class religion. Spurred by the pioneering efforts of scholars such as Leslie Woodcock Tentler, Elizabeth Fones-Wolf, and Ken Fones-Wolf, a number of senior labor historians have engaged in deeply reflective studies of religion. Michael Kazin's empathetic portrait of William Jennings Bryan, Robert Bruno's analysis of working-class religiosity, and Nick Salvatore's ruminations on the impact of faith on labor scholarship stand out as preeminent examples. At the same time, the enthusiasm that historians of religion show for the concept of "lived religion" has often placed working-class religious culture at the center of the historical narrative. James Terence Fisher's expansive study of the Irish-Catholic New York City waterfront, David Chappell's nuanced analysis of the African American civil rights movement, and depictions of southern religion by Darren Dochuk, Jarod Roll, and Richard Callahan have brought a deepened appreciation for working-class culture and politics to the fore in religious history. Additionally, the journal *Religion and American Culture* featured a special forum on religion and class, while *Labor* and the *Radical History Review* have focused special issues on the question of religion. Clearly, the desire for rapprochement and greater integration of working-class studies and religious history runs through the recent scholarship.[3]

[2] Evelyn Savidge Sterne, "Bringing Religion into Working-Class History: Parish, Public, and Politics in Providence, 1890–1930," *Social Science History,* 24 (Spring 2000), 151.

[3] Leslie Woodcock Tentler, "Present at the Creation: Working-Class Catholics in the United States," in *American Exceptionalism? U.S. Working-Class Formation in an International Context,* ed. Rick Halpern and Jonathan Morris (New York, 1997), 134–35; Ken Fones-Wolf, *Trade Union Gospel: Christianity and Labor in Industrial Philadelphia, 1865–1915* (Philadelphia, 1989); Elizabeth Fones-Wolf and Ken Fones-Wolf, "No Common Creed: White Working-Class Protestants and the CIO's Operation Dixie," in *Rethinking U.S. Labor History,* ed. Donna T. Haverty-Stacke and Daniel J. Walkowitz (New York, 2010), 111–36; Michael Kazin, *A Godly Hero: The Life of William Jennings Bryan* (New York, 2006); Robert Anthony Bruno, *Justified by Work: Identity and the Meaning of Faith in Chicago's Working-Class Churches* (Columbus, 2008); Nick Salvatore, *Faith and the Historian: Catholic Perspectives* (Urbana, 2007). On "lived religion," see Robert A. Orsi, "Everyday Miracles: The Study of Lived Religion," in *Lived Religion in America: Toward a History of Practice,* ed. David D. Hall (Princeton, 1997), 3–21. James T. Fisher, *On the Irish Waterfront: The Crusader, the Movie, and the Soul of the Port of New York* (Ithaca, 2009); David L. Chappell, *A Stone of Hope: Prophetic Religion and the Death of Jim Crow* (Chapel Hill, 2004); Darren Dochuk, *From Bible Belt to Sunbelt: Plain-Folk Religion, Grassroots Politics, and the Rise of Evangelical Conservatism* (New York, 2011), esp. 79–111; Jarod Roll, *Spirit of Rebellion: Labor and Religion in the New Cotton South* (Urbana, 2010); Richard J. Callahan Jr., *Work and Faith in the Kentucky Coal Fields: Subject to Dust* (Bloomington, 2009). David G. Hackett, et al., "Forum: American Religion and Class," *Religion and American Culture,* 15

The Texas-based Southern Baptist J. Frank Norris leads a flag-burning rally in Detroit during the 1940s. Norris's politicized fundamentalism alarmed liberals and union leaders, who saw shades of fascism in Norris. *Courtesy Walter P. Reuther Library, Wayne State University.*

This essay builds from this developing scholarship but also suggests new questions and issues. The first step, however, is to identify clearly the proper historical actors. Demographically, as Liston Pope and others have observed, the phrase *working-class religion* in early to mid-twentieth-century America referred primarily to three specific groups: Catholics, African American Protestants, and white evangelicals (principally Baptists and Pentecostals) with roots in the rural South. Such an observation may seem obvious, but it remains surprisingly unexamined. For decades historians concerned with the impact of industrialization on religion focused on the rise of the Social Gospel within northern, middle-class Protestant churches. While useful, this approach reveals very little about the religion of working people themselves. Herbert Gutman's landmark essay on working-class religion redressed that omission, but Gutman too looked primarily at northern Protestant workers. To be sure, the worlds of immigrant Catholic devotionalism, African American evangelicalism, and southern white revivalism were varied and distinct—but they were also unmistakably the three dominant cultures of working-class religiosity throughout the twentieth century. To construct a more comprehensive picture of working-class religion, we must begin to put these people into a common narrative.[4]

(Winter 2005), 1–29; *Labor: Studies in Working-Class History of the Americas,* 6 (Spring 2009); *Radical History Review,* 99 (Fall 2007).

⁴ Liston Pope, "Religion and the Class Structure," *Annals of the American Academy of Political and Social Science,* 256 (March 1948), 84–91. Liston Pope's assessment is reevaluated in Christian Smith and Robert Faris, "Socioeconomic Inequality in the American Religious System: An Update and Assessment," *Journal for the Scientific Study of Religion,* 44 (March 2005), 95–104. The terms of the discussion on working-class religion were established by Henry F. May and reassessed by Herbert Gutman. See Henry F. May, *Protestant Churches and Industrial*

Detroit offers a useful case study because the city encapsulated that national demographic phenomenon. By the late 1930s over 600,000 Catholics lived in the arch-diocese of Detroit—by far the single largest denomination in the city. Polish immigrants—over 250,000 strong—fully dominated communities such as Hamtramck, where four large Polish parishes surrounded the nearby Dodge Brothers Company auto-mobile manufacturing plant, but Poles were just the largest of many ethnic groups. Indeed, by 1933 Detroit's Catholics could hear the faith celebrated in twenty-two differ-ent languages. African American Baptists counted themselves as the third-largest reli-gious group in the city during that year. By the early 1950s black migrants had established more than two hundred churches plus dozens more places of worship in storefronts and residences to hold many of the believers among the city's 300,000 African Americans who had come north to fill the foundries at the Ford plant. South-ern-born whites had been seasonal migrants since the 1920s and were already reshaping Detroit's religious geography: three Pentecostal Assemblies of God congregations, forty-one non–Northern Baptist congregations, and at least six enterprises such as the Detroit Foursquare Gospel, Detroit Gospel Tabernacle, and Missionary Tabernacle flourished throughout the city. Observing some of the 250,000 new arrivals streaming north during the 1940s for war-industry jobs, one excited investigator declared that Detroit "is in a 'Bible Belt' . . . just as devout" as its more famous southern cousin. Before the war ended, Detroit had evolved into a virtual laboratory of working-class religiosity in which European Catholicism met evangelistic Protestantism, South invaded North, and black jostled white.[5]

Working-class religion, then, is partially a demographic term. More importantly, however, it is also a politicized construct of language and ideology invented by outside observers who ascribed social meanings, intellectual values, and political implications to working-class religious practices. Most of the civic and religious leaders who shaped this discourse in the early twentieth century were committed to a liberal, progressive modernism and were ill at ease with the seemingly alien religious practices of working-class "others." Consequently, critics employed a common vocabulary of culturally freighted keywords—*cultish, clannish, docile, fatalistic, otherworldly, overly emotional,* and *authoritarian*—to describe working-class religions. These terms constructed a narrative that placed working-class religion on the margins of modernity and allowed critics to question whether workers' religion posed a basic threat to democratic, open societies. Historians should approach this vocabulary with interest but also with caution. It does

America (New York, 1949); and Herbert Gutman, "Protestantism and the American Labor Movement: The Chris-tian Spirit in the Gilded Age," *American Historical Review,* 72 (Oct. 1966), 74–101.
    [5] U.S. Department of Commerce and Labor, Bureau of the Census, *Census of Religious Bodies: 1926,* vol. I: *Summary and Detailed Tables* (Washington, 1930); Leslie Woodcock Tentler, *Seasons of Grace: A History of the Catholic Archdiocese of Detroit* (Detroit, 1990), 3. For additional statistics on African American churches, see Ulysses W. Boykins, *A Hand Book of the Detroit Negro* (Detroit, 1943), 31. For statistics on southern white churches, see "Interview with Rev. E. L. Hughes," [ca. 1937], typescript, Summaries of Interviews and Observa-tions file, box 3, Milton Kemnitz Papers, 1932–1995 (Bentley Historical Library, University of Michigan, Ann Arbor). On African American and southern white churches in cultural context, see Richard Walter Thomas, *Life for Us Is What We Make It: Building Black Community in Detroit, 1915–1945* (Bloomington, 1992); and James N. Gregory, *The Southern Diaspora: How the Great Migrations of Black and White Southerners Transformed America* (Chapel Hill, 2005). "The Religious Ferment in Detroit," Sept. 1943, typescript, Survey of Racial and Religious Conflict Forces in Detroit folder, box 71, Civil Rights Congress of Michigan Collection (Walter P. Reuther Library, Wayne State University, Detroit, Mich.).

not reveal much about the actual beliefs or religious world views of working-class people, but it does reveal, quite starkly, that Catholics, African Americans, and southern whites were scrutinized through the same discursive lens and that contemporaries of the time worried about the likelihood that working-class religion would foment fanaticism, divisiveness, and political corruption.[6]

The UAW worried about the reactionary potential of working-class religion, but the union simultaneously offered a more optimistic narrative and hoped to tap into what it saw as positive religious values: social equalitarianism, communalism, and prodemocracy. Even more importantly, during the 1930s Detroit's working-class religious communities were producing a generation of progressive religious leaders eager to escape the stereotypes that had long hounded their traditions. Among Catholics, Fr. Raymond S. Clancy led a new generation of "labor priests" in founding the Archdiocesan Labor Institute (ALI), while several hundred lay people became involved with the Catholic Worker movement and the Association of Catholic Trade Unionists (ACTU). The southern Presbyterian minister Claude C. Williams moved north to Detroit in 1942 to found the Peoples Institute of Applied Religion (PIAR), one of the most radical religious organizations of the twentieth century. African American ministers such as Charles Hill, Malcolm Dade, and Horace White turned their congregations into hotbeds of union and civil rights activism. Not quite a fully integrated "spiritual front," these religious progressives were nevertheless an ecumenical group energized by the populist, multicultural Americanism of the New Deal and the industrial union movement. Seeking to reimagine the political possibilities of their faiths, these leaders and their liberal allies were forced to engage and resist the existing tropes of working-class religious discourse. In its place, they articulated a prolabor, antiracist, and broadly tolerant version of working-class religion as the authentic, democratic faith of America's workers.[7]

As World War II loomed, however, working-class religion became increasingly politicized on the right and on the left. In fact, Detroit had emerged as an epicenter of reactionary and antimodernist religion by the late 1930s. J. Frank Norris, the "radio priest" Fr. Charles Coughlin, and the former Huey Long protégé Gerald L. K. Smith were all active in the city; Coughlin and Smith even joined forces in a series of political campaigns. In this cultural hothouse, the discourse on working-class religion was pushed to new ideological extremes and was no longer seen as merely obscurantist or escapist. Many leftists now linked the fundamentalism and religious ethnocentrism of Norris, Coughlin, and Smith to fascism and racism. Nervously confronting race-driven "hate

---

[6] My thinking about religion as a social and political discourse has been influenced by Callum G. Brown, *The Death of Christian Britain: Understanding Secularisation, 1800–2000* (New York, 2001); Robert A. Orsi, *Between Heaven and Earth: The Religious Worlds People Make and the Scholars Who Study Them* (Princeton, 2005); and Sean McCloud, *Divine Hierarchies: Class in American Religion and Religious Studies* (Chapel Hill, 2007).

[7] On the Archdiocesan Labor Institute and Raymond Clancy, see Matthew Pehl, "The Remaking of the Catholic Working Class: Detroit, 1919–1945," *Religion and American Culture,* 19 (Winter 2009), 37–68. On the Association of Catholic Trade Unionists, see Steve Rosswurm, "The Catholic Church and the Left-Led Unions: Labor Priests, Labor Schools, and the ACTU," in *The CIO's Left-Led Unions,* ed. Steve Rosswurm (New Brunswick, 1992), 119–38; and Pehl, "Remaking of the Catholic Working Class." On Claude Williams, see Cedric Belfrage, *A Faith to Free the People* (New York, 1944); and Robert H. Craig, *Religion and Radical Politics: An Alternative Christian Tradition in the United States* (Philadelphia, 1992). On Charles Hill, see Angela D. Dillard, *Faith in the City: Preaching Radical Social Change in Detroit* (Ann Arbor, 2007). The "spiritual front" is James T. Fisher's term for the mid-twentieth-century liberal interfaith alliance, built on the twin bases of anticommunism and social justice. See Fisher, *On the Irish Waterfront,* 131–35.

strikes" in defense plants and racial violence on city streets, progressives feared they saw the foot soldiers of fascism lurking under clerical cover.[8]

Yet in a sign of just how contested the discourse had become, Coughlin, Smith, and Norris articulated a potent counternarrative that was diametrically opposed to that of progressives. According to this alternate discourse, working-class Christianity was under deadly assault by secularists, unionists, modernists, and communists. The pernicious influence of clerical progressives such as Clancy, Williams, and Hill seemed most insidious to religious antimodernists. A corrupted religion, rightists were convinced, prepared the working class for the eventual political triumph of communism or a similar anti-American statism. Particularly within the dispensational, premillennial world views of Norris and Smith, communist tyranny was foretold by scripture and was not merely a flawed economic system but was also a portent of the end times. For fundamentalists, communism was synonymous with religious modernism (which denied the literalism of scripture) and the hand of government (which threatened God's chosen remnant). As such, a minister suspected of smuggling communism into America under the guise of religion threatened the destruction of both democracy and Christianity.[9]

Those examples suggest a divergence from what historians have generally portrayed as the "unifying" effect of religion during the war years. In Detroit—arguably America's most important industrial center—the Right and the Left agreed on only one point: the cultural and ideological shape of a postwar America would be determined by the rapidly shifting religious consciousness of a diverse working class. "All patriotic Americans are agreed that we must win this war," Gerald L. K. Smith conceded in 1942, but, he insisted, "we are not agreed on what must follow." Any veneer of consensus, as Smith indicated, was thin and conditional. On the shop floors and in the neighborhoods of Detroit, religion remained central to working-class identity, but its social consequences were unpredictable. Defining the political character of this religion—as a bulwark for democracy, a wedge for fascism, or a stalking-horse for communism—was one of the most urgent cultural projects of the war years.[10]

Demarcating Christian Discourse

Christian discourse in early twentieth-century Detroit was influenced by currents of progressivism in political culture and modernism in religious culture. Within this framework, religion was expected to meet certain ideological expectations: espousing universalistic doctrines of social ethics, promoting civic responsibility, and nurturing a

---

[8] On Charles Coughlin, see Alan Brinkley, *Voices of Protest: Huey Long, Father Coughlin, and the Great Depression* (New York, 1982); and Michael Kazin, *The Populist Persuasion: An American History* (New York, 1995). On Gerald L. K. Smith, see Glen Jeansonne, *Gerald L. K. Smith: Minister of Hate* (New Haven, 1988); and Leo P. Ribuffo, *The Old Christian Right: The Protestant Far Right from the Great Depression to the Cold War* (Philadelphia, 1983). On hate strikes, see Beth T. Bates, "Double V for Victory Mobilizes Black Detroit, 1941–1946," in *Freedom North: Black Freedom Struggles outside the South, 1940–1980,* ed. Jeanne Theoharis and Komozi Woodard (New York, 2003), 17–40.

[9] Joel A. Carpenter, *Revive Us Again: The Reawakening of American Fundamentalism* (New York, 1997); Daniel K. Williams, *God's Own Party: The Making of the Christian Right* (New York, 2010); Joseph C. O'Mahoney, "New Deal Fascism," *Cross and the Flag,* 2 (Aug. 1943), 1–3. Matthew Avery Sutton, "Was FDR the Antichrist? The Birth of Fundamentalist Antiliberalism in a Global Age," *Journal of American History,* 98 (March 2012), 1052–74.

[10] For an example of the "unity" thesis, see Martin E. Marty, *Modern American Religion,* vol. III: *Under God, Indivisible, 1941–1960* (Chicago, 1999). Gerald L. K. Smith, "My Hat Is in the Ring," *Cross and the Flag,* 1 (May 1942).

capacity for intellectual individualism. The religion preached at Central Methodist Church, for example, contained "a sort of civic aspect," according to the religious sociologist H. Paul Douglass. St. John's Episcopal Church added "an admirable series of lectures on civic topics" and employed professional social workers with an unusually high "technical competency." Detroit's mainline churches also supported that most emblematic of Progressive Era institutions: the settlement house. First Presbyterian Church, for example, founded the Dodge Community House to deliver essential social services for the immigrants of Hamtramck, while the Congregational Men's Club sponsored the Franklin Street settlement (Detroit's oldest). These and other middle-class, mainline congregations promoted a religion that enriched democratic social functions, and hence they received praise and encouragement.[11]

Working-class religions, however, often fell short of these discursive ideals because they were allegedly socially unengaged, insular, preoccupied with supernatural matters, fueled by emotional excesses, and susceptible to exploitation by crafty demagogues. African American religion—with its long tradition of exuberant music and powerful preaching—was especially susceptible to charges of "over-emotionalism." In 1918, when large numbers of black migrants began settling in Detroit, mainline church leaders expressed alarm over "forms of religious fervor" among these newcomers. A 1926 mayor's report (from a committee chaired by the young Detroit clergyman Reinhold Niebuhr) similarly worried that African American migrants suffered from a "lack of emotional stability." Consequently, working-class migrants found their spiritual needs met by "irresponsible religious organizations which experience mushroom growth in the city." Storefront churches, in particular, "lack stability and discipline in their group life; the moral fruits of their religious fervor are frequently jeopardized by a type of hysteria which issues in social phenomena of dubious ethical value. The leadership in these groups is usually without adequate educational equipment and free of any kind of supervision or discipline." In denouncing working-class black religion as "irresponsible" or "hysterical," the report reinforced the idea that "appropriate" religion should be both emotionally disciplined and socially beneficial.[12]

Critics of working-class Catholicism picked up the same theme. Hungarian Catholics were described by one sociologist as "emotionally unstable and very suggestible." Similarly, the supposedly "peasant mind" of Sicilian and southern Italian Catholics found cathartic release during celebrations of St. Joseph's Day, when boisterous brass bands marched through Detroit's Italian neighborhood carrying religious icons. Additionally, the church's strong support for devotional culture generated a deep emotional response among lay people who, in the words of Detroit's Catholic newspaper, embraced patron saints with "gratitude and zeal." Southern white evangelicals, meanwhile, exhibited what

[11] H. Paul Douglass, *The Church in the Changing City: Case Studies Illustrating Adaptation* (New York, 1927), 151–59, 177, 287, 290; "Report of the Dodge Community House," 1930, folder 353, box 227, Series 8: Member Settlement Houses, Records of the National Federation of Settlements and Neighborhood Centers (Social Welfare History Archives, University of Minnesota, Minneapolis); "The Franklin Scene: An Informal History of Detroit's Oldest Social Settlement," 1948, folder 354, *ibid.*

[12] George Edmund Haynes, *Negro New-Comers in Detroit, Michigan: A Challenge to Christian Statesmanship; A Preliminary Survey* (New York, 1918), 31–35; "Report of the Mayor's Committee on Race Relations," 1927, in *Papers of the NAACP: Selected Branch Files, 1913–1939,* ed. John H. Bracey and August Meier (microfilm, 18 reels, University Publications of America, 1991), part 12, series C, reel 12.

one scholar described as a "deep drive for individualistic expression" in their religious lives, often through rollicking revival services.[13]

In addition to being too fervent, working-class religion was also accused of producing a sullen resignation toward the disappointments of earthly life. Polish immigrants, for instance, were described as suffering "low standards of living . . . revealed in fatalism." Southern whites were "trained to a stoic concealment of their emotions" by a "rigid, patriarchal morality." In response, critics said, workers turned toward otherworldly "superstitions," especially folk medicine. Various investigators found the widespread use of charms, curses, herbs, and folk elixirs, along with a generalized acceptance of faith healing, among Poles, Hungarians, Mexicans, African Americans, and southern whites. The problem, as Reinhold Neibuhr told his friend Fred Butzel, was that this type of religion "excites the people but doesn't do them any good, doesn't give them any leadership." Reflecting the broader modernist belief, Neibuhr suggested that religion was "good" when it directly engaged the serious problems of society. Churches that substituted otherworldly exuberance for social ethics were, in Neibuhr's words, "the lowest form of religious life."[14]

Outsiders also worried about the clannish insularity and authoritarian tendencies of working-class religion. Catholics, in particular, were presumed to lack intellectual independence. To one observer, Detroit's Hungarian Catholics seemed "sheep-like," locked in helpless thrall to the parish priest. The lives of tens of thousands of Polish immigrants who surrounded the Dodge Brothers plant were "enveloped in religion," and the authority of the parish priest was rarely questioned. African Americans, too, formed "cults," built around the intense and supposedly authoritarian charisma of particular ministers. As the Detroit Urban League president John Dancy described them, cults depended on an "emotional attitude for holding on to [their] membership" and served "no real worthwhile purpose in the community." Dancy criticized the Church of God and Saints of Christ in particular on these grounds; the congregations were "for the most part very poor . . . [and] made up of people who are tremendously emotional and usually below the average in intelligence."[15]

The story that modernists told about working-class religion flattened and simplified what were complex and often-ambiguous cultural systems. Nevertheless, the description of the social dangers posed by working-class religion was powerful, and in the context of

---

[13] Erdmann Doane Beynon, "Crime and Custom of the Hungarians of Detroit," *Journal of Criminal Law and Criminology,* 25 (Jan.–Feb. 1935), 772; Lois Rankin, "Detroit Nationality Groups," *Michigan History Magazine,* 23 (Spring 1939), 115; Ida M. Santini, "The Preservation of St. Joseph's Day and Something about the Sicilian Colony in Detroit," 1953, typescript 37 (Folklore Archive, Reuther Library); *Michigan Catholic,* July 3, 1930. On Catholic devotionalism, see Robert A. Orsi, *Thank You, St. Jude: Women's Devotion to the Patron Saint of Hopeless Causes* (New Haven, 1996). D. K. Wilgus, "Country-Western Music and the Urban Hillbilly," *Journal of American Folklore,* 83 (April–June 1970), 158.

[14] Albert J. Mayer and Sue Mark, "Social Change, Religion, and Birth Rates," *American Journal of Sociology,* 62 (Jan. 1957), 384; Elmer Akers, "Southern Whites in Detroit," 1937, typescript, p. 7, Summary of Individual Interviews folder, box 3, Kemnitz Papers; Wilgus, "Country-Western Music and the Urban Hillbilly," 165; Victoria W. Wolcott, *Remaking Respectability: African American Women in Interwar Detroit* (Chapel Hill, 2001), 113–26; Reinhold Niebuhr, "The Reminiscences of Reinhold Niebuhr: Oral History, 1953," 1953, transcript, p. 24 (Columbia Center for Oral History, Columbia University, New York, N.Y.).

[15] Beynon, "Crime and Custom of the Hungarians of Detroit," 774; Arthur Evan Woods, *Hamtramck, Then and Now: A Sociological Study of a Polish-American Community* (New York, 1955), 34. John Dancy to F. Marion Woods, Sept. 28, 1928, in *Microfilm Edition of the Detroit Urban League Papers,* ed. John M. R. Chavis and William McNitt (microfilm, 18 reels, Michigan Historical Collections, 1973), reel 3; Dancy to Julius Hadley, Feb. 25, 1930, *ibid.*

Gerald L. K. Smith, a one-time follower of Huey Long, used Detroit as his publishing, political, and organizational base during World War II. *Courtesy Walter P. Reuther Library, Wayne State University.*

the early 1930s the message grew even more urgent. Detroit was hammered mercilessly by the Great Depression, which pushed unemployment for factory workers to 50 percent. For those who were able to keep their jobs, the demands of the increased speed of production combined with lower wages to increase stress and cause industrial accidents. Tensions culminated in 1932 when the Detroit Unemployed Councils and the UAW organized a hunger march against the Ford factory to protest job losses; the march met violent police resistance. A year later, a massive strike wave exploded throughout area factories. Meanwhile, Catholics began recounting apocalyptic appearances of a "ghostly figure"—perhaps St. Joseph—across the city, and African Americans embraced the militant Nation of Islam. Religious responses, like political ones, were becoming desperate.[16]

The UAW surged to the forefront of the national labor movement at this deeply uncertain moment. Union leaders recognized that they could hardly ignore working peoples' religion; instead, they hoped to capitalize on it by offering their own creed—a synthesis of the modernist middle-class Social Gospel with a working-class vision of industrial democracy. The union made numerous symbolic gestures to the importance of such a religion. Homer Martin, the UAW's first president, was chosen in part because as a former Baptist minister he "made men feel that in organizing a union they were going forth to battle for righteousness and the word of God." R. J. Thomas, Martin's successor as UAW president, was also a one-time divinity student and member of the Christian Endeavor movement. Although Walter Reuther was no churchgoer, his brother Victor argued that "religion had a good deal to do with the shaping of our family life." The pages of Reuther's first UAW newsletter, the *West Side Conveyor,* often celebrated prolabor religious

[16] On the 1932 hunger march and the 1933 strike wave, see John Barnard, *American Vanguard: The United Auto Workers during the Reuther Years, 1935–1970* (Detroit, 2004), 40–72; Tentler, *Seasons of Grace,* 411–13; Erdmann Doane Beynon, "The Voodoo Cult among Negro Migrants in Detroit," *American Journal of Sociology,* 43 (May 1938), 894–907.

leaders and articulated a version of working-class Christianity. Later, as the UAW president from 1946 to 1970, Reuther maintained strong alliances with ecumenical organizations such as the National Religion and Labor Foundation.[17]

Even so, the UAW faced a difficult cultural balancing act. Some workers required convincing that the new and untested union could be reconciled with their powerful, preexisting religious identities. The shop steward J. K. Paulson, for example, encountered "a few workers who seem to believe that to be a member of a union . . . would conflict with their religious views." He dismissed those beliefs as "rather absurd" and insisted that union leaders were "most sincere in worship of their Lord and Master." Simultaneously, some local industrialists offered generous financial support to antiunion preachers and often assailed the UAW as an atheistic front of un-American radicalism. Clearly, the union needed to persist in attempting to meet workers on their own cultural ground. It repeatedly paid for full-page advertisements in the *Michigan Catholic* encouraging Catholic workers to join, and it loudly promoted Archbishop Edward Mooney's statement that "no Catholic Church authority has ever asserted that the C.I.O. [Congress of Industrial Organizations] is incompatible with Catholicity." African American ministers—many of whom received needed financial assistance from Henry Ford—remained almost uniformly opposed to the union. Therefore, when the UAW hired William Bowman in 1937 as one of its first black organizers, the organization highlighted Bowman's role not only as an iron molder but also as the pastor of a local church.[18]

If the union hoped that religion might unify workers around common moral and political goals, such hopes were sometimes cruelly frustrated. When the UAW ran a "labor slate" of candidates in the 1937 Detroit common council elections, it was counting on the class consciousness of striking workers at the Dodge plant to reshape city government. Fueled in part by anti-Semitism, however, workers decisively rejected Maurice Sugar, the UAW-supported Jewish labor lawyer. In the middle of a sit-down strike, frustrated organizers angrily harangued their own members: "Your rotten with racial and religious intolerance."[19]

Experiences such as these caused unionists to retreat into familiar discursive tropes about the clannishness of working-class religion, but the swiftly changing context of the late 1930s pushed this discourse to more extreme conclusions. The UAW member Harry Cruden epitomized this shift when he expressed alarm about the Detroit triumvirate of the "three little stools": Coughlin, Smith, and Norris. For Cruden and others the rise of mass media added a dangerous new element to the pitfalls of working-class religion. Collectively, the radio sermons and newspapers that Coughlin, Smith, and Norris

[17] On Homer Martin, see Irving Howe and B. J. Widick, *The UAW and Walter Reuther* (New York, 1949), 51. "Labor's Program Is True Christianity," *United Automobile Worker*, Oct. 22, 1938; Edgar DeWitt Jones, "Congress Attacks Church Reaction," *Christian Century*, Oct. 4, 1944, pp. 3–4; Victor G. Reuther, *The Brothers Reuther and the Story of the UAW: A Memoir* (Boston, 1975), 35–36; *West Side Conveyor*, Aug. 10, Sept. 21, 1937; "The Religion and Labor Council of America: A Precis of Its Service to the American Labor Movement," May 2, 1960, typescript, folder 1, box 519, UAW President's Office: Walter P. Reuther Records (Reuther Library).

[18] J. K. Paulson, "Unions and Churches," *United Automobile Worker*, Nov. 26, 1938; *Michigan Catholic*, Aug. 3, Aug. 12, Oct. 7, Dec. 8, 1937; August Meier and Elliott M. Rudwick, *Black Detroit and the Rise of the UAW* (New York, 1979), 43.

[19] *Dodge Main News*, March 27, 1937; Bruce Nelson, "Autoworkers, Electoral Politics, and the Convergence of Class and Race: Detroit, 1937–1945," in *Organized Labor and American Politics, 1894–1994: The Labor-Liberal Alliance*, ed. Kevin Boyle (Albany, 1998), 121–56. On the impact of ethnoreligious traditionalism on the labor movement, see Peter Friedlander, *The Emergence of a UAW Local, 1936–1939: A Study in Class and Culture* (Pittsburgh, 1975), 130–32.

disseminated widely broadcast a hyperpatriotic, antilabor message to tens of thousands of Detroit-area Catholic and Protestant workers. The UAW organizer Joseph Ferris, for example, was convinced that Coughlin "controlled the people ... from the radio." This militant, religiously tinged nationalism was piped through a vast media network into working-class homes and provoked in modernists a nightmarish comparison to the fascism simultaneously spreading across Europe. Cruden forcefully pleaded with workers to recognize that "the Bible of those preachers is not the Word of God, but an Americanized version of 'Mein Kampf.'" T. McNabb, a worker at Detroit UAW Local 227, agreed, arguing that Coughlin and Smith enabled "the mass mania that precedes totalitarianism." With the rise of European fascism, the discourse surrounding working-class Christianity became increasingly divisive and remained deeply contested during the war years.[20]

Catholicism and the Struggle for Democracy

Few individuals influenced the parameters of Christian discourse in the 1930s and early 1940s more decisively than Charles Coughlin. While the priest's early sermons espoused a vision of ecumenism and social justice, these pronouncements were uneasily nestled within his countervailing tendency toward demagoguery and intolerance. By the mid-1930s Coughlin had veered far to the right, earning the enmity of liberals and unionists and causing more than a few observers to worry about the compatibility of Catholicism and democracy. At the same time, however, a strong prolabor Catholic coalition took shape within Detroit's parishes, union locals, and archdioceses. Prolabor Catholics diligently worked to extricate themselves from Coughlin's shadow and articulated a "democratic," pro–United Automobile Workers vision of Catholicism to stand against the "fascist" faith that was increasingly championed by Coughlin. In the process, working-class Catholicism came to serve as a mirror for the larger cultural and political struggles of the late New Deal era.

By the mid-1930s Coughlin loomed as a towering figure revered by many working people. They took solace from Coughlin's sympathetic descriptions of a blue-collar Jesus, "born in the cradle of the laboring class." Coughlin began translating these sentiments into concrete political results, including the formation of labor organizations. In 1936 Coughlin allied with the labor organizer Richard Frankensteen to create the Automotive Industrial Worker Association in the Dodge Brothers Hamtramck plant (later United Auto Workers Local 3). He was even an invited speaker at the first UAW convention.[21]

By later in the year, however, Coughlin's sympathy to unionism had become clouded by hostility to strikes and a certainty that the Congress of Industrial Organizations had opened the gates for communism. He angrily repudiated Franklin Roosevelt and supported the Union party presidential campaign of William Lemke. Anti-Semitism increasingly colored Coughlin's denunciations. In 1938, his newsletter *Social Justice* printed the anti-Semitic *Protocols of the Elders of Zion,* an authorless document purporting to be an actual, secret Jewish plan for world domination. Coughlin even called for the formation

[20] Letter to the editor, *United Automobile Worker,* Nov. 29, 1939, p. 7; *ibid.,* May 1, 1940, p. 7.

[21] Charles E. Coughlin, *Father Coughlin's Radio Discourses, 1931/32* (Royal Oak, 1932), 176; Steve Jefferys, "'Matters of Mutual Interest': The Unionization Process at Dodge Main, 1933–1939," in *On the Line: Essays in the History of Auto Work,* ed. Nelson Lichtenstein and Stephen Meyer (Urbana, 1988), 100–128; "Coughlin Makes Unity Appeal," *United Automobile Worker,* May 1936, p. 1. This was a special convention issue.

of "platoons," and shortly afterward founded the Christian Front to mobilize his follow-ers. With his intolerance exposed and his intentions unclear but possibly dangerous, his incompatibility with the UAW was unquestionable.[22]

To progressive critics, Coughlin embodied and confirmed the worst characteristics of working-class religion, epitomizing both clerical "authoritarianism" and socially destruc-tive "emotionalism." When Joseph Ferris sought to explain Coughlin's popularity with workers, he concluded that the priest "was an outlet for [people's] emotions." The labor organizer John Zaremba also noted Coughlin's authoritarian power, complaining that Polish autoworkers obstinately viewed him as "infallible." Wyndham Mortimer, the UAW's first vice president, made the obvious political connection: Coughlin was no more than a "fascist demagogue." The UAW newspaper articulated the indictment in 1938: "Fascism brazenly hurls defiance at Christianity and crucifies the faithful. The bible is being rewritten to conform with what Hitler 'thinks' of God. And in Detroit, a priest looks at this modern spectacle of Christ being crucified in Europe and applauds the barbarian horde."[23]

Even so, many liberal priests and working-class lay people in Detroit rejected Cough-lin's views. The social vision of the UAW seemed more appropriate and appealing to a largely post-immigrant, more assimilated generation of workers who urgently sought to reconcile their deep-seated religious identities with "democratic" unionism. Between 1937 and 1939 Catholic Action—a church-sponsored movement to unite spirituality with social engagement—unleashed a flood of activity. In 1937 Detroiters founded a cell of the Catholic Worker movement that pulsed with energy and excitement. In July of the next year lay workers founded Detroit's chapter of the ACTU, which boasted over 2,500 members by the early 1940s; as one member put it, the organization was devoted to "a Christian platform in the U.A.W." In 1939 a group of labor priests led by Fr. Clancy established the Archdiocesan Labor Institute. By 1940 the institute had founded more than forty labor schools in local parishes to discuss Catholic social teachings and instruct unionists in the nuts and bolts of parliamentary procedures. Additionally, Detroit became home to two nationally circulating Catholic labor newspapers.[24]

Many Detroit Catholics coalesced around this prolabor culture. When Joe Zarella, a member of the Catholic Worker movement from New York City, toured Detroit's Cath-olic high schools, students "bombarded him with questions, and promised support for the Catholic Worker ideal." The movement's "houses of hospitality" quickly became important neighborhood gathering places and resources. Fr. Clare Murphy, meanwhile, sought to enlist workers who were "profoundly in love with God, who . . . have zeal, courage, and real attack" to advance Catholicism within the city's unions. A sizeable vanguard of lay Catholics responded. According to ACTU leaders at the Chrysler Motor

[22] On Coughlin's later career, see Brinkley, *Voices of Protest,* 242–67.

[23] Joseph Ferris interview by Jack W. Skeels, 1961, transcript, p. 8, United Auto Workers Oral Histories Col-lection (Reuther Library); John A. Zaremba interview by Skeels, 1961, transcript, pp. 15–16, *ibid.*; Wyndham Mortimer, *Organize! My Life as a Union Man* (Boston, 1971), 75, 96–97; "Father Coughlin's Anti-Semitism," *United Automobile Worker,* Nov. 26, 1938, p. 5.

[24] *Catholic Worker,* Oct. 1937; *Michigan Catholic,* Nov. 18, 1937; "Constitution of ACTU," July 15, 1938, type-script, folder 1, box 1, Association of Catholic Trade Unionists of Detroit Records (Reuther Library). For Association of Catholic Trade Unionists membership statistics, see John C. Cort, *Dreadful Conversions: The Making of a Catholic Socialist* (New York, 2003), 160. On a "Christian platform," see student evaluation, [n.d.], folder 16, box 1, Father Raymond S. Clancy Papers (Reuther Library); "Minutes of the Meeting of January 26, 1939, to Plan Parish Labor Schools," typescript, folder 15, *ibid.* Raymond Clancy, "Detroit ALI," *Christian Social Action,* Dec. 1939.

Corporation plant, "the welfare of Local 7 . . . is PART OF OUR RELIGION!" For lay Catholics—so often accused of submitting to an "authoritarian" religion—the ACTU visibly emboldened many to combine evangelical enthusiasm and democratic activism. "*You* can do more than any priest, bishop, or Pope," an ACTU speaker told members, "toward bringing your non-Catholic fellow-worker back to the faith of their fathers!"[25]

Prolabor Catholics needed to prove their commitment to industrial democracy and to distance themselves from the image of an obscurantist, authoritarian religious culture. Catholics faced an additional challenge in this task because not only did they not seek to define themselves against the "fascist" strain in American Catholicism but they also asserted a fervently anticommunist Christian discourse. While many prolabor activists in the 1930s gravitated to the communist Popular Front, Catholic laborites hoped to chart a third course that celebrated democracy and unionism while unequivocally opposing communism. Thus while the ACTU outlined a detailed plan for what it termed "economic democracy," the organization also frankly rebuffed potential alliances with communists. "No good thing need be opposed because it happens to have the unsolicited support of Communists," the group delicately declared. "But no reciprocal political relations can rightfully exist between Catholics and the Communist Party for any cause."[26]

The ALI labor schools were critical because communist-trained activists often dominated the operations in the early days of many locals. George Merrelli, who organized Polish and Italian workers at the Detroit Chevrolet Gear and Axel Division plant, recalled walking into a Polish social club for the union local's first meetings and finding portraits of Joseph Stalin on the walls. It was "through the educational effort of the Catholic group," Merrelli said, that ordinary ethnic Catholics learned "how to spot a Commie" and manage a local. Frank Marquart, a socialist in the education department of the UAW, recalled that activists would "point out the line which was being peddled, and make it clear to the workers" when a policy was for the narrow good of communists. The ACTU, according to Marquart, "served as a training ground. Where else did the people who had leadership abilities acquire them in those days except in radical groups or in the ACTU?"[27]

Thus Catholics found themselves taking sides in the often-brutal factional infighting that bedeviled the UAW for its first several years. The ACTU's relationship with George Addes is revealing in this regard. Addes, the first UAW secretary-treasurer, was raised a Catholic and even cited papal labor encyclicals to legitimate UAW efforts at arbitrating work speed. Politically, however, Addes was a thoroughgoing leftist, and his loyalty and

[25] *Catholic Worker*, Jan. 1938; *ibid.*, May 1938; Fr. Clare Murphy to members of Catholic Study Clubs, July 16, 1938, folder 6, box 17, F. J. Patrick McCartney Papers (Archives of the University of Notre Dame, Notre Dame, Ind.); Newsletter, ca. 1938, Chrysler Local 7 folder, box 23, Association of Catholic Trade Unionists of Detroit Records. Emphasis in original.

[26] On the Catholic-communist conflict, see Douglas P. Seaton, *Catholics and Radicals: The Association of Catholic Trade Unionists and the American Labor Movement; From Depression to Cold War* (Lewisburg, 1981); and William Issel, "'A Stern Struggle': Catholic Activism and San Francisco Labor, 1934–1958," in *American Labor and the Cold War: Grassroots Politics and Postwar Political Culture*, ed. Robert W. Cherney, William Issel, and Kieran Walsh Taylor (New Brunswick, 2004), 154–76. Resolution, Aug. 5, 1938, UAW folder, box 34, Association of Catholic Trade Unionists of Detroit Records.

[27] ACTU Bulletin, folder 3, box 1, Association of Catholic Trade Unionists of Detroit Records; George Merrelli interview by Patricia Pilling, 1982, transcript, pp. 18, 37–38, Polish-American Autoworkers Oral Histories Collection (Reuther Library); Frank Marquart interview by Skeels, 1960, transcript, pp. 9, 11–12, United Auto Workers Oral Histories Collection.

proximity to prominent communists caused many Catholics to recoil. When Addes joined the leftist ticket in the pivotal 1946 UAW presidential election, the ACTU backed the anticommunist platform of Walter Reuther, cementing what one scholar has termed an "informal alliance" between Reuther and the Catholics. In the wake of Reuther's victory, ACTU president Paul Weber sought to assure worried outsiders that there was no "Catholic bloc" within the UAW. The group's decision to back Reuther, Weber said, "was made freely, and individually, without direction or pressure from any source." More interestingly, Weber pointed out that the ACTU supported Reuther because his policies "have been consistently in harmony with the principles laid down in the Papal Encyclicals," and they offered the best chance of enacting something resembling the group's "industry council" plan. In an interview after Reuther's election, Weber explained, "We are not campaigning for the election of Catholic officials but for the adoption of Catholic principles." The ACTU viewed the policies of the Protestant-bred Reuther as more "Catholic" than those of their coreligionist George Addes.[28]

Communists and their leftist allies naturally pushed back against Catholic laborites with words that had become stock-in-trade for critics of working-class religion. In 1938 the ACTU chaplain in Detroit, Sebastian Erbacher, complained that "laborers are being filled with hatred for the church," and accused communists of painting all Catholics with the brush of fascism. Two years later the ACTU warned its members that a "fake handbill" insinuating a link between the organization and European fascism was floating through various factories. Again in 1942 the former *Christian Social Action* editor Richard L. G. Deverall—at the time an official in the UAW Education Department—was accused of being a closet fascist. When *In Fact* magazine published the charge (even after the UAW executive board had already dismissed the accusation), Deverall wrote to the magazine's editor with barely contained rage. "As a member of the liberal element within the Catholic Church," he fumed, "I very bitterly resent being attacked as a fascist, when I have suffered for years because of the fact that I HAVE battled Fascism." In fact, prolabor Catholics agreed with the modernist premise that religion might serve as fascism's American handmaiden. Rev. Frederick Siedenburg—appointed by President Franklin D. Roosevelt to the Detroit branch of the National Labor Relations Board—concluded in 1939 that "if Fascism arises in the United States it will come in a sugar-coated form" like an escapist religion.[29]

Some workers remained suspicious of Catholic laborites. Secular workers often distrusted any religious involvement in working-class institutions, while Protestants, prizing traditions of religious individualism, worried about the hierarchical nature of the Catholic Church. Ultimately, however, prolabor Catholics made strides in distinguishing themselves from Coughlinites and in building alliances with secular unionists. The Socialist Frank Marquart, for example, appreciated the activism of the ACTU in defending

[28] George Addes to Raymond Clancy, Nov. 29, 1939, folder 2, box 4, Clancy Papers; George Addes, n.d., untitled speech, George Addes 1941–1946 folder, box 7, Association of Catholic Trade Unionists of Detroit Records; Edward Duff, S. J., "Activation in ACTU," *Queen's Work,* May 1946, p. 1; *Detroit News,* Aug. 3, 1941; Statement of support for Reuther, UAW folder, box 3, Association of Catholic Trade Unionists of Detroit Records.

[29] Sebastian Erbacher to Norman McKenna, Feb. 25, 1938, folder 6, box 1, Norman C. McKenna Papers (American Catholic History Research Center and University Archives, Catholic University of America, Washington, D.C.); *Wage Earner,* Oct. 14, 1940; Richard Deverall to George Seldes, April 6, 1942, folder 14, box 1, McKenna Papers. Emphasis in original. Industrial Conference Reports, Season 1939: The Detroit Meeting, folder 13, box 36, Records of the Social Action Department, United States Conference of Catholic Bishops Collection (American Catholic History Research Center and University Archives).

"democratic unionism." The African American unionist Horace Sheffield added, "There's no question about it . . . [the ACTU] made some positive contributions." Meanwhile, Coughlin became anathema within Catholic circles. In late 1939 the ACTU chaplain Raymond Clancy publicly rebuked Coughlin on behalf of the archdiocese, and by 1943 two well-regarded priests asserted that "90% of the clergy [in Detroit] have no use for Coughlin."[30]

Yet as the United States entered World War II, Coughlin remained a popular parish priest and still represented to modernists a dangerous manifestation of working-class religion. The priest's apparent alliance with Gerald L. K. Smith was especially disconcerting for liberals. Smith, a Disciples of Christ pastor, joined many evangelical southern whites by relocating to Detroit in the late 1930s. In 1941 he launched the newspaper *The Cross and the Flag*—a title indicative of Smith's admixture of Christianity and politics—and a year later ran for the Senate on the Republican ticket. He lost but subsequently ran for president three times as the Christian Nationalist party candidate—perhaps the first explicitly political program premised on Christian fundamentalism since the schism between modernists and fundamentalists in the 1920s. By the onset of World War II this budding political activism among fundamentalists coincided with a new willingness to form interdenominational coalitions; both developments emerged largely from an increasing sense of panic that "communistic" modernism had infected American religion. "We Christians must continue to enjoy our liberty to disagree theologically," Smith wrote in a 1945 defense of Coughlin, but, "when it comes to Communism and Atheism the lovers of Christ must stand together as one solid body." In this populist political theology, the bastions of American democracy—private property, the traditional family, and white Christianity—were under siege by the forces of secularism, communism, unionism, and pluralism. Smith hoped to enlist other southern-born white evangelicals for the cause; in Claude Williams, one of the fiercest religious progressives of the twentieth century, he would find a formidable antagonist.[31]

Southern Evangelicals and Christian Discourse

The surge of southern evangelicals into Detroit's booming industrial plants left religious modernists stunned and puzzled. Edward DeWitt Jones, one of Detroit's leading Protestant luminaries, announced with bewilderment in 1942 that "no other city . . . has so many flourishing 'Tabernacle churches' as Detroit." Ellsworth Smith, director of the War Emergency Commission for the Detroit Council of Churches (DCC), was initially optimistic about the "church-minded" migrants, but by 1945 he was worried. "It cannot be said too emphatically," he warned, that "Detroit is a center of terrific religious energy." Moreover, a "very disturbing proportion of this energy is being drawn off by independent groups which offer a poor and often destructive religious education." Smith feared that "vast areas of population" might be "surrendered to these nondenominational, but very

[30] "Father Coughlin's Errors," *Michigan Catholic,* Nov. 16, 1939; Marquart interview; Judith Stephan-Norris and Maurice Zeitlin, *Talking Union* (Urbana, 1996), 173; "Conversations with Father J. L. Cavanaugh and Father John Coogan," Survey of Racial and Religious Conflict Forces in Detroit folder, box 71, Civil Rights Congress of Michigan Collection.
[31] "Protestants and Catholics Beware," *Cross and the Flag,* 4 (Sept. 1945), unpaginated; Jeansonne, *Gerald L. K. Smith,* 64–79; Carpenter, *Revive Us Again,* 89–107.

energetic, groups." In fact, by 1943 only 400 out of the city's 1,600 churches belonged to an established denomination.[32]

Committed to biblical literalism, revivalist worship, and a premillennialist belief in the imminence of end times, southern white evangelicals typically rejected both the theology and the social activism of modernist Christianity. For modernists, these cultural concerns were rapidly translated into political concerns. Writing of Detroit in *The Churchman,* Wilbur Larremore Caswell worried that "fanatical sects," once under the influence of a Norris or a Smith, represented "one of the most serious perils to both our religious and our political life." The Michigan Civil Rights Congress concurred, warning that vast numbers of newly arriving southern fundamentalists were "susceptible to leadership by dangerous demagogues" and bluntly concluding that "there is probably more American fascist, reactionary, and downright sedition propaganda generated in Detroit than in any other city."[33]

Liberals' tropes, while heightened by the war, had some validity. In 1942 Smith announced that he had received support from 50,000 Detroit-area CIO members—proof, he averred, that there are "still millions of Bible-reading, church-going, prayerful workers in America" who remained untouched by "Communists" such as Walter Reuther. Southern evangelicalism was also transforming the workplace. By late 1943 multiple sources estimated that between 3,000 and 3,500 shop-floor preachers were working in defense industry plants; UAW president R. J. Thomas counted more than a thousand preachers in Ford factories alone. Hoping to reach these industrial workers, the Presbyterian Church made a daring departure: it arranged for Claude Williams, a fiery evangelist and political radical from Arkansas, to serve as the presbytery's "minister to labor."[34]

Williams read the Bible as a manifesto of progressive political causes. His ministry, he explained to Studs Terkel, consisted of translating the "democratic impulse of mass religion rather than its protofascist content into a language then understood." In his booklet "The Galilean and the Common People," Williams taught that the "religion OF the prophets and the Son of Man is a religion OF, BY, and FOR the toiling masses of humanity." In another lesson, "The Carpenter," Williams contrasted the "false" religion of rulers and priests with the "true" religion of Moses, Jeremiah, and the prophets. These lessons were frequently rendered in quasi-mathematical formulas such as "the Labor Movement : Government = True Religion : Real Democracy." Williams always attempted to ground his political points with scriptural references or biblical parallels. Only this radically democratic religion, he believed, could pull southern evangelical workers away

[32] Edgar DeWitt Jones, "Strange Churches Rise in Detroit," *Christian Century,* Dec. 9, 1942, pp. 3–4; Ellsworth Smith, "Mobilization for War-Time Services and Reconstruction," [ca. 1943], typescript, folder 1, box 5, Series II: Metropolitan Detroit Council of Churches Records (Reuther Library); Ellsworth Smith, "Report for the Summer, 1945," typescript, folder 2, *ibid.*

[33] Wilbur Larremore Caswell, "Educating the 'Bible Christian,'" *Churchman,* Feb. 15, 1944; "The Religious Ferment in Detroit," Survey of Racial and Religious Conflict Forces in Detroit folder, box 71, Civil Rights Congress of Michigan Collection; "The Hill-Billies as Strikebreakers," Sept. 1943, *ibid.*

[34] Gerald L. K. Smith, "We Take Our Stand," *Cross and the Flag,* 1 (April 1942); Claude Williams, "The Hell-Brewers of Detroit," folder 14, box 111, Series II: Topical Files, RG 73, Social Ethics Pamphlet Collection (Special Collections, Yale University Divinity Library, New Haven, Conn.); "First Report of Peoples' Congress of Applied Religion," July 22–24, 1944, folder 5, box 19, Series III: Peoples Institute for Applied Religions, 1939–1977, Claude Williams Papers (Reuther Library); Claude Williams to Henry Jones, April 3, 1942, folder 19, box 2, Series I: Correspondence, 1929–1979, *ibid.*

from "the Detroit apostles of fascism" who used "the King James Bible as their *Mein Kampf*."[35]

By the early 1940s Williams had identified a number of "shop tabernacles" at area plants, likely established with the support of management. The UAW rightly worried about the content of industry-sponsored religion, suspecting that it countered the union's religious discourse. Williams agreed that employers had been "attempting to take advantage of the religious sentiment of their employees and of the uncritical preachers among them to foster under the guise of religion" an antiunion scheme. Williams sought to counter this influence by establishing what he called a Gospel Preacher's Council of Applied Religion. The initial group consisted of twenty-five preachers employed in war plants, but members believed that "there are hundreds of us preachers who toil with their hands as we do." Joining together for fellowship, Bible study services, and publication of a newsletter, the council was intended to serve as Williams's main conduit into working-class religious communities. In 1943 councils were operating at General Electric, Hudson Motor Car Company, U.S. Tire and Supply Company, and Murray Body Corporation, with organizing efforts underway elsewhere.[36]

In 1944 Williams founded the Detroit Council of Applied Religion. In May of that year he hosted an "ordination" ceremony for his working-class ministers that unabashedly mixed radical politics and religious ritual. Held at the Lucy Thurman branch of the Young Women's Christian Association, the gathering's participants were an interracial fellowship. Williams provocatively chose to hold the ceremony on May 1, a day of international workers' solidarity. In the sermon he presented that day, he urged the participants to "return to vital religion" and "return to the people." While receiving their ordination, Williams's ministers were instructed not to kneel as if before a bishop "in a submissive way" but to stand as ready to fight. Music and song had long been key to Williams's ministry, and "old tunes with new content" were liberally used on that day as well. Appropriately, the ceremony's closing "hymn" was the labor ballad "Joe Hill."[37]

A month later, Williams convened the Peoples' Congress of Applied Religion, to, as he put it, "map action, not debate issues" in the "fight for democracy." Out of this gathering grew the umbrella organization Peoples' Institute of Applied Religion (PIAR). Williams sought to fuse together representatives from organized labor, youth groups, "grass-roots" preachers, and the "middle-class preacher and laymen." To further its ministerial aims, the congress designed Bible study courses to teach that the "history of the labor movement will never be completely written until it begins with Moses," and labor

---

[35] Studs Terkel, *Hard Times: An Oral History of the Great Depression* (New York, 1970), 380; Claude Williams, "The Galilean and the Common People," folder 15, box 18, III: Peoples Institute for Applied Religions, Williams Papers. Emphasis in original. Claude Williams, "The Scriptural Heritage of the People," folder 11, box 111, Series II: Topical Files, RG 73, Social Ethics Pamphlet Collection; Claude Williams, "The Man Who Has an Answer," *ibid.*; Claude Williams, "Anti-Semitism, Racism, and Democracy," *ibid.*; Belfrage, *Faith to Free the People*, 260–61.

[36] "Gospel Preachers' Council," 1944, typescript, folder 10, box 18, Series III: Peoples Institute for Applied Religions, Williams Papers; Williams, "The Man Who Has an Answer"; Williams to "Sponsors and Friends," 1943, box 8, United Presbyterian Church in the U.S.A. Presbytery of Detroit Records (Bentley Historical Library).

[37] Williams to Herbert Hudnut, March 9, 1944, folder 12, box 19, Series III: Peoples Institute for Applied Religions, Williams Papers; Undated typescript, [ca. May 1944], folder 22, box 18, *ibid.* On the labor ballad "Joe Hill," see Donald E. Winters Jr., *The Soul of the Wobblies: The I.W.W., Religion, and American Culture in the Progressive Era, 1905–1917* (Westport, 1985).

"will never enlist and retain the bulk of American workers until it recognizes and approaches them in terms of their deep religious conditioning."[38]

Williams obsessively measured the PIAR against the machinations of Gerald L. K. Smith's America First party. The reasons were clear: for both men, the political shape of working-class religion was at stake. "Smith would distort and pervert the Bible, exploit the faulty religious conditioning of the masses and prostitute religion to develop shock troops at the behest of an industrial baron who aspires to be the Thyssen of an American fascism," Williams emphatically wrote to one of his supporters in the presbytery. He hoped to "appeal to the very deep and genuine religious sentiment of the masses, to enlist them as democratic elements in the dynamic movements of a free society."[39]

Just as Williams and his allies worried that fascist religion could spell the end of democracy, however, those on the right accused Williams and his organization of serving as a communist front. Even so, for Williams's gathered ministers, communism presented just as grave a danger to the intertwined future of Christianity and democracy as fascism posed for liberals and leftists. To J. Frank Norris, Williams was part of a "MODERNIS-TIC, COMMUNISTIC ECCLESIATSICAL CONSPIRACY" and "one of the rankest Communists in America." The National Laymen's Council of the Presbyterian Church described Williams as a "militant agitator for a *new social and economic order.*" The council claimed to have a document from the files of the House Committee on Un-American Activities proving Williams's connection to the Communist party, and the council even claimed to know Williams's party name.[40]

Smith likewise began his campaign against Williams by describing him as the "Communist on the Presbyterian payroll" and claimed to possess a confidential memo showing that Williams was a paid Soviet agent. By 1945 Smith had upped the rhetorical ante, referring to Williams as "Satan's Apostle to the American Church." One of Smith's followers infiltrated a conference that Williams held at St. Paul's Episcopal Church in Detroit, decried the presence of "Satan in God's House," and claimed that Williams's followers "crawled over the pews and actually saturated the place." For Smith and his fundamentalist followers, the threat of communism was literally demonic.[41]

Williams did little to stifle rumors of his political unorthodoxy. In fact, his defiance regarding the issue only heightened emotions. According to one credible report, Williams often made allusions to communist rhetoric, referring to himself as a "fellow-traveler with the Man Who Went to the Cross." In a letter to Henry Jones, one of his supporters, Williams dismissed the communist charge as "irrelevant" and turned the tables to aggressively accuse his own church benefactors of complicity in the "evils" that communists confronted. Williams ultimately admitted that he paid dues to the Communist

[38] "First Report of Peoples' Congress of Applied Religion"; Claude Williams, "Report on Work under War Emergency Program," Aug. 31, 1944, typescript, folder 12, box 18, Series III: Peoples Institute for Applied Religions, Williams Paper.

[39] Williams, "Report on Work under War Emergency Program."

[40] Belfrage, *Faith to Free the People,* 283–88; Williams, "Man Who Has an Answer"; National Laymen's Council, "Special Report—Involving the Rev. H. P. Marley," [ca. 1944], typescript, box 8, United Presbyterian Church in the U.S.A. Presbytery of Detroit Records. Emphasis in original.

[41] "Red Preachers," *Cross and the Flag,* 3 (Nov. 1944); "Satan in God's House," *ibid.,* 3 (Feb. 1945); "Claude Williams," *ibid.,* 4 (Sept. 1945); Kenneth Goff, "Christians, Beware!" *ibid.,* 4 (Nov. 1945); "Red Preacher Slurs the Cross," *ibid.,* 4 (March 1946). On apocalyptic beliefs, see Paul S. Boyer, *When Time Shall Be No More: Prophecy Belief in Modern American Culture* (Cambridge, Mass., 1992).

party for a few months in 1937, but that he never strayed from his firm religious beliefs. Williams's deep religiosity likely solidified his political absolutism.[42]

Williams was profoundly committed not just to the labor movement but also to the ideal of racial equality. In a typical pamphlet, he declared that "prejudice or discrimination" constituted "a *transgression at the very heart of true religion.*" Williams's fierce support for equality dovetailed with a swelling civil rights movement within black Detroit. Not coincidentally, two of Williams's earliest and most loyal Detroit supporters, John Miles and Charles Hill, were progressive African American clergymen who viewed Williams as a leader of the "spiritual front" against racism and reactionary politics. Williams's gatherings were almost always biracial, and he often recruited Owen Whitfield, a prominent African American religious radical from the South, to address PIAR audiences. As Williams understood, race was becoming increasingly central to Christian discourse during the war years; it added an entirely new dimension to the struggle between reactionary and progressive visions of working-class religion.[43]

Racial Ideology and Christian Discourse

By the early 1940s racial ideology had emerged as perhaps the most crucial element in the discourse surrounding working-class religion. For those who had built and supported the UAW, "fascist" religion became inextricably linked with "racist" or anti-Semitic religion. Contrarily, for right-wing religious leaders who condemned the UAW and its religious allies as "communist," communism became virtually synonymous not only with unionism but also with promiscuous race mixing. African Americans were naturally at the heart of these changes and debates, and African American ministers played a decisive role in bringing racial justice to the forefront of Christian discourse. In particular, the Congregationalist Horace White, the Episcopalian Malcolm Dade, and the Baptist Charles Hill hoped to diminish the stereotype of "overly-emotional" black religiosity, to promote a progressive politics of interracial solidarity within the UAW, and to tighten the discursive links between "fascist" and racist religion.[44]

These developments emerged haltingly at first. In the early 1930s black churches and workers were slow to warm to the UAW. Most churches remained the recipients of corporate gifts (especially from Henry Ford), and many black workers knew unions to be bastions of white privilege. Moreover, the individualistic theology of evangelical religion caused some black workers to view secular collective action suspiciously, but as the UAW

---

[42] Sourlock, "The Peoples Institute of Applied Religion," July 1945, private report typescript, folder 14, box 111, RG 73, Social Ethics Pamphlet Collection; Royal Wilbur France, "The Case of Claude Williams," [ca. 1953], typescript, *ibid.*; Williams to Jones, Feb. 3, 1945, folder 12, box 19, Series III: Peoples Institute for Applied Religions, Williams Papers.

[43] Williams, "Anti-Semitism, Racism, and Democracy"; Williams to Leslie A. Bechtel, Aug. 18, 1945, box 8, United Presbyterian Church in the U.S.A. Presbytery of Detroit Records; Erik S. Gellman and Jarod H. Roll, "Owen Whitfield and the Gospel of the Working Class in New Deal America, 1936–1946," *Journal of Southern History,* 72 (May 2006), 303–48.

[44] For the context of the liberal, antiracist alliance during the 1940s, see Alan Brinkley, *The End of Reform: New Deal Liberalism in Recession and War* (New York, 1995), 164–70. On the countervailing conflation of racial and economic conservatism, see Glenn Feldman, "Southern Disillusionment with the Democratic Party: Cultural Conformity and 'the Great Melding' of Racial and Economic Conservatism in Alabama during World War II," *Journal of American Studies,* 43 (Aug. 2009), 199–230.

achieved major victories and began a concerted recruitment effort, African Americans reconsidered unionism. Religion occupied a central place in this process.[45]

Horace White, a graduate of the Oberlin College Divinity School, was one of the earliest black pastors to push churches in the union's direction. A Social Gospel advocate, White was deeply impressed with the social potential of the labor movement, and he immediately turned his Plymouth Congregational Church into a meeting place for aspiring black unionists. Malcolm Dade's story neatly paralleled White's. Dade, similarly steeped in the Social Gospel, arrived from New England to pastor St. Cyprian's Church in 1936; he found the situation of black workers "just flagrantly bad, wrong, certainly not good." Together, both churches drew the most progressive and socially engaged element of Detroit's black middle class, while also becoming social, spiritual, and organizational resources for the swelling ranks of UAW supporters. Dade understood the significance of this development. Union leaders, Dade explained, "wanted to put their finger on Negro life. And, Negro life . . . is in the Negro church."[46]

The Reverend Charles A. Hill loomed even larger, combining a universalistic vision of human rights, a commitment to radical politics, and the passion of his Baptist pulpit to become black Detroit's preeminent prophetic voice. A Detroit native, Hill became assistant pastor at the huge and influential Second Baptist Church in 1918. In 1920 he established his own congregation, Hartford Avenue Baptist Church, which would become one of the ten largest black churches in Detroit by 1926. When the UAW mounted its first organizing campaigns in the 1930s, Hill turned the church into one of the most vital social resources at black unionists' disposal.[47]

By early 1941 UAW efforts to transform Detroit into a "union town" approached a defining crisis point. The union needed recognition from the last unorganized auto giant, the Ford Motor Company. The company employed by far the largest number of African Americans of any auto company; for Ford to be organized—and the union to survive—the UAW needed the support of black workers. In April, during the decisive strike against the River Rouge plant in Dearborn, the union's black clerical supporters proved crucial. White delivered speeches and sermons from the UAW's sound truck outside the plant. When a contingent of black workers resisted joining the strike, Hill "went out to the Ford factory and . . . pleaded with them to come out; [he] told them that they could not afford to make any advance by themselves; they had to learn to work with other workers." He was happy to host union meetings in the basement of the church, making it "difficult for [Ford spies] to prove that we were just discussing union matters. And so . . . [unionists] got together regardless of their race and nationality." Although Ford tried once again to divide the black clergy by promising exclusive access to jobs for members of loyal church bodies, Hill happily reported in 1943 that "the majority of the colored clergy worked hand in hand with the CIO and blocked the move. . . . The colored clergy tell their flocks to obey the Lord and obey the CIO." Gloster Current of the National Association for the Advancement of Colored People

[45] Meier and Rudwick, *Black Detroit and the Rise of the UAW.*
[46] Horace A. White, "Who Owns the Negro Church?" *Christian Century,* Feb. 9, 1938, p. 177; Malcolm Dade interview by Jim Keeney and Roberta McBride, Sept. 17, 1969, transcript, pp. 7, 17, Blacks in the Labor Movement Collection (Reuther Library).
[47] Rev. Charles Hill interview by McBride, May 8, 1967, transcript, Blacks in the Labor Movement Collection; Dillard, *Faith in the City,* 27–40.

agreed with Hill, observing that "many colored deacons who were previously anti-CIO have now swung around and are all out for the CIO."[48]

This political shift among many black churches and worshippers also signaled a discursive shift in the construct of working-class religion. Although some observers continued to dismiss working-class African American religion as excessively emotional and dangerously obscurantist, this language steadily retreated as religion became a potential bridge linking black workers, CIO unionism, and New Deal politics. Reorienting both the political culture of black churches and the discourse surrounding black religion was a central preoccupation of the prophetic preachers. By presenting black religion as progressive, universalistic, and "rational," these clerics linked it with the culture of contemporary liberalism. Such a connection, especially made in the context of World War II, permitted the ministers to make an additional contribution to the discourse surrounding the politics of religion: "fascist" religion was really "racist" religion, and both needed to be opposed in the name of democracy.

Progressive whites quickly accepted this analogy. Among Catholics, the ACTU president Paul Weber acknowledged in 1943 that the "race problem in Detroit" had become critical, and he placed the "greater part of the blame . . . upon white people who persist in a totally undemocratic and un-American attitude of discrimination toward colored people." The ACTU chaplain Raymond Clancy agreed, reiterating the theme that racism was both un-American and un-Christian. The lay people most committed to this doctrine soon erected an organization network linking Catholicism and racial equality. A small but lively chapter of the Catholic Interracial Council of Detroit distributed thousands of pamphlets and lectured before tens of thousands of area Catholics. At a remarkable service in 1943, Sacred Heart Church established an "interracial shrine": mass was followed by a program on "Catholic action and race relations," cosponsored by the ACTU and the United Automobile Workers Local 600. Such religious rituals and social performances tightly interwove the threads linking religious identity with political commitments to racial justice, industrial unionism, and democracy.[49]

Mainline Protestants agreed. In 1942 Protestants took a leading part in the Metropolitan Detroit Fair Employment Practice Council because equal opportunity laws presented a chance for "translating Judeo Christian principles and democratic ideals into practice." In 1944 the Detroit Council of Churches issued an "interracial code"—the first of its kind in the country—that sanctioned member churches for excluding African Americans, citing "Christian, democratic, and scientific principles." An interracial workshop, sponsored by the city of Detroit in 1945, demonstrated the growing pervasiveness of such discourse. Representatives of one hundred churches attended, and many speakers expounded the theme that had come to define the war for many: democracy needed Christianity, and both needed to advance an agenda of racial equality. Herbert Hudnut, the pastor of the Woodward Avenue Presbyterian Church, made the connection explicit:

[48] Hill interview, 4–6; "Conversation with Charles A. Hill," Sept. 1943, Survey of Racial and Religious Conflict Forces in Detroit folder, box 71, Civil Rights Congress of Michigan Collection; "Conversation with Gloster Current," *ibid.*

[49] Paul Weber, "Editorial," *Wage Earner,* June 11, 1943; *ibid.,* June 25, 1943; *Michigan Catholic,* July 15, Oct. 28, 1943; Catholic Interracial Council, "Bulletin," Sept. 1946, Catholic Interracial Group folder, box 11, Association of Catholic Trade Unionists of Detroit Records.

"We are Nazis to the extent that we possess degrees of hate within us against our fellow men."[50]

This discourse reflected the desire to ameliorate very real social tensions simmering within workplaces and neighborhoods throughout the city. The politics of race rather than the boundaries of denomination increasingly shaped both Christian discourse and religious identity during World War II. As Detroit's African American population continued to increase, black workers found themselves slowly advancing into some previously "all-white" factory jobs and positions of leadership in the UAW. As a growing, avidly Democratic constituency, they represented a rising political threat to conservatives. Throughout the city, new African American neighborhoods were established and older ones grew, persistently challenging the highly segregated racial geography. And the promise of a "double victory" over fascism abroad and racism at home produced a more confident, militant, and confrontational attitude among many blacks. For all these reasons, the religion of conservative and antimodernist working-class whites became fixated on preserving racial hierarchies at the same moment that progressives were linking Christianity to racial equality.[51]

Progressives especially worried about the local volatile Packard Motor Car Company plant, which became a highly contested battleground between antithetical religious and cultural forces. In October 1941 white workers at Packard launched an unauthorized strike over the transfer of two African American metal polishers to what was considered "white" work on defense products; the strike spiraled on for six months. When twenty-five thousand Packard workers launched a second hate strike in June 1943, working-class unity seemed elusive at best. Religion exacerbated these disputes. Offering his considerations on the troubles at Packard, the *Michigan Chronicle* reporter Theodore Wood observed that "conflicts in plants between whites and blacks were more frequent where revivalist influence was strong."[52]

Frank Norris was the most notable influence. He hosted popular "Packard days" services on Thursday and Friday nights at Temple Baptist Church, using the opportunity to excoriate communism, the UAW, and racial integration. According to Williams, Norris operated sixteen different religious programs at the Packard plant, plus a shop-floor radio show. Williams described the content of Norris's gospel to a Civil Rights Congress investigator: "Sunday after Sunday, both from his pulpit and on the air, [Norris] preaches that it is an insult that white men should be compelled to work along side of 'niggers' in plants. For the 'protection' of white women, he demands that the whole Negro population of 'rapists' and 'primitives' be separated in schools, in homes, in theatres, in parks, in shops, in jobs." Yet simultaneously Norris cultivated a handful of African American preachers on the shop floor. The case of the African American Pentecostal preacher and

---

[50] "'Of One Blood All Nations': An Interracial Code for Protestant Churches," Feb. 17, 1944, typescript, folder 14, box 29, United Community Services Central Files (Reuther Library); "Summary of the Interracial Workshop Conference Sponsored by City of Detroit Interracial Committee," June 1, 1945, typescript, folder 14, box 101, *ibid.*

[51] For studies of racial conflict in World War II–era Detroit, see Robert Korstad and Nelson Lichtenstein, "Opportunities Found and Lost: Labor, Radicals, and the Early Civil Rights Movement," *Journal of American History,* 75 (Dec. 1988), 786–811; and Thomas J. Sugrue, *Origins of the Urban Crisis: Race and Inequality in Postwar Detroit* (Princeton, 1996), 33–57.

[52] Meier and Rudwick, *Black Detroit and the Rise of the UAW,* 125–36; Robert H. Zieger, *The CIO, 1935–1955* (Chapel Hill, 1997), 155; "Race Conflicts in Detroit Riots," Sept. 1943, Survey of Racial and Religious Conflict Forces in Detroit folder, box 71, Civil Rights Congress of Michigan Collection.

Packard worker Robert Hill vividly illustrates the cultural trench warfare that was waged over religious ideology. Hill, described by Williams as "the most dynamic speaker in the plant," had been courted by Norris and even had appeared on Norris's radio show. Williams's protégé, the African American Packard shop preacher Virgil Vanderburg, approached Hill and apparently convinced his fellow evangelist that "he was being used." Flipped to Williams's position, Hill addressed hundreds of workers each week and, "being the most influential speaker, the anti-Negro forces are check-mated in their religious programs."[53]

While it is difficult to directly correlate religious influences, Norris's hostility to the UAW likely won a generous hearing among recently resettled southern whites, especially after the union threatened the jobs of those who participated in racially inspired walkouts. Even so, incendiary religious conflict was not limited to Protestants. According to Leroy Spradley, an African American committeeman in the UAW, one Polish American priest also visited the Packard plants and urged an alliance between white Protestants and ethnic Catholics toward "maintaining Christian civilization there"—essentially creating an interfaith black-white dyad that would thwart the promotion of blacks into previously all-white shop departments.[54]

Beyond the workplace, many ethnic Catholics viewed home ownership as a sacred duty, and perceived threats to these Catholic communities—often established through heavy sacrifice from working-class parishioners—were greeted with hostility. The small-scale riots surrounding occupancy of the Sojourner Truth Housing Project in February 1942 offers the most vivid example. Designed to house two hundred African American defense workers, the project—federally funded, but locally administered—was designed for a northeast section of the city near previous black settlements. Whites in the adjacent neighborhoods reacted swiftly to the construction. Led by the Polish American realtor Joseph Buffa, residents formed the Seven Mile–Fenelon Improvement Association (SMFIA) to lobby officials to keep "their" neighborhoods—and public housing in general—white.[55]

To the dismay of liberal Catholics, priests and parishioners became a driving force in the SMFIA. In December 1941 the Detroit Council of Social Agencies complained that Fr. O'Mara was "one of the most bitter factors" opposing the housing project. Even more important was Fr. Constantine Dzink, whose overwhelmingly Polish parish—Saint Louis the King—became a headquarters for SMIFA meetings. Described by one reporter as "an aged, bald, Polish peasant," Dzink personified liberal fears that working-class religion nurtured fascism. Employing long-standing discursive categories, the report described Dzink as "a virtual dictator over the lives and thoughts of several thousand Poles." During the 1920s the supposed "authoritarian" culture and emotional

[53] "Interview with the Rev. Claude Williams," Sept. 1943, Survey of Racial and Religious Conflict Forces in Detroit folder, box 71, Civil Rights Congress of Michigan Collection; Williams to Hudnut, March 9, 1944, folder 12, box 19, Series III: Peoples Institute for Applied Religions, Williams Papers.

[54] "Talk with Leroy Spradley," Sept. 1943, Survey of Racial and Religious Conflict Forces in Detroit folder, box 71, Civil Rights Congress of Michigan Collection.

[55] "Visit to Bishop Stephen Woznicki," Sept. 1943, Survey of Racial and Religious Conflict Forces in Detroit folder, box 71, ibid.; "Relations between Poles and Jews," ibid. On conflicts between Catholics and African Americans, see John T. McGreevy, Parish Boundaries: The Catholic Encounter with Race in the Twentieth-Century Urban North (Chicago, 1996), 74–77; and Dominic J. Capeci, Race Relations in Wartime Detroit: The Sojourner Truth Housing Controversy of 1942 (Philadelphia, 1984).

susceptibility of immigrant Catholics was considered socially unhealthy; by the early 1940s it had morphed into something inherently political and downright dangerous.[56]

Thus, racial ideology divided black workers from white workers as well as progressives from conservatives within the same religious traditions. When Louis Murphy and Marie Conti of the Catholic Workers movement visited fellow Catholics protesting the Sojourner Truth project, they came away deeply troubled. Conti, noting the ubiquity of American flags on the protest line, wondered whether "the Negro can help but doubt democracy." Although the pair tried to stimulate conversation and reflection, they instead found themselves in bitter disagreement with other "good Catholics" from the parish of St. Louis the King. "I said to a Catholic, self-called, that Christ died for both white and Negro—and he actually denied it," Conti lamented. Tellingly, another "good Catholic" accused the members of the Catholic Workers movement of not being "real" Catholics, but rather Communists and "nigger-lovers"—a painful contrast to Conti's own dismissal of a racist as a "self-called" Catholic and a revealing conflation of "communism" with racial pluralism. As Murphy and Conti retreated, a group of men followed them menacingly, one uttering threats. "I have never in my life seen hate personified as I did in the persons of these Catholics," Conti morosely concluded.[57]

Black clerical leaders naturally supported the Sojourner Truth homes and used their churches as spaces to hold rallies and discuss strategy. For Charles Hill, who led the Sojourner Truth Citizens' Committee, the conflict was an opportunity to plead for working-class solidarity. African Americans and Polish Americans, he wrote, were "in the same boat together." Piercing through decades' worth of Christian discourse, Hill recognized that immigrant Catholics and African Americans had *both* been the subject of demeaning stereotypes: that "Polish people are stupid and uncouth and unfit for anything except manual work," or that "Negroes make poor neighbors." Hill urged Poles to "refuse to listen any longer to these stories."[58]

Unfortunately, as Hill later admitted, his arguments did not seem to change any minds. Indeed, the riots at the Sojourner Truth Housing Project was just a prelude to the much more serious violence that erupted in June 1943. According to a state investigative committee, tensions between black and ethnic (likely Catholic) youth sparked the violent eruption. Trouble allegedly started days before the riot began, when African American boys were pelted with stones at an amusement center and decided to retaliate by "[taking] care of the Hunkies." This "retaliation" began on Belle Isle, an island park in the middle of the Detroit River. Hot, irritable, and overcrowded whites and blacks in the park engaged in scuffles that eventually spread through the city and produced a wave of racial violence that raged virtually uncontrolled until federal troops arrived two days later. Thirty-four people, twenty of them African American, lay dead after three days of vicious street fighting.[59]

[56] Charles Livermore to Robert MacRae, Dec. 5, 1941, folder 9, box 110, United Community Services Central Files; "Conversation with Father Constantine Djuik," Sept. 1943, Survey of Racial and Religious Conflict Forces in Detroit folder, box 71, Civil Rights Congress of Michigan Collection; "Detroit: A Survey and a Program of Action," [ca. 1944], typescript, folder 13, box 101, United Community Services Central Files.

[57] *Catholic Worker,* March 1942.

[58] Capeci, *Race Relations in Wartime Detroit,* 93–99; Charles Hill, "To Loyal and Patriotic Polish-Americans Living Near Sojourner Truth Homes," 1942, typescript, 1942, folder 11, box 110, United Community Services Central Files; "A Statement of a Point of View regarding the Sojourner Truth Homes Controversy," *ibid.*

[59] "Factual Report of the Detroit Race Riot of June 20–21, 1943," typescript, folder 2, box 1, Michigan Governor's Committee to Investigate the Detroit Race Riots Records 1943 (Special Collections Research Center, University of Chicago, Chicago, Ill.).

Responses to the race riot perfectly capture the politicized shape of Christian discourse heading into the postwar period. For Gerald Smith, the riot was a textbook example of the failure of interracialism, the fruits of moral dissolution, and the mendacity of communists. He believed that northern "screwballs and sentimentalists" had upset the "natural" order of racial separation and hastened the disintegration of traditional sexual mores. Once in the North, African Americans were "encouraged by politicians and Communists to make dates with white girls and to flirt with white girls on the street." Communists employed white women to bait gullible black men, thus artificially fomenting black discontent. The only solution, Smith averred, was "Christian statesmanship," which might preserve the hierarchies of race and gender, oppose communism, and in the process save "traditional" American democracy.[60]

Louis Martin of the *Michigan Chronicle* also invoked Christian rhetoric to draw diametrically opposite political conclusions. The riot alluded to efforts by reactionaries to preserve an antidemocratic racial caste system. When the state investigative committee concluded that the riot had been provoked by the African American bid for equality, Martin angrily compared the report to anti-Semitic fascist propaganda. "By a similar procedure," Martin observed, "passages could be taken out of the Holy Bible which would make the Scriptures equally inflammatory." Indeed, Martin concluded, had committee members read the Bible, "their report would have repudiated the principle of brotherhood of man as an incitement for oppressed Negroes to riot." Martin, like Claude Williams and other religious leftists, linked "true" religion to political democracy and racial equality; "false" religion, or simple godlessness, produced both racial oppression and fascism.[61]

As World War II ended, the discourse surrounding working-class religion cooled considerably. Fears of a "fascist" insurrection led by a religious demagogue shriveled away in the glow of Axis defeat. The most vituperative religious antimodernist was once again scuttled to the margins of cultural life, replaced by the more moderate and telegenic evangelism of Billy Graham. Leftist religious radicals suffered a more certain defeat. Charles Hill found himself before the House Un-American Activities Committee in 1952; the ACTU struggled against the "apathy" of Catholic workers; and Claude Williams was even convicted of heresy (charged with being a communist). Moreover, by the early 1960s increasing numbers of Catholics, Pentecostals, and Southern Baptists were enjoying a measure of upward mobility while their churches embraced an aura of respectability. Moderation and consensus, it seemed, had prevailed in religious culture, and working-class religion had become, simply, American religion.[62]

Even so, the legacy of Christian discourse from the 1930s and 1940s would not fade away so easily. The war years had deeply politicized religious language and ideas while eroding traditional denominational barriers. Various iterations of a religious Left reemerged beginning in the mid-1950s, pursuing political goals rooted in the values of the war-era Social Gospel: progress, justice, and equality. The activists and organizations

[60] Gerald L. K. Smith, "Race Riots: An Interpretation," *Cross and the Flag,* 2 (July 1943).

[61] "The Famous Report," *Michigan Chronicle,* Aug. 21, 1943, p. 4.

[62] On postwar religion, see Patrick Allitt, *Religion in America since 1945: A History* (New York, 2003); Dillard, *Faith in the City,* 186–91; Untitled manuscript, [ca. 1957], Father Hubble ACTU Report to Cardinal Mooney folder, box 4, Association of Catholic Trade Unionists of Detroit Records; and France, "Case of Claude Williams."

that pursued these goals—from the Southern Christian Leadership Conference to Concerned Clergy and Laity against the War to Interfaith Worker Justice—sought to create religiously pluralistic coalitions of the politically like-minded, and they usually linked their moral goals to some vision of direct government action. Conservatives, meanwhile, also hearkened to the values of their war-era antecedents: a preference for limited government, a respect for long-held traditions, a suspicion of social change, and an idealization of the nuclear family. By the 1970s new conservative coalitions—from the Stop ERA movement to the Christian Coalition to Evangelicals and Catholics Together—had politicized theses values across the denominational spectrum.

More startlingly, the discursive categories of the 1930s survived remarkably intact. Conservative critics continued to denounce civil rights activists as communists well into the 1960s. More recently, suspicions of socialism leveled against liberals have carried meanings not dissimilar from the accusations from Coughlin or Smith: that an intrusive state and modernist elite are dismantling traditional Christianity and "true" democracy. Progressive critics have maintained their discursive categories as well. The religious Right, for example, has been denounced as a would-be theocracy, undermining American political values in the name of an obscurantist, end-time theological authoritarianism. Recent journalists have even revived the term *fascist* to describe the political theology of far-right Christian groups.[63]

As historians continue to integrate religion into the narrative of the American twentieth century, World War II–era Detroit offers useful insights. First, it illustrates that class identity and class politics cannot be ignored in studies of religion. It also provides a model for placing the most significant and populous working-class religious groups inside a larger, more transformative story. Finally, as the contemporary world continues to assess the promises and pitfalls of politicized religion, wartime Detroit offers one important example of people simultaneously coming together and moving apart in the context of a rapidly changing world.[64]

[63] Politicized religious language has reemerged in, for example, Jim DeMint, *Saving Freedom: We Can Stop America's Slide into Socialism* (Nashville, 2009); Michelle Goldberg, *Kingdom Coming: The Rise of Christian Nationalism* (New York, 2006); and Chris Hedges, *American Fascists: The Christian Right and the War on America* (New York, 2006).

[64] On religion's ambiguous political impact, see Robert D. Putnam and David E. Campbell, *American Grace: How Religion Divides and Unites Us* (New York, 2010), 493–550.

Closing Doors: Hollywood, Affirmative Action, and the Revitalization of Conservative Racial Politics

Eithne Quinn

When the Equal Employment Opportunity Commission (EEOC) held a one-day hearing in Hollywood in March 1969, it was a high moment in the struggle for minority jobs in the film industry. At the close of the hearing, the EEOC's general counsel Daniel Steiner stated: "I think we have established on the record today clear evidence of a pattern or practice of discrimination in violation of Title VII of the Civil Rights Act of 1964." The testimony given to the EEOC committee had uncovered "gross underutilization" of minority workers and "recruiting systems that have as their forseeable effect the employment only of whites," his statement read. On the basis of these findings, the Justice Department took the extraordinary step of preparing lawsuits under Title VII (which prohibited employment discrimination based on "an individual's race, color, religion, sex, or national origin") against practically the entire industry: the Association of Motion Picture and Television Producers (AMPTP), six of the seven major motion picture studios, the International Alliance of Theatrical Stage Employees (IATSE), and "a good number of craft unions."[1] Had it gone to trial, it would have been the first case against industry-wide discrimination since the 1964 act was passed.

However, following lobbying by the film industry, the EEOC head Clifford Alexander, who had chaired the hearing, was summoned to appear before a Senate Justice subcommittee, where he was "subjected to a tongue-lashing," as one journalist described, by the

Eithne Quinn teaches American studies at the University of Manchester, England.

For their suggestions and support, and invitations to present this paper, I would like to thank Bridget Byrne, Mel Donalson, Cliff Frazier, Jeff Geiger, Lee Grieveson, Richard Heffner, David Hesmondhalgh, Jan-Christopher Horak, Mark Jancovich, Steven Jones, Peter Knight, Steve Neale, Anamik Saha, Jill Solomon, William Van Deburg, Brian Ward, Craig Watkins, Howard Winant, and especially Peter Krämer. Thanks also to Frank Mackaman at the Dirksen Congressional Center, Clare Denk and Joan Cohen at the Margaret Herrick Library, and Greg Cumming and Rob Olguin at the Nixon Presidential Library for help in accessing papers. Special thanks to Ed Linenthal, Kevin Marsh, and the *Journal of American History* reviewers for full and thought-provoking feedback, and to the editorial staff at the *JAH*. I am indebted to the Leverhulme Trust and the Arts and Humanities Research Council for supporting this research.

Readers may contact Quinn at eithne.quinn@manchester.ac.uk.

[1] U.S. Equal Employment Opportunity Commission, *Hearings before the U.S. Equal Employment Opportunity Commission on Utilization of Minority and Women Workers in Certain Major Industries: Hearings Held in Los Angeles, Calif., March 12–14, 1969* (Washington, 1969), 227, 228. See also A. D. Murphy, "Gov't Charges: Pix Discriminate in Jobs," *Daily Variety*, March 14, 1969, pp. 1, 22–23; Vincent J. Burke, "U.S. Plans to Prod Film Industry on Job Discrimination Charges," *Los Angeles Times*, Oct. 19, 1969, pp. 1, 14; "Gov't Crackdown on H'Wood," *Daily Variety*, Oct. 20, 1969, pp. 1, 8; Dan Knapp, "An Assessment of the Status of Hollywood Blacks," *Los Angeles Times*, Sept. 28, 1969, Calendar section, pp. 1, 17–18. "Transcript of Civil Rights Act (1964)," *Our Documents*, http://www.ourdocuments.gov/doc.php?flash=true&doc=97&page=transcript.

doi: 10.1093/jahist/jas302

powerful Senate Republican minority leader Everett Dirksen. "Stop some of this harassment of the business community," stormed Dirksen, "like your carnival hearing out there in Los Angeles . . . or I am going to the highest authority in this government to get somebody fired." A week later, President Richard M. Nixon announced that Alexander was to be replaced. The film industry's political lobbying was complemented by a savvy public relations campaign. Jack Valenti, the head of the Motion Picture Association of America (MPAA), organized a high-profile luncheon in honor of Roy Wilkins, the director of the National Association for the Advancement of Colored People (NAACP). In his opening remarks at the April 1969 event, Valenti characterized advances in African American participation in the film business as "a curve reaching a new high in a road that is up." The industry's purported openness, he continued, "is most heartening and most important to me because the door is open to the black people without it being forced."[2]

While the EEOC's assault on white privilege in Hollywood was indicative of the period's progressive interventionism, the industry's response crystallized forces of backlash that were gathering great momentum. Historians have focused strongly on the rise since the early 1970s of modern conservatism and the role that racial identity politics played in conservatism's resurgence. Of particular relevance for this article is Nancy MacLean's exploration of how the civil rights struggle for equal employment spurred conservative activism. As she and others detail, a new "color-blind" discourse was first fomented by intellectuals and policy advisers around the turn of the 1970s. These influential advocates, many of whom became known as neoconservatives by the late 1970s, came from the right of the Democratic party and the left of the Republican party and turned sharply away from the black freedom struggle, which they had supported, after the mid-1960s civil rights victories. Proceeding from the assumption that discrimination had more or less ended with civil rights reforms, these new conservatives championed a laissez-faire approach to racial equality. That strategy was to have far-reaching implications. As Jacquelyn Dowd Hall summarizes: "Largely moribund by the 1960s, the conservative movement reinvented itself in the 1970s, first by incorporating neoconservatives who eschewed old-fashioned racism and then by embracing an ideal of formal equality, focusing on blacks' ostensible failings, and positioning itself as the true inheritor of the civil rights legacy."[3]

This article examines race politics and the film industry during the early years of affirmative action, focusing on the role that studio management played in the formation and propagation of "color-blind" conservatism. Valenti's upbeat interpretation of Hollywood's

    [2] Burke, "U.S. Plans to Prod Film Industry on Job Discrimination Charges," 14; Everett Dirksen quoted in "Dirksen Threatens 'to Get' Black 'Fired' for Bias Fight," *Jet,* April 10, 1969, p. 6. Jack Valenti quoted in Bill Ornstein, "Black Employment Pics, TV Up," *Hollywood Reporter,* April 22, 1969, p. 1.
    [3] On the rise of modern conservatism since the early 1970s, see, for example, Matthew D. Lassiter, *The Silent Majority: Suburban Politics in the Sunbelt South* (Princeton, 2006); Kevin M. Kruse, *White Flight: Atlanta and the Making of Modern Conservatism* (Princeton, 2005); Michael Lind, "Conservative Elites and the Counterrevolution against the New Deal," in *Ruling America: A History of Wealth and Power in Democracy,* ed. Steve Fraser and Gary Gerstle (Cambridge, Mass., 2005), 256–61; Lisa McGirr, *Suburban Warriors: The Origins of the New American Right* (Princeton, 2001); George Lipsitz, *The Possessive Investment in Whiteness: How White People Profit from Identity Politics* (Philadelphia, 1998); and Dan T. Carter, *From George Wallace to Newt Gingrich: Race in the Conservative Counterrevolution, 1963–1994* (Baton Rouge, 1996). Nancy MacLean, *Freedom Is Not Enough: The Opening of the American Workplace* (Cambridge, Mass., 2006), esp. 185–261. Jacquelyn Dowd Hall, "The Long Civil Rights Movement and the Political Uses of the Past," *Journal of American History,* 91 (March 2005), 1237.

open door for minorities painted a picture of an industry rapidly creating a level playing field and in no need of federal intervention to "force doors." Here and elsewhere the rhetoric of Hollywood management provided a rationale and a cover for the industry's attacks on state intervention and minority activism. This article establishes the bad faith of management's discursive stance by describing the entrenched exclusion of minorities in the film industry. Despite the formal end of hiring bias, Hollywood was still over-whelmingly white at the end of the 1960s and generally showed "no concrete evidence of a willingness to change the employment pattern," stated Steiner.[4] While the EEOC committee exposed underrepresentation of all minority groups (as well as women) in Hollywood, its sharpest focus was on African Americans—reflecting their very high rates of exclusion from film jobs and the particular civil rights import of Title VII for black Americans. The industry's reaction regarding the issue of race was, in turn, energized by a repudiation of African American, rather than other minority group, demands. Although job exclusion and concerns about racial representation in the film industry affected all minority groups, the preponderance of discussions about race in the 1960s and 1970s centered on African Americans. For this reason, black-white racial politics stands as the central frame for this article.

While the racial themes of Hollywood films of this period have been discussed exten-sively by scholars, attempts to break down racial barriers in the Hollywood labor market are underdocumented, as are the responses of Hollywood management and labor organi-zations. Film scholarship on race in this period has tended to neglect white industry and production politics, which risks normalizing and/or totalizing the industry's racial power relations.[5] This article focuses on the two principal flash points created when minorities and their allies demanded fuller entry into the industry during the early post–Civil

---

[4] U.S. Equal Employment Opportunity Commission, *Hearings before the U.S. Equal Employment Opportunity Commission on Utilization of Minority and Women Workers in Certain Major Industries,* 228.

[5] On black representation in films of the period, see James Murray, *To Find an Image: Black Films from Uncle Tom to Super Fly* (New York, 1973); Thomas Cripps, 'The Dark Side of Whiteness: *Sweetback* and John Dollard's Idea of 'the Gains of the Lower Class Negroes,'" in *The Persistence of Whiteness: Race and Contemporary Hollywood Cinema,* ed. Daniel Bernardi (New York, 2008), 269–91; Ed Guerrero, *Framing Blackness: The African American Image in Film* (Philadelphia, 1993), esp. 9–111; Mark A. Reid, *Redefining Black Film* (Berkeley, 1993); Donald Bogle, *Toms, Coons, Mulattoes, Mammies, and Bucks: An Interpretive History of Blacks in American Films* (New York, 1997), esp. 231–66; William L. Van Deburg, *Black Camelot: African-American Culture Heroes in Their Times, 1960–1980* (Chicago, 1997), esp. 127–96; and Keith M. Harris, *Boys, Boyz, Bois: The Ethics of Black Masculinity in Film and Popular Media* (New York, 2005), esp. 21–77. On Latino representation in Hollywood films, see, for example, Chon A. Noriega, ed., *Chicanos and Film: Representation and Resistance* (Minneapolis, 1992); Rosa Linda Fregoso, *The Bronze Screen: Chicana and Chicano Film Culture* (Minneapolis, 1993); and Charles Ramirez Berg, *Latino Images in Film: Stereotypes, Subversion, Resistance* (Austin, 2002). On black filmmaking, see Lindsay Patter-son, ed., *Black Films and Film-Makers: A Comprehensive Anthology from Stereotype to Superhero* (New York, 1975); Gladstone L. Yearwood, "The Hero in Black Film: An Analysis of the Film Industry and the Problems in Black Cinema," *Wide Angle,* 5 (Spring 1982), 67–81; Thomas Cripps, *Making Movies Black: The Hollywood Message Movie from World War II to the Civil Rights Era* (New York, 1993), esp. 250–94; Robert E. Weems, *Desegregating the Dollar: African American Consumerism in the Twentieth Century* (New York, 1998), esp. 80–99; Melvin Donal-son, *Black Directors in Hollywood* (Austin, 2003); S. Craig Watkins, *Representing: Hip Hop Culture and the Produc-tion of Black Cinema* (Chicago, 1998), esp. 77–103; David James, "Chained to Devilpictures: Cinema and Black Liberation in the Sixties," in *The Year Left 2: An American Socialist Yearbook,* ed. Mike Davis et al. (London, 1987), 125–38; Jesse Algeron Rhines, *Black Film, White Money* (New Brunswick, 1996), esp. 36–50; and Tommy L. Lott, "Hollywood and Independent Black Cinema," in *Contemporary Hollywood Cinema,* ed. Steve Neale and Murray Smith (London, 1998), esp. 211–28. Although whiteness studies is a fertile field in film studies, it almost always attends to textual representation and/or critical and audience reception. See, for example, Richard Dyer, *White: Essays on Race and Culture* (London, 1997); Diane Negra, *Off-White Hollywood: American Culture and Ethnic Female Stardom* (London, 2001); Hernan Vera and Andrew Gordon, *Screen Saviors: Hollywood's Fictions of Whiteness* (Lanham, 2003); and Bernardi, ed., *Persistence of Whiteness.*

Rights Act period. The first was the federal action of 1969–1970, and the second came in the summer of 1972 when black groups—galvanized by the failure of the Justice Department to exact long-lasting changes—took a direct-action approach in the fight for jobs and control. The racial rhetoric of Hollywood management in 1969 occurred notably early in the intellectual gestation of the new "color-blind" laissez-faire discourse—1972 marks the beginning of the mainstream political emergence of this discourse. The powerful film business, this article argues, not only disseminated incipient neoconservative ideas but it was also an important site where the discourse and its policy implications were tested and ultimately made normative.

Closed Doors

The Hollywood film industry had always been a bastion of whiteness. Its decision makers and workers were the same color as the heroes and heroines who populated its film narratives. Racial minorities were represented in films through stereotypical regimes that reproduced white-dominated racial norms for vast audiences. Starting most notoriously with *The Birth of a Nation* (1915), African Americans have figured prominently in Hollywood's racist symbolic relations because of their unique history of material and cultural oppression as well as their rich expressive resources. Excluded from Hollywood production, African Americans, beginning in the 1910s, set up their own small companies to make films for black audiences. However, by the mid-1960s this segregated sector had died off, a casualty, as the film historian Thomas Cripps explains, of audience integration and, ironically, of Hollywood's liberal postwar "message movies": "as the films reinforced hope, they diverted black attention away from the goal of an independent black cinema."[6] Fast developing a new sense of popular-cultural self-identity and of their own box-office clout as consumers, African Americans in the late 1960s were left without a meaningful independent film industry or any real foothold in mainstream production.

From this low starting point, Valenti's characterization of "a road that is up" referred to two main advances in participation by African Americans in film: the on-screen progress achieved by message-movie black actors and the imminent release of Hollywood's first black-directed studio picture of the sound era, Gordon Parks Sr.'s *The Learning Tree* (1969). These developments—particularly the extraordinary stardom of Sidney Poitier following his three hit studio pictures of 1967, *Guess Who's Coming to Dinner, In the Heat of the Night,* and *To Sir, with Love*—were indeed remarkable. However, they presented a highly misleading image of the industry's distribution of jobs and power that was compounded by filmic narratives of race progress and black occupational success. In fact, Hollywood remained starkly exclusionary. The evidence prepared for the EEOC hearing revealed that the studios' behind-the-scenes utilization of blacks, Latinos, and other minorities was well below the average rates for industries in the rest of the Los Angeles area. The six major studios that were referred by the EEOC to the Justice

---

[6] *The Birth of a Nation,* dir. D. W. Griffith (Epoch Film Co., 1915). Thomas Cripps, *Black Film as Genre* (Bloomington, 1979), 9. On "race film" production and its decline, see Cripps, *Making Movies Black,* esp. 126–50; Jacqueline Najuma Stewart, *Migrating to the Movies: Cinema and Black Urban Modernity* (Berkeley, 2005), esp. 189–244; and Cedric J. Robinson, *Forgeries of Memory and Meaning: Blacks and the Regimes of Race in the American Theater and Film before World War II* (Chapel Hill, 2007).

Department (Warner Bros.–Seven Arts, Twentieth Century–Fox, Columbia, Walt Disney, Paramount, and Metro-Goldwyn-Mayer) had work forces that comprised only 2.1 percent blacks in 1967 (well short of the Los Angeles area's 7.4 percent). The situation was little better for other racial minority groups. Latinos, who represented 10.1 percent of the area's work force, made up only 4.2 percent of all studio employees. The same audit showed that Native Americans and Asian Americans, notwithstanding their much smaller work force numbers, were also underrepresented at the studios.[7]

Even more troubling than the raw numbers was the fact that the industry's minority employees usually worked the lowest-paying, lowest-skill jobs—many of the studios' black employees were janitors and messengers. At the EEOC hearing, Warner Bros.–Seven Arts labor relations executive Arthur Schaefer stated that the only African American of the eighty-one officials and managers at the company headed the building's janitorial department. In an unguarded moment that followed, Schaefer agreed that his studio's employment opportunity program was "pretty dismal." At some studios, such as notoriously conservative Walt Disney, there was no African American manager, official, or even technician in 1969. An exchange between the EEOC's Clifford Alexander and Disney personnel manager Kenneth Sieling ran as follows:

"How many officials and managers do you have at Walt Disney now?" . . .

"A total of 238."

"Of that number how many are black?"

"We have no black employees."

Asked about the company's 157 technicians, Sieling replied, "we reported 'no black.'" To the knowledge of all the studio representatives who gave evidence, summarized the *Hollywood Reporter* the next day, "there had never been any blacks or Mexican-Americans on any studio board of directors or in any policy-making position."[8]

The industry's craft unions were no better than the studios, built as they were on a seniority structure known as the "experience roster" set up in 1948 that all but excluded minorities. Overall figures of minority union membership in the motion picture crafts in 1967 showed blacks representing 2.9 percent and Spanish-surnamed Americans 5.3 percent. Prestigious creative and technical areas such as sound, camera work, and illustration were almost exclusively white, with some union locals having no minority members at all. The roster system was overseen by the AMPTP, which represented the interests of studios and producers in labor negotiations, and was maintained through collective bargaining agreements—thus both studios and unions were responsible for its institutional arrangements. They maintained a system in which everyone in the union must be employed or offered a job before an outside recruit could be hired. This structure led to

[7] *The Learning Tree,* dir. Gordon Parks Sr. (Warner–Seven Arts, 1969); *Guess Who's Coming to Dinner,* dir. Stanley Kramer (Columbia, 1967); *In the Heat of the Night,* dir. Norman Jewison (United Artists, 1967); and *To Sir, with Love,* dir. James Clavell (Columbia, 1967). Figures from U.S. Equal Employment Opportunity Commission, *Hearings before the U.S. Equal Employment Opportunity Commission on Utilization of Minority and Women Workers in Certain Major Industries,* 537–49. For the figures in summary form, see California Advisory Committee to the U.S. Commission on Civil Rights, *Behind the Scenes: Equal Employment Opportunity in the Motion Picture Industry* (Washington, 1978), 11–12. See also Knapp, "Assessment of the Status of Hollywood Blacks," 17–18.

[8] Arthur Schaefer, Clifford Alexander, and Kenneth Sieling quoted in U.S. Equal Employment Opportunity Commission, *Hearings before the U.S. Equal Employment Opportunity Commission on Utilization of Minority and Women Workers in Certain Major Industries,* 179, 185, 211–12. Collette Wood, "Blast H'Wood 'All-White' Hiring," *Hollywood Reporter,* March 14, 1969, p. 3.

what critics called a "double refusal": an individual needed a studio job to join the union, but needed to be in a union to get a studio job.[9]

Nepotism was often inscribed in union admissions procedures. Questions on the membership applications of the International Alliance of Theatrical Stage Employees, the powerful union consortium that covered all film industry technical crafts, were depressingly reminiscent of Jim Crow grandfather clauses. A question that regularly appeared asked, "What type of vocation did your father and/or guardian pursue for a livelihood?" Josef Bernay, representing IATSE at the hearing, attempted to explain the purpose of the question (intimating gendered as well as racial possessive investments): "Maybe for background purposes as far as, let's say, persons who are engineers, and then maybe his son becomes one, or a person is an artist and the son takes the artistic trend, something similar to that, so maybe his background is more imbued with more knowledge so he is more apt to know about it." Far from exemplifying Valenti's "open door," this policy not only ran afoul of Title VII but also contravened National Labor Relations Act laws.[10]

The studios had the legal power, following civil rights legislation, to force the unions to include minorities when presenting their lists of applicants for craft jobs on particular productions or, failing that, to look beyond the local unions for personnel. Universal City Studios, as the hearing testimony of its vice president Anthony J. Frederick detailed, was the only major studio that made efforts to circumvent the "double refusal" for minority workers by not automatically referring all applicants to relevant union locals. That policy, coupled with the studio's local minority-training initiatives, resulted in somewhat higher levels of nonwhite employees across a range of job categories at Universal than at the other studios, enabling Universal to be the one major not listed as a prospective defendant by the Justice Department. Studio executives at the other majors, however, were disinclined to intervene in processes that afforded systematic advantages to whites. As the commentator Charles Allen, who had been involved in minority training in the film industry, remarked tartly: "If labor unions provide Jim Crow crews, management has an option to insist on integrated ones—but doesn't."[11]

Given the deep legacies of racism and exclusion, the persistent underrepresentation of blacks, Latinos, Asian Americans, and Native Americans in this and other industries in the years immediately following the 1964 Civil Rights Act was hardly surprising. Building a minority presence was going to take some time, as procedures were implemented and personnel identified and trained. As Clifford Alexander explained, the genesis of the

[9] Figures from U.S. Equal Employment Opportunity Commission, "EEOC Reveals Statistics on Minority Membership in Unions," Sept. 28, 1969, press release, p. 2, EEOC 1969 [CFOA 7730] (4 of 4) folder, box 84, Leonard Garment files, Staff Member and Office Files, White House Central Files (Richard Nixon Presidential Library, Yorba Linda, Calif.). On the institutional arrangements of the film crafts' experience rosters, see U.S. Equal Employment Opportunity Commission, *Hearings before the U.S. Equal Employment Opportunity Commission on Utilization of Minority and Women Workers in Certain Major Industries,* 151–53; California Advisory Committee to the U.S. Commission on Civil Rights, *Behind the Scenes,* 41; Vance King, "Hiring Check Worries H'Wood: Gov't Probers Seen Creating Cliffhanger for Producers, Unions," *Film and Television Daily,* July 7, 1969, pp. 1, 4; Leonard Feather, "Hollywood: Inglorious Black and White," *Entertainment World,* Dec. 12, 1969, p. 14; Knapp, "Assessment of the Status of Hollywood Blacks," 17–18; and Jack Jones, "U.S. Board to Ask Suit Charging Film Job Bias," *Los Angeles Times,* March 14, 1969, sec. 2, pp. 1, 10.

[10] U.S. Equal Employment Opportunity Commission, *Hearings before the U.S. Equal Employment Opportunity Commission on Utilization of Minority and Women Workers in Certain Major Industries,* 158, 159, 228.

[11] For Anthony J. Frederick's testimony, see U.S. Equal Employment Opportunity Commission, *Hearings before the U.S. Equal Employment Opportunity Commission on Utilization of Minority and Women Workers in Certain Major Industries,* 113–39. Charles Allen, "Boris Karloff ... Too Dark?," *New York Times,* Feb. 28, 1971, p. D13.

industry's union seniority system "wasn't directly to keep chicanos and blacks out; it was to include relatives and those in an in-group." He describes a process of white opportunity hoarding that points to the complexities and challenges of affirmative action in an industry built on informal hiring patterns. Nonetheless, the testimony of the studios' labor relations executives (with the partial exception of Universal's Anthony Frederick) and the IATSE's Bernay revealed that they had very little knowledge of affirmative action procedures or even the broad implications of the Civil Rights Act. As *Daily Variety* reported: "What really tripped up the studio execs was a repeated question about an 'affirmative action plan.' The studio reps, to a man, apparently figured the words were casually phrased. Actually, the expression 'affirmative action' is used in the 1964 law, and on-going programs in other industries utilize the standard nomenclature."[12]

Indeed, it was in comparison with other industries that Hollywood came off so badly. The EEOC committee had, in all, held three days of hearings in Los Angeles, with one day devoted to the motion picture business. The industries chosen were those with the greatest discrepancy between the minority work force numbers available in the area and the representation of those minorities in a given industry—we "tried to isolate some that were particularly venal, if you will, in their practices via those statistics," explained Alexander. Thus, of those isolated for the California hearings, the motion picture industry was the only one "venal" enough to be referred to the Justice Department. "Hollywood is the most exclusionary of all, not only in ownership, where there is [no minority representation], but in the entire mechanism of distribution of motion pictures, [and] the production of motion pictures," asserted Alexander in the early 1970s.[13] Aside from the arrival of a couple of feted African Americans such as Poitier and Parks, Hollywood had shown little intention of changing its exclusionary practices and was even largely oblivious of the new laws. In 1969 the push for enforcement of Title VII—to force doors—was therefore absolutely necessary to change the industry's employment pattern. In response to such compromising exposure, studio management fashioned truly remarkable rhetorical reversals.

"Open Doors"

The Justice Department investigators began gathering testimony in late spring 1969, poring over union books and records of studio hiring practices in preparation for a showdown with Hollywood's labor associations and big management—amassing, as one commentator described, "a five-foot shelf of signed affidavits from victims of discrimination." Management and unions feared that the probe might result in a consent decree, such as the ones that employers in other industries were facing around this time. If violated, these decrees could lead to company executives being held guilty of contempt and result in punitive court judgments.[14] Although in the firing line, the film industry rapidly

[12] Clifford Alexander interview by Joe B. Frantz, June 4, 1973, transcript, p. 13, Lyndon Baines Johnson Oral History Collection (Lyndon B. Johnson Library, Austin, Tex.). On the lack of awareness of affirmative action procedures, see U.S. Equal Employment Opportunity Commission, *Hearings before the U.S. Equal Employment Opportunity Commission on Utilization of Minority and Women Workers in Certain Major Industries*, 184, 200, 228. Murphy, "Gov't Charges," 23.

[13] Alexander interview, 3, 7.

[14] Feather, "Hollywood," 14. On consent decrees, see, for example, Robert H. Zieger, *For Jobs and Freedom: Race and Labor in America since 1865* (Lexington, Ky., 2007), 175–207. On Hollywood's apprehension, see King,

began to regroup. Both Hollywood management and the national Republican leadership seemed to see opportunity in the wake of the EEOC's assault, amid the dramatic changes in the national political climate on race.

The EEOC's public hearings in Los Angeles set off an immediate and far-reaching counterattack. When Clifford Alexander was summoned to appear at the Senate subcommittee the following week, his heated exchange with the Republican Everett Dirksen showcased the two conflicting interpretations of Title VII of the Civil Rights Act. Along with outlawing employment discrimination, Title VII also created the EEOC to enforce this new law. Title VII was certainly far-reaching: if workers believed they were being discriminated against by employers (governmental and nongovernmental), labor unions, or employment agencies, they could file a complaint with the federal government. However, this new legislation was deeply contested from its inception. Indeed, it was Dirksen, as the Senate minority leader in 1964, who had extracted important concessions to curtail Title VII's power as the price of his support for the Civil Rights Act. The "Dirksen amendments" helped end the longest filibuster (534 hours) in U.S. Senate history, but weakened the bill. The restraints deprived the EEOC of the power to issue the cease-and-desist orders that could have immediately halted illegal practices of discrimination. Dirksen also required a prohibition of "preferential treatment" to remedy hiring and promotion imbalances. As Nancy MacLean explains: "While seekers of inclusion focused on the spirit of the bill for which they had worked so hard for so many years, the restraints built into Title VII emboldened its critics." An EEOC committee could set the terms of debate in "the spirit of the bill" at public hearings, such as those in Los Angeles, but the agency knew that its demands for compliance were not fully enforceable, due to the restraints authored by Dirksen. "We sort of gummed them to death if we could, but we had no enforcement powers," Clifford Alexander remarked.[15]

At the 1969 Senate subcommittee hearing, responding to Dirksen's "emboldened" pronouncements about the EEOC's "punitive harassment of the Los Angeles business community," Alexander stated that the "people who are being harassed [are] the blacks, Mexican-Americans, and other minorities, who are subjected to segregated housing facilities, hiring and promotional policies." The subcommittee's chairperson, Democratic senator Edward Kennedy, stepped in to defend Alexander following Dirksen's tirade, asserting, "those who threaten your job because you do it well are going to have trouble getting rid of you." However, a week later, on March 28, President Nixon announced that Alexander would be replaced as the EEOC head. His position untenable, Alexander announced his resignation in April, more than two years before he was due to step down as leader. He was replaced by African American EEOC member William Brown—who, in a press interview at the time, described himself as a Republican "all my life." The White House made, at best, a half-hearted attempt to deny the connection between Dirksen's tirade and Alexander's removal. But in a May 1969 letter Dirksen wrote that at the Senate subcommittee hearing he had told Alexander "what an irrational, harassing

---

"Hiring Check Worries H'Wood," 1; Collette Wood, "Justice Dept. Here on Probe," *Hollywood Reporter,* May 15, 1969, pp. 1, 11; and "Gov't Crackdown on H'Wood," 1, 8.

[15] MacLean, *Freedom Is Not Enough,* 71. On Title VII and the built-in restraints, see Charles W. Whalen and Barbara Whalen, *The Longest Debate: A Legislative History of the 1964 Civil Rights Act* (Washington, 1985), 200–201, 149–93; and Robert D. Loevy, ed., *The Civil Rights Act of 1964: The Passage of the Law That Ended Racial Segregation* (Albany, 1997), 97–101, 226. Alexander interview, 8.

approach was taken [at the hearings in California]. The next day he resigned as Chairman." The letter ends: "The President is fully aware of what I am doing and I regard my services to him as extremely helpful." In another letter also partly concerning "the Los Angeles vendetta and carnival EEOC put on," Dirksen described the federal agency as a "tribe."[16]

Getting rid of Alexander, a Lyndon B. Johnson appointee who, as the historian Hugh Davis Graham states, was "uniformly regarded as exceptionally bright, energetic, and capable," was a victory for anti–affirmative action Republicans. With Alexander replaced by William Brown, the rate at which the EEOC processed complaints dropped sharply. By 1971 the backlog of discrimination complaints was "19,000 and increasing." The EEOC continued to achieve victories—notably the forcing of the American Telephone and Telegraph Company to pay a settlement of $15 million to past victims of bias—but with Brown's appointment, the legislative push to give the EEOC cease-and-desist powers lost a key advocate. In summer 1969 the newly promoted Brown, who had previously supported granting the EEOC cease-and-desist powers, not only began to favor the court-enforcement approach strongly supported by Dirksen but also drafted the court-enforcement bill. "I'm very happy that Senator Dirksen . . . is thinking the way I'm thinking," he stated, facing difficult questions about his own about-face. The court-enforcement legislation would hand to the beleaguered EEOC responsibility for pursuing federal court action on behalf of complainants, forcing the agency into protracted lawsuits that were difficult to bring to resolution. Alexander called the system "a cruel hoax."[17] The eventual failure of the cease-and-desist legislation, a law strongly pursued by liberals in Congress, civil rights groups, and all EEOC members except Brown, was a major blow.

Alexander was called to the Senate subcommittee after film industry complaints about the EEOC hearing "were relayed to" Dirksen, reported the *Los Angeles Times*. It is highly likely that a key relayer was Jack Valenti, the dynamic boss of the MPAA (a post he held from 1966 to 2004). Headquartered in Washington, D.C., the MPAA represented the business interests of the major studios. Valenti was its leading public relations spokesperson and "a hard-nosed, charismatic lobbyist for the uninhibited distribution of Hollywood motion pictures stateside and abroad," as the film historian Kevin Sandler describes. He had arrived at the MPAA direct from the White House, where he had worked for President Johnson coordinating speechwriting and lobbying Congress. Although Valenti retained his close association with Johnson in his new post, he nonetheless brokered productive alliances with Republicans. Following Nixon's 1968

[16] Alexander quoted in U.S. Congress, Senate Committee on Interior and Insular Affairs, *Committee Prints, Volume 3* (Washington, 1971), 801–2; Dirksen and Edward Kennedy quoted in "Dirksen Threatens 'to Get' Black 'Fired' for Bias Fight,'" 6, 7. William Brown quoted in James Batten, "Equal Employment Boss: Slaying a Dragon with a Pea-Shooter," *Miami Herald*, Oct. 23, 1969, p. B9. Everett M. Dirksen to Irene Leander, May 26, 1969, Clifford Alexander file, Alphabetical File 1969, Everett M. Dirksen Papers, Everett M. Dirksen Collection (Dirksen Congressional Center, Pekin, Ill.); Dirksen to Bryce N. Harlow, April 7, 1969, *ibid.*

[17] Hugh Davis Graham, *The Civil Rights Era: Origins and Development of National Policy, 1960–1972* (New York, 1990), 238. Figures from "Civil Rights Preview: Progress, 1954–71," [n.d.], p. 3, Civil Rights Preview (Black Box) folder, box 1 Late Accretion, 1969–1974 collection: Bradley H. Patterson, Staff Member and Office Files, White House Central Files (Nixon Presidential Library). On the American Telephone and Telegraph Company settlement, see Dean J. Kotlowski, *Nixon's Civil Rights: Politics, Principle, and Policy* (Cambridge, Mass., 2001), 118–21. William H. Brown press conference, Aug. 29, 1969, transcript, p. 11, EEOC 1969 folder, box 84, Garment files, Staff Member and Office Files, White House Central Files (Nixon Presidential Library). Alexander quoted in Batten, "Equal Employment Boss," B9. See Graham, *Civil Rights Era*, 420–21, 428–30.

presidential victory, Valenti gave an interview to *Daily Variety:* "Valenti Feels Easier in Approaching Republicans on Film Trade's Behalf," read its title. Published in February 1969, just before the Hollywood hearing, the piece reported that "Valenti considers it fortunate that he counts several top Republicans among his personal friends." One of the two mentioned by name was Everett Dirksen. Valenti would later recall that, during his White House days, he would "service [Dirksen's] account" with the president and "got to know him famously." "The day would hardly pass without at least one phone call from Dirksen," boasted Valenti. The speed and strength of the political reaction to the EEOC hearing was most likely facilitated by the film industry's top representative and his "friendship" with the probusiness Senate minority leader.[18]

Whatever complaints Hollywood management quietly relayed, its luncheon on April 21 honoring the NAACP's Roy Wilkins was all about publicity. In attendance were many industry executives, stars (Wilkins is pictured with the actress Julie Andrews in the *Hollywood Citizen News*), and journalists. Using the example of *The Learning Tree* in his opening remarks, Valenti made the specious claim that, of the forty-seven people working on the film, "all but five [were] black." In fact, as Arthur Schaefer of Warner Bros.–Seven Arts, which released the film, reported at the EEOC hearing, the film had eight black crew members, in addition to its African American director/co-producer: an assistant cameraman, men's wardrobe stylist, women's hair stylist, lamp operator, painter, transportation driver, publicist, and a special photographer. Thus, though the film was a landmark in the black struggle for film industry integration, the crew was still majority white. The MPAA boss heaped on the flattery as he introduced Wilkins, whom he had known since his White House days: "When it comes to integrity, I know of no better example than Roy Wilkins," who was "one of the great men in this generation." At lunch, the NAACP leader made a thoughtful speech that touched on the "educational role" of the entertainment industry in overcoming discrimination and the "slow pace" of progress in its minority hiring.[19]

However, perhaps buoyed by Valenti's feel-good rhetoric, the moderate NAACP leader also felt moved to make positive comments about Hollywood, leading to a *Daily Variety* cover story: "Roy Wilkins Praises Pic Biz: NAACP Leader Asserts Film-TV Industry 'Has Done a Very Satisfactory Job.'" Wilkins's public endorsement, which may very well have been taken out of context, represented a coup for industry management just as the Justice Department launched its probe. Such headlines ("Black Employment Pics, TV

---

[18] Burke, "U.S. Plans to Prod Film Industry on Job Discrimination Charges," 14. Kevin S. Sandler, "The Future of U.S. Film Censorship Studies," *Velvet Light Trap,* 63 (Spring 2009), 69. "'Valenti Feels Easier in Approaching Republicans on Film Trade's Behalf,'" *Daily Variety,* Feb. 16, 1969, p. 3; Jack Valenti interview by Frantz, July 12, 1972, transcript, p. 11, Johnson Oral History Collection. On Valenti's relationship with Dirksen, see also Jack Valenti, *This Time, This Place: My Life in War, the White House, and Hollywood* (New York, 2007), 46–47.

[19] Roy Wilkins and Julie Andrews photograph in "Negro Film Roles Show Sharp Increase," *Hollywood Citizen News,* April 22, 1969, clipping, Blacks and Film (1969) file, subject files (Margaret Herrick Library, Academy of Motion Picture Arts and Sciences, Los Angeles, Calif.). Valenti's opening remarks quoted in Ornstein, "Black Employment Pics, TV Up," 1. Schaefer testimony in U.S. Equal Employment Opportunity Commission, *Hearings before the U.S. Equal Employment Opportunity Commission on Utilization of Minority and Women Workers in Certain Major Industries,* 177. On the racial politics of the making of *The Learning Tree,* see Eithne Quinn, "Sincere Fictions: The Production Cultures of Whiteness in Late 1960s Hollywood," *Velvet Light Trap,* 67 (Spring 2011), 3–13. Valenti quoted in Jim Mullen, "Roy Wilkins Praises Pic Biz: NAACP Leader Asserts Film-TV Industry 'Has Done a Very Satisfactory Job,'" *Daily Variety,* April 22, 1969, p. 1; Valenti and Wilkins quoted in Ornstein, "Black Employment Pics, TV Up," 1, 11.

Roy Wilkins, the director of the National Association for the Advancement of Colored People, talks to the film star Julie Andrews at a luncheon held in Wilkins's honor in Hollywood on April 21, 1969. The event was organized by Jack Valenti, the head of the Motion Picture Association of America, and attended by many industry executives and journalists. This photo appeared in the *Hollywood Citizen News,* April 22, 1969. *Courtesy Academy of Motion Picture Arts and Sciences, Los Angeles, Calif., Margaret Herrick Library, subject files, Blacks and Film (1969) file.*

Up" declared the cover of the *Hollywood Reporter* on the same day) repaired some of the damage to Hollywood's image inflicted by the dramatic EEOC press stories the previous month. The industry's cultivation of Wilkins offers a striking example of the cooptation of civil rights leaders during this period. After the lunch, Wilkins commented that Valenti had been "very kind and appreciative" but had "made no promises." Like Clifford Alexander, Wilkins strongly supported the antidiscrimination record of the Johnson administration, and Valenti's association with the former president no doubt worked to Valenti's advantage. As Wilkins reflected, "I met Valenti in Washington, we got to know each other and when he got the new job with the Motion Picture Association he said he would like to have me come out here." This was the second time Valenti had invited him out to Hollywood. The first came a year earlier in the aftermath of Martin Luther King Jr.'s assassination—another critical moment to showcase the centrist black leader. The film historian Stephen Vaughn describes Valenti's great facility for cultivating politicians: "His flamboyance and flair for dramatization and hyperbole, his enthusiasm and energy, and his willingness to flatter others effusively all went over well in Hollywood and in Washington, two places where fantasy and politics intermingle."[20]

[20] Mullen, "Roy Wilkins Praises Pic Biz," 1; Wilkins quoted in Ornstein, "Black Employment Pics, TV Up," 11; Stephen Vaughn, *Freedom and Entertainment: Rating the Movies in an Age of New Media* (New York, 2006), 24. On Lyndon B. Johnson's equal employment record, see Alexander interview, 8–11; Roy Wilkins, *Standing Fast: The Autobiography of Roy Wilkins* (Cambridge, Mass., 1994), 295–307, 329.

It is worth noting that Wilkins publicly condemned the removal of Alexander, perhaps chagrined by the proindustry press headlines he had generated. A statement by Wilkins read:

> A case of anti-Negro racial policy with a minimum amount of fuzziness has risen in the Nixon Administration with the resignation of Clifford L. Alexander, Jr. . . . No matter how much gloss is applied, Negro citizens and their allies will remember that Republican Senate leader Everett M. Dirksen of Illinois publicly rebuked Alexander for allegedly "harassing" businessmen to secure conformity with the 1964 Act outlawing discrimination in employment and threatened to get him fired.

Despite his centrist politics—marked by his public rejection of Martin Luther King Jr.'s anti–Vietnam War stance and his strong repudiation of the black power movement—Wilkins maintained a critical stance on Nixon's civil rights record and the ousting of Alexander. Whatever Wilkins's private thoughts at the Hollywood lunch may have been, within a month or so of the EEOC's journey to Hollywood, one national affirmative action leader had been removed and another had been publicly co-opted—indicating the film industry's political salience and the virulence of its image management.[21]

During and after the Wilkins lunch, Valenti repeated his key message: "We have the desire to open the door for new Negro talent rather than have someone force it open."[22] This metaphoric refrain was clearly a counterproposal to the antidiscrimination initiatives under way: the "someone" in the message was the EEOC, Justice Department, and minorities—especially African Americans. This repudiation of affirmative action, as with the removal of Alexander, was energized by a growing backlash against federal intervention that was beginning to affect the policies of the new Nixon administration (1969–1974). A significant point to highlight is Valenti's discursive sleight of hand. The industry, so recently revealed as an exclusionary bastion of whiteness, became, in Valenti's statements, the moral champion of labor-market equality, endangered by the coercive threat of the courts. By suggesting that racial discrimination was of little significance, Valenti intimated that statist measures to facilitate racial redistribution were unnecessary and illiberal. This was the signature discursive move of what would soon be called racial neoconservatism: the roles of victim and perpetrator—those opening and those obstructing doors—were reversed.

Though the term *neoconservatism* did not emerge until several years after Valenti fashioned his anti–affirmative action metaphor, its various discursive contours began to coalesce around the turn of the 1970s. As a leading neoconservative proponent, Irving Kristol, later explained: "neoconservatism emerged as an intellectual tendency in the late 1960s and 1970s." Similarly, the scholar Peter Steinfels explains that neoconservatism was "in many ways a product of the sixties." Key intellectuals who began propounding what became known as the neoconservative critique included the senior editor at Basic Books, Irving Kristol; scholar and politician Daniel Patrick Moynihan; public intellectual Nathan Glazer; and *Commentary* magazine editor Norman Podhoretz. Moynihan, who had worked for John F. Kennedy and Johnson before becoming a close Nixon adviser,

---

[21] Wilkins statement quoted in "Alexander's Resignation Forced by Bias," *Crisis*, 76 (May 1969), 217. On Wilkins's criticism of Richard M. Nixon and Dirksen, see Wilkins, *Standing Fast*, 333–34. On his public rejection of black power, see *ibid.*, 315–21. On his criticism of Martin Luther King Jr.'s antiwar stance, see, for example, Adam Fairclough, *Better Day Coming: Blacks and Equality, 1890–2000* (New York, 2001), 314.

[22] "Negro Film Roles Show Sharp Increase"; Ornstein, "Black Employment Pics, TV Up," 1.

disseminated the new thinking in high-profile speeches and in a widely leaked memorandum from January 1969 in which he called for a period of "benign neglect" of African Americans. As with any "racial project," according to the scholars Michael Omi and Howard Winant, neoconservatism was "simultaneously an interpretation, representation, or explanation of racial dynamics, and an effort to reorganize and redistribute resources along particular racial lines." This budding interpretation of America as basically nondiscriminatory legitimated the existing distribution of resources as a route to achieving equality, undermining calls for progressive redistribution along racial lines. As Steinfels argues, such interpretations "vastly overestimate the degree to which meritocratic standards already operate in institutions."[23]

Like the Italian American Jack Valenti, the other key neoconservative proponents were white ethnic, and this factor, in most cases, overtly informed their value frameworks. Neoconservative thinking was characterized, as Matthew Frye Jacobson has explored in his book subtitled "white ethnic revival in post–civil rights America," by skepticism toward state intervention on behalf of blacks; by individual (rather than structural) interpretations of racism; and by an image of America as a land of immigrants who pull themselves up by their bootstraps, in which newly enfranchised and empowered blacks should be treated as merely the latest wave of incoming strivers. The white ethnic group most associated with neoconservatism is also the one most associated with civil rights activism: Jewish Americans. And this group held many decision-making positions in Hollywood. Jews, in general, have been disproportionately liberal in social and political terms, and some inside the industry of the early 1970s continued strongly to support the black freedom struggle as it became more radical. Such support is exemplified by the minority employment initiatives of the producers Hal De Windt and Hannah Weinstein, and by BBS Productions' Bert Schneider, a vocal supporter of the Black Panther leader Huey P. Newton.[24]

[23] Irving Kristol, *Reflections of a Neoconservative: Looking Back, Looking Ahead* (New York, 1983), xii; Peter Steinfels, *The Neoconservatives: The Men Who Are Changing America's Politics* (New York, 1979), 3. On the genesis of the neoconservative critique around the turn of the 1970s, see Howard Winant, *The World Is a Ghetto: Race and Democracy since World War II* (New York, 2001), 150–51, 171–72; Michael Omi and Howard Winant, *Racial Formation in the United States: From the 1960s to the 1990s* (New York, 1994), 128–32; Angela D. Dillard, *Guess Who's Coming to Dinner Now? Multicultural Conservatism in America* (New York, 2001), esp. 56–98; Matthew Frye Jacobson, *Roots Too: White Ethnic Revival in Post–Civil Rights America* (Cambridge, Mass., 2006), esp. 177–205; and MacLean, *Freedom Is Not Enough,* 196–99. For seminal texts that fed into the neoconservative racial project, see the 1960s writing in *Commentary* magazine, starting with Norman Podhoretz, "My Negro Problem—And Ours," in *The Commentary Reader: Two Decades of Articles and Stories,* ed. Norman Podhoretz (New York, 1967), 376–87; and Nathan Glazer, "Negroes and Jews: The New Challenge to Pluralism," in *Ethnic Dilemmas,* by Nathan Glazer (Cambridge, Mass., 1983), esp. 70–93. See also Daniel Patrick Moynihan, *Coping: Essays on the Practice of Government* (New York, 1973); and Nathan Glazer, *Affirmative Discrimination: Ethnic Inequality and Public Policy* (New York, 1975). Daniel P. Moynihan to Richard Nixon, Jan. 16, 1970, memorandum, p. 7, Civil Rights Preview folder, box 84, Patterson files, Staff Member and Office Files, White House Central Files (Nixon Presidential Library). Omi and Winant, *Racial Formation in the United States,* 56; Steinfels, *Neoconservatives,* 228. See also Howard Winant, *The New Politics of Race: Globalism, Difference, Justice* (Minneapolis, 2004), 39–49.

[24] Jacobson, *Roots Too,* esp. 177–205. On black-Jewish relations in Hollywood during these years, see Thomas Cripps, "African Americans and Jews in Hollywood: Antagonistic Allies," in *Strangers and Neighbors: Relations between Blacks and Jews in the United States,* ed. Maurianne Adams and John H. Bracey (Amherst, 1999), 457–70; and Michael Rogin, *Blackface, White Noise: Jewish Immigrants in the Hollywood Melting Pot* (Berkeley, 1996). On Bert Schneider's support of the Black Panthers, see Peter Biskind, *Easy Riders, Raging Bulls: How the Sex-Drugs-and-Rock 'n' Roll Generation Saved Hollywood* (New York, 1998), 60–61, 123–24, 177. Public opinion surveys at the end of the 1960s show a reasonably large minority of whites continuing to explain black disadvantage principally in terms of discrimination and to be sympathetic to black activism—no doubt many Jews were among this number. See Howard Schuman et al., *Racial Attitudes in America: Trends and Interpretations* (Cambridge, Mass., 1997), 153–64.

However, in that period of dramatic flux in race relations, many white ethnics, including Jews, cleaved increasingly to the ethnic allegiances and racial resentments that were being propounded in incipient neoconservative discourses of the day. Since early 1969, Moynihan had been briefing Nixon on the growing fractures in the black-Jewish civil rights alliance. As calls by African Americans and their federal allies for proportional representation in employment gained steam, they started to sound alarm bells for some Jewish Americans when it affected sectors in which Jews were well-represented. As Nancy MacLean details, the budding neoconservatives were already framing the issue in zero-sum terms: more black representation meant less Jewish representation. Along with higher education recruitment and academe, the good jobs in the film industry into which African Americans sought entry were occupations in which Jewish Americans had long enjoyed a strong presence. Following his arrival in Hollywood, Valenti established close links with the Beverly Hills lodge of B'nai B'rith, which had as members many entertainment industry executives and which held fund-raisers attended by the MPAA boss. In the month that the Justice Department dropped its suit, April 1970, Valenti was honored with two awards from the organization: the Man of the Year award from the local Beverly Hills Lodge, given annually "as a salute to American industry for its furtherance of forward-looking social and cultural programs," and also the President's Medal, a national B'nai B'rith honor awarded every few years by special recommendation. Given the timing, the Beverly Hilton dinner dance to mark this double honor likely provided an occasion to propagate Valenti-style anti–affirmative action identity politics. This was the beginning of the period, after all, when "'white ethnics' and 'white backlash' became interchangeable terms," as the historian Bruce Nelson argues in his influential study of race and class in the workplace.[25]

Valenti's meritocratic language of "open doors" stands in rhetorical distinction to the response of Hollywood's union leaders to the EEOC charges. The IATSE head and the industry's top union leader Richard Walsh sounded much more racially trenchant, stating that there was "no discrimination in any of the laws and policy of the IATSE, and where any charges are made we intend to defend the IA to the extreme." Though the tones of the rhetoric differed sharply, the content of Valenti's and Walsh's statements were more or less the same: a denial of discrimination and a defense of the realm. In fact, the union locals represented by the IATSE covered a vast array of crafts, most of which were highly exclusionary; but a few were racially progressive and "swam against the tide." Substance aside, however, studio management saw the strategic advantage of creating distance between the studios and the unions by exploiting the latter's more embattled tone. A *Los Angeles Times* article in October 1969 titled "Film Executive Blames Hiring Bias on Unions" typified management's public relations campaign. The piece quotes the industrial relations director for Columbia Pictures Howard Fabrick: "'I'm the last guy in the world who would try to maintain that Hollywood has clean hands in the question of minority group employment. . . . But it's not the fault of the studios. The real question

---

[25] Graham, *Civil Rights Era,* 310–11. MacLean, *Freedom Is Not Enough,* 196–99. "Jack Valenti BevHills B'nai's 'Man of Year,'" *Daily Variety,* March 26, 1970, Jack Valenti, Biography files, core collection (Herrick Library); "Film Boss Jack Valenti Wins Man of Year Award," *Los Angeles Herald Examiner,* April 20, 1970, *ibid.*; "Jack Valenti Gets Two Awards from B'nai B'rith," *Hollywood Reporter,* April 21, 1970, *ibid.* Bruce Nelson, *Divided We Stand: American Workers and the Struggle for Black Equality* (Princeton, 2001), 291.

for the Justice Department to handle is challenging a union seniority structure that has for 20 years prohibited a studio in hiring in the manner it might, in all good conscience, want to." The disarming admission at the beginning of the statement directs attention away from its stark moral order: the unions have dirty hands, the studios have a clean conscience. As Clifford Alexander later remarked, "the effect... of all that violently opposing [by the unions] was exactly the same as the polite corporate executive who has all the lingo down but still doesn't employ or doesn't promote."[26]

Overriding all other considerations was the desire of studio management to fend off its own threatened Justice Department suit. Exerting pressure on unions to integrate their labor force might aid this primary struggle by deflecting attention from studio hiring practices. Once the interests of the major studios were protected, this volatile situation could provide unintended opportunities. If government agencies forced unions to open jobs to minorities, the agencies would be helping dismantle the crafts' high wages and strong bargaining position that were maintained by restrictions on labor supply. The combination of big-budget flops, a shortage of credit, and a national economic downturn triggered the film industry's near collapse around the turn of the 1970s. Management was desperate to bring down production costs, and labor was an obvious target.[27]

This triangulation between studio management, affirmative action advocates, and unions paralleled dynamics in another high-profile struggle to integrate a different craft union work force. The Philadelphia Plan, devised by the Johnson administration and backed by Nixon in September 1969, sought to integrate that city's construction workers when they were employed on federal projects—the first time substantive employment targets were to be used in a systematic attempt at industry integration. As with film crafts, construction was full of prestigious blue-collar jobs fiercely defended by industry's overwhelmingly white work force. Since the public purse was bankrolling Philadelphia's building program, the government held the role of employer, who, like Hollywood studio management, was interested in reducing labor costs. The motives behind Nixon's backing of the Philadelphia Plan, despite his general hostility to antidiscrimination policy, have been widely debated. As the historian Robert Zieger explains, "Nixon's political strategists believed that programs such as the Philadelphia Plan could not help but drive a wedge between two of the Democratic Party's core constituencies—organized labor and African Americans." According to the Nixon aide John Ehrlichman, unions and antidiscrimination proponents were indeed soon "locked in combat" and "the Nixon Administration was located in the sweet and reasonable middle." In Hollywood, the likes of Valenti and Fabrick were also trying to position themselves as the holders of the reasonable middle ground in a bid to further the industry's public relations image and business interests. When national union leader George Meany charged that Nixon was "trying to make a whipping boy out of the Building Trades" in Philadelphia, his claims

[26] Richard Walsh quoted in Bill Ornstein, "Walsh Rips Race Bias Charge," *Hollywood Reporter*, April 10, 1969, p. 1; King, "Hiring Check Worries H'Wood," 4. See also Dave Kaufman, "Unions Prep Seniority Defense," *Daily Variety*, July 11, 1969, p. 1. Howard Fabrick quoted in Robert Kistler, "Film Executive Blames Hiring Bias on Unions," *Los Angeles Times*, Oct. 19, 1969, p. A14; Alexander interview, 14.

[27] David A. Cook, *Lost Illusions: American Cinema in the Shadow of Watergate and Vietnam, 1970–1979* (New York, 2000), 3–6, 64; Janet Wasko, *Movies and Money: Financing the American Film Industry* (Norwood, 1982), 176–89; Jon Lewis, *Hollywood v. Hard Core: How the Struggle over Censorship Saved the Modern Film Industry* (New York, 2000), 151–56.

echoed Hollywood's labor leaders who "accused management of a ploy to make the unions the heavies in the delicate situation."[28]

The Justice Department's antidiscrimination initiative in Hollywood ultimately went the same way as the Philadelphia Plan: by 1970 both had been extremely watered down. Philadelphia's construction industry targets were all but abandoned, following popular backlash and an abrupt shift in government policy. Following protracted negotiations in Hollywood, a conciliatory Justice Department dropped its threatened legal action in April 1970, settling instead on a two-year voluntary agreement proposed by the industry that established a goal of 20 percent minority employment in the film business. The agreement instructed union locals, including those for sound, camerawork, and film editing, to set up minority labor pools and specified that a minimum of 20 percent of union referrals to the studios should come from those pools. The agreement also stipulated that the unions set up a program to train seventy minority members in specific crafts. These measures did create a short-term rise in minority behind-the-camera employment, but the dispute had been, reported Dave Kaufman in *Daily Variety*, "resolved in a manner sought by the industry"—the increases were not binding, and, after the "specified period, the rosters will operate as in the past." "While no one involved claimed victory, and the official release was couched in diplomatic terms, there is no question that government acceptance of the voluntary agreement represents a triumph for the industry," wrote Kaufman with only a little overstatement.[29]

The agreement stipulated that at the end of the two-year period, in spring 1972, the minority labor pools were to be merged with the union rosters. But this proposed outcome was delayed because not enough minority members had yet qualified. As a congressional report stated: some "could not afford the expensive initiation dues; and overall the unions were not enthusiastic about receiving them." Thus, aside from excising the nepotistic questions on the application form, the roster system continued largely unabated. As the agreement ended, black activists from an array of organizations mounted one of their most high-profile campaigns for film-industry integration. Having pursued and exhausted federal channels to bring about change, these organizations challenged Hollywood directly. However, their antagonists were ready, having developed and finessed the backlash racial discourses that were about to go mainstream.[30]

"Semantic Infiltration"

During the outcry following the summer 1972 release of *Super Fly*, many African American groups assailed Hollywood demanding more jobs and power. Anger at the film's controversial romanticization of a heroic black cocaine dealer led to the coining of the

---

[28] Zieger, *For Jobs and Freedom*, 186; John Ehrlichman quoted in Terry H. Anderson, *The Pursuit of Fairness: A History of Affirmative Action* (New York, 2004), 120. See also Thomas J. Sugrue, "Affirmative Action from Below: Civil Rights, the Building Trades, and the Politics of Racial Equality in the Urban North, 1945–1969," *Journal of American History*, 91 (June 2004), 145–73. George Meany quoted in Anderson, *Pursuit of Fairness*, 120; Kaufman, "Unions Prep Seniority Defense," 1.

[29] California Advisory Committee to the U.S. Commission on Civil Rights, *Behind the Scenes*, 13–14. "Justice Backed Down on 'Race,'" *Daily Variety*, April 8, 1970, p. 1; Dave Kaufman, "More Pic-TV Jobs for Minorities," *ibid.*, April 1, 1970, pp. 1, 7.

[30] U.S. Congress Subcommittee on Equal Opportunity, *Oversight Investigation of Federal Enforcement of Equal Opportunity Laws* (Washington, 1976), quoted in California Advisory Committee to the U.S. Commission on Civil Rights, *Behind the Scenes*, 14.

Priest (played by Ron O'Neal) and Eddie (Carl Lee) are the heroic Harlem business partners in the summer 1972 hit *Super Fly,* directed by Gordon Parks Jr. Anger at the film's romanticization of black cocaine dealers led to the coining of the term *blaxploitation* to describe and critique a new production trend of black action films and to the forming of the Coalition against Blaxploitation, which lobbied for more black jobs and control in the film business. *Courtesy* BFI *Stills, British Film Institute, London.*

term *blaxploitation* to describe and critique a new production trend of black action films such as *Cotton Comes to Harlem* (1970) and *Shaft* (1971), which typically featured urban crime, sex, and violence. Protests came from Jesse Jackson's Operation PUSH (People United to Save Humanity) and an alliance called the Coalition against Blaxploitation (CAB) led by the Beverly Hills–Hollywood branch of the NAACP (though not fully supported by its national leadership) and that also included the Congress of Racial Equality, the Southern Christian Leadership Conference, and the newly formed Black Artists' Alliance. Consternation about some of these black action films was genuine and intense; at the same time, the controversy and profitability of the films provided a platform for action. Through public statements, protests outside major studios, meetings with executives, and the threat of box-office boycotts, activists forwarded their demands for more black jobs, more positive images, and a say in decision-making processes. According to CAB's head Junius Griffin, who was the NAACP's Beverly Hills–Hollywood branch president, the protestors were struggling "against the power exploitation of the black condition in America by the white owned, white controlled, and white financed motion picture industry." Despite the heightened rhetoric, the campaigns of CAB and Operation PUSH were pragmatic, emphasizing inclusion within, rather than transformation of, the film business.[31]

---

[31] *Super Fly,* dir. Gordon Parks Jr. (Warner Bros., 1972); *Cotton Comes to Harlem,* dir. Ossie Davis (Metro-Goldwyn-Mayer, 1970); *Shaft,* dir. Gordon Parks Sr. (Metro-Goldwyn-Mayer, 1971). On the racial politics of *Super Fly,* see Thomas Doherty, "The Black Exploitation Picture: *Super Fly* and *Black Caesar,*" *Ball State University Forum,* 24 (Spring 1983), 30–39; Eithne Quinn, "'Tryin' to Get Over': *Super Fly,* Black Politics, and Post–Civil Rights Film Enterprise," *Cinema Journal,* 49 (Winter 2010), 86–105. The growing body of scholarship on early 1970s black action films includes Novotny Lawrence, *Blaxploitation Films of the 1970s: Blackness and Genre* (New York, 2008); Yvonne D. Sims, *Women of Blaxploitation: How the Black Action Film Heroine Changed American Popular Culture* (Jefferson, 2006); Stephane Dunn, *"Baad Bitches" and Sassy Supermamas: Black Power Action Films* (Urbana, 2008); and "Blaxploitation Revisited," special issue, *Screening Noir,* 1 (Fall/Winter 2005). "Fight

For the black protest groups, as for the EEOC, remedying past and continuing injustice required the initiation of a system of preference in industry hiring and promotion practices. These groups shared a basic demand, most fully articulated in Jesse Jackson's statements, for economic "redress." As he and others were at pains to point out, the idea of special treatment was not a new one: for hundreds of years, through slavery and Jim Crow, whites had been the official beneficiaries of a preferential racial system. Echoing arguments powerfully presented in Kwame Ture and Charles Hamilton's 1967 manifesto *Black Power,* activists contended that preferential policies were essential to counteract the profoundly color-conscious legacy of white supremacism, which was everywhere evident in the institutional exclusions of Hollywood. The charged neologism *blaxploitation* could hardly have been more resonant of this interpretive frame. As the film scholar Ed Guerrero remarks: the term "Blaxploitation might as easily and accurately describe the cruel injustice of slavery or, for that matter, much of the historical sojourn of black folk in America."[32]

But the protest groups were met by powerful counterforces. In August 1972 claims of "reverse discrimination" gained legitimacy in mainstream political debate when the president of the American Jewish Committee (AJC) Philip Hoffman wrote a widely publicized open letter to the presidential candidates, Richard Nixon and George McGovern, on behalf of a number of major U.S. Jewish organizations. The letter, which came from groups that had actively supported the civil rights movement, called on the candidates to "reject categorically the use of quotas and proportional representation." It argued that race-conscious policies stood against liberal individualism, sparking a scare about racial quotas that helped instigate a dramatic turnabout in the terms of debate. "Never before had charges of 'reverse discrimination' against whites been made by people with such credibility as proponents of fairness," argues Nancy MacLean. It was "a setback from which the quest for inclusion never recovered its earlier momentum." Nixon quickly responded by publicly eschewing proportional representation and ordering government agencies to prohibit quota hiring. "Criteria for selection will be based on merit," and "numerical goals . . . must not be allowed to be applied in such a fashion as to, in fact, result in the imposition of quotas," read Nixon's memorandum to department and agency heads.[33]

The specific focus of the open letter was recruitment and hiring in higher education, but in the film industry a strikingly similar rhetoric was deployed to reject black demands for inclusion. In September 1972 Hollywood management offered its first official response to the black film protests, charging that the demands amounted to a bid for unfair preference. The statement came, as before, from Valenti, and he outright rejected

'Black Exploitation' in Pix," *Daily Variety,* Aug. 16, 1972, p. 1. On Operation PUSH, see Will Tusher, "Black Capitalism Big Factor in PUSH Drive on Hollywood," *Hollywood Reporter,* Sept. 18, 1972, p. 3. "NAACP Takes Militant Stand on Black Exploitation Films," *ibid.,* Aug. 1, 1972, p. 1.

[32] Will Tusher, "Blackbuster Drive for Share of Industry Power Structure," *Hollywood Reporter,* Sept. 15, 1972, p. 1; Tusher, "Black Capitalism Big Factor in PUSH Drive on Hollywood," 3. Kwame Ture and Charles V. Hamilton, *Black Power: The Politics of Liberation in America* (1967; New York, 1992); Guerrero, *Framing Blackness,* 69.

[33] Philip E. Hoffman to the President, Aug. 4, 1972, quoted in Graham, *Civil Rights Era,* 446. MacLean, *Freedom Is Not Enough,* 187, 218. Robert Hampton to Heads of Departments and Agencies, Aug. 18, 1972, memorandum, p. 1, EEOC Policy—Remedies (Merit Systems) folder (1 of 4), box 85, Patterson files, Staff Member and Office Files, White House Central Files (Nixon Presidential Library).

the demands of Operation PUSH and some of the groups in the Coalition against Blaxploitation. The *Hollywood Reporter* headline declared: "Valenti Calls Black's Bluff; Rejects 'Special' Treatment." In this article, he states: "I'm deeply concerned not just about the movie business, but about any part of the society when, with threats of any kind, some group or some organization demands something that nobody else has." Rather than reasonable demands to confront historic and continuing exclusion, the activists' calls for redress were instead construed by Valenti as requests for a handout. By intimating that the case had wider valency ("any part of society"), Valenti signaled his participation in a broader debate then taking place: black demands were presented as an assault on national interests and liberal values. By claiming that African Americans were demanding "something that nobody else has," Valenti echoed the sentiments of nascent neoconservatives, who, in their writings, were insisting that white ethnics had not shared in the historic "white privilege" on which the black power critique was predicated.[34]

At the heart of the emerging neoconservative discourse was a reduction of race to ethnicity. As Michael Omi and Howard Winant have explored, neoconservative advocates reinvigorated ethnicity-based paradigms of race, premised on individual rights, to combat black nationalist and class-based paradigms that were based on group rights. The latter collectivist perspectives were interpreted as attacks on American liberal pluralism. In his industry response, Valenti stated: "I feel uneasy about any segment of the population demanding for itself what other segments of the population don't have. There are Italians, Catholics, Jews, Poles, Chicanos, Chinese, Japanese, blacks, northerners and southerners. I don't know where you draw the line." By naming blacks alongside other ethnic, racial, and regional groups working in film, Valenti discounted the impact of institutional racism on black employment prospects. With his populist roll call of pluralist America, he rhetorically leveled unequal power relations by reducing racial difference to a matter, merely, of competing ethnic and regional "segments" in healthy rivalry. Valenti's language echoed white ethnic writing of the time, which, as Jacobson describes, "interpret[ed] the African-American experience through the lens of Ellis Island's huddled masses" and "la[id] claim to a kind of just-off-the-boat innocence in its rendition of white-black social relations." Embedded in Valenti's misleading assumption that all groups had an equal shot was the implication that racial imbalances in the film industry were the result of a lack of black aptitude or ability. Scholars have pointed to the invidiousness of such positions that tacitly tend, as Winant puts it, "to rationalize racial injustice as a supposedly natural outcome of group attributes in competition."[35]

Evidence suggests that Valenti was an architect rather than merely an early adopter of white ethnic revival. In the summer of 1965, White House aide Valenti was fashioning a new kind of ethnic identity politics in response to black civil rights gains. He lobbied for an audit to be taken of white ethnic employment in the executive branch, remarking to

[34] Will Tusher, "Valenti Calls Black's Bluff; Rejects 'Special' Treatment," *Hollywood Reporter,* Sept. 29, 1972, pp. 3, 23. For an influential example of white ethnic revival writing, see, for instance, Michael Novak, *The Rise of the Unmeltable Ethnics: Politics and Culture in the Seventies* (New York, 1972), 71, 301. For an overview of white ethnic backlash against the civil rights movement, see Jacobson, *Roots Too,* 187–97.

[35] Omi and Winant, *Racial Formation in the United States,* 14–23, 113–36. See also Christopher Newfield and Avery F. Gordon, "Multiculturalism's Unfinished Business," in *Mapping Multiculturalism,* ed. Avery F. Gordon and Christopher Newfield (Minneapolis, 1996), 80–83; Gary Peller, "Race-Consciousness," in *Critical Race Theory: The Key Writings That Formed the Movement,* ed. Kimberlé Crenshaw et al. (New York, 1995), 127–58, esp. 128–33. Tusher, "Valenti Calls Black's Bluff," 23. Jacobson, *Roots Too,* 194–95. Winant, *New Politics of Race,* 43.

Johnson: "We have made no significant Italo-American appointments." "While you have made some spectacular Negro appointments, let us not forget that the largest ethnic group in this country (larger than the Negro) is the Italian," he continued. At a time widely viewed as the zenith of Great Society liberalism, Valenti was already vying to position African Americans as just another ethnic group, whose gains were potentially at the expense of his own group. He proposed to Johnson putting on the fast track the promotion of Italian Americans already in office and asking "all the Italo-American congressmen to submit to us the name of the best qualified Italo-American they know and from that pool draw . . . appointments to key jobs in government."[36] His suggestions for achieving greater Italian American representation were thus precisely the kinds of preferential measures that were unavailable to minorities in Hollywood who had no representatives in leadership roles. Where the AJC in 1972 sought to defend Jewish representation in higher education from the perceived threat of preferential policies for underrepresented minorities, Valenti, some seven years earlier, had been lobbying on behalf of Italian Americans in the face of African American advances.

In his 1972 press statement, Valenti mused: "I think it's bad to polarize a society by trying to segment it. I'm very much for integration because I think segregation is bad, segregation of anybody." The slippage from *segmentation* to *segregation* is telling. By calling out black activists as segregationist, Valenti was participating in a far-reaching rearticulation of the terms of debate. Perhaps the single most powerful contribution of the neoconservatives was to rehabilitate conservatism (from a 1960s low point) in large part through the appropriation of the language of civil rights. The most notorious example of this is the reinterpretation of the term *color blind*. Martin Luther King Jr. expressed its previous political meaning when, in 1963, he famously envisioned a future, built on substantial social reorganization, in which his children would "not be judged by the color of their skin." "Amazingly," remarks the historian Robin Kelley, neoconservatives "have couched their opposition to affirmative action and welfare in terms of Dr. Martin Luther King, Jr.'s dream for a 'color-blind' society. In other words, they have seized the language of the Civil Rights movement and turned it on its head." Valenti inverted public understandings of segregation, which in recent popular memory conjured shameful images of angry white southerners and police setting dogs on black people—images that had mobilized Americans of all races against Jim Crow. Daniel Moynihan later described this process as "'semantic infiltration': if the other fellow can get you to use his words, he wins." By detaching color blindness from its civil rights moorings and linking it to opposing ones, neoconservatives managed to steal a good deal of the movement's moral capital.[37]

In his comments, Valenti placed total faith in the ability of a free-labor market to produce conditions of racial equality. The disingenuousness of this neoliberal rhetoric becomes clear when one contrasts his repudiation of government intervention on behalf of minority workers with the film industry's aggressive solicitation of government help

[36] Jack Valenti to Lyndon Baines Johnson, July 13, 1965, Human Rights 2-1 file, box 43, White House Central Files (Johnson Library). See also MacLean, *Freedom Is Not Enough*, 244.

[37] Tusher, "Valenti Calls Black's Bluff," 3. Martin Luther King Jr., "I Have a Dream," 1963, reprinted in *Heath Anthology of American Literature, Volume 2*, ed. Paul Lauter (Lexington, Mass., 1994), 2483–86; Robin D. G. Kelley, *Yo' Mama's Disfunktional! Fighting the Culture Wars in Urban America* (Boston, 1997), 89–90. Daniel Patrick Moynihan, "Notable and Quotable," *Wall Street Journal*, April 18, 1985.

Film industry leaders lobby President Richard M. Nixon at the Western White House in San Clemente, California, on April 5, 1971. Jack Valenti is seated at the far corner of the table facing the camera. The Revenue Act of 1971 that followed this meeting provided government subsidies and tax shelters for the film industry. *Courtesy National Archives. Nixon Presidential Library,* WHOP, *roll 5981, image 10.*

on behalf of the industry. In 1971 Nixon met with an array of top industry leaders, including Valenti, organized by the MCA/Universal executive Taft Schreiber, who had headed Nixon's fund-raising campaign for California in the 1968 presidential election. The representatives complained about the industry's dire financial straits, while insisting, as recorded in the meeting's minutes, that "U.S. films deserve support as they prove U.S. freedom." They lobbied for measures including federal tax relief and the imposition of import duties on foreign films to enhance Hollywood's competitive advantage. "Two major developments assisting recovery . . . were expedited by the Nixon administration at the urgent request of industry leadership," explains the film historian David Cook: income tax credits on losses that created profit shelters and, written back into legislation, an investment tax credit on domestic production. Built into the Hollywood-friendly Revenue Act of 1971 that followed soon after the Hollywood meeting with Nixon was a provision for the creation of offshore studio subsidiaries that could avoid taxes on profits made from exports by reinvesting them in domestic production. Thus, at the same time that motion picture executives were lambasting calls for special treatment for blacks, they sought and won government subsidies, tax shelters, and tax-leveraged investment that greatly aided their domestic and international corporate competitiveness.[38]

[38] Peter M. Flanigan to the President's File, April 5, 1971, pp. 1–4, esp. 2, box 84, President's Office Files, White House Special Files (Nixon Presidential Library); Cook, *Lost Illusions,* 9–14, esp. 11; Connie Bruck, *When Hollywood Had a King: The Reign of Lew Wasserman, Who Leveraged Talent into Power and Influence* (New York, 2003), 270–76; A. D. Murphy, "Tax Break to Ease Pix Crisis: 'Schrieber Plan' to Cut Charges," *Daily Variety,* Sept. 15, 1971, p. 3; A. D. Murphy, "U.S. Grant Pushed for Pic Jobs," *ibid.,* Sept. 24, 1971, pp. 1, 6. On the

While the film business quietly went about instituting a new corporate order, many white film workers, facing high levels of unemployment, began to feel besieged. The few minority entrants helped by the voluntary agreement were an obvious target for their frustration. With many whites out of work, what George Lipsitz calls "the possessive investment in whiteness" was only more acute. Valenti's comments lent validation to gathering racial resentments. Repeatedly stating in his press comment that he rejected the activists' "basic premise" and did not "buy the notion" that you can divide filmmaking along racial lines, Valenti drew attention to the rearticulative force of his statement. He was coaching his executive peers, white film workers, and the media in a wholesale rejection of the color-conscious racial project—providing a vocabulary that allowed them to defend privileges and express resentments without sounding racist.[39]

Valenti was perfectly placed to help create and popularize this new language. Before his two-year stint as special assistant to President Johnson, he ran his own advertising agency. Both jobs allowed him to develop skills in the manipulation and control of information. The writer Connie Bruck remarks that Valenti "had a facility for translating abstractions into human terms." President Johnson's assistant Larry Levinson recalls that "The President would often say about some speech, 'I want it Valenti-ized! I want it made human!'" Richard Heffner, who worked under Valenti for nearly two decades as the head of the film ratings administration, recalls that the former Houston adman felt "his power came not from dialogue with the public, but from *telling* the public something, *conning* it, not from trying to *inform* it." Valenti combined his extrovert facility for press exposure with a very secretive corporate operating style—he was renowned for his curtailment of information about the internal functioning of the MPAA. Under Valenti, according to Heffner, it became "the tradition of the MPAA, through the years, to try to do things sub rosa, not openly." Valenti would later assert: "The fact, too long in the closet, is that politicians and Hollywood are sprung from the same DNA. They both deal in illusions whose machinations are oftentimes unseen by and unknown to the public." Thus, bringing together the skills of public relations with behind-the-scenes lobbying, and a facility for populist language with a flair for covert operations, he was a formidable corporate advocate.[40]

But just as Valenti and others were declaring race an irrelevant anachronism in the early 1970s, the industry was producing and profiting from egregiously color-conscious film products. Heightened racial themes were central to the black action (or blaxploitation) film cycle, from the "black-is-beautiful" heroes and heroines and the white villains to what the film scholar Paula Massood terms the "black ghetto chronotope" of their settings. For the scholar Guerrero, a "surge in African American identity politics" was

---

industry's financial reconfiguration around this time, see Tino Balio, "Retrenchment, Reappraisal, and Reorganization," in *The American Film Industry,* ed. Tino Balio (Madison, 1976), 329–31; Thomas H. Guback, "Hollywood's International Market," *ibid.*, 367–409; and Wasko, *Movies and Money,* 176–89.

[39] Lipsitz, *Possessive Investment in Whiteness,* 2. In 1971 unemployment in the International Alliance of Theatrical Stage Employees locals ranged from 40% to 85%, as reported by Walsh in Flanigan to the President's File, April 5, 1971, p. 1, President's Office Files, White House Special Files. On white worker resentment, see, for example, Dave Kaufman, "Laborers Exec Says Minority Hiring Distressing His IA Local," *Daily Variety,* May 21, 1970, pp. 1, 11; and Dave Kaufman, "Minority Hiring Goes to Court: Labor Group Seeks to Void Industry's Agreement with the Justice Dept.," *ibid.,* Nov. 4, 1971, pp. 1, 8. Tusher, "Valenti Calls Black's Bluff," 3, 23.

[40] Bruck, *When Hollywood Had a King,* 234. Richard Heffner quoted in Vaughn, *Freedom and Entertainment,* 25. Emphasis in original. Jack Valenti, "It's Lights, Camera, Politics," *Los Angeles Times,* Sept. 6, 1996, p. 9.

one of the cycle's "broad, overdetermining conditions of possibility." Given the youthfulness of the baby boom populace and the white-flight exodus to the suburbs, the black urban youth audience became a very significant niche market for the film industry. Hollywood moved quickly to produce and distribute black action narratives such as *Shaft* and *Super Fly* that dramatically overturned previous race-representational norms.[41]

Indeed, Valenti had played a key role in enabling the circulation of the new risqué themes portrayed in blaxploitation, which typically included scenes of racialized sex and violence. What Valenti is most renowned for during this period of his MPAA leadership was the 1968 introduction of a new rating system. Stephen Vaughn comments of Valenti that people "who were seeking principled leadership against excessive violence, sex, and profanity . . . found him a disappointment." Valenti helped instigate a liberalization of motion picture standards that gave rise to the very kinds of racial imagery that were so at odds with his postracial industry declarations. As "an ardent opponent of censorship," in the words of the film historian Thomas Doherty, Valenti was thus assuredly a neoliberal. In this regard, he parted company with the fledgling neoconservatives, who generally held the permissive culture epitomized by Hollywood partly responsible for the deterioration of the social order.[42]

The CAB activists, undermined by hostile discursive currents, rapidly lost steam. Their meeting with industry management, shortly after the storm over quotas and Valenti's intervention, captures the forced retreat. The first of the activists' "demands" agreed to at the meeting concerned industry jobs, and it was inordinately attenuated, asking the industry only to: "Work toward establishing an affirmative level of minority emphasis of employment." The idea of racial preference was suddenly so stigmatized as to be off the agenda. In the same month, Clifford Alexander remarked, "the politically sensitive term 'quota' is being used to pit Black against white, worker against worker." Other grassroots initiatives to increase minority employment in the film industry, notably a deeply progressive black-Jewish alliance called the Third World Cinema Corporation set up in 1971 by Cliff Frazier, Ossie Davis, and Hannah Weinstein continued to make headway, training workers and producing films. However, the tide was generally turning against minority activism in the film industry. At the CAB meeting, Hollywood management, which was well represented by the likes of Lew Wasserman, who headed the AMPTP—though not by Valenti—were more than happy to pay lip service to the CAB's downgraded demands.[43]

Of course, Valenti's laissez-faire stance was not representative of all studio executives, and the voluntary agreements Hollywood negotiated with the Justice Department in 1970 and the CAB in 1972 were acted on in diverging ways. On the conservative wing,

[41] Paula Massood, *Black City Cinema: African American Urban Experiences in Film* (Philadelphia, 2003), 84–93, 117; Guerrero, *Framing Blackness*, 69.

[42] Vaughn, *Freedom and Entertainment*, 25. On the introduction of the new rating system, see also Kevin S. Sandler, *The Naked Truth: Why Hollywood Doesn't Make X-Rated Movies* (New Brunswick, 2007), esp. 42–82. Thomas Doherty, *Hollywood's Censor: Joseph I. Breen and the Production Code Administration* (New York, 2007), 330. On the conflicting cultural perspectives of neoconservatives and neoliberals, see David Harvey, *A Brief History of Neoliberalism* (Oxford, 2005), 166.

[43] Steve Toy, "Meeting with Coalition against Blaxploitation on 12 Demands Deemed 'Very Good,'" *Daily Variety*, Oct. 16, 1972, p. 11; "Clifford Alexander Attacks Federal Job Discrimination," *Jet*, Oct. 12, 1972, p. 24. Ronald Gold, "Community Film Exec Says Majors Must Face Down Unions on Crew Bias," *Daily Variety*, Nov. 10, 1971, pp. 1, 22; Cliff Frazier interview by Eithne Quinn, April 17, 2007, digital recording and transcript (in Eithne Quinn's possession).

Walt Disney and Twentieth Century–Fox, who had refused even to participate in the Justice Department probe of 1969, were basically free to carry on as usual. By contrast, on the more progressive wing, Warner Bros., for instance, fulfilled promises for more minority representation with concrete jobs. Of 144 new office employees put on the payroll at the Warner studio during 1973, an impressive 35 percent were from minority groups. Accepting a Corporate Image Award for this achievement, Warner chairman Ted Ashley offered an eloquent rejoinder to Valenti's nonredistributive version of job-market equality: "Corporations have a responsibility to make certain that equal opportunity in employment is not merely a slogan, but rather a reality. In doing so, we're not doing anybody here a favor. People of the minority groups are talented, are skilled and dedicated. Bringing more of them into our offices and into our studios serves our company as much as it serves broader goals." Warner's minority employment initiatives in 1973 were a long way from its self-described "pretty dismal" state in 1969—being "gummed to death" by the EEOC had paid dividends.[44]

Though there was no consensual view on race among the studio bosses in this polarized and transitional period, the encroaching discourse of laissez-faire color blindness began to subsume other positions. Studios soon learned that they could defend the status quo far more effectively by espousing neoconservative postracialism than by adopting an old-fashioned defense of privilege. Disney, for instance, has been renowned since the 1970s for both its hard-nosed corporate operations, including keeping a tight rein on labor and wages, and for flagship animated features such as *The Lion King* and *Aladdin* that present, as many scholars have argued, racially conservative politics under a thin veil of multiculturalism. Meanwhile, the time of the more proactive corporate response, such as Universal's and Warner's, had reached its peak in the early 1970s. By the mid-1970s Warner was no longer operating its own studio lot, instead leasing facilities and employees from other studios. Thus, readily auditable in-house staff numbers had dropped precipitously. Thereafter, the idea of redress lost much of its mainstream purchase, attended by diminishing public concern for equal employment.[45]

In 1976 the California Advisory Committee to the U.S. Commission on Civil Rights tried to assess the progress made on minority utilization. The seniority roster system, overseen by the unions and the studios, persisted almost entirely unabated, and many creative openings were still advertised through word of mouth. Consequently, minorities were still very underrepresented on the industry's rosters. In 1977 blacks still only represented a paltry 2.8 percent of the overall work force (based on figures from twenty-four union locals), with even lower percentages in prestigious crafts. The figures volunteered by major studios about their in-house staff were somewhat better, suggesting there

---

[44] Burke, "U.S. Plans to Prod Film Industry on Job Discrimination Charges," 14. Ted Ashley quoted in Will Tusher, "Industry Tops U.S. on Minority Hiring," *Hollywood Reporter,* Jan. 22, 1974, p. 1.

[45] *Aladdin,* dir. Ron Clements and John Musker (Walt Disney, 1992); *The Lion King,* dir. Roger Allers and Rob Minkoff (Walt Disney, 1994). Corporate Disney has developed a reputation for "controlling labor" and "tough tactics," with salaries for its workers typically below industry standards. See Janet Wasko, *Understanding Disney: The Manufacture of Fantasy* (Malden, 2001), 89–99, esp. 70, 89, 98. For critiques of neoconservative multiculturalism in Disney's animated features, see, for example, Erin Addison, "Saving Other Women from Other Men: Disney's *Aladdin,*" *Camera Obscura,* 31 (Jan.–May 1993), 4–25; Robert Gooding-Williams, "Disney in Africa and the Inner City: On Race and Space in *The Lion King,*" *Social Identities,* 1 (no. 2, 1995), 373–79; and Derek T. Buescher and Kent A. Ono, "Civilized Colonialism: *Pocahontas* as Neocolonial Rhetoric," *Women's Studies in Communication,* 19 (no. 2, 1996), 127–54. California Advisory Committee to the U.S. Commission on Civil Rights, *Behind the Scenes,* 26–27.

had been at least a doubling of the employment percentage of minorities (and of women) between 1969 and 1976. Although representing progress, these statistics were a limited and underverified achievement for several reasons. First, the reliability of these studio-devised figures was questioned by the committee, which itself found "conflicting data." The committee reported that few studios had made real efforts to produce an affirmative action plan, and some even refused to offer information to the commission. Very little evidence pointed to minority representation in decision-making positions—despite claims by the studios to the contrary. Studios had focused much of their minority hiring, as in the case of Warner, on administrative and clerical positions. Many of the gains were thus far away from the symbol creators of motion picture making who are, as the media scholar David Hesmondhalgh stresses, "the primary workers in the making of texts"—and thus in film's role in the production of social meaning. Moreover, contraction in the size of the film industry's work force between 1969 and 1976 coupled with a surge in minority numbers in the local population rendered any net gains "negligible," according to the Commission on Civil Rights. The committee concluded that "sporadic and weak enforcement efforts by the Federal Government have allowed the industry to shirk its responsibilities."[46]

Conclusion

With its entrenched white work force and as the producer of hugely influential texts, Hollywood was a natural target for the mobilized EEOC under the able Clifford Alexander. However, precisely because of the film industry's heightened importance, both as a hallowed industry that favorably affected the U.S. balance of trade and as preeminent image factory, attacking it galvanized virulent reactions. Dirksen and Nixon saw the Title VII challenge to the movie industry (a business with which Nixon was apparently infatuated since his childhood in Yorba Linda) as an opportunity to defang the EEOC.[47] The industry lobbied Dirksen, the architect of the Title VII amendments, and Valenti assisted with the war of ideas. Valenti skilfully deployed budding neoconservative arguments, which complemented his own sense of white ethnic revival and his status as an ex-Democratic adviser turned corporate leader, on behalf of motion picture management.

The historian Dan Carter asserts: "even though the streams of racial and economic conservatism have sometimes flowed in separate channels, they ultimately joined in the political coalition that reshaped American politics from the 1970s through the mid-1990s."[48] An early point of confluence was Hollywood and the struggle for minority jobs. By forging a rhetorical alliance between white business interests and white workers in the industry, management helped delegitimize government agencies and black

[46] California Advisory Committee to the U.S. Commission on Civil Rights, *Behind the Scenes,* 5–6. On the studios' in-house figures, see *ibid.,* 41–42, esp. 42. David Hesmondhalgh, *The Cultural Industries* (London, 2002), 5–6. The mid-1970s demise of the black action-film cycle all but ended the short run of African American directors and scriptwriters in Hollywood—a trend that did not improve until the arrival of Spike Lee in the late 1980s and the hip-hop-inspired ghetto action-film cycle in the early 1990s. On labor and racial diversity in contemporary Hollywood, see Mark Wheeler, *Hollywood Politics and Society* (London, 2006), esp. 117–38; and Susan Christopherson, "Beyond the Self-Expressive Creative Worker: An Industry Perspective on Entertainment Media," *Theory, Culture, and Society,* 25 (nos. 7–8, 2008), 73–96.

[47] On Nixon's personal investment in Hollywood, see Bruck, *When Hollywood Had a King,* 275; and Mark Feeney, *Nixon at the Movies: A Book about Belief* (Chicago, 2004).

[48] Carter, *From George Wallace to Newt Gingrich,* xiv.

protestors. At the same time, by stigmatizing organized labor as die-hard discriminators, industry executives positioned themselves as the centrist liberals in ways that valorized their bid to reduce union organization. Although, in material terms, this latter attempt was unsuccessful—the experience rosters were not dismantled—it worked well discursively by neutralizing attacks on the studios.

The color-blind racial discourse, first conceived by the neoconservatives, became a new national consensus in the 1980s and 1990s.[49] It captured the center ground of thinking on race, underpinning profound policy change as U.S. politics shifted to the right. The film industry was a key early site where, during profound post–civil rights restructuring, new ideas about race, equality, and discrimination were shaped and legitimized. While individual African Americans achieved extraordinary advances, Hollywood's employment infrastructure changed little and its management gained new cohesiveness from the civil rights assault it confronted. From a performance characterized by racial embarrassment, defensiveness, and ignorance at the 1969 public hearing, Hollywood rapidly transformed, or perhaps reprised, its image into one of expansive liberal centrism. While some studios made efforts to integrate aspects of their work force, Hollywood generally managed to rehabilitate its racial reputation with little reform of its institutions and practices.

---

[49] See, especially, Winant, *World Is a Ghetto,* 169–76; and Michael K. Brown et al., *Whitewashing Race: The Myth of a Color-Blind Society* (Berkeley, 2003).

Jewish Urban Politics in the City and Beyond

Lila Corwin Berman

By the late 1960s, Detroit's Temple Beth El was in the final stages of planning its move to the suburbs. Housed since 1922 in a colonnaded neoclassical building on Woodward Avenue, the Reform synagogue had long served as a visible anchor for Jewish life in midtown Detroit. Now, almost a half century after the building had been erected, the congregation leaders were amassing their resources to construct a modernist synagogue in a suburb seventeen miles to the northwest. As of 1965 almost half of all Detroit Jews lived in the suburbs, and the vast majority of Jews who remained in the city occupied a series of middle- and upper-middle-class neighborhoods that abutted the northwest suburbs. Yet Temple Beth El did not go gentle into the postwar suburbs. In the summer of 1967, mere weeks after the Detroit riots spread through the blocks around the synagogue, the rabbi and synagogue president issued a statement describing their congregants as "ambassadors of reconciliation" and depicting the synagogue's physical location as a "source of strength and stability . . . to our city." As late as 1969, when relocation to the suburbs had become a near certainty, synagogue leaders assured the congregation that "a new edifice in the suburbs" would not undermine Temple Beth El's "commit[ment] to the problems of the inner-city."[1]

Well before the Detroit riots, and well before Temple Beth El, other synagogues, Jewish institutions, and Jews left the city, Jews had created a new politics of urban investment that was intensified, not diminished, by urban flight and upheaval. Jewish leaders and activists did not equate Jews' migration from the city with Jewish abandonment of

Lila Corwin Berman is an associate professor of history and the director of the Feinstein Center for American Jewish History at Temple University. The author wishes to thank Patricia Becker, Matt Lassiter, Jennifer Mittelstadt, Deborah Dash Moore, Bryant Simon, and Heather Thompson; the *JAH,* its reviewers, including Beryl Satter and Kenneth Waltzer, and its careful and patient editors; the Frankel Institute for Advanced Judaïc Studies and the Metropolitan History Workshop, both at the University of Michigan; and the University of Washington Institute for the Study of Race, Ethnicity, and Sexuality.

Readers may contact Berman at lcberman@temple.edu.

[1] Sidney Bolkosky, *Harmony and Dissonance: Voices of Jewish Identity in Detroit, 1914–1967* (Detroit, 1991), 300. "Beth El to Continue in Present Location, Pastoral Letter Asserts," *Detroit Jewish News,* Aug. 11, 1967, p. 5. Archie Katcher to Oscar Zemon, Jan. 3, 1969 (Rabbi Leo M. Franklin Archives, Temple Beth El, Bloomfield Hills, Mich.) The July 1967 Detroit riot left 43 people dead (30 of whom were killed by law enforcement personnel), more than 2,500 buildings looted or burned, and more than 7,000 people arrested. See Thomas J. Sugrue, *The Origins of the Urban Crisis: Race and Inequality in Postwar Detroit* (1996; Princeton, 2005), 259; and Sidney Fine, *Violence in the Model City: The Cavanagh Administration, Race Relations, and the Detroit Riot of 1967* (Ann Arbor, 1989).

doi: 10.1093/jahist/jas260

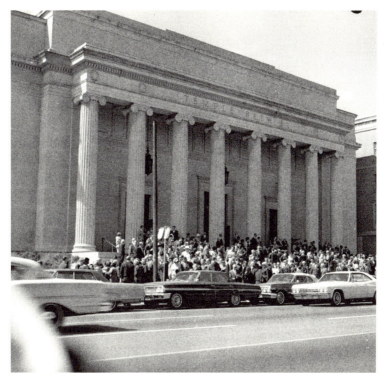

Temple Beth El, pictured above in a 1963 photograph, remained in the central-city area of Detroit longer than most other synagogues. Designed by Louis Kahn, the building on Woodward Avenue and Gladstone Street was completed in 1922. The new Temple Beth El building, pictured on the facing page in the final stages of construction, opened in 1973 in suburban Bloomfield Hills and was designed by Minoru Yamasaki. *Courtesy Walter P. Reuther Library, Wayne State University.*

the city. Rather, they asserted that one did not have to live in the city to care about it or be an urban activist.

The depth of Jews' postwar urban investment has been clouded by the striking demographics of Jewish suburbanization and the persuasive scholarship on white flight that correlates the journey away from the city with detachment from the city. Roughly one out of every three Jews in the United States moved to the suburbs in the two decades after World War II. Historians often note that Jews left cities more rapidly than other whites, and some scholars attribute this difference to historical patterns of Jewish mobility and portability that served as survival strategies for Jews in hostile lands. Otherwise, historians tend to view Jewish urban flight as consonant with the trends of white flight more generally. Yet a close analysis of Jews' political activism from World War II through the 1960s reveals the limitations of the current historical discussion on white flight and demands that historians rethink the correlations they have drawn between space, identity, and politics.[2]

[2] Gerald Gamm, *Urban Exodus: Why the Jews Left Boston and the Catholics Stayed* (Cambridge, Mass., 1999); Thomas Kessner, *The Golden Door: Italian and Jewish Immigrant Mobility in New York City, 1880–1915* (New York, 1977); Louis Wirth, *The Ghetto* (Chicago, 1928); Arthur Hertzberg, *The Jews in America: Four Centuries of an Uneasy Encounter; A History* (New York, 1989), 321.

Influenced by a theoretical interest in space (the "spatial turn"), a rich historiography draws attention to the landscape of the suburbs as a fortification against urban problems and as the setting for a new form of anti-urban, white conservatism. In his book about postwar Atlanta, Kevin Kruse asserts that "White flight, in the end, was more than a physical relocation. It was a political revolution." In similar fashion, Thomas Sugrue and Robert Self explain, "The mass migration of tens of millions of Americans to suburban areas realigned American politics." Sugrue, Self, Kruse, and other historians have shaped a white-flight scholarship that connects individuals' decisions to leave cities with the structural realities of racist federal housing policy. As David Freund illuminates in his study of suburban Detroit, "New racial thinking was decisively shaped by the powerful new institutions and private practices that fueled postwar suburban growth while also successfully excluding most black people from its benefits." White conservative politics, invested in shielding white middle-class life from problems perceived as urban and non-white, may have gestated in cities, but it thrived in suburban sites of urban removal.[3]

Woven into accounts of the new suburban politics of ex-urbanites is the history of the transformation of European immigrants into white ethnic Americans. As George Lipsitz writes, "The suburbs helped turn European Americans into 'whites' who could live near

[3] Barney Warf and Santa Arias, eds., *The Spatial Turn: Interdisciplinary Perspectives* (New York, 2009), 1–10. Kevin M. Kruse, *White Flight: Atlanta and the Making of Modern Conservatism* (Princeton, 2005), 6. For a similar discussion of white flight that gives more attention to the variety of suburbanites' politics, see Matthew D. Lassiter, *The Silent Majority: Suburban Politics in the Sunbelt South* (Princeton, 2006). Robert O. Self and Thomas J. Sugrue, "The Power of Place: Race, Political Economy, and Identity in the Postwar Metropolis," in *A Companion to Post-1945 America*, ed. Jean-Christophe Agnew and Roy Rosenzweig (Malden, 2002), 28. David M. P. Freund, *Colored Property: State Politics and White Racial Politics in Suburban America* (Chicago, 2007), 8. On black suburbanization, see Andrew Wiese, *Places of Their Own: African American Suburbanization in the Twentieth Century* (Chicago, 2004).

each other and intermarry with relatively little difficulty. But this 'white' unity rested on residential segregation and on shared access to housing and life chances largely unavailable to communities of color." For European immigrants, admission into the suburbs served as a geographic marker of acceptance into a white power structure that defined itself by the distance it maintained from a black, urban underclass.[4]

As valuable as historians' spatialization of white-flight politics and identity is, it does not satisfactorily account for the enduring urbanism that accompanied Jewish urban flight. In this article I draw attention to Jews' collective and public politics as communicated through their leaders, institutions, and press in postwar Detroit to illustrate how Jews transformed their politics from local urbanism to remote urbanism. In the immediate postwar years, Jews located their politics in their urban neighborhoods and pursued local, individual, and communal methods to improve their urban existences and to address the perceived challenges of racial integration. In the decades that followed, however, they shifted the focus of their urbanism away from the neighborhood and toward a more geographically remote legislative and policy-oriented form of political activism. Whether as elected officials, lobbyists, or members of a courted voting constituency, Jews gained faith that their voices would be heard even when they spoke from beyond their neighborhood. They came to perceive the problems of urbanism and, especially, urban race relations as much larger than their individual or communal responses to them. So if in the midst of their new efforts to reform urban policy and law, Jews left the city (as they did), moved their synagogues and institutions to the suburbs (as they did), and stopped voting in city elections and referenda (as they did), they could still maintain they were activists for the cause of urban betterment.

Detroit Jews knew they were not alone in reinventing their urbanism in spaces geographically remote from cityscapes. They communicated with Jewish leaders throughout the United States. From west Philadelphia to Newark to Boston to Baltimore to Chicago's Hyde Park and Lawndale to Queens to Brooklyn's Brownsville and Crown Heights to Shaker Heights in Cleveland to Boyle Heights in Los Angeles to Detroit, Jews invested energy initially in maintaining their local urbanism and later in preserving their remote urbanism through legislative as well as policy- and coalition-oriented politics that connected them to urban concerns and urban identities.[5]

---

[4] George Lipsitz, "The Possessive Investment in Whiteness: Racialized Social Democracy and the 'White' Problem in American Studies," *American Quarterly,* 47 (Sept. 1995), 374. On whiteness, see also Karen Brodkin, *How the Jews Became White Folks and What That Says about Race in America* (New Brunswick, 1998); Matthew Frye Jacobson, *Whiteness of a Different Color: European Immigrants and the Alchemy of Race* (Cambridge, Mass., 1998), 171–99; David R. Roediger, *Working toward Whiteness: How America's Immigrants Became White; The Strange Journey from Ellis Island to the Suburbs* (New York, 2005), 157–98; and Michael Rogin, *Blackface, White Noise: Jewish Immigrants in the Hollywood Melting Pot* (Berkeley, 1996), 209–50.

[5] For studies of Jews in other U.S. cities, see Lloyd P. Gartner, *History of the Jews of Cleveland* (Cleveland, 1978); Henry Goldschmidt, *Race and Religion among the Chosen Peoples of Crown Heights* (New Brunswick, 2006); Arnold R. Hirsch, *Making the Second Ghetto: Race and Housing in Chicago, 1940–1960* (New York, 1983); William B. Helmreich, *The Enduring Community: The Jews of Newark and MetroWest* (New Brunswick, 1999); Hillel Levine and Lawrence Harmon, *The Death of an American Jewish Community: A Tragedy of Good Intentions* (New York, 1992); Sylvie Murray, *The Progressive Housewife: Community Activism in Suburban Queens, 1945–1965* (Philadelphia, 2003); Antero Pietila, *Not in My Neighborhood: How Bigotry Shaped a Great American City* (Chicago, 2010); Wendell Pritchett, *Brownsville, Brooklyn: Blacks, Jews, and the Changing Face of the Ghetto* (Chicago, 2002); George J. Sánchez, "'What's Good for Boyle Heights Is Good for the Jews': Creating Multiracialism on the Eastside during the 1950s," *American Quarterly,* 56 (Sept. 2004), 633–61; Beryl Satter, *Family Properties: Race, Real Estate, and the Exploitation of Black Urban America* (New York, 2009); and David Varady,

Jews' local and remote urban politics were rife with contradiction and hypocrisy that white-flight and whiteness scholarship has helped expose. As urban dwellers, Jews often championed the ideals of integration while personally benefiting from a racist housing system that exploited black Americans' desperation for and exclusion from decent housing and mortgages. And when Jews left cities in the second half of the twentieth century, they materially disinvested in urban life in the same way as countless white Americans. Yet Jews' migration away from cities must be reconsidered within the framework of an ongoing urban Jewish consciousness that did not simply acquiesce to a white, suburban, conservative politics.[6]

Jews' urban activism, whether local or remote, tended to follow the shifting terrain of civil rights–era liberalism. In the 1940s leftism and liberalism still found common cause around issues of individual rights and class betterment. Yet with the rise of the Cold War, many Jewish institutions purged their leftist members and participated in a nationwide assault on the Left. Liberals, strengthened by the diminished Left, placed their faith in the state to protect individual and group rights. Simultaneously, rising strains of black radicalism and white conservatism challenged the efficacy of civil rights liberalism, guiding some Jews toward a neoconservative politics that rejected the idea of state-based group protections in favor of individual rights. Most Jews, however, eschewed white conservatism and remained committed to a liberal belief in the power of the state to protect individual rights alongside group interests.[7]

Jews' liberalism alone does not explain the contours of their postwar politics and identity. The lines dividing leftists, liberals, and, eventually, neoconservatives were often blurry and the wide range of issues related to Israel or the Holocaust disrupted neat political taxonomies.[8] Rather, we must also pay close attention to Jews' urbanism and their shifting relationship to the city to gain a more complete appreciation of postwar politics across the ideological spectrum. Simply put, one's location in space is not necessarily coterminous with one's politics or identity.

What follows has broad implications for our understanding of postwar cities and politics, but it is not a mere proxy for the history of urban politics. Importantly, my discussion of Jews' relationship with urban space and politics is concerned with how Jews perceived the presence and proximity of African Americans, and it is not intended to illuminate the equally complicated subject of how African Americans thought about their entrance into spaces that Jews claimed as Jewish or white. American Jews' attachment to cities stemmed from their particular investment in maintaining space for Jewish

---

"Wynnefield: Story of a Changing Neighborhood," in *Philadelphia Jewish Life, 1940–2000,* ed. Murray Friedman (Philadelphia, 2003), 101–12.

[6] On Jews' roles, both exploitative and reformist, in urban real estate, see Pietila, *Not in My Neighborhood;* and Satter, *Family Properties.* On Jews' ambivalence about whiteness, see Eric L. Goldstein, *The Price of Whiteness: Jews, Race, and American Identity* (Princeton, 2006).

[7] On the shifting nature of liberalism during the civil rights era and the growing distance between liberal attitudes and activism, see Thomas J. Sugrue, *Sweet Land of Liberty: The Forgotten Struggle for Civil Rights in the North* (New York, 2008), 540. On ethnic politics and liberalism, see Joshua M. Zeitz, *White Ethnic New York: Jews, Catholics, and the Shaping of Postwar Politics* (Chapel Hill, 2007). For a groundbreaking study of suburban liberalism, see Lily Geismer, "Don't Blame Us: Grassroots Liberalism in Massachusetts, 1960–1990" (Ph.D. diss., University of Michigan, 2010).

[8] Michael E. Staub, *Torn at the Roots: The Crisis of Jewish Liberalism in Postwar America* (New York, 2002).

life to survive and thrive in the United States. Jews, whether they were religious or not religious, generally perceived cities as more hospitable to Jews than other environments. During eras of European enlightenment and liberalization, progressive policies to integrate Jews into civic life tended to originate in urban areas and benefit urban Jews most. Furthermore, in the United States, Jewish intellectuals crafted new models for American citizenship grounded in clearly urban perspectives; theories of cultural pluralism and dual civilizations valorized the kinds of public space that cities offered, where diverse groups could interact and still stake out spaces defined by ethnic propinquity.[9]

The vast majority of Jews in the United States first settled in cities and found relative success in them. Even as Jews moved away from the postwar city, many persisted in the belief that cities offered freedom, security, and a sense of possibility for them and, by extension, all Americans. Jews' urbanism resided at the heart of postwar Jewish politics, though this urbanism did not manifest itself in a singular political perspective. Jews on the left, Jews on the right, and the large pool of postwar Jews who were somewhere in the liberal center all drew upon visions of enduring urbanism to animate their political ideals.

The Jewish Neighborhoods of Detroit

With notable frequency historians have looked to Detroit for explanations of twentieth-century urban transformations. Its rise and fall as an urban industrial center and its demographic shift from a white city to a black city parallel similar shifts in many other urban locales. The unique texture of Detroit—the role that the automobile industry played in defining the city, its distance from either coast, and the eventual thoroughness of its segregation and deindustrialization—has also attracted historians interested in documenting urban tensions and politics. Yet historians of Jewish urban politics have almost entirely neglected Detroit. In the neighborhoods of Detroit, one finds an unexplored slice of American Jewish life that is connected to postwar experiences of urban Jews throughout the United States and speaks powerfully to the relationship between urban politics and space.[10]

The approximately 35,000 Jews who lived in Detroit by 1920 experienced the triumphs of a city that had grown astronomically over the last half decade. Detroit had become the fourth largest city in the United States and, by 1937, with 71,000 Jews, the sixth largest Jewish city. More than 80 percent of those Jews lived a few miles to the

---

[9] For overviews of Jews' relationship to urbanism, see Ezra Mendelsohn, ed., *People of the City: Jews and the Urban Challenge* (New York, 1999); and Yuri Slezkine, *The Jewish Century* (Princeton, 2004), 1, 10, 40–104. See also special issues devoted to Jews, geography, and identity in *Jewish Social Studies,* 11 (Spring–Summer 2005); and *Prooftexts,* 26 (Winter–Spring 2006). On Jewish theories of national citizenship, see Lila Corwin Berman, *Speaking of Jews: Rabbis, Intellectuals, and the Creation of an American Public Identity* (Berkeley, 2009), 93–118; and Daniel Greene, *The Jewish Origins of Cultural Pluralism: The Menorah Association and American Diversity* (Bloomington, 2011), 63–90.

[10] On Detroit, see Kevin Boyle, *Arc of Justice: A Saga of Race, Civil Rights, and Murder in the Jazz Age* (New York, 2004); Freund, *Colored Property;* Sugrue, *Origins of the Urban Crisis;* Jon C. Teaford, *Cities of the Heartland: The Rise and Fall of the Industrial Midwest* (Bloomington, 1993); Heather Ann Thompson, *Whose Detroit? Politics, Labor, and Race in a Modern American City* (Ithaca, 2001); and Olivier Zunz, *The Changing Face of Inequality: Urbanization, Industrial Development, and Immigrants in Detroit, 1880–1920* (Chicago, 1982). On Detroit's Jews, see Bolkosky, *Harmony and Dissonance;* Henry J. Meyer, "The Structure of the Jewish Community in the City of Detroit" (Ph.D. diss., University of Michigan, 1939); Robert A. Rockaway, *The Jews of Detroit: From the Beginning, 1762–1914* (Detroit, 1986); and Kenneth Waltzer, "East European Jewish Detroit in the Early Twentieth Century," *Judaism,* 49 (Summer 2000), 291–309.

north and west of the city center in the Twelfth Street–Linwood–Dexter neighborhood, so called for its major thoroughfares. The neighborhood was populated by middle-class Jews and white ethnic Catholics, with predominantly two-flat (or two-family) homes and a smattering of single-family dwellings.[11]

Even though as many non-Jews as Jews lived in the neighborhood, Jews perceived the neighborhood as Jewish space and identified its terrain and meaning as firmly located within the Jewish community. The demographics and geography of the neighborhood drove this sense; some blocks housed almost exclusively Jewish families, and Jews knew where other Jews lived. Additionally, the neighborhood's streetscape reflected Jewish life. Reform, Conservative, and Orthodox synagogues, the Jewish Community Center, a United Hebrew School building, and Jewish bakeries and stores lined the central arteries. Finally, the almost entirely Jewish student body at the local public schools confirmed Jews' perception that they inhabited a Jewish neighborhood. Because most Catholic children attended parochial schools, Jews experienced neighborhood elementary schools and high schools as Jewish institutions.[12]

Jews' perception of Jewish space, however, was mutable. As in most other cities, Jews in Detroit had first settled in a downtown neighborhood, the Hastings Street neighborhood, adjacent to the city center and industry. Jews clustered in a handful of blocks and established Jewish institutions and shops. Over time, many Jews left Hastings Street for better housing stock and public services, gradually settling in the Twelfth Street–Linwood–Dexter neighborhood. A stream of newcomers, however, kept the population of Jews in Hastings Street constant until the 1920s, when a community study found that "with the steady increase of the Negro population and their pressure upon the Jewish districts for housing facilities," the Jewish population was waning. That trend was exacerbated by new restrictions on immigration that slowed the influx of new Jews into the neighborhood. According to the authors of the community study, the demise of the Hastings Street neighborhood "created a serious problem for the Jewish community" and its ability to maintain stable institutional life.[13] Nonetheless, there is no evidence that community leaders attempted to persuade Jews to stay in the neighborhood. Instead, these leaders directed the bulk of their efforts to reconstituting Jewish life in the section of the city where the majority of Jews were now settling.

Among Jewish business owners, however, one can observe the stirrings of a new consciousness about the relationship between neighborhood stability and the politics of race in the United States. While most Jewish residents left the Hastings Street neighborhood,

[11] Zunz, *Changing Face of Inequality*, 285–371; Bolkosky, *Harmony and Dissonance*, 17–19, 185, 437.

[12] On the concept of a Jewish neighborhood, see Goldschmidt, *Race and Religion among the Chosen Peoples of Crown Heights*, 76–115; and Deborah Dash Moore, "On the Fringes of the City: Jewish Neighborhoods in Three Boroughs," in *The Landscape of Modernity: Essays on New York City, 1900–1940*, ed. David Ward and Olivier Zunz (New York, 1992), 252–72. On neighborhood geography and identity, see Bryant Simon, *Boardwalk of Dreams: Atlantic City and the Fate of Urban America* (New York, 2004), 63–82. On Jews and knowledge of other Jewish urban residents, see Mandell ("Bill") Berman interview by Judy Cantor, Oct. 9, 1990, transcript, p. 13, (Congregation Shaarey Zedek, Southfield, Mich.). On the Jewish predominance in neighborhood schools, see Bolkosky, *Harmony and Dissonance*, 185. On parochial schools in Detroit, see Leslie Woodcock Tentler, *Seasons of Grace: A History of the Catholic Archdiocese of Detroit* (Detroit, 1990), 443–44.

[13] On Jews and the Hastings Street area, see "The Shifting Jewish Districts," 1923 survey of Detroit Jewish community, attached to Zeldon Cohen to CRC [Community Relations Committee] Neighborhoods Committee Members, Sept. 24, 1965, folder 2, box 23 (Jewish Community Council Archives, Walter P. Reuther Library, Wayne State University, Detroit, Mich.); and Waltzer, "East European Jewish Detroit in the Early Twentieth Century." On the influx of blacks into Detroit in the 1920s, see Zunz, *Changing Face of Inequality*, 287.

many Jewish-owned shops remained there. In the mid-1930s the black press accused Jewish merchants of hostile conduct toward black customers and employees and of edging out black retail competition. Jewish leftists and liberals, in concert with black leaders from communist and noncommunist organizations, sought to ameliorate the situation. In 1937 local Jewish leaders concerned with the negative publicity persuaded a handful of Jewish shopkeepers who still owned stores in the neighborhood but for the most part no longer resided in it to organize the East Side Merchants Association. According to the group's publicity, "The purpose of this organization [is] to promote a better relationship between Jewish merchants and their Negro customers." In Brownsville, a densely Jewish neighborhood in Brooklyn, Jewish and black reformers similarly targeted shopkeepers, most of whom no longer dwelled in the area, to convince them that easing racial tensions would stabilize the economic well-being of the neighborhood and their stores.[14]

In the immediate postwar years, greater numbers of Jews and Jewish institutions turned toward similar forms of local activism to help control the rapidly shifting economic, political, and cultural landscape within their neighborhoods. The massive wartime population shifts that brought well over 1 million African Americans to northern industrial centers, the postwar slowing of industrial production, and a burgeoning national discussion about prejudice and discrimination all fueled new urban tensions. Housing shortages, compounded by racist federal and state policies, squeezed African Americans into limited and exploitative housing markets while also stimulating new real estate growth on the fringes of cities.[15]

In cities across the United States, Jews distinguished themselves from other ethnic and religious groups by the rapidity with which they disbanded once-Jewish neighborhoods. Historians explain that a combination of Jews' cultural patterns and real estate practices enabled Jews to act quickly once they perceived changes in the socioeconomic and racial landscape of their neighborhoods. Much evidence supports these explanations. Detroit had a much higher rate of homeownership by midcentury than did other urban centers, but, even so, only half of all Jews owned homes compared with 70 percent of white Protestants and Catholics. And Jewish institutions, especially synagogues, moved away from city neighborhoods in Chicago, Cleveland, Newark, Philadelphia, Detroit, and many other cities much faster than did Catholic churches bound to the geography of the parish. Historians have allowed these facts to eclipse the ambivalence that postwar Jews felt about leaving their urban neighborhoods, however, and the attachment they felt to urbanism.[16]

[14] "Facts for Your Information," n.d., folder 9, box 66 (Jewish Community Council Archives). On Jewish-black relations in Detroit, see also Marshall Field Stevenson, "Points of Departure, Acts of Resolve: Black-Jewish Relations in Detroit, 1937–1962" (Ph.D. diss., University of Michigan, 1988), 97–100. On Jewish liberal and leftist alliances in Detroit in the 1930s and early 1940s, see Steve Babson, Dave Riddle, and David Elsila, *The Color of Law: Ernie Goodman, Detroit, and the Struggle for Labor and Civil Rights* (Detroit, 2010), 34–36, 199–232. Pritchett, *Brownsville, Brooklyn*, 60–62, 72.

[15] For an overview of the federal policies that stimulated suburban development, see Adam Rome, *The Bulldozer in the Countryside: Suburban Sprawl and the Rise of American Environmentalism* (New York, 2001), 19–43. On black migration to the North, see Isabel Wilkerson, *The Warmth of Other Suns: The Epic Story of America's Great Migration* (New York, 2010). On postwar economic shifts, see Barry Bluestone and Bennett Harrison, *The Deindustrialization of America: Plant Closings, Community Abandonment, and the Dismantling of Basic Industry* (New York, 1982). On national attitudes toward discrimination, see Gary Gerstle, *American Crucible: Race and Nation in the Twentieth Century* (Princeton, 2001).

[16] On homeownership, see David Goldberg and Harry Sharp, "Some Characteristics of Detroit Area Jewish and Non-Jewish Adults," in *The Jews: Social Patterns of an American Group*, ed. Marshall Sklare (Glencoe, 1958), 115; Gamm, *Urban Exodus*, 51–55; Hirsch, *Making the Second Ghetto*, 189–94; and John T. McGreevy, *Parish Boundaries: The Catholic Encounter with Race in the Twentieth-Century Urban North* (Chicago, 1996), 18. On

Most postwar Jewish urban communities established local- and individual-oriented campaigns, often filtered through local community councils, to save what was always termed the "changing" Jewish neighborhood. Such campaigns unfolded in the context of a new liberal post-Holocaust discourse about racism that located the origin of prejudice in individuals' attitudes and the remedies to prejudice in education-based efforts to reform the individual. Accordingly, one's behavior (for instance, how one reacted to a new black neighbor) and the existence or absence of racism in the United States was assumed to be in close alignment. Only beginning in the late 1950s did liberal discourse shift to embrace broader remedies to racism, where law and policy, not individuals' attitudes and decisions, were identified as the agents of urban transformation. In the 1940s, however, Jews imagined their political framework as a local and Jewish one and believed that they could affect political change through the sum of their actions.[17]

Grassroots Politics, Jewish Survival, and Integration in "Changing" Neighborhoods

A survey in the late 1940s found that only 49 percent of Detroit Jews lived in the Twelfth Street–Linwood–Dexter neighborhood compared with 80 percent less than a decade earlier. An accompanying report described Jewish homeowners as "in a state of near hysteria," fearful of being unable to sell their homes and becoming stranded in a nonwhite and non-Jewish neighborhood.[18] Throughout the 1940s and early 1950s prominent and often outspokenly liberal Jews committed themselves to persuading fellow Jews to stay put and embrace a racially integrated yet still Jewish vision of the Twelfth Street–Linwood–Dexter neighborhood. In 1947 they formed the Midtown Neighborhood Council. Blurring the language of Jewish survival and racial justice, local campaigns to preserve Jewish urban neighborhoods were a critical though short-lived stage in the development of a new Jewish urban politics.

Central to the local campaign to save the Jewish neighborhood was Detroit's Jewish Community Council, an organization in which many of the neighborhood activists had long been members and leaders. Founded in 1936, the Jewish Community Council answered the needs of predominantly Yiddish-speaking, leftist, Eastern European–born Jews who felt marginalized by the German-Jewish elite in Detroit. By the 1940s Jewish community councils throughout the urban United States provided organizational homes for Jewish leaders invested in preserving a Jewish urban presence and committed to a liberal urban politics of racial justice and integration.[19] That many of the leading Jewish

---

urban attachment among city dwellers more generally, see Amanda I. Seligman, *Block by Block: Neighborhoods and Public Policy on Chicago's West Side* (Chicago, 2005).

[17] For a list published by the National Community Relations Advisory Council of over 20 cities with active Jewish community councils involved in efforts to stem neighborhood change, see *A Guide to Changing Neighborhoods: A Manual of Guidance for Dealing with Intergroup Relations Problems in the Neighborhood Undergoing Change* (New York, 1956), 15, folder 1, box 86 (Jewish Community Council Archives). On the shifting rhetoric of race, see Berman, *Speaking of Jews*, 96–98; Kirsten Fermaglich, *American Dreams and Nazi Nightmares: Early Holocaust Consciousness and Liberal America, 1957–1965* (Waltham, 2006), 24–57; Susan A. Glenn, "The Vogue of Jewish Self-Hatred in Post–World War II America," *Jewish Social Studies,* 12 (Spring–Summer 2006), 95–136; and Stephen Steinberg, *Turning Back: The Retreat from Racial Justice in American Thought and Policy* (Boston, 1995).

[18] *Guide to Changing Neighborhoods,* 15. On neighborhood demographics, see Bolkosky, *Harmony and Dissonance,* 185, 298.

[19] Kurt Peiser and William Boxerman, "Forward Steps in Jewish Community Organization: Recent Experiences in Detroit," *Jewish Social Service Quarterly,* 14 (Dec. 1937), 240–50. On the Jewish Community Council,

organizations supporting local efforts for residential integration were at least as committed to Jewish survival as they were to racial justice created a situation that was complicated at best, untenable at worst. Could a Jewish neighborhood endure as a racially integrated neighborhood, and was this question as seemingly absurd as asking whether a white neighborhood could endure as a racially integrated neighborhood?

The Midtown Neighborhood Council resembled in form hundreds of other white neighborhood and homeowners associations that emerged in postwar Detroit and across the United States. The formation of a neighborhood association was a common response to property owners' fears that their neighborhood was losing its status and stability, often because of the entrance of nonwhites into it. Community meetings at homes and school auditoriums, homegrown leadership, and neighborhood-based activities were typical of these associations. Neighborhood associations generally thrived on social coercion and peer pressure. For example, a 1947 publicity flyer explained, "The Midtown Neighborhood Council is a representative group of your friends and neighbors who have joined hands to help improve the area in which we live."[20]

While the Midtown Neighborhood Council resembled other white urban neighborhood associations in form, its ideals made it distinctive. Unlike many surrounding neighborhood associations, it repudiated intimidation and violence against African Americans as strategies for preserving the character of the neighborhood. A report generated almost a decade later celebrated the Twelfth Street neighborhood as "the only area in the city where in-migration of Negro families produced no violence, no picketing and no threats."[21] Instead of turning to physical intimidation, supporters of the Midtown Neighborhood Council used their organizing skills to build an emotionally percussive case that equated Jews' collective commitment to the neighborhood with their commitment to Jewish survival and racial justice. Yet in its actions, the Midtown Neighborhood Council appeared to be weighing the relative value of residential integration against the goal of maintaining a Jewish neighborhood. Never able to articulate a clear vision of how those two goals would be reconciled, the leaders of the group often fell prey to contradictory and even racist statements about the relationship between black and Jewish life. Furthermore, the leaders failed to acknowledge the racist structures—beyond individual attitude—in which Jews were implicated, particularly through their real estate transactions.

Throughout the mid-1940s the Jewish Community Council dispatched teams of graduate student interviewers to collect data about residents of the Twelfth Street neighborhood, especially those displaying For Sale signs on their property. Interviewers were given specific instructions not only to find out why Jews were selling their homes but also to convince these homeowners to take their homes off the market and join the nascent Midtown Neighborhood Council. Interviewers were directed to tell homeowners that the

see also Walter E. Klein, "The Jewish Community Council of Metropolitan Detroit: The Organizing Years," *Michigan Jewish History*, 18 (Jan. 1978), 20–34; and Amy Shevitz, "Civil Rights, White Flight, and the 'Jewish Quest for Inclusion,'" paper presented at the 2008 Biennial Scholars' Conference on American Jewish History (in Lila Corwin Berman's possession).

[20] "Midtown Neighborhood Council: A Community Service," [1947], folder 9, box 67 (Jewish Community Council Archives). On neighborhood associations, see Freund, *Colored Property*, 243–83; Stephen Grant Meyer, *As Long as They Don't Move Next Door: Segregation and Racial Conflict in American Neighborhoods* (New York, 2000), 172–96; and Sugrue, *Origins of the Urban Crisis*, 209–58.

[21] Report by S. J. Fauman and Eleanor Wolf, [mid-1950s], folder 2, box 552 (Jewish Community Council Archives).

drop in real estate values was a temporary one, exacerbated by "fear and panic," and they were armed with data to prove that the neighborhood was neither becoming too black nor depreciating, two issues that white homeowners perceived as intimately connected. According to Jewish Community Council reports, only one hundred African American families had settled in the broad vicinity of the neighborhood, and even fewer nonwhites resided in the core of the neighborhood. With these statistics interviewers reassured homeowners that the neighborhood was still white, Jewish, and a sound investment.[22]

Yet the guidelines also provided another set of rhetorical cues to convince Jews to stay in the neighborhood. Interviewers were encouraged to analogize Jewish experiences with the struggles of African Americans. To the question, "Is what they say about Negroes true?" interviewers were told to respond, "No! Remember, the *same things* are said about Jews." The last line of the interviewers' guide reiterated, "Remember—Prejudice against Negroes is part of the same social disease as anti-Semitism." The belief that residential discrimination was a slippery slope—if white Americans practiced it against African Americans they also would eventually sanction it against Jews—undoubtedly drove many Detroit Jews to support integration and distinguish the pathway of Jewish politics from that of many other American ethnic groups.[23]

When contemplating the integration of their neighborhoods, however, Jews were compelled to define what, precisely, made a neighborhood a Jewish neighborhood. After all, Jews had lived alongside Catholics hailing from many European nations without worrying about whether the neighborhood was still Jewish. Assumed Jewish spaces were rarely entirely Jewish, a reality often inconsequential to how Jews thought about those spaces. Still, the presence of African Americans fundamentally changed how Jews imagined their neighborhood. By the middle of the twentieth century, lending codes, property-assessment practices, zoning ordinances, and restrictive covenants militated against mixed-race residential space. Furthermore, those policies deprived blacks of legal protections against duplicitous and unregulated home-financing schemes and led to massive fluctuations in home values that offered quick gain for some and rapid loss for others. A Jewish real estate agent, for example, wrote the Jewish Community Council in 1947 with a list of Jewish agents (including himself) who had recently sold homes to black families. He suggested that these agents were willing to weather the ire of local Jewish homeowners, in part, because their profits for a sale to a black person far exceeded what they could make from selling the same home to a white person. The Jewish Community Council received other reports that year of Jewish landlords evicting white tenants in favor of black ones who would pay higher rents. Contrary to what liberal Jews hoped to prove, the housing market was not race blind, a reality that Jewish liberals only started to confront in the 1950s when they sought to reform real estate agents' behavior.[24]

In a later assessment, the Jewish Community Council deemed their house-to-house interviews a success. Some property owners were convinced to take their homes off the market or at least remove For Sale signs, which "gave visible evidence to the passer-by of

[22] *Manual for Interviewers in 12th Street Area,* Nov. 6, 1946, pp. 1–2, folder 6, box 15, *ibid.*; "Instructions to Interviewers Midtown Facilities Survey," [late 1940s], folder 5, box 584, *ibid.*; John Feild to Director, July 17, 1947, memo, *ibid.*

[23] *Manual for Interviewers in 12th Street Area,* 2; Marc Dollinger, *Quest for Inclusion: Jews and Liberalism in Modern America* (Princeton, 2000), 164–90.

[24] B. Edelman of Edelman Realty to Jewish Community Council, May 7, 1947, folder 5, box 15 (Jewish Community Council Archives); S. Stahle to Jewish Community Council, June 2, 1947, *ibid.*

preparation for flight." However, the Jewish Community Council likely inflated the demographic stability of the neighborhood by including newly settled displaced persons from World War II in its statistics and by extending the boundaries of the neighborhood to include wealthier Jewish areas to the north and west.[25] Time would show that these efforts did not keep Jews in the neighborhood. In the short term, however, the interviews helped galvanize a local movement among Jews to preserve and save their neighborhood.

In the spring of 1947 posters and five thousand flyers publicized a massive clean-up campaign that drew attention to the role individuals played in stemming the tide of neighborhood decline. With special attention to newcomers, mainly black families that leaders imagined might not know how to maintain middle-class homes, the Midtown Neighborhood Council distributed a list of "Ten Do's" and "Ten Don'ts" about neighborhood and home maintenance. While its efforts concentrated on individual remedies to neighborhood deterioration, the Midtown Neighborhood Council was at least aware that actions by the city could thwart individuals' attempts to stabilize their neighborhoods. Residents repeatedly complained about rat infestations and linked the problem to the city's increasing negligence regarding trash collection. In the late 1940s neighborhood leaders lobbied the city for more efficient garbage disposal, new traffic lights, better playgrounds, and more parking facilities near commercial areas. There is no evidence that the city responded to these pleas, but the requests indicate a growing awareness among neighborhood leaders of the limits of local activism.[26]

As historians have noted, neighborhood-based politics relied heavily on the participation of women. Of the individuals mentioned in the coverage by the Jewish press of the Midtown Neighborhood Council, roughly one-third were women. These generally middle-class women tended to have more flexible schedules and more knowledge about daily neighborhood life than did men. They noticed when the racial composition of their children's classes shifted and the number of children per classroom increased or when, as one woman observed, nearby stores appeared to be "catering to the colored," and they also talked regularly to their neighbors. Furthermore, they were almost always the ones who answered the door when interviewers and surveyors knocked during the day. Thus their involvement in neighborhood politics corresponded to the role they played in maintaining the neighborhood and assessing whether it was remaining a Jewish space.[27]

[25] Report by Fauman and Wolf. *Guide to Changing Neighborhoods,* 16. On criticism of the Jewish Community Council's demographic statistics, see Bernard Rosenberg, "Afro-Jewish Americans: The Case of Twelfth Street Detroit," [1950], folder 5, box 584 (Jewish Community Council Archives). On postwar displaced persons in Detroit, see Sidney M. Bolkosky, "Detroit's Reactions to the Holocaust and the New Immigrants," *Judaism: A Quarterly Journal of Jewish Life and Thought,* 49 (June 2000), 309–22.

[26] "Midtown Council to Hear Talk by Citizen of Month," *Detroit Jewish News,* Jan. 9, 1948, clipping, folder 6, box 15 (Jewish Community Council Archives); "Neighborhood Sub-committee," Jan. 21, 1947, meeting notes, *ibid.* On press coverage for clean-up drives, see Louis Fraiberg to Benedict Glazer and Lawrence Crohn, April 16, April 25, 1947, *ibid.* On lobbying the city for improvement, see Midtown Neighborhood Council minutes, June 1, June 8, 1948, folder 9, box 67, *ibid.*; *Midtown Facilities Study Questionnaire,* [1949], folder 5, box 584, *ibid.*; and *Guide to Changing Neighborhoods,* 15–18. On city governments' neglect of neighborhoods with growing black populations, see Will Cooley, "Moving on Out: Black Pioneering in Chicago, 1915–1950," *Journal of Urban History,* 36 (July 2010), 489.

[27] "Action Planned by New Mid-town Council," *Detroit Jewish News,* Nov. 11, 1947, clipping, folder 6, box 15 (Jewish Community Council Archives); Danny Raskin, "Listening," *Detroit Jewish News,* April 11, 1947, clipping, *ibid.*; "12th Street Area 'Model' in Cleanup Campaign," *Detroit Jewish News,* April 4, 1947, clipping, *ibid.*; "Midtown Council to Hear Talk by Citizen of Month"; "Council Calls Owners of 12th Street Property," *Detroit Jewish Chronicle,* [1947], clipping, *ibid.* Nathan Shur to Jewish Community Council, Nov. 19, 1947, *ibid.* On

Nevertheless, these local efforts relied on the active involvement of prominent community leaders—almost entirely men—who lent the movement credibility and authority. In this regard, rabbis, whose synagogues dotted the Twelfth Street neighborhood, were crucial participants in the Midtown Neighborhood Council's efforts. In a letter sent to neighborhood rabbis in the fall of 1947 the president of the Jewish Community Council requested that the rabbis use their upcoming High Holiday sermons to "promote harmony between the various groups living in the Twelfth Street area" and advise their congregants against panic selling and abandoning the neighborhood. Rabbis were also asked to deny rumors that their synagogues were planning exit strategies from the neighborhood. Most neighborhood rabbis took an active role in the Jewish Community Council's work since they knew that their institutions' survival depended upon the ongoing presence of Jews in the neighborhood, and many were firm believers in the ideals of integration. At the same time, synagogue records prove that rabbis and congregational leaders quietly made plans to leave the neighborhood and the city, discreetly buying tracts of land in the suburbs in the early 1950s.[28]

Even as Jewish Community Council leaders realized that neighborhood synagogues were ambivalent allies in the effort to preserve the Jewish neighborhood, they also understood the instrumental value of having religion on their side during the Cold War years. By the late 1940s groups advocating integration and fair housing were under increased governmental scrutiny for sowing seeds of national discord and aligning with communist interests. In 1947 the director of internal relations for Detroit's Jewish Community Council cautioned leaders that a "strong left wing element . . . is ready to step in and take control unless we are careful." In earlier years the Jewish Community Council had collaborated with leftist organizations on many civil rights initiatives. Yet when the House Committee on Un-American Activities began investigating communist activity in Detroit in the early 1950s, the Jewish Community Council strongly admonished its members to sever ties with Jewish-dominated leftist civil rights and labor groups. Liberal Jewish organizations across the country took similar steps.[29] The impact on interracial politics was profound; for the previous two decades, whites, among them a disproportionate number of Jews, and blacks had found common ground in leftist (communist and noncommunist) politics, yet the anticommunism crusade eroded this terrain. Likewise, Cold War anticommunism created an ever-widening chasm between liberals and leftists.

---

women's participation in neighborhood politics, see Lila Corwin Berman, "Gendered Journeys: Jewish Migrations and the City in Postwar America," in *Gender and Jewish History*, ed. Marion A. Kaplan and Deborah Dash Moore (Bloomington, 2011), 336–49; Lisa McGirr, *Suburban Warriors: The Origins of the New American Right* (Princeton, 2001), 87; Murray, *Progressive Housewife;* and Becky Nicolaides, *My Blue Heaven: Life and Politics in the Working-Class Suburbs of Los Angeles, 1920–1965* (Chicago, 2002), 41.

[28] Aaron Droock to rabbis, Sept. 11, 1947, folder 6, box 15 (Jewish Community Council Archives). For examples of denying rumors, see announcement from Congregation Beth Yehudah (in Yiddish), Dec. 1947, *ibid.;* and Fraiberg to Shmarya Kleinman, A. C. Lappin, Morris Lieberman, and Louis Rosenzweig, Jan. 6, 1948, *ibid.* Congregation Shaarey Zedek (Conservative) and Temple Beth El (Reform) bought land in the suburbs in the early 1950s. See Irving Katz to Rabbi Richard Hertz, June 4, 1953 (Franklin Archives); and Shaarey Zedek board meeting minutes, April 19, 1948 (Congregation Shaarey Zedek).

[29] Samuel Zipp, *Manhattan Projects: The Rise and Fall of Urban Renewal in Cold War New York* (New York, 2010), 125–29. On concerns about leftists and the Jewish Community Council, see Fraiberg to Oscar Cohen, Oct. 24, 1947, folder 6, box 15 (Jewish Community Council Archives); and *Guide to Changing Neighborhoods,* 36. On purges in Detroit, see Babson, Riddle, and Elsila, *Color of Law,* 201–9. More generally, see Stuart Svonkin, *Jews against Prejudice: American Jews and the Fight for Civil Liberties* (New York, 1997), 113–34.

Over time, Jewish leaders came to appreciate the many advantages of attaching them-selves to liberal political movements beyond their neighborhoods. In the 1940s Jews had regarded the racial change occurring in Jewish neighborhoods as a Jewish issue and attempted to address it through local and Jewish means. Yet by the early 1950s Jewish leaders saw less and less to recommend this approach. Most Jews had moved away from "changing" neighborhoods, and those Jews who had vocally welcomed black families and sought to create a viable politics of integration had become targets of anticommunist suspicion. Increasingly, Jewish leaders perceived the individual, the neighborhood, and the local as far less powerful political tools for affecting change in American life than the new urban politics of liberal coalition building, and legislative and policy reform.

The Problem with Neighborhood Politics

By the early 1950s Detroit Jewish activists were frustrated with the meager results their local politics appeared to be yielding in the Twelfth Street–Linwood–Dexter neighbor-hood. During a 1950 meeting Jewish Community Council leaders expressed their exas-peration: "There are probably few areas in the city where there is a higher proportion of people endowed with a liberalism . . . with respect to racial, religious, and cultural differ-ences. . . . If there is any place in town where a stable, cosmopolitan community can be maintained this should be it." But it was not. For Sale signs and the constant parade of moving vans marred activists' vision of an effective local campaign to save the Jewish neighborhood and create a stable integrated community. Over the course of the 1950s, the neighborhood shifted from housing 49 percent of Detroit's Jewish population to no more than 9 percent of it.[30] The Midtown Neighborhood Council did not give up, but its faith in local activism was waning.

A comparison of two neighborhood manifestos, one from 1947 and the other written in the early 1950s, reveals the gradual shift in Jewish political activism away from local and individual methods and toward remote political activism that neither blamed indi-viduals for neighborhood transformations nor believed that their actions could ameliorate those changes. In 1947 the Jewish Community Council, in concert with the emerging Midtown Neighborhood Council, had papered the neighborhood with a leaflet printed in English and Yiddish entitled "Let's Think Clearly." A call to action for the neighbor-hood, it maintained that rumors alone were fueling a real estate panic and averred, "Jews should and can live in harmonious relationship with our neighbors and at the same time continue to utilize the cultural and spiritual advantages of Jewish group life in this area." The leaflet ended with an announcement of a community meeting and a stirring affirma-tion of the power of local action: "Friendly relationships with and understanding of one's neighbors and the combating of prejudice are attributes of the truly American way of life. These are also the precepts which make for Jewish living. Actions based on these principles will result in a better and more wholesome neighborhood."[31]

A few years later, the Jewish Community Council released a new statement called "Neighbor, Where Are You Running?" Distributed throughout the neighborhood and

[30] Jewish Community Council minutes, Sept. 14, 1950, folder 1, box 68 (Jewish Community Council Archives). Bolkosky, *Harmony and Dissonance,* 298.
[31] "Let's Think Clearly," leaflet attached to *Statement about the Twelfth Street Area by the Jewish Community Council of Detroit,* Dec. 1947, folder 6, box 15 (Jewish Community Council Archives).

also reprinted in the local press, the leaflet struck an ominous tone. No longer were residents beseeched to "think clearly"; they were now told to stop "running." And no longer were Jewish individuals assured that they could combat prejudice by cultivating friendly relationships with their nonwhite neighbors. Instead, they were informed that whether or not they realized it, "unscrupulous real estate dealers" were manipulating them "into leaving a good home [and] neighborhood near the downtown area for another of very doubtful value and probably overpriced." Less reliant on goodwill than the earlier document, the 1950s statement invoked constitutional law—recent Supreme Court rulings on fair housing and citizenship—as a means of intimidation, warning residents not to do anything "foolish" that would put them on the wrong side of the law. Printed on the back of the leaflet was a Not for Sale sign that Jews were encouraged to display in their front yard.[32]

By the early 1950s, Jewish leaders in urban neighborhoods throughout the United States were waging a battle against real estate agents, many of whom, not coincidentally, were Jews. These leaders feared that the good intentions of individuals were no match for the profiteering of real estate agents who sowed the seeds of panic to reap the rewards from home sales. Portraying residents as helpless in the face of real estate mendacity, a Detroit correspondent to the *Jewish Daily Forward* reported, "Residents of the area have informed Council representatives that they have been visited daily, solicited by daily phone calls and have received abundant literature from [real estate agents]." According to the reporter, real estate agents profited from getting homeowners to believe that their neighborhood was "changing in its racial character" and that their home values would plummet if they did not sell quickly. In tandem with the local chapter of the National Association for the Advancement of Colored People (NAACP), the Jewish Community Council collected data on advertisements for homes in the Twelfth Street–Linwood–Dexter area in the late 1940s and discovered that Jewish and African American agents persistently characterized the properties they were selling as suited for "colored" people. Furthermore, a survey in the mid-1950s found that 60 percent of residents living in a particular enclave of the neighborhood that remained heavily Jewish received solicitations from real estate agents "once a week or just about every day." These "blockbusting" tactics were common, and real estate agents across the country used them to purchase homes below market value from panicked whites and then sell them at an inflated price, often through exploitative financing, to house-hungry black buyers.[33]

[32] "Neighbor, Where Are You Running?," reprinted in *Michigan Chronicle*, July 15, 1950, clipping, folder 1, box 68, *ibid.* "Neighbor, Where Are You Running?," leaflet, 1950, folder 4, box 68, *ibid.* Though they did not mention particular Supreme Court cases, the authors of the statement were likely referring to *Shelley v. Kraemer*, which struck down the legal enforcement of racially motivated restrictive covenants in housing, and possibly *Knauer v. United States*, a case that examined naturalization policy and argued that the United States did not grant "second-class citizenship." *Shelley v. Kraemer*, 334 U.S. 1 (1948); *Knauer v. United States*, 328 U.S. 654, 658 (1946).

[33] David Naimark, "This Week in Detroit," *Jewish Daily Forward*, June 12, 1950. For a translation of this article, see folder 4, box 68 (Jewish Community Council Archives). Joseph Fauman to Ed Swan (of the National Association for the Advancement of Colored People), [1950], folder 1, box 68, *ibid.* Eleanor K. Caplan and Eleanor P. Wolf, "Factors Affecting Racial·Change in Two Middle Income Housing Areas," *Phylon*, 21 (no. 3, 1960), 230. Jeffrey M. Hornstein, *A Nation of Realtors: A Cultural History of the Twentieth-Century American Middle Class* (Durham, N.C., 2005), 84–117. On similar patterns in Philadelphia, Baltimore, and Chicago, see Sheryll Cashin, *The Failures of Integration: How Race and Class Are Undermining the American Dream* (New York, 2004), 45–52; Pietila, *Not in My Neighborhood*, 89–210; Ellsworth Rosen, "When a Negro Moves Next Door," *Saturday Evening Post*, April 4, 1959, pp. 32–33, 139–42, reprint, folder 1, box 552 (Jewish Community Council Archives); and Satter, *Family Properties*, 171.

In the mid-1940s George Schermer, a non-Jew, had been appointed by Republican mayor Edward Jeffries as the director of the Mayor's Interracial Committee. He worked alongside African American leaders to highlight the sources of black-white tension and, particularly, housing discrimination. In a report documenting the role of white ethnic groups in housing discrimination, Schermer contended that although Jews were rarely hostile to black settlement, they nonetheless bore a special burden and responsibility to quell racial tension over housing issues. He found that anti-Semitism pervaded both white and black responses to housing problems, so Jews were consistently perceived as central actors. He also understood that Jews' real estate dealings often caused racial tension, convincing whites that Jews brought blacks into the neighborhood and convincing blacks that Jews took advantage of blacks' powerlessness in the housing market. In private conversations with Jewish leaders in 1950, Schermer encouraged them to confront Jews involved in the real estate industry.[34]

In 1950 the Jewish Community Council invited a handful of Jewish real estate agents to discuss the Twelfth Street–Linwood–Dexter neighborhood. A council leader chastised the agents for endangering "communal property and institutional investments" through their "immoral" efforts to "creat[e] artificial panic for financial gains." Yet those words rang hollow when another council leader backpedaled to reassure the group that the council "eagerly" supported integration and that the meeting should not "be interpreted as an anti-Negro one."[35] Yet how could it not be?

Jewish leaders lacked the language to explain what distinguished selling a property to a black family from destroying a Jewish neighborhood. Thus most leaders focused only on the problem of panic selling. They did not interrogate the racist structures that enabled individuals to profit from driving whites out of neighborhoods and selling homes at inflated prices and with exploitative financing schemes to blacks. A Detroit Jewish real estate agent fumed in a letter to the Jewish Community Council that its leaders were hypocrites for endorsing "biracial housing" while vilifying agents who sold to nonwhites as "blockbusting."[36] Indeed, the same Not for Sale sign that Jewish Community Council leaders had hoped would communicate a local commitment to an ongoing Jewish urban presence could also be read as a populist attack against integration—a de facto restrictive covenant.

As Schermer witnessed the growing power of the Republican Albert Cobo's conservative and racist mayoral administration that took office in 1950, he became disillusioned with liberals' local efforts to preserve stable neighborhoods. In the early 1950s the NAACP filed a lawsuit charging the mayor and the housing commission with discrimination. At the same time, Schermer spoke out against the entrenched racism in the housing system that was impervious to individual- and neighborhood-based reform. Schermer urged Jews in particular to be leaders in establishing a "free open unrestricted housing market" across the city. After writing a scathing report that exposed the depths of racism in Detroit's private and public housing system and gained attention from housing activists nationwide, Schermer resigned under pressure in 1952. The following year, Mayor Cobo

[34] "Process Record of a Meeting Called to Explore the Current Social Situation in the Mid-town Area and to Determine the Most Effective Use of the Community Council Staff Assigned," April 18, 1950, folder 9, box 67 (Jewish Community Council Archives); Stevenson, "Points of Departure, Acts of Resolve," 164–67.

[35] Julius Weinberg, memo, June 6, 1950, folder 68, box 1 (Jewish Community Council Archives).

[36] Bernard Edelman to Jewish Community Council, [1950–1951], folder 8, box 68, *ibid.*

dissolved the Interracial Committee.[37] Yet cynicism about local neighborhood politics and demands for large-scale Jewish-led urban reform came to characterize a new mode of Jewish urban politics remote from the Jewish neighborhood.

Urban Politics beyond the Neighborhood

By the mid-1950s the northwest area, named for its location in relation to downtown, had become the new center of Jewish settlement in Detroit. People strolling the streets of northwest Detroit could easily think they were in the suburbs—after all, the neighborhood was just about as close as one could get to the suburbs without leaving the city limits. The homes were large and the lawns ample; families owned cars; men generally commuted downtown to white-collar jobs; and the local high school prepared young people for college. The Jewish Community Center, along with several synagogues, established satellite facilities in the northwest area, and rumors circulated that many of these institutions were planning to sell their Twelfth Street–Linwood–Dexter buildings. Until the early 1960s the northwest area remained a white bastion and housed approximately 60 percent of Detroit's Jews.[38]

Northwest Detroit served as a transitional political space. Here Jews turned the focus of their politics away from the local neighborhood efforts that had marked their lives in the more southern regions of the city and toward a remote and policy-oriented strategy. The problems of race and neighborhood stability, they came to believe, would be solved neither by communal browbeating and organizing nor by staying in increasingly African American neighborhoods suffering from infrastructural neglect, overcrowding, and other signs of deterioration. Rather, the community could address these problems by lobbying for legislative and policy changes to equalize the treatment blacks and whites received, especially regarding issues òf housing. This form of political activism was more public and far reaching than local neighborhood activism, but it also demanded less perceived sacrifice from individual Jewish families or the Jewish community as a whole.

Jews' fervent embrace of the principle of open occupancy resembled that of other white liberals' investment in the issue yet was driven by specifically Jewish motivations. In the 1950s and 1960s Jews in Detroit and other northern industrial cities came to see their neighborhoods as special targets of black settlement. A 1956 manual addressed to Jewish urban leaders dealing with "Problems in the Neighborhood Undergoing Change" asserted plainly, "Jews are more often involved in changing neighborhood problems [than other groups]." Published through the New York City–based National Community Relations Advisory Council (NCRAC), the manual included contributions from Jewish urban activists throughout the nation. Relying on population studies, the authors explained that fifteen of the eighty-seven substantial U.S. Jewish communities (defined

---

[37] On George Schermer and calls for an unrestricted housing market, see George Schermer, "New Neighbors and Property Values," Feb. 11, 1952, speech to the Study Conference for Women of the Metropolitan Detroit Area, folder 3, box 284, *ibid.*; "Report of the Changing Neighborhoods Subcommittee," Oct. 26, 1955, folder 5, box 534, *ibid.*; Stevenson, "Points of Departure, Acts of Resolve," 380–84; Sugrue, *Origins of the Urban Crisis,* 225; and "George Schermer, Rights Expert, Dies at 78," *New York Times,* June 6, 1989, p. D22.

[38] Phillip Applebaum, *A Tour of Jewish Detroit* (Detroit, 1975), 9; Bolkosky, *Harmony and Dissonance,* 298; Changing Neighborhoods Committee, informal meeting of special personnel minutes, Aug. 5, 1959, folder 3, box 6 (Jewish Community Council Archives); Abraham Citron to Kleinman and the Changing Neighborhood Committee, Aug. 11, 1959, *ibid.*

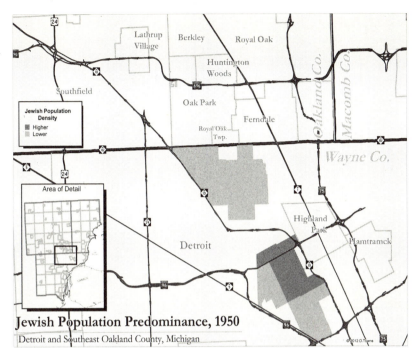

Jewish Population Predominance, 1950

Detroit and Southeast Oakland County, Michigan

The maps on these facing pages show northwest Detroit and the suburban communities in Oakland County situated north of the Detroit/Wayne County border. Despite efforts by Jewish leaders to slow migration away from the central city, from 1950 to 1960 large segments of the Jewish population of Detroit moved to the northwest corner of the city and also began to establish a presence in the inner suburbs to the north. *Data from United States Bureau of the Census,* U.S. Census of Population, 1950 *(Washington, 1952); United States Bureau of the Census,* U.S. Censuses of Population and Housing, 1960 *(Washington, 1962); and Albert J. Mayer,* Jewish Population Study: 1963; Number of Persons, Age, and Residential Distribution *(Detroit, 1964). Maps by Patricia Becker and Douglas Towns.*

as communities with populations over four thousand) had experienced a doubling of their nonwhite population from 1940 to 1950, and another thirteen had seen their non-white population increase by one-third. These rates, the authors implied, far outpaced the rates in non-Jewish communities.[39]

Urban Jewish leaders offered many reasons why African Americans settled in Jewish neighborhoods, including perceived Jewish liberalism and the fact that Jews tended to live in areas marked by high rates of mobility and turnover. Urban leaders also suggested that African Americans were not simply attracted to Jewish neighborhoods; rather, they were directed to those neighborhoods by city and state policies that pushed black home buyers and renters out of the open housing market.[40]

Jewish urban leaders in the 1950s started to advocate political activism that was not confined to their local neighborhood. Responding to their growing belief that their neighborhoods were subject to forces beyond their control and owing to their reluctance to confront the implications of Jews' involvement in racist real estate practices, many leaders

[39] *Guide to Changing Neighborhoods*, 46, 48.
[40] On black buyers and renters being directed to Jewish neighborhoods, see Levine and Harmon, *Death of an American Jewish Community*, 66–91.

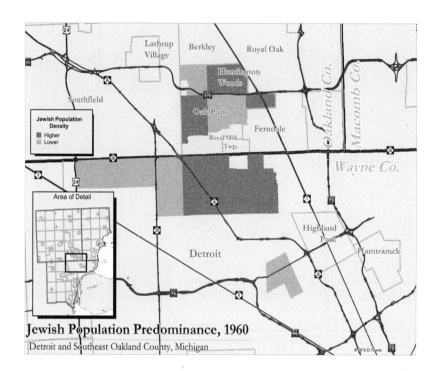

Jewish Population Predominance, 1960
Detroit and Southeast Oakland County, Michigan

turned toward citywide remedies to reform housing policy. A leader of Detroit's Jewish Community Council demanded that revisions be made to an early draft of the 1956 manual published by the NCRAC to highlight "the stake of the Jewish community in . . . helping to achieve equality of opportunity in acquiring housing *throughout* a city." The final version of the manual did indeed frame the issue of Jewish neighborhood stability in a broad discussion of housing discrimination. It stated, "An increasing number of cities today face serious problems caused by changes in the racial character of particular neighborhoods. These problems would be substantially lessened if the housing market were not restricted by discriminatory practices. Such practices prevent the natural and gradual movement of families . . . in all parts of the city in accordance with their means and desires."[41]

Jews were leading voices in the effort to remake housing policy. Many other liberal whites echoed Jews' commitment to open-occupancy legislation, but Jews positioned themselves as intimately and emotionally invested in the policy, explaining that their neighborhoods in particular bore the scars of racist housing policy, even if most Jews had long left these neighborhoods. At meetings in the early 1960s Jewish Community Council leaders committed to policy activism, premised upon coalition politics and broad-scale campaigns for fair-housing practices. Dr. Shmarya Kleinman, the chair of the Jewish Community Council's Changing Neighborhood Committee, explained, "It has now been universally recognized that work in neighborhoods, in blocks, even in areas of the city, will not alone be effective in normalizing housing patterns and in stabilizing neighborhoods on an integrated basis. . . . Times have changed." In the fall of 1961,

[41] "Detroit Comments on Draft of the Guide for Dealing with Changing Neighborhoods," [1955–1956], folder 4, box 82 (Jewish Community Council Archives). *Guide to Changing Neighborhoods*, 9.

reviewing the accomplishments of the Jewish Community Council's recently renamed Neighborhoods and Housing Committee (formerly Changing Neighborhood Committee) over the past two years, Kleinman declared that a "major shift in orientation and practical aims" had occurred, palpable even in the new name of the committee, which had been the subject of passionate discussion over the past year. "We are no longer in the patch-up or remedial business to stop panic, but are working to destroy all the props of discrimination in housing," Kleinman explained, adding, "We consider that this is not only a Jewish issue, nor just a neighborhood issue, but a city, state and national issue."[42]

Instead of implementing neighborhood clean-up drives, Jewish leaders devoted themselves to meeting with "tri-faith" and "city-wide" religious leaders, establishing the Greater Detroit Committee for Fair Housing Practices, and issuing public statements trumpeting nationwide open-occupancy and fair-housing policies. They asserted that new policies, with broad-based support, would destroy the "props of discrimination" that they believed had doomed their local neighborhood activism.[43]

Throughout the early 1960s urban Jewish community groups across the country pledged themselves to the cause of fair housing, maintaining that if the law prohibited homeowners and landlords from using race as a factor in sale or rental decisions then black settlement would occur equally across urban landscapes, eventually dismantling urban discrimination. That Jewish activists committed themselves to policy and legislative remedies for urban housing and discrimination just as they were leaving their urban neighborhoods is no irony—it reveals the contours of a new Jewish geography of remote urban politics.

Remote Urban Activism

In 1961 Jews living in northwest Detroit formed a new neighborhood association, the Bagley Community Council. It operated from one of the last significant Jewish settlements in the city, yet served as a site for political mobilization on issues such as housing policy and racial discrimination that moved Jews well beyond neighborhood politics. On its face, the organization emerged from a local political sensibility. Much like the founders of the Midtown Neighborhood Council, the active members of the Bagley Community Council were predominantly Jewish homeowners concerned with preserving the character of their neighborhood. The Bagley neighborhood, a roughly one-square-mile area, was residential, with stately single-family, two-story homes. Of the four thousand families who lived there in 1962, 66 percent were Jewish and less than .05 percent were African American. Similar to the Midtown Neighborhood Council, the Bagley Community Council organized neighborhood meetings, encouraged residents to tidy up their homes and lawns, and attempted to stop real estate agents from stirring up panic among homeowners. And just as it had for the Midtown Neighborhood Council, the Jewish Community Council played a critical role in supporting the Bagley Community Council, providing staff and helping sculpt its agenda.[44]

[42] Changing Neighborhood Committee minutes, March 9, 1960, folder 4, box 4 (Jewish Community Council Archives). Neighborhoods and Housing Committee minutes, Nov. 28, 1961, *ibid.*

[43] Neighborhoods and Housing Committee minutes, Nov. 28, 1961, *ibid.*, 1; Jewish Community Council, "Statement on Open Occupancy," Feb. 1961, *ibid.*

[44] On the Bagley neighborhood, see Eleanor Paperro Wolf and Charles N. Lebeaux, *Change and Renewal in an Urban Community* (New York, 1969); and Damon Stetson, "Community Finds Integration Key: Detroit Neighborhood Group Is Hailed for Approach," *New York Times,* April 22, 1962, p. 64.

Yet the two neighborhood associations, separated by more than a decade and about five miles, pursued very different political strategies. Whereas the Midtown Neighborhood Council had focused on convincing individual homeowners to remain in the neighborhood, the Bagley Community Council tied itself and the stability of urban Jewish neighborhoods to efforts to reform city, state, and federal housing policies. Bagley's leaders were enmeshed in city and state politics and knew well the vocabulary of open and nondiscriminatory housing practices. Starting in the early 1960s the national offices of the American Jewish Committee and the Anti-defamation League kept local leaders abreast of developments in housing law with periodic memos on new rulings across the country, and the National Community Relations Advisory Council asked all of its local Jewish community council affiliates for copies of their statements about housing discrimination and fair housing.[45]

With a deft political touch, the president of the Bagley Community Council, a Jewish man who was also the executive assistant to the Michigan State Highway Commission, explained, "We are not for integration and we are not against integration. We are for an open housing market all through the city." He assured Jewish residents that the "climate of opinion is changing in favor of fair housing practices," and, thus, by getting involved with open-occupancy politics, Jews were able to fight for a policy that did not hinge upon their individual willingness to live in integrated neighborhoods.[46] The Bagley Community Council hoped to prove that it was in everyone's interest—liberal and nonliberal, Jewish and non-Jewish—to support fair-housing measures.

Echoing similar proposals in dozens of other U.S. cities to reform housing policy and create open-occupancy laws, Detroit's city council crafted a Fair Neighborhood Practices Ordinance in 1962, and the Bagley Community Council immediately voted to uphold the measure. The ordinance was initially intended to punish real estate agents and sellers who employed racially discriminatory practices in their transactions, but the final version offered a very limited definition of discrimination. In response, two members of Detroit's city council proposed a broader and more enforceable open-occupancy law. The measure promised to mandate nondiscriminatory selling practices throughout the city, a promise that Bagley Community Council and Jewish Community Council leaders believed would ease the pressure of black settlement in Jewish neighborhoods and, more importantly, create a more viable and sustainable future for middle-class urban life.[47]

The transformation in Jewish politics away from local neighborhood activism and toward the broad, more spatially detached goal of fair-housing policy was made possible by Jews' growing economic and political power in the postwar years. The characteristics that historians suggest turned Jews into whites also served as the foundation for a new Jewish urban politics. Data culled from the University of Michigan Detroit Area Study of the early 1950s found that almost three-quarters of Detroit's Jewish household heads

[45] Paul Hartman (Anti-defamation League), memo, March 13, 1961, folder 2, box 533 (Jewish Community Council Archives); Theodore Leskes (American Jewish Committee), memo, March 30, 1961, *ibid.*; Samuel Spiegler (Director of Information, National Community Relations Advisory Council), memo, Dec. 28, 1959, folder 1, box 533, *ibid.*; Jewish Community Council press release, Oct. 3, 1960, folder 6, box 569, *ibid.*
[46] Neighborhood and Housing Committee minutes, Nov. 28, 1961, folder 4, box 4 (Jewish Community Council Archives).
[47] On the Fair Neighborhood Practices Ordinance, see Jack Walker, "Fair Housing in Michigan," in *The Politics of Fair-Housing Legislation: State and Local Case Studies,* ed. Lynn W. Eley and Thomas W. Casstevens (San Francisco, 1968), 353–82; and Wolf and Lebeaux, *Change and Renewal in an Urban Community,* 70.

Photographed in 1964, this family stands on a street in the heart of Jewish northwest Detroit, very close to the Bagley neighborhood. *Courtesy Leonard N. Simons Jewish Community Archives, Jewish Federation of Metropolitan Detroit.*

(all men) held white-collar jobs. Furthermore, Jews in the city had attained levels of education commensurate with the white Protestant population. Finally, a greater number of Jews than ever before held political posts, due, in part, to gubernatorial and judicial appointments made in the late 1950s. With access to more power, Jews entered into civic discussions about urban reform; at the same time, their access to power also distanced them from the centers of urban poverty and neglect.[48]

It was no coincidence that one of the sponsors of the new measure for fair-housing practices was a Jewish man, Mel Ravitz (the other was William Patrick, a black city councilor). Ravitz, a committed member of the Jewish Community Council's Neighborhoods and Housing Committee and a Wayne State University sociologist, had won a seat on the Detroit city council in 1961. In his role in the Jewish community and his elected position on the city council, he became an activist for legislation barring discrimination in housing. Attempting to persuade fellow Neighborhoods and Housing Committee members to turn their attention beyond the Jewish neighborhood, he argued, "All neighborhoods must be opened [through fair-housing measures] if pressure is to be relieved on any one neighborhood." Echoing Schermer, he charged, "It is up to the Jewish community to furnish leadership on this pressing problem of American communities."[49]

[48] Goldberg and Sharp, "Some Characteristics of Detroit Area Jewish and Non-Jewish Adults," 113–15; Sidney Fine, *Expanding the Frontiers of Civil Rights: Michigan, 1948–1968* (Detroit, 2000), 98.
[49] Thompson, *Whose Detroit?*, 25. On Mel Ravitz, see the finding guide of the Mel Ravitz Collection Papers, 1939–2001 (Reuther Library), http://www.reuther.wayne.edu/files/UP001720.pdf. Neighborhoods and Housing Committee minutes, Nov. 28, 1961, folder 4, box 4 (Jewish Community Council Archives).

The new open-occupancy proposal, the Patrick-Ravitz ordinance, was met with a counterproposal for a Homeowner's Rights Ordinance. Though the Homeowner's Rights Ordinance was clearly grounded in racism, attempting to justify discrimination through the language of individual rights and private property, it resembled the Patrick-Ravitz ordinance in its focus on the individual behaviors of buyers, sellers, and their agents and its tacit tolerance for a racist and unequal economic structure. Yet in the early 1960s few whites in Detroit, whether Jewish or not, voiced the radical critique that open occupancy perpetuated the structural economic inequalities ingrained in American capitalism.[50]

In the fall of 1964 the Homeowner's Rights Ordinance came to voters as a city referendum. The Jewish Community Council provided staff, equipment, and publicity to the campaign waged against the ordinance by the relatively liberal city leadership. Nonetheless, the measure passed by 23,000 votes, reflecting the rising strength of white conservatism in the city. A court judgment overturned it two years later. When the ordinance passed, the Jewish Community Council emphasized in a press release that "areas containing substantial numbers of Jewish residents voted heavily against the ordinance." The press release did not mention that substantial numbers of Jews no longer lived in the city or voted in city referenda. Council leaders may have thought this irrelevant owing to the fact that Jews, whether they lived in the city or not, still remained vital participants in discussions about urban housing policy. But the nature of their participation had clearly shifted from one characterized by geographic enmeshment to one of remote, if still passionate, commitment.[51]

In 1963, as the citywide debate about fair-housing legislation was reaching a fevered pitch, the Jewish Community Council, alongside white and black Protestant pastors and representatives of the Archdiocese of Detroit (Catholic), organized the Metropolitan Conference on Open Occupancy. The conference embodied the interfaith coalition politics that liberal groups throughout the city were embracing in their move toward legislative and policy understandings of urban politics. Even the choice of the word Metropolitan in the title, rather than City or Detroit, indicated a new scale of urban commitment beyond the city limits. According to the conference program, the gathering came at the impetus of leaders from various religious groups who had thought, "This is not our problem alone, what are the others doing?" The organizers of the conference explained, "Privately and independently, we were often shocked to realize that we felt more in common with those of other faiths who were dedicated and working on [fair-housing issues], than we did with members of our own faith who were apathetic or negative." Building on a postwar trend in which religious leaders saw religion more as the material of coalition-building politics than as a specific set of theological premises, Detroit religious leaders joined politicians and social researchers in a plea for open occupancy.[52]

[50] Citizens for a United Detroit, pamphlet, [1964?], folder 4, box 83 (Jewish Community Council Archives). On Jews and open occupancy, see also Meyer, As Long as They Don't Move Next Door, 177–78; Sugrue, Origins of the Urban Crisis, 227; and Sugrue, Sweet Land of Liberty, 243.

[51] Harold Dubin to Walter Klein, [1964–1965?], folder 4, box 83 (Jewish Community Council Archives); Robert Kirk, "Court Kills Homeowners Law," Detroit News, Dec. 30, 1966, clipping, folder 6, box 83, ibid. Jewish Community Council press release, Sept. 17, 1964, ibid.; Dubin to Klein, [1964–1965?], folder 4, box 83, ibid.

[52] "Program for the Metropolitan Conference on Open Occupancy," Jan. 2–3, 1963, p. 1, folder 3, box 83, ibid. Mark Silk, Spiritual Politics: Religion and America since World War II (New York, 1988), 108–35.

Liberal Jewish leaders such as Ravitz and Rabbi Richard Hertz of the Woodward Avenue Temple Beth El, who both spoke at the conference, believed the more that unfair housing policies were understood as everyone's problems, the better for Jews. The truth, however, was that fewer and fewer Jews lived in city neighborhoods, so while their politics remained focused on Detroit, their stake in the city had changed from a concrete interest in making the city livable for their community to a more abstract ideal of racial justice and urban stability.

When Rabbi Hertz addressed the audience at the Metropolitan Conference on Open Occupancy, he studiously avoided drawing any connection between Jews' commitment to racial justice and their willingness to remain in integrated urban areas. The rabbi explained, "My people have had a long history in the battle for open occupancy. We have lived in some of the foulest ghettos of the world. We know what it means to be harried and haunted and harassed, the last to benefit and the first to be denied. . . . The freedom to live where one wants is a precious privilege of first class citizenship devoutly cherished by Jews of this country."[53] Now that Jews finally had gained the right to live where they wished, they would work hard to ensure others possessed it, but they would not curtail their own freedom of movement in the name of fulfilling a vision of integration. This logic made sense to a man who simultaneously supported open occupancy and encouraged his congregation to leave the city for an all-white suburb. Countless Jewish institutions across the country made the same journey, many under the leadership of people who openly defended open occupancy and fair housing.

For Jewish leaders in Detroit, the fight for open occupancy had two effects. First, it confirmed their belief that only a large-scale policy-oriented campaign could save Jewish life in the city. A researcher studying the Bagley Community Council, who was an active member herself, reported that council members' support for the open-occupancy campaign came on the heels of their growing sense of the "futility of confining activity to the Bagley area . . . [and solving] problems on a neighborhood basis."[54] Second, and rather contradictorily, the fight for open occupancy stoked a sense of cynicism about the city and its politics. After all, the reactionary Homeowner's Rights Ordinance had passed. A sense of fatalism—the feeling that Detroit was a lost cause—only grew as Bagley Community Council members strayed further from local neighborhood politics and attempted to reform larger urban policies.

Jews found it far more difficult to feel sanguine about reforming a whole city, let alone an entire system, than to feel hopeful about making a difference on a particular block. By 1964 Bagley residents reported growing skepticism with the community organization's ability to save the neighborhood. Although empirically the neighborhood had changed only slightly in its racial composition over the past four years, residents interpreted the slow but steady increase of black families in the neighborhood (now 10 percent, up from 1–2 percent in 1962) as foreshadowing unwanted changes to come. Many homeowners continued to describe the neighborhood as a good place to live, but fewer answered affirmatively when surveyors asked if they would recommend it to friends, and many expressed

---

[53] "Challenge to Conscience: Conclusions, Recommendations, Major Messages," [1963], p. 12, folder 3, box 83 (Jewish Community Council Archives).
[54] Wolf and Lebeaux, *Change and Renewal in an Urban Community,* 85.

concerns about safety and crime that they linked directly to the arrival of more black families.[55]

Jewish residents' sense of impending doom was less about actual conditions in the neighborhood—home values appeared to be holding steady, and residents still believed that the local schools offered high-quality education. Instead, their sense of foreboding drew upon history. They were certain that without significant changes to housing policy or legislation, the same patterns of neighborhood and school decline and home deprecia- tion that they had already witnessed would continue because of the arrival of black fami- lies. By 1965 almost half of all the Jews in Detroit lived outside the city in the northwest suburbs.[56] Yet from their outposts in the suburbs, many Jews continued to base their politics and identities on the city, lobbying for urban policies that they hoped could change the city's longstanding racial patterns.

Urban Politics, Suburban Space

Well before the urban uprisings of 1967, Detroit Jews had created a remote urban poli- tics that could weather their move away from the city. At a meeting in January 1966, the Jewish Community Council's newly formed Education and Housing Committee pledged to "work toward the establishment of quality education throughout the Metro- politan area whether or not there is a portion of the Jewish community in residence" and to "continue to utilize the resources of the Jewish community as a force to support these programs which stress quality education, open occupancy and education for living in integrated communities."[57] This statement was a far cry from issuing a demand that Jews inhabit integrated neighborhoods. Jewish leaders were instead speaking from a new polit- ical terrain fundamentally removed from neighborhood space: the suburbs.

Local neighborhood politics had given Jews a sense that there was larger meaning in whatever individual sacrifices they endured to stay in the neighborhood, and that sense of meaning was not easily replicable. Indeed, the politics of remote urban activism often took the form of a kind of abnegation of responsibility, a claim that the real problems existed outside of the Jewish purview and that the Jews could only lobby others for change. This logic imprinted itself on white liberalism more generally. Writing in the *Atlantic Monthly* in 1963, Murray Friedman, a onetime socialist turned neoconservative, explained, "Liberal whites are . . . caught in the dilemma of believing in equal rights for Negroes . . . while at the same time attempting to escape from the real and fancied disad- vantages of desegregation."[58] For Jews, Friedman explained, the dilemma was even more intense because they found it very difficult to disengage from urban concerns, even after they had dismantled the lived space of Jewish urbanism. Yet one cannot dismiss Jews' enduring investment in urbanism as the vestiges of white liberal guilt or a form of nostal- gia. Rather, Jews' enduring connection to urbanism had real political consequences for Jews and their relationship to American civil society. Far from imagining themselves as

[55] *Ibid.*, 20–32.

[56] Bolkosky, *Harmony and Dissonance,* 300.

[57] Joint meeting of Neighborhoods and Education Committee minutes, Jan. 11, 1966, folder 8, box 590 (Jewish Community Council Archives).

[58] Murray Friedman, "The White Liberal's Retreat," *Atlantic Monthly,* 21 (Jan. 1963), 43. On Jews and liber- alism, see also Murray Friedman, *The Neoconservative Revolution: Jewish Intellectuals and the Shaping of Public Policy* (New York, 2005).

blending seamlessly into white suburban life, American Jews worked to distinguish their politics and their identities from the suburban spaces they occupied.

The shift toward remote urban activism allowed Jews to leave the city and still believe that they were taking their city politics with them. In the aftermath of the 1967 riots, the *Detroit Jewish News* scrambled to document just how active Jews remained in urban affairs, and the Jewish Community Council formed an Urban Affairs Subcommittee charged with maintaining and publicizing the "real involvement of the Jewish Community" in city affairs through programs such as clothing drives, tutoring, and employment-training services.[59] A concern for "neighborhood change," once the catch phrase of Jewish efforts, gave way to a new commitment to solve the "urban crisis," a phrase that appeared on the Jewish agenda only after 1967 and then with striking frequency. When the locus of Jewish concern had been the neighborhood, the stakes had been much more immediate; after all, the neighborhoods to which Jews directed their attention were the neighborhoods where Jews lived. In the climate of the perceived "urban crisis," Jews' investment was not in saving a particular space of the city—rather, their goal, more abstract yet also more ambitious than before, was to save the city. Since the early 1950s Jews had honed a form of political activism to take on this task, and the 1967 riots put their politics to a new test.

Jewish leaders studiously sought partners with liberal black leaders in the city and worked to enmesh these leaders into urban and suburban initiatives. Almost all of their formal coalitions with black leaders, whether in the city or the suburbs, were formed under the auspices of interfaith alliances with black liberal Protestant clergy. For example, Jewish leaders supported the creation of interfaith Suburban Action Centers that would engage with black leadership to educate suburbanites about city conditions and serve as nodes of support for city reform efforts. In the months after the riots, Jewish and black liberal clergy joined in interfaith efforts to disseminate "an interpretation of the riot" that neither validated the "Radical Right" nor fanned the fires of black power politics. Along these lines, liberal Jewish leaders endorsed initiatives that black clergy proposed to add more blacks to the police force and limit the number of gun permits issued in white areas.[60]

Although leftist Jews such as the famed labor lawyer Ernest Goodman were committed to defending black radical politics, most hoped to find a way to harness separatist, nationalist, and other forms of black radical politics to a liberal vision for the city and its reform. A 1968 report sponsored by the Interfaith Emergency Council noted that a "group of militant and moderate Afro-American leaders have met with a group convened by the American Jewish Congress for the purpose of formulating a developmental assistance program through the Jewish community." For a time, Jews in Detroit, like other white and black middle-class liberals, attempted to salvage a strong liberal urban presence by placating black nationalists with financial support for some of their neighborhood

[59] "Riot Victims Get Aid . . . 'No Let-Down in Rebuilding Detroit,'" *Detroit Jewish News,* Aug. 11, 1967, p. 5; "Responses of Jewish Community Agencies and Organizations to the 'Urban Crisis,'" May 7, 1968, folder 1, box 591 (Jewish Community Council Archives); Community Relations Council Urban Affairs Subcommittee minutes, Jan. 9, 1969, *ibid.*

[60] Steering Committee, Interfaith Emergency Council minutes, Sept. 22, 1967, folder 6, box 29 (Richard C. Hertz Papers, Jacob Rader Marcus Center of the American Jewish Archives, Cincinnati, Ohio). Interfaith Action Council, report, April 5, 1968, *ibid.*

initiatives. As the historian Heather Thompson explains, "if black faith could be restored, peace would return and liberal leadership would be secure."[61]

Jews' remote urbanism was premised upon a willed blindness to the structural critique increasingly embedded in black protest politics. For example, in the spring of 1969, several rabbis received notice of a "black manifesto" circulating that decried capitalism; blamed white religious groups, including Jews, for perpetuating societal inequity; and demanded from them monetary compensation for years of exploitation. Detroit's Jewish Community Council urged rabbis not to "over-react" if individuals requested permission to read the manifesto in front of their congregations. The council explained that the manifesto revealed "a power struggle within the black community rather than a serious attempt to extract 'reparations' from religious institutions." Summarily dismissing the manifesto, council leaders concluded, "This in no way affects our basic commitment and responsibilities and the validity of our involvement in urban problems."[62]

Jews' attachment to urbanism fueled their tendency to flatten the varieties of black politics and to dismiss black radicalism as either irrelevant or outlandish. Politically engaged Jews wanted to believe that their policy and legislative-oriented activism could reform the city without a major structural revolution. In the weeks and months following the riots, the *Detroit Jewish News* reported on African American leaders' anti-Zionist statements and on black efforts to eject Jews from civil rights organizations. Characterizing these activities as stemming from "black power controlling elements," the editors of the paper berated black leaders for "weaken[ing] the force that are striving for unity in the ranks of the freedom loving people." Black radicalism did not spring anew from the 1960s, nor was it univocal. Yet many Jewish leaders, alongside other liberals, hoped to marginalize radical voices and re-create a liberal urban center, even if Jews no longer inhabited the city. To be certain, other Jews perceived black radicalism as such a threat to Jewish security that they eschewed liberalism, characterizing it as pandering to radical forces. Still, one can see the pulsating power of urban reformist politics even in these Jews' disavowal of liberalism. For example, a decidedly antiliberal, pro–Richard M. Nixon Jewish man served as a representative on New Detroit, a biracial committee of private citizens invested in rebuilding the city, and he joined with other wealthy Jews in bankrolling programs for the redevelopment of Detroit. These Jews clearly wanted to protect their material investments in the city, but they perceived their economic investments in the city as inextricably tied to their ideological commitment to urban reform and sustainability.[63]

---

[61] Arthur Cryns and Franklin Zweig, "To Change the Climate of Violence in Detroit: A Crisis-Oriented, Inter-University Training Institute as a Supportive and Consultative Arm to Community Efforts toward Tension Reduction, Racism Reform and Community Development in the Detroit Area," draft manuscript, March 20, 1968, *ibid.* On Ernest Goodman's defense of black radical politics, see Babson, Riddle, and Elsila, *Color of Law,* 366–443. Thompson, *Whose Detroit?,* 75, 87–100. On attempts by Jews to salvage a strong liberal urban presence in other U.S. cities, see Matthew J. Countryman, *Up South: Civil Rights and Black Power in Philadelphia* (Philadelphia, 2006), 160–62; and Suleiman Osman, *The Invention of Brownstone Brooklyn: Gentrification and the Search for Authenticity in Postwar New York* (New York, 2011), 244.

[62] Dubin (of Jewish Community Council) to Rabbis, May 22, 1969, memo, folder 10, box 31 (Hertz Papers).

[63] "Irresponsible Bigots' 'Power' Pressures," *Detroit Jewish News,* Sept. 15, 1967, p. 4. On anti-Zionist statements made by African American leaders, see also "SNCC Attack on Zionism, Israel Branded 'Anti-Semitic Tragedy,' Affecting Race Relations in U.S.," *ibid.,* Aug. 18, 1967, p. 1. On black radicalism in the 1960s, see Robert O. Self, *American Babylon: Race and the Struggle for Postwar Oakland* (Princeton, 2003), 217–20. On Jews and ties between urban economic investments and ideological commitments, see Peter Golden, *Quiet Diplomat: A Biography of Max M. Fisher* (New York, 1992).

As misguided as the effort by Jews to reform the city remotely may have been, this strategy also constituted a new form of Jewish urban activism. Most significantly, the city continued to exist in Jews' consciousness as a place that mattered, even when Jews felt disillusioned and disappointed with it. By the end of the twentieth century and beginning of the twenty-first century, pockets of urban activists, many of whom were Jewish, insisted that a more grounded, local urban involvement replace the remote urban engagement of the past. In 2010 Quicken Loans moved its headquarters from Livonia, a suburb to the northwest of Detroit, to Detroit's central business district. Dan Gilbert, the Jewish, Detroit-born chairman and founder of the company, led the way for other business ventures and foundations to invest in Detroit. David Carroll, a Quicken Loans vice president and also a Jewish native of Detroit, explained in 2012, "We are committed to transforming Detroit—from a shrinking, so called 'rust belt' city of high unemployment to a thriving commercial hotbed that is the envy of all." For Gilbert, that commitment included purchasing cheap real estate in the downtown core and providing incentives for employees who chose to live in the city. The company also benefitted from substantial tax abatements and federal and state subsidies. Several other Jewish-led initiatives, including the Live Detroit Fund to subsidize rents sponsored by the Jewish Federation of Metropolitan Detroit, the revitalization of the Isaac Agree Downtown Synagogue, and the creation of Moishe House, a communal living space for Jews in their twenties, targeted a small swathe of downtown Detroit as the foundation for a new cultural and technological corridor. Despite failing public schools, thousands of abandoned homes, astronomical unemployment rates, and rampant poverty, the corridor was envisioned to attract creative, affluent, predominantly white people to an approximately six-square-mile section of a 144-square-mile city. New development plans aside, Jews' early twenty-first-century investments in the city replicated patterns to negotiate and remake urban space that had characterized their politics over the last six decades.[64]

Historians who think that urban politics of city dwellers were checked at the entrance ramps to the highways that led millions of Americans to the suburbs must reexamine their narrative. Well before most Jews left the city, they were already crafting a new form of politics that changed their relationship to the physical space of their lives. Local activism mandated a grounded and individual-oriented attachment to the neighborhood and the city; remote policy politics offered a way to engage with urban issues from afar. Each form was flawed, and neither solved the problem of racial segregation. Nonetheless, urban flight must be understood as more complicated than a journey away from urban liberalism and toward white suburban conservatism. For many Americans, this formulation works, but for others it does not. If we are to understand American cities of the past and present, we must train our eyes on the expanses of American urbanism, well into the heart of the suburbs and, perhaps most recently, back into the city.

[64] David Carroll, "Detroit Initiatives," Jan. 23, 2012, report (in Berman's possession); David Carroll telephone interview by Lila Corwin Berman, Feb. 22, 2012. On the Jewish Federation of Metropolitan Detroit's Live Detroit, see http://www.livedetroitfund.org/; and Scott Kaufman (CEO of the Jewish Federation) telephone interview by Berman, March 22, 2012. On recent efforts by Jews in other cities to reinvest and reinhabit urban spaces, see "New Early Learning Experience Coming Soon to Center City," *Jewish Exponent*, July 15, 2010, p. 18; Anthony Weiss, "On the Jersey Waterfront, Jews Return, but Jewish Community Still Struggles," *Jewish Daily Forward*, April 24, 2009, p. 1; and Jill Jacobs, "Unlocked Gates: Steps toward a Jewish Urban Theology," *Tikkun*, 21 (July–Aug. 2006), 53–62. Present-day urban-focused Jewish organizations include Jewish Council on Urban Affairs, Bend the Arc (formerly Progressive Jewish Alliance and Jewish Funds for Justice), Jews United for Justice, Jewish Community Action, Avodah: The Jewish Service Corps, Jewish Organizing Initiative, Tikkun Ha-Ir, Jews for Racial and Economic Justice, and Urban Adamah.

Interchange: The War of 1812

Introduction by Nicole Eustace

Centennial anniversaries provide unique opportunities for commemorating the past while characterizing the present. In some cases anniversaries may remind us of things we would rather forget—a point that is especially true when the date in question marks a war. Of all wars in American history, the War of 1812 enjoys the dubious distinction of being the one least likely to be remembered. In a freewheeling conversation, the contributors to this interchange have tried to determine why the War of 1812 in North America has so often been a forgotten conflict and whether or not that situation needs to be remedied. At its bicentennial, does the memory of the war deserve to be exhumed or should all discussion of the conflict be buried once and for all?

Considering the war from a variety of analytical and geographical angles, these historians debated whether people in the United States often fail to remember the conflict because it was inconsequential or because the memories it evokes are uncomfortable. Was the war popular in its day but insignificant in history, or were its effects important but ultimately unpalatable? How does the war look different when viewed from varied cardinal directions: south from Canada, north from the United States, west from Britain, or east from Indian country? In what areas—from economics to politics to diplomacy to society and culture—should the impact of the war be measured?

If these discussions led to any point of convergence, it was perhaps to the agreement that the war has been hard to remember because it is so difficult to define. The meaning of the war was and is as diffuse as the nations that fought it: Americans with their divided and localized loyalties, Britons spread thin by global conflicts, Canadians of diverse origins, and Indians with multiple imperial ties. Yet if something that is "diffuse" is indistinct and obscure, it is also, by definition, widespread and well dispersed. The scholars whose thoughts are gathered here range considerably in their assessments of the war. Collectively, however, their comments on topics as diverse as patriotism, nationalism, imperialism, localism, sovereignty, citizenship, trade policy, and Indian rights suggest that the War of 1812 can claim greater significance in myriad historical realms than its usual obscurity would suggest.

This online discussion took place during the last two months of 2011. The *JAH* is indebted to all of the participants for their willingness to contribute to this "Interchange":

doi: 10.1093/jahist/jas236

RACHEL HOPE CLEVES is an associate professor of history at the University of Victoria. Her book *The Reign of Terror in America: Visions of Violence from Anti-Jacobinism to Antislavery* (2009) won the 2010 Gilbert Chinard Prize from the Society for French Historical Studies and the French Institute of Washington. Readers may contact Cleves at rcleves@uvic.edu.

NICOLE EUSTACE is, with the *Journal of American History* editors, a co-convenor of this interchange and an associate professor of history and the codirector of the Atlantic World Workshop at New York University. She is the author of *Passion Is the Gale: Emotion, Power, and the Coming of the American Revolution* (2008) and *1812: War and the Passions of Patriotism* (2012). Readers may contact Eustace at nicole.eustace@nyu.edu.

PAUL GILJE is the George Lynn Cross Research Professor at the University of Oklahoma. His books include *The Road to Mobocracy: Popular Disorder in New York City, 1763–1834* (1987); *Rioting in America* (1996); *Liberty on the Waterfront: American Maritime Society and Culture in the Age of Revolution, 1750–1850* (2004); and *The Making of the American Republic, 1763–1815* (2006). He is working on two book manuscripts: "Free Trade and Sailors' Rights in the War of 1812" and "'To Swear like a Sailor': Language, Meaning, and Culture in the American Maritime World, 1750–1850." Readers may contact Gilje at pgilje@ou.edu.

MATTHEW RAINBOW HALE is an assistant professor of history at Goucher College. His article "On Their Tiptoes: Political Time and Newspapers during the Advent of the Radicalized French Revolution, circa 1792–1793" (*Journal of the Early Republic,* Summer 2009) won the 2010 Ralph D. Gray Best Article Prize from the Society for Historians of the Early American Republic. His study of the impact of the French Revolution on American political culture will be published by the University of Virginia Press. Readers may contact Hale at mhale@goucher.edu.

CECILIA MORGAN is a professor of cultural and social history in the Department of Curriculum, Learning, and Teaching at the University of Toronto. Her books include *Public Men and Virtuous Women: The Gendered Languages of Religion and Politics in Upper Canada, 1791–1850* (1996); *Heroines and History: Representations of Madeleine de Verchères and Laura Secord* (2002, with Colin M. Coates); and *"A Happy Holiday": English Canadians and Transatlantic Tourism, 1870–1930* (2008). Readers may contact Morgan at cecilia.morgan@utoronto.ca.

JASON M. OPAL is an associate professor of history at McGill University. He is the author of *Beyond the Farm: National Ambitions in Rural New England* (2008) and *Avenging the People: Andrew Jackson, the Southern Borderlands, and the Ordeal of American Democracy* (New York, forthcoming). Readers may contact Opal at jason.opal@mcgill.ca.

LAWRENCE A. PESKIN is an associate professor of history at Morgan State University. He is the author of "Conspiratorial Anglophobia and the War of 1812" in the *Journal of American History* (Dec. 2011). His books include *Manufacturing Revolution: The Intellectual Origins of Early American Industry* (2004) and *America and the World: Culture, Commerce, Conflict* (coauthored with Edmund F. Wehrle, 2011). Readers may contact Peskin at lawrence.peskin@morgan.edu.

ALAN TAYLOR is a professor of history at the University of California, Davis. His books include *The Divided Ground: Indians, Settlers, and the Northern Borderland of the American Revolution* (2006) and *The Civil War of 1812: American Citizens, British Subjects, Irish Rebels, and Indian Allies* (2010). Readers may contact Taylor at astaylor@ucdavis.edu.

JAH: **A bicentennial inevitably heightens public interest in historical events. As a result, academic historians all become "public historians" in ways intentional and not. How can scholars make the best use of the anniversary of the War of 1812? How does the new scrutiny change the way we will research, write, and teach about this often-overlooked war?**

LAWRENCE A. PESKIN: I think the War of 1812 is overlooked because the story surrounding it is not very uplifting nor are the causes of the war easy to understand. I know that it is gradually disappearing from my survey lectures and, I think, from textbooks. (Two to four pages of coverage seem to be the norm.) At least the American Revolution, the Civil War, and World War II offer positive lessons and can be fit into the public's general sense of historical progress. The story of the War of 1812 is often sordid—containing venomous politics, American aggression, racism, and a general sense of futility. There is little that can be sold as triumphalism beyond Andrew Jackson's decisive victory in the Battle of New Orleans. Perhaps the idea of treating the conflict as a "second war for independence" comes closest. Even here in Baltimore, Maryland, where there are a number of public celebrations planned to mark the bicentennial, the tenor is usually more along the lines of "the city was not burned down" and Francis Scott Key wrote a nice poem because of the defense of Fort McHenry. As scholars, we walk a difficult road here because the lessons we take from the war are not lessons that the public wants to hear.[1]

RACHEL HOPE CLEVES: In Canada there is strong public interest in the War of 1812. Prime Minister Stephen Harper recently allocated $11.5 million to commemorate the two hundredth anniversary of the war, and I have fielded questions about the conflict from students in my classes. Perhaps the explanation for this interest connects to the general sense here that Canada won the war. According to a Harper government press release, "the War of 1812 helped define who we are today. . . . Against great odds, it took the combined efforts of Canadians of all ancestries to repel the American invasion and defend Canada in a time of crisis." Or, as my students put it, "we burned down the White House." A recent class discussion of Alfred Young's *The Shoemaker and the Tea Party* became sidelined by a spirited refutation of Young's contention that the United States won the war. However committed my students and the prime minister may be to this memory of the war (especially surprising here in British Columbia, far from the fields of battle), their historical knowledge is glancing. A recent poll found that many Canadians could not name the parties to the war, and when I explained to my students that Americans remember the war as a victory over the British because of Jackson's triumph in the Battle of New Orleans, they were utterly confused about what New Orleans could have to do with a war that they understand as having taken place in Canada.[2]

[1] On the War of 1812 as a "second war for independence," see Donald R. Hickey, *The War of 1812: A Short History* (Urbana, 1995); and A. J. Langguth, *Union 1812: The Americans Who Fought the Second War of Independence* (New York, 2006). Francis Scott Key, "Defense of Fort McHenry," *Baltimore American,* Sept. 21, 1814, p. 2.

[2] "Commemorating Canadian History: The War of 1812," Oct. 11, 2011, *Here for Canada,* http://www.conservative.ca/press/news_releases/commemorating_canadian_history_the_war_of_1812; Alfred F. Young, *The*

In answer to the opening question, I think historians have a responsibility to correct the nationalizing narratives of public memory. As the anniversary of the war's commencement raises public interest, I would like to complicate questions about who won with discussions of dissent, the ethics of warfare, historical contingency, and the fluidity of identity—all of which make the war interesting to me.

CECILIA MORGAN: I agree with Rachel Hope Cleves that in Canada at present there is a strong interest in the War of 1812, partly generated by Harper's federal conservative government. Such encouragement is, I think, of a piece with the government's desire to make the military—and emblems of loyalty to Britain—more prominent in Canadian social, cultural, and political life. The desire to fund commemorative activities also comes with promises of funding for events linked primarily to political, military, and sports history and is accompanied by a decline in federal funds for other humanities research. That nation-building aspect of War of 1812 commemoration troubles me.

I also agree that any detailed historical knowledge is all too often inaccurate or anachronistic, as exemplified by statements from the Canadian prime minister's office that the War of 1812 was a pivotal moment in the creation of Canada—an eerie echo of statements made by Canadian commemorators in 1912. Therefore, I agree that historians need to be involved in public debate and discussion about the meanings of the war as an intensely local affair and as a manifestation of larger imperial and transatlantic processes. There are, though, strong local attachments to the war and its meanings that I would argue predate the federal government's involvement. On the Niagara Peninsula, where I live, I have been struck by the ongoing interest in and fascination with the war. The existence of such local interest, however, does not mean that we should not be trying to counter the state's narratives, as they do have weight and do resonate with local groups, but it also seems to me that the war's meaning and significance have also played a role in regional and national identities within the Canadian context. Another interesting aspect of the historiography of this war—at least in British Canada—is that so much of it has been produced by public or popular historians, and it has generally received little scrutiny from academic historians.[3]

NICOLE EUSTACE: My hope is that that the anniversary of the War of 1812 can prompt us to a new consideration of the idea of empire in American history. The conflict's most profound losers were not the Americans who saw their capitol burned to the ground or the Canadians who successfully repelled weak efforts at invasion, but rather were the Indians who lost their last best hope of a British-backed barrier state in the Northwest Territory. True, the War of 1812 has long been a forgotten conflict, but as Fred Anderson and Drew Cayton have reminded us, sometimes we need to pay closest attention to the wars that seem easiest to forget. In my work on emotion and patriotism, I am interested in understanding how Americans leveraged the moral power of emotion to glorify

Shoemaker and the Tea Party: Memory and the American Revolution (Boston, 1999), 33; "Harper's 1812 Overture: Study Shows Canadians Unfamiliar with War's Details," *Toronto Globe and Mail,* Oct. 5, 2011, p. 5.

[3] Statements on the War of 1812 by Canadian commemorators in 1912 can be found in W. L. Grant, *Ontario High School History of Canada* (Toronto, 1914); and Elizabeth Thompson, "Laura Ingersoll Secord," in *Niagara Historical Society and Museum Papers,* comp. Janet Carnochan (Niagara-on-the-Lake, 1912).

battle and vilify opponents—the better to justify controversial political actions such as going to war in 1812.[4]

PAUL GILJE: The year 2012 presents a once-in-a-century opportunity for American and Canadian historians to examine the War of 1812 and help the public remember this forgotten war. As is clear in the comments from Rachel and from Cecilia Morgan, Canadians are busy seizing this opportunity. Americans, it seems, could not care less. There are modest efforts to commemorate the war in the United States—in those areas that are near the Canadian border or in those areas, such as Baltimore, that played a special role in the war and in forming the American national identity. So far, however, these efforts have been drowned out by commemoration of the sesquicentennial of the Civil War.

The great tragedy of brother fighting brother from 1861 to 1865 continues to capture the American imagination in a way that the War of 1812 does not. Alan Taylor has reminded us in his book *The Civil War of 1812* that the conflict indeed cast brother against brother, but as important as Alan's book has been among academics, its message has not had mass public appeal in the United States. Perhaps the problem is, as Lawrence A. Peskin has suggested, that the War of 1812 was a sordid affair in which the Americans did not behave in ways that fit easily into the exceptionalist model—portraying Americans as always triumphantly standing for ideals over interest and good over evil—that to this day captivates the popular imagination. Even so, all wars are sordid, and what was not won on the battlefield was gained after the peace as the Americans declared victory and convinced themselves—in part because of Andrew Jackson but also because of the battle of Baltimore and the battle of Lake Champlain—that they had once again beaten the most powerful military machine in the world. In the decades after 1815 Americans looked to the War of 1812 and remembered only the glory—even electing presidents (Jackson, William Henry Harrison, John Tyler, and Zachary Taylor) who had won battles during the conflict—until the expansionism of the 1840s and the coming sectional conflict in the 1850s focused national attention elsewhere. What is a historian to do? We definitely should not feed the national mythology either in Canada or the United States. We should remember, as Nicole Eustace says, part of the tragedy of the war was that Native Americans were its biggest losers. Likewise, we should try to encourage our readers to think about empire in America and, I would add, in Canada. We must make our books accessible to that broader readership and avoid speaking only to ourselves.[5]

CLEVES: The commemoration funding in Canada is designated for military-related purposes such as reenactments, the erection of battlefield monuments, and honoring Canadian militias and regiments. How much room does this framework allow for asking questions about the necessity of war? Which historical interpretations can we effectively advance within the framework of doing commemorative public history? If I see the War of 1812 as unnecessary, expansionist, and devastating to indigenous communities, would

---

[4] Fred Anderson and Andrew Cayton, *The Dominion of War: Empire and Liberty in North America, 1500–2000* (New York, 2004).

[5] Alan Taylor, *The Civil War of 1812: American Citizens, British Subjects, Irish Rebels, and Indian Allies* (New York, 2010).

I serve my interpretation better by protesting the commemorations than by joining them?

EUSTACE: As a scholar, I can imagine neither participating as a reenactor nor protesting those who engage in reenactments. My task is to investigate how the war was defined by its contemporary supporters and how it continues to be described today. I have great respect for those who serve in the military (and for those who seek to honor that service), but I do have concerns about how the War of 1812 was and is being chronicled. My job is to offer a critical interpretation of the narratives surrounding the war (the stories that helped generate the war and those that commemorate it). Despite its many failures and problems, the War of 1812 ushered in an "era of good feelings" in the United States—a phrase coined in the Boston newspaper *Columbian Centinel* in 1817 and quickly picked up by dozens of other papers eager to describe the national atmosphere in the wake of the war. My task is neither to counter nor to countenance those emotions but rather to analyze them. In the process, I think I can demonstrate the power of pleasurable feelings to lend positive moral coloration to questionable and even objectionable events. If that kind of critical analysis rains on a few (commemorative) parades, so be it.[6]

MATTHEW RAINBOW HALE: From an American perspective, I think historians need to avoid excessive hand-wringing when it comes to the general lack of interest in the War of 1812. I agree with Lawrence that the War of 1812 is not an uplifting story, yet that is not the only reason the War of 1812 is overshadowed. The American Revolution, the American Civil War, and World War II receive more attention than the War of 1812 in large part because they were bigger, more transformative conflicts. I cannot imagine a day when the level of American popular interest in the War of 1812 will equal or surpass the level of interest in those other conflicts. In fact, I think historians do the public a service by carefully evaluating the relative impacts of military conflicts. I am fascinated by "Mr. Madison's war" because it illuminates important developments in the early United States. In addition, the problem that Cecilia pointed to—the insufficient attention paid to the War of 1812 by academic historians—is more compelling to me than the relative lack of interest in the conflict among the general populace.[7]

PESKIN: I wonder about the impact of the war on the United States versus the impact of social, economic, and political trends. What I am getting at here is that 1815 (the year the war ended) remains an important hinge date in textbooks and scholarly works, marking a general transition between the revolutionary era and the classic antebellum period. After 1815 the political scene certainly shifts as the Federalist party collapses and new leaders take power. After 1815 we see the rise of industry in the North and the heyday of cotton culture in the South, as well as a transportation revolution and a market revolution. Diplomatic historians can also point to increased national confidence and

---

[6] "Era of Good Feelings," *Boston Columbian Centinel,* July 12, 1817, p. 2.

[7] On the origins of the concept of "Mr. Madison's war," see John Lowell, *Mr. Madison's War: A Dispassionate Inquiry into the Reasons Alleged by Mr. Madison for Declaring an Offensive and Ruinous War against Great-Britain, Together with Suggestions as to a Peaceable and Constitutional Mode of Averting that Dreadful Calamity, by a New England Farmer* (Boston, 1812).

expansionism. I suppose aspects of the War of 1812 can be connected to these developments (such as the rise of the war hawks, the collapse of antiwar Federalism, and the push for domestic manufacturing), but I am skeptical that these occurrences would have unfolded much differently had the war never occurred.[8]

CLEVES: That is an interesting question, Lawrence. I frequently tell my students that wars produce social transformations (and I reinforce that point in my women's history classes where war often seems to shuffle gender and sexual norms). But is that truism actually true for the War of 1812? I would argue that the conflict led to the emergence of antiwar movements in the United States, which helped redefine attitudes to violence in the antebellum era.[9]

JASON M. OPAL: Teaching at an Anglophone school in Quebec, I am allowed a unique look at the ways the present conservative government tries to move Canadian social and political life to the right. As Cecilia notes, a historical narrative emphasizing military struggle as shared national sacrifice is central to that project. Most Francophones seem to dismiss such efforts, even though the government stresses that *all* Canadians helped repel the Americans. The crucial element missing in Quebec is any kind of veneration for the British Empire: Prime Minister Harper's national narrative embraces Canada's connection to the larger global historical mission of the empire, while most Francophones have little good to say about that same empire.

For me, the War of 1812 was a victory for all the major white interest groups in the southeast region of the United States, many of which had previously been at odds. In particular, speculators—who tended to be political and military leaders—and poor settlers—who were often seeking to escape governments run by such men—"won" enough land not to have to worry about who got what. In western North Carolina, for example, poorer settlers had long struggled to gain title to lands they had originally purchased in 1783 and 1784 but that had been transferred to state and federal authority and retroceded, in part, to the Cherokee. This caused considerable tension between and among settlers, borderland elites, and the federal government. The devastation of Cherokee and Creek lands that culminated during the War of 1812 not only opened up huge tracts of land for all kinds of white migrants but also convinced large numbers of them that their government, or at least parts of it, shared their fundamental interest in landed independence.[10]

Whether or not those migrants had slaves, and even whether they claimed one hundred or one thousand acres, mattered less than it had a generation previously. That is, the sheer availability of land and the shared narrative of wartime suffering muted the many conflicts of interest between emigrant streams. Combined with the U.S. defeat of

---

[8] The "war hawks," led by Henry Clay, Felix Grundy, and John C. Calhoun, are a staple of War of 1812 historiography, but there has been discussion about whether the term is appropriate. On the concept, see *Indiana Magazine of History,* 60 (June 1964). This was a special issue devoted to the war hawks.

[9] On the idea that support for the War of 1812 led to a general antiwar movement, see Rachel Hope Cleves, *The Reign of Terror in America: Visions of Violence from Anti-Jacobinism to Antislavery* (New York, 2009), esp. 104–52.

[10] David S. Heidler and Jeanne T. Heidler, *Old Hickory's War: Andrew Jackson and the Quest for Empire* (Baton Rouge, 2003); Angela Pulley Hudson, *Creek Paths and Federal Roads: Indians, Settlers, and Slaves in the Making of the South* (Chapel Hill, 2010).

the Mississippi Territory Creek Indians in the Creek War of 1813–1814, the War of 1812 made the rapid expansion of slavery not only possible but also blameless; the race-nation, rather than any one territory or polity, had won the right to make of the Gulf Coast what it wished. The victors also did not have to tolerate any possible threat to slavery, which is why, in many respects, the Seminole War of 1818 followed quite naturally from the aftermath of the war in 1815. Put another way, we should consider the War of 1812 as a turning point in the history of slavery in its broadest sense, and we should link the long-term results of the conflict to the rise of the militant slave owners of the antebellum period.[11]

HALE: Jason M. Opal and Nicole have outlined two important, interwoven developments—the accelerated appropriation of Indian lands and the accelerated expansion of slavery—that stemmed from the War of 1812. Another related development that drew strength directly from the war was the emergence and legitimization of backcountry settlers and politicians on the American national scene. Two decades before the signing of the Treaty of Fort Jackson to end the Creek War, residents in the nation's backcountry participated in a series of revolts now known as the Whiskey Rebellion. Easterners of almost all stripes responded to the uprising by rallying together to crush it, in part because they held intense disdain for backcountry settlers. Yet after Jackson's victory in the Battle of New Orleans in 1815, backcountry residents and politicians gained a foothold in American public life. Supposedly uncivilized settlers were transformed into hardy, courageous American frontiersmen—patriotic "Hunters of Kentucky." This new—albeit still-contested—image of backcountry settlers and politicians helped propel Jackson to the U.S. presidency in 1828, and less than two decades after that, James K. Polk—another individual with backcountry roots—became the president. Not coincidentally, both Jackson and Polk were militant slaveholders and ardent expansionists from the Southeast. Would backcountry residents have gained cultural legitimacy in American public life without the War of 1812? Most likely yes; their numbers and vitality suggest that it would have been very difficult to ignore them or prevent them from gaining incredible sway. Still, the larger point is that contingent events during the War of 1812 were the specific medium through which many backcountry individuals acquired their new reputation and power on the national stage. "Mr. Madison's war" mattered.[12]

OPAL: I agree with Matthew Rainbow Hale's comment, and I want to add a regional twist. We are not sure—aside from in Pennsylvania—when and how (or even if) backcountry settlers won claims to Indian lands based on "right of conquest" or "extinguished" claims in the Southeast. Understanding how settlers connected their particular claims and titles to a national story of wartime trial and redemption would offer a better read on what postwar nationalism was and was not. I think this is a concrete way to get at the cultural and political ascent of the western settlers. One medium that definitely lionized settlers as nationals was the frontier atrocity narrative, many of which were published in the immediate aftermath of the war. Not unlike earlier tales of capture and

[11] Heidler and Heidler, *Old Hickory's War*.
[12] On the song "Hunters of Kentucky," see John William Ward, *Andrew Jackson: Symbol for an Age* (New York, 1962), 13–29.

murder by the ruthless Indians, these were remarkably graphic tales of butchered families, often avenged by women rather than men.[13]

MORGAN: These comments point to important similarities and significant distinctions concerning the war's effect on British North America and the United States. One similarity is that the war's outcome was calamitous for indigenous people in both areas: the death of the Shawnee Tecumseh at the Battle of Moraviantown in 1813, the end of the prospect of a pan-indigenous confederacy, and the end of indigenous peoples' role as military allies of the Crown. In the 1820s British policy toward natives shifted to assimilation, setting the stage for future nineteenth-century developments. The influx of British immigrants after the end of the Napoleonic Wars had a significant impact on the ability of aboriginal peoples, especially in Upper Canada, to hold onto lands and resources. Immigration also brought a fresh wave of British missionaries to the region (replacing those unwelcome ones from the United States) seeking to change native practices and values and who—at times—supported aboriginal opposition to the colonial government's attempts to move them from their traditional territories.[14]

Jason also raises an important point about settlers becoming heroes through the medium of atrocity and captivity narratives. In the context of Upper Canada, patriotic service during the War of 1812 became a political bargaining chip. It is not a coincidence that members of the legislative assembly, for example, usually served in the militia or that militia service was noted in petitions to the Crown as proof of the would-be patronage recipient's worth. Not surprisingly, there were other implications for such military service. Military and patriotic discourse about service in 1812, both during and after the battles, helped reinforce existing notions of the political realm as masculine, and marked by virtue, honor, and patriotic service to the Crown. (Any sense that Upper Canadian men might have participated in atrocities or simply been unwilling to fight was absent.) Moreover, although historians have not yet tackled the links between settler colonialism in British North America and the military, that same influx of British immigrants in the 1820s, 1830s, and 1840s also lived through imperial wars—both as civilians and, in a number of cases, as members of the military in European and imperial conflicts.[15]

ALAN TAYLOR: I am pessimistic that there will be much public attention paid to the War of 1812 in the United States (except in Baltimore) and perhaps too much of the wrong type of attention will be paid to the war in Canada. Although the light cast on history

---

[13] On the processes of "right of conquest" and "extinguished" claims to obtain Indian lands, see Stuart Banner, *How the Indians Lost Their Land: Law and Power on the Frontier* (Cambridge, Mass., 2005). Among the most important captivity narratives informing readers that the murderous savages it described had been exterminated by Gen. Andrew Jackson is Eunice Barber, *Narrative of the Tragical Death of Darius Barber and His Seven Children* (Boston, 1819).

[14] On the calamitous effect of the War of 1812 on indigenous peoples, see, for example, Carl Benn, *The Iroquois in the War of 1812* (Toronto, 1998); Colin G. Calloway, *The Shawnees and the War for America* (New York, 2007); and Guy St-Denis, *Tecumseh's Bones* (Montreal, 2005).

[15] On the political realm as masculine, see Cecilia Morgan, "Gender, Loyalty, and Virtue in a Colonial Context: The War of 1812 and Its Aftermath in Upper Canada," in *Gender, War, and Politics: Transatlantic Perspectives, 1775–1830*, ed. Karen Hagemann, Jane Rendall, and Gisele Matelle (New York, 2010), 301–24; and Cecilia Morgan, *Public Men and Virtuous Women: The Gendered Languages of Religion and Politics in Upper Canada, 1791–1850* (Toronto, 1996).

will be dim, it will be a bit brighter than usual, so I hope that we would do whatever we can to exploit this brief (and limited) opportunity to reach a broader public. Having seen the master narratives of nations continue to thrive among the public despite a generation of historical criticism, I do not hope to topple them, but I do think we have a chance to encourage a wider slice of the public to recognize them as narratives with particular purposes. Given that much of the public does want to feel good about its nation, my strategy is to acknowledge openly the (limited) value of the nationalist narratives. Then we have a chance to identify elements left out of traditional narratives—and to identify alternative stories that can also be told. This may be setting my sights too low, or it may be the best strategy for subtly opening a few minds, which I suspect is the best that we can do.

To the elements of significance (and relevance) already on the table, I would add three others. First, the war strikes me as fundamentally about citizenship: who should have it and who should not. Many of our students have to confront the shifting boundaries of citizenship in their own lives and in their parents' lives. There is an ongoing, never-complete struggle over the rights and benefits of citizenship in the United States and Canada that has roots in the War of 1812. Second, the war is obviously about collective violence, invasion, and occupation, and so it invites comparisons with how the United States and its allies (including Canada) now deal with occupied peoples and their territories. The mainstream media sanitizes most of the violence of war today or presents it in the style of a video game. Even so, those of us who teach about any war in the past have a chance to reveal the human costs and the tangled relationships invariably created by any invasion and occupation. Third, the war reveals a bitter (and recently much-inflamed) conflict within the United States about the proper boundaries of federalism. That the United States fought the War of 1812 so badly has everything to do with the limited state and decentralized union that sought to maximize the individual pursuit of happiness. I do not know whether a strong or a decentralized union is better today. (It depends for me, as I suspect it does for many others, on who holds the national power.) But the War of 1812 certainly highlighted the flaws that existed on the decentralized and defunded nation side of the ledger.

EUSTACE: Another point of significance to add to the list is that for all practical purposes, the War of 1812 was the first constitutionally declared war in the history of the United States. It bears reexamination exactly for what it can tell us about the formation of American public opinion toward support for or opposition to the war. Few people at the time saw immediate physical hardship or benefit from the war; most experienced it not first-hand through service or suffering but secondhand through the culture of print. The war was not without real costs, but—in part because the U.S. population as a whole suffered few casualties—American evaluations of the war generally were markedly positive. I think the patriotic culture of the War of 1812 era may be one of the most significant facets of the conflict.[16]

---

[16] While the war generated considerable controversy, it led to national political success for the Republican party at the expense of the Federalist party. For a study of public opinion on the war, see Nicole Eustace, *1812: War and the Passions of Patriotism* (Philadelphia, 2012).

OPAL: I have recently found myself trying to calculate and estimate how many Americans (perhaps I should label them "Americans," as they sometimes resided in territories with unclear jurisdictions) actually experienced or saw frontier warfare firsthand, especially in the southwestern territories. Historians could make similarly futile but interesting efforts for the War of 1812. My sense is that in certain concentrated areas, such as what became central Tennessee, the white population was thoroughly traumatized by the war experience. In some of these places the number of women and children killed almost matched the number of men killed. In mid-Tennessee, for example, at least one-third of those killed during a 1793–1794 war with the Chickamauga faction of the Cherokee were women and children—a dramatic change from earlier years, when warriors clearly targeted white men while sparing and capturing women, children, and slaves. Newspapers such as the *Knoxville Gazette* dwelled on the mutilation and display of pregnant women's bodies. (Of course the carnage on the Native American side was greater and perhaps more indiscriminate.) How and why did these experiences become so central to the self-image of the American—and, to some extent, the Canadian—population as a suffering, avenged "nation"? As Nicole points out, the war is as much a story of public opinion and print culture as of social experience, but reading and talking about violence and atrocity is an experience all its own, and evidently a convincing one.[17]

PESKIN: Jason's point is well taken, but I think the important question is why such literature was being produced. Certainly 1811–1812 newspaper reports of violence, which are just ubiquitous, always seem to have a political valence to them. In my reading of them it often seems that the British are more responsible than Native Americans—that is, their hidden (or not-so-hidden) hand lies behind everything, particularly for Democratic-Republicans. I would posit that political figures were very cleverly using an existing popular literary trope (and, to a lesser extent, a lived experience of violence) to sway public opinion against Britain (and the Federalists).[18]

CLEVES: It is striking how extensively the political debates about the War of 1812 were framed by rivaling charges of brutality. To the stacks of anti-Indian and anti-English atrocity literature produced during the war, add the reams of gothic antiwar writings produced by Federalist dissenters, as well as the anti-American literature produced in Great Britain and Canada. On the Sunday after the United States declared war, the Federalist minister David Osgood denounced the conflict as merely "violence against the lives and properties of our fellow-beings." Matthew Mason has written about how British propagandists attacked the United States as a land of violent slaveholders where "a negro may be flogged till he expires under the lash." Canadians represented Americans as vicious invaders. Of course, the War of 1812 was hardly the first or last war to be legitimated by claims about the brutality of the enemy. What seems remarkable to me, from an Americanist perspective, is the extent to which domestic political debates in the

<hr />

[17] Jason M. Opal, *Avenging the People: Andrew Jackson, the Southern Borderlands, and the Ordeal of American Democracy* (New York, forthcoming); Tom Kanon, "The Kidnapping of Martha Crawley and Settler-Indian Relations prior to the War of 1812," *Tennessee Historical Quarterly,* 64 (Spring 2005), 3–23; Cynthia Cumfer, "Local Origins of National Indian Policy: Cherokee and Tennessean Ideas about Sovereignty and Nationhood, 1790–1811," *Journal of the Early Republic,* 23 (Spring 2003), 30–31, 40–41.

[18] For an example of the popular literary trope, see "Speech by Felix Grundy," *Annals of Congress,* 12 Cong., 1 sess., Dec. 12, 1811, p. 426.

United States were framed around charges of brutality. In my own research I was continually surprised by the content and extent of American antiwar rhetoric directed against American soldiers. A mass antiwar movement attacking ordinary American soldiers as murderers is not plausible today. Between 1812 and 1815, however, people such as Osgood felt no compunction to make gestures of respect toward soldiers or veterans. As a consequence, Osgood and his ilk have been treated as villains by many historians. Even so, I wonder if the stigmatization of antisoldier rhetoric comes at a cost to movements against war.[19]

HALE: Viewing violence and conceptualizations of violence through a transnational lens suggests new ways of thinking about the War of 1812. David Bell's *The First Total War: Napoleon's Europe and the Birth of Warfare as We Know It* brilliantly demonstrated that the French Revolution and the Napoleonic Wars sparked a new culture of war, and I would argue that something similar occurred in the United States. I have found that many Americans—especially those on the democratic side of the political aisle—were enthralled by Gallic military campaigns and the ways they supposedly opened up new arenas of human activity and ambition. (As Jason noted, "reading and talking about violence and atrocity is an experience all its own.") The popular, romantic investment in French revolutionary and Napoleonic conflict in turn yielded a tendency to exalt victorious warfare for its own sake rather than for any moral, social, or political good that might result, perhaps prompting us to reevaluate the origins of that conflict. In their treatments of the war's causes, historians have generally focused on impressment, commercial rights, desire for Native American and Canadian lands, and republican and anti-British conspiracy theories. But we cannot fully understand the coming of the War of 1812 without taking into account the generalized thirst for military combat that emerged in the early nineteenth century. Steven Watts broached this theme in his thought-provoking book *The Republic Reborn: War and the Making of Liberal America, 1790–1820.* In my opinion, however, the emphasis in that work on the republicanism-liberalism debate limited its reach.[20]

The time seems ripe for a new account of the origins of the War of 1812. In that vein, one potential starting point might be the fact that in the years before the war, some Americans exhorted the United States to declare war against *both* Britain and France. Consideration of the new, transatlantic culture of war that emerged in the early nineteenth century should also spur us to consider the possibility that Americans gauged

[19] On anti-American literature produced in Great Britain and Canada, see Matthew Mason, "Battle of the Slaveholding Liberators: Great Britain, the United States, and Slavery in the Early Nineteenth Century," *William and Mary Quarterly,* 59 (March 2002), 665–96, esp. 678; and Taylor, *Civil War of 1812,* 145. David Osgood, *A Solemn Protest against the Late Declaration of War in a Discourse Delivered on the Next Lord's Day after the Tidings of It Were Received* (Exeter, 1812), 8–10. On the villainous historiographical treatment of David Osgood and his ilk, see George Dangerfield, *The Era of Good Feelings* (New York, 1952), 87–88; Roger H. Brown, *The Republic in Peril: 1812* (New York, 1964), 158; Steven Watts, *The Republic Reborn: War and the Making of Liberal America, 1790–1820* (Baltimore, 1987), 276, 292; and Len Travers, *Celebrating the Fourth: Independence Day and the Rites of Nationalism in the Early Republic* (Amherst, Mass., 1997), 194.

[20] David A. Bell, *The First Total War: Napoleon's Europe and the Birth of Warfare as We Know It* (New York, 2007). Works that emphasize impressments, commercial rights, desire for Native American and Canadian lands, and Republican and anti-British conspiracy theories in discussing the War of 1812 include Reginald Horsman, *The Causes of the War of 1812* (New York, 1962); Bradford Perkins, *Prologue to War, 1805–1812: England and the United States* (Berkeley, 1968); Brown, *The Republic in Peril;* and Lawrence A. Peskin, "Conspiratorial Anglophobia and the War of 1812," *Journal of American History,* 98 (Dec. 2011), 647–69. Watts, *Republic Reborn.*

success in the War of 1812 differently than we might at first think. Nicole correctly noted that "American evaluations of the war generally were markedly positive," which has baffled historians who look at the invasion of Canada and the British Chesapeake campaign and see nothing but American failure. Yet if a popular desire for war—or perhaps, more specifically, an eagerness to prove the military capacity of the United States against Britain—was at the heart of the march toward and willingness to engage in war, then many Americans' positive, self-centered, and prideful evaluation of events between 1812 and 1815 appears much more understandable—or at the very least, a bit less ridiculous. Dan Hicks's essay "Broadsides on Land and Sea: A Cultural Reading of the Naval Engagements of the War of 1812" is helpful in this regard. Hicks shows that many residents in the United States enthusiastically celebrated American victories in single-ship engagements, despite their strategic irrelevance, because they supposedly vindicated the nation's honor. He notes that Americans were so preoccupied with the symbolic meaning of ship-to-ship warfare that they turned an unmitigated maritime disaster, the engagement between the USS *Chesapeake* and the HMS *Shannon* in 1813, into an emblem of U.S. greatness by claiming that the battle had not been fair and that Britons' jubilant reaction to the contest was a backhanded tribute to American military prowess. My David Bell–inspired emphasis on a new, transatlantic culture of war fits nicely, of course, with Rachel's work on the ways conservatives were ultimately seduced by the violence they feared and condemned. Some Federalists in the era of the War of 1812 celebrated Horatio Nelson and his naval victories in a manner that showed the bipartisan allure of Napoleonic military conflict, and more research on conservatives' fondness for British martial activity must be conducted.[21]

EUSTACE: I agree with Lawrence that politicians of the 1812 era made deliberate use of the conventions of the atrocity tale. One of the chapters in my book is a case study of the remarkable synergy and symmetry between William Henry Harrison's political letters and speeches during the War of 1812 and the wartime literary captivity narratives that draw on his exploits. One especially fascinating aspect of this process is that it is not a matter of purely top-down manipulation by leading political figures. Rather, there seems to be a feedback loop in which mass participation in political culture becomes possible through the production of anti-Indian literature, while ambitious politicians can advance by capitalizing on these same cultural preoccupations. Significantly, as Matthew notes, on the pro-war side, this is not simply a matter of invoking horror but is also a process of producing pleasure. Part and parcel of proarmament arguments is a remarkably romantic view of war as the means of experiencing transcendent feelings of love. For every condemnation of savage cruelty and British barbarity there is an exhortation to American men and women to prove their romantic ardor for each other by enacting their love of country. Women are presented in captivity tales published during the war as Anglo-American heroines and objects of desire even as they prompt readers to revile Indians. In

---

[21] Dan Hicks, "Broadsides on Land and Sea: A Cultural Reading of the Naval Engagements of the War of 1812," in *Pirates, Jack Tar, and Memory: New Directions in American Maritime History*, ed. Paul A. Gilje and William Pencak (Mystic, 2007), 180–84.

the patriotic pro-war rhetoric of 1812, pleasure and horror work together in a sort of back-to-back motivational system.[22]

JAH: In what realms did the War of 1812 have its most significant impact?

PESKIN: I am fairly skeptical about the impact of the war itself, but I do think two events occurring immediately after it ended did help U.S. leaders feel much more confident about expansion and, arguably, imperialism both on the North American continent and abroad. The first was Jackson's victory at the Battle of New Orleans. The second, lesser-known event was the smashing victory of the relatively new U.S. Navy along the Barbary Coast in 1815, which made Commodore Stephen Decatur arguably an even bigger hero than Jackson. I have sometimes called this Second Barbary War the "second War of 1812" in that it was prompted by the Algerian capture of American merchant ships in 1812. The United States was convinced that the capture was actually prompted by Britain although no evidence I know of supports that contention. Decatur's great victory was more unambiguous and easier to celebrate than the outcome of the War of 1812. Combined with Jackson's victory, it allowed Americans to contemplate the idea of the nation becoming a more influential global power on land and sea. So I would argue that 1815 marks the point at which the United States begins to see itself (and to act) as a world power. That being said, I still suspect that the end of the Napoleonic Wars in 1815 ultimately had more of an effect on America's post–War of 1812 position in the world than did either of the wars of 1812.[23]

MORGAN: My contribution here involves not so much the larger, transatlantic landscape as it does the local and the regional. Inasmuch as they have been concerned with the War of 1812, historians of British North America have pointed to the war's most immediate impact on the economy of Upper Canada, the area that bore the brunt of the American, British, and aboriginal conflict so far as land battles and occupation were concerned. George Sheppard, whose work is to date the only in-depth study of the war's social history, has pointed out that while some Upper Canadians benefited during the war from government contracts in the colony's towns, the war brought a number of merchants close to financial disaster. Moreover, rural colonists saw their crops destroyed and livestock taken; compensation claims and the records of the Loyal and Patriotic Society of Upper Canada, which provided relief to those Upper Canadians who could prove their loyalty and suffering, paint a picture of a war intertwined with domestic and intimate issues.[24]

---

[22] Eustace, *1812*, 118–67. For an example of a captivity tale, see Eliza Swan, recounted in Eliza Swan, *An Affecting Account of the Tragical Death of Major Swan, and of the Captivity of Mrs. Swan and Infant Child, by the Savages* (Boston, 1815). The book portrays Eliza as an alluring mother figure by contrasting her with a grotesque caricature of her Indian antagonists. The story repulsed readers with its repeated references to savages and its descriptions of torment but also enticed them with a steady stream of sensual images of Eliza.

[23] On the Second Barbary War, see Frank Lambert, *The Barbary Wars: American Independence in the Atlantic World* (New York, 2005), 179–202; Frederick C. Leiner, *The End of Barbary Terror: America's 1815 War against the Pirates of North Africa* (New York, 2006); and Lawrence Peskin, *Captives and Countrymen: Barbary Slavery and the American Public, 1785–1816* (Baltimore, 2009), 187–210.

[24] George Sheppard, *Plunder, Profit, and Paroles: A Social History of the War of 1812 in Upper Canada* (Montreal, 1994); Loyal and Patriotic Society of Upper Canada, *The Report of the Loyal and Patriotic Society of Upper*

However, as Alan pointed out and as I have suggested elsewhere, the war's most significant and lasting impact in Upper Canada was on residents' claims to the status of loyalty and patriotism as British subjects. In the war's more immediate aftermath, most of these claims were framed in the language of suffering, of wounds—corporeal and material—endured, for which Upper Canadians deserved recompense. This language was most often deployed by men in an idiom of masculine sacrifice, although women employed it at times, stating that the well-being and sanctity of the domestic realm had been violated by the war. (They were, perhaps, indirectly cloaking incidents of sexual abuse and rape, although that point is difficult to push further).

Another language emerged, one closer to what Nicole has described as a language of love or, at least, of a romanticism that surrounded the war's history. Upper Canadian men represented themselves as having triumphed over a brutal invading force. This sense of triumph was personified by the Canadian militiaman Isaac Brock as the epitome of the militarily and intimately virtuous, self-sacrificing Christian soldier who could serve as a symbol for all Upper Canada militia members' contributions. Brock's image drew on the commemorations of Gen. James Wolfe and Horatio Nelson but was one with a particularly local resonance and meaning as expressed in his burial, in the dedication (and rededication) of the Queenston Heights monument to Brock in Ontario, and in the colony's schools. While historians—myself included—have been critical of the "militia myth" and the ways Brock's commemoration fed into it, the myth exercised a powerful hold on representations of the War of 1812 in Upper Canada, including as a "better story" that countered the Loyalist narrative of flight, loss, and trauma. No matter that Brock died at the start of the war; for those who mourned his death, such an early demise probably helped them celebrate him, because then they did not have to deal with his possible incompetence or acts of brutality.[25]

EUSTACE: Lawrence rightly pointed out that the War of 1812 was not transformative in the sense of ushering in major changes in domestic policy or Euro-American diplomacy. However, the war did foster many casual presumptions about the morality and practicality of continental warfare in North America. Transition from the stage of revolutionary generals such as William Hull cleared the path for a far more bombastic set of leaders— from Jackson to John C. Calhoun to William Henry Harrison—to set an opportunistically belletristic tone for the nation during the next half century. Thus one key form of war impact was a certain militarization of popular culture and politics, and this observation, in turn, gets back to the other half of Matthew's point: after the War of 1812, a new style of leader steeped in the lure of the backcountry, rose to power. Matthew speculates that this shift toward pugilistic, imperialistic patriotism would have happened even without the War of 1812. I wonder if that is so.

Canada (Montreal, 1817); Loyal and Patriotic Society of Upper Canada, *Explanation of the Proceedings of the Loyal and Patriotic Society of Upper Canada* (Toronto, 1841).

   [25] On Isaac Brock, see Wesley B. Turner, *The Astonishing General: The Life and Legacy of Isaac Brock* (Toronto, 2011). On the Queenston Heights monument, see Robert Shipley, *To Mark Our Place: A History of Canadian War Memorials* (Toronto, 1987); Norman Knowles, *Inventing the Loyalists: The Ontario Loyalist Tradition and the Creation of Usable Pasts* (Toronto, 1997); and Sheppard, *Plunder, Profit, and Paroles*, 208–43. For criticism of the "militia myth," see Colin M. Coates and Cecilia Morgan, *Heroines and History: Representations of Madeleine de Verchéres and Laura Secord* (Toronto, 2002); and Sheppard, *Plunder, Profit, and Paroles*, 208–43.

When I think back to work on the eighteenth-century origins of this culture in Pennsylvania (my own work, that of Peter Silver or Jane Merritt, for example), I am most struck by how little immediate political power was gained by violently anti-Indian frontier folk between 1754 and 1812. In that sense, the military and political achievements of men such as Harrison and Jackson (and John Tyler, who also served in the War of 1812) truly stand out.[26]

GILJE: There is nothing like a war—even a regionally unpopular one—to cement bonds, stir emotions, and forge national identity. Herein lies the importance of those naval battle victories (even the "unfair" defeats that Lawrence has mentioned). The defense of honor at sea—in a war that many saw as being fought to protect commerce and end impressment—played to the nation's emotions and helped mold a stronger identity with the United States. The spate of land victories toward the end of the war at Baltimore, on Lake Champlain, and at New Orleans added to the sense of American pride and nationalism. Oddly, however, it was the sense of victory at the end of the war, despite the abysmal overall performance during the conflict, that provided the greatest impetus for American national identity. By declaring victory—it is difficult not to think of George W. Bush's unsuccessful declaration of mission accomplished in 2003—James Madison and the Republicans molded American memory of the war for the next generation.[27]

American national identity had a maritime component, but it also had a backcountry component thanks in part to Andrew Jackson and his Tennessee Volunteers. The emergence to power of the previously marginal American backcountry thus became part and parcel of the new nationalism. That nationalism had a political component in the American political system, pushed by men such as Henry Clay, John C. Calhoun, and John Quincy Adams, but nationalism also faced resistance from strong identities linked to state and region that would create the tensions that ultimately led to the Civil War. I would not go so far as to say that without the War of 1812 there would have been no Civil War, but the appeal to the union in 1861 by a rail-splitting frontiersman built upon an American nationalism that owed much to the experience of fighting the War of 1812.

CLEVES: Like Laura Ingalls in *Little Town on the Prairie,* I have been busy "thinking about the War of 1812." I wish I knew what Laura was thinking! Did she connect her family's settler saga to the legacy of the war? Was she memorizing the names and dates of battles for her teaching examination? What I have been thinking about the war comes from Paul Gilje's suggestion that "without the War of 1812 there would have been no Civil War." Granted, he was unwilling to push his point quite that far, but I wish he had.[28]

One of the reasons I like teaching the War of 1812 is because it opens up such great counterfactual provocations. My own particular counterfactual slant on the war has to do

[26] On the eighteenth-century origins of the culture of imperialistic patriotism in Pennsylvania, see Nicole Eustace, *Passion Is the Gale: Emotion, Power, and the Coming of the American Revolution* (Chapel Hill, 2008); Peter Silver, *Our Savage Neighbors: How Indian War Transformed Early America* (New York, 2007); and Jane Merritt, *At the Crossroads: Indians and Empires on a Mid-Atlantic Frontier, 1700–1763* (Chapel Hill, 2007).

[27] On "mission accomplished," see "President Bush Announces Major Combat Operations in Iraq Have Ended," May 1, 2003, speech, *The White House,* www.whitehouse.gov/news/releases/2003/05/20030501-15.html.

[28] Laura Ingalls Wilder, *Little Town on the Prairie* (New York, 1941), 236.

with its end. So much of the war's impact and remembrance hinges on the circumstances of its final days. In short order, news of the Treaty of Ghent, the Battle of New Orleans, and the report of the Hartford Convention reached the U.S. capital—a perfect storm that cemented the war hawks' hold on American culture while delegitimizing the antisouthern, antiexpansionist, antiwar opposition. If these events had been more staggered in time, if the peace treaty had taken another season to seal, if the British had succeeded in capturing New Orleans, if the demands of the Hartford Convention had circulated within a nation still burdened by an ongoing unpopular war, how differently might American history have progressed? In other words, accepting no change to the timeline between June 1812 and November 1814, is it possible to amend Paul's claim to read "without *the end of* the War of 1812 there would have been no Civil War"? Could a secessionist movement have taken hold in the spring of 1815 if the Treaty of Ghent had not been signed? Could the loss of New Orleans have definitively delegitimized the position of the war hawks and led to a more geographically restricted American republic in the post-1815 era? Could a shift in the balance of power away from the war hawks have limited the expansion of slave power and led to a negotiated abolition of slavery (as in the British Empire)?[29]

OPAL: It is a commonplace in American historiography that the War of 1812 brought about or encouraged a new, more assertive form of nationalism in the United States. In his massive synthesis of American democracy, for example, Sean Wilentz devotes a chapter to nationalism and the War of 1812. What the word "nationalism" conceals and implies is frustratingly vague and even misleading, so let me suggest two ways we might unpack the commonplace. First, certain printers and newspapers, perhaps most notably Hezekiah Niles's *Niles Weekly Register,* were crucial in announcing that a new national feeling had been born, and that anyone who did not share in those feelings was something less than American. Niles published about nationalism precisely in terms of emotion, describing how a larger national self felt insulted, angry, and righteous. Such publications also blurred the chronology of events that led to the war's end, suggesting, for example, that Jackson's victory at the Battle of New Orleans had led to the Treaty of Ghent. I do not think we should underestimate the extent to which particular persons and publications created narratives and formed public opinion rather than the other way around. Second, when discussing nationalism we could all benefit from a bit of comparative political science and sociology. Nationalism relies on some new articulation of an "other" against which an imagined community can be contrived or perceived. It seems to me, as well, that some forms of nationalism imbue a given plot of earth with special or semidivine meaning. The nationalism that came out of the War of 1812 certainly valued and valorized American soil as something to be defended from foreign attack, but it seems positively opposed to any territorial limit, oriented instead to a personal and communal right to expand across western geographies and global markets. To the extent that

---

[29] The Treaty of Ghent is covered in most histories of the War of 1812, but has not received much independent attention. See, for example, Donald R. Hickey, *The War of 1812: A Forgotten Conflict* (Urbana, 1989), 281–99. Views on the Hartford Convention include Theodore Dwight, *History of the Hartford Convention with a Review of the Policy of the United States Government, which Led to the War of 1812* (New York, 1833); James Banner, *To the Harford Convention: The Federalists and the Origins of Party Politics in Massachusetts, 1789–1815* (Boston, 1970); and Sean Wilentz, *The Rise of American Democracy: Jefferson to Lincoln* (New York, 2005).

the war was about the rise of a militant settler/frontier nationalism, it seems to me to be about the conquest of land not by the political community or the state but by individuals in rebellion against the state—by people, such as Jackson, who were always willing to organize and initiate violence without any authorization other than their own.[30]

GILJE: Let me add to the list another important and often-overlooked impact of the War of 1812. Traditionally, the war has been viewed as a watershed moment in American foreign policy, marking a major change in direction. Before the war, so the old argument went, the United States faced the Atlantic Ocean and was consumed with diplomatic problems connected to conflicts in Europe. Impressment and neutral rights transfixed American diplomats, and the war in many ways was fought to solve these issues. The Treaty of Ghent, however, ignored these issues and merely established *in statu quo ante bellum*. Likewise, the peace also meant the end to American hopes for expansion into Canada. This peace that changed nothing, again following the old line of thinking, also changed everything. Without war in Europe, neutral rights and impressment were nonissues. If the invasions of Canada failed, the United States could do an about-face into Texas and move on to the Pacific Ocean. Americans even proclaimed a protective umbrella for the entire Western Hemisphere in the Monroe Doctrine. It made a great story. Unfortunately, it was not true. The War of 1812 did not mark a major turning point and redirection of American foreign policy. Instead—and herein lies an important and overlooked significance—it marked the success of the Atlantic foreign policy goals that had been pursued since the American Revolution. Those goals were the protection of neutral rights and the establishment of reciprocal trade agreements (often lumped together under the rubric of free trade), and the safeguarding of its citizenry from impressment—or in the catch phrase of the era, sailors' rights.[31]

In every treaty the United States negotiated in the antebellum era, the diplomats sought to include some provisions that would guarantee the rights of neutrals to trade with belligerents unmolested by the warring parties. Sometimes they were successful and sometimes less so. More importantly, in March 1815 Congress passed a bill that declared that it was American policy to seek reciprocal trade agreements—in which merchants from each signatory country would be treated equally in terms of import duties and tonnage duties.[32]

That measure, the proclaimed goal of John Adams's Model Treaty of 1776, would change the way the world would do business and has become standard in international trade relations. No sooner had the United States established this policy by law than a reciprocal agreement was included in the commercial accord with Great Britain called the Convention of 1815 (which should be considered an extension of the Treaty of Ghent). The reciprocal provision of the convention was renewed in subsequent agreements with Great Britain, and during the 1820s and 1830s it became embedded in every major trade accord signed by the United States. In other words, the War of 1812

---

[30] Wilentz, *Rise of American Democracy,* 141–78.

[31] On the Treaty of Ghent as a turning point in American diplomatic history, see Thomas A. Bailey, *A Diplomatic History of the American People* (New York, 1969), 163; Samuel Flagg Bemis, *A Diplomatic Story of the United States* (New York, 1965), 179; Dangerfield, *Era of Good Feelings,* 105; and George Dangerfield, *The Awakening of American Nationalism, 1815–1828* (New York, 1965), 1.

[32] Act of March 3, 1815, 3 Stat. 229 (1815).

marks the triumph of revolutionary-era American trade policy—a policy that persists to this day.[33]

Likewise, American diplomats may have walked away from impressment while patching together the peace at Ghent, but before the end of 1815 they were pushing the British for a settlement on the issue. Although impressment was excluded from the Convention of 1815, American diplomats continued to raise the issue into the 1840s. By that time, although the British still refused to concede officially their so-called right to search American ships, the Royal Navy had long given up the idea that it could forcefully recruit British subjects from American ships. My point here is twofold. The United States did not surrender its prewar foreign policy goals concerning trade and impressment to turn around and concentrate on expansion. Thus the War of 1812 does not represent a break with the past whereby the United States ignored the Atlantic and concentrated on North America. Yet this corrective to an older interpretation does not alter the significance of the war: it remains a crucial watershed in American history because it marked the successful implementation of revolutionary diplomacy.

HALE: I am intrigued by Paul's ideas regarding the War of 1812 and the evolution of American foreign policy, yet I am somewhat skeptical. Specifically, my sense is that Paul's story fails to take into account critical conceptual changes regarding the law of nations. As various scholars have argued, the American Revolution and subsequent events helped propel a shift in the law of nations from naturalism to positivism. The mere assertion of American independence prompted—perhaps not initially but by the mid-1780s—new ways of thinking about international recognition, statehood, and the idea of international law itself. Equally critical to the shift from naturalism to positivism was popular elite advocacy of the Constitution as a new form of federal union that would not only enable the American states to harmonize intrastate relations and protect citizens' rights and interests but would also enable them to act more energetically in an international world that was purportedly (ideally) becoming more rational, stable, and civilized. Hopes for a new and improved Vattelian world were completely demolished, however, on the rocks of the French Revolution and Napoleonic rule. To be sure, visionary Republicans such as Joel Barlow continued well into the 1790s to advocate for a utopian reformulation of European diplomacy along the lines of the American federal system. Increasingly, however, leading Republicans eschewed visions of a new world order and instead promoted neutral maritime rights as a means of securing American sovereignty and union. Secretary of State James Madison's relatively moderate efforts to curb British commercial abuses were accordingly based not on natural rights but on well-established legal principles. Madison's attempts failed, of course, and in 1812 as president he led the country into war. The emphasis on neutral rights and trade agreements in the 1810s and 1820s may seem like the fulfillment of American revolutionary diplomatic principles, but in many ways it represented a wholesale transformation of those

---

[33] On John Adams's Model Treaty, see Felix Gilbert, *To the Farewell Address: Ideas of Early American Foreign Policy* (1961; Princeton, 1970); and Vernon G. Setser, *The Commercial Reciprocity Policy of the United States, 1774–1829* (Philadelphia, 1937). On the Convention of 1815, see Hunter Miller, ed., *Treaties and Other International Acts of the United States of America* (8 vols., Washington, 1932), II, 595–600.

principles. Rather than forging a path for American revolutionary internationalism, the War of 1812 helped clear a path for liberal positivism.[34]

JAH: **As many have noted, a key issue that came up on many fronts during the War of 1812 was that of citizenship. Another was the rise of nationalism. To what degree were these developments intertwined? How did a culture of nationalism shape ideas about citizenship and, conversely, how did debates about the boundaries of citizenship delimit the character of American and Canadian nationalism? What role did race and gender play in defining these concerns?**

HALE: Before we think about the relationship between nationalism and citizenship, I think we should return to Jason's skeptical comment about the rise of American nationalism during the War of 1812 era. As he notes, and as David Waldstreicher made clear fifteen years ago, many individuals in the early republic tried to create a particular version of national spirit by celebrating in print and ritual a new and purportedly common feeling of nationalism. But that does not necessarily mean that nationalism was weak in the three decades between 1780 and 1810 nor does it mean that nationalism was on the rise during and in the aftermath of the War of 1812. I wonder how we would measure something like the rise of American nationalism in this era. Do we attempt to quantify the usage of terms such as *nationalism, nation,* and *America*? Even if it could be shown that there was an increase in references to certain words traditionally associated with nationalism, that would not necessarily mean that there was a rise in nationalism. It could instead mean that the idea of the nation was increasingly contested, ambiguous, and fluid—especially in the world of print. It could mean that sectional attempts to shape the nation in the image of a particular region were on the rise. Or it could mean that partisan attempts to manipulate the language of nationalism were on the rise.[35]

As Jason argued, we need to do a better job of contextualizing nationalism and delineating its historical evolution. One possible subject for research—and one that is quite obvious when talking about the War of 1812—is the emergence of the postrevolutionary generation. Historians have often written about that cohort and the challenge it faced in terms of following its American revolutionary predecessor, but they have not always done a good job of thinking about the particular formative experiences of those who never really knew King George III as their sovereign. In that vein, it might be fruitful to think about the ways the "big" events of the 1790s and early 1800s—including the rise of party and newspaper politics; the French Revolution and Napoleonic rule; wars with Native Americans and Barbary corsairs; the expansion of slavery; alterations to family life, sensibility, and republicanism; and the War of 1812—helped shape the postrevolutionary generation's understanding and practice of American nationalism. My sense is that large numbers of postrevolutionary Americans articulated a view that war alone was

---

[34] David Armitage, "The Declaration of Independence and International Law," *William and Mary Quarterly,* 59 (Jan. 2002), 39–64; Peter Onuf and Nicholas Onuf, *Federal Union, Modern World: The Law of Nations in an Age of Revolutions, 1776–1814* (Madison, 1993). On James Madison's shift to liberal positivism, see Onuf and Onuf, *Federal Union, Modern World,* 201–20.

[35] David Waldstreicher, *In the Midst of Perpetual Fetes: The Making of American Nationalism, 1776–1820* (Chapel Hill, 1997).

the realm in which national spirit and character could be forged. Perhaps, in that regard, it is not coincidental that a postrevolutionary American—Francis Scott Key—wrote a somewhat gory war anthem that celebrated not only the Battle of Fort McHenry but also the divine "power that hath made and preserved us a nation!"[36]

CLEVES: Let me contribute another skeptical note to our discussion of the significance of the War of 1812. Alan argues that American and Canadian nationalisms solidified in the context and in the aftermath of the war, but I would like to point out that understandings of American-Canadian differences in the postwar era also had significant continuities with constructions of those differences in the prenational past. Prior to the American Revolution, Anglo colonists differentiated their societies from the French colonies to the north largely on the basis of religion and morality. According to New Englanders in particular, Puritanism had laid the basis for sound morals in their colonies that contrasted sharply with the moral licentiousness of the French Catholics (and indigenous converts) to the north. The moral failings of the Canadians were further conflated in the colonial imagination with the northerners' material poverty—seen as the consequence of their insufficient spiritual and physical discipline.[37]

During the nineteenth century, as Québécois traveled south to New England in pursuit of wage labor, New Englanders met the migrants with a nationalist hostility that bore the distinct imprints of their prenational past. Laura Ingalls's writing can again be used to illustrate some of the sentiment. The volume in her series of books that describes the upbringing of her future husband, Almanzo Wilder, in upstate New York during the 1860s and 1870s includes a set of French Canadian characters named Lazy John and French Joe, who "had no farms," "sang and joked and danced," and liked to drink "red wine instead of cider."[38] Poverty and licentiousness seem to be the distinguishing characteristics of (French) Canadians in the American mind.

I did finally discover Laura's thoughts about the War of 1812 in *Little Town on the Prairie*. She gives the following narrative during a school exhibition in 1882: "Next came Madison, the war of 1812, the invasion, the defeat, the burning of the Capitol and the White House in Washington, the brave sea-battles fought by American sailors on America's few ships, and at last the victory that finally won independence."[39] I wonder how significantly this narrative has shifted during the past 130 years. When we talk about emerging nationalism, are we still talking about that "finally won independence" by another name?

MORGAN: Even if we consider the shaping of nationalist sentiments and attachments to be an ongoing process, I think it fair to say that the war simply did not play the same role in, for example, New Brunswick, Nova Scotia, where narratives of the Loyalists were more influential and prominent in discussions of patriotism, and certainly not in Quebec, which throughout the nineteenth century (and well into the twentieth century)

[36] The historiography of the "revolutionary generation" includes Steven J. Novak, *The Rights of Youth: American Colleges and Student Revolts, 1798–1815* (Cambridge, Mass., 1977); and Glenn Wallach, *Obedient Sons: The Discourse of Youth and Generations in American Culture, 1630–1680* (Amherst, 1997). Francis Scott Key, "Defense of Fort McHenry."

[37] Taylor, *Civil War of 1812*, 458.

[38] Laura Ingalls Wilder, *Farmer Boy* (New York, 1933), 67.

[39] Wilder, *Little Town on the Prairie*, 195.

displayed great ambivalence and at times hostility to the British Empire and the kind of English-Canadian nationalism that was linked to it. To be sure, in English-speaking Canada well into the twentieth century, school textbooks were often written and published in Ontario and distributed across the country from that province so that the story of the War of 1812 as a defense against American aggression and a vindication of ties to empire and Canada was widely disseminated. Whether this narrative had meaning for those in the western provinces or British Columbia is another question, although patterns of mid-nineteenth-century migration within Canada (for example, from Ontario to the West) might have helped shape particular families' and communities' constructs of nationalism. (Such a question, to the best of my knowledge, has yet to be explored.)

I would argue that at this point in our understanding of the war and Canadian nationalism, it is in Upper Canada/Canada West/Ontario that memory played a prominent role in definitions of nationalism. Certainly Ontario's commemorations of the war—whether of particular battles or of individuals—proliferated in the late nineteenth and early twentieth centuries, culminating in the war's centenary; there really was not an equivalent flurry of commemorative activities in the other Canadian provinces. To some extent this came about because Ontario could claim particular sites and events—such as Queenston Heights, Lundy's Lane, Moraviantown, the burning of Niagara—as places where, commemorators claim, the war was most intimately and traumatically experienced. Yet, as we know, public memory is selective: the creation of particular historical narratives, their rise to prominence within concepts of nationalism, and the silencing or forgetting of other narratives is not just a feature of what happened or of physical proximity to historic sites. The celebration of the War of 1812 as a triumph of English Canadian nationalism was also shaped by an ongoing nineteenth-century discourse of loyalty to Britain in Ontario society, sharpened and made more pressing by late Victorian-period and Edwardian-period imperialism. It is no coincidence, for example, that commemorating the War of 1812 became popular at the same time that English Canadians (many of them in Ontario) were celebrating Canada's involvement in the South African War (1899–1902).[40]

I am intrigued by the thought that the war's initial impact on concepts of loyalty was not just the result of the resurgence of imperialism. I wonder if celebrating military valor—especially as tied to masculinity—might be seen as a continuity in English Canadian and, especially, in Ontario history, starting with the commemorations of Isaac Brock in the war's aftermath and continuing with the arrival of a number of British half-pay officers (officers who were retired or not in active service) in Upper Canada in the 1830s and 1840s, local militia support for the government in the rebellions of 1837–1838, resistance to the Fenian raids in 1866, and the enthusiasm with which Ontario men joined the expedition to suppress the Riel resistance (also known as the Northwest Rebellion) of 1885.[41]

[40] On the intimate and traumatic experiencing of 1812 events, see Janet Carnochan, *History of Niagara* (Toronto, 1914). On English Canadian imperialist thought during the War of 1812 era, see Carl Berger, *The Sense of Power: Studies in the Ideas of Canadian Imperialism, 1867–1914* (Toronto, 1970); and Carman Millar, *Painting the Map Red: Canada and the South African War, 1899–1902* (Montreal, 1997).

[41] On the rebellions of 1837–1838, see Colin Read, *The Rebellion of 1837 in Upper Canada* (Ottawa, 1988). On Fenian's raid of 1866, see Brian Clarke, *Piety and Nationalism: Lay Voluntary Associations and the Creation of an Irish-Catholic Community in Toronto, 1850–1895* (Montreal, 1993), 188, 194–97, 200, 202. On the Riel resistance, see Olive Patricia Dickason with David T. McNab, *Canada's First Nations: A History of Founding Peoples*

I am particularly interested in the ways participation in 1812 became part of family histories, told and repeated within the realms of domesticity and intimacy so that, in addition to public commemorations and school texts, familial memory also fed into narratives of masculine heroism and nationalistic endeavor. How did supposedly distinct sites—the family and warfare—potentially reinforce each other? One such example is the Merritt family. William Hamilton Merritt, a St. Catharines, Ontario, businessman and a major force behind the building of the Welland Canal, was a young militia member in 1812; his descendants went on to fight for the government in western Canada in 1885 and in South Africa. One of his female descendants, Helen Merritt, was a staunch imperialist, English Canadian nationalist, patriotic playwright and songwriter, and a member of a women's rifle club in Toronto.[42]

I am speculating here, since there is very little scholarship on the social and cultural role of the military in British North America or in nineteenth-century Canada. It is telling that a recent and significant collection of essays on the importance of liberalism in nineteenth- and early twentieth-century Canada does not mention the War of 1812. However, the history of commemoration in English Canada suggests that there was a certain amount of enthusiasm for remembering these events: for example, the monuments that were erected to the repulsion of the Fenian raids and the tributes paid to Canadians' involvement in the events of 1885 and the South African War.[43]

OPAL: This discussion puts to rest any doubts I ever had about the value of cross-border comparative analysis, especially when exploring nationalism and citizenship. I agree that a key component of this "new" nationalism was the open embrace of military glory. As Matthew has shown, this marked a qualitative change from the neostoic, republican traditions of the revolutionary era. I also think that the popular and official description of the United States as a long-suffering victim of European intrigue and Native American brutality—echoed in newspapers, presidential addresses, grand jury presentments, patriotic letters to John Adams in 1798 and James Madison in 1812—enabled a new kind of nationalism rooted in vengeance against the rest of the world rather than membership in the "civilized world." That emphasis made possible a new vision of the nation, or union, as a kind of frontier household, writ large, utterly exposed and engaged in heroic violence against unspeakable foes all around and against the natural world. That strikes me as quite new and somewhat distinctive to the United States (although the works of Lisa Ford and Elizabeth Elbourne provide comparisons with Australia and South Africa) and directly linked to the War of 1812. Residents were now citizens not only because of their white skin, American birth, and Protestant religion but also because of their role in a

from Earliest Times (New York, 2009); Blair Stonechild and Bill Waiser, *Loyal Till Death: Indians and the North-West Rebellion* (Calgary, 1997); and J. R. Miller, *Skyscrapers Hide the Heavens: A History of Indian-White Relations in Canada* (Toronto, 1991).

[42] On the Merritt family, see J. J. Talman, "Merritt, William Hamilton," in *Dictionary of Canadian Biography*, ed. Jean Hamelin and Francess G. Halpenny, (19 vols., Toronto, 1976), IX, 544–48.

[43] Jean-François Constant and Michel Ducharme, eds., *Liberalism and Hegemony: Debating the Canadian Liberal Revolution* (Toronto, 2009); Shipley, *To Mark Our Place*; Millar, *Painting the Map Red*; Sarah Carter, *Capturing Women: The Manipulation of Cultural Imagery in Canada's Prairie West* (Montreal, 1997).

historical epic in which virtuous settlers endured injury and insult before finally avenging themselves, God-like, on their enemies.[44]

GILJE: One of our problems as historians is that we have a tendency to examine the concepts of nationalism and citizenship as constants. In the context of the early nineteenth century, however, both ideas were still developing. As such, the War of 1812 marked an important signpost in the evolution of American nationalism and citizenship.

It is difficult to discuss any real sense of nationalism as the American Revolution began, especially since that conflict had so many of the earmarks of a civil war. Once the new nations—the government under the Articles of Confederation had merely loosely united the states together to fight a war—gained independence, the idea of a singular nation began to coalesce. This cohesion was a process built on a shared ideology and vocabulary that emphasized words such as *republic, liberty,* and (sometimes) *equality.* Whatever individual religions were espoused by Americans (as we can start to call the people of the United States at that time), they all joined in a civil religion even as they debated how that civil religion would be manifested in the political arena. The creation of the U.S. Constitution represented another step in this direction, as did the politics of the 1790s and early 1800s, and as Matthew has suggested, as did the various conflicts with the British, French, Barbary states, and Native Americans. The War of 1812 fits into this narrative not as just another marker but also as a major milestone since the nation almost did not survive the conflict and the last remnants of the Federalist party, which seemed to be denying aspects of the shared anti-British experience, was all but wiped out. The role of the second generation of Americans in facing the test of the war was also important in this process. Nationalism may not have ruled the day in 1815, 1826, 1840, or 1848 (and it certainly did not in 1861), but it had evolved toward its nineteenth-century form within the United States.

Citizenship, too, was in a state of transition during the late eighteenth and early nineteenth centuries. In 1776 Americans occasionally used the term. By 1787 they used it frequently enough for it to be mentioned in the Constitution. No one at the Philadelphia constitutional convention bothered to define it, however. (The term would not be defined until the creation of the Fourteenth Amendment after the Civil War.) Only in the 1790s, inspired by the French Revolution, did the word emerge as central to American parlance. However frequently used and important the concept of citizen had become when Thomas Jefferson was sworn in as president in 1801, it was also a contested idea. The Federalist party clung to older British ideas about subjecthood (an awkward neologism, but one that gets to the point), whereby birth dictated national allegiance. Many Federalists argued that naturalization did not erase earlier obligations to the British crown and that the British had a right to claim the service of those who had been born in Great Britain and who were not in North America at the time of the Revolution. The Republicans disagreed and asserted that individuals could choose through immigration and naturalization to become "citizens" of the United States and be protected by the flag. By

---

[44] Lisa Ford, *Settler Sovereignty: Jurisdiction and Indigenous Peoples in America and Australia, 1788–1836* (Cambridge, Mass., 2010); Elizabeth Elbourne, *Blood Ground: Colonialism, Missions, and the Contest for Christianity in the Cape Colony and Britain, 1799–1853* (Montreal, 2002).

1796 the issue had become important enough to lead to the passage of the Seamen's Protection Act and, of course, it lay at the heart of the debate over impressment.[45]

Here the War of 1812 was central. Once that conflict broke out, the only agreed-upon cause after the British repealed the Orders in Council in June 1812 was impressment and the ability of the American flag to protect its citizens—including those who were naturalized. As it turns out, Madison ultimately was willing to abandon those rights to gain peace. By the end of 1814, however, as the Republicans noted, the issue had become moot with the defeat of Napoleon Bonaparte at the Battle of Nations in the War of the Sixth Coalition. Even so, Republicans did not forget about impressment at the end of the War of 1812. By the summer of 1815 the former secretary of the treasury Albert Gallatin and Speaker of the House of Representatives Henry Clay were pushing the issue in their negotiations over a commercial agreement, and impressment would emerge almost every time the British and American diplomats negotiated anything for the next thirty years. For all intents and purposes, the British never impressed another sailor from an American ship after the war.[46]

The question also asks about gender and race. As far as I know, the War of 1812 did not speak to the relationship between citizenship and gender, although I can imagine that women participated in the sense of national identification that was strengthened by the war. There is some evidence, however, concerning race. After the passing of the Seamen's Protection Act, African American and European Americans received certificates of citizenship from the government. Although I have not seen any specific evidence concerning how blacks viewed these documents, the fact that so many—perhaps thousands—were given a piece of paper stating that they were Americans must have had some impact on the way they viewed themselves as citizens. Once the War of 1812 broke out, African Americans fought on both sides. During the British incursions into the Chesapeake Bay region many African American slaves ran to the British to gain their freedom. Blacks fought on both sides in the other southern campaigns. There were also African American sailors serving on American and British ships in the war. At Dartmoor Prison in Princetown, England, African American prisoners of war were segregated into their own prison building, but that prison also became the center of entertainment for whites and blacks there. Many years later, abolitionist newspapers occasionally mentioned the sacrifices of African American sailors in opposing the British in the War of 1812. The evidence that I have seen is scant, but it suggests that the issue of impressment and the War of 1812 had some impact on American blacks, enhancing the sense of citizenship and nationalism for some and weakening it for others.[47]

An extensive and complex literature has been developed on race and gender in the early republic. How, then, do we fit the War of 1812 into this literature? The story of gender is multilayered as both male and female gender roles underwent dramatic changes in the United States (and elsewhere) from the eighteenth to the nineteenth centuries.

[45] "An Act for the Protection and Relief of American Seamen" 1 Stat. 477 (1796).

[46] "The Acts, Orders in Council, &c. of Great Britain [on Trade], 1793–1812," *American State Papers: Documents, Legislative and Executive, of the Congress of the United States,* vol. I: *Foreign Relations* (Washington, 1832), http://www.napoleon-series.org/research/government/british/decrees/c_britdecrees1.html.

[47] James Fulton Zimmerman, *Impressment of American Seamen* (Port Washington, 1966), 56–57, 68, 80–81; W. Jeffrey Bolster, *Black Jacks: African-American Seamen in the Age of Sail* (Cambridge, Mass., 1997), 102–30. For instances of African Americans discussing notions of citizenship thirty years after the war, see *Emancipator,* Dec. 1, 1842, March 9, 1843.

During the period of the early republic women who clung to older notions of more open sexual activity were increasingly condemned as marginal and lower class, while the middle class became more closed—even repressive—sexually. In short, Anglo-Americans moved from the world of Daniel Defoe and *Moll Flanders* to the world of Louisa May Alcott and *Little Women*. Simultaneously, there was an increasing sentimentalization of women's role in society—a sentimentalization that had an impact on both male and female gender identities. What I would like to see is a study that addresses these transformations in relation to the War of 1812. About twenty years ago I read a letter written to a sailor's sister by an American prisoner of war in Jamaica. The writer dripped with sentiment even while cockroaches scampered across his page. This source, and others like it, would be a good place to begin a study of this kind.[48]

Likewise, there is a great deal that can be said about race in the War of 1812. Few subjects have attracted more scholarly attention in the last forty years than the history of race and slavery. Scholars have demonstrated that the American Revolution had a huge impact on both areas: many African Americans seized the opportunity of the war to gain their freedom, both white and black Americans trumpeted the cause of liberty, and legislatures and courts set in motion emancipation in the North and manumissions in the South. During the early republic, however, southerners became increasingly committed to their peculiar institution and pushed a racial explanation of slavery. Northern society, where most African Americans had gained their freedom by 1830, also became more racist as expressed through limited economic opportunities for blacks and vicious race riots perpetrated by whites. These changes have been well studied, but there has been little done to place the War of 1812 into this larger narrative. Instead we have little snippets of stories about black activity during the war. Thus, as had occurred during the American Revolution, the British offered freedom to slaves who joined their ranks in the Chesapeake region. Further south, some blacks escaped to Florida and established a safe haven at the so-called Negro fort that American troops destroyed after the war ended. Blacks formed part of the hodgepodge army under Andrew Jackson at the Battle of New Orleans, and many African Americans fought for both the British and the Americans during the war, but there has been little discussion about what all this meant. Most of the standard histories of race and slavery seem to jump over the war as if nothing important happened.[49]

Historians have written extensively on race in Indian-white relations vis a vis the War of 1812. If Patrick Griffin and others are correct, hardened racial attitudes between Native Americans and European Americans reached a point of intense hostility during the War of 1812. Despite later European American views of Tecumseh as a noble Indian defending his "declining" race, several American soldiers at the battle of the Thames, where Tecumseh was killed, claimed to have skinned and tanned his dead corpse, using the strands of human skin as mementos of the war. This gruesome keepsake must

---

[48] Daniel Defoe, *Moll Flanders* (London, 1721); Louisa May Alcott, *Little Women* (Boston, 1868); "A Sailor Prisoner of War during the War of 1812," *Maryland Historical Magazine*, 85 (Spring 1990), 58–72.

[49] Leon F. Litwack, *North of Slavery: The Negro in the Free States, 1790–1860* (Chicago, 1961); Gary B. Nash, *Forging Freedom: The Formation of Philadelphia's Black Community, 1720–1840* (Cambridge, Mass., 1988); Gilje, *Rioting in America;* Robert L. Anderson, "The End of an Idyll," *Florida Historical Quarterly*, 42 (July 1963), 35–47; Frank Lawrence Owsley Jr. and Gene A. Smith, *Filibusters and Expansionists: Jeffersonian Manifest Destiny, 1800–1821* (Tuscaloosa, 1997), 103–17.

certainly represent a watershed in ongoing racial attitudes that left a deep and unfortunate legacy for the rest of the nineteenth century.[50]

MORGAN: I mentioned the possibility that the memory of the war might have intersected with particular constructs and performances of masculinity for men in Upper Canada, particularly those with lived experiences and/or family histories of the war—a point about which I must be speculative. However, Upper Canadian women's position vis a vis the war is also worth mentioning. Not surprisingly, these women were not only victims of the war, but some were also active supporters of the British: making and presenting banners to the York militia, demonstrating direct support for troops involved in battles or skirmishes around homesteads, helping male family members evade American patrols, and, in Laura Secord's case, passing on information. Some of their activities resembled those of the British women studied by Linda Colley in the Napoleonic Wars. Yet at war's end and in the decades following there was little or no public discussion of women's contributions to the British cause. For example, there is no female figure of patriotic and loyal discourse in Upper Canada who might in any way have been a counterpart to the "republican mother" (even in a conservative way). Even so, by the late Victorian period a number of historians of women, such as the prominent British-born Canadian women's rights campaigner Sarah Curzon, turned to women's participation in the War of 1812 and particularly to Secord as examples of female patriotism and loyalty that justified the expansion of civil society to white, middle-class women. Even those women who were not particularly interested in their own enfranchisement looked to the war—and narratives of pioneers and Loyalists—as examples of women's sacrifices and contributions to the (British) Canadian nation.[51]

Although members of the Haudenosaunee (Six Nations) along with other aboriginal allies can, I think, be described as having lost the most in the war, the memory of the conflict (and its relation to concepts of citizenship and nationalism) is persistent among various members of the community. Such remembrance is far from a straightforward process, given the government's increasing exclusion of aboriginal peoples from concepts of Canadian nationalism and, eventually, citizenship. Even so, delegations from the Six Nations showed up at gatherings of the Ontario Historical Society in the 1890s and early 1900s and at 1912 commemorative ceremonies of the war to insist that their participation as allies be remembered. That discourse persisted into the twentieth century and made the case for natives' civic participation and for their treatment as a sovereign nation (or, at the very least, for not subjecting them to Indian agents' surveillance and supervision).[52]

---

[50] Patrick Griffin, *American Leviathan: Empire, Nation, and Revolutionary Frontier* (New York, 2007). On what was done to Tecumseh's body after the Battle of the Thames, see R. David Edmunds, *Tecumseh and the Quest for Indian Leadership* (Boston, 1984), 214–17; and Donald R. Hickey, *Don't Give Up the Ship: Myths of the War of 1812* (Urbana, 2006), 68.

[51] Linda Colley, *Britons: Forging the Nation, 1707–1837* (New Haven, 1992). On republican motherhood, see Linda K. Kerber, *Women of the Republic: Intellect and Ideology in Revolutionary America* (Chapel Hill, 1980); and Linda K. Kerber, *No Constitutional Right to Be Ladies: Women and the Obligations of Citizenship* (New York, 1988). Sarah Curzon, *The Story of Laura Secord* (Welland, 1895).

[52] On the Six Nations presence in War of 1812 commemoration ceremonies, see Michelle A. Hamilton, *Collections and Objections: Aboriginal Material Culture in Southern Ontario* (Montreal, 2010); and Cecilia Morgan, "History and the Six Nations: The Dynamics of Commemoration, Colonial Space, and Colonial Knowledge," in *Placing Memory and Remembering Place in Canada* (Vancouver, 2010), 57–80.

EUSTACE: It is not clear that there is any a point at which we can say "nationalism ruled the day" in the United States any time before the close of the Civil War. This is an argument that has recently been made powerfully and persuasively by Trish Loughran. From the Revolution to the Civil War, the "united" states were united in name only; they were divided not only by sectionalism and political factionalism but also along lines of race, class, and gender. While scholars have often written as if the creation of a unified national identity was a clear goal sought (if not met) by inhabitants of the early United States, we need to reconsider all the ways that national divisions were deliberate and desired in early America.[53]

This is where the intersection of citizenship and nationalism becomes quite interesting. Before the American Revolution, all the inhabitants of British North America—regardless of race, sex, class, or age, and irrespective of any other ties of identification or affiliation—were considered subjects of the British Crown, a status that was not retractable. As the work of Jenny Hale Pulsipher has recently highlighted, Indians understood this notion of equal subjection to the Crown, and they sought to turn it to their advantage. Yet with the creation of the United States, a new form of affiliation—national citizenship—emerged: a consensual and contractual status determined less by birth than by allegiance. Paradoxically, subjecthood (which was coerced) was universal, whereas citizenship (which was volitional) was restricted, largely to adult white male property owners. One of the distinguishing features and confounding factors of early American nationalism, then, was that it rested on a model of political participation that did as much to limit affiliation as to encourage identification.[54]

In my current work to understand the emotional basis of American patriotism during the War of 1812, I have found far fewer calls for brotherly love to inspire love of country than claims that the romantic ardor of American men and women would spur them to support the nation. Whereas brotherly love has been defined by Benedict Anderson and understood by many to invoke "horizontal comradeship," romantic love has more ambiguous political overtones. On the one hand, free choice in marriage related to ideals of democratic political consent in the early American republic. On the other hand, just as early nineteenth-century marriages did not make equals of husbands and wives, so a patriotic rhetoric based on romantic love did not promise all members of the population the opportunity to participate in the nation on an equal basis.[55]

While nationalism is often said to require a unified sense of identity, it may also proceed from a more easily achieved—and more readily restricted—commitment to joint action. In searching for the emotions of early American nationalism, then, we might do well to focus less on those emotions that are supposed to advance the formation of "identity" and more on those that might enhance instrumentality. In the United States in 1812, the nation needed to draw strength from the actions of its entire population, but its leaders

---

[53] Trish Loughran, *The Republic in Print: Print Culture in the Age of U.S. Nation Building, 1770–1870*. An example of work suggesting that the development of U.S. nationalism required the creation of a unified identity is Joyce Oldham Appleby, Lynn Avery Hunt, and Margaret C. Jacob, *Telling the Truth about History* (New York, 1995), esp. 93–94.

[54] Jenny Hale Pulsipher, *Subjects unto the Same King: Indians, English, and the Contest for Authority in Colonial New England* (Philadelphia, 2006).

[55] On Benedict Anderson's concept of brotherly love versus the American emphasis on patriotic romance, see Eustace, *1812*, 52, 238n7, 258n48; and Benedict Anderson, *Imagined Communities: Reflections on the Origin and Spread of Nationalism* (London, 1991), 7, 154.

neither needed nor desired to grant every member of the populace the same kind of status. All Americans were not citizens; in this way, their unity was sharply limited. Yet by acting cooperatively to support the country in an hour of crisis, they could coordinate their interests. Patriotism may arise from shared pursuits just as often as from shared personhood. Nothing makes this clearer than emotional calls for wartime mobilization.

By the era of 1812, American expansionists sought above all to foment military action: to force Indians to relinquish lingering territorial rights to the lands of the Great Lakes and the Mississippi basin and to compel the British to abandon all diplomatic and trading ties to American Indians. They needed, ultimately, to fuel lust for geographic gains. Quite conversant with the notion that there is an inherent connection between passion and action, Americans at the turn of the nineteenth century knew that they had to stoke longing before they could stake claim to new lands. It was no accident, then, that the love that underlay early American nationalism was an explicitly romantic kind that grew out of ordinary desires to create families and acquire farms.

JAH: **What do you think of the substitute titles for the War of 1812 (such as "the Second War of Independence" or "Mr. Madison's War")? Are there others worth considering for the second bicentennial?**

OPAL: Let me begin by posing a simple question: When did people (Americans? Canadians? Historians?) begin using substitute titles for the war? One of the big blank spots in my understanding of the period is how Americans came to recall the War of 1812 and other conflicts associated with it—especially the settler-Indian violence along the southwestern borderlands and the Florida invasion (also known as the First Seminole War) of 1818. Alan Taylor's *The Civil War of 1812* is a masterly book, and so I am tempted to say that the war should be named for the multisided conflict within and around the British Empire that it clearly was. I have been reading some of Andrew Jackson's messages to the Tennessee Volunteers in the spring of 1812, and they readily confirm what Alan stresses: impressment and the underlying theory of a subject's (or a colony's) lifelong loyalty was the heart of the matter, at least for those who led the war on the U.S. side. (It should also come as no surprise that these same messages soon evolve from enthusiastic war cries to disappointed finger wagging about desertion and prolonged absences from duty.) However, as Alan notes, the civil war paradigm works best for the northern borderlands where the bulk of the fighting took place. Indeed, in the spirit of splitting rather than lumping, I would stress how the fighting in the Southeast and the Gulf Coast region followed a very different trajectory, pitting Creek Indians against fellow speakers of Muskogee, Upper Creek towns against Lower Creek towns, and various American warlords (Jackson most prominently) against most natives and their occasional British and Spanish allies.[56]

So why not call the conflict "the Great Lakes War"? The war was between and within the republic and the empire, but the fighting was also about control of these bodies of water and their surrounding river valleys and basins. It was about which sovereigns or groups of sovereigns would control the passage of people and materials through the region and the use of water, timber, and soil around the Great Lakes. It ended, somewhat

---

[56] Taylor, *Civil War of 1812*; Andrew Jackson, "To the Second Division. March 7, 1812," in *The Papers of Andrew Jackson*, vol. II: *1804–1813* (Nashville, 1984), 290.

remarkably, with the hardening of national borders and the demilitarization of the dividing line. Naming the war by its geographical heartland would also disentangle it from the bloodshed far to the south, which, to my mind, is best named "the Creek Civil War" or "the Creek War." These conflicts shared what Americans claimed as the common denominator of victory: a second triumph over the British Empire and a new assurance not only of independence (the absence of external control) but also of sovereignty (supremacy and absolute freedom of choice, including the use of violence). They also shared what Americans, especially, came to remember as a second founding and a war of national unification.

CLEVES: I would argue that lumping serves us better because it reveals how the War of 1812 fits into a long historical trend: Wars between empires fought in North America have long been associated with simultaneous wars of expansion. For example, the Seven Years' War may have been an imperial conflict fought between France and England on American soil, but it was simultaneously a war of expansion waged by settlers in western Pennsylvania against the Delaware Indians. The Revolution likewise was a conflict between the new United States and Great Britain and simultaneously a war of expansion fought by western settlers against the Cherokee people in North Carolina. The fact that the War of 1812 was simultaneously a war between the United States and Great Britain and a settler war against the Creek nation in Alabama seems entirely in keeping with this tradition. I would argue that from the perspective of someone such as Col. James Smith, the author of *An Account of the Remarkable Occurrences in the Life and Travels of Col. James Smith During His Captivity with the Indians in the Years 1755–1759,* the imperial wars from 1755 onward blended together into one long settler war against a variety of native groups extending to the War of 1812 when Smith's role in the story ended with his death. Perhaps one way to express this relationship is by arguing that as the United States gained power through imperial wars, it increased its ability to displace native peoples from the frontiers.[57]

MORGAN: Being flippant, some Canadians tend to call the War of 1812 "the war nobody won," especially when trying to explain the conflict to visitors from outside Canada. Although I think that should be modified to "the war that some white folks sort of won but one that aboriginal people definitely lost." That name is less pithy and catchy, of course, but it is more honest.

Based on memory of my own research on the Upper Canadian press, in British North America use of "the War of 1812" emerged in the 1830s and 1840s (perhaps even earlier). David Thompson published *A History of the Late War between Great Britain and the United States of America* in 1832; ten years later the British military officer, journalist, and novelist John Richardson published in book form his newspaper articles about his war experiences as *John Richardson's War of 1812.* This may suggest the kind of naming of the war that I have seen in the middle of the nineteenth century and certainly thereafter.[58]

[57] James Smith, *An Account of the Remarkable Occurrences in the Life and Travels of Col. James Smith During His Captivity with the Indians in the Years 1755–1759* (Cincinnati, 1870).

[58] David Thompson, *A History of the Late War between Great Britain and the United States of America: with a Retrospective View of the Causes from Whence It Originated; Collected from the Most Authentic Sources. To which Is Added an Appendix, Containing Public Documents &c. Relating to the Subject* (Niagara, 1832); Alexander Clark Casselman, *John Richardson's War of 1812* (1842; Toronto, 1902).

HALE: I agree with Rachel that "the Great Lakes War," while compelling in certain ways, is, in the end, not a sufficiently encompassing moniker to characterize what we now call the War of 1812. One alternative name for the War of 1812 would be "the Napoleonic War in America." Placing the War of 1812 in an international context allows us to see links not only between what happened in the Great Lakes region and the American Southeast but also between American commercial activities in the Baltic Sea, diplomatic intrigue in London, and naval conflict off the coast of Valparaiso.

I am somewhat uncomfortable with the idea that the War of 1812 is best character-ized as a civil war, in large part because that concept implies to me a formal military conflict between different segments of one political-constitutional community. Denver Brunsman's 2010 article on impressment makes clear that the very existence of the American "nation-state provided the American people with an arsenal of new logistical and ideological tools for resisting British press gangs." Whereas Americans in the colonial era generally resisted the particular methods and economic rationale of impressment, Americans in the early national era resisted the very idea of impressment because they increasingly imagined, championed, and elaborated a distinct American national identity. What resulted was an enhanced emphasis on volitional citizenship, which points us back to the last discussion topic on the ways the War of 1812 intersected with debates about citizenship.[59]

Pondering the continuities and differences between British impressment in the colo-nial and early national eras leads us to the idea of the War of 1812 as "the Second War of Independence" because that title portrays the Anglo-centric orientation of many Americans and the ways they compared what happened in the 1810s with what hap-pened in the 1770s and 1780s. Another name that was used in the immediate aftermath of the war and another that indicates Americans' preoccupation with Britain was "the Late War," which Colin McCoy suggests was perhaps the most commonly used phrase. McCoy also provides an answer to Jason's question about when exactly the conflict became known—at least to Americans—as the War of 1812. According to McCoy, the label was used as early as 1816, but it did not take hold in the popular imagination until the late 1830s when numerous writers responded to John M. Armstrong's polemical *Notices of the War of 1812.* Jason's larger point about the mystery surrounding the popular memory of the War of 1812 still remains, of course.[60]

PESKIN: My inclination is to focus regionally and float the idea of renaming the War of 1812 "the Canadian War" to go along with the great frontier struggle of the nineteenth century: the Mexican War. I might even flippantly call it "the War of Southern Aggres-sion." In all seriousness, however, this interchange (in addition to Alan Taylor's work) has done such a great job of showing how important the war is to Canadian historiogra-phy and national identity that none of us should ever glide over Canada again when we teach this subject. Obviously, later battles of the war were far removed geographically from Canada, but the British would never have retaliated if the United States had not

[59] Denver Brunsman, "Subjects vs. Citizens: Impressment and Identity in the Anglo-American Atlantic," *Journal of the Early Republic,* 30 (Winter 2010), 571.
[60] Colin McCoy, "Democracy in Print: The Literature of Persuasion in Jacksonian America, 1815–1840" (Ph.D. diss., University of Illinois, 2001), 83; John M. Armstrong, *Notices of the War of 1812* (2 vols., New York, 1836).

invaded Canada. This idea might also prompt consideration of American militaristic expansionism to the north and south coupled with traditional consideration of western expansion during the nineteenth century.

OPAL: I also hope that this interchange and recent scholarship helps put Canada at the center of U.S. historians' accounts of the postrevolutionary period. I am teaching a mid-level course, The Age of the American Revolution, to a primarily Anglo-Canadian audience but with many Quebecois and Americans also in attendance, and I make more and more reference to Upper Canada and Lower Canada throughout. I also ask my students to consider the everyday differences between being a subject of the empire and a citizen of the republic. While seemingly a simple distinction, it is among the most important and elusive.[61]

I would like to conclude by wondering why the northern border of the United States became pacified and settled, at least as far as the two European-American polities were concerned. Much recent scholarship—perhaps most provocatively Carroll Smith-Rosenberg's *This Violent Empire*—emphasizes the aggressiveness of the early United States. In some renderings, the American nation—however defined—*required* war, in part, as Smith-Rosenberg argues, because of an elite quest to stabilize its own identity and hold over political and economic power. Besides, American settlers increasingly understood their right to take over new soil as natural, God-given, and nonnegotiable. It is therefore worth wondering why, or to what extent, the concept of Manifest Destiny accepted a northern national boundary. Abolitionist historians such as Joshua Giddings were eager to provide an answer: slavery made regions and cultures so dangerous to their neighbors since no master could tolerate any space of freedom nearby lest that invite his chattels to run away. Of course there were legions of northern expansionists who were as eager as their southern compatriots to conquer and subdue the West. Were they more willing to fight over the boundaries of Oregon territory than we generally assume? Were the various border incidents during and after the 1830s more than just regional curiosities? Had the idea of a Canadian border to American "destiny" become ingrained in the popular culture?[62]

GILJE: The War of 1812 is the War of 1812; there is ultimately a certain utility in convention. For almost two hundred years, Americans have referred, rightly or wrongly, to the conflict that lasted from June 1812 to February 1815 as the War of 1812. Whether or not we like the name, we are stuck with it.

The phrase was used early in American history. Although there was at least one reference to "the war of 1812" shortly after the war broke out, the phrase began to appear regularly in toasts and newspaper articles immediately after the war ended. An advertisement for a prisoner of war memoir published in 1816 states that the book covered "the beginning and the end of what may be called the war of 1812" and in that same year a bookstore advertised *The History of the American War of 1812*. Usually cited in newspapers without

---

[61] Jason M. Opal, "The Age of the American Revolution," syllabus, Spring 2012, McGill University, Montreal, Canada (in Jason Opal's possession).

[62] Carroll Smith-Rosenberg, *This Violent Empire: The Birth of an American National Identity* (Chapel Hill, 2010); Joshua R. Giddings, *The Exiles of Florida: The Crimes Committed by Our Government against the Maroons Who Fled South Carolina and Other Slave States* (Columbus, 1858).

capitalization, the phrase "the war of 1812" appeared intermittently thereafter, until, as Cecilia and Matthew state, the 1830s and 1840s, when it was used with greater frequency. The search engine for *America's Historical Newspapers* lists seventeen references to "the war of 1812" (regardless of capitalization) in 1820; fifty-eight in 1830; and ninety-one in 1840. Such a gradual increase suggests a growing acceptance of the term.[63]

Many people in the postwar period called the conflict "the war for free trade and sailors' rights." I must confess, however, that this label paled in usage when compared to the other label mentioned by Matthew: "the Late War." That was the appellation used most frequently in the years after 1815. Compare, for example, its usage in newspaper citations versus the use of "the war of 1812": the label "late war" appeared 2,672 times in 1820; 1,143 in 1830; and 928 in 1840. This frequency, however, is not a case for changing the name. While "the Late War" made sense during those decades (ignoring the more persistent and frequent Indian conflicts and the Second Barbary War in 1815), it is useless now. One might compare "the Late War" to my father's generation's use of "the war" when referring to World War II. That label ignored the Korean War and other military conflicts after 1945, but everyone who had lived through the 1940s, and even those of us born in the 1950s, knew what was encompassed by "the war." This distinction, several wars removed and after the deaths of so many of the "greatest generation," is no longer so clear. Likewise, Americans in the 1820s could refer to the War of 1812 as "the Late War" because it was such a searing experience for them. As the conflict grew more distant and as other wars took its place, however, a more specific name was needed. The War of 1812 seemed apropos, especially since it distinguished the conflict from the other major early American war, the war of 1775, or the war of 1776, which we refer to as the American Revolution. Ultimately, then, as I said, the War of 1812 is the War of 1812![64]

EUSTACE: I agree with Cecilia's point that we must consider the War of 1812 as "the war that some white folks sort of won but one that aboriginal people definitely lost." As she admits, that title is not exactly catchy, but it does have the virtue of echoing an equally unmelodic contemporary title bestowed by the war opponent and Congregationalist minister John Lathrop: "The Late War . . . between the American and the British Forces and Indians in the Years 1811, 1812, 1813, 1814, 1815." By dating the conflict from 1811 (the year of William Henry Harrison's victory at the Battle of Tippecanoe) and including Indians as well as the British in his title, Lathrop made clear that he viewed the fight first and foremost as a struggle to secure U.S. territorial claims against Indians and to eliminate the British as Indian allies. Expanding settlement was both a cause and an effect of U.S. wars in North America. In what many Euro-Americans saw as a virtuous cycle— but which many Native Americans and their British and Canadian allies viewed as a vicious circle—the continent's wide-open grounds supported demographic expansion even as an increasing U.S. population enabled the seizure and settlement of new land. Reporting on "the fears and apprehensions, which the Indians on the western borders have long entertained," Lathrop claimed that one had told him, "you white people,

---

[63] *Baltimore Patriot*, Jan. 5, 1816; *Wilmington American Watchman*, Nov. 16, 1816. *America's Historical Newspapers*, Series I: 1690–1922, available at Readex.
[64] *America's Historical Newspapers*, Series I: 1690–1922.

intend to make us poor Indians, remove, little by little, and then push us into the water where the sun goes down."[65]

In my current work on patriotism I am looking closely at the relationship between population expansion and territorial aggression in the 1812 era—an analysis that has necessitated close attention to gender. Reproductive work represented a critical stage in the U.S. cycle of continental warfare. Women peopled the land won by men. From the beginning of the War of 1812 to the end, war boosters urged U.S. men and women to show their love of country by siring and bearing children for the nation. This emphasis on the power of population allowed inhabitants of the United States to differentiate themselves from both the British and the Indians. Whereas British critics of the United States such as Thomas Malthus urged Americans explicitly to reduce their family sizes to diminish their demand for Indian territory, American commentators such as Thomas Jefferson contradicted him directly. Upon reading Malthus, Jefferson insisted that the ample lands of the American continent guaranteed U.S. inhabitants complete freedom to raise families and break land for farms. Whereas Indians drew pity from many U.S. commentators for their low fertility levels and for their supposed failure to properly cultivate the land, all U.S. inhabitants from enfranchised white men to enslaved black women could procreate and populate the country.[66]

Strange as it may seem to tie love of country to romantic love, reproduction was a defining element of patriotism during the War of 1812. I have found that in much pro-war rhetoric from high politics to popular prints, rearing children featured as the first obligation and the finest privilege of American patriots. Making romantic love and reproduction central to American liberty relocated the site of Americans' most basic rights from the public to the private realm and helped make simple population membership—not formal legal citizenship—the most fundamental form of national belonging. All the nation's inhabitants—male and female, black and white—could be patriots even though only a few enjoyed the full legal rights of citizens. (The actual systematic disruption of black family life did not figure into white men's articulation of such ideals.) Only Indians were left out of this equation entirely; in this sense their status as noncitizens differed fundamentally from that of white women and from that of free and enslaved blacks. What set Indians apart from the patriotic population was that, unlike U.S. residents, they could never be mothers or soldiers for the American nation unless and until they gave up allegiance to their own tribal nations.[67]

Addressing Matthew's point that conflicts over British recognition of U.S. citizenship rights were an important impetus for the war, I will say that one of the most far-reaching effects of the conflict was to clarify the way citizenship was viewed at home. The war allowed elite white male leaders to articulate a powerful vision of partial national

---

[65] John Lathrop, *A Compendious History of the Late War; Containing an Account of all the Important Battles, Many of the Smaller Actions, between the American, and the British Forces, and Indians in the Years 1811, 1812, 1813, 1814, 1815* (Boston, 1815), esp. 8.

[66] T. R. Malthus, *An Essay on the Principle of Population; or, A View of Its Past and Present Effects on Human Happiness with an Inquiry into Our Prospects Respecting the Future Removal or Mitigation of the Evils Which It Occasions* (Washington, 1809), 9–10; Thomas Jefferson to Jean Baptiste Say, Feb. 1, 1804, Series 1, General Correspondence Collection, 1651–1827, Thomas Jefferson Papers (Library of Congress, Washington).

[67] By bearing and raising children, American women and men lent strength to the nation in all its foreign competitions, from Indian conflicts to British contests. See Jefferson to William Short, Nov. 28, 1814, Series 1, General Correspondence Collection, 1651–1827, Jefferson Papers. Popular embrace of such ideas can be seen in "Early Marriage, an Extract," *Carlisle Gazette*, Nov. 1, 1815, p. 4.

inclusion. Ultimately I think that the real significance of the war lies with the (temporary but decades-long) solution to this citizenship problem: how to draw on the strength of the nation's full population without granting universal rights to political participation. The real victory in the war was twofold. First, the wartime crisis crystallized the definition of patriotism as a love that encompassed the entire national family without bringing all inhabitants the recompense of legal citizenship. Second, the crisis unified the nation's population in the intensifying pursuit of new land and large families—actions that benefited all at the expense of Native Americans.

PESKIN: I have an observation about Nicole's fascinating find of a contemporary (John Lathrop) who described the conflict as the War of 1811 rather than 1812. Dating the war back to 1811 does not necessarily diminish the British role, as I find that a large number of Americans saw the British as the real enemy in the Indian conflict of 1811, or at least as the sinister force behind Tecumseh and others. So dating the war back to 1811 could be a recognition of perceived British perfidy as much as a sign that the war was primarily about Native Americans and western territory.

EUSTACE: Thanks, Lawrence. I like your suggestion that one useful way of thinking about how the War of 1812 fits into history is to consider its analogs and coordinates, so that the War of 1812 is to the Old Northwest as the Mexican War was to the Southwest, making "the Canadian War" one logical choice for an alternate name.

Coming from an eighteenth-century studies background my impulse was to reach back in time to think about the ways this war related to another war named for a time period: the Seven Years' War. In some sense, the War of 1812 solidified changes and resolved instabilities put into motion in 1763. Only with the signing of the Treaty of Ghent and the abandonment of any idea of a British-backed Indian buffer zone did the British effectively cease to offer any imperial counterweight to Indians confronting the United States. Tracing the beginning of the War of 1812 back to the end of the Seven Years' War (also known as the French and Indian War) suggests another possible coordinating title for the 1812 conflict: "the British and Indian War."

HALE: Consider one last label: "Mr. Madison's War." This contemporaneous moniker is helpful because it reveals the highly partisan nature of the conflict. Federalists not only opposed the war in principle but, as Richard Buel has made clear, they also went to great lengths to subvert the government and its prosecution of the war. It should also be noted that the Federalists, for all their pettiness and selfishness, had a point. Without Madison as president, there may not have been a conflict known as the War of 1812. The way Madison drove the nation to war is similar to the way post–World War II presidents have taken the nation to war through strong executive action. Yet a major difference is that the War of 1812 began with a congressional declaration of war. The term "Mr. Madison's War" does not, in that sense, account for relatively widespread public approval—in the form of affirming votes by popularly elected representatives—of the conflict.[68]

[68] Richard Buel Jr., *America on the Brink: How the Political Struggle over the War of 1812 Almost Destroyed the Young Republic* (New York, 2005), 170–235.

This brings us back to Nicole's earlier point that the War of 1812 is the first declared war in the history of the United States. Even though the American republic had gone to war against Native Americans and the Algerines, those two groups apparently did not merit congressional authorization of formal military action. I am not sure anyone has explored at length why some foreign groups merited an official declaration of war while others did not, but I suspect it has something to do with certain white Americans' assumptions that natives and Algerines, in contrast to the British, existed outside the pale of civilization. No matter how much Americans may have despised Britons and imagined them in conspiratorial terms, they nonetheless seemed to consider it a given that a war against the United Kingdom must be officially declared, even if rallying congressional support for a declaration of war would be arduous and politically expensive.

I raise this observation because I wonder if it has something to do with Jason's point about the way the War of 1812 helped pacify the Canadian American border. More specifically, does a declaration of war help set the terms of peace in the sense that it implicitly calls for military victory (and future peace) or a formal, negotiated settlement (and future peace)? Thus, whereas Americans felt compelled to make a treaty with the British, they felt no need to make a treaty with the Indians except when it suited them and when terms could be dictated. Likewise, because Native Americans were not objects of a declaration of war, their interests had no standing (and no representatives) at the Treaty of Ghent negotiations. Finally, while American wars with Britain seemed to have rather well-defined starting and ending points, conflicts with Native Americans seemed to spring forth before official Anglo-American war had begun (as Lawrence's and Nicole's observations about 1811 suggest) and spill over after Anglo-American war had officially ended (as evidenced by Jackson's forays in the Southeast in the late 1810s). Perhaps this type of speculation about a link between formally declaring war and the nature of the postwar peace too easily glosses over various facts on the ground, including the proximity of natives to western Americans and the common commercial interests of British and American traders. Still, I would venture that an extended consideration of the way the presence or absence of a declaration of war reveals attitudes about various foreign groups and shapes the postwar settlement would be quite illuminating.

Book Reviews

Shifting Grounds: Nationalism and the American South, 1848–1865. By Paul Quigley. (New York: Oxford University Press, 2012. xii, 325 pp. $34.95.)

Paul Quigley examines an old issue—the nature of southern nationalism—through a new and somewhat improved wide-angle lens. *Shifting Grounds* not only shifts (along with the people whose voices are heard in the text) from broad to narrow views of its subject but also ranges widely, connecting topics such as moral criticism of dancing to the character of the Confederate experiment. Quigley anchors the study in the various currents of nineteenth-century nationalism. As in David M. Potter's classic essay on the subject ("The Historian's Use of Nationalism and Vice Versa, *American Historical Review,* July 1962, pp. 924–50), Quigley argues that Americans' national loyalties were far from simple. Allegiance was almost always plural rather than singular.

In probing the foundations of nationalism in the antebellum South, Quigley cites the usual suspects—southern intellectuals (especially South Carolinians)—who wrestled with questions of both national and southern identity. After all, white southerners were also American nationalists who celebrated the Fourth of July and watched with great interest the emergence of nationalist movements and revolutions in Europe. Although nationalism was often associated with ideas about democracy and progress, ethnic and less inclusive forms of nationalism proved equally important. History and constitutionalism likewise came into play because despite memories of the American Revolution that tended to cement national identity, federalism reinforced state claims to loyalty and at times weakened sectional ones. Quigley acknowledges racial and gender issues at play but generally avoids a presentist critique of nineteenth-century Americans. *Shifting Grounds* strikingly recaptures the emotional and visceral side of topics that have too often been treated in a highly abstract fashion.

Not surprisingly, Quigley finds a close connection between proslavery ideology and southern nationalism even as he acknowledges that radicals or so-called fire-eaters represented only a small if vociferous minority. In some cases, personal losses and feelings of social isolation fueled a passion for separatism and a tendency to lash out at enemies real and imagined. The intellectual dilemmas involved, however, were serious and tangible. Separatist nationalism in Europe, along with distinctions drawn between nations and governments, might prove appealing, but there were also tensions between state sovereignty and southern nationhood—tensions that would become famously apparent during the Civil War. Ethnic foundations for southern independence proved weak, and calls for cultural independence often failed to resonate beyond intellectual circles. Secessionists found appeals to the American Revolution more useful even as southerners at times sought to stake out their own particular claims to the historical symbols and ceremonies of American nationalism.

During the sectional controversies of the 1840s and 1850s, southerners embraced what Quigley terms "a shifting and conditional unionism" (p. 87). At the same time, the Wilmot Proviso and other perceived assaults on southerners and slavery produced a powerful language of "victimhood, humiliation, and oppression" (p. 90). Amid the secession crisis, disunionists talked about bonds of affection and kinship as opposed to cold politics and interests, the insufficient glue barely holding together a tottering American union. Many southerners reacted with a deeply aggrieved belligerence to John Brown's 1859 raid on Harpers Ferry and Abraham Lincoln's call for troops after the firing on Fort Sumter in 1861. Yet many southern whites could not abandon their deep affection for the American Union, and the pain and distress even for those who became loyal Confederates often remained palpable.

Lacking much of a blueprint for their "nation," Confederate leaders stumbled into the future and into a war. Proving legitimacy to the world and even to their own citizens became a real challenge. What role would slavery play in the new nation? What would happen to the symbols and ceremonies of American nationalism? What did Confederate citizenship mean? These and other difficult questions plagued but did not destroy the Confederacy. Likewise, worries about the character of the Southern nation and its people persisted but hardly proved fatal. Quigley's treatment of these issues is generally sound and persuasive, though he never grapples with the contemporary debates about whether Confederate nationalists were revolutionaries. On occasion, he strains for significance. When Lucy Wood lowered a U.S. flag in Virginia, she may have "tested the meanings and boundaries" of "citizenship and womanhood," but she may have been simply lowering a flag (p. 167).

Quigley recognizes that defining the enemy became part of Southern national identity, making his brief discussion of Yankee barbarism quite useful. So too does his emphasis on both blood and sacrifice prevent the material on national identity, citizenship, and patriotism from becoming bloodless (pun intended). Recently, historians have recognized how suffering among civilians and soldiers can be unifying as well as demoralizing, and Quigley follows this trend. He acknowledges the shifting nature of wartime loyalties—a theme nicely developed in Judkin Browning's book on the Union occupation of eastern North Carolina (*Shifting Loyalties*, 2011). *Shifting Boundaries* pays attention to divisions, doubts, and demoralization without exaggerating them. Even religious ideas about sin and divine chastisement could actually make the penitent more committed to the Confederate cause. War inevitably drew the citizen closer to the state—a conclusion that takes into account both the weaknesses and persistence of the Confederacy and its people.

Shifting Grounds is a learned book that wears its learning lightly. Quigley has carefully organized his material and presents important ideas in a clear way that generally avoids academic buzzwords and needless complications. A good deal of the information will be familiar to scholars, but the book also presents a number of fresh insights in a pleasing manner.

George C. Rable
University of Alabama
Tuscaloosa, Alabama

doi: 10.1093/jahist/jas295

The American Family: From Obligation to Freedom. By David Peterson Del Mar. (New York: Palgrave Macmillan, 2011. x, 211 pp. Cloth, $85.00. Paper, $27.00.)

David Peterson Del Mar's *The American Family* is not a history; it is, rather, an extended essay about broad cultural factors that shaped American families since the colonial period. The subtitle, *From Obligation to Freedom,* labels the main change over time that Peterson Del Mar stresses.

When English people migrated to North America and founded colonies they did so within a cultural context that valued common relations over individual rights or liberties. They regarded society as a hierarchical construct with predetermined places for everyone and an interlocking system of obligation and appropriate deference. In support of this view, Peterson Del Mar cites the famous sermon delivered in 1630 by John Winthrop on the ship *Arabella.* Between the colonial period and the present, the sense of mutual obligation declined as the concepts of individualism and especially individual freedom expanded. This evolution, the author argues, shaped the dynamics of American families both in terms of their internal structures and also in terms of social policy affecting families.

This major transformation in social values happened slowly over two centuries. The prosperity of the colonies helped undermine the rigid social order and patriarchy. On the American Revolution, Peterson Del Mar observes that "the process of revolution served to undermine patriarchal assumptions" (p. 42). The prosperity of the nineteenth century helped transform families through greater economic efficiency. Among the emerging middle-class families, women and children no longer had to engage in productive work, and this in turn resulted in greater focus on their individual needs. At the same time birth rates began their long decline. Once the family evolved from a small self-sufficient factory into a collection of individuals, the nature of the relationships within the family changed as well. By the twentieth century people chose their mates primarily for emotional rather than economic reasons.

By the end of the twentieth century, the social obligations of the colonial period had all but disappeared; individual freedom was now a primary cultural value and a new sense of "the self" had emerged. As Peterson Del Mar's chronological account reaches the twenty-first century, his commentary on the social forces becomes more trenchant as he finds much to deplore in contemporary patterns. Families today, he believes, are in serious trouble because the decline of obligations and the rise of individualism have gone too far.

This brief summary cannot do justice to a much more nuanced and inclusive discussion. Peterson Del Mar does discuss variations among American families, including those of African Americans and American Indians. Still, the dominant theme of this slim volume is one of cultural evolution rather than family changes over time.

The author offers brief discussion of demographic changes, but this is a work about influences on the family rather than the families themselves. The work includes both a substantial body of notes, referencing recent secondary literature, and an extensive bibliography.

Joseph M. Hawes, *Emeritus*
University of Memphis
Memphis, Tennessee

doi: 10.1093/jahist/jas285

America Walks into a Bar: A Spirited History of Taverns and Saloons, Speakeasies, and Grog Shops. By Christine Sismondo. (New York: Oxford University Press, 2011. xviii, 314 pp. $24.95.)

In *America Walks into a Bar,* Christine Sismondo traces the evolution and functions of taverns and other drinking establishments through American history, from the earliest European settlers to current controversies over affluent mothers taking their toddlers into bars for "Mommy and Me" cocktail hours. She argues for the importance of taverns as political spaces, asserting that individuals and groups excluded from formal political institutions have historically used commercial drinking spaces to develop political consciousness and organize political actions. Although she includes a few counterexamples, she generally assumes that campaigns launched from taverns will be politically progressive, following from the outsider status of many who frequent them. Sismondo is particularly good at setting the stage concisely and relaying engaging anecdotes that advance her interpretation. While some of her examples, such as the Whiskey Rebellion (1791–1794) and the 1886 Haymarket affair, are already well known, she recounts less familiar episodes as well. Especially effective are Sismondo's analyses of cases where access to the tavern or bar is a contested issue, such as New York City's Stonewall Inn (the focus of the 1969 Stonewall riots) or efforts of women to enter drinking establishments as customers and workers.

Sismondo provides detailed typologies of taverns, saloons, and speakeasies in specific historical periods, but she is less successful at analyzing how and why such institutions changed form and function over time. While she notes that national Prohibition in 1920 contributed to the rise of the speakeasy, Sismondo fails to explain the earlier demise of the tavern and the rise of the saloon or why the frontier saloon remained "an apolitical haven" while urban saloons in the eastern United States became intensely political (p. 104). Sismondo also does not engage very extensively with the fact that alcohol is a psychoactive drug and its possible implications, except for a brief discussion of drunkenness in her comparison of taverns with coffeehouses (p. 47). Her focus on the political implications of taverns as gathering places means that this is not a book about drinking as such. Still, it would be worth asking how, if at all, the substance of alcohol and its effects made this kind of public space different from others.

Although the book is occasionally repetitive, its broad chronological coverage is a strength, allowing Sismondo to examine commercial drinking spaces and campaigns against them, and to show many intersections with political, social, and cultural developments. The book's intriguing anecdotes and thematic connections to other issues in American history suggest that this work can be drawn on to enliven the U.S. history survey and will also entertain general readers. Sismondo uses diaries, songs, cocktail recipes, and other primary materials to add rich details, while relying on secondary scholarship for context and framing. Unfortunately, the notes are not very comprehensive, limiting the usefulness of the book for scholars. Some of the most fascinating stories and most multifaceted arguments about change over time lack detailed citations, although the bibliography lists a wide range of resources.

Michelle Lee McClellan
University of Michigan
Ann Arbor, Michigan

doi: 10.1093/jahist/jas264

Second Cities: Globalization and Local Politics in Manchester and Philadelphia. By Jerome I. Hodos. (Philadelphia: Temple University Press, 2011. xvi, 246 pp. $65.00.)

Global cities get a lot of attention these days. The great ancient ones, such as Rome and Constantinople, were engaged in extensive empire trade, made possible by a labor pool bolstered by both free and slave foreigners. A millennium later, London and New York emerged on top of the global list. In between, smaller cities grew out of market and university towns. But it was in the eighteenth century that new cities proliferated, a result of population shifts caused by economic and geopolitical changes ushered in by the industrial revolution and New World exploration.

Those new cities and their role in the modernizing world are at the center of Jerome I. Hodos's *Second Cities.* He investigates not the great global city but those emergent "second cities" that he defines as something between the world capital and "the hopelessly marginalized city," those urban areas antithetical to change and expansion (p. 7). Such a perspective, as well as his transnational approach, is compelling: Manchester and Philadelphia were at the brink of greatness, but never quite achieved it. Hodos seeks an answer to an intriguing question—why did some cities rise to the top while others did not despite having many of the necessary characteristics?

At the start of the eighteenth century, Philadelphia was a core colonial city, the center of the American republic. By the end of the nineteenth century, it had slipped into Hodos's definition of a secondary city, marked by loss of international financial dominance, weaker cultural influence, and declining immigration. New York, a smaller city at the time, quickly outpaced the "city of brotherly love" to become the global city. Manchester, which did not exist in 1700, was by 1800 one of the largest manufacturing centers of the world, home to extraordinary wealth and influence. Though never London's rival, it also lost its primacy as a major city during the nineteenth century in much the same way as Philadelphia.

Hodos's clearly written and well-supported argument explores the intricacies of these changes while highlighting the similarities of the two cities' paths. Philadelphia's decline in status was brought on by its loss of dominance in global finance, coinciding with New York's ascension in this area. Manchester's decline in status came as its manufacturing sector migrated externally, and new challenges strained its internal government. Such second cities, Hodos argues, replaced their losses with more specialized and limited manufacturing as well as focused and advanced service industries, such as education and hospitals.

Immigration, the focus of chapter 4, is particularly significant, Hodos says, because second cities have different migration patterns indicative of racial, ethnic, and class differences within them. Philadelphia and Manchester "have many migrants but few migrant communities," the result of having more internal migration than external (p. 15). Cities that do not welcome immigrants tend to falter and become static, whereas cities that welcome foreigners tend to thrive. A second city, Hodos says, is middle class by nature, bereft of innovation and world culture. Can these cities even stay in the second rung? Only if they seek greater international contact and become masters of their fate in an increasingly competitive modern world.

Lisa Keller
Purchase College
State University of New York
Purchase, New York

doi: 10.1093/jahist/jas313

Weeds: An Environmental History of Metropolitan America. By Zachary J. S. Falck. (Pittsburgh: University of Pittsburgh Press, 2010. xvi, 256 pp. $40.00.)

Weeds have been ubiquitous in American cities throughout their history, and metaphorical references to "human weeds" have been nearly as common in American culture. In *Weeds,* Zachary J. S. Falck traces two interconnected histories—the environmental history of urban plants labeled as weeds and the cultural history of attempts to condemn and control certain urban residents by referring to them as "weeds."

Weeds relates the history of urban plant life to broader trends in urban and suburban development. Building cities unintentionally created the ecological conditions for unwanted plants to thrive there. Ironically, expansion of American cities often fostered the growth of weeds in both neglected urban neighborhoods and unevenly developed suburban spaces. Because of the cultural association of weed-filled lots with decline and neglect, the abandonment of particular urban areas could become a self-fulfilling prophecy as the ecological success of unwanted plants was perceived as an indicator of urban decay. As Falck explains, the residents of such neighborhoods—whether they were tramps in the early twentieth century or residents of housing projects in the latter half of the century—were also the people most likely to be criticized as undesirable "human weeds." Such analogies between people and plants naturalized

contempt and essentialized poverty and other social ills, although more progressive groups of Americans seized on this language as well, such as African Americans who labeled racism and segregation as weeds to be eradicated.

Weeds covers territory from the old cities of the eastern seaboard to the newer cities of the sun belt, and Falck's impressive research has uncovered fascinating information and anecdotes from all over the country, including municipal ordinances, neighborhood and court battles over plant life, and the research of both professional and amateur ecologists studying urban plants. At times, the wide-ranging examples can be disorienting for the reader, and some of the most fascinating parts of the book are those in which Falck develops his analysis through detailed examples. One such section traces the history of cannabis cultivation and efforts to police its growth since the 1920s, while another focuses on campaigns to eradicate ragweed and their unintended consequences.

The book moves roughly chronologically, from Progressive Era weed laws that transformed plants into nuisances to the twenty-first century, in which an increasing interest in native plants has come into conflict with persistent negative perceptions of unruly urban landscapes. However, the book might have been better served by a topical structure. Chapters jump from ecological to cultural analysis and back, which can be confusing. Falck also finds a great deal of continuity over the course of the twentieth century, both in the persistent ignorance of ecological processes and in the cultural realm. Overall, *Weeds* represents an original approach to urban environmental history and a valuable contribution to the field.

Joanna Dyl
University of South Florida
Tampa, Florida

doi: 10.1093/jahist/jas268

American Property: A History of How, Why, and What We Own. By Stuart Banner. (Cambridge: Harvard University Press, 2011. 355 pp. $29.95.)

What is property? This simple question animates Stuart Banner's history of "an institution at the root of our political and economic life" (p. 2). As with many simple questions, however, the answer is rather complicated, but Banner brings a remarkable degree of clarity to this sprawling subject.

His central claim is that definitions of property are neither natural nor timeless but are forever in flux. He opens the book by showing how long-standing English laws and precedents evaporated in the decades after independence. Out went archaic obligations that required landowners to perform certain tasks, permit others to use their land, or pay tithes; doctrines such as primogeniture and fees tail likewise disappeared. Some customs vanished because they "seemed inconsistent with republican principles"; others fell to a "desire not to deter development" (pp. 20, 18).

None of this, Banner argues, happened by design but instead took place on a haphazard, case-by-case basis. This was particularly true in the way that intangible things—product trademarks, price data, and celebrity portraits—went from the public domain to the domain of private ownership. Banner brings these developments to life with well-crafted vignettes: a woman who sued after a flour company used her portrait in its advertisements without permission, and the machinations of a player-piano company to monopolize music.

Banner traces these new forms of property in specific chapters, but he also addresses several larger trends that gathered steam toward the end of the nineteenth century. Judges began to abandon the idea that property was a discrete thing; instead they saw it as a "bundle of rights." That observation in turn protected landowners from government incursion. As Banner explains, "if value resided not in land itself but in the right to do things with land, regulation of the use of land should require compensation at least as much as physical confiscation of the land" (pp. 60–61).

Progressive judges also rejected the idea of property as a commodity, positing instead that it was a function of what a property owner could or could not do vis-à-vis other people. This conclusion opened the door to more government, not less: "the more one thought about property as relations between people, the less likely one was to oppose regulation that adjusted those relations" (p. 104). In

subsequent chapters, Banner shows how that idea came to fruition in progressive form (zoning ordinances, for example) as well as in less celebrated forms of regulation (racial covenants).

Banner's final chapters address twentieth-century developments: the rise of de facto ownership of the air waves; judges' struggles to define corpses as a form of "quasi property" that "split the difference between . . . calling the body property and allowing others to defile it" (p. 241); liberals' attempts to broaden the definition of property to encompass welfare payments; and conservative campaigns to reaffirm individual property rights in the face of environmental regulations.

While Banner acknowledges that some groups pushed to redefine property to make money, he rejects the idea that the legal system self-consciously promoted capitalist development by redefining property rights. Rather, this is a book about how "small decisions had big consequences"—how petty squabbles over ownership helped push the definition of property in new if unintended directions, benefiting elites and ordinary people alike (p. 120).

American Property is a model work of scholarly synthesis. Banner has taken a dry, somewhat forbidding subject and made it his own; indeed, other claimants to this piece of historiographical property will have a tough time surpassing this lucid, thoughtful work.

Stephen Mihm
University of Georgia
Athens, Georgia

doi: 10.1093/jahist/jas275

Thrift and Thriving in America: Capitalism and Moral Order from the Puritans to the Present. Ed. by Joshua J. Yates and James Davison Hunter. (New York: Oxford University Press, 2011. x, 622 pp. $35.00.)

Joshua Y. Yates and James Davison Hunter, their twenty-three contributors, and their publisher have produced an important new book. The anthology addresses a wide range of historical themes and poses exciting and productive new lines of inquiry into the study of modern mass consumerism, capitalism, and moral order (an awkward yet accurate phrase for a title). Yates and Hunter's provocative introduction and ambitious conclusion will soon be required reading for aspiring cultural, economic, and intellectual historians interested in assaying the shifting character of American life.

To the editors' credit, the diverse volume holds close to their central thesis—a bold, innovative, and interdisciplinary argument best explained in three parts. First, they argue that the concept of thrift is far more complex and persistently relevant to Americans than many might assume. Traditionally linked to profound generational spokespeople, such as the Puritans, early nineteenth-century capitalists, and those who survived the Great Depression, thrift too often suggests a static, simple, and reactionary social habit. It offers nostrums that provide only the *means* to persist: frugality, sobriety, self-denial. By contrast, this volume shows how this fixed characterization completely ignores the capacious social, economic, and ethical meanings behind thrift. Rather than simply the act of being thrifty, thrift is here presented as a process that privileges the ends of thriving rather than the means. This approach enervates the concept with new analytical life: thriving as an ongoing socioeconomic condition and thriving by a reflexive assessment about life in America. The editors want to show "how the enduring question of thriving has always been the subtext of thrift" and how this subtext "in turn, has repeatedly inspired . . . powerful forms of social critique and movements of social reform" (p. 32). Significantly (yet subtley) the volume blends traditional empirical scholarship with powerful textual and postmodern analysis.

Freed from both Merriam Webster and Poor Richard, thrift "well-understood" animates the volume's second argument: that the ethos of thrift remains a fairly consistent, if overlooked, expression of America's civic ideology. Morphing from its Puritan and classical roots into more modern ideals—such as consumer, collective, reactionary, and even green thrift—the idea is historicized in the bulk of the essays within the context of relentless economic change. Given the proficiencies of the contributors—including Joyce Appleby, T. J. Jackson Lears, Daniel

Walker Howe, and Steven Fraser—one could turn to almost any chapter to find intriguing reassessments of the dominant historiography on classical republicanism, religion, the rise of new corporate orders, consumer debt and credit, mass advertising, class, and globalization.

But a close review of any individual contribution runs the risk of losing the importance of the volume as a whole. *Thrift and Thriving in America* arranges the essays into three chronological eras. The first, spanning from 1630 to 1880, witnessed the transformation of thrift from an unremarkable virtue (rarely observed) to one of the central tenets of middle-class respectability. As the late Stephen Innes shows, perhaps the most remarkable feature of this transformation was the rise of "an appropriate institutional context," which drove the concept deep into the national debates over civil society, just governance, and rational economic growth (p. 117). The most dramatic change occurred during the second epoch, from 1880 to 1950. Just as industrial capitalism refashioned the relationship between capital and labor, so too did it accentuate the institutional prominence of thrift. No longer relevant in a world of abundance (and easy credit), the ethos of thrift provided both capitalists and consumers a virtue ready-made for new habits. In Lendol Calder's essay on consumer credit, for example, the husbanding of time replaced penny-pinching as the updated justification for installment payments. As the perceived need to protect critical new resources, such as time, "became urgent" the ethos of thrift became "irresistible," a comforting virtue for people with modern desires (p. 330).

The volume's third theme is explored more fully in the final chronological section, from 1950 to the present. In an era characterized by both phenomenal material abundance and a voracious appetite for nonrenewable resources, thrift appears about as relevant as sabbatarianism. While the editors admit that the book offers no "definitive theoretical synthesis," the essays firmly support the argument that thrift continues to regulate the moral ambiguity of economic exploitation and to provide a normative vocabulary for modern economic reality (p. 16). Some may disagree with Yates and Hunter's faith that a reappraisal of thrift can help contemporary society address its struggles with sustainability. But few can deny that this volume poses fresh and stimulating questions about the "evolving and contrasting visions of the good life and society" (p. 572).

David Blanke
Texas A&M University–Corpus Christi
Corpus Christi, Texas

doi: 10.1093/jahist/jas238

U.S. Army Doctrine: From the American Revolution to the War on Terror. By Walter E. Kretchik. (Lawrence: University Press of Kansas, 2011. xvi, 392 pp. $39.95.)

Walter E. Kretchik, an associate professor at Western Illinois University, traces the evolution of U.S. Army doctrine from 1779 to the present by examining the army's "keystone" publications, "the dominant manuals that have shaped army operations for over two centuries" (p. 4). He discerns five separate stages and devotes a chapter to each. First, between 1779 and 1845 the army imitated British and then French models. Doctrine emphasized infantry drill and conventional operations while "informal practice" prevailed in frontier warfare (pp. 24–25). During the second period, from 1855 to 1898 and particularly after the Franco-Prussian War, German influence gradually supplanted French models. Third, between 1905 and 1945 field service regulations promoted a combined arms warfare approach while elaborating upon the battlefield roles of corps, divisions, brigades, and, during the latter stages, army groups and numbered armies. Just prior to World War II, these regulations began to cover the operation of U.S. Army Air Force units in conjunction with the ground arms. Fourth, during the period of the Cold War, from 1945 to 1991, successive editions of the U.S. Army Field Manual 100-5 paid increasing attention to joint and combined operations. These publications also gave attention to low-intensity conflict for the first time, but too little in the view of many critics. In the fifth and final period, 1991 to the present, the various editions of Field Manual 3-0 (which replaced the 100-5 series) emphasized all levels of conflict, from peace operations to high-intensity

conventional warfare. While continuing to emphasize joint and combined operations, army doctrine has devoted increasing attention to information operations and to the importance of working with civilian organizations, both governmental and nongovernmental.

Although readers might quibble with some details, the last two chapters, reflecting the author's army career, are very well done. These chapters are essential reading for anyone concerned with military development since 1945. The first three chapters, however, are a major disappointment. While they contain useful material, they must be approached with extreme caution.

Kretchik lacks any genuine feel for historical context. The first three chapters suffer from the author's attempts to impose current definitions on the past. What results is a profoundly anachronistic analysis. While doctrinal manuals provide the reader with a picture of the army's vision of operations on and off Cold War and post–Cold War battlefields, they do not provide a similar overview for the army of the eighteenth, nineteenth, or early twentieth centuries. The author rejects concepts and practices not contained in such manuals as "informal." He notes specifically that he does not discuss Continental army artillery or cavalry because Friedrich Wilhelm von Steuben's *Regulations* (1779) only concerned infantry, but when manuals for those other arms begin appearing in the 1830s he ignores them without explanation. Practice often precedes concepts, concepts often precede terms that capture their essence, and the meaning of those terms often evolve over time. By trying to put the past into the straitjacket of the present, the author missed an opportunity to tease out meanings that reveal much about the changing nature of the army—in other words, the kind of intellectual *tour de force* that could have defined our understanding of the institution for current and future generations. Unfortunately, Kretchik's deep understanding of the present has stunted his analysis of the past.

Edgar F. Raines Jr., *Emeritus*
U.S. Army Center of Military History
Washington, D.C.

doi: 10.1093/jahist/jas210

The Reactionary Mind: Conservatism from Edmund Burke to Sarah Palin. By Corey Robin. (New York: Oxford University Press, 2011. xiv, 290 pp. $29.95.)

The Reactionary Mind is a collection of previously published book reviews and articles, divided into two parts, rather weakly related to each other. Part 1, "Profiles in Reaction," begins with the counterrevolutionary drive of conservative politics from the French Revolution to the present. Along the way are discussions of Thomas Hobbes, Ayn Rand, Barry Goldwater, conservatives who moved left, and Supreme Court justice Antonin Scalia. Part 2, "Virtues of Violence," consists of essays on the Cold War in Latin America, the neoconservative rejuvenation of America's imperial vision ("We're an empire now, and when we act, we create our own reality," said an aide to President George W. Bush [p. 165]), the September 11, 2001, attacks and the wars that followed, before ending with the argument that conservatism is "enlivened" by violence—"War is life, peace is death" (p. 219).

Historians who want greater complexity will be troubled that Corey Robin uses the words *conservative, reactionary, revanchist,* and *counterrevolutionary* interchangeably. In addition, he seats "philosophers, statesmen, slaveholders, scribblers, Catholics, fascists, evangelicals, businessmen, racists, and hacks at the same table" (p. 34). Counterrevolution, he argues, is the animating spirit of conservatism—"the felt experience of having power, seeing it threatened, and trying to win it back" (p. 4).

The central problem of this collection is that not all expressions of conservatism fall within so simplistic a formulation. In examining the past two hundred years, historians find innumerable conservatives moved by issues not inherently counterrevolutionary. Conservatives may be impressed with the freedom-enhancing work of the marketplace and of limited government, or they may push for lower taxes because they feel government has failed them in some way. Following World War II, most liberals were anticommunist without being reactionary. These are essential convictions, not the consequence of one basic counterrevolutionary impulse.

Lumped awkwardly together under the large banner of counterrevolution are Hobbes and Ronald Reagan, Edmund Burke and Rand. Perhaps as a marketing gimmick, Sarah Palin is placed in the book's title but is seldom mentioned and never substantively discussed. Moreover, Robin misreads Burke as a reactionary who, deep-down, celebrated violence. But the Irish political theorist who distrusted all ideologies is best remembered as a proponent of organic political and social reform. Although he did not immediately condemn the French Revolution, he soon arose to write lyrically in opposition to it, foreseeing dangers in a confiscating and bloody democracy.

This volume has strengths. Several chapters are especially interesting and can be read as the stand-alone articles they once were about Hobbes, Rand, neoconservatives, and American purpose, for example. It is also well written. Yet the essays read more like a public intellectual engaged in contemporary disputes than a historian objectively engaged in historical analysis. Irritated at some of his subject matter, Robin frequently emulates his combative online personality in arguing his case, but in doing so he risks becoming part of the present polarized culture he attempts to explain.

Ronald Lora
University of Toledo
Toledo, Ohio

doi: 10.1093/jahist/jas181

Nationalism in Europe and America: Politics, Cultures, and Identities since 1775. By Lloyd Kramer. (Chapel Hill: University of North Carolina Press, 2011. xii, 260 pp. Cloth, $65.00. Paper, $24.95.)

Lloyd Kramer in *Nationalism in Europe and America* examines political culture in Europe and America since the late eighteenth century— the point at which he contends modern nationalism emerged. For Kramer, nationalism is still the major organizing concept in modern politics, shaping wars, personal and group identities, religion, and cultural discourse generally. His book offers a sweeping survey of the birth and development of modern nationalism, including identification of iconic symbols and events such as "Marianne" (the personification of republican France), Nazi propaganda posters of the Aryan family, and Emanuel Leutze's painting *Washington Crossing the Delaware* (1851). But his focus rests primarily with nationalist political theorists—ranging from Philip Freneau and George Bancroft (in the United States) to Guiseppe Mazzini (in Italy), Johann Gottlieb Fichte (in Germany), Adam Mickiewicz (in Poland), and Emmanuel-Joseph Sieyes (in France)—since he contends nationalism is heavily dependent on the construction, maintenance, and revision of historical narratives.

This survey effectively illustrates the core features of nationalist discourse and helps explain its endurance in the face of new global cultural and technological initiatives. The colonization of primordial relationships that reflect "strong emotional desires to belong to social groups" and the constant "cultural education" that is employed by nationalists to link basic features of human life such as grief and sacrifice to a cause make nationalism one of the few remaining sources of cohesion in the modern world (p. 5).

When Kramer extends these generalizations to argue that these similarities erase any attempts to distinguish national projects, his case is much weaker. He correctly emphasizes the attempt by nationalist writers to emphasize their differences from each other. To Kramer, these social constructions are designed to solidify national identity. He rejects a distinction between "civic" and ethnic or racial national formulations on the grounds that there are extensive overlaps between the two. It is certainly true that resting beneath, and sometimes alongside, American definitions of nationhood as adherence to a set of propositions regardless of other identities are the beliefs of what Louis Hartz once identified as thousands of American "drugstore Gobineaus" (*The Liberal Tradition in America*, 1955, p. 291). Yet to offer an approach that conflates this formulation with the Nazi definition of racial purity is to miss an important point about the very ingenuity of nationalism that Kramer has identified. Similarly, Kramer rejects the concept of American exceptionalism despite acknowledging that the United States lacked an "ancient history, unique language, or exclusive ethnic identity"

that forced nationalists to identify distinctiveness in political and economic spheres (p. 126). Nevertheless, he contends that American nationalists tend "to exemplify rather than differ from nationalist movements and political cultures in almost every modern of 'Western' or 'Eastern' society" (p. 124). His primary evidence for this conclusion is from an analysis of Indiana senator Albert Beveridge's racial imperialism. This formulation, however, was severely contested in America—so much so that President William McKinley was forced to assert in his second inaugural address (in 1901) that American values "will not abate under tropic suns in distant seas."

Despite an overemphasis on common characteristics, *Nationalism in Europe and America* is a useful, succinct introduction to the creation and development of nationalism in the Atlantic world context.

Philip Abbott
*Wayne State University
Detroit, Michigan*

doi: 10.1093/jahist/jas290

Religion in America: A Political History. By Denis Lacorne, trans. George Holoch. (New York: Columbia University Press, 2011. xxii, 225 pp. $29.50.)

Denis Lacorne, a distinguished student of American politics at the Paris Institute of Political Studies (informally known as Sciences Po), has written a fascinating and noteworthy study of American religion. Its primary focus is the historiography of the relationship between religion and American politics and identity as seen through the rich literature of French reflections on that subject. The book's chronology consists of five critical moments or "historiographical regimes" in which two competing narratives of identity formation play out—the origins of one is in the secular Enlightenment; the other's origin is in a romantic Puritan/Protestantism (p. xix). This division, while replicating the tensions explored in Robert A. Ferguson's *The American Enlightenment, 1750–1820* (1997) and J. David Greenstone's *The Lincoln Persuasion: Remaking American Liberalism* (1993), is deepened and complicated when viewed from the perspective of French writings. French intellectuals then and now have often expressed a deep ambivalence about America, seeing it either as a vanguard nation of enlightened democracy or as a godless, hypocritical, money-obsessed nation that is also (paradoxically) an intolerant Anglo-Protestant theocracy. This ambivalence played out in mid-eighteenth-century French portrayals of America as a land of religious utopias—especially William Penn's Quaker Pennsylvania. First pictured by Voltaire, the Marquis de Jaucourt, and Abbé Raynal as reincarnations of ancient republican virtue, by the end of the eighteenth century, these Quaker/Protestant virtues were transformed by French writers into hypocritical covers for expansionism and exploitation; these authors portrayed America itself as dominated by a Puritanism that recalled the fanaticism of barbarians.

The collapse of the French Revolution and its successor regimes not only softened French views of the role of religion in politics but also occasioned a new look at the role that Puritanism and Protestantism generally played in the formation of American democracy. Parallel with British and American writers, French writers came to see the "spirit of Puritanism" as the seedbed of the American Revolution and its state and national constitutional consolidations. This rediscovery of religion, seen most vividly in Alexis de Tocqueville's *Democracy in America* (1835), was shaped into a romantic/historicist narrative first by Whig clergymen and then by the German-trained historian and New England Democrat George Bancroft. Bancroft's *History of the United States* (1834), a providential work that combined American exceptionalism with the progress of European civilization, was seconded by French liberals such as François Guizot and Benjamin Constant.

The remainder of the study, from American revivalism through nativism and anti-Catholicism to the rise of the religious Right, contemporary church-state issues, and President Barack Obama's adroit balancing act of "faith-friendly secularism," is more familiar to American readers (p. 161). Less known, however, are the views of the French writers of the 1930s and 1940s who portrayed America as the morally bankrupt enemy of Europe, a continent with a culture and civilization that must be protected from American hyperindividualism and national hubris. French intellectuals have since oscillated in their opinions of America, often depending upon how they view the power of enthusiastic Protestantism in American political culture. The French-trained Harvard University historian Patrice Higonnet codified this love-hate oscillation almost perfectly in his *Attendant Cruelties: Nation and Nationalism in American History* (2007).

Eldon J. Eisenach
University of Tulsa
Tulsa, Oklahoma

doi: 10.1093/jahist/jas208

Prophetic Encounters: Religion and the American Radical Tradition. By Dan McKanan. (Boston: Beacon, 2011. 326 pp. $34.95.)

In tracing the life histories of individuals, organizations, and movements of the American radical tradition over the course of two hundred years, Dan McKanan maintains that there are "prophetic encounters" during which people in their struggle to create a more just and equitable society are empowered "to tell new stories and build new communities" (p. 3). *Prophetic Encounters* comprises twenty-one chapters that capture how "we can glimpse the face of the divine and change the world" (p. 15). McKanan's telling of the history of American radicalism (he assumes the descriptors *left* and *radical* are interchangeable) is guided by three insights: "the Left is a tradition, the Left is thoroughly intertwined with religion, the Left is itself analogous to religion" (p. 5). The claim that there is a "radical tradition" is important to McKanan, for it is an acknowledgment that each generation is shaped and inspired by those who have gone before it. Equally important is the extent to which religion and radicalism are "intertwined," which calls into question the often-artificial distinction between religious and secular radicalism. Finally, the insight that "the Left is itself analogous to religion" is for McKanan a way of stressing that radicalism, like religion, binds people together with shared values, ideals, and commitments that forge new identities and communities.

McKanan weaves together a rich tapestry that extends from an examination of the religious roots of the early nineteenth-century Working Men's movement to the future of a broad-based American radicalism. His understanding of religion is inclusive and connects people of various hues and stripes, be they traditional-believing Christians or Jews, spiritualists, free-thinkers, or religious dissenters and those usually not thought of as religious such as Eugene V. Debs, who understood the dehumanizing impact of capitalism on human life and held to an alternative vision of human society in which human community and solidarity could be kindled, fostered, and sustained. McKanan lifts up a range of voices: we encounter radical aboli-tionists, black and white, nineteenth- and twen-tieth-century female radicals, socialists, Catholic radicals, and people involved in nonviolent resis-tance to war and institutional racism, along with student radicals, feminists, environmentalists, and lesbian, gay, bisexual, and transgendered activists. Particularly noteworthy is McKanan's analysis of the rise of the religious and political Right, especially at a time when many Ameri-cans identify "Christian" with conservative evan-gelical Protestantism, overshadowing other expressions of the Christian tradition that adhere to a more radical understanding of Christian faith and practice.

McKanan has joined together stories, such as the crucial role of black churches throughout American history, that speak as much to success as failure. For McKanan, failure needs to be seen in light of the daunting task that confronts all American radicals who seek a kingdom marked by justice. *Prophetic Encounters* is well worth reading and a needed corrective to limited understandings of both the history of American radicalism as well as the pivotal role that religion has played in the struggle for a pol-itics demarked less by an obsession with power and more about how to conceive the world dif-ferently and create new human possibilities.

Robert H. Craig
College of St. Scholastica
Duluth, Minnesota

doi: 10.1093/jahist/jas184

The City on the Hill from Below: The Crisis of Prophetic Black Politics. By Stephen H. Marshall. (Philadelphia: Temple University Press, 2011. xii, 235 pp. $64.50.)

Would Martin Luther King Jr. have been suc-cessful without a vision of a covenanted America: citizens separated by race but able to be called to reconciliation, higher purpose, and God's love? Without this, there would have been no "I Have a Dream" speech. King's role as a prophetic social critic who envisioned a "beloved community" created through the Christian principle of nonviolence left behind a long legacy. And now we learn from Stephen H. Marshall that his role also had a long prehistory.

The City on the Hill from Below traces a tra-dition of African American political thought that is prophetic and grows out of "covenant" thinking that envisions civic life as "a sacred errand" (p. 2). It emphasizes the bond of love between citizens and searches a language of sacrifice to overcome "self-interestedness" (p. 13). Marshall explains that "prophets are a distinguished group of inspired social critics who remind the community of their constitu-tive covenanted obligations to God and inter-pret prevailing social contradictions in light of these originary covenanted obligations" (p. 18). All of this had the sort of moral pull and conviction capable of addressing the mis-treatment of African Americans throughout history.

Marshall divides his book into chapters on David Walker, Frederick Douglass, W. E. B. Du Bois, and James Baldwin. There is not a great deal of new material on any of these figures, but Marshall does well at drawing con-nections between them. The historical con-texts of these figures are so different: Walker was writing when slavery solidified throughout the South; Douglass when the Civil War approached; Du Bois in the wake of Recon-struction and the rabid racism of the 1890s; Baldwin during and after the successes of the 1950s–1960s civil rights movement. Yet even with their differences, Marshall shows how patterns of thought repeat. Ironically, it is when he loses the thread of the work that Marshall is most insightful—for instance, in discussing Douglass's idea of slavery as "social death" (p. 67). Marshall is especially astute on Du Bois's antimaterialism and his hatred of the excesses of the Gilded Age mattering as much as his dismay at Booker T. Washington's leadership. Du Bois linked "philosophical wisdom and civic virtue" and came up with an "aristocratic civic republicanism" (p. 121) that feared demagoguery as much as abject racism. Marshall's discussion of Baldwin is also intriguing, emphasizing the theme of love. "Love is," Marshall writes, "an activity of revelation, an activity in which the lover discloses himself or herself to the beloved as a condition of pushing the beloved to self-disclosure" (p. 154).

Historians might bristle at the sweep of such a work that brings together differences under one rubric. Others will find Marshall's prose clunky, piled-on, and pretentious: We hear about "heteronormative, patriarchal norms of society" and Harvard University's "productive constitutive imperfection" (pp. 24, 118). In addition, Marshall ends this short book not by tying things together but by exploring Barack Obama's "post–civil rights" generation and the professionalization of politics (p. 170). It is not clear how or if the tradition of prophecy has disappeared or been co-opted by the Right or has just lost steam. Still, even with these weaknesses, Marshall's book makes for a fine treatment of black political thought.

Kevin Mattson
Ohio University
Athens, Ohio

doi: 10.1093/jahist/jas310

Black in Latin America. By Henry Louis Gates Jr. (New York: New York University Press, 2011. xii, 259 pp. $26.95.)

This is an accessible account of a respected public intellectual's encounter with the histories of African chattel slavery and its legacies in the Americas today. It is the companion volume to the PBS documentary series of the same name and, like the films, leans heavily on the persona of its author, structuring itself as a travelogue of Henry Louis Gates Jr.'s flight plans, hotels, and meetings. An entertaining alternative to the chronologically framed textbook, this approach has its advantages. In a folksy vernacular it recounts a great range of historical events and actors, offering a wonderful level of detail without overly challenging the novice audience.

The book extends the first-person narrative of discovery into a sort of historical whodunit. Is Brazil really a racial democracy? How did

Mexico's African heritage disappear? "I felt as if I were investigating a great mystery," Gates affirms in Peru (p. 91). Each puzzle is resolved into a digestible nugget: Brazil's racial harmony is desired but still distant; Mexico's caste categories have left deep denial there; Afro-Peru was long muzzled, but recent cultural and political triumphs offer hope for multiculturalism; the Dominican Republic's vehement differentiation from Haiti distances it from its blackness, while Haiti is strong and proud, if beset by troubles; and Cuba is full of fighters whose spirit will emerge into the next revolution.

Along the way to these nutshells are subtle takes on historical issues. Gates wrestles with the dilemma that faces every scholar in the classroom: how to convey complexity at an introductory level. He aims high, promising to pose a sophisticated, useful question: "what does it mean to be 'black'" (p. 3)? The answers redound, alas, to the myriad color categories in play in Latin America (including a ten-page appendix listing terms) in contrast to North America, where the answer is apparently self-evident. "In the United States, everyone just sees me as black," Gates explains in Brazil, refusing any sense of the relevance of class, eschewing the pressing task of analyzing the ongoing, interlinked construction of race and nation everywhere (p. 38). In Mexico, Gates asks his hosts, "why were your white people more willing to sleep with black people than my white people" (p. 75)? This stunning amnesia, a thoroughgoing naturalization of the one-drop rule, is the fruit of the comparative gesture.

In a move designed to reassure the ill-informed, Gates confesses that he was astonished to realize that the United States was not the only place in the Americas to import African slaves. Offered as a rejection of U.S. exceptionalism, this familiar ritual of proclaiming innocent ignorance is exceptionalist in effect, as is Gates's consistent positing of U.S.-style black consciousness as the best solution to racism anywhere. Is the United States' brutal racialization of black, brown, and poor via the criminal justice system—even if it does produce stars such as Gates—the best our visionaries can imagine?

Framing the work as national comparison, in tandem with the fraternal embrace extended to the ignorant, defines a recognizably imperial reading position and compromises the lessons the book aims to teach about race. For instructors willing to risk or counter those effects, the book has much to offer.

Micol Seigel
Indiana University
Bloomington, Indiana

doi: 10.1093/jahist/jas169

Representing the Race: A New Political History of African American Literature. By Gene Andrew Jarrett. (New York: New York University Press, 2011. x, 262 pp. Cloth, $70.00. Paper, $22.00.)

Gene Andrew Jarrett, in his first book, *Deans and Truants: Race and Realism in African American Literature* (2007), did such a fine job with his arguments that by book's end readers might well have experienced a figure-background shift, finding themselves not simply with a new appreciation for those "truant" works of the book's title but regarding them as central to African American letters. *Representing the Race* would seem to signal an even more ambitious project in its subtitle, but it is important to register that indefinite article; Jarrett is not attempting *the* political history of African American literature. Still, in the space of 209 pages, Jarrett reaches from the colonial era and the first days of the republic to the writings of President Barack Obama and the court case involving Alice Randall's parodic novel *The Wind Done Gone* (2001).

There is much to learn from this project, for both experienced scholars and more casual readers. I am embarrassed to say that I have not yet read President Obama's first book, *Dreams from My Father* (1995), and so it came as a surprise to learn that in his youth he had known, by way of his grandfather Stanley Dunham, the African American poet Frank Marshall Davis. Many readers, I imagine, will be in the reverse position, learning of Davis, his remarkable career as a writer, and his contacts with Obama. It is to be hoped that this information might have the effect of sending more readers to Davis's poetry even as it illuminates our understanding of Obama as an author.

The book opens with a superb meditation on Thomas Jefferson's writings (once we get past the insistence that Jefferson was a "black president" [p. 2]) in the context of his senseless dismissal of Phillis Wheatley, followed by a critical reading of David Walker's responses to Jefferson and Jeffersonian racial ideology. Subsequent chapters offer analyses of Frederick Douglass's third autobiography, *Life and Times of Frederick Douglass* (1881), as well as critical writings of Anna Julia Cooper, Alain Locke, Pauline Hopkins, Rudolph Fisher, Claude McKay, Langston Hughes, and others. But, as rewarding as those chapters are, the final two chapters truly have something original to offer. Jarrett's study of the case of *Suntrust Bank v. Houghton Mifflin Co.* (U.S. Court of Appeals, 2001), in which the trustees of the Margaret Mitchell copyrights sought to prevent publication of Randall's *The Wind Done Gone,* opens onto a vital discussion of the racial politics of copyright law, and the final section on Obama is surely one of the more astute discussions of his work as a writer.

"Hopefully, my book signals a watershed moment in thinking about the political history of African American literature," Jarrett writes in his introduction (p. 17). In a sense, the book *is* filled with hope, and while *Representing the Race* never quite gets around to answering a question posed at the outset—how does "one measure the political value of African American literature"?—it provides a series of analyses that may be most useful when we find ourselves at that watershed.

Aldon Nielsen
Pennsylvania State University
University Park, Pennsylvania

doi: 10.1093/jahist/jas165

Whiting Up: Whiteface Minstrels and Stage Europeans in African American Performance. By Marvin McAllister. (Chapel Hill: University of North Carolina Press, 2011. xvi, 330 pp. $39.95.)

This study of whiteface minstrelsy and the performers (the stage Europeans in the title) who appropriated "white dramatic characters crafted initially by white dramatists and, later, by black playwrights" explores the careers and contributions of African American actors, singers, dancers, comedians, playwrights, and performers in many media who challenged American cultural stereotypes in theater and popular entertainment from the eighteenth through the twenty-first centuries (p. 1).

Marvin McAllister investigates the "dual Afro-Diasporic tradition of whiteface minstrels and stage Europeans that . . . operated for centuries just beneath America's representational radar" and allowed African Americans to "reach beyond traditional artistic practices to play with or subvert white ways and cultural meanings" (pp. 1, 5).

Using Joseph Roach's definition of white [face] minstrelsy as an "extra-theatrical, social performance in which people of African descent appropriate white-identified gestures, vocabulary, dialects, dress, or social entitlements," McAllister identifies, analyzes, and interprets several dozen representations of race, gender, ethnicity, political inequality, and social injustice by "historicizing" his thoughtfully chosen examples to reveal that whiting up was "an underappreciated African American tradition" (p. 1).

McAllister focuses on several African American performers who played stage Europeans, such as James Hewlett in John Home's *Douglas,* Paul Robeson in Shakespeare's *Othello,* Canada Lee as Daniel de Bosola in John Webster's *The Duchess of Malfi,* and Evelyn Preer in Oscar Wilde's *Salome.* Those artists were only a few who chose their stage vehicles from European and American dramas or entertainments rather than accommodating themselves to the audience's insistence on common stereotypes or conventional representations of black men and women.

Whiting Up, with its iconic cover photo of Bob Cole in costume as Willie Wayside (the red-haired white tramp), interrogates the many contributions of African Americans to popular American entertainment. From vaudeville and the creation of all-black touring companies to early twentieth-century African American musical comedy to workshop theater (the Ethiopian Art Theatre and Negro Ensemble Company), and from the direct-address monologue comics to the successful television comedians who appealed to white

and black audiences, each of the institutions and artists mentioned "created a foundation for . . . creating, mastering, and potentially transforming unwieldy racial imagery" (p. 214).

After McAllister considers Adrienne Kennedy's *Funnyhouse of a Negro* (1964), Anna Deavere Smith's *Fires in the Mirror* (1992), David Hwang's *Yellow Face* (2007), and Halle Berry's performance in the film *Frankie and Alice* (2010), he concludes that

> when we respectfully appropriate whiteness, blackness, yellowness, or brownness, we can transform our social deconstructions and reconstructions into new universals . . . where difference is celebrated and racism is a problem vigilantly relegated to the past. (p. 264)

McAllister hopes that his examination of African American whiteface performance will encourage "more racially transcendent casting decisions that force audiences to operate on multiple and sometimes conflicting levels" (p. 17). He accomplishes that goal by providing a deeper understanding of racial representations, contributing an excellent addition to recent studies committed to reversing the negative stereotypes in American popular culture, and increasing the opportunities for black artists to demonstrate the full range of their creativity for audiences of all races, colors, and cultural traditions.

William J. Mahar, *Emeritus*
Penn State Harrisburg
Middletown, Pennsylvania

doi: 10.1093/jahist/jas314

Fighting for America: The Struggle for Mastery in North America, 1519–1871. By Jeremy Black. (Bloomington: Indiana University Press, 2011. xx, 470 pp. $39.95.)

In *Fighting for America,* Jeremy Black follows the contours of various contests of empires in North America over four centuries. The book starts with military engagements and diplomatic confrontations involving Indian, Spanish, French, Dutch, and British governments in a multipolar North America but graduates into a detailed examination of a century-long bipolar contest (1783–1871) featuring the United States and Great Britain. In this respect, the structure of *Fighting for America* reflects the declining American fortunes of other imperial powers in the late eighteenth and early nineteenth centuries.

Black concludes with a thought-provoking methodological essay on historians' approaches to the study of America and its relation to Britain, Europe, and the world. His intention in this book is to counter deterministic explanations of the United States' emergence in the mid- to late nineteenth century as the dominant power in North America. Rather than portraying a steady march to predestined and, in retrospect, foreseeable preeminence, Black emphasizes that the growth of American power in North America was a product of both chance and policy choices made by national and imperial governments. Thus, the U.S. rise to power was haphazard, precarious, and even reversible—a product of momentous decisions of the British, French, Spanish, Mexican, and U.S. governments at critical points in time. Indeed, Black points out that the United States' dominance in North America was not conceded, nor recognized, until quite late in the game.

Black examines the evolution of continental influence, control, and consolidation in North America as a factor and outcome of interactions between empires. Challenges to governments' influence and control that emanated from within their own jurisdictions are generally viewed through the prism of diplomacy. Critics will point out that such internal challenges—specifically, peripheral populations' effective resistance to central governments—often proved more vexing, persistent, and threatening than those posed by foreign governments. To Black, however, these challenges implicitly or explicitly invited foreign intervention.

Black's account of imperial contests over territory and influence is a purposeful effort to undermine Turnerian narratives of exceptionalism and Manifest Destiny—narratives that focus more on overcoming internal challenges. He thus emphasizes the role of diplomatic and military contingency (or opportunity) over structural advantages enjoyed by the United States. Historians who point to such structural demographic, social, economic, political,

environmental, and strategic factors in America's march of progress—prodigious population growth, class mobility, cheap and abundant land, a booming economy, disunited enemies at home and overstretched rivals abroad, and oceanic buffers that offered the United States effective defense for free—likely do not see themselves as Manifest Destiny Turnerians. Nevertheless, Black cautions against elements of Turnerian determinism in those historians' approach to American history. He argues that the advantages bestowed on the United States by providence or circumstance were not decisive in its emergence as the supreme North American power. In doing so, Black asks critics and others to identify the degree to which U.S. dominance in the late nineteenth century was a product of internal strengths or actions taken and avoided by the nation's rivals.

Guy Chet
University of North Texas
Denton, Texas

doi: 10.1093/jahist/jas244

A Distinct Judicial Power: The Origins of an Independent Judiciary, 1606–1787. By Scott Douglas Gerber. (New York: Oxford University Press, 2011. xxii, 413 pp. $95.00.)

This is a delightful book. Scott Douglas Gerber acknowledges from the start that he has been an active participant in debates about the proper role of the federal judiciary in the American system of government. He opposes what he identifies as a heavily supported contemporary concept of "popular constitutionalism" (p. 3). Thus, he writes: "The principal aim of my book is to shed light on the federal model by exploring the experiences of the original states. My objective, quite simply, is to identify the origins of Article III" (pp. xiv–xv). He has a secondary purpose, one that follows closely after the origins, the matter of defining judges' duties, with special attention to their power of judicial review. From that general intention, Gerber moves easily into a history of the notion of judicial review. Beginning with Aristotle, Gerber tracks the emergence of that notion and concludes with John Adams. Of Adams, Gerber writes that he was "the American founding's most sophisticated, political theorist" (p. 24). Thus, even though Adams was not at the 1787 Philadelphia convention, Gerber closes the first part of his book by noting the important role that Adams played in the debates about the Constitution.

In the almost three hundred pages that follow, Gerber describes in detail the processes by which each state reached the conclusion that an independent judiciary was a critical part of its new status. That it took some states into the nineteenth century (Connecticut in 1818, for example) should not be a surprise to anyone. Others, such as New Jersey (1947) and Rhode Island (2004), may be a surprise, though their lateness serves to support what Gerber notes near the start of the book—that debate about the judiciary is ongoing.

In the end, Gerber presents a short appendix "to demonstrate that popular constitutionalism is wrong." Like in most of Gerber's other books, the appendix is divided into topical sections, each containing the core of a response to an argument or another discrete point. The encyclopedic character of the book places it comfortably within Oxford University Press's collection.

Having Gerber return to his own participation in the debate brings us back to the beginning of this review, where the book is described as "delightful." Another description might have been "charming." On a level separate from Gerber's debate is the prodigious amount of research evidenced in the long middle of his book. Anyone doing research on early American constitutionalism will undoubtedly be directed to this book, for both content and argument. Those starting their work with this book would also be wise to note the textual material. Repeatedly, Gerber thanks someone on the opposing side, in the "popular constitutionalism" camp. He offers thanks and appreciation for those who read the manuscript and offered comments, even those who have different conclusions than his. To say that is an example for all to follow is an understatement.

Walter F. Pratt
University of South Carolina
Columbia, South Carolina

doi: 10.1093/jahist/jas175

The Empire Reformed: English America in the Age of the Glorious Revolution. By Owen Stanwood. (Philadelphia: University of Pennsylvania Press, 2011. x, 277 pp. $45.00.)

Conspiracy! A seventeenth-century Puritan asked, "if God be with us, who can be against us?" (Francis Higginson, *New England's Plantation,* 1630). Readers of Owen Stanwood's engrossing analysis of English America in the age of the Glorious Revolution might answer: "Everyone!" Conspirators against English liberties included the French, who represented the brutal, arbitrary, and absolutist Catholic world; their even more brutal papist Indian allies; and England's internal enemies, namely, English Catholics and radical dissenters from the Church of England. These conspirators ran rampant through the British Isles and the evolving English American colonies. England's conspiratorial enemies, more than any other factor, helped define the early reformed empire Stanwood so ably describes. This tale of reforming an emerging empire is a complex and, at times, tedious tale of repetitive missteps and miscalculations that prevented meaningful solutions by imperial managers.

Stanwood is sympathetic to efforts at imperial reforms. Although he does not dwell on this point, the story of failed imperial reform in the post-Restoration period eerily parallels the imperial failures of the pre–War for Independence era. Imperial managers never seemed to get it right.

As the story unfolds beginning in the 1660s, Stanwood presents the necessities for a more centralized (read, effective) empire. The tensions between entrenched local autonomy in the colonies and the need for more centralized control from London became the dominant and constant theme of empire formation. Reluctant colonial leaders recognized that it was in their self-interest to yield some authority to London but gripped tenaciously their cherished concept of local autonomy. Imperial leaders conceived well-thought-out plans but generally appointed the most inept minions to carry them to the colonists. It was not the brilliant plans of imperial leaders but the ever-growing fear of the French and their Indian allies that moved English colonists. Imperial reform looked most attractive to colonists when these threats escalated, whether in New England, the Chesapeake, or the West Indies. Those who ventured forth to the plantations, unfortunately for imperial reform, squandered their advantages by their ineptitude as politicians and their lack of understanding of the locals they tried to govern. Some of Stanwood's most obscure examples of reform prove to be his most instructive, those from New Hampshire and Bermuda, for example.

Perhaps Stanwood's greatest contribution results from his systematic focus on anti-Catholicism. Rumors of papist plots (beginning with the fictional Titus Oates plot in 1678) became the great motivator for mobilizing public support. Some, Edwyn Stede in Barbados, for example, saved their careers by learning how to play the anti-Catholic card. Others, most notably the Catholic third Lord Baltimore and his papist officials in Maryland, proved hapless in the face of Catholic-Indian conspiracies. A Protestant rebellion fueled by rampant anti-Catholicism destroyed Baltimore's efforts to "promote religious understanding" (p. 62). This constant struggle between good (Protestants) and evil (Catholics) defined religion and empire for the English. Stanwood has admirably pulled together disparate sources to show how these papist/Indian conspiracies helped define the empire and thwart attempts to make it effective.

John D. Krugler
Marquette University
Milwaukee, Wisconsin

doi: 10.1093/jahist/jas185

One Family under God: Love, Belonging, and Authority in Early Transatlantic Methodism. By Anna M. Lawrence. (Philadelphia: University of Pennsylvania Press, 2011. 282 pp. $42.50.)

Anna M. Lawrence, who teaches at Florida Atlantic University, subtly challenges the argument of Lawrence Stone and E. P. Thompson that eighteenth-century evangelicals, especially the Methodists, promoted the repression of sexuality and companionate marriage. She contends that Methodists in England and America lived out an elastic idea of family in which "brothers," "sisters," "fathers," and "mothers" in the faith provided an alternative form of family that relativized the biological

family unit and prompted a reconsideration of gender roles. The Methodist inclination toward intimacy among believers also strengthened emotional bonds in a manner that accelerated rather than hindered evangelical participation in the eighteenth-century turn toward romantic marriage. Methodist "family values" in the eighteenth century had little in common with the family values that have insinuated themselves into twenty-first century politics.

Through studies of Mary Bosanquet Fletcher, Hester Ann Roe Rogers, and Catherine Livingston Garretson, Lawrence illustrates how early Methodists found that their conversion into John Wesley's community often required a break from their birth families. The Methodists, however, offered them a new family of fictive kin who used emotional, erotic, and romantic language to express their ecstatic love for each other. Their love feasts and watch-night services offered anti-Methodist critics repeated opportunities to accuse them of sexual improprieties, and there were a few missteps, but Methodists were more likely to learn, through their experiences of God, how to make more independent decisions about marriage and family.

Some chose celibacy, but that choice was prominent only among the circuit riders who carried the Methodist gospel through large geographical "circuits," forming family-like "bands" and "classes" in which others learned a language that helped them adapt to the emerging romantic ideal of companionate marriage. Even the circuit riders lived celibate lives for only a short while. John Wesley's disastrous forays into the marital state contributed to his suspicion of the institution, but Charles Wesley not only found a loving marriage but also wrote hymns that popularized the language of intimacy. Unlike some predecessors, the Methodists began to think even of heaven as an opportunity to rejoin family members who had already crossed over into death. Meanwhile, Methodist families became nurseries of piety that often included the visiting circuit rider as virtually another member of the family. In the American South, Black slaves not only found "family" in Methodism as well as biological families, but they also sometimes became part of paternal, hierarchical, and oppressive but also strikingly intimate "family" circles in the plantation household.

The interpretation of the American Revolution as a family break-up might overstate the force of metaphors, but the argument that the split between American and British Methodists resembled, even exemplified, a family dispute is more plausible. Lawrence also minimizes the "family fights" through which Methodists divided into multiple antagonistic groups, but her well-researched investigation of the Methodist family offers a fresh angle of vision on an important religious movement.

E. Brooks Holifield, *Emeritus*
Emory University
Atlanta, Georgia

doi: 10.1093/jahist/jas202

Martyrs' Mirror: Persecution and Holiness in Early New England. By Adrian Chastain Weimer. (New York: Oxford University Press, 2011. x, 218 pp. $55.00.)

Adrian Chastain Weimer begins *Martyrs' Mirror* with a sketch of the English Protestant martyr tradition. Fueled by the Marian martyrs, this tradition assumed that Antichrist would persecute the true church until his kingdom finally fell, and the tradition passed over to New England with many consequences. It heightened local religious conflicts by raising their stakes. Perhaps, Weimer suggests, in the long term it helped bring about practical tolerance, since people's willingness to suffer for their beliefs could be read as validation of them, or at least of the inappropriateness of acting as persecutors. Martyrdom also fed into devotional ideals, and it was conceptually elastic enough for Congregationalists to convince themselves that the discomforts of colonization were forms of martyrdom (although in one of Weimer's examples [p. 6], Cotton Mather is probably referring to Huguenots killed by the Spanish).

One chapter is devoted to the Separatist martyr tradition. Roger Williams appears in his debate with John Cotton in which each of them affirmed the validity of his respective stance toward the Church of England by asserting that its proponents had suffered more genuine persecution. William Bradford invoked Separatism's martyrs in the 1640s as he attempted to preserve a distinctive Separatist identity at a time when little distinguished Separatist practices from those of other New England Congregationalists.

Three chapters focus on New England's intra-Protestant disputes. "Performances of Martyrdom in the Antinomian Controversy" spottily explores how parties in that dispute embraced the rhetoric of persecution. Weimer's unreflective use of the nineteenth-century label *Antinomian Controversy* perhaps explains why she underplays the extent of fear about the allegedly murderous Family of Love (*Familist* and its cognates were more widely used terms in the controversy than *antinomian*). A few people were banished, not the "dozens" that Weimer claims (pp. 15, 63); the rest left by choice. English Baptists had their own martyrdom traditions, but in New England, as Weimer shows, their affinities with Congregationalism often muted the apocalyptic rhetoric of their protests against the local establishment. Those same affinities hindered the sustained repression that some Congregationalists attempted against them. Quakers sought out persecution as a witness to the righteousness of their cause and the anti-Christian nature of their opponents. Congregationalists were happy to oblige, even while arguing that it was they who were being persecuted by the Quakers, whom they were whipping, mutilating, and executing. Unlike with the Baptists, there is little evidence to support Weimer's speculation that widespread local revulsion against Quaker executions led to their cessation.

A final chapter is devoted to King Philip's War (1675–1676). During that conflict, Congregationalists invoked the devil's war against the church and praised their soldiers as martyrs to deflect their own responsibility for the fighting and Quaker claims that the devastating war was divine vengeance for persecution. Daniel Gookin used tropes of martyrdom and persecution to defend the praying Indians against his fellow hostile English. Native converts may have been slow to invoke martyrdom because of cultural differences.

Martyrs' Mirror is an adventurous, thoughtful, and well-written survey of an important aspect of New England piety.

Michael P. Winship
University of Georgia
Athens, Georgia

doi: 10.1093/jahist/jas247

From Jamestown to Jefferson: The Evolution of Religious Freedom in Virginia. Ed. by Paul Rasor and Richard E. Bond. (Charlottesville: University of Virginia Press, 2011. x, 203 pp. $40.00.)

From Jamestown to Jefferson is a collection of six commissioned essays that outline the process by which Virginia transitioned from being a place with uneasy religious toleration and an established church to one of disestablishment and religious liberty. Despite a multiplicity of authors, the volume achieves a cohesiveness and integration often lacking in such collections.

Brent Tarter and Edward L. Bond provide a good grounding in the new Anglican history, which documents a strong vein of spirituality and lived religion in Virginia from its earliest founding. Virginians lived in a religious culture built upon the church seasons, the Book of Common Prayer, folk customs, and an established church that overcame shortages of clergy and a scattered population to create a lived faith on terms different than the familiar New England models.

Philip D. Morgan and Monica Najar pick up the story by showing that Virginia always had a diverse religious culture (thanks to indigenous populations, the importation of enslaved Africans, and the recruitment of non-English immigrants). English dissenters and the Great Awakening added further layers of diversity. The Anglican majority reacted to threats to social order and hierarchy with both legal and extralegal harassment and violence. Groups that did not seem to challenge the social order were treated with tolerance. Before 1776 Presbyterians were successful in avoiding most persecution by working within

the bounds of the Act of Toleration (1689). Baptists faced persistent persecution and violence because they rejected toleration in favor of religious liberty.

Thomas E. Buckley covers the struggle for disestablishment during the last three decades of the century and shows how a coalition of liberals and evangelicals developed an argument that religious liberty and healthy competition among religious groups were positive for the new republic. Anglicans, distracted by the formation of the Episcopal Church and an internal struggle between liberals and traditionalists, did not mount a strong defense of their own position and gutted the power of their church leaders.

The final essay, by Daniel L. Dreisbach, draws conclusions from the other essays while making a pointed distinction between religious liberty and a secular state. Virginians believed that religion was necessary for good morals, and good morals for good government. The best way to achieve this system, they argued, was through a vibrant competitive religious environment rather than a state church. Religion was expected to influence the state, but the state was not to favor one religion over another.

Overall, the volume is successful. Both Morgan and Najar, however, failed to absorb all of Bond and Tarter's findings, falling back on statements about the lack of a daily religious practice among Anglicans and adopting a definition of morality that lacks understanding of an Anglican culture that emphasized good works and saw a sabbath used for both worship and leisure as a well-spent day. While Bond points out that communion Sundays were exceptionally well attended, Morgan repeats old statements about low participation in communion. Morgan classified the Manakintown Huguenots as dissenters when noting that over time they baptized 150 of their slaves, but he does not recognize that the baptisms were recorded in the records of Anglican parishes and that Anglican clergy were doing the baptizing (p. 98). Najar forgets that Anglican parishes were funded by taxes before 1776 rather than by contributions of attendees (p. 116).

Despites these quibbles, this slim volume is a good read and has food for thought for both historians and the larger public.

Joan R. Gundersen, *Emerita*
California State University, San Marcos
San Marcos, California

doi: 10.1093/jahist/jas243

Early Modern Virginia: Reconsidering the Old Dominion. Ed. by Douglas Bradburn and John C. Coombs. (Charlottesville: University of Virginia Press, 2011. xii, 350 pp. $39.50.)

Inspired by the editors' article, "Smoke and Mirrors: Reinterpreting the Society and Economy of the Seventeenth-Century Chesapeake" (*Atlantic Studies*, Oct. 2006), the essays in this volume were originally presented in 2007 to mark the anniversary of the settlement at Jamestown. Researching Virginia's early history can be challenging. Unlike those of neighboring Maryland, many Virginia records were lost to haphazard storage conditions, occasional fires, and the chaotic conditions of military campaigns. The relative completeness and convenience of Maryland records have attracted more scholarly attention—especially from museum and public history professionals. Consequently, many scholars have been tempted to accentuate the similarities of the two Chesapeake colonies. Contributors to this volume convincingly argue that the history of the Old Dominion is sufficiently different to deserve closer scrutiny, regardless of the difficulties involved.

The editors Douglas Bradburn and John C. Coombs reject the adjective *colonial* in favor of the more useful *early modern* to emphasize interpretive frameworks that connect Virginia with the Atlantic world of the seventeenth century. An introduction by Lorena S. Walsh and conclusion by Philip D. Morgan provide a useful overview of the Chesapeake school's methodologies and analytical tools, while placing the volume's essays within historiographical and multidisciplinary context.

The Old Dominion of this volume is familiar and yet intriguingly foreign. New England's oft-assumed distinctiveness is complicated by Bradburn's essay, "The Eschatological Origins of the English Empire." He examines a common cast of characters and their shared intentions for Virginia and New England. Camilla Townsend analyzes the familiar struggles of Jamestown from the perspectives of the region's native inhabitants and the court of King Philip of Spain, while Edward DuBois Ragan delineates the evolving identities of Native Americans in the Rappahannock valley as they became surrounded by English settlements.

"The Rise and Fall of the Virginia-Dutch Connection in the Seventeenth Century," by Victor Enthoven and Wim Klooster, substantiates a greater and more complicated series of interactions between Virginia, England, and the Netherlands—including the English administration of several Dutch towns—than is commonly recognized. Their essay provides a nuanced examination of Dutch influences as they analyze interactions ranging from free trade to illicit smuggling, through familial ties and business partnerships, to occasional open warfare. This essay—like several others—also explores the evolving nature of identity.

Terri L. Snyder employs legal records to scrutinize the lives of unfree women at a time when "boundaries between acceptable and unacceptable violence were increasingly blurred, while those between free and enslaved were made increasingly clear" (p. 147). Essays by Coombs and William A. Pettigrew add to our understanding of slavery in the Old Dominion even as they challenge many accepted views on the characteristics of slavery's origins and practice there.

Rather than view deference and defiance as a dichotomous framework, Alexander B. Haskell sees both as integral to the political discourse of early Virginia. "Deference," he argues, "was inevitably the product of negotiation, or rather of the myriad negotiations that took place in" a variety of social and legal interactions (p. 176). Haskell distinguishes between the office and the officeholder and clarifies the seemingly contradictory views of individuals such as the Reverend Devereux Jarratt.

The scholars contributing to this collection exhibit a solid grounding in the historiography of early modern Virginia, while effectively employing new sources and methodologies to offer compelling new interpretations of the Old Dominion. As Philip Levy notes in his essay, "the change that made Middle Plantation was not chaotic, violent, or the result of failure . . . instead it was local, gradual, and remarkably steady" (p. 201). This impressive and highly recommended volume conveys the nuance of complexity and diversity that was the evolving society of early modern Virginia.

L. Scott Philyaw
Western Carolina University
Cullowhee, North Carolina

doi: 10.1093/jahist/jas259

Assumed Identities: The Meanings of Race in the Atlantic World. Ed. by John D. Garrigus and Christopher Morris. (College Station: Texas A&M University Press, 2010. xii, 152 pp. $29.95.)

This collection consists of an introduction and five essays examining issues of racial identification and classification in several Atlantic contexts from the seventeenth to the nineteenth century. Franklin W. Knight's introductory essay offers useful contextualization of the contributions, although assertions such as race has been "notoriously unreliable as a principal identifier" (p. 4) and "the United States has an unusual fixation on race" (p. 11) seem to miss the fundamental nature of what Elsa Goveia identified as the structuring principle integrating of Caribbean (and North American) societies (Elsa Goveia, "The Social Framework," *Savacou*, Sept. 1970, pp. 7–15).

John D. Garrigus's "'Thy Coming Fame, Ogé! Is Sure'" seeks to establish a significant historical place for Vincent Ogé, a wealthy merchant belonging to the *gens de couleur* social strata of Haiti. In October 1790 Ogé led a revolt to secure voting privileges for property-owning free people of color, which, while usually acknowledged in standard narratives of the Haitian Revolution, still remains overshadowed by the actions of figures such as Toussaint Louverture. Using the underutilized transcript of Ogé's January 1791 interrogation, Garrigus makes a compelling argument for such a reconsideration. He illustrates how Ogé had been planning to organize a free colored militia months before his revolt and, in so doing, attempted to extend the scope of citizenship across the racial barrier in the context of a "new Parisian definition of the militiaman-as-citizen" (p. 38).

Rebecca Goetz's "'The Child Should Be Made a Christian'" examines the 1667 Virginia law that disrupted the long-standing tradition in which baptism and conversion to Christianity conferred freedom on the enslaved. Rather than situating the case in the usual historical trajectory—as part of the transition from indentured servitude to permanent enslavement—Goetz argues for "its unique place in the history of Christianity in the Chesapeake and in the construction of race in the early South" (p. 47). Indeed, the act constituted "an exercise in self-definition and in racial categorization for the English" and thereby played a "singular role in defining the English understanding of human difference" and "what it meant to be Christian" (*ibid.*). In other words, being Christian would come to mean being English, white, and of free social status (p. 65).

Trevor Burnard's contribution focuses on the shaping of white identity in the Caribbean. While noting the centrality of the paradigmatic musings of Edward Long and Bryan Edwards, he also argues that Benjamin Franklin's *Observations concerning the Increase of Mankind* (1755) had a significant influence in creating "a chasm ... between British West Indian and British North American colonial societies," whereby the former could never be sufficiently (and properly) English (p. 73). Moreover, in this context, issues of gender were related to understandings of whiteness, evidenced by the struggle in the absence of sumptuary laws to mark racial identity. Yet the assertion that "Whiteness was endangered by the dereliction of gender rules" might be a bit of an overstatement, given the systematic way that the plantocratic allocation of gender roles buttressed the social system (p. 84).

Sidney Chalhoub, also reexamining a well-established issue, analyzes the 1831 Brazil law prohibiting the African slave trade, which was passed due to British pressure. Noting that historians have often pointed to the lack of enforcement of this law, Chalhoub focuses instead on what became the "customary seigneurial right" of randomly enslaving smuggled Africans (and later their descendants) (p. 89). As a result, a paradox emerged whereby public authorities *did* enforce the privilege to enslave illegally, a development that undermined freedom for all blacks in Brazil and led to the construction of racial codes to make all blacks and Africans "natural slaves" (p. 91).

The last essay, by Rebecca J. Scott and Jean M. Hébrard, traces the story of a family descended from an enslaved Haitian woman, identified as Rosalie of the Poulard Nation, whose family history traversed Haiti, Cuba, France, and the United States, with one descendant becoming a delegate for the state of Louisiana during congressional Reconstruction. The complex struggle to negotiate slavery and revolution provide, as the authors assert, a lens through which to view the "history of vernacular concepts of rights and dignity in the Atlantic world" (p. 117). Overall, this provocative collection of essays should generate new streams of thinking about well-established topics.

Demetrius L. Eudell
Wesleyan University
Middletown, Connecticut

doi: 10.1093/jahist/jas168

Cabin, Quarter, Plantation: Architecture and Landscapes of North American Slavery. Ed. by Clifton Ellis and Rebecca Ginsburg. (New Haven: Yale University Press, 2010. x, 294 pp. $45.00.)

The built environment of North America cannot be fully understood without taking slavery into account, argue the architectural and landscape historians Clifton Ellis and Rebecca Ginsburg in their edited volume *Cabin, Quarter, Plantation*. This excellent collection of twelve scholarly essays reveals the impact of the institution of chattel bondage on the *built landscape,* a term that refers to not only buildings but also to "yards, streets, fields, alleys, obscure trails, dusty lanes, fences, tree lines and all other elements of our surroundings that are the product of human intervention" (p. 2). Drawing from seven original and five reprinted studies from various disciplines, the editors have produced a fine collection that represents "scholars' best understandings to date of the interplay between slavery and the design, construction, and use of North America's built environment" (p. 9).

Central to the essays are three interrelated theoretical concepts. The first is slave agency. Several of the studies chosen for this collection illuminate the ways bondspeople appropriated or actively manipulated space and the material

world in response to slavery. Garrett Fesler's essay, for example, illustrates how the "swept yard" in front of slaves' houses reveals mechanisms of cultural survival that allowed Africans to apply traditional notions of outdoor communal spaces to the plantation setting (pp. 32–33). Barbara Heath's essay on the use of space on Virginia plantations similarly analyzes the existence of subfloor pits in slaves' houses, used to hide prohibited wares.

Another thread in the essays is the concept of racialization. The built environment allowed white slaveholders to reinforce their claim to racial superiority and mark their slaves as different or inferior. An example is the way planters modeled their plantations after small villages, with an elegant "big house" to shelter the white family and rude quarters to house slaves, as Dell Upton argues in a classic essay on plantation layout and social structure in eighteenth-century Virginia. Studies by Ellis, Edward A. Chappell, and William Chapman further reveal that the gradual improvement of slave housing in Bermuda, the Danish West Indies, and Virginia served to reinforce planters' paternalist ideology.

Finally, a third theoretical concept that runs throughout this volume is standpoint theory: "the enslaver and the enslaved perceived different geographies" (p. 6). An example is Ginsburg's essay on the ways American fugitive slaves utilized the "black landscape" to effect their flight (p. 54). She reveals how slaves secretly infused their surroundings with coded meanings that contradicted the hierarchical landscape systems of whites.

Cabin, Quarter, Plantation can easily be adapted for classroom use because its essays are well written, interesting, and openly suggest further research. A minor drawback is an almost exclusive focus on the United States and the English Caribbean (with no studies of Spanish or French colonies). Nevertheless, this volume is an excellent introductory overview of scholarship on the critical relationship between slavery and space.

Damian Alan Pargas
Utrecht University
Utrecht, Netherlands

doi: 10.1093/jahist/jas188

Ulster to America: The Scots-Irish Migration Experience, 1680–1830. Ed. by Warren R. Hofstra. (Knoxville: University of Tennessee Press, 2012. xxviii, 263 pp. $45.00.)

Readers interested in colonial and early American life will be delighted by the work of Warren R. Hofstra and his team of contributing writers that includes the notable historians Patrick Griffin, Kerby A. Miller, Richard K. MacMaster, Marianne S. Wokeck, and linguist Michael Montgomery. They form quite an impressive lot of Scots-Irish scholars. The authors have crafted a series of temporally situated case studies to cast light on one of the most amorphous ethnic groups ever to set foot on the mid-Atlantic area of the American colonies. One of the authors' objectives is to dispel myths associated with the group. Because of the absence of a common ethnic identity among the settlers and the different push and pull factors that affected successive waves of immigrants from Ulster, it is inviting to accept the authors' contention that these folk were indeed less stereotypical than the buckskinned frontiersman of popular imagination. However, dispelling the image of backcountry pioneers in search of natural liberty, which David Hackett Fischer so boldly described in *Albion's Seed: Four British Folkways in America* (1989), is an ambitious aim for such a small book. The writers succeed in showing that early American settlers from Ulster were a diverse lot made up of frontier-oriented homesteaders, adventurers, and well-educated clergy and business folk.

However, a number of the essays rely too much on secondary sources, which in many cases were used by the authors in earlier publications. Of particular note is Griffin's chapter on searching for independence. One is hard pressed to find a source in it published after 2005. He relies on his *People with No Name: Ireland's Ulster Scots, America's Scots Irish, and the Creation of the British Atlantic World* (2001), James G. Leyburn's *The Scotch-Irish: A Social History* (1962), Kerby Miller's body of work, and other secondary sources while virtually ignoring primary sources. A similar problem limits David W. Miller's chapter on searching for a new world.

While Griffin and David Miller rely heavily on their own work and other secondary sources,

MacMaster successfully harvests primary sources from the Donegal area of Pennsylvania. Among the records he used were minutes from the Donegal Presbytery, Rev. John Roan's account books, and several wills.

The book has two other limitations. One issue pertains to the political events that forged an Ulster Scots identity in Ireland during the 1600s as well as a schismatic culture area that straddled the Irish Sea. The authors are correct in pointing out that the migrants' experiences in America as well as their intermingling with other politically persecuted folk such as German and English Baptists affected their sense of Scots-Irishness. The book misses an opportunity, however, to explain their sense of political oppression and how that perception may have shaped their new American identity. Indeed, David Miller misses the mark in describing their experiences with the Crown. The ebb and flow of political policies such as the implementation and then elimination of the *regium donum* (an annual stipend made by the Crown to Presbyterian ministers in Ireland) and the adoption of discriminatory test acts in the late 1690s were political push factors. The other issue that detracts from the book is the lack of work on settlements in South Carolina, Georgia, and Tennessee, where Scots-Irish educators built colleges to train backcountry ministers.

The collection of essays in *Ulster to America* shows how groups of Scots-Irish folk settled in Delaware, Pennsylvania, Virginia, North Carolina, and Kentucky. It succeeds in describing the settlers' search for a sense of community, land, social order, peace and prosperity, freedom, security, and independence. The authors' list of pull factors is certainly reasonable.

Barry A. Vann
University of the Cumberlands
Williamsburg, Kentucky

doi: 10.1093/jahist/jas186

Revolutionary Founders: Rebels, Radicals, and Reformers in the Making of the Nation. Ed. by Alfred F. Young, Gary B. Nash, and Ray Raphael. (New York: Knopf, 2011. x, 452 pp. $32.50.)

Separately, the coeditors Alfred F. Young, Gary B. Nash, and Ray Raphael have long led the charge to remind Americans that there were more people involved in the American Revolution than those who signed the Declaration of Independence. Now they have joined forces to present a collection of twenty-two short essays written by the leading historians of the period, each nominating a new person or group of people to enter into the revolutionary hall of fame, whether as political "radicals," military "rebels," or social "reformers." These men and women deserve even more attention than the "traditional founders"; the editors argue that the "protagonists" of *Revolutionary Founders* "wanted to extend the lofty principles expressed" in the declaration (p. 4).

The book is divided into three sections, each dedicated to a particular phalanx of "founder." The essays that make up the section on political "radicals" include Young's piece on the Boston cobbler and street leader Ebenezer Makintosh, Raphael's examination of the political skills of the Worcester blacksmith Timothy Bigelow, T. H. Breen's piece on the career of the New Hampshire insurgent Samuel Thompson, Nash's profile of Philadelphia's radical caucus, Jill Lepore's overview of Thomas Paine's place in radical historiography, and David Waldstreicher's excellent contextualization of the involvement of the poet Phillis Wheatley in Boston's imperial crisis.

The second section, on military "rebels," features essays by Philip Mead on Joseph Plumb Martin's adventures in the Continental army; Michael A. McDonnell on two militia leaders in a Virginia county fighting against the revolutionary visions projected by the planter elite; Cassandra Pybus on three African Americans who fled American slavery and eventually helped found Sierra Leone; Jon Butler on James Ireland, John Leland, and John "Swearing Jack" Waller, three Baptist ministers fighting for religious toleration in Virginia; Colin G. Calloway on the efforts of the Chickamauga Indian leader Dragging Canoe to resist American encroachment; and James Kirby Martin on the Oneida leaders Han Yerry and Tyona Doxtader, heroic supporters of the patriot cause who tragically lost out just the same.

The third and final section, on social "reformers," includes Gregory Nobles's article on the legend surrounding Daniel Shays and Job Shattuck, the supposed leaders of the 1786

Massachusetts Regulation; Terry Bouton's comparison of how William Findley and David Bradford channeled resistance to the federal government during the so-called Whiskey Rebellion; Wythe Holt's fascinating portrayal of how the radical visionary Herman Husband imagined an egalitarian frame of government far different from that provided in the U.S. Constitution; a superb analysis by Woody Holton of just how revolutionary the act of simply writing a will was for Abigail Adams; Sheila Skemp's essay on Judith Sargent Murray and women's ideas of equal rights after the Revolution; Richard S. Newman's account of three "black founders" in Philadelphia; Melvin Patrick Ely's explication of how emancipation affected individuals in postrevolutionary Prince Edward County, Virginia; Seth Cotlar's description of Robert Coram, a former soldier who sent President George Washington a pamphlet containing radical ideas about populist economics and education reform; Jeffrey L. Pasley's work on Thomas Greenleaf, a headstrong printer who saw himself as a defender of press freedom; and Alan Taylor's description of Jedediah Peck's embrace of the new democratic possibilities unleashed by the Revolution.

Scholars of the Revolution will find little new in these contributions. In fact, most of the essays are distillations of larger works, very familiar to experts of the period; here are miniatures of prizewinning interpretations already forwarded by Taylor, Holton, and Ely, for example. Moreover, many of the individuals identified as "revolutionary founders" are not surprising; the usual suspects of the neo-Progressive interpretation of the era are all found inside, and most are well known to historians. There are, however, interesting new nominees (by Cotlar) and stellar contributions on more established subjects (by Waldstreicher, Holton, and Holt).

The importance of *Revolutionary Founders* lies in the act of collecting. It is a compendium that is meant to replace other catalogs of leading figures, such as Bernard Bailyn's *Faces of Revolution* (1990) and Joseph J. Ellis's *Founding Brothers* (2000). In this implicit argument, the editors are wholly successful. Though the editors surely hope for public influence, this book will also find traction in the classroom. Undergraduate teachers of the Revolution will find this a tremendous resource for increasing students' understanding (and for keeping their attention) of who made the Revolution, why they took action, and how they imagined it might improve their lives. Although the book is still a testament to the persistent need for syntheses about the American Revolution, *Revolutionary Founders* is another excellent effort in, as Eric Foner writes in the epilogue, "setting the record straight about the American Revolution and the ongoing struggle it unleashed for liberty and equality" (p. 395).

Robert G. Parkinson
Shepherd University
Shepherdstown, West Virginia

doi: 10.1093/jahist/jas217

Unfinished Revolution: The Early American Republic in a British World. By Sam W. Haynes. (Charlottesville: University of Virginia Press, 2010. xii, 378 pp. $29.95.)

When did the United States become independent? The answer is not nearly as straightforward as it might at first seem. In 1776 Congress declared the thirteen British colonies to be free and independent states. However, Americans had to wait another two years for France to become the first major European power to accept their claim; Britain and Spain took even longer. The date when American sovereignty was formally recognized is also not a satisfactory answer. Although the Anglo-American Treaty of Paris (1783) brought the first phase of the union's struggle for international rights and recognition to a close, Americans labored for decades to escape the perception that Britain, in particular, viewed them as something less than a great nation with the same rights and capacities as their former colonial masters.

Following an arc that stretches from the battle of New Orleans to the onset of the American Civil War, Sam W. Haynes argues in this splendid book that Britain was both the European nation that Americans most hoped to emulate and the one that posed the greatest obstacle to the realization of those ambitions. Britain had this dual role, moreover, not just because of its unsurpassed political and commercial power, but because of the broad appeal—matched, at times, by an equally strong repulsion—of British culture.

For wealthy Americans, Britain embodied the principles of aristocratic *noblesse oblige;* for African Americans and abolitionists, Britain was the world's leading humanitarian power; and for American workers, Thomas Paine, Frances Wright, and Robert Owen were a source of inspiration, even as Americans worried about Lancashire's satanic mills. Wherever Americans looked, Britain was both a beacon of hope and a harbinger of danger. Most of the things that Americans admired—including Britain's aristocratic traditions, its humanitarianism, and its radicalism—were things that they also found deeply alarming. "American attitudes . . . defied simple analysis and broad generalization," writes Haynes in one of the book's many well-turned phrases (p. 11).

Ironically, in the decades following the War of 1812 Americans probably had less to fear than the Anglophobes who populate Haynes's book might lead us to believe. Although Albion's commercial and diplomatic power was very real, so too was the British desire to avoid conflicts that could expose the nation's transatlantic interests to American filibusters and adventurers. As Haynes notes, the decade-long crisis over Texas proved to be the moment when Americans finally awoke to this reality. During the mid-1830s, fear of British intervention was a crucial factor in the U.S. government's decision not to annex the Lone Star Republic; in 1848, Americans seized Texas and the rest of northern Mexico with scarcely a nod in John Bull's direction.

Although the broad contours of this story are well known, few historians have told it with the elegance and insightfulness that Haynes achieves here. Americans, Haynes reminds us, shaped their nation during the early nineteenth century not just in their own image but also in the image of their former colonial master. If we have difficulty remembering the extent of that influence today, it is at least in part because Americans ultimately succeeded in making so much of Britain's example their own.

Eliga H. Gould
University of New Hampshire
Durham, New Hampshire

doi: 10.1093/jahist/jas307

Relieve Us of This Burthen: American Prisoners of War in the Revolutionary South, 1780–1782. By Carl P. Borick. (Columbia: University of South Carolina Press, 2012. xiv, 170 pp. $29.95.)

Carl P. Borick's *Relieve Us of This Burthen* delves into a previously ignored and marginalized aspect of the American Revolutionary War—the treatment of American prisoners of war (POWS) captured during the British southern campaigns of 1780–1782. These southern captives faced brutal conditions, including outbreaks of disease, poor food, and an abject disregard by authorities tasked with overseeing their welfare. In particular, other authors have overlooked the important role of Lord Charles Montagu, who utilized the terrible conditions as a recruitment tool, enticing American prisoners to fight for the British in the West Indies to escape captivity.

Borick, the assistant director of the Charleston Museum, has an exceptional understanding of the history of the city and its environs. He breathes life into the individual subjects of his study, and through extensive examinations of manuscript sources, allows their words to convey the plight of the war captive. The book brings to light many previously ignored stories, rather than rehashing the more well-known, and occasionally discredited, prisoners' tales. There is a nice mix of regulars and militia, as well as a balance between officer and enlisted perspectives. Borick has used both American and British sources to minimize the understandable bias that might otherwise intrude upon the story. Most unique to this work is the use of pension and bounty land applications held in the National Archives, a painstaking microfilm journey that yields substantial new descriptions of the captivity experience.

Unfortunately, Borick's grasp of the overall POW history of the conflict is flawed, at best. For example, he asserts that Sir Henry Clinton expected to exchange Americans captured at Charleston for John Burgoyne's army, taken at Saratoga. The British argued they were not POWS, did not require exchange, and refused any compensation for their return. This "Convention Army" has been well-chronicled and represents one of many holes in Borick's examination of secondary works, particularly those produced in the last three decades and focused on the war in the southern colonies. Linkages to broader issues of the war, including the difference between conventional and irregular warfare, the rivalry between the states and Congress, and the treatment of British and Loyalist POWS all merit much deeper examination than is presented in this short work.

Overall, the work's flaws do not overshadow its value as an analysis of a unique group of American military personnel, and as such, it is a worthy addition to the library of any professional or enthusiast interested in the war, captivity narratives, or the history of South Carolina. It is not the definitive work on prisoners of the Revolution, but it presents an interesting companion to volumes dedicated to the more well-known prison hulks of New York Harbor.

Paul J. Springer
*Air Command and Staff College
Maxwell Air Force Base, Alabama*

doi: 10.1093/jahist/jas241

A Merciless Place: The Fate of Britain's Convicts after the American Revolution. By Emma Christopher. (New York: Oxford University Press, 2010. viii, 432 pp. $29.95.)

The major theme of oceanic history that has emerged over the past generation has been the interconnectedness of people, objects, and ideas. It is fitting that historians living and operating in a transnational world of instantaneous communication and social media should discover the roots of globalization in the eighteenth century, when so many key elements of the modern world came into focus through trade, revolution, and violence. This oceanic approach makes it impossible to confine major events, such as the American Revolution, within the narrow parameters of national historiographies. Emma Christopher's *A Merciless Place* is a notable contribution to this literature.

The story Christopher tells is relatively straightforward. During the closing stages of the American War of Independence, the British experimented with sending convicts to the west coast of Africa. The first convicts were sent as members of two army units, raised to defend the interests of the Company of Merchants Trading to Africa. The convict soldiers were used to attack Dutch trading forts on the Gold Coast. Disease, indiscipline, and conflict with the company—which feared the convicts might disrupt and undermine the slave trade—rendered the experiment a failure. After the American war the British again tried to send convicts to Africa, without a clear idea of what they would do when they arrived. This effort, too, ended in failure. With America no longer an option and having failed in Africa, the British sought another destination for their felons. In 1788 the British began sending convicts to Botany Bay in eastern Australia where they helped colonize New South Wales.

The strength of this fine book is the wealth of detail and the subtle and sensitive reading of the evidence that Christopher brings to the subject. *A Merciless Place* provides a detailed analysis of subjects ranging from crime and criminal justice in eighteenth-century London to the operation of the slave trade in West Africa. She does so through a close reading of the sources, especially court records, and by providing compelling portraits of many of the people involved in convict transportation. Two of the most memorable figures in the story are William Murray, a career criminal, and Capt. Kenneth Mackenzie, who commanded the convict soldiers in Africa during the ill-fated experiment. Murray, who went by a number of aliases during his criminal career, had cheated the gallows several times and survived deportation to Virginia before being sent to Africa. Mackenzie was a Highland Scot who had fought in America and faced severe financial hardship when he agreed to accept the command in Africa. He proved to be an incompetent martinet driven by greed. He eventually executed Murray without trial by tying him to the mouth of a cannon and firing it. Mackenzie was eventually convicted of murdering Murray (and later pardoned).

A Merciless Place is an important book that tells the story of the convicts themselves— swept from the streets, often for trifling crimes, and shipped far from home: Virginia, the Gold Coast, and Botany Bay, to name but the most prominent destinations. Their stories epitomize the capricious and peripatetic nature of life and justice for those on the margins of the British Empire during the eighteenth century.

Frank Cogliano
University of Edinburgh
Edinburgh, Scotland

doi: 10.1093/jahist/jas171

Repressive Jurisprudence in the Early American Republic: The First Amendment and the Legacy of English Law. By Phillip I. Blumberg. (New York: Cambridge University Press, 2010. xiv, 410 pp. $120.00.)

In this fine comprehensive study, Phillip I. Blumberg surveys repressive state and federal judicial decisions regarding freedom of expression from the founding era through the 1830s. He looks at seditious libel, criminal libel, the imposition on defendants of bonds that could be forfeited by further improper speech before trial, contempt of court by criticism of decisions in the press, contempt of the legislature, antislavery speech, and blasphemy.

Repressive jurisprudence on these issues, inherited from Blackstone and English common law, "was fundamentally incompatible with the political ideals of the Revolution incorporated into the new Constitution" (p. 2). Still, "the constitutionality of the doctrines so dramatically restricting the range of criticism of the established institutions of the society [was] routinely upheld for more than 150 years" (*ibid.*). The political revolution was not matched by a legal revolution.

Blumberg's great contribution is to put the repressive, politically motivated Sedition Act prosecutions (and related state and common-law prosecutions) in the context of a larger set of repressive doctrines and attitudes and to show how they often functioned synergistically to repress political critics. Contempt of court for out-of-court criticisms of judicial decisions was another powerful weapon in political battles.

After the demise of the Sedition Act (1798) and of federal criminal common law, politically motivated state prosecutions for criminal libel continued for years, with Federalists prosecuting

Jeffersonian Republicans, Republicans prosecuting Federalists, and one faction of Pennsylvania Republicans prosecuting another. How is this to be explained? With the reception of English common law in the new American states, Blumberg says, "Blackstone . . . became the authoritative source of American constitutional law" (p. 379).

Still, free discussion often flourished, and the law evolved. Blumberg's account of repression includes several victories for freedom of expression: colonial juries that refused to convict (pp. 56–57); the Continental Congress's refusal to punish the press when faced with free-press objections (p. 66); the broad shock when Chief Justice Francis Dana of Massachusetts charged a jury with Blackstone's definition of freedom of the press (p. 69); the Sedition Act's acceptance of truth as a defense, and of an expanded role for the jury, and its rejection of free press as only a protection against prior restraint (guarantees that were ineffective in the face of packed juries and Federalist judges); grand juries that refused to indict; remarkable decisions and reforms in Pennsylvania (pp. 197, 201); and gradual reform in the states.

Blumberg discounts remarkably modern free-speech and free-press anti–Sedition Act arguments of Republicans in Congress because many of those politicians suggested that states could deal with libels. Still, some Republicans rejected repressive doctrines for the states, too. As one Republican put it, independent and upright state judges and juries would recognize that criticism of public officials was not criminal but a public duty and that truth could never be a libel (Michael Kent Curtis, *Free Speech, "The People's Darling Privilege,"* 2000, p. 74). In one Massachusetts common-law seditious-libel prosecution, the lawyer defending a Republican newspaper argued that seditious libel was not received by Massachusetts because it was inconsistent with republican government—that free press was not limited to protection against prior restraint and that great latitude was allowed for criticism of public men and public measures.

Blumberg's study shows that common-law seditious libel, criminal libel, and similar repressive doctrines facilitated politically inspired prosecutions and that the doctrines are inconsistent with democracy.

Michael Kent Curtis
Wake Forest University School of Law
Winston-Salem, North Carolina

doi: 10.1093/jahist/jas249

Reborn in America: French Exiles and Refugees in the United States and the Vine and Olive Adventure, 1818–1865. By Eric Saugera, trans. Madeleine Velguth. (Tuscaloosa: University of Alabama Press, 2011. xii, 572 pp. $30.00.)

Reborn in America traces the history and circumstances surrounding the efforts of French émigrés to establish what became known as the Vine and Olive colony in Alabama. This book, by the French professor Eric Saugera, provides a meticulously researched, flowing history of an intriguing settlement project that featured unexpected twists of fate and ultimately fell far short of its goals. In addition to being definitive, *Reborn in America* also provides a captivating narrative, featuring lively prose for which both the author and the translator Madeleine Velguth should be commended.

The author sensibly organizes the book into five parts corresponding to successive stages of the colony's establishment, and each presents different source and organizational challenges for Saugera. The first section lays the groundwork by explaining the circumstances surrounding the major leaders of this effort, some of whom were Bonapartist officers. The Hundred Days (March 1–June 18, 1815) forced the restored royalist government to revoke its amnesty for Napoleon's supporters; many of them had few options but to flee to the United States. Meanwhile, the political situation surrounding the colony's founding, on both sides of the Atlantic Ocean, was mercurial. With the emperor exiled to St. Helena, real and imagined conspiracies menaced the stability of several key Latin American governments, while the Monroe administration in the United States faced a delicate situation in its diplomatic relations with the new royalist French government in the wake of war with Britain. Relying primarily on French sources (including government archival material)

Saugera deftly explains a hugely complicated situation with exceptionally lucid prose.

The circumstances in Europe provide an essential context for this venture launched in Alabama, and events there continued to impact the effort launched in America. By 1817 several hundred French exiles had joined together on the East Coast in the Colonial Society of French Emigrants to establish a republican settlement in the western regions of the United States that had been recently seized from Native American groups. Meanwhile, Congress debated the wisdom of selling the settlers large quantities of land, as fears continued to circulate of a multi-continental conspiracy to place the banished Napoleon Bonaparte at the head of a new American Empire.

Saugera shows how the participants were a far more mixed group than traditional history has suggested. While some of the leaders were indeed leading Bonapartist generals—who had varied intentions—the Colonial Society of French Emigrants represented a wide range of social classes, skills, resources, and even political views. Among its numbers was Jacques Lajonie, a lieutenant in Napoleon's army who had fortuitously avoided the Russian campaign due to war wounds. Lajonie's perceptive letters are a main source and provide an essential perspective on the history of this colony.

By the late 1820s, because of the unsuitability of Alabama for viticulture and because of a revived amnesty for Bonapartists in France, most of the original French settlers had sold their interests to the English-speaking settlers who were moving into Alabama to establish cotton plantations. However, while the longterm impact of the Vine and Olive colony was limited, its history was frequently astounding. This book does it full justice, revealing great insights about the era and the people who lived in it.

John T. McGrath
Boston University
Boston, Massachusetts

doi: 10.1093/jahist/jas276

The People of the Standing Stone: The Oneida Nation from the Revolution through the Era of Removal. By Karim M. Tiro. (Amherst: University of Massachusetts Press, 2011. xxiv, 247 pp. Cloth, $80.00. Paper, $26.95.)

Karim M. Tiro's *The People of the Standing Stone* contributes to discussion of the interplay between the Oneida (a Native American tribe in northeastern North America) and European colonists. Sufficient primary sources have survived to enable Tiro to provide a well-documented picture of the interaction between these two cultures from the mid-eighteenth century (when the Oneida were loyal to the Iroquois Confederacy) to the late eighteenth century (when they separated from the confederacy to support the patriot cause in the American Revolution) to the early nineteenth century (when they suffered the same fate as their confederates in losing what they considered their ancestral territory to incoming floods of colonists).

Tiro's work expands on the conclusions drawn by other historians including Jack Campisi, William N. Fenton, Barbara Graymont, Joseph T. Glatthaar, Laurence M. Hauptman, Francis Jennings, Daniel K. Richter, and Alan Taylor, who have conducted in-depth investigations of the Oneida in the same time period. There are moments when Tiro's analyses of specific areas of interest, such as the reasons why the Oneida departed in different directions in the 1830s and 1840s, provide thought-provoking insight. In addition, he rightly identifies community leaders by their Oneida names rather than replacing them with English substitutes as has been the custom in the past. Tiro offers broad vistas of the Oneida nation's journey from being one of the Iroquois Confederacy's "younger brothers" (along with the Tuscarora and the Cayuga), whose influence rested on their mandate of counseling the "older brothers" (the Mohawk, the Onondaga, and the Seneca), to eventually being an increasingly landless and bewildered refugee band seeking asylum in distant American and Canadian settlements. Tiro corrects past scholarly misconceptions that the negative influence of their resident missionary, the Reverend Samuel Kirkland, created factions that weakened Oneida unity; he focuses instead on divisive elements of an economic, cultural, religious, and political nature that were of their own making.

However, there are some things Tiro does not address. The choice of Oneida chiefs and the relationship between chiefs and warriors begs elucidation. Nowhere does Tiro explain the rise and function of the significantly influential Pine Tree chiefs. Clans are occasionally mentioned but not discussed even though after the American Revolution Oneida speakers at conferences and signatories of treaties with the American government and with New York State were often shown in the records as representing their clan affiliations. Tiro is similarly silent on the choice and role of clan mothers, and he does not address why later treaties were signed by swelling numbers of Oneida community members. Tiro supports his argument that the federal government offered the Oneida recompense for losses they sustained despite their loyalty to the patriot cause in the American Revolution with documents that indicate that many Oneida homes were constructed and furnished with European commodities. This situation could have been discussed as evidence of increasing Oneida involvement with the Albany Committee of Safety, and hence the patriot cause. Nevertheless, Tiro succeeds in providing a very readable account of a tumultuous century for the Oneida.

David Norton
King's University College
London, Ontario, Canada

doi: 10.1093/jahist/jas206

Phillis Wheatley: Biography of a Genius in Bondage. By Vincent Carretta. (Athens: University of Georgia Press, 2011. xvi, 279 pp. $29.95.)

Students of early African American literary history have long operated without adequate understanding of the lives and worlds of African American writers. That situation is starting to change, though slowly, and it is revealing that we are only now getting a biography of the writer often considered the founding mother of this literary tradition, Phillis Wheatley (1753?–1784). Fortunately, Vincent Carretta's biography is quite good. Carretta's previous work includes the authoritative if somewhat controversial biography of Olaudah Equiano, and he knows the historical period well, on both sides of the Atlantic Ocean. He has pieced together

as full a story as can be told about Wheatley; indeed, he tells an engaging and informative story, including a careful accounting of those parts of Wheatley's life currently lost to the historical record. Moreover, he advances our knowledge of Wheatley's life considerably. As Carretta notes in the preface, his research produced a range of discoveries, including

> more writings by and attributed to Wheatley; new information about her origins, her upbringing in Boston, her likely role in the production and distribution of her works, the way she gained her freedom, her religious and political identities, and her marriage to John Peters, including the fact that they lived together for months before the wedding; and a plausible explanation for why she disappeared from the public record for several years during the 1780s. (p. x)

As Carretta's overview suggests, his discoveries provide not only new information but also newly broadened avenues for exploring Wheatley's unique development as a writer.

Wheatley's writings are in fact central to the story Carretta tells—their improbable emergence (given her situation as a slave and as a young black woman in a white supremacist world) and their shifting reception over time. Other studies, particularly the work of John C. Shields, have established the richness, depth, and reach of Wheatley's literary imagination. Carretta has something to say on such matters, but his focus is more on writing than on literature, and on literature as cultural capital more than literature as aesthetic achievement. "We have increasingly come to appreciate Wheatley as a manipulator of words," Carretta observes, adding, "perhaps we should have more respect for her as a manipulator of people as well" (p. 137). This is the story of a writer and not just the story of writings that emerged from a young, enslaved black woman. In that distinction lies the real value of this book: the way Carretta transforms Wheatley—who sometimes has been portrayed as almost a hapless accident of history, a young slave who happened to write poems of uncertain literary quality—into a knowing actress on the historical stage, a literary artist who anticipates Emily Dickinson as well as Frances Ellen Watkins Harper, someone who knew how it felt to "dwell in possibility" (Dickinson, "I Dwell in Possibility").

John Ernest
West Virginia University
Morgantown, West Virginia

doi: 10.1093/jahist/jas263

Love's Whipping Boy: Violence and Sentimentality in the American Imagination. By Elizabeth Barnes. (Chapel Hill: University of North Carolina Press, 2011. x, 211 pp. $49.95.)

Since September 11, 2001, scholars have addressed with renewed fervor the central role of violence in American culture. With *Love's Whipping Boy* Elizabeth Barnes advances the conversation by reaching back to nineteenth-century literature, mapping an essential national dialectic between violence and sentiment. Drawing on Sigmund Freud's theories of sadism and masochism, Barnes posits that U.S. Protestant theology contributes to the white male's internalization of both aggressor and victim identities, which in turn enables democratic involvement through the promotion of empathy.

Historically, a whipping boy received the punishment warranted by a young sovereign-to-be. Nineteenth-century literature contains any number of Christlike disciplined surrogates, but Barnes observes how the disciplining father figures, much like Abraham when ordered to sacrifice Isaac, "are recast . . . as the *sufferers* of the violence they deploy, thereby potentially redeeming violence itself from scandalous ends" (p. 7, emphasis in original). Within this salvific structure, the murderous father and the sacrificial son are one, punishment serves as the deepest expression of love, and aggression is the surest sign of empathy.

Barnes's opening chapter on Charles Brockden Brown's *Wieland* (1798) reveals how the titular patriarch's familicide casts him as a divine sacrifice in the development of a sensibility that was essential to the new republic. From the transformation of a murderer into a martyr, Barnes turns to the "fraternal melancholy" of Herman Melville, especially as expressed in *White-Jacket* (1850) and in the short story "Bartleby, the Scrivener: A Story of Wall Street" (1853), but also demonstrated in Melville's role as domestic abuser. Melville makes plain how fraternity based on shared suffering places the individual in an "emotional double bind" where empathy constitutes humanity, but "*too fully* feeling another's pain and powerlessness" could harm a sense of self (p. 12, emphasis in original). In chapters 3 and 4 Barnes teases out the implications of the emotional double bind in the conflict over slavery and in the aftermath of the Civil War. She concludes that John Brown serves as the nation's whipping boy because his race indicates empathetic submission rather than inherent abjection, but Frederick Douglass, in the short story "The Heroic Slave" (1853) and *My Bondage and My Freedom* (1855), must wed the black man's pursuit of freedom to acts of violence associating him with the master. Barnes's closing chapter on Louisa May Alcott's March family trilogy (encompassing the books *Little Women* [1868], *Little Men,* [1871], and *Jo's Boys and How They Turned Out* [1886]) explores the postbellum attempt to redirect the aggression of boys (or boyish girls) through the cultivation of empathy with things they harm, yet insofar as that attempt depends on an understanding of doomed "savagery," it underwrites lethal Indian policy.

I find in Barnes's forceful interpretive work a deep resonance with the writings of Richard Slotkin, especially his *Regeneration through Violence* (1971), though Slotkin offers an encyclopedic account of the bloody frontier while Barnes produces a tightly spun meditation on the nation's persistent urge to "feel right." Both Slotkin and Barnes find Melville their most insightful, if tortured, guide to the national psyche. In closing her book, Barnes draws on Melville's *Billy Budd* (1886–1891, published 1924) to frame the question raised by the spectacles of the Abu Ghraib prison: "To what extent can we recognize and experience the intra- and intersubjective nature of our worlds without the penetrating aid of violent enactments?" (p. 169). As she indicates, we find no satisfactory answers—only additional evidence of an America dependent on feeling deeply the pain it inflicts.

Laura L. Mielke
University of Kansas
Lawrence, Kansas

doi: 10.1093/jahist/jas195

Pío Pico: The Last Governor of Mexican California. By Carlos Manuel Salomon. (Norman: University of Oklahoma Press, 2011. xiv, 233 pp. Cloth, $24.95. Paper, $19.95.)

Pío Pico (1801–1894) was an important figure in California during the Mexican era (1821–1846). As governor during the American conquest and a well-known businessman in Los Angeles after the U.S.-Mexican War, he was an important transitional figure in nineteenth-century California, and his name is now attached to, among other things, a major Los Angeles boulevard, a school, and an apartment complex. This work is the first full-scale biography of Pico.

The book is fairly equally divided into a consideration of the Mexican period and the post-1850 American period. Descended from members of the 1776 colonizing expedition of Juan Bautista de Anza, Pico came of age during the time when Spanish rule was giving way to Mexican independence. He served in the territorial legislature, was granted extensive lands, and became a leading figure in southern California. He was appointed commissioner of Mission San Luis Rey after it was secularized. Carlos Manuel Salomon demonstrates that as commissioner, Pico cared little about the Indians whose livelihood he was supposed to ensure. Pico was an active figure in the factional struggles that plagued California during the 1840s and that prevented effective resistance to the American invaders. He fled to Baja California and Sonora during the war but returned to Los Angeles in 1848.

In the second half of the book, Salomon examines Pico's life as a southern California rancher and real estate investor. He maintains that Pico's experiences challenge Leonard Pitt's argument in *Decline of the Californios* (1966) that the *californio* community quickly diminished during the American period. Pico was able to do very well selling cattle and acquiring land into the 1870s. He was able to use the American system of courts to his advantage and often initiated lawsuits against others. These practices eventually proved to be his undoing, as he lost virtually everything in a series of court actions in the 1880s and early 1890s. But Salomon argues that these misfortunes resulted from Pico's "complex mix of ambition and recklessness" (p. 134). At his death, Pico (a Mexican of Afro-mestizo background) was ironically celebrated as one of the last Spanish dons.

The book focuses on Pico as an individual, and at times it left me wishing for a broader view of the social context in which Pico lived. He was a key figure in the secularization of the missions and the development of the California *rancho* economy, but Salomon says little about these wider developments. He might have also placed Pico's entrepreneurial activities in the 1850s and after in the context of what other *californios* around Los Angeles and San Diego were experiencing.

On the whole, however, the biography successfully presents a nuanced picture of a complicated and significant figure. This volume should be read by anyone interested in nineteenth-century California. It joins Robert Ryal Miller's *Juan Alvarado: Governor of California, 1836–1842* (1998) as an important contribution to nineteenth-century California and Mexican American history.

Robert M. Senkewicz
Santa Clara University
Santa Clara, California

doi: 10.1093/jahist/jas189

The Accidental Slaveowner: Revisiting a Myth of Race and Finding an American Family. By Mark Auslander. (Athens: University of Georgia Press, 2011. xvi, 383 pp. Cloth, $69.95. Paper, $24.95.)

This study seeks to answer questions about the myths of slavery in the southern states and what meanings they hold for us today. In focusing on a story about a female slave named Kitty, or Miss Kitty, held by the Methodist bishop James Osgood Andrew, the first president of Oxford College's Board of Trustees (the precursor of Emory University), Mark Auslander examines her brief life (1822–1851) and uncovers the lives of her children and later kin down to the present day. The myth surrounding Kitty and Andrew emerged from an 1844 letter to the General Conference of the Methodist Episcopal Church in New York City, likely written in Andrew's behalf by his close friend Augustus Longstreet, a lawyer, to show how the bishop never wished to be a slave owner but through circumstances beyond his control was forced to become one. Part of the myth was how much the bishop loved his slaves and how much Kitty loved her owner. The author points out that African Americans viewed the myth differently than most whites, at the time and in later years.

In seeking the myth's meaning for today's audience, the author became "embedded in the complex tapestry of race and the unresolved legacies of slavery" (p. 2). He and his wife traveled to several states in search of Kitty's ancestors, researching in courthouses, archives, and household attics. They also interviewed descendants, searching for the meaning and legacy of slavery. The author probed questions important to public historians: How is slavery represented and remembered in American society and what does slavery mean regarding our current racial difficulties? To answer these questions Auslander employs what anthropologists call historical ethnology, as well as sociology. He also summarizes the writings of anthropologists, ethnologists, novelists, poets, artists, and others to examine the meaning of kinship across racial lines and over time. For example, he describes the 1876 painting by Winslow Homer, *A Visit from the Old Mistress,* deemed by the author as the greatest American painting of the nineteenth century, to reveal the attitudes of African Americans toward a former slaveholding mistress.

It is clear, however, that this book is not meant for historians, except in the broadest sense. The myths are interesting and tracing them can tell us certain things about the past, but untangling them is nearly impossible, and their significance in addressing current racial problems is at best problematic. Seeking to uncover them in this instance produced a number of lengthy quotes, a tendency to use the first person singular, abstract discussions of kinship found in the works of anthropologists, and a good deal of emphasis on Auslander and his wife's personal, decade-long journey. Nonetheless, by tracing the current descendants of Kitty, the author has made a contribution to African American genealogy, no small undertaking.

Loren Schweninger
*University of North Carolina at Greensboro
Greensboro, North Carolina*

doi: 10.1093/jahist/jas300

The Allstons of Chicora Wood: Wealth, Honor, and Gentility in the South Carolina Lowcountry. By William Kauffman Scarborough. (Baton Rouge: Louisiana State University Press, 2011. xiv, 204 pp. $35.00.)

The Allstons of Chicora Wood is a biographical study of Robert F. W. Allston (1801–1864), a rice planter, state legislator, and governor of South Carolina (1856–1858). It incorporates vignettes of Allston's charismatic wife, Adele Petigru, and their children, especially Ben, a military officer and Episcopal priest, and Bessie, the author of *A Woman Rice Planter* (1913). Robert Allston was a figure of regional importance, noted chiefly for his essays on rice culture and for his unsuccessful attempts to expand South Carolina's public school system in the 1830s and 1840s. William Kauffman Scarborough notes that Allston's political activities played second fiddle to his agricultural interests and emphasizes family history, estate management, and cultural and charitable activities in his account of Allston's career. His research is meticulous, and he tells his story clearly and well, though sometimes with a veneer of sentiment.

Curiously, Scarborough skims over the central puzzle in Allston's life story: why a man whose wealth and prominence gave him full access to all that the antebellum United States had to offer ultimately chose to cast his lot with his state instead of his nation. The grandson of a Revolutionary War officer, Robert Allston was educated at West Point and served briefly as an ordnance officer, surveying harbors from Plymouth, Massachusetts, to Mobile, Alabama. He traveled extensively in the northern states, where two of his uncles had settled, and his eldest son, also a graduate of West Point, served in Pennsylvania, Missouri, Utah, and California in the 1850s. His brother-in-law James Petigru was a prominent Unionist. Yet Allston became a nullifier and a secessionist; moreover, he evaded pressure to run for the U.S. Congress, preferring to remain a big fish in the vibrant yet relatively small pond of South Carolina politics. He prioritized estate management and development of his local community above service to the nation and encouraged his son to do the same. Why did Allston set his priorities as he did?

The Allstons of Chicora Wood is essentially the story of a family's romance with its locale:

its rootedness in the South Carolina low country and its relative indifference to the nation burgeoning around it. Scarborough's approach to his subject is similarly localist. He does not situate the Allstons' experiences within the framework of larger trends in southern planter families or estate management; works such as Lorri Glover's *Southern Sons: Becoming Men in the New Nation* (2007), which might have enriched Scarborough's discussion of the experiences of the Allston men at West Point, and Laura Kamoie's *Irons in the Fire: The Business History of the Tayloe Family and Virginia's Gentry, 1700–1860* (2007), which might have shed light on Robert Allston's commitment to developing local infrastructure, are not addressed. *The Allstons of Chicora Wood* is thus a narrow, though finely drawn and suggestive account of a prominent South Carolina family.

Darcy R. Fryer
Brearley School
New York, New York

doi: 10.1093/jahist/jas246

Slavery and Sin: The Fight against Slavery and the Rise of Liberal Protestantism. By Molly Oshatz. (New York: Oxford University Press, 2011. x, 183 pp. $49.95.)

In this provocative and elegantly written book, Molly Oshatz provides an important reframing of the theological significance of the antebellum debate over slavery. Oshatz focuses on the intellectual history of moderate antislavery Protestants who sought to preserve both Protestant orthodoxy and moral opposition to slavery in the face of an aggressive proslavery biblical argument and an abolitionist movement that elevated conscience above scripture. To resolve this dilemma, antislavery moderates became reluctant theological innovators. They developed ideas about moral progress and the ongoing, historically situated nature of revelation that anticipated the ideas of liberal Protestantism in the postbellum period. By connecting the stories of these two movements Oshatz provides a framework for understanding both as part of a religious and intellectual history that spans the great historiographical divide of the American Civil War.

Oshatz takes the moderates seriously. Although current historians tend to dismiss them as prevaricating defenders of the status quo, she argues that the moderates' position was awkward but "morally honest" (p. 58). The biblical record condoning slavery was too compelling for them to ignore, and the "weak, contorted, and highly selective biblical exegesis" of Christian abolitionists who tried to argue otherwise merely confirmed proslavery accusations (p. 45). To explain slavery's sinfulness in more acceptable terms, moderates began to argue that the appropriate application of God's law could change as societies progressed. Slavery was not declared to be sinful in the Bible, but the gradual unfolding of Christian principles revealed it to be so. Without acknowledging it, moderates had begun the turn toward historicism.

Oshatz occasionally notes the moderates' limitations. Their distaste for abolitionism sometimes seems as much a social aversion to abolitionists' confrontational style as it does a matter of principle. More importantly, moderates "saw slavery as a moral issue between slaveholders and abolitionists, not between Christians and black slaves" and thus failed to emphasize "the antibiblical racist nature of Southern slavery" (pp. 73, 74). In this they were perhaps more complicit than Oshatz usually grants in narrowing the terms of the debate that created their interpretive dilemma.

After the Civil War and emancipation, slavery's sinfulness seemed self-evident to northern Protestants. As they responded to new challenges, including evolutionary theory and historical biblical criticism, liberal Protestants built upon antislavery moderates' ideas about moral progress, revelation in and through history, and the role of Christian experience in determining the meaning of the Bible, but they did so without fully recognizing their source. The debate over abolition became an object lesson in the demands that moral progress placed on Christians, and the moderates had failed that test. The very events that confirmed their theological ideas made the moderates seem morally blinkered and irrelevant. But like the antislavery moderates, liberal Protestants discovered how difficult steering a middle course could be. Rather than preserving Protestant orthodoxy's relevance in a rapidly changing world, Protestant liberalism often "served as a spiritual halfway house between orthodoxy and secular humanism" (p. 145). With a fine sense of such ironies, Oshatz's excellent work highlights the formative influence of slavery in American Protestantism, even after the Civil War, as well as the persistent theological and moral challenges posed by political, cultural, and social change.

Randolph Scully
George Mason University
Fairfax, Virginia

doi: 10.1093/jahist/jas316

The American Crucible: Slavery, Emancipation, and Human Rights. By Robin Blackburn. (New York: Verso, 2011. x, 498 pp. $34.95.)

Robin Blackburn's *The American Crucible* is the latest installment of his extended treatment of African slavery in the Atlantic world. Chronologically and thematically it overlaps his two previous works, *The Making of New World Slavery: From Baroque to Modern, 1492–1800* (1997) and *The Overthrow of Colonial Slavery, 1776–1848* (1988). Here, Blackburn intertwines the history of slavery with that of abolition from the fifteenth century through the nineteenth century. He also tracks the legacy of abolitionism into twentieth-century struggles to establish international recognition of fundamental human rights.

Blackburn argues that times of instability in the capitalist world system had negative repercussions for slave regimes. One such period was the age of revolution during the late eighteenth and early nineteenth centuries. Another occurred later in the nineteenth century, beginning with the United States in the 1850s and 1860s, and then Cuba and Brazil in the 1870s and 1880s. Although regional and international conflicts often affected plantation regimes, only in Haiti, the United States, and Cuba (and to a lesser extent in Brazil) did war destroy slavery. To succeed, emancipation required pressure "from below as well as from above, with slave de-subordination destroying plantation discipline while legislation denied the slave order the force of law within a given territory" (p. 392). Emancipation also drew on the actions of free descendants of the enslaved and citizens of the metropoles who considered slavery incompatible with humanitarian sensibilities.

This brief summary scarcely does justice to the astonishing breadth of the book. Blackburn

writes authoritatively across centuries and continents. Although his propensity for historiographical debate does not always serve the greater good, he readily engages specialists on their home turf. His assessment of the recent trend in scholarship on Haiti is chilling. A quarter century ago, as the bicentennial anniversaries of the revolution and independence approached, Haiti enjoyed a "brief moment of glory in the literature of the 'age of revolution,'" but recent historiography has relegated Haiti "back to the shadows" (p. 218). In Blackburn's view, Haiti is the key to understanding slavery and abolition in the entire Atlantic basin during the nineteenth century.

Interpretive breadth exacts a price. Maintaining balance among chronology, place, and people within a dynamic world system at times overtaxes the narrative vignettes that must carry the analysis. Specialists may find the vignettes' sweep too broad or their emphases slightly misplaced. Such phrases as "the forward march" of abolition and the "triumph" of emancipation, for instance, approach a whiggish tone of inevitability that the overall analysis refutes (pp. 278, 283). A number of minor errors escaped copy editing, such as Blackburn's reference to the Federal Works Project instead of the Federal Writers' Project (p. 352).

Both here and in his prior work, Blackburn repeatedly invokes two classics—C. L. R. James's *The Black Jacobins: Toussaint L'Ouverture and the San Domingo Revolution* (1938) and Eric Williams's *Capitalism and Slavery* (1944)—arguing their profound influence on scholarship. *The American Crucible* belongs in the same select company.

Joseph P. Reidy
Howard University
Washington, D.C.

doi: 10.1093/jahist/jas196

A Nation within a Nation: Organizing African-American Communities before the Civil War. By John Ernest. (Chicago: Ivan R. Dee, 2011. xii, 214 pp. $35.00.)

This is a book about black efforts to organize collectively before the Civil War. In six thematic chapters (on mutual aid societies, churches, fraternal orders, the black convention movement, schools, and the black press), John Ernest charts the institutions and arguments through which "people of African heritage who were identified as black in the United States founded, forged, and learned to improvise a collective identity" (p. 20). Over time, Ernest argues, free people of color shifted from an externally defined to an internally defined concept of community, from one defined by shared oppression or African heritage to one defined by "a common sense of history, shared goals . . . and lives interconnected by religious, educational, economic, and political forums for mutual assistance and debate" (pp. 131–32, ix). The result, he concludes, quoting Martin Delany, was "a nation within a nation" (p. 137).

There are valuable insights to be gained from framing African American identity as contingent rather than fixed, and though it does not break new ground, *A Nation within a Nation* delivers on much of that promise. It reminds us that there was nothing automatic about "the black community" and directs our attention to the hard work of community formation, efforts that are especially vivid in Ernest's discussion of the black convention movement. It expands our sense of the geography of antebellum black America, and Ernest repeatedly brings in evidence from places such as Indiana and even California. The book wonderfully communicates the richness of black institutional life and the often-breathtaking scope of its ambitions: to end slavery, counter racist representations, even reform whites' morals. And it cogently lays bare the tensions that such a diversity of aims stirred up. There are also costs to this framing. Ernest restricts his study mainly to free blacks in the North and does not try to incorporate enslaved people into his narrative—an entirely understandable decision but one that limits his ability to innovate on the concept of nation, to compare free black life across different regions, or to bring into view the integral links between free communities and enslaved ones. Perhaps the most valuable potential of the community-as-process framing—tracing change over time—is blunted by the book's thematic organization.

Ernest sharply critiques "scholarly and popular" writing on black life for assuming the existence of black community and for emphasizing the achievements of notable individuals over any serious appreciation of the complexities of white repression and black response (pp. 5, 19–20). At least as far as historical scholarship is concerned, these criticisms badly miss their mark. They do not do justice to the best public history institutions or creative fiction on the topic, either. Because the book has no footnotes, it is difficult to know what works Ernest has in mind. But occasional nods to current affairs and a preface that positions antebellum black history as the forerunner of Barack Obama's community organizing suggest that popular culture is Ernest's real target. And on that score, sadly, his lament still rings all too true.

Dylan C. Penningroth
Northwestern University
Evanston, Illinois and
American Bar Foundation
Chicago, Illinois

doi: 10.1093/jahist/jas167

Money over Mastery, Family over Freedom: Slavery in the Antebellum Upper South. By Calvin Schermerhorn. (Baltimore: Johns Hopkins University Press, 2011. viii, 286 pp. Cloth, $60.00. Paper, $30.00.)

Calvin Schermerhorn has written a compelling, finely grained study of how enslaved and free people shaped—and were shaped by—the sometimes-wrenching economic transformations that remade the antebellum upper South. His thesis rings clearly and convincingly throughout the book: slaveholders were less concerned with the paternalistic trappings of mastery than with finding new ways of wringing profits from their human chattels. Whether by selling their bondspeople to the Deep South, allowing them to earn wages, or by employing them in industries, slaveholders in the upper South used bound labor to resuscitate the local economy. The enslaved were quick to sense the dangers and opportunities created by these new commercial activities. The same market that exposed them to sale also allowed slaves to cobble together human and financial resources, which they used to insulate themselves and their kinfolk from the devastating effects of interstate trade. The result of the unequal struggles between modernizing masters and slaves "is what manned . . . and financed the revival of the coastal upper South's economies" (p. 207).

Schermerhorn's work complements other studies that underscore the extent to which antebellum southerners—black and white, free and enslaved—were inured in a modern, market-driven society. Schermerhorn suggests that slavery in the upper South bore the indelible marks of two streams of modernity. The first was the interstate slave trade, which undercut any paternalist ties between slaveholders and their human chattels and revealed the "peculiar institution" to be nothing more than a property relationship. The second modernizing impulse was the attempt of slaveholders to resurrect the upper South's moribund plantation economy as a market society complete with canals, factories, and railroads. Schermerhorn shows that masters embraced slavery, modernity, and the market revolution without sensing any contradictions. Indeed, the three were inextricably linked. "The upper South," Schermerhorn concludes, "became more economically diverse as . . . the capital generated by selling slaves to distant owners was used to support the intensification of commercial activity" (p. 202). The economic changes envisioned by slave owners did not herald slavery's death. If anything, masters and mistresses grew more adept at exploiting their bondspeople.

The commercial transformation of the upper South created new threats to the enslaved. Traders and kidnappers scoured the countryside, telegraphs carried news from distant slave markets, and bondsmen were torn from their families to work in distant and often-dangerous railroad camps. Still, slaves embraced the market and learned to bend it to their needs. New employments allowed slaves to become networkers; they used their jobs and newfound mobility to form relationships that sometimes yielded capital, information, influence, or protection. Networks gave bondspeople a stake in the system, compelling them to work harder and also mitigating against forms of resistance such as flight or rebellion. Schermerhorn shows that people such as Charles Ball, despite having ample opportunities to escape, tarried in bondage because their families were enslaved and because they were marshaling the financial resources and personal connections that would liberate—or at least protect—their kin. As he succinctly concludes, "the enslaved chose family over freedom" (p. 210).

There is much to admire in Schermerhorn's book, but it is not without its shortcomings. The author focuses almost entirely on enslaved people who were employed as domestic servants or in industrial settings. The upper South may have been the most urban and heavily industrialized region within the Old South, but many of its bondspeople continued to labor on farms and plantations. I wonder how the personal histories of these more obscure—but perhaps more typical—bondspeople would complicate Schermerhorn's interpretation.

Max Grivno
University of Southern Mississippi
Hattiesburg, Mississippi

doi: 10.1093/jahist/jas197

Weirding the War: Stories from the Civil War's Ragged Edges. Ed. by Stephen Berry. (Athens: University of Georgia Press, 2011. xiv, 385 pp. Cloth, $69.95. Paper, $24.95.)

Frequently, books claim to challenge the master narrative of the Civil War in one way or another. Rarely do you find a book that challenges the very notion of a master narrative. *Weirding the War,* a collection of essays edited by Stephen Berry, claims to do just that. "Weirding" is, according to Berry, "the historians' equivalent of 'freakonomics' (the use of economic theory to investigate atypical subjects in the hope of yielding fresh insights into typical social dynamics)" (p. 5). In a historical sense, Berry explains it as "a way of alienating the past from its present purposes, releasing the past from its present work, and returning to the past a measure of its original 'foreignness'" (*ibid.*).

Berry and his contributors manage to accomplish their goal and weird the Civil War. As part of this effort, Berry plunders coroner reports for dead Southerners and Michael DeGruccio loots dead soldiers. Megan Kate Nelson describes how Northerners reveled in ruins, while Rodney J. Steward explains how Southerners did not destroy property; instead, officials confiscated it. Amy

Murrell Taylor examines African Americans who froze to death after being turned out of Northern refugee camps. Andrew L. Slap chronicles the story of African Americans who turned themselves out of camp and deserted the Union army. While Diane Miller Sommerville discusses Confederate soldiers who lost their minds, Brian Craig Miller examines Southerners who lost their limbs. On a lighter note, both Anya Jabour and Steven E. Nash find that Southern girls just wanted to have fun—and boyfriends—during wartime. LeeAnn Whites examines women who were literally prostrate for their cause: prostitutes during Missouri's guerilla war. Some essays examine real soldiers: Peter S. Carmichael discusses how Civil War soldiers thought, Lesley J. Gordon assesses how some Connecticut soldiers remembered and forgot after the war, and Daniel E. Sutherland examines an imaginary soldier—reimagining the painter James Abbot Whistler as a Civil War general. Joan E. Cashin describes real hunger.

Most Americans remember the honorable men in Civil War armies; these essays remind us of the flexible nature of honor. Kenneth W. Noe discusses the court-martial and acquittal of a Confederate officer who left his command in battle. Barton A. Myers explains how nineteenth-century men justified torturing women. Southern civilians and soldiers of the era also enjoyed ring jousting; Paul Christopher Anderson examines how this relic of medieval chivalry may have facilitated the rise of the Ku Klux Klan.

Traditionally, a review of an edited collection selects certain essays as more valuable than others; in this instance that seems inappropriate. My response to these essays and the responses of most readers will be bound by their willingness to accept the essays' unique interpretations of Civil War history. While scholars will find many of these essays valuable, I believe that the greatest value of this collection may be its use in undergraduate courses. These short essays and their rather postmodern approach to Civil War studies might be more attractive to twenty-first-century undergraduates than other, more traditional Civil War narratives. Ironically, it is by breaking Civil War history from the limitations of the Civil War narrative that we can introduce twenty-first-century Americans to their counterparts in the nineteenth century—weird.

Barbara A. Gannon
University of Central Florida
Orlando, Florida

doi: 10.1093/jahist/jas225

Confederate Minds: The Struggle for Intellectual Independence in the Civil War South. By Michael T. Bernath. (Chapel Hill: University of North Carolina Press, 2010. xvi, 412 pp. $39.95.)

In the spring of 1861 the new Confederacy faced a number of shortages, but who would have thought that among the most pressing needs, according to Confederate partisans, was literature? They believed that the new nation-state would never be fully independent until it could boast of its own writers who could produce the highest quality novels, scientific papers, religious tracts, and political theory. Confederates further argued that, until 1860 at least, the South, much to its detriment, had depended on the North and Europe for its leading ideas. Therefore, in the coming war, it would be necessary not only to defeat Northern armies but also to supplant Northern ideas. To that end, Confederate leaders urged the establishment of new magazines and the publishing of more books by Southern authors, as well as setting up the institutional infrastructure to support such activity—printing houses, schools, booksellers, newspapers. According to Michael T. Bernath, those efforts should be interpreted as part of a larger project of nation building—a key element in the creation of Southern nationalism.

In the end, the Confederate effort to establish an independent intellectual life during the Civil War failed, according to Bernath. But not for lack of effort. Southerners wrote and published an avalanche of books and poems and articles on virtually all conceivable subjects, despite a shortage of printing paper, ink, and presses. Still, as Confederates lamented by the end of the war, the quality of these productions was often poor. Poetry hastily written by school girls and published in Southern newspapers came in for special abuse at the hands of

Confederate critics. Confederates recognized that, however well these intellectual effusions might serve to unite rebels in the South, real intellectual progress remained a long-term project well beyond their reach. Although the war years saw an impressive increase in the number of Southerners purchasing books and magazines, the market for those goods remained weak. And the institutions that supported intellectual life in the Civil War South remained small and ineffectual, despite efforts to improve schools, particularly in North Carolina.

Bernath thoroughly documents intellectual activity in the Civil War South, which he contends has been undervalued by Civil War historians. Yet how all these books and articles impacted the war effort remains unclear. That Confederates read a great deal, despite the odds against such a trend, does not prove that all this new intellectual activity contributed to the building of Confederate nationalism, regardless of what Confederates partisans might have hoped. In part, this weakness in the book flows from an unwillingness by the author to grapple with ideas themselves. Bernath mentions the leading arguments of the works from which he quotes, but he seldom subjects those ideas to rigorous questioning and analysis, as Eugene Genovese and Michael O'Brien have done recently for ideas in the antebellum South. As a result, Bernath is able to describe what Confederates did to produce new ideas during the war but is unable to assess the significance of those ideas. Still, this valuable work finally puts to rest the notion that the Confederacy was an intellectual wasteland and that Confederates had nothing to say aside from their rebel yell.

Wayne K. Durrill
University of Cincinnati
Cincinnati, Ohio

doi: 10.1093/jahist/jas239

The Enemy Within: Fears of Corruption in the Civil War North. By Michael Thomas Smith. (Charlottesville: University of Virginia Press, 2011. x, 229 pp. $35.00.)

Michael Thomas Smith's insightful new book raises important and provocative questions about Northern political culture in the 1860s. Smith revives an oddly neglected question:

Why were wartime Northerners obsessed with fears of corruption and conspiracy? His response (because they had been raised in a culture steeped in the premodern ideology of republicanism) would have been self-evident a generation ago; today it is a striking claim that risks instant, eye-rolling dismissal but in fact demands careful consideration.

Smith argues that at the heart of Northerners' overheated outrage surrounding ambitious and scheming war profiteers, generals, bounty brokers, bounty jumpers, and cotton traders lay a culture bred on republican fears of centralization, abuse of power, aristocratic privilege, and the "'dissipations' and 'wanton extravagance'" that attended luxury and wealth (p. 19). Most recent historians have discarded republicanism as a useful interpretive tool, yet Smith finds too much otherwise irrational conspiracy rhetoric and too great a preoccupation with moral decline and its impact on civic health to ignore. He wisely refrains from rendering republican ideology a magic bullet, instead presenting a balanced and nuanced tapestry in which republicanism was interwoven with partisan politics, evangelical Protestantism, anxieties over economic development and urbanization, and fiercely contested ideals of manliness—all intensified by the pressures of a war for national survival. The result leaves the reader hard put to deny that republicanism continued to be a central facet of Northerners' outlook into the 1860s.

The chief significance of this, Smith argues, is that popular depictions of the Civil War North as moving rapidly toward centralization and modernity—*à la* Alan Nevins, George M. Fredrickson, and James McPherson—vastly overstate the eagerness with which Northerners embraced that trend; many, at least, had serious misgivings. Similarly, depictions of the Civil War as the first modern war fail to take into account the extent to which "the continuing influence of republican suspicion of government power" prevented a "truly efficient mobilization of either the nation's human or financial resources"—a process Smith describes well in his analyses of the overblown Northern responses to the half-dozen scandals presented here (p. 176).

The argument is compelling, but the book sorely needs an opening chapter providing historical context for Northerners' wartime fears. While the author refers broadly in his introduction to the slave power and abolitionist conspiracies of the 1850s as well as antebellum concerns with Freemasons, Catholics, and others, his discussion is historiographical, not historical; rooting wartime anticonspiracy ideology in prewar culture would have made it more comprehensible and linked it more firmly to the republicanism of the American Revolution. On a similar note, tying the book's anticorruption themes to recent studies on antiparty feeling, such as Mark Voss-Hubbard's *Beyond Party: Cultures of Antipartisanship in Northern Politics before the Civil War* (2002) and Adam I. P. Smith's *No Party Now: Politics in the Civil War North* (2006), would also have rested its claims on a firmer foundation.

Even so, Smith's *The Enemy Within* is an engaging, thought-provoking study that will force students of Civil War–era politics and political culture to rethink their overly hasty abandonment of the republican synthesis.

Russell McClintock
St. John's High School
Jefferson, Massachusetts

doi: 10.1093/jahist/jas218

Lincoln's Forgotten Ally: Judge Advocate General Joseph Holt of Kentucky. By Elizabeth D. Leonard. (Chapel Hill: University of North Carolina Press, 2011. xiv, 417 pp. $40.00.)

Joseph Holt is a fairly obscure figure even for Civil War scholars. Holt was involved in President James Buchanan's administration, served as judge advocate general for President Abraham Lincoln, and played a part in the trial of Lincoln's assassins, but the details of his participation in all three roles have been hazy. Elizabeth D. Leonard brings Holt's participation into much sharper focus by contending that

no member of Abraham Lincoln's administration or the postwar federal government—indeed, no Civil War–era political figure—has been more unjustly neglected by historians, more misrepresented by Americans' collective historical 'memory,'

and, in the end, more completely forgotten than Joseph Holt. (pp. 1–2)

Holt's obscurity may be explained partially by his choice never to run for a single local, state, or federal office. In that regard, his career may reveal a much larger pool of significant politicians who never held judicial, elective, or military positions. Perhaps his success in government came about because contemporaries felt reassured by his lack of desire to gain elective office.

Leonard concentrates on Holt's service to Buchanan and Lincoln, his prosecution of Lincoln's assassins, and his role in the administrations of Andrew Johnson and Ulysses S. Grant. As Buchanan's commissioner of patents, postmaster general, and then secretary of war during the administration's final sixty-four days, Holt increasingly despised southern Democrats who abandoned Buchanan and the nation. This sentiment led him to keep his native Kentucky out of the Confederacy in 1861 and thereby gain Lincoln's trust to the extent that Lincoln appointed him judge advocate general in September of 1862, a post he would hold until 1875. Largely because Holt did not seek elective office and, as Leonard emphasizes, because he and Lincoln worked so well together on presidential pardons for federal soldiers, the two established a strong bond. As Holt increasingly realized the need to use the military to counter Copperheads, as seen in his role in *Ex parte Milligan* (1866), this bond only grew. Turning to Holt's role as chief prosecutor in the trial of Lincoln's assassins, Leonard argues convincingly that while Holt was deceived by some informants, a fact he later conceded, he truly believed that those charged were guilty and deserved execution. Leonard's most intriguing coverage concerns the growing rift between Holt and President Johnson. Johnson wanted Holt to take full responsibility for the assassins' execution after realizing that this event would hinder his leadership of a conservative political movement that increasingly doubted the guilt of those executed and also desired to prevent the trial of Jefferson Davis. Holt devoted the rest of his life to defending his role and asserting that Johnson had supported the trials and executions.

In addition to providing extremely effective coverage of Holt's governmental career, Leonard also insightfully traces his private life, revealing much about his two marriages (both of which ended in premature death), his relations with family members (most of whom were Confederate sympathizers), and even his links with other single and married women. As a result of Leonard's skillful research and careful assessment, this book was a cowinner of the 2012 Lincoln Book Prize, awarded by the Gilder Lehrman Institute of American History. Surely, Joseph Holt will no longer remain an obscure figure.

Robert C. Kenzer
University of Richmond
Richmond, Virginia

doi: 10.1093/jahist/jas199

Spain and the American Civil War. By Wayne H. Bowen. (Columbia: University of Missouri Press, 2011. 188 pp. $40.00.)

"Spain is the natural ally of the South," declared the *Richmond Daily Dispatch* in February 1862. "If the South has had a friend, from the beginning of her troubles, it has been Spain" (p. 1). With that thought in mind, Wayne H. Bowen uses Spanish, U.S., and Confederate sources to examine why Spain and the Confederacy failed to develop an alliance in the American Civil War and whether Spanish intervention would have made a difference in the outcome. Spanish leaders thought the division of the American republic into two nations would provide the opportunity to solidify their imperial interests in the Caribbean region and in Hispanic America and would help return their nation to the status of a great power. The government in Madrid followed Britain and France in announcing neutrality and extending belligerent rights to the Confederacy; it allowed Confederate blockade-runners and smugglers into its ports, including in' Cuba; prominent Spanish military and political figures sympathized with the South, as did most Spanish officials in Cuba; and Spain's foreign minister, Saturnino Calderón Collantes, assured the Confederate agent Pierre Rost that the Spanish government was the "natural ally and friend" of the Confederacy (p. 78). Yet, alas, Spain and the Confederacy never became allies.

To justify his study, Bowen insists that Spanish intervention "could have changed the course of the war," but he then concedes that if Spain had decided to extend military or diplomatic assistance, "it had little means to do so" (pp. 7, 82). With a weak army, navy, and economy, how could Spain's intervention have altered the outcome of the Civil War? The presence of the Spanish fleet in Havana Harbor might have raised questions about the legitimacy of the Union blockade, but this type of courtroom challenge was no more threatening to the Union's warships than was Spain's wooden fleet. It is difficult to believe that Spanish intervention could have made a difference—even if Britain and France had taken the lead.

If Spain's intervention ever had a chance, that chance disappeared when the British and French ultimately decided that the South had nothing to offer that was worth a war with the Union. To drive home the same point to the Spanish, the Union invited their embassy in Washington, D.C., to send a naval representative to observe the construction of ironclads in the Brooklyn Navy Yard. This thinly veiled threat convinced the Madrid government that it was incapable of countering the Union ironclad.

This is a useful though overly detailed account, much of it extraneous material dealing with the period long before the Civil War. A few corrections are in order. There was no exchange of money in the Adams-Onís Treaty of 1819. The U.S. Senate does not ratify treaties, nor does the president declare war. And it was Secretary of State William H. Seward who called for war with Spain in 1861 in an attempt to unite all Americans; President Abraham Lincoln killed the proposal by a pocket veto. Bowen nonetheless provides the first extended study of Spain's decision against intervention, thereby drawing more attention to the· international dimension of the Civil War.

Howard Jones
University of Alabama
Tuscaloosa, Alabama

doi: 10.1093/jahist/jas222

Demon of the Lost Cause: Sherman and Civil War History. By Wesley Moody. (Columbia: University of Missouri Press, 2011. xii, 190 pp. $30.00.)

Wesley Moody correctly states in his introduction that William T. Sherman is a figure who still elicits a profound level of emotion, particularly in southern popular memory of the American Civil War. Moody is seeking not to correct the record but rather to investigate the creation of the Sherman myth. This is a worthwhile endeavor because digging beneath the thick crust of mythology that surrounds Sherman and his march through the Confederate heartland can create the foundation for a better historical understanding of the development of the Lost Cause—a phenomenon that also continues to influence American perceptions of the war years and affect intersectional relationships. However, the author's claim that scholars have too frequently accepted the mythology surrounding Sherman is simply unfounded.

Moody is best in showing that Sherman's reputation was demonized over the years as the result of southern apologists and the work of military men and politicians. Unfortunately, his discussion of the scholarship is outdated, as is evident early when he examines Sherman's Atlanta campaign. Similarly, Moody's claim that historians focus too much on the eastern theater of war has not been the case for some years, and his assertion that the vast majority of historians still associate Abraham Lincoln's reelection with the fall of the city is based on a single citation from a book that is almost thirty years old.

The greatest shortcoming of *Demon of the Lost Cause* is its discussion of Sherman's treatment of Southern civilians, a vital component in the general's demonization. Moody examines one of the first histories of Sherman's march, published by his aide-de-camp, George Nichols. Although Nichols makes frequent mention of encountering angry Southern women, Moody argues that it cannot be established whether these were "true accounts or a literary device" (p. 37). This is simply untrue. Abundant sources establish the veracity of Nichols's account, sources I used heavily in my own work, which covers a great deal of what Moody states historians have neglected.

In fact, Moody ignores the vast scholarship that has focused on southern women, both those who encountered Sherman and those who were fundamental in the creation of his memory as the scourge of the South.

In his final chapter, "Sherman and the Modern Historians," Moody gives a historiographical overview, arguing that while academics may have been "well-meaning" they have neglected to seek out "what" Sherman actually did and have instead concentrated on "why" (p. 147). Moody discusses Mark Grimsley's paradigm-shifting book, *The Hard Hand of War* (1995), but misrepresents Grimsley's argument by claiming that Grimsley compared Sherman's tactics to those of earlier, brutal European warfare. In fact, Grimsley differentiated Sherman's tactics as far more circumscribed by Victorian ideals and argued that Sherman conducted "hard war" rather than "total war." This, according to Grimsley, may have been "as systematic and extensive as anything Europe had seen" but was also more enlightened as it was conducted by men "with strong moral values that stayed their hands" (p. 204).

In his concluding paragraph Moody somewhat condescendingly offers forgiveness to scholars for accepting the pervasive mythology surrounding Sherman (p. 151). I would direct readers instead to Carol Reardon's recent essay, "William T. Sherman in Postwar Georgia's Collective Memory, 1864–1914," which covers much of Moody's argument in a tightly focused and deeply insightful twenty pages (Joan Waugh and Gary W. Gallagher, eds., *Wars within a War,* 2009). While this book may appeal to a general audience, it offers nothing new to the academic community.

Jacqueline Glass Campbell
Francis Marion University
Florence, South Carolina

doi: 10.1093/jahist/jas254

Sing Not War: The Lives of Union and Confederate Veterans in Gilded Age America. By James Marten. (Chapel Hill: University of North Carolina Press, 2011. xii, 339 pp. $39.95.)

In *Sing Not War,* James Marten explores the lives of Civil War veterans, the way the American public viewed those veterans, and the tensions between veterans and nonveterans in the last third of the nineteenth century. Marten makes the case for Civil War veterans' prominence in—and even separation from—American society, partly because of their large numbers but also because the problems of a relative few of them (physical and mental disabilities, institutionalization in asylums or soldiers homes) became mapped onto the public perception of all veterans (represented in numerous archetypes including the begging old soldier, the empty sleeve, and the mentally ill veteran). Indeed, much of the book's focus is on those most affected by their time in the military. Marten convincingly argues that these extreme examples provide insight into the long-term impact of Civil War service more broadly; for example, while few veterans were actually begging, many men scraped "by on paltry pension checks, odd jobs, and charity" (p. 6).

Marten explains that for reasons of sources, time, and analytical framework, the book does not address black veterans or Confederate veterans as much as it might. This narrowing of focus at times to Northern white veterans is a potential area for criticism, though Marten includes Confederate examples for each section. In chapters on disabled veterans, soldiers' homes, pensions, the commercialization of veteranhood, and the struggle over what it meant to be a veteran in Gilded Age America, Marten uses veterans' newspapers, investigations of (Northern) soldiers' homes, newsletters from southern homes, accounts from northern home inmates, surveys of veterans, Sanitary Commission reports, travel accounts, and a wide array of period fiction. He highlights throughout an ongoing conflict between public patriotic gratitude toward soldiers for their sacrifices and an increasing sense of separation of veterans from civilians (one that began with separate wartime experiences and then became exacerbated by the failure of some veterans to match up to an ideal and by fights over the size and scope of pensions).

Marten also notes a remarkable divergence in the public perceptions of Civil War veterans in the North and South. While the veteran as idealized hero can be seen in both regions, Marten argues that the northern image became entangled with the veteran as social problem. Marten attributes this regional distinction in perceptions of veterans to several factors, including the greater percentage of southern white men who served, the varied economic opportunities in the two regions, and the politicization of the Grand Army of the Republic and federal pensions (and the relatively small size and scope of Confederate pensions). Marten is also rightly concerned with how veterans fulfilled societal expectations regarding manhood. Military service traditionally offered a claim to manhood, but postwar critiques of veterans were framed in a language that challenged their masculinity. Ultimately, Marten demonstrates the many ways the war impacted Civil War veterans' postwar lives and defined them to themselves and to others. *Sing Not War* is an important contribution to the growing literature on Civil War veterans.

Jeffrey W. McClurken
University of Mary Washington
Fredericksburg, Virginia

doi: 10.1093/jahist/jas240

"We Will Be Satisfied with Nothing Less": The African American Struggle for Equal Rights in the North during Reconstruction. By Hugh Davis. (Ithaca: Cornell University Press, 2011. xx, 209 pp. $45.00.)

Reconstruction reached beyond the defeated South; the North also faced challenges to its racial practices after the Civil War. The states there had made slavery a dead letter before the war. Yet the advent and aftermath of the Thirteenth Amendment, ratified in December 1865, revived angry arguments about race in the meaning of liberty and democracy. The Fourteenth Amendment in 1868 and the Fifteenth Amendment in 1870 further exposed irritating racial issues. The North, no less than the South, struggled over extending equal protection of the law and the right to vote to blacks. For example, a New York statewide referendum in 1869 rejected equal voting rights for black men.

Too little attention has focused on blacks' struggles for equal rights in the Reconstruction North, Hugh Davis insists. "By emphasizing the northern black contributions to the debate on interracial democracy and identifying links between events in the North and the South, my book helps to meet the needs," Davis writes at the outset in identifying his aims, "for positing a national, not just a southern, vision of what Reconstruction could accomplish and for connecting local and state agitation for equal rights to a national Reconstruction" (p. xi).

Focusing on voting rights and segregated public schools, Davis narrates local and national campaigns for equal rights that African Americans mounted outside the South from the 1860s to the 1880s. In a prologue, five chapters, and an epilogue, he tracks the National Equal Rights League which was founded in 1864, as well as its auxiliaries and successor, the National Executive Committee of Colored Persons, which was founded in 1869. Coordinating concerted action among blacks from New England to the West Coast, the organizations revealed the common condition and quest of "colored people" across the United States (pp. 45–46).

In tracing African Americans' agency and arguments for equal access to the franchise and public schools, Davis exposes divisions and frustrations. He especially bares most white Republicans' shallow commitment to emancipation. Neither blacks nor whites could completely agree on exactly what equal rights meant or on the best ways to realize them. Advocates achieved highs in the ratification of the Fifteenth Amendment and the Civil Rights Act of 1875. But lows came too. The act, for example, failed to include a long-sought ban against segregated schools. Davis's narrative thus becomes one of failure in black and white. The collapsed promise of Reconstruction abandoned blacks North and South to a national majority uninterested in compromising white supremacy.

Davis contributes significantly to intensifying interest in moving beyond misplaced regionalism to understand the embedded power of racism nationwide in America. He has broadened the more local focus provided, for example, in Daniel R. Biddle and Murray Dubin's *Tasting Freedom: Octavius Catto and the Battle for Equality in Civil War America* (2010). Davis nicely connects blacks' postwar activism with their antebellum abolitionism and their wartime military service. His Reconstruction emphasis, however, sometimes clouds the continuity of blacks' persistent struggle against racist, antidemocratic elites, and white masses bent on preserving their race-based preferences and privileges.

Thomas J. Davis
Arizona State University
Tempe, Arizona

doi: 10.1093/jahist/jas201

Radical Reform: Interracial Politics in Post-emancipation North Carolina. By Deborah Beckel. (Charlottesville: University of Virginia Press, 2011. xii, 298 pp. $45.00.)

Postemancipation politics in the South was a mess of inchoate collective actors, shifting aims and allegiances, and unstable coalitions, and nowhere was this more evident than in North Carolina. The state had remarkably competitive elections and high voter turnout (including for black men) through 1896, a stunning cross-class and biracial coalition that won power temporarily from the white-dominated Democratic party, and a just-as-stunning elite-dominated virulent white supremacy campaign in 1898 that violently shut down black political activity in the name of "progress."

In *Radical Reform* Deborah Beckel tries to make sense of this mess by analyzing many disparate political elements as having a common impulse to reform politics. This reform impulse can best be understood, she argues, not by starting the story with Reconstruction. Rather, one must reach back to the antebellum period to appreciate the antecedents of the impulse and therefore its trajectory: "by focusing on antebellum reform movements, Civil War dissidence, and the postwar interracial Republican Party, I explore the interplay of racial, class, and geographical divisions" (pp. 6–7).

Antebellum North Carolina politics, Beckel suggests, were riven by class and regional divisions as lower-class white men, disproportionately concentrated in the mountain and piedmont regions, struggled for full suffrage rights and other reforms against entrenched landed interests more characteristic of the eastern counties and coastal plain. Unlike most other antebellum southern states, North Carolina had lively two-party political competition, but those seeking reform were never unified, crosscut as they were by divisions.

of Mexico region. He compares the architectural descriptions in the memoir of thirteen-year-old Mexican Olga Betriz Torres (*Memorias de mi viaje* [Recollections of my trip], 1918) as she moves north with her family in 1914, with the travelogues of the Anglo-American Richard Harding Davis (*Three Gringos in Central America and Venezuela,* 1896, and *Soldiers of Fortune,* 1897) as he roams south of the border.

In his final chapter, just as the "oriental style" in Western home decor resulted from meandering all over Asia for pickings, so too does Gleason meander all over American spaces as he deals with a hodgepodge of readings from pulp fiction (Charlie Chan in Hawaii and Fu-Manchu in San Francisco) to serious architectural history (Frank Lloyd Wright). Gleason's book proved overwhelming, and the sites remain still unseen.

Helen Bradley Foster
University of Minnesota
Minneapolis, Minnesota

doi: 10.1093/jahist/jas270

Out on Assignment: Newspaper Women and the Making of Modern Public Space. By Alice Fahs. (Chapel Hill: University of North Carolina Press, 2011. 360 pp. $37.50.)

Alice Fahs argues that women newspaper reporters working between roughly 1885 and 1910 carved out new public space for women both by roaming across urban space searching for the "woman's angle" in American public life and by writing about the wide new world for women. Even the "woman's pages" in which they chronicled the emerging public woman staked out new public space for women.

Fahs's engaging exploration of this symbiotic relationship offers a fresh perspective for evaluating the history of women in journalism partly because it traces the unheralded culture of women reporters who personified the "bachelor girls" they wrote about. This new breed of independent young working women lived on their own in hotels or apartment houses, defying traditional notions of home. "They live alone, depend upon no one for livelihood, mentality, or entertainment, and in fact paddle their own canoe with all the nerve

and independence of a full-fledged bachelor," the journalist Margherita Arlina Hamm wrote in 1892 (p. 138). Fahs, a professor of history at the University of California, Irvine, argues that the zestful newspaper accounts of bachelor girls connected to the embryonic suffrage movement "by enabling women to imagine themselves as independent actors in metropolitan life" (p. 161).

Hamm wrote "Among the Newspaper Women" for the *New York Journalist,* one of numerous diverse sources Fahs scoured (including new databases that enabled her to examine the long reach of obscure syndicated columnists) for evidence that challenges myths about early newspaperwomen. She reframes the exploits of many unsung stunt reporters who followed the legendary Nellie Bly. Usually recalled as an embarrassing excess of yellow journalism, stunt journalism showcased female reporters on center stage of an exciting new culture of leisure and entertainment, in Fahs's view.

Fahs similarly reevaluates the contributions of the denigrated "woman's page" as "a lost world of women's writings that placed women at the heart of a new public life" (p. 13). She argues that this section in newspapers served as a public forum that legitimated new public roles for women and connected female communities that transcended geography. Contributors and readers of these pages debated such vital issues as suffrage, labor, and education.

Many newspaperwomen belonged to the first generation of middle-class New Women who desired independence, meaningful work, and self-fulfillment. Fahs cannot avoid romanticizing her subjects, but she does document the discrimination in pay and assignments and the strains on private life and family they experienced. Most lasted only about four years in the profession. Fahs acknowledges that perhaps her book's greatest weakness, the minimization of women writing for ethnic, black, and foreign-language newspapers, results from her emphasis on mainstream metropolitan newspapers. Yet she does describe acts of resistance performed by the black press as well as the counterhegemonic journalism of activist labor journalists such as Eva Valesh.

Fahs argues that much of women's print culture has been lost because newspapers are so often ignored as literary history. *Out on*

Assignment shows that however ephemeral newspapers may be, their conversations carried across generations that propelled women into public life.

Linda J. Lumsden
University of Arizona
Tucson, Arizona

doi: 10.1093/jahist/jas312

Boll Weevil Blues: Cotton, Myth, and Power in the American South. By James C. Giesen. (Chicago: University of Chicago Press, 2011. xvi, 221 pp. $40.00.)

The boll weevil is an important component of the history of the South, but in James C. Giesen's view, the boll weevil is even more significant as a character in southern mythology. In *Boll Weevil Blues,* Giesen treats the reader to a wide-ranging geographic and chronological journey that includes lessons in entomology, discussions of music, and close analyses of southern culture. Giesen wrote this study to correct what he views as a serious misunderstanding of the impact of the boll weevil on the cotton-growing regions of the South. The *actual* impact of the boll weevil on cotton production, he asserts, was far less important than the rise and power of the *myth* of the boll weevil on the southern psyche.

While the boll weevil did create significant problems for southern farmers, it hardly altered the South's reliance on cotton as the most important cash crop. The weevil did not disrupt the Mississippi delta plantation system, nor did it create a diversified agricultural economy in southeastern Alabama. In Georgia, the weevil offered a convenient explanation for the decline of an already-ailing cotton economy. Thus despite much writing and oratory that attributed a fundamental transformation in the South to the boll weevil, the changes wrought because of the weevil were for the most part superficial. It was not until after World War II that southern rural life was truly revolutionized, and factors other than the boll weevil catalyzed those changes.

As the myth of the boll weevil grew apace with its trek across southern cotton fields, various groups within the South attempted to control and employ the myth of the weevil to their own ends. Planters in the Mississippi delta, U.S. Department of Agriculture (USDA) scientists and bureaucrats, Delta and Pine Land Company corporate operators, landowners, and even sharecroppers saw in the boll weevil's destructive power opportunities to further their respective visions of the South. No matter the goals that these competing interests had in mind, however, Giesen argues that the myth of the boll weevil's destructive power was greater than the damage the insect inflicted. The USDA special agent Seaman Knapp, for example, perceived the weevil's invasion as an unmatched opening to remake the southern agricultural landscape. Knapp used the boll weevil's arrival as the impetus for funding demonstration farms and demonstration agents. In a way, then, Knapp and the weevil did remake the southern countryside, but it was a countryside still planted in cotton.

Boll Weevil Blues is a good read and an example of the importance of balancing the reality of the boll weevil with the rhetoric surrounding it. It is impossible to understand the cotton South without understanding its agriculture; it is likewise impossible to understand cotton culture without understanding the boll weevil's role in the region's history and myth. Giesen offers an integrated treatment that contributes to understanding both of these points.

George B. Ellenberg
University of West Florida
Pensacola, Florida

doi: 10.1093/jahist/jas191

A Mess of Greens: Southern Gender and Southern Food. By Elizabeth S. D. Engelhardt. (Athens: University of Georgia Press, 2011. xiv, 265 pp. Cloth, $59.95. Paper, $24.95.)

The relative scarcity of research on the history of southern foods is surprising, especially given how strongly food is bound up in the region's identity. Elizabeth S. D. Engelhardt's study of the social, political, and economic significance of southern women and food between the 1870s and the 1930s is, therefore, a welcome addition to the literature. She argues that gender, class, and race shaped women's acquisition, production, and consumption of food in the American South.

An American studies and women's studies scholar, Engelhardt situates her own southern family's foodways in the region's long-standing association between cuisine and status. She acknowledges, for instance, that her family more often ate dove and squirrel than the archetypal markers of southern identity, barbecued pork and fried chicken. Contextualizing her family's customs in the broader southern experience enables Engelhardt to analyze the private world of women and food that centered on knowledge and experiences shared in the kitchen, and to expose women's public roles and influence in shaping the importance of food to identity.

Engelhardt draws on a wealth of sources, including novels, scrapbooks, letters, cookbooks, and newspapers, to serve up a series of case studies. In one of the strongest, she considers how and why educated, southern, white, middle-class women sought to persuade their poorer, rural sisters to forego easily grown and prepared corn in favor of wheat in their baking, insisting that corn bread "imperiled the morals, the health, and the future prospects of your entire family" (p. 51). She argues for the logic of rural women's preference for corn bread and complicates our romantic connection to biscuits by underlining the arduous labor and expense they demanded. Another wonderful study illuminates how the Tomato Clubs of the 1910s empowered 500,000 girls, giving them "a course in reading, science, public speaking, and socializing" and the opportunity to earn money (p. 84). Mentoring girls as they grew their tomatoes, canned them, and brought them to market enabled women across the South to assert women's value to their community.

In a surprising chapter on the region's transition from farming to mill work, Engelhardt contends that despite the abundance around them, low-wage workers and their families found themselves sickened and dying from malnutrition. The lack of niacin (vitamin B-3) in the impoverished workers' diet of meat, meal, and molasses caused an epidemic of pellagra, which affected hundreds of thousands of southerners. In her chapter on local cookbooks and curb markets, Engelhardt subtly measures women's relationship with food and their

community by analyzing recipes and the importance of shared space. Throughout, the author's reading of fiction enriches her social and cultural analysis and is the primary basis for her study of women moonshiners. While it is questionable whether moonshine can be analyzed as food, she raises important questions about women's involvement in its production.

Engelhardt makes strong, compelling observations about the centrality of food in the lives of women and southerners.

Katherine Parkin
Monmouth University
West Long Branch, New Jersey

doi: 10.1093/jahist/jas252

God and the Atlantic: America, Europe, and the Religious Divide. By Thomas Albert Howard. (New York: Oxford University Press, 2011. xiv, 256 pp. $45.00.)

"That's OK, McDonald's will be there." This was one of the teasing remarks German friends and family made to me in response to news that the United States would not have an exhibition at the World's Fair in Hanover over a decade ago. While intended mostly as lighthearted humor, such comments contain a critique of American culture that, as this book reveals, emerges from a vast historical landscape of anti-American attitudes held by intellectuals across the political spectrum in Europe. Thomas Albert Howard provides a detailed tour through this nuanced terrain of anti-American attitudes, focusing on European views of American religion. The author expertly demonstrates that Europeans' assessment of American religion is not *simply* negative. He systematically points out the reasons for their disdain by marshaling evidence from two dozen intellectuals—mostly from Germany and France in the nineteenth century. In the final third of his book Howard also brings into focus two European scholars—Philip Schaff and Jacques Maritain—who have more positive assessments of American religion and evaluates why this is the case.

This book is valuable for scholars interested in the intellectual history of the embattled but remarkably resilient "secularization thesis."

While *God and the Atlantic* is clearly intended as a history of European intellectuals' views on American religion, readers may still be frustrated by Howard's tendency to note only briefly the wider social context of many of the intellectuals to whom he refers. For example, in his otherwise excellent discussion of Maritain, he does not mention that Maritain's call for a "new Christendom" in the mid-1930s was an important part of the intellectual framework for Christian intellectuals' participation in creating the United Nations Universal Declaration of Human Rights (1948). Historical variations in European popular religion are also not assessed to tease out the extent to which the practice of nineteenth-century European religion differed from American practice. It surely was different but perhaps not to the extent that intellectuals thought it was.

While mostly a book for specialists in European and American intellectual history, it would appeal to others as well. To help European students of American religion understand their sometimes-unexamined assumptions, for example, this book would be a helpful companion to determine the extent to which their attitudes toward American religion are based on the empirical reality of American religious experience or on inherited European assumptions. Scholars of American diplomacy who read this book will more fully appreciate the nuances of European attitudes toward American religion regardless of who sits in the Oval Office. *God and the Atlantic* also complements popular books such as Dick Martin's *Rebuilding Brand America* (2007). While Martin sought to demonstrate the value of advertising research for improving America's image, Howard demonstrates that when European and American views of religion are concerned, the differences are much more substantive than a passing remark about McDonald's as America might suggest.

Benjamin L. Hartley
Palmer Theological Seminary
Eastern University
Wynnewood, Pennsylvania

doi: 10.1093/jahist/jas172

The Independent Orders of B'nai B'rith and True Sisters: Pioneers of a New Jewish Identity, 1843–1914. By Cornelia Wilhelm. (Detroit: Wayne State University Press, 2011. xii, 361 pp. $44.95.)

Cornelia Wilhelm places the oldest American Jewish fraternal order, B'nai B'rith (founded 1843), and its smaller, shorter-lived sister order, the Independent Order of True Sisters, into the context of German Jewry's struggle for modernity and "desire for civil emancipation" in both Germany and the United States (p. 1). According to Wilhelm, B'nai B'rith embodied an attempt to align Judaism with Enlightenment rationalism and humanistic universalism, an effort that sometimes conflicted with a concurrent impulse toward ethnic particularism. She argues persuasively that the motivation for the establishment of the orders originated in Germany but became "intensified" in the United States, with its atmosphere of religious freedom and philo-Semitism (p. 8). In the later years of the period covered by the book, B'nai B'rith brought its hybrid German-Jewish American sensibility back across the ocean through branches in Europe.

Wilhelm ties B'nai B'rith directly to the Reform movement in Judaism, with which it shared dual German and American origins. She rejects the label "secular synagogue" that historians of the order have given it, because the order was not secular and it was too universalistic to be a synagogue (p. 7). In fact, she shows that radical reformers who hoped that B'nai B'rith would become a direct institutional expression of their movement battled within the order against moderate reformers led by Isaac Mayer Wise who sought to emphasize the order's kinship with Masonic-style fraternal ritual and thereby keep it above sectarian religious conflicts within the Jewish community. As Wilhelm points out, B'nai B'rith had an advantage over the synagogue in that membership was transferable and it had the ability "to bridge religious differences," especially for those who rejected traditional Judaism but wanted to retain a connection to the community (p. 67).

Wilhelm makes a further contribution by discussing the history of the Independent Order of True Sisters, a women's order closely aligned with B'nai B'rith. The True Sisters remained a small organization of a couple of thousand members, unlike its brother order, which enrolled tens of thousands. Wilhelm might have done more to explain this failure to grow in terms of American fraternalism's overwhelmingly male constituency. But she does well to point out the disproportionate influence of the True Sisters, the first national organization to bring American Jewish women into the public sphere and therefore a precursor to larger organizations such as the National Council of Jewish Women.

This is an exceptionally well-researched book, often drawing on previously unknown sources in English and German. (Each chapter averages over two hundred notes.) But, perhaps because the book has been translated from German, it is not an easy read. Too many pronouns lack clear antecedents. Some sentences take several reads to discern their meanings. Occasionally, an assertion does not make sense within the context of the book's argument, and one wonders whether something was lost in translation. Nevertheless, Wilhelm has made an important contribution to the history of the modernization and Americanization of Jewish culture and religion.

Daniel Soyer
Fordham University
Bronx, New York

doi: 10.1093/jahist/jas179

All Together Different: Yiddish Socialists, Garment Workers, and the Labor Roots of Multiculturalism. By Daniel Katz. (New York: New York University Press, 2011. xiv, 298 pp. $39.00.)

Daniel Katz weaves together the fields of racial/ethnic, gender, and labor history to reveal the centrality of multiculturalism to the early years of the International Ladies Garment Workers Union (ILGWU). Katz argues that a particularly Jewish brand of socialism, born in the Russian Empire and transplanted to the United States in the early twentieth century, significantly influenced how activists conceptualized racial/ethnic, or—in their terms—"national," identity and the importance of those identities to building a strong, multiethnic labor organization. Delving into the records of ILGWU, including several of

its most militant locals, Katz uncovers the crucial roles played by women in institutionalizing "social unionism," centered not solely on shop-floor activism but also on creating bonds among workers through cultural and educational programming. Social unionism did not seek a monolithic worker culture but instead highlighted the distinctiveness of each national group recruited by the union. Reaching a peak in the New Deal era, social unionism declined during the war years, evolving into a moderate Jewish liberalism.

Katz locates the origins of what he terms "mutual culturalism" in tsarist Russia among socialists in the General Union of Jewish Workers (the Bund). These radicals, drawing on the ideas of Chaim Zhitlowsky, crafted a radical Jewish identity centered on Yiddish language and culture. They forged a path between socialisms that focused too narrowly on class identity and, in the case of Herzlian Zionism, Jewish nationalisms devoid of class consciousness. Bundists envisioned a class-based socialist movement composed of many nationalities. Immigrants brought these ideas to the United States and, specifically, to the ILGWU, where local activists created programs devised to, in Katz's terms, promote political, social, and multicultural education. By the 1920s the union had broadened these offerings to recruit new workers, including Italians, African Americans, and Puerto Ricans, to the union. These programs helped sustain the union during the doldrums of the 1920s and early 1930s when the labor movement was fiercely divided between Communists and Socialists. Mutual culturalism reached a high-water mark in the early 1930s, bringing together workers across racial lines to forge a union identity that never suppressed individual national or racial/ethnic identities.

With the advent of the New Deal, power dynamics shifted away from the locals and toward the national led by David Dubinsky. While many locals eyed the National Recovery Administration (NRA) warily, Dubinsky felt the NRA could augment union power. By 1937 the international branch began to move further away from mutual culturalism, replacing female educators, who were generally most committed to these ideas, with men. In an engaging chapter on the revue *Pins and*

Needles, Katz illustrates these transformations with scenes of female militancy shifting to images of the workplace as marriage market. Moreover, African Americans were marginalized, Hispanics were invisible, and Jews were encouraged to act less "Jewish." The emerging liberalism, while still committed to racial justice, abandoned the multiculturalism that had built the union. In this fine study, Katz provides a model for how to integrate labor, racial/ethnic, immigration, and gender history.

Mary McCune
State University of New York Oswego
Oswego, New York

doi: 10.1093/jahist/jas291

The Borders of Integration: Polish Migrants in Germany and the United States, 1870–1924. By Brian McCook. (Athens: Ohio University Press, 2011. xxii, 270 pp. Cloth, $55.00. Paper, $26.95.)

The harsh world of coal mining in the years around 1900 serves as the setting for Brian McCook's comparative study of Polish workers in the German Ruhr valley and in northeastern Pennsylvania. McCook examines what he calls the "borders of integration": both Poles' adaptation to novel environments and their efforts to preserve their ancestral culture. Further, McCook argues that these Poles' experiences are comparable to those of recent migrants and that their story offers insights for contemporary newcomers and state authorities.

After a brief overview of the Polish homeland, McCook focuses on the coalfields, showing that both areas had great population diversity, with ethnic Poles the most numerous migrants. These newcomers began residence in both locales at the bottom of the ethnic hierarchy, but in environments that offered contrasting possibilities. In Germany, pervasive police oversight and an interventionist state created more limits on ethnic institutional development and public participation than in the United States. Nativism in both areas served to gratify native-born workers living a precarious existence and to foster an inward-looking inclination among Poles, which promoted ethnic institutional elaboration and a sharpened consideration of identity.

The role of strikes was crucial to creating a sense of solidarity that transcended ethnicity, and in both areas Poles participated with growing enthusiasm and effect. In the Ruhr valley they had to form their own union, but in Pennsylvania the multiethnic United Mine Workers of America adopted a policy of inclusivity in the 1890s. Multiple identities emerged as ethnic identity was supplemented with union membership and, increasingly, participation in citizenship.

Because faith was important in fostering identity and cohesion in both settings, McCook pays substantial attention to religion. While Poles in both areas were overwhelmingly Catholic, the Roman Catholic Church in Pennsylvania allowed for separate Polish parishes while the bishops in the Ruhr valley simply added Polish priests and services to existing congregations. The author tends to overemphasize contrasts in polity since Polish American parishes actually frequently had elected parish committees paralleling the councils in German churches. Nevertheless, Americanization did coexist with a broad toleration of ethnicity as the bishops in Pennsylvania allowed, even if sometimes grudgingly, numerous Polish (and other ethnic) parishes to form.

World War I and its aftermath had important consequences for Polish immigrants in both areas. The loyalty of Poles in the Ruhr valley became suspect despite their support for the German war effort, and after the war the democratic Weimar government was intolerant of ethnic pluralism. Most Poles therefore left for France or the restored homeland. In contrast, the continuation of a limited pattern of state oversight and greater possibilities for citizenship in Pennsylvania impelled Poles there, especially the second generation, to enter more and more into the larger society.

McCook offers an insightful comparative study that carefully situates in time Polish immigrant communities in the Ruhr valley and in Pennsylvania and demonstrates well their social and political evolution. He makes a strong case for the modern relevance of the Polish experience in discussion of immigration and government policy today.

William J. Galush, *Emeritus*
Loyola University Chicago
Chicago, Illinois

doi: 10.1093/jahist/jas198

Untimely Ruins: An Archaeology of American Urban Modernity, 1819–1919. By Nick Yablon. (Chicago: University of Chicago Press, 2009. xvi, 380 pp. Cloth, $70.00. Paper, $25.00.)

Henry James famously complained that Americans had nothing to write about: "no castles, nor manors, nor old country-houses, nor parsonages, nor thatched cottages, nor ivied-ruins" (p. 259). Nick Yablon, however, reveals no shortage of written and visual depictions of American ruins, many generated by anxieties such as James's. What made New York so disturbing in 1904, when James returned after two decades abroad, was the rapidity of urban transformation. Skyscrapers replaced his childhood haunts. Capitalism's premium on novelty was hardly offset by cheap gestures to previous architectural styles.

This engaging, densely typeset book analyzes ruins—and meditations on them—ranging from Alexis de Tocqueville's encounters with abandoned frontier cabins to Herman Melville's "Bartleby, the Scrivener" (1853) to postapocalyptic science fiction serials in early twentieth-century magazines. Such real and imagined ruins are "untimely": most involve deliberate demolition or disaster, not deterioration over time. Produced instantly, modern ruins are quickly mourned, spoiling the nostalgic pleasures associated with classical decay. By 1900 it seemed modern buildings would never have the pleasure of becoming ancient. Americans worried that any surviving ruins would be incoherent to future archaeologists. Furthermore, the media depicting them had become ephemeral. Yablon follows Walter Benjamin in reading for the anxieties and utopian fantasies of earlier urban dwellers: "suppressed voices, secret hopes, and lived experiences of everyday people, even marginalized ones" (p. 16).

The century-long shift from Thomas Cole's paintings to pulp magazines might suggest a narrative of cultural decline, but Yablon focuses more on how America's imagined ruins tell key stories about urban modernity. In the early nineteenth century, Americans fretted less about urban life than about their lack of a heroic past, and so they rendered America's mountains and forests as ancient and equated Native America with vanished antiquity. But as immigration and industrialization reshaped urban life, emphasis shifted to the transient nature of modern architecture, constantly demolished and replaced. In imagined futures, mixed-race hordes would inhabit American ruins (most often a dystopian scenario, but in at least one case framed as a desirable state). Huge buildings hastily erected were hastily demolished, either by humans or, in the case of the San Francisco earthquake, by nature. Buildings rose and fell in a single generation, underscoring mortality. Unlike James, New York would never grow old. Yablon cites James's brother, William, on the "permanent earthquake conditions" of the twentieth-century city while arguing that the photographic snapshot and cheap print were fitting media to capture and disseminate such a world (p. 220). Yablon does not find this mind-set antimodern so much as capturing the experience of urban modernity.

From start to finish, this impressive study performs its own work of mourning. Long before the World Trade Center appears in the epilogue, descriptions of spectacular urban disaster conjure up ground zero. In the book's final paragraphs Yablon reads Alexis Rockman's painting *Manifest Destiny* (2004), which depicts a polluted, underwater future Brooklyn, as a counterpoint to Cole's series of paintings *The Course of Empire* (1833–1836). There is no reconciliation of culture and nature here; capitalist modernity, it turns out, will only serve to create untimely ruin.

Bryan Waterman
New York University
New York, New York

doi: 10.1093/jahist/jas176

An Immigrant Neighborhood: Interethnic and Interracial Encounters in New York before 1930. By Shirley J. Yee. (Philadelphia: Temple University Press, 2012. xii, 243 pp. Cloth, $74.50. Paper, $26.95.)

The immigrant residential enclaves in New York City at the turn of the twentieth century are often portrayed in literature and remembered in the popular imagination as places where newcomers lived, worked, socialized, and worshipped with those from the same home country, region, or ethnic group. Yet as Shirley J. Yee reminds us, to leave the narrative at that is to miss part of the story. In this highly readable book, she explores the relationships that developed across ethnic lines in lower Manhattan neighborhoods during the late nineteenth and early twentieth centuries in a range of social and economic contexts from shops and tenements to schools, missions, saloons, and settlement houses. Some of these interethnic and interracial relations were fleeting and superficial; others were of greater consequence. They emerged, she notes, out of necessity—conducting business, finding employment, caring for the sick, burying the dead—as much as out of personal desire.

While Irish, Jewish, and Italian immigrants all appear in the book, Chinese residents of New York City are especially prominent in the chapters focusing on intermarriage, commercial relations in stores, restaurants, and laundries, and care for the living (by physicians, pharmacists, nurses, and midwives) and the dead (by undertakers). Fewer than five thousand Chinese lived in Manhattan in 1910; their small numbers as well as existing exclusionary barriers prevented them from entering certain trades and professions and brought them into contact with other ethnic and racial groups. As the book moves on to consider urban reform institutions and organizations, Yee looks at antivice committees targeting prostitution, illegal gambling, and "white slavery," and at settlement houses through a cross–ethnic relations lens, arguing that these were places where interactions took place across ethnic, racial, and class lines.

In seeking to redress the balance by highlighting interethnic and interracial encounters, and in challenging the notion of isolated ethnic enclaves in lower Manhattan, there is a risk of going overboard in the other direction. After all, many New York City immigrant neighborhoods a century ago were associated with one ethnic group that had a particularly strong influence, most famously the Jewish Lower East Side and Little Italy in southern Manhattan. For the overwhelming majority of immigrant New Yorkers, the most significant relations were with coethnics with whom they felt most comfortable and shared cultural, religious, and linguistic bonds. This said, *An Immigrant Neighborhood* provides a window onto economic and social interactions among immigrants in different ethnic groups. For this

reason, the book will be of interest not only to those concerned with the immigrant past but also to scholars seeking to understand better the nature and consequences of interethnic relations in immigrant neighborhoods today.

Nancy Foner
*Hunter College and Graduate Center
City University of New York
New York, New York*

doi: 10.1093/jahist/jas211

In Pursuit of Gold: Chinese American Miners and Merchants in the American West. By Sue Fawn Chung. (Urbana: University of Illinois Press, 2011. xxxiv, 258 pp. $55.00.)

Since the nineteenth century, Chinese immigrants have braved their way to the American western frontier in pursuit of gold, better economic opportunities, political freedom, and personal fulfillment. They played a dynamic role in western frontier life and contributed significantly to the socioeconomic and cultural development of the region. Yet little is known about them and their history. Sue Fawn Chung's *In Pursuit of Gold*, a welcomed addition to studies on Chinese in the American West, contributes much to our knowledge of the Chinese in small mining towns in Nevada and eastern Oregon. By using a variety of sources, including immigration records, census manuscripts, legal documents, newspapers, memoirs, and archival manuscripts, the author depicts small multiethnic communities with strong interdependence at a time when Chinese were severely persecuted in most areas of the American West.

Chung's study focuses on miners and merchants in the three mining towns of John Day, Oregon, and Tuscarora and Island Mountain, Nevada. She explains that the Chinese were among the early miners there and constituted the majority of the residents of those towns. The harsh conditions of these frontier towns, such as inhospitable weather and rugged terrain, forced residents to become interdependent, and the towns were not too much affected by the anti-Chinese rhetoric prevalent in larger Euro-American–dominated mining towns.

Chung recognizes the economic contributions the Chinese made in these towns. They helped build the towns and irrigation ditches and made the area productive in mining and in agriculture. Chung further notes the social interactions between the Chinese and the Euro-Americans. The Chinese taught other ethnic groups in the communities about Chinese culture, foods, and beliefs. They also had more opportunities to be exposed to American ways than did Chinese who lived in areas with larger Chinese populations.

In the book's best nuance, Chung keenly observes that although the Chinese miners and merchants in the three relatively small, isolated towns faced situations similar to those in other mining towns elsewhere in the Chinese diaspora—for example, in British Columbia, Canada, and New South Wales, Australia—their experiences sharply contrasted with those of their counterparts in South Africa, where the Chinese were "coolie laborers" and suffered harsh treatment during their short tenure there. In fact, the Chinese miners in the three U.S. mining towns, with assistance from Chinese merchants, had advantages over Euro-American miners in working abandoned claims. The interaction between the Chinese and other settlers helped the Chinese miners and merchants work and live together with non-Chinese settlers in relative harmony. *In Pursuit of Gold* will serve as a valuable reference to those interested in Chinese American and immigration studies.

Huping Ling
Truman State University
Kirksville, Missouri

doi: 10.1093/jahist/jas160

Finding Oil: The Nature of Petroleum Geology, 1859–1920. By Brian Frehner. (Lincoln: University of Nebraska Press, 2011. xvi, 232 pp. $50.00.)

Finding Oil sweeps through the first sixty years of the history of the American petroleum industry, analyzing change over time in oil exploration. Brian Frehner's account begins in 1859, when surface indications such as oil seeps determined where to drill; it ends in 1920 with the emergence of professional petroleum geology. The result is a good book that provides interesting insights into an important though neglected aspect of oil history.

The most entertaining section of the book surveys the earliest approaches to finding oil. The scramble for oil in the late nineteenth century attracted charismatic explorers who employed divining rods, electrical impulses, and even mysterious black boxes to convince others that they could find oil—and at times to swindle investors. Frehner contrasts them to practical oil men who observed nature to develop local knowledge for finding oil. Some used creekology, studying the flow of creeks on the surface to try to identify likely locations for oil deposits under the surface. Others drilled on the high ground in and around cemeteries after noting the frequency of discoveries near graveyards. Belt-line theories led to drilling at the same elevations where oil had been previously discovered in a region. Such theories bring smiles a century later, but Frehner notes that they often contained a kernel of geological truth.

As practical oil men gained experience searching for oil in numerous locales, careful observation and instinct combined to increase their understanding of what might lie beneath the earth's surface. Their knowledge, plus information generated by topological surveys by federal and state governments, prepared the way for the emergence of professional geology in the years from 1890 to 1920. University professors in Oklahoma and other oil-producing states helped create a geology that combined scientific theory with knowledge gained in the successful exploration for oil. Searching for oil—and higher salaries than those earned by university professors—their students entered the oil business and demonstrated that professional geologists could increase the odds of finding oil. Oil companies such as Henry L. Doherty's Cities Services began the final act of this historical drama by hiring a large staff of professional geologists.

Throughout his convincing analysis of the roots of professional geology, Frehner regularly returns to the theme that "nature and culture shaped one another" in a process marked by "contestation for control of knowledge and of nature" (pp. 17, 15). He provides little discussion, however, of a central cultural force in the United States: the pursuit of profit. Early oil often was hiding in plain sight, with ample surface indications of good places to drill. As oil became more difficult, more expensive, and riskier to find, investments in the training and employment of professional geologists made economic sense to practical oil men bent on creating global scientific knowledge of the best places to explore. *Finding Oil* is an excellent introduction to this fascinating history.

Joseph A. Pratt
University of Houston
Houston, Texas

doi: 10.1093/jahist/jas284

The Making of Yosemite: James Mason Hutchings and the Origin of America's Most Popular National Park. By Jen A. Huntley. (Lawrence: University Press of Kansas, 2011. xiv, 232 pp. $34.95.)

In *The Making of Yosemite,* the environmental historian Jen A. Huntley provides a worthwhile biography of the late nineteenth-century publisher, hotelier, and businessman James Mason Hutchings and his contribution to the early history of Yosemite National Park. Huntley situates her task as moving beyond the traditional image of Hutchings as "the selfish, narrow-sighted businessman" that attempted to hamper the public preservation of Yosemite with his private land claims (p. 2). She instead reveals a complicated individual who strove to combine the promotion of nature with its preservation.

Huntley does much to flesh out and reconfigure the historical persona of Hutchings and show a man very much caught up in frontier California. The book charts Hutchings's immersion in (and commentary on) the plunder, violence, chaos, and opportunity of the gold rush, his successful foray into print culture and the letter sheet business, and his fervent promotion and hoteling of Yosemite. After a summer trip to Yosemite in 1855 (frustratingly, without recording a word in his diary), Hutchings gave up minerals for mountains and dedicates himself to promoting the California wilderness, or, in his words, opening "a sealed book to the general public" (p. 66). Hutchings contributed to the

unfolding visual and experiential relationship with Yosemite through his colorful magazine publications and a successful tourism business (with John Muir at one point cutting lumber at his hotel).

Throughout the book, Huntley does well to promote Yosemite, crafting the wilderness as "not merely a reflective surface but a creative and dynamic force in the evolution of American environmental attitudes and policy" (p. 9). She shows how Yosemite became a next stage for the Golden State following the gold rush—a new cultural symbol for San Francisco and later a beacon for the nation as a whole. Like other park scholars, Huntley remains adamant that "Yosemite represents a powerful tipping point in American concepts of land use" (p. 6). But Huntley also revises expectations surrounding the mythic "origin story" of the national park, noting the complexity of motives surrounding its preservation, fighting in Hutchings's corner against accusations of him turning Yosemite into "another Niagara," and highlighting the fallacy of separating consumer tourism from land preservation.

The Making of Yosemite provides great insight into early promotions of California and the fashioning of park imagery. Huntley successfully recasts Hutchings in the historical narrative, revealing interesting inconsistencies in the historical record as well as challenging conventional notions of binaries (such as nature versus culture, business versus environment). The book is beautifully written, reflective, and nuanced. While some may take issue with the closing comments that business and environment can sit comfortably together, *The Making of Yosemite* is a valuable addition to California history.

John Wills
University of Kent
Canterbury, England

doi: 10.1093/jahist/jas299

Main Street Public Library: Community Places and Reading Spaces in the Rural Heartland, 1876–1956. By Wayne A. Wiegand. (Iowa City: University of Iowa Press, 2011. xiv, 244 pp. Paper, $25.95.)

The historiography on American public libraries has long been characterized by institutional and biographical works, many of them commemorative in nature. From the mid-twentieth century onward, scholars inside and outside the library field have tried to be more comprehensive, integrating current theory into their perspectives. Wayne A. Wiegand—a notable and prolific library historian and the author of the definitive biography of Melvil Dewey—culminates here his long-standing examination of the multiple roles public libraries played in four upper midwestern small towns—Sauk Centre, Minnesota; Osage, Iowa; Lexington, Michigan; and Rhinelander, Wisconsin. Each community was settled by middle-class, white, Protestant folk of New England heritage and remained relatively homogeneous throughout the period under study.

The author questions the conventional paradigm of libraries as a positive and neutral influence and "the 'library faith' that assumes that without an informed and educated citizenry democracy cannot exist [and] that without libraries available to all citizens Americans cannot be fully educated or informed" (p. 3). Both of these premises grew from nineteenth-century roots, and he regards them as top-down assumptions, which contrast with his bottom-up perspective. Wiegand argues that public libraries have been shaped by not only their managers and benefactors but also by the people who have voluntarily used them. Applying recent scholarship of the history of reading and the history of public space to the institutions he studies leads him to read popular fiction, present-day "fictional media," as a prime factor that explains the enthusiasm, real and symbolic, for public libraries. This conclusion required a century's worth of primary data from the four libraries, including the catalogs of book collections and circulation-use records—as well as library and local archival records.

Following an introduction where Wiegand lays out his case, four chapters supported by meticulous scholarship narrate the unique stories of each small-town library with lively writing. A final chapter compares, contrasts, and analyzes these "Main Street Public Library" collections. An epilogue concludes that public library users indeed engaged the institution "sometimes as place, sometimes as source of information, most often as a source of reading

materials"—or all three (p. 179). The bottom line is that the libraries' collections reflected constant and changing demands and did not challenge the status quo, but rather reinforced the values of the majority. The libraries were occupants more than contributors to Main Street society, Wiegand maintains. Neither arsenals of democracy nor instruments of social control, these small-town libraries were agents that promoted social harmony for their communities. Rejecting both the received romantic consensus and the views of progressive cynics, the author seems profoundly moved by the simple fact that public libraries reflect the values and tastes of those who plan and use them. This work complements the classic histories of major public research libraries and biographies of major figures. It succeeds brilliantly in its intent—to elucidate "the overall history of the small-town public library" in America (p. 1). We could hope that this project will be a model for other, and perhaps corroborating, regional studies.

Donald G. Davis Jr.
University of Texas
Austin, Texas

doi: 10.1093/jahist/jas203

Heaven's Bride: The Unprintable Life of Ida C. Craddock, American Mystic, Scholar, Sexologist, Martyr, and Madwoman. By Leigh Eric Schmidt. (New York: Basic, 2010. xvi, 335 pp. $28.95.)

In *Heaven's Bride,* Leigh Eric Schmidt sensitively explores the unusual life and ideas of the mystical sexologist Ida C. Craddock (1857–1902). Craddock held that "religion and sex-love, indeed, are but two reservoirs of emotion," with deep and overlapping connections, and her life's work focused on promoting rapturous sexual energy as an exalted sacred force (p. 265). She has been known principally as the eccentric (even crackpot) victim of the infamous vice reformer Anthony Comstock, but Schmidt, a professor of religion, takes Craddock's religiosity seriously.

The book creatively sets aside strict chronology and opens with Craddock's first challenge to Comstockery, a publication championing belly dancing at the 1893 Columbian Exposition as valuable premarital instruction. Schmidt next describes her daring intrusion into the male domain of the anthropological study of phallic worship, before looping back to Craddock's childhood and education in Philadelphia to show her indomitable ego in the making. An only child raised by a widowed mother, Craddock was a star pupil at a rigorous academy. She aced the demanding entrance exams for the all-male University of Pennsylvania, impressing the faculty examiners to push for her admission, but the board of trustees turned her down—repeatedly, as her persistent challenges went on for nearly two years.

In the late 1880s Craddock gravitated to the freethinkers in the American Secular Union and Liberal League groups. She was never an infidel, however; she forged her own amalgam of religion, drawing on Bible mysticism, spiritualism, theosophy, and Indian Tantrism. At the same time, she made a thorough study of the physiology of sex, claiming that "the sexual act is . . . in its last analysis, a religious act" in which God also participated (p. 163). To put distance between herself and her anxious mother, bent on institutionalizing her, Craddock resided in a string of major cities, offering sex therapy for married clients and frank advice pamphlets for sale. And all the while she worked on a long and explicit manuscript titled "The Marriage Relation," which forms a cornerstone of Schmidt's analysis.

Four times Comstock hounded and entrapped Craddock, with charges ranging from obscenity to blasphemy. Supporters from the secular and free speech crowd raised money for her legal defense, but at trial Comstockery prevailed. Craddock got the last word by choosing suicide instead of the penitentiary and by leaving remarkable suicide notes that finally put Comstock on the defensive.

Schmidt strategically saves for last the question many readers will be pondering: How did the unmarried Craddock obtain her sexual expertise? Craddock's explanation—from frequent intimate relations with a spirit-world husband—fails to convince. Schmidt then shows what a 1910s psychoanalyst made out of Craddock's "erotomania," insisting she must have had an actual sexual guru. Schmidt offers his own intriguing solutions to this mystery and concludes with an assessment of how Craddock's mystical union stacks up against the largely secularized sexualities of our day. This highly engaging book offers new ways to situate sex in an era that was tipping from religious to secular.

Patricia Cline Cohen
University of California
Santa Barbara, California

doi: 10.1093/jahist/jas187

Neurasthenic Nation: America's Search for Health, Happiness, and Comfort, 1869–1920. By David G. Schuster. (New Brunswick: Rutgers University Press, 2011. xvi, 203 pp. $42.95.)

Neurasthenic Nation reignites an interesting debate: Does medical history study imaginary or real diseases? For David G. Schuster, neurasthenia is a cultural figment that helped Americans deal with the growing stresses of the late nineteenth century: "Neurasthenia recast many unpleasant aspects of life as undesirable byproducts of a nation trying to evolve and improve faster than the natural abilities of its citizenry could keep pace" (p. 1). So the term, literally meaning tired nerves, was a diagnosis of convenience for people who really had nothing wrong with them but who complained of overwork and stress.

An alternative view postulates that a form of low-level psychiatric illness, involving depressed mood, anxiety, fatigue, somatic symptoms, and preoccupation with such symptoms, has always existed. This approach argues that nervous illness, as we might call it, is real and has probably not changed substantially from one era to another. Investigating neurasthenia as a chapter in the larger history of nervous illness exemplifies this alternate perspective.

I cannot fault Schuster for adopting the first approach, as many other scholars have; and this volume, which originated as a doctoral dissertation, is solidly based on archival research. The first chapter takes us over familiar territory: Schuster presents the *dramatis personae* Edwin Van Deusen, the psychiatrist who coined the term *neurasthenia,* then George Beard, the New York electrotherapist who popularized the diagnosis in 1869.

The next chapter demonstrates the imprint of the diagnosis on American life: the use of nerves and neurasthenia for merchandising everything imaginable. Yet this happened in other countries as well, especially in Germany, where spas offering Silas Weir Mitchell's "rest cure" were filled with nervous cases. Schuster displays parochialism in asserting that these international developments were somehow particularly American.

The chapter on neurasthenia and spirituality breaks new ground in linking the diagnosis to religious movements such as Christian Science. Even so, it is discouraging to see the obligatory chapter on neurasthenia and gender, rehashing the worn-out suggestion that both men and women could become neurasthenic by failing to "meet expectations" about "their expected roles" (pp. 85–86). This chapter, nonetheless, has the virtue of drawing on case records from the Cooper Medical Clinic and Amelia Gere Mason's correspondence with Mitchell.

Chapter 5, on how "neurasthenia prompted people to search for new ways of living to improve their quality of life," transports us completely from the realm of actual illness into that of disembodied cultural representations (p. 113). Here again I am concerned that medical history is being sawed into a branch of intellectual history spiced with illustrations from the Sears, Roebuck, and Co. catalog.

A final chapter on the decline of neurasthenia ascribes its disappearance in part to "changes within the American medical profession" (p. 142). Here I simply disagree with the author. Neurasthenia vanished as a diagnostic term in the 1920s as the concept of mood disorders such as "neurotic depression" supplanted that of "nervous illness." Yet I doubt that the subjective experience of people with what had been "nerves" and was now "depression" changed greatly, though Schuster argues otherwise.

It is somewhat unfair to treat Schuster's excellent study as a whipping boy for my own views. The book is a worthy addition to the voluminous literature on neurasthenia, but at the same time it is legitimate to argue for a necessary change of course in U.S. social and medical history.

Edward Shorter
University of Toronto
Toronto, Canada

doi: 10.1093/jahist/jas281

The Collapse of American Criminal Justice. By William J. Stuntz. (Cambridge: Belknap, 2011. x, 413 pp. $35.00.)

This is a difficult book to review. The problem arises partly from the tragic circumstances of its publication, which occurred shortly after its author died at a much too early age. Partly, the difficulties are a product of its subject: the depressing failures of the American criminal justice system and the impact of those failures on modern society. But, ultimately, reviewing this book is difficult because the author's efforts to use history to prove that the choices of the past determined the problems of the present weaken his diagnosis and proposed cure (also based on his view of history).

That is not to say that the problems of the present cannot be explained by reference to the past. On the contrary, many students of American criminal justice have argued that understanding how criminal justice functioned in the past is crucial to discussions of how and why it works, or fails, today. But this study engages very little of the historical work by students of law, crime, or punishment. To give just a few examples: The book makes claims about the prevalence of lynching in the nineteenth- and early twentieth-century South without reference to W. Fitzhugh Brundage's exploration of the significant variations on lynching, and the law's response to it, within that region (*Lynching in the New South,* 1993). The book asserts that lynching practices in the North and West declined, without consideration of Michael J. Pfeifer's comprehensive study of the prevalence of rough justice throughout the United States (*Rough Justice,* 2006). The study makes claims about the nature of punishment North and South without discussing Michael Meranze's study of imprisonment in the early republic (*Laboratories of Virtue,* 1996) or Rebecca McLennan's work on imprisonment in the nineteenth and twentieth centuries (*The Crisis of Imprisonment,* 2008). The book argues that rights claims in the late nineteenth century were limited to white-collar criminals and their "high-quality lawyers," apparently without being aware that I, and others, have studied cases in which lawyers for poor, immigrant, or African American defendants charged with "core crimes of murder and rape" made rights-based claims in that period (p. 127). And so on.

I would be the first to agree with William J. Stuntz's basic premise that tensions between law and justice, and the often-related conflicts between local forces and state powers, are crucial to understanding criminal justice in the United States and its constitutional framework. Similar claims have been made from a variety of perspectives by Lawrence M. Friedman, Eric Monkkonen, and Jennet Kirkpatrick, to say nothing of the authors mentioned above. Similar assumptions play a significant, if more implicit role in Laura F. Edwards's *The People and Their Peace* (2009), Philip J. Ethington's *The Public City* (2001), and Allen Steinberg's classic *The Transformation of Criminal Justice* (1989). By failing to enter into a dialogue with these works or the many others that also engage those problems across U.S. history, this book does not do justice to its premise or the critical problems it identifies.

Elizabeth Dale
University of Florida
Gainesville, Florida

doi: 10.1093/jahist/jas163

Who Gets a Childhood? Race and Juvenile Justice in Twentieth-Century Texas. By William S. Bush. (Athens: University of Georgia Press, 2010. xii, 257 pp. Cloth, $59.95. Paper, $24.95.)

In *Who Gets a Childhood?*, William S. Bush historicizes a thorny issue for those championing the idea that the United States has developed into a color-blind society in which the forces of racial discrimination no longer have a significant impact. If most people generally agree that children and adolescents are not entirely responsible for the predicaments in which they sometimes find themselves, numerous indicators suggest that the juvenile justice system frequently denies this protected status from youths of color. This situation, as Bush's meticulously researched study shows, characterized juvenile justice in Texas for most of the twentieth century.

Indeed, *Who Gets a Childhood?* recounts a tragic story of repeated missed opportunities

to remake a juvenile justice system that would "deliver on its promises of treatment, rehabilitation, and most significantly, protection" (p. 5). Even as legislators and advocates for children were creating favorable conditions for reforming the excessively punitive Texas juvenile justice system, particularly in the 1910s and 1920s and then again between the 1940s and 1970s, significant barriers blocked their efforts at every step. In fact, the chronological scope of *Who Gets a Childhood?* is more limited than its title advertises. Regrettably, we hear precious little about the 1980s and 1990s, a period in which the Reagan revolution took the politics of law and order to a new level. Nonetheless, Bush's multilayered analysis of some seven decades of Texas juvenile justice breaks new ground in a number of ways, and it should be required reading for anyone working at the intersection of race and juvenile justice in the twentieth century.

The book constitutes an important contribution to a field in which local- and state-level histories are scarce—though its greatest value lies in its breadth, which extends far beyond the institutions of the juvenile justice system. To be sure, institutions are at the center of the story. Bush's research uncovers abusive conditions inside some of the state's most notorious juvenile training schools, reveals how the state agency empowered to eradicate training school abuses and bring about a more rehabilitative approach ended up advocating more prison-like facilities, and demonstrates how both juvenile courts and antidelinquency programs adhered to a racial double standard that treated African American and Mexican delinquents as irredeemable and white youths as salvageable. However, the book's most important innovation involves its handling of the social, political, and cultural forces—local, state, and national—that shaped the conditions within these institutions. Bush convincingly demonstrates how the staffs of juvenile training schools, with strong support from ordinary townspeople in the schools' vicinity, stubbornly resisted giving up corporal forms of disciplinary control. They did so, in part, because a disproportionate number of youths under their supervision were African Americans and Latinos, a phenomenon related to broader shifts—the emergence of southern civil rights activism, increasing anxieties about the problem of black and Mexican gangs, and the widespread appeal of "culture-of-poverty" conceptions among policy makers and juvenile justice professionals.

Unfortunately, *Who Gets a Childhood?* deals with some of these issues in a somewhat schematic manner. For example, the role of gangs in juvenile training schools receives surprisingly little attention, and Bush makes no attempt to theorize how the rise of black power consciousness played into the construction of the "dangerous" black youth in the mid-1960s and thus contributed to the increasing fervor to commit youths of color to prison-like facilities. Moreover, Bush is even vaguer about how Mexicans came to fit into this category of irredeemable delinquents. Yet these are somewhat minor shortcomings, which by no means diminish the importance of this very timely book.

Andrew J. Diamond
*Center for International Studies and Research
Paris, France*

doi: 10.1093/jahist/jas219

Sustaining the Cherokee Family: Kinship and the Allotment of an Indigenous Nation. By Rose Stremlau. (Chapel Hill: University of North Carolina Press, 2011. xvi, 320 pp. Cloth, $65.00. Paper, $24.95.)

The allotment policy carried out in Indian Territory from 1887 to 1934 divested tribes of their common landholdings despite treaty guarantees. While Angie Debo's *And Still the Waters Run* (1940) is the definitive text exposing the resulting "orgy of exploitation," Rose Stremlau's *Sustaining the Cherokee Family,* a community study of three-dozen families in Chewey, Oklahoma, points out "that is not the whole story, at least not for Cherokees" (p. 5). Stremlau argues that allotment was not simply a policy aimed at dividing communal lands into individually owned tracts, but it was a "profoundly gendered" program that targeted the most intimate aspects of Indian peoples' lives—their families (p. 18). Yet, despite this, Cherokee households remained "egalitarian, flexible, inclusive, and decentralized" (p. 22). Instead of stripping Cherokee

people of the most basic features of their society—kinship, hospitality, reciprocity, and communalism—allotment led Cherokee people, both those who participated and those who resisted, to draw upon traditional Cherokee values and respond in a calculated and informed manner.

Stremlau's first two chapters, "Arriving" and "Belonging," examine the pre-allotment patterns among Cherokee families. Intermarriage with whites "'ran' in families," but many Cherokees defied this practice and showed no preferences for Cherokee or white marriage partners (p. 50). "Serial monogamy" persisted among Cherokee men and women; extended maternal relatives, particularly elderly women, remained central to Cherokee families and their decision-making processes; and literacy in Cherokee and/or English continued as the norm (p. 52). Chapter 3, "Debating," provides a detailed analysis of the strategies employed by Cherokee national officials to resist allotment and protect Cherokee communal landholdings on the grounds that this arrangement supported a communitarian ethic. Further, most officials viewed common land ownership as effective at preventing the poverty and homelessness that plagued the United States.

The final five chapters—"Enrolling," "Dividing," "Transforming," "Adapting," and "Sustaining"—emphasize the creative and ordered responses of the Cherokee people to a chaotic and poorly implemented policy. Stremlau describes the practical realities that made allotment policy a failure, including flawed maps, inconsistent census records, requirements for marriage, death, and birth certificates when none existed, noncompliance by those who opposed allotment (particularly male and female Nighthawk Keetoowahs), officials' reliance on community informants, travel constraints of allotees, and uncooperative witnesses. Yet Cherokees challenged maps, produced documents, and used nonviolent activism to resist the policy, and informants and witnesses acted out of care and respect for neighbors.

Stremlau's methods challenge scholars to move beyond the racist language of blood quantum to understand the decision-making processes of Cherokee people who privileged their kinship responsibilities. The greatest strength of *Sustaining the Cherokee Family* is also arguably its greatest weakness: agency can be misinterpreted as political or social power when very little of either existed. Stremlau works hard to perform a scholarly balancing act; her work demonstrates the "affection and joy" of Cherokee families who adapted to and survived a policy that despite their resilience resulted in the exploitation and economic devastation of Cherokee communities (p. 243).

Julie L. Reed
University of Tennessee
Knoxville, Tennessee

doi: 10.1093/jahist/jas255

The Northern Cheyenne Exodus in History and Memory. By James N. Leiker and Ramon Powers. (Norman: University of Oklahoma Press, 2011. xiv, 258 pp. $34.95.)

James N. Leiker and Ramon Powers add important insight to the voluminous scholarship on the Northern Cheyenne who fled Oklahoma to return to their northern homeland in 1878. Instead of simply relating historical facts about military movements and federal Indian policies, the authors focus on how the memory, commemoration, and retelling of this history reshaped the narrative. They start with the exciting premise that for both Euro-American settlers and the Northern Cheyenne, new group identities formed through cultural memory and the act of telling. Each group narrates from different perspectives, only relating a part of the history. Descendants of settlers commemorate the violence perpetrated on their ancestors through oral histories, museums, and reenactments. The Northern Cheyenne commemorate their struggle through oral history, naming places, and reenacting the journey. The authors explore how such commemoration of "memories of shared violence and shared victimhood . . . aid in creating new peoples" for both groups (p. 72).

Leiker and Powers skillfully delve into the changing constructions of the violence of this history and the struggles over who deserves the title of victim. In comparing the violence perpetrated on both sides, they make a useful distinction between the individual violence perpetrated on settlers by young Cheyenne men and the state-sanctioned violence inflicted on Cheyenne people by the United States. They thoroughly explore the settlers' memory, relating many personal narratives, but are sparser in their treatment of Cheyenne perspectives, relating few memories of the flight and massacre.

Although the authors portend to focus on both Euro-American and Cheyenne perspectives, the follow-through could benefit from more indigenous voices. The authors make the case that the shared memories of flight created a new Northern Cheyenne group identity, but they supply limited evidence. The narrative privileges a Euro-American perspective: for example, calling the Cheyenne removed to Oklahoma "immigrants" instead of the more apt "refugees" or "internees" and explaining Cheyenne raids on settlers as the result of culture shock (pp. 36, 100). They conclude that frontier mythology celebrates both the perseverance of Euro-American pioneers and of Native American people defending their homes, but they fail to acknowledge that both of these narratives serve a Euro-American perspective. The authors clearly demonstrate that the larger American culture shifts their sympathy from the settlers to the Northern Cheyenne, but they do not demonstrate that this becomes possible through the extinction narrative that argues that Native American people were destined to leave their land, despite their noble struggle. They detail how Euro-Americans enshrined the noble savage stereotype around the Northern Cheyenne flight, but they could expand their exploration of Cheyenne uses of the same history.

Leiker and Powers significantly add to the conversation about how a shared experience of violence solidifies a group and reshapes their identity, particularly for Euro-American settlers. Importantly, they attempt to demonstrate this for both sides, but a complete exploration of the Cheyenne perspective might necessitate a book of its own.

Christina Gish Hill
Iowa State University
Ames, Iowa

doi: 10.1093/jahist/jas282

Lessons from an Indian Day School: Negotiating Colonization in Northern New Mexico, 1902–1907. By Adrea Lawrence. (Lawrence: University Press of Kansas, 2011. x, 309 pp. $34.95.)

A strange beginning to a work entitled *Lessons from an Indian Day School*: "This book is an education history, but it is not about the school" (p. 1), writes Adrea Lawrence, a non-Indian (p. 13) assistant professor at American University in Washington, D.C. Rather, she uses the "school as a prism for looking at the educative processes associated with colonization and racialization in the New Mexico Territory" around 1900 (p. 1). Drawing on the methodology of the historian Richard Storr, she positions her study as inductive micro-history, examining the many implications of the U.S. Office of Indian Affairs (OIA) campaign to transform Indians, specifically those of Santa Clara Pueblo. To achieve her "ethnographic reconstruction" Lawrence utilizes multi-disciplinary sources, including Indian voices, yet relies heavily on the wide-ranging correspondence of two OIA employees (*ibid.*). From 1902 to 1907 Clara D. True was a teacher in the day school at Santa Clara, and from 1900 to 1912 Clinton J. Crandall, her superior in the OIA hierarchy, was superintendent of the Santa Fe Indian School.

The day school serves as a prism to examine the increasingly complex and changing relationships between different individuals and ethnic groups—Indians, Hispanics, and Anglos—along with their relationships to the land. Gender issues also emerge, between a bureaucratic man and an independent woman. True's culturally ignorant attempts to confront student disease, for example, provoked both Pueblos and Crandall. Questions of citizenship were especially problematic: unlike many Indians at that time, Pueblos were citizens (under the 1848 Treaty of Guadalupe Hidalgo). Yet with Crandall's encouragement they accepted a more paternalistic wardship status and a reservation to protect their lands and life-style. The Santa Clara day school is the focus of only one chapter—and then mostly through the letters of True, revealing little about activities inside the classroom. Might autobiographies have helped (even those by ex-pupils of other schools); or pupil essays, as appended by Gertrude Golden to *Red Moon Called Me: Memoirs of a Schoolteacher in the Government Indian Schools Service* (1954)?

Lawrence suggests lessons missed, especially in cross-cultural understanding. But, as she fairly concludes, lessons were also learned. True defied Crandall by refusing to compel pupil attendance until after the Pueblo harvest. And she later criticized depictions of "the Indian" "as a thing to be robbed and converted rather than as a being with intellect, sensibilities, and will, all highly developed," a victim of "degradation at our hands" (p. 204).

This is a deeply and widely researched study, enriched by maps and photographs. Lawrence contextualizes the school within debates about law, land ownership, citizenship, disease, gender, alcohol consumption, and other issues rarely examined so intensively in such educational studies. Above all, she conveys how individuals and groups, especially Santa Clara people, negotiated and manipulated federal designs. With unintentional irony, perhaps, she ends by validly calling for greater scholarly attention to Indian day schools, rather than boarding schools. The work is a major contribution, yet one perhaps requiring a better title, such as "Santa Clara Pueblo and Its Day School: Negotiating Colonization in Northern New Mexico, 1902–1907." This is not a criticism, just a suggestion.

Michael C. Coleman, *Emeritus University of Jyväskylä Jyväskylä, Finland*

doi: 10.1093/jahist/jas180

The Rise of the Federal Colossus: The Growth of Federal Power from Lincoln to FDR. By Peter Zavodnyik. (Westport: Praeger, 2011. xx, 544 pp. $54.95.)

Relying on a thorough survey of published papers, laws, court decisions, and the proceedings and debates of the U.S. Congress, Peter Zavodnyik presents an encyclopedic account of the growth of federal authority between the Civil War and the Great Depression. He asserts that "by the time the New Deal arrived all of the precedents necessary for the establishment of an all-powerful central government were available," arguing that the revolutionary phase in the development of American federalism was not the New Deal and the period that followed it, but the preceding 72 years when national government began regulating banks, overseeing labor relations in critical industries, and providing aid to the downtrodden. (p. xix)

Zavodnyik divides his account into five chapters that hew to a traditional periodization (the Civil War, Reconstruction, the Gilded Age, the Progressive Era, and the 1920s).

Readers in search of an exhaustive account of the activities of the federal government and the expansion of its impact on society will find value in Zavodnyik's narrative. The author seemingly leaves no piece of evidence behind in his attempt to document carefully the different ways that federal authority operated between 1865 and 1933. Topics such as the use of federal police power to intervene in strikes; the roles played by federal patronage, river and harbor appropriations, Civil War pensions, and farm policy in winning the affections of voters; and the federal role in mobilizing the nation for war all receive attention.

Readers familiar with the work of such scholars as Theda Skocpol, Richard John, William J. Novak, Mark Wilson, and Brian Balogh (or, for that matter, with the older work of C. K. Yearley and Harry Scheiber) will find much that is familiar in Zavodnyik's history. In a number of respects, the book reads as a libertarian-inflected account that responsibly reinforces the main findings of political and legal historians since Stephen Skowronek published *Building a New American State: The Expansion of National Administrative Capacities* in 1982. Zavodnyik generally refrains from intervening historiographically, but at points his choice of words reveals a point of view, as when he describes interest groups as engaging in "mutual exploitation" and a search for "places at the trough" between 1921 and 1933 (p. 357). For the most part though, Zavodnyik sticks relentlessly close to his sources, an approach that ultimately renders this book useful to historians mainly as a kind of primary-source concordance.

Was the New Deal just a postlude to the expansion of federal authority between 1860 and 1932? While Zavodnyik emphasizes the range of federal activity in the years before Franklin D. Roosevelt took office, he does not answer this question in full, in large measure because his book ends before the New Deal begins. Although Zavodnyik's account will be of some interest to political historians of the late nineteenth and early twentieth centuries, scholars unfamiliar with the field should first consult Balogh's *A Government Out of Sight: The Mystery of National Authority in Nineteenth-Century America* (2009), as well as the classic histories by Morton Keller.

Jason Scott Smith
University of New Mexico
Albuquerque, New Mexico

doi: 10.1093/jahist/jas205

The Door of Hope: Republican Presidents and the First Southern Strategy, 1877–1933. By Edward O. Frantz. (Gainesville: University Press of Florida, 2011. xii, 295 pp. $74.95.)

Edward O. Frantz's fascinating book tells the story of the Republican party's abandonment of southern blacks to Jim Crow in post–Civil War America through an examination of the southern tours of Republican presidents from Rutherford B. Hayes to Herbert Hoover. These tours, though choreographed to generate spectacle and political capital, were not merely showpieces; they bore, as was written of Theodore Roosevelt's 1905 tour, an "organic relation to the course of events" (p. 154). Frantz demonstrates that during trips to the South, presidents appealed to whites by signaling tacit approval of the southern racial hierarchy; behind the pomp and parades lay strategic calculations designed to hold off African American criticism and develop southern electoral support. He thus helps explain one phase of the sad pattern of reversal and retrenchment in the development of civil rights in America.

In focusing on these tours as expressive of substantive policy positions, Frantz also helps unpack the oft-simplified concept of the modern presidency. Scholars sometimes speak of presidential modernity as if it sprang fully formed out of the twentieth century. In reality it was forged through generations of sometimes-tentative efforts to maximize presidential political capital by drawing on the strengths of the office. This book lays important ground-work for understanding the granularity of that evolution.

Frantz's attention to the African American press, which brings editors such as Timothy Thomas Fortune and William Calvin Chase into dialogue with their readers and with presidents, is also important work. I was also enthralled by the series of rhetorical duels between Republican presidents and southern politicians over racial violence. Both of the topics show that the aban-donment of southern African Americans took place as the result of a debate in which the terms were clearly and publically articulated. The stories of the evolution of presidential modernity and of national acceptance of Jim Crow thus become richly intertwined.

I would have liked to have seen these southern strategies placed into the context of the presidents' national political environments to provide a better sense of why they pursued such quixotic and dangerous southern goals. Frantz more often references broader policy agendas than explains them. Examination of these agendas would not excuse presidents from making poor moral choices but would clarify how they viewed their southern strate-gies in the context of a nonsouthern public—almost the entirety of the Republican electorate—which was increasingly disinter-ested in civil rights and had never been completely sold on what Frantz calls "the lib-eration legacy of the party" (p. 203).

A good account of the relation between the Republicans of the "system of 1896" to those of the 1970s and 1980s should be written. Frantz clearly wants to begin that story, but his comparisons of Richard M. Nixon and his predecessors such as Hayes and Hoover are more evocative than established. In both cases the party faced tough choices about race, and in both cases they made regrettable decisions, but the book does not prove that they did so for the same reasons, in the same way, or in the same spirit. In conflating the two periods one risks obscuring historical nuance with contemporary assumptions.

Daniel Klinghard
College of the Holy Cross
Worcester, Massachusetts

doi: 10.1093/jahist/jas279

William Howard Taft: The Travails of a Pro-gressive Conservative. By Jonathan Lurie. (New York: Cambridge University Press, 2012. xvi, 214 pp. $90.00.)

Jonathan Lurie traces the life of President William Howard Taft from his birth in 1857 to his appointment as chief justice of the Supreme Court in 1921. (His nine years in that office will be the subject of another volume.) Lurie writes that this book is "intended neither as a new biography nor as a detailed study of Taft's presidency," and he frequently cites Henry F. Pringle's *The Life and Times of William Howard Taft* (2 vols., 1939), Lewis L. Gould's *The William Howard Taft Presidency* (2009), and other standard works, almost always approvingly (p. xiii). Referring readers to Gould's books for further bibliography, Lurie also relies on the papers of the Taft family friend Mabel Boardman (held at the Library of Congress), the journalist Gustave Karger (held at the Cincinnati Museum Center), and many other manuscript collections.

In one major respect, however, Lurie strives to revise the conventional view of Taft as a deep-dyed conservative. Lurie's Taft was a "progressive conservative"—on correct terms with the Republican "old guard," unsympa-thetic to such insurgents as George Norris or Robert M. La Follette, and hostile to Woodrow Wilson and Louis D. Brandeis. Yet Taft's policies, as Lurie paints them, were usually as progressive as Theodore Roosevelt's (except for popular recall of judicial decisions, which Taft abhorred), and his antitrust prose-cutions and withdrawals of public lands went well beyond Roosevelt's. On the one hand, no incoming president had as much judicial or administrative experience; on the other hand, Taft's experience (and interest) in politics was very narrow and his desire for the presidency was never great. The result was a presidential term characterized by administrative action and the creation of progressive-favored expert commissions but one inept at tariff revision and negatively affected by the Richard Ballinger–Gifford Pinchot controversy and the overthrow of Speaker of the House Joseph G. Cannon. Ultimately, Taft won only eight electoral votes in his bid for reelection.

Lurie has written extensively and authoritatively on legal, military, and constitutional subjects. With Taft he has chosen a biographee very suited to his own talents. Taft was appointed to the Ohio Superior Court at the age of thirty and to the federal appellate court at thirty-five, "with the uncanny luck that sometimes comes to those who don't work for it" (p. 23). There he made his mark on corporate conduct, antitrust matters, and labor cases: he "was not uniformly hostile to labor" or the right to strike but "he deplored any resulting violence" (p. 30). As the civilian governor of the Philippines he stood his ground against the authoritarian generals Arthur MacArthur and Adna Chaffee. Taft could be indecisive in personal matters but decisive on the bench and as colonial administrator (pp. 41–49).

Lurie devotes considerable space throughout this too-short book to tracing the apparent political love affair between Taft and Theodore Roosevelt and its deterioration after the 1908 election. Less on that and more on Taft as the man who "modernized the presidency" might have been preferable (p. xiii).

Lurie makes a very good case for Taft as a "progressive conservative." On environmental conservation, antitrust matters, and in his 1912 acceptance speech statement that it had become "the duty of government to protect the weaker classes by 'positive law'" (p. 170), Taft would likely be much too progressive for today's conservatives.

Walter Nugent, *Emeritus*
University of Notre Dame
Notre Dame, Indiana

doi: 10.1093/jahist/jas326

Southern Prohibition: Race, Reform, and Public Life in Middle Florida, 1821–1920. By Lee L. Willis. (Athens: University of Georgia Press, 2011. xii, 209 pp. Cloth, $59.95. Paper, $24.95.)

In this book, Lee L. Willis chronicles the rise of prohibition in middle Florida during the nineteenth and twentieth centuries. Like previous scholars, Willis argues that white, middle-class townspeople emerged as the leading advocates for prohibition, fearing that alcohol and other drugs (such as cocaine and opium) impeded the region's moral and economic prosperity. But, as Willis discovers, opposition to these substances was not confined to middle-class whites. African Americans, in particular, endorsed prohibition because they believed that alcohol posed a threat to their families and communities. They joined forces with their white counterparts, an alliance that helped pave the way for the enactment of prohibition laws in several Florida counties.

Prohibition sentiment first emerged in middle Florida during the antebellum period. Condemning drunkenness for promoting social discord, white evangelicals led the initial fight against "King Alcohol" and managed to gain the support of Whigs (and later Democrats), most of whom hoped to use the issue of temperance to curry favor among townspeople. Nonetheless, the call for legal prohibition fell on deaf ears. Most whites, Willis explains, were only willing to unite "under the banner of racial prohibition" (p. 65). As such, when the General Assembly enacted a law in 1854 that banned all blacks from consuming alcohol, white support for legal suasion declined. That said, the antebellum temperance movement in Florida was important. According to Willis, it helped change "the state's political culture" by gentrifying drinking establishments and strengthening white supremacy (p. 66).

It was not until after the Civil War that the crusade for prohibition in middle Florida began to make significant headway. An increase in alcohol consumption among former Confederate soldiers, along with the abolition of laws that prohibited African Americans from drinking alcohol, encouraged many whites to embrace legal prohibition. For them, alcohol (and drug) consumption threatened not only to stymie economic and moral progress but also to weaken the racial status quo. Meanwhile, African American politicians and ministers increasingly endorsed prohibition as well. "Black reformers viewed prohibition as a means to social improvement, not social control," Willis explains, "They believed that supporting prohibition would be an opportunity to prove their respectability and establish themselves as leaders who inculcated discipline and responsible behavior within the black community" (p. 104). In the end, white and black reformers united in support of prohibition. Such an alliance played a vital role in the passage of local-option laws at the turn of the twentieth century, especially in Florida counties that had large African American populations.

Willis broadens historical understandings of prohibition in the American South. His interpretation of African American reformers is original and will influence how scholars interpret the prohibition movement. Unlike other historians, Willis does not limit his analysis of legal prohibition to alcohol. Prohibitionists, he reminds readers, targeted cocaine and other drugs as well. Students of southern and alcohol history will find this book of great interest.

Bruce E. Stewart
Appalachian State University
Boone, North Carolina

doi: 10.1093/jahist/jas182

Eugene Kinckle Jones: The National Urban League and Black Social Work, 1910–1940. By Felix L. Armfield. (Urbana: University of Illinois Press, 2012. xii, 116 pp. $55.00.)

In this slim volume, Felix L. Armfield illuminates the life and work of Eugene Kinckle Jones, the executive secretary of the National Urban League during the organization's first three decades. Guichard Parris and Lester Brooks's *Blacks in the City: A History of the National Urban League* (1971), Nancy J. Weiss's *The National Urban League, 1910–1940* (1974), and Jesse Thomas Moore Jr.'s *A Search for Equality: The National Urban League, 1910–1961* (1981) have already documented Jones's work leading the league, and there is little here that goes beyond or takes issue with these accounts. Nevertheless, Jones's life story has not been told in the detail that Armfield assembles, and his role in the effort to professionalize black social work has never been developed this fully. These emphases make this book a contribution to the literature in its field.

Born in 1885 in Richmond, Virginia, where his parents were college teachers, Jones grew to maturity in a world where educated blacks—W. E. B. Du Bois's "talented tenth"—were expected to provide leadership for the advancement of the race. Jones was educated at Virginia Union College before attending Cornell University, where he played a key role in founding the nation's first black fraternity, Alpha Phi Alpha, and earned a master's degree in economics and social science. Jones's first job was as a teacher in black schools in Louisville, Kentucky. There he met George Edmund Haynes, a black sociologist on the faculty of Fisk University who had co-founded the Committee on Urban Conditions among Negroes, which became the National Urban League. In 1911 Haynes invited Jones to come to New York to work for him as assistant director of the league. Jones and Haynes were both named executive secretaries of the league in 1916, and by 1917 Jones was fully in charge of the organization.

During his tenure, Jones focused on gaining employment and providing social services for blacks in American cities, especially in the North. The National Urban League established a research division to document the needs of urban blacks and a fellowship program to prepare blacks to become social workers. Jones personally led the Social Workers' Club, the first black social work organization in New York City, and he "worked tirelessly to integrate the profession of social work" (p. 23). He pressed for the legitimization of the professional authority of black social workers, for their inclusion in the American Association of Social Workers and the National Conference of Social Work (NCSW), and for the NCSW and urban settlement houses to focus attention and energy on the services blacks required. During this process Jones became the first black executive officer of the NCSW.

An attentive copy editor would have saved Armfield from some embarrassing misspellings and factual mistakes and could have helped him avoid frequent repetition. It also would have been good for Armfield to draw more heavily on the rich array of manuscript materials that he lists in his bibliography and to spend less time quoting from the work of other historians.

Nancy Weiss Malkiel
Princeton University
Princeton, New Jersey

doi: 10.1093/jahist/jas233

African American Civil Rights: Early Activism and the Niagara Movement. By Angela Jones. (Santa Barbara: Praeger, 2011. x, 281 pp. $44.95.)

There is a scholarly consensus that early histories of the postwar civil rights movement focused too much on Martin Luther King Jr. Those works were also preoccupied with the period 1955–1968, neglecting earlier developments. Angela Jones argues that similar misconceptions have marred our understanding of the Niagara Movement, a group founded in 1905 to fight segregation and disfranchisement. The Booker T. Washington–W. E. B. Du Bois rivalry is another example of the "tendency to reduce African American civil rights history to a few key leaders" (p. 3). In reality, Washington and Du Bois were figureheads in a wider debate within African American society between competing radical and conservative publics. The Niagara Movement was not just an extension of Du Bois's personality; it was also a communications hub that engaged in democratic decision making by numerous local power brokers.

The perception of the Niagara Movement as a well-intentioned failure is also unjust. Its achievements cannot be measured solely by the goals accomplished during its lifetime. It must be judged by its long-term contribution to the civil rights struggle. In generating dialogue within the black community on how to challenge racial injustice, the group's formation was a precondition for later legal attempts at reform by the National Association for the Advancement of Colored People.

In a balanced analysis Jones acknowledges the shortcomings of the Niagara Movement as well as its strengths. From the outset it was beset by internal divisions and was chronically underfunded. Moreover, even Niagara Movement members admitted that it did too little because "all they did was talk" (p. 34). At the same time the group achieved much. In addition to promoting debate, its emphasis on cultural pride was a forerunner to the New Negro movement of the 1920s. Jones challenges Kami Fletcher's 2008 findings in *The Niagara Movement: The Black Protest Reborn* that the Niagara Movement marginalized women. Although women were not allowed to become members until 1906 the group supported women's rights, as reflected in its backing for female suffrage.

More consideration could have been given to certain issues. Given the recent focus on class divisions within the civil rights movement, readers would have benefited from more discussion on the extent to which the well-educated, professional backgrounds of Niagara Movement members hindered their ability to develop grassroots support. Although by 1906 the group had secretaries in twenty-six states, more analysis is needed to show whether this is evidence of broad local activism as opposed to small clusters of individuals.

The author rightly notes the repressive racial climate of the day as a limitation on what the Niagara Movement could achieve. At the same time, her observation that "by the time the Movement dissolved, the strategic need . . . to work with whites was obvious" begs the question of how to account for the success of the Marcus Garvey movement just a few years later (p. 101).

Overall, however, Jones's study is a welcome addition to an underresearched area of African American history and one likely to encourage further work in the field. No mean achievement.

Kevern Verney
Edge Hill University
Ormskirk, England

doi: 10.1093/jahist/jas269

Politics and Partnerships: The Role of Voluntary Associations in America's Political Past and Present. Ed. by Elisabeth S. Clemens and Doug Guthrie. (Chicago: University of Chicago Press, 2010. 329 pp. Cloth, $55.00. Paper, $19.00.)

With the diminishment of public social programs in the United States over the past thirty years, nonprofit and voluntary organizations have taken on new visibility and significance in debates about the maintenance of the social safety net. These political and policy shifts have invited scholarly analysis of the contemporary and historical role of such organizations. The eleven historians, sociologists, and anthropologists assembled by Elisabeth S. Clemens and Doug Guthrie in *Politics and Partnerships* remind us that voluntary associations—rather than acting as a "third sector" that is distinct from both government and the market—have been deeply imbedded in politics and markets for decades if not centuries.

The collection has a distinctively twentieth-century cast to it, with the exception of Johann N. Neem's examination of the complex interplay between the state and civil society in the early republic that initially fostered—then ultimately fragmented—Americans' sense of nationalism prior to the Civil War. This modernist focus is appropriate given the authors' goal of using the essays to "inform contemporary efforts to understand and transform contemporary systems of governance" (p. 2). The systems of intellectual and social provision by nonprofits that the contributors to the volume analyze have their closest analogues in the urban industrial economy and polity of the twentieth century. Mark Hendrickson's and Alice O'Connor's chapters demonstrate how nonprofit organizations incubated policy ideas outside of the political mainstream during the 1920s and 1970s, respectively. In Hendrickson's most striking example, the National Urban League rescued a group of African American researchers who were financially abandoned with the elimination of the U.S. Department of Labor's Division of Negro Economics and allowed them to continue to undermine stereotypical views of "the Negro labor question" in northern industries. O'Connor reveals how, half a century later and on the other side of the political spectrum, conservative philanthropists, incensed by the seemingly liberal activism of the Ford Foundation in particular, funded a series of emphatically conservative foundations aimed at liberating businesses from the regulatory apparatus of the New Deal.

Another common theme across the essays is the remarkable flexibility of voluntary organizations in adapting to new political and economic regimes. For instance, Clemens shows in her chapter how the Red Cross, despite serving as one of the depression-era symbols of a voluntary system gone wrong, accommodated itself to new areas of public social provision during the New Deal. By World War II it had reemerged as a direct collaborator with the government in overseas relief and a progenitor of a new system of state-voluntary relationships. Similarly, Michael McQuarrie traces

how, during the rollback of the New Deal state in the 1980s, nonprofit local development corporations controlled by business leaders in Cleveland took advantage of the shift in federal policy from direct provision of public housing to tax incentives to encourage private-sector housing provision. Those corporations allied themselves with neighborhood community development corporations to promote the literal rebuilding of Cleveland's neighborhoods—all outside the formal political structures of governance.

The sheer heterogeneity of voluntary, nonprofit organizations will continue to present a difficult obstacle for theorizers of the role they play and have played in American politics. The links between the nonprofit research institutes examined in James A. Evans's chapter, for example, and the suburban megachurch discussed in Omri Elisha's chapter, are tenuous at best. Even so, one of the many strengths of Clemens and Guthrie's engaging collection is the way the case studies challenge facile generalizations about the political behavior, then and now, of these significant American institutions.

Andrew Morris
Union College
Schenectady, New York

doi: 10.1093/jahist/jas274

Miss Cutler and the Case of the Resurrected Horse: Social Work and the Story of Poverty in America, Australia, and Britain. By Mark Peel. (Chicago: University of Chicago Press, 2012. xiv, 325 pp. $49.00.)

What can the case files of the Charity Organization Societies (cos) and similar groups tell us about the treatment of the poor and the attitudes of charity workers and their "clients"? The societies were private groups in many cities in the English-speaking world, whose goals were to substitute "scientific charity" for "indiscriminate giving" to distinguish the "deserving" from the "undeserving" poor.

Mark Peel starts his book with a discussion of the possibilities and problems in using these sources, then goes on to a nuanced, "transnational" (rather, he insists, than comparative), detailed examination of case files in Melbourne, Australia; London, England; and selected cities in the United States. He has looked at some two thousand files, with about half from Australia (his home at the time he began the project). He focuses on the interwar years, with an occasional glance backward or forward.

Peel starts each section with a dramatized version of a case file that he thinks illustrates an attitude in that particular country. In the file he picks from Australia, Miss Cutler investigates a request for aid from a client because his horse had died. She visits the home, and in the yard she discovers a living horse. She and her colleagues tended to regard themselves as detectives, revealing chicanery among the applicants.

In London, the drama centers on a woman seeking money to redeem her bedclothes from pawn. The visitor from the cos says she can have the money if she will deliver her soon-to-arrive baby at the hospital, rather than at home. The applicant rejects the deal and is dismissed by the visitor as "stupid." The London cos tended to regard the poor as permanently inadequate and incapable of changing.

In the United States, Peel investigates several cities' child-saving organizations, although they were not quite the same as the cos. In Boston, the dramatized case concerns Jerzy Koziorek, the son of Polish immigrants who wants to be known as George and to become American. He runs away from home frequently to live with foster parents, but after some years of help and guidance by the Children's Aid Association (CAA), George has a good job in a store, and the CAA closes the file. In other words, the CAA hoped their applicants could change, and in some cases the clients did so.

These oversimplified encapsulations do not do justice to the subtle, complex, and detailed analyses that Peel provides for these and other case files. He has not written a monograph with a thesis, evidence, and conclusion. Instead he has a series of random anecdotes that are always insightfully analyzed. He does, however, have a sharp conclusion: "too many well-intentioned people make a tenacious mistake" in not listening to the poor (p. 279). He might have

provided a glimpse into what else was going on in society's dealings with the poor. In the United States, at least, settlement houses (a term not in his index) considered themselves an alternative, even an opposition to the cos. Yet within the bounds Peel set for himself, he does a marvelous job.

Daniel Levine
Bowdoin College
Brunswick, Maine

doi: 10.1093/jahist/jas309

Nothing Less Than War: A New History of America's Entry into World War I. By Justus D. Doenecke. (Lexington: University Press of Kentucky, 2011. xii, 394 pp. $40.00.)

Justus D. Doenecke, best known for his classic study of the anti-interventionists just before World War II (*Storm on the Horizon: The Challenge to American Intervention, 1939–1941,* 2000), turns his attention here to the domestic controversy leading to American participation in World War I. This is a thrice-told tale, and Doenecke does not aim to break new archival ground. Instead, he offers a comprehensive and elegantly written synthesis of existing scholarship, informed by his own use of the Woodrow Wilson Papers, the *Congressional Record,* and the contemporary press. In scarcely more than three hundred pages of text, Doenecke chronicles the debates over German and British violations of neutrality that persuaded President Woodrow Wilson to intervene in April 1917—not as an ally, but as a reluctant associate of the entente powers. Graduate students seeking to master the topic quickly will find Doenecke an informed and generally dispassionate guide.

In an era when the United States repeatedly sends forces abroad without a formal declaration of war, Wilson's concern for the niceties of neutral rights a century ago seems anachronistic, even quaint. Yet Doenecke confirms the consensus view that, in the American public mind, violations of so-called international law by German submarines and British surface ships loomed larger than either commercial interests or the bonds of sentiment. Although Wilson made a point of not reading the newspapers, he believed in his own genius for leadership and, according to Doenecke, "possessed an uncanny ability to articulate the fears and aspirations of his people" (p. 4). This may be true; still, public discourse and Wilson's interpretation of it remained astonishingly unsophisticated. In retrospect it is astounding that the president stood convinced that "nothing in particular" except a disembodied interlacing of alliances had started the war and that the two sides sought virtually the same objectives (pp. 230, 304).

Doenecke makes a valiant effort to give every major stateside historian of the conflict his due. In the end, though, he cannot escape the imprint of his mentor, Arthur Link. Although Wilson may have chosen poor advisers, even with all his faults he figures as the hero of the tale. Doenecke opposes the realists and rejects out of hand Robert Osgood's observation that a German victory would have imperiled American national security. He finds Theodore Roosevelt, Henry Cabot Lodge, and Elihu Root all "strident" and venomous. He denounces Secretary of State Robert Lansing—who came to favor intervention—as inept, irresponsible, and disloyal. He dismisses Col. Edward House as a "rank novice" in diplomacy, a negotiator who became far more dangerous than William Jennings Bryan (p. 302). He does not mention the pernicious influence of Edith Galt Wilson on the president.

Doenecke doubtless portrays accurately how the American public regarded the European conflict before 1917, but this remains, in Sally Marks's phrase, "the world according to Washington" (*Diplomatic History,* July 1987, pp. 265–82). Doenecke provides an exemplary critical bibliography of American books, articles, and dissertations on the run up to intervention, but he does not cite a single foreign source either on the origins or the conduct of the war. Although the United States would soon become the dominant world power, only a tiny minority of Americans, on the evidence here, understood what the struggle was about.

Stephen A. Schuker
University of Virginia
Charlottesville, Virginia

doi: 10.1093/jahist/jas303

Margaret Sanger: A Life of Passion. By Jean H. Baker. (New York: Hill and Wang, 2011. 349 pp. $35.00.)

Goucher College history professor Jean H. Baker, biographer of Mary Todd Lincoln, the Adlai Stevenson family, and American suffragists, among others, explicates the life and accomplishments of a controversial birth control advocate in *Margaret Sanger.* Baker claims that Sanger "has been written out of history" and that this biography presents "a more nuanced view of [Sanger's] perspectives" than we have at present (pp. 4, 5). This book clearly demonstrates the lifelong, unflagging, single-minded passion that Sanger held for her cause. That passion led directly to a major advance for women: oral contraception.

In addition to mining the usual historical sources, Baker scours the copious other resources available on Sanger, including Margaret Sanger Papers Project publications edited by Esther Katz and Sanger's papers at Smith College and the Library of Congress. Baker's sole reliance on Sanger's own writing for many facts presents a problem, however. Early in the text, Baker notes that her subject stretched or fabricated many facts of her life (pp. 35, 114n37). She gives the example of Sanger re-creating her in-laws in *Margaret Sanger: An Autobiography* (1971). The Sangers were Jewish refugees who lived in New York's garment district, but their daughter-in-law turned them into an English sheep rancher and the daughter of a European mayor living in Australia. After acknowledging this predilection toward inventiveness, however, Baker often supports her own statements with Sanger's autobiographical writings. References to her autobiography or her *My Fight for Birth Control* (1931), or both, represent almost 30 percent of the notes for the first five chapters (almost half) of this book. Many of these references stand alone, with no supporting works listed. The researcher looking for in-depth documentation should turn to Ellen Chesler's *Woman of Valor* (1992).

In three hundred pages, Baker explores the private life of Sanger from birth to death, through one failed marriage, to another marriage for money and status, to the death of one of Sanger's children and the suffering of the other two, due to their mother's absences and inattention. She explores the advocate's public life, from her Greenwich Village and socialist ties to her arrests for violating obscenity laws to her frontline provision of birth control to her push for funding and developing the birth control pill. Baker sees Sanger's actions as feminist and her disturbing alliance with eugenicists as opportunist rather than racist. Baker does not flinch from Sanger's less attractive qualities—marital infidelity and conflicts with other movement leaders, for example. The book notes Sanger's wry sense of humor. In the 1930s, while unsuccessfully lobbying Congress to make it legal for doctors to dispense contraception, Sanger concluded, "The more I have to do with Congressmen, the more I believe in birth control and sterilization" (p. 205).

Baker quotes the author Pearl S. Buck as saying in a 1935 speech, "In the future people will be astonished . . . that the things for which Margaret Sanger fights should ever have been opposed or wondered at or taken for anything else than a matter of inevitable human right and reason" (pp. 225–26). Would that Buck's prediction had come true.

Jimmy Wilkinson Meyer
Shreve, Ohio

doi: 10.1093/jahist/jas266

The White Negress: Literature, Minstrelsy, and the Black-Jewish Imaginary. By Lori Harrison-Kahan. (New Brunswick: Rutgers University Presss, 2011. x, 229 pp. Cloth, $65.00. Paper, $24.95.)

In *The White Negress,* Lori Harrison-Kahan argues that existing understandings of the making of white identity in the interwar period among American Jews of European descent change when we include Jewish women actors and authors. The author positions her work in critical dialogue with "whiteness studies" books by Michael Rogin, Toni Morrison, and David Roediger—all of whom argue that first- and second-generation European Americans staked their claim to whiteness by creating and consuming obviously stereotypical blackface performances. Harrison-Kahan instead favors authors who have troubled Jewish racial transformations and negotiations, such as Matthew Frye

Jacobson, Karen Brodkin, and Jonathan Freedman. She contends that her inclusion of female authors and performers allows us to see that particular Jewish women created interracial imaginaries "to fashion a pluralistic, rather than purely white, American identity, while simultaneously asserting her sexual independence in defiance of traditional gender roles" (p. 13).

A work of cultural and textual criticism, *The White Negress* has four chapters, each featuring a different subject: the vaudevillian Sophie Tucker, who belted out "coon songs" and sometimes performed in blackface; the author of *Show Boat* (1926), Edna Ferber; Fannie Hurst, the author of *Imitation of Life* (1933) and a friend and employer to Zora Neale Hurston; and Hurston, who had a longtime fascination with biblical and contemporary Jews. Hurston's book *Moses, Man of the Mountain* (1939), which focuses on the Exodus from Egypt, features racially ambiguous Israelites who speak in a black vernacular.

The book's Jewish women subjects not only described and depicted blackness but they also commonly had longstanding working relationships with black women whom they employed, while also sometimes striking up friendships fraught with the differences of race, class, and artistic achievement. It was not unusual for Tucker to develop friendships with black women from the theatrical world. One, Mollie Elkins, became a fast friend and actually helped support Tucker at a low point in her career. In other cases, Tucker employed black women as maids. Hurst once employed Hurston as a maid, and that relationship was similarly fraught with class tension and keen racial differences.

The White Negress makes precious few attempts to tie its representations of Jewish race and gender into larger historical narratives. In one of the few instances when the author tries to do so, her salvo seems off the mark: Harrison-Kahan contends that Hurston's version of Moses was "best embodied" (p. 170) by Joel Spingarn, the white Jewish professor of literature, who became chairman of the board of the National Association for the Advancement of Colored People in 1914 and died in 1939. In the same era, there were many African American leaders, from Marcus Garvey to A. Philip Randolph to Ida B. Wells and Walter White, who could claim more impressive credentials as the Moses of the black race. Still, this is a fine book, filled with expertly hewn close readings of a small but important group of female actors and authors, women who made significant contributions to how African Americans and Jews of European descent imagined one another.

Jacob S. Dorman
University of Kansas
Lawrence, Kansas

doi: 10.1093/jahist/jas306

Color in the Classroom: How American Schools Taught Race, 1900–1954. By Zoë Burkholder. (New York: Oxford University Press, 2011. xii, 252 pp. $34.95.)

Color in the Classroom describes the efforts of school reformers who worked to change American attitudes toward race during the first half of the twentieth century. Despite dense prose, the book effectively demarcates different phases in the effort to promote tolerance and combat bigotry.

At the dawn of the twentieth century, when many Americans used the word race as a synonym for ethnicity, schools sought to Americanize immigrants recently arrived from Europe. Some teachers tried to suppress every vestige of non-Anglo ethnicity, while others fostered assimilation by encouraging respect for carefully selected aspects of immigrant heritage. After immigration was restricted in the 1920s, the latter approach came to prevail.

The more tolerant approach had an unintended effect: it reinforced the belief that all European Americans were members of the Caucasian race. According to Zoë Burkholder, this "recasting [of] previously racialized white minorities as members of the dominant racial majority" led to a "hardening [of] the racial distinction between 'white' people and those who were 'colored'" (p. 13).

It was not until the World War II era that many schools began teaching tolerance of "colored" minorities. Despite that late start, Burkholder maintains, "this new tolerance pedagogy reconstructed the dominant discourse on race in American schools in an extremely short time" (p. 100). Even students who clung to ethnically and racially conscious

views they had formed in their home communities came "to recognize, and if necessary, to mimic the lessons they were taught in school, if only to cash in on the cultural capital of performing as educated American citizens" (p. 10).

Changing the way American schools taught about race was not a chance occurrence. Burkholder describes the roles that the anthropologist Franz Boas, educator Rachel Davis DuBois, and many others played in designing and leading "one of the most audacious antiracist initiatives ever undertaken in American history" (p. 5). She praises her protagonists as "early civil rights warriors" who taught "lessons on scientific racial equality to young children, years before the height of the popular civil rights movement" (p. 11).

In assessing this undertaking, Burkholder points to the perceived need for unity in wartime and the increased emphasis on culture, rather than biology, in several branches of social science. When she emphasizes the wartime context, she is on solid ground. But the jury is still out when it comes to the relative importance of nature and nurture. Burkholder shows that the pendulum swung from the social sciences favoring nature in the first decades of the twentieth century to emphasizing nurture in the 1930s, 1940s, and 1950s. But science did not end in 1954, the terminal date for this monograph, and in recent decades the pendulum has swung back toward nature. Genetic information is making its way out of the laboratories and showing that people with different continental ancestries have different distributions of DNA (deoxyribonucleic acid). This poses a challenge to those who assume, as Burkholder does, that race is just a social construct.

Raymond Wolters
University of Delaware
Newark, Delaware

doi: 10.1093/jahist/jas166

Mary Turner and the Memory of Lynching. By Julie Buckner Armstrong. (Athens: University of Georgia Press, 2011. xiv, 255 pp. Cloth, $59.95. Paper, $24.95.)

Over the course of a week in May 1918, mobs of whites in Brooks and Lowndes

Counties in southern Georgia murdered eleven African Americans after the murder of a white farmer. Among the victims of the white lynch mob were Mary Turner and her unborn child. When the mob heard that Turner intended to press charges against the lynchers who had killed her husband, Hayes, they hanged her upside down from a bridge over the Little River, shot her, set her on fire, removed the fetus from her womb, and stomped the unborn child to death in front of a crowd of several hundred people. The mob murder of Mary Turner and her unborn child surely rank among the most brutal in the sadly prolific and sordid record of lynching violence in American history. In this book, Julie Buckner Armstrong provides a significant service by comprehensively grappling with the cultural history of this event and telling us much about the role of collective memory and art in mediating the trauma of genocidal violence.

Strongly attentive to race, gender, and the unstable, shifting strands of detail and meaning, Armstrong painstakingly traces successive narratives of the lynching of Turner. These include contemporaneous accounts in the white and black press; Walter White's investigation for the National Association for the Advancement of Colored People (NAACP); the response of Georgia governor Hugh M. Dorsey; and artistic responses by the sculptor Meta Warrick Fuller, from the fiction writers and poets Angelina Weld Grimkè, Carrie Williams Clifford, Anne Spencer, and Jean Toomer, from the filmmaker Oscar Micheaux, and from the social scientist and NAACP executive secretary John Shillady. Armstrong then turns to more recent representations of the mob murder of Turner at the National Great Blacks in Wax Museum in Baltimore; in the work of the artist Kara Walker and the writer Honorée Fannone Jeffers; in annual reenactments of the lynching staged by activists in recent years; in a state historical marker erected in 2010 near the site of the lynching; and in the collective memory of the local black and white communities and among Turner's descendants. Armstrong argues that the myriad artistic representations of the lynching "may not provide facts or clear-cut outlets for redemption, but if art records agony, it offers testimony of spiritual survival" (p. 185). Similarly, in summing up the multiplicity of narratives of the mob killing, Armstrong holds that "Mary Turner's lynching is about black women, about national shame, about forgotten voices, about hidden trauma, about the potential for healing" (p. 204).

The book is well researched and thoughtfully written. Cloying excursions into painfully punchy literary jargon are few and far between, and short passages of autobiography-as-analysis risk resembling to the self-absorbed side of the blogosphere, but ultimately Armstrong's charting of her intellectual journey in writing the book is more a strength than a weakness. I would have preferred that Armstrong provide more context on Jim Crow and World War I–era Georgia, but overall, as a cultural studies and literature scholar, she is commendably cognizant of the contours of historical change. Her book joins the important work of scholars such as Sherrilyn Ifill in seeking to address the painful memory and legacy of lynching in American history.

Michael J. Pfeifer
John Jay College of Criminal Justice
City University of New York
New York, New York

doi: 10.1093/jahist/jas213

Gospel According to the Klan: The KKK's Appeal to Protestant America, 1915–1930. By Kelly J. Baker. (Lawrence: University Press of Kansas, 2011. xvi, 326 pp. $34.95.)

How often do students of the second Ku Klux Klan (KKK) use Protestant religious themes as their primary interpretive tool? Fundamentalist and evangelical connections are often noted in passing, but the Klan's broader religious appeal is seldom analyzed. Kelly J. Baker addresses this issue in her unconventional yet informative history of the Ku Klux Klan of the 1920s. The book is simultaneously an extended historiographical essay and a narrowly focused examination of the Klan's print culture. As the title suggests, the emphasis is on the essential role of Protestantism as both catalyst and cohesive bond for Klan members. Baker is concerned that by emphasizing the theatrically visual symbols of robed and masked men and women, burning crosses, and lynch mobs, historians and popular writers obscure the significant religious content of Klan doctrines and activities.

Baker cautions that older studies of the KKK are often incorrect and that newer revisionist studies emphasizing a strain of populism appealing to ordinary people can be misleading. With chapters arranged thematically rather than chronologically, the book relies heavily on examination of the textual content and religious meaning of the Klan's print culture. The basic sources are the group's official publications, the *Imperial Night-Hawk* and *Kourier Magazine,* state Klan newspapers, pamphlets, official documents, and cartoons. Chapter topics include religious themes in the Klan's early organization, KKK Protestantism, nationalism, gender, and whiteness, and the legacy of the Klan.

Readers without much knowledge of Klan history might be confused at times, and specialists in Klan history will benefit from the author's insights even as they may question her methodology. To better understand the significance of "the sacred aspects of Klan life" and "world view," Baker adopts modified "ethnographic methods to document, describe, and interpret" the religious meaning of Klan doctrines, rituals, and activities (p. 28). This ethnographic approach requires the author to reject stereotypical images and empathize with the men and women of the Klan to better understand their beliefs and motivations. This approach requires an act of faith for both the interpreter and the reader. Citing Harry Stout's *Upon the Altar of Nation* (2006), Baker also advocates using moral history to measure "the distance between what historical actors ought to have done and what they actually did" (p. 240).

Aside from printed material, the book relies heavily on archival sources and KKK history in Indiana and Georgia. Although Baker recognizes the significance of regional variables in Klan leadership and behavior, there are few examples. It would be easy to dismiss the author's approach as too theoretical and limited, but to do so would be a mistake. Unfortunately, there is considerable repetition from chapter to chapter, and the attempt in the afterword to link the 1920s Klan's religious and social themes to Rev. Terry Jones, Glenn Beck, Comedy Central channel humorists, political bloggers, and Tea Party movement factions suffers from hasty writing and a brief lapse in editing. Still, the book has value for both students of the Klan and scholars seeking the roots of modern conservatism, and the University Press of Kansas should be applauded for extending its reach.

Eckard Toy Jr.
Parkdale, Oregon

doi: 10.1093/jahist/jas235

The Listener's Voice: Early Radio and the American Public. By Elena Razlogova. (Philadelphia: University of Pennsylvania Press, 2011. 216 pp. $39.95.)

The thesis of *The Listener's Voice* is that radio listeners "participated in the formation of radio" in the United States during the 1920s and 1930s. The book offers a different emphasis in American radio history. It goes beyond business and legal histories, and also audience histories, to show how the latter affected the former previously overlooked ways, perhaps precisely because they were informal and unorganized and thus not explicitly documented. Even so, Elena Razlogova has found them by reading numerous listener letters in a new light.

The book documents a range of ways audiences affected the shape of radio in these decades. Razlogova effectively shows that large corporations did not have their way unimpeded. Instead, she describes multiple ways listeners at first countered the concentrated power of radio corporations and networks, as well as the Federal Radio Commission, in efforts to influence radio development. In the 1910s and 1920s audiences provided feedback to experimental broadcasters to help them develop better technologies. In the 1920s local stations welcomed and responded to listener letters about their programs. When the 1927 Radio Act reallocated broadcast frequencies and licenses from small to large stations and networks, listeners wrote to support local stations and protest the changes. Radio magazines for radio amateurs in the 1920s, like local radio stations, forged a mutual relationship with their readers. Eventually, they were displaced in the 1930s by fan magazines published by large "pulp" houses, more interested in leading than listening to readers. Still they retained letter-to-the-editor columns where listeners could voice their opinions. Radio serial writers attended to listener letters and drew from them ideas for scripts. However, Razlogova finds that by the late 1930s radio's moral economy broke down as network concentration and audience measurement took hold. But the story did not end there. After the war, the arrival of television, and the decline of network radio, there was a revival of listeners' voices and of local stations listening to those voices.

She thoroughly documents her findings, using listener letters and recounting responses from radio personnel and radio magazines. In so doing, she reveals a history of informal activities, relationships, and accomplishments that contrast and complement the corporate organizational and legal histories of radio. She balances the formal structures of power with another kind of power arising from the informal and individual actions of audiences and customers.

There is one flaw, although it does not diminish the value of the book's findings: the volume does not convincingly show that this is an example of a moral economy. When E. P. Thompson discussed the concept of moral economy, he was referring to collective action on the part of the lower classes who did not have the vote and for whom such action was their principal means of political participation ("Moral Economy of the English Crowd in the Eighteenth Century," *Past and Present*, Feb. 1971, pp. 76–186). The concept implies a community and culture behind the collective action, legitimating and enabling the less powerful to forestall the workings of a market economy. However, most of what Razlogova describes involves listeners acting individually as customers and as personal, even intimate letter writers. Many listeners wrote, but not in unison, yet they affected social and organizational change. This is an important, alternate force of development. While not intentional or collective, their cumulative effect shaped radio. These were

individuals going about their daily business in the interstices of dominant structures, or people circumventing formal organizational structures sometimes by developing informal working arrangements with others inside radio organizations. Such mundane informal actions that complement or circumvent formal rules, are less dramatic—and much less obvious—than planned collective action but are no less important in their impact.

Richard Butsch
Rider University
Lawrenceville, New Jersey

doi: 10.1093/jahist/jas287

Will Rogers: A Political Life. By Richard D. White Jr. (Lubbock: Texas Tech University Press, 2011. xxix, 347 pp. $29.95.)

The title of Richard D. White Jr.'s important study might seem odd at first. Sadly, Will Rogers's "political life" is largely unknown to Americans today, who remember him—if at all—as the "hayseed cowboy comedian" whose folksy quips are sprinkled over after-dinner speeches and whose benign smile now seems the antithesis of political relevance (p. xxi). After all, is this not the fellow who famously declared he never met a man he didn't like? Such affability strikes us now—and again, sadly—as quaintly apolitical. It was not always so, and largely because Rogers's incredible political life reminds us of that fact, this is a welcome and necessary book.

White has vitally contributed to the literature on Rogers's significance to twentieth-century American life. Biographies have long described Rogers the celebrity and folk hero, and more recent work has examined his groundbreaking influence on the performance of political humor. White effectively complements these themes by tracing the Oklahoma cowboy's metamorphosis from a politically inquisitive vaudeville entertainer into a potent political force whose folksy humor belied his serious effect on public opinion and frequently on domestic and foreign policy. He asks how such an entertainer could "become the foremost political critic of his era" (p. xxvii), and while his analysis rarely confronts this fundamental question directly, his engaging narrative answers it incrementally, inviting readers into a deepening familiarity with Rogers reminiscent of the process by which Americans came to know and listen closely to him a century ago. White shows how Rogers earned the nation's trust as an intermediary between the American public and the shifting political landscape that accompanied the nation's involvement in World War I, then the illusory prosperity of the 1920s, and the disastrously genuine depression that followed. The down-home familiarity of Rogers's honest humor, combined with his formidable intelligence, empowered him and his audiences to negotiate the dynamic tensions between isolationism and internationalism, conservatism and progressivism, and those of a country challenged by modern industrialization to abandon its rural past. Rogers's ability to articulate these tensions and to ease them through laughter that was at once clarifying and cathartic, established him among millions as an everyman expression of Americans' best selves.

White's study is meticulously researched. He makes particularly fine use of periodical literature and archival material at the Will Rogers Memorial Museum in Claremore, Oklahoma, to animate Rogers's political life through his correspondence and the profusion of talks, syndicated columns, articles, and radio broadcasts that quickly made his words nearly as likely to appear in the *Congressional Record* as over the radio or in the hundreds of newspapers that carried his columns. If Rogers was still known primarily as a stage and film star in the early 1920s, by 1928 his friend H. L. Mencken was marveling at his ability to alter foreign policy and to make and unmake political candidates (pp. 136–37). The Hollywood director Cecil B. DeMille declared him "the American who least can be spared." When Rogers was killed in a 1935 plane crash, Hollywood and Broadway closed down, and so did Congress.

"Everything is changing," Will Rogers wrote in 1932. "People are taking their comedians seriously and the politicians as a joke" (p. 79). White's valuable and timely study will reintroduce a wide range of readers to the man who modeled this cultural inversion and

exercised the political power of laughter borne not of cynicism or enmity, but celebratory democracy.

Peter M. Robinson
College of Mount St. Joseph
Cincinnati, Ohio

doi: 10.1093/jahist/jas248

Setting the Table for Julia Child: Gourmet Dining in America, 1934–1961. By David Strauss. (Baltimore: Johns Hopkins University Press, 2011. xvi, 324 pp. $45.00.)

Before Julia Child burst onto the American scene in the early 1960s, a burgeoning gourmet food movement "set the table" for her success. Despite the lean times and food rationing during the Great Depression and World War II, many affluent citizens— enticed by glossy magazines, charismatic chefs, travel agents, wine purveyors, and recreational dining societies—participated in a subculture of luxury consumption centered on classic French cuisine.

In his thoroughly researched, cogent, sometimes overly specialized book, David Strauss chronicles the evolution of gourmet dining in the mid-twentieth-century United States. He considers the significance of this gastronomic milieu, especially for those who could afford its cosmopolitan mode of "good living." Yet Strauss also connects his subject to broader themes, including class and gender relations, international affairs, the mass media, and transformations in American foodways.

Strauss deftly explains how gourmet advocates during the first half of the twentieth century positioned themselves against a utilitarian "nutritionist ethos" that emphasized health-giving properties (vitamin, minerals, calories) and efficient preparation of meals for the masses. While these two approaches were (and are) not mutually exclusive, culinary connoisseurs viewed cooking and dining as aesthetic, sensual experiences—pathways to pleasure, exploration, and edification.

To study the rise of epicurean eating is necessarily to focus on elites, especially upper-middle-class white men whose participation in posh food and wine clubs enhanced their social capital. Strauss devotes three chapters to these societies, which began in 1934 after the repeal of Prohibition allowed wine importers to tap new markets. Eager to share his archival bounty, he serves up a stew of information studded with mouthwatering menus and photographs of toque-wearing gourmands. For decades, these clubs remained "strongholds of masculinity" that privileged gourmet cuisine as the province of professional male chefs and excluded women and other ethnic and racial groups (p. 110). Strauss analyzes these clubs' exclusivity with references to Thorstein Veblen other theorists. In the end, however, the allocation of ninety pages to the details of these banquets is not warranted by their narrow demographic or limited social impact:

> The equation of gourmet dining with lavish meals for special occasions was a poor way to challenge the dominant nutritionist approach. Priced beyond the means of the average American . . . [it] isolated the activities of gourmet societies from the lives of middle-class Americans. (p. 132)

Subsequent chapters explore intersections among chefs, food writers, and readers of *Gourmet* magazine. Founded in 1941 as the nation mobilized for the war effort, *Gourmet*'s celebration of French food—the "dishes of an ally" against the Nazis—dovetailed with patriotic sensibilities (p. 161). After the war, Julia Child's prickly collaboration with chef Simca Beck, which Strauss reads as a microcosm of Franco-American diplomatic relations, helped make gourmet cuisine more accessible to home cooks. These developments, in turn, spurred trends, such as a proliferation of various ethnic eateries and the expansion of popular food journalism, that reached broader ranks of consumers.

Yet by the 1960s the gourmet movement had "exacerbated a divide in American society that will be difficult to bridge" (p. 254). Today, progressive food writers including Marion Nestle, Mark Bittman, and Michael Pollan aim to democratize access to fresh, flavorful ingredients and sociable mealtimes as cornerstones of a nutritious, environmentally sound approach to feeding the nation. With over 45 million Americans now receiving food stamps and countless others scarcely able to maintain a well-balanced diet, the "foodie" scene at four-star restaurants today is as out of touch with predominant bread-and-butter realities as were the decadent soirees of the Depression era. Historical scholarship will not solve this problem, of course, but it can shed light on the cultural roots of these grievous disparities.

Lori Rotskoff
Barnard Center for Research on Women
New York, New York

doi: 10.1093/jahist/jas283

A Great Leap Forward: 1930s Depression and U.S. Economic Growth. By Alexander J. Field. (New Haven: Yale University Press, 2011. x, 387 pp. $45.00.)

Alexander J. Field presents a convincing case for a "novel claim: potential output grew dramatically across the Depression years" (p. 1). As a result, his book is a compelling argument that the record-high total productivity gains (or total factor productivity [TFP]) of 1929–1941 were the real bases for the successes of the war economy and for the "golden age" (1948–1973) of mass consumer prosperity (p. 106). The first and longest part of this important book is a significant revision of economic history since the Civil War titled "A New Growth Narrative." Its six chapters are an exemplary demonstration of how careful and imaginative use of statistical information can revise deeply entrenched ideas about the past. Ordering his data into business-cycle peak-to-peak periods, Field is able to make a series of meaningful comparisons that highlight the positive developments of 1929–1941 usually overlooked by historians seeking to explain the persistent high levels of unemployment that justify labeling those years the *Great Depression.*

Gross domestic product and the productivity of nonfarm workers grew strongly during the New Deal era. Indeed, a record-setting peacetime recovery from the collapse of 1929–1933 was the essential foundation for the political successes of Franklin D. Roosevelt and the Democratic party in the 1934 and 1936 elections. Field also shows that the remarkable TFP growth in the 1930s was concentrated in three areas: transportation, especially road building and trucking; electrical power generation and distribution; and continuing innovations in manufacturing technique and technology. Field's disaggregation and description of the major components of the surge in TFP during the depression thus reveal how it was possible for American businesses to produce and distribute the steady stream of "next new things" that was the essence of the war economy and the golden age of mass consumption.

The second half of the book is broken into two parts: "Extensions and Reflections" and "Historical Perspectives on 2007–2010." The publisher's decision to fuse these two very different sets of essays with the six narrative chapters in part 1 will undoubtedly please scholars and graduate students, but it will also severely limit the book's readership. Part 2 is a complex, highly technical examination of various alternative theories economists have used to explain changes in productivity and output. Its three chapters reach the following conclusions: first, there is "a striking empirical regularity in U.S. economic history" that can be best explained by the procyclical character of TFP growth (p. 190); second, the equipment-investment thesis developed by Brad DeLong and Larry Summers to explain the recent information-technology boom is not an effective explanation for TFP growth in other periods; third, general-purpose-technology transformations are infrequent and very long-lasting, and are therefore ineffective for explaining most business cycles of the last 150 years. Part 3 is very present minded and policy oriented. Field seeks but does not find much evidence in the history he has written for a hopeful "silver-lining" claim that we are, in the wake of the financial collapse of 2008, building the potential for a great increase in productivity.

There is one very significant problem in Field's revision of the history of American economic growth. He fails to recognize the importance of the political policy changes created by the New Deal; indeed, he virtually denies the connections between politics and the economy. For example, Field breezily dismisses the unprecedented character of the road-building and other infrastructure projects created by the Public Works Administration and Works Progress Administration, saying that "they probably would have been undertaken (with a supply-side rather than make-work justification) had the economy not headed south" (p. 72). Unlike so many other important assertions made in the book, this one is not carefully interrogated; it is simply repeated. We later find this remarkable ahistorical conclusion: "With or without the depression, Wallace Carothers would have invented nylon. Similarly . . . it is highly probable that the buildout of the surface road network would have continued at roughly the same pace in the absence of the Depression" (p. 297).

The lack of political-economic analysis is the most serious flaw in *A Great Leap Forward*. Nonetheless, as a study of the private nonfarm economy this book breaks new ground. Teachers of twentieth-century American history should read Field's book for its totally convincing demolition of the folklore history idea that World War II was good for the American people because it ended the Great Depression and created the basis for the mass consumer prosperity that followed the war.

Ronald Edsforth
Dartmouth College
Hanover, New Hampshire

doi: 10.1093/jahist/jas245

Corporate Dreams: Big Business in American Democracy from the Great Depression to the Great Recession. By James Hoopes. (New Brunswicks: Rutgers University Press, 2011. xii, 234 pp. $24.95.)

Because we live in a society where corporate-speak—*customer* for *patient* or *student,* for example—has gone mainstream, the business ethicist James Hoopes believes we need to understand the differences between valid "entrepreneurial leadership in politics and government" and tired versions of corporate fluff (p. 188). He argues that simplistic president-as-chief-executive-officer equations of politics and business are dangerous because top-down corporate managerial and monetary sovereignty are very different from political institutions based on egalitarian values and popular sovereignty. Further, he posits that corporations have at best an ambiguous relationship to a free political order, as they can "insidiously corrupt democratic values" if corporate managers claim "the mantle of moral leadership" in society (p. 2).

Elaborating on previous work, Hoopes tries to offer brief and pithy generalizations that will help students who have only vague understandings of recent economic and industrial changes appreciate "the tension between corporatism and democracy in the national character" and comprehend the ways the "dangerous" but "useful" legal creation of the modern corporation has underwritten much of the modern world as we know it (pp. 16, 4). Preprofessional students will find this short book informative, and a few hardy souls will move on to other works that have covered the same ground in history, sociology, economics, and political science. Professors with students bathed in the soothing ideological balm that government is a foregone disappointment or that business and economics do not matter as much as the identity and social issues central to most recent academic discussion will find this book useful for survey classes where discussions of dollars-and-cents issues are otherwise largely absent. Historians, too, are among those ignorant of the dead economists whose ideas undergird their world.

Especially useful is Hoopes's examination of the "intellectual assumptions and bases" of modern management thinking as opposed to the superficial and self-serving digests of this thinking to which most businessmen, politicians, or students are exposed (p. 160). Hoopes also makes good, understandable points about the comparative advantages of different types of industrial structure. More than a few historians will find many of the arguments unfamiliar. Big business is created when the costs of managerial hierarchies within a firm are less than the transaction costs among larger numbers of smaller firms not normally operating in concert. The Internet era's recent lowering of both transaction costs among firms and the managerial costs within firms, therefore, does not automatically give the advantage to small entrepreneurs at the expense of larger corporate dinosaurs. Walmart, International Business Machines (IBM), General Electric, and Amazon.com are all the wave of the future simultaneously. Though he can only selectively sample a vast literature in a short survey such as this, Hoopes seeks to educate modern young people who find names such as John F. Kennedy or C. Wright Mills barely recognizable to the increased importance of modern managerial thinking in both its simplistic and complex aspects. Corporations, he concludes, are only likely to be more responsible if citizens have improved understandings of them as key social institutions.

Kim McQuaid
Lake Erie College
Painesville, Ohio

doi: 10.1093/jahist/jas256

A Short History of Physics in the American Century. By David C. Cassidy. (Cambridge: Harvard University Press, 2011. 211 pp. $29.95.)

A brief, nontechnical history of twentieth-century physics aimed at nonphysicists is highly desirable: in that era, physics revolutionized our picture of nature, reshaped geopolitics, and bequeathed now-unavoidable ethical dilemmas. Yet such a story is difficult to tell. Its plot includes a host of characters, laboratories, and machines; seminal episodes include the Great Depression, the Manhattan Project, *Sputnik,* and the failed attempt to "throw deep" with the Superconducting Supercollider (President Ronald Regan's football-metaphor instructions to the developers of the supercollider in 1987). Fortunately, this book is largely successful.

The title—which suggests uniform American dominance during the twentieth century—is misleading; "The Rise and Fall of American Physics"—the headline of the book's press release—better captures the spirit. This tale is less a story of a dominance than of a trajectory: the crude beginnings of American physics, its rapid ascent to its apex, and the loss of its leading role. In the first chapter, David C. Cassidy covers the early focus of American physics on applied teaching and research and how figures such as Henry Rowland of Johns Hopkins University helped inculcate a spirit of "pure" physics research.

Cassidy relays key institutional developments such as the formation of the American Physical Society and the *Physical Review,* and the first American Nobel Prizes in physics.

Chapters 2 and 3 cover the period between the world wars, which witnessed accelerators becoming must-have tools, the maturation of physics institutions, and the rise of physicist-administrators such as George Ellery Hale and Ernest O. Lawrence, who skillfully maneuvered government, industry, the military, philanthropists, and research institutions into powerful alliances. Cassidy discusses the discipline's curious and often-puzzling patterns of discrimination against women, Jews, and ethnic minorities. A landmark of sorts came in 1931, when *Physical Review* for the first time began to get more citations in physics literature than its chief German rival, the *Zeitschrift für Physik.* Chapter 4 gives a well-told short version of wartime physics, including the Manhattan Project, "the world's largest and—at $2.2 billion—most expensive research and development effort until the advent of the Apollo Space Program" (p. 84). Cassidy remarks that many veterans look back on this project "as a later generation would look back upon Woodstock" (*ibid.*). Still, it is regrettable that Cassidy did not spend more time discussing the Massachusetts Institute of Technology Radlab, which developed the radar that helped win World War II, rather than so much space to the Manhattan Project, which ensured the war's end.

The remaining chapters discuss the decline of American physics, focusing less on the outcome of mistakes than on globalization and increasing scale. Inevitably, the drawbacks of packing everything into a single short story are most evident in these chapters. For instance, we miss a discussion of the rise and fall of reactors, which were, for a time, another must-have instrument. Cassidy also neglects the recent vast upsurge in physics subfields and interdisciplinary research, which has transformed physics and its cultural niche. The only comparable book is Daniel J. Kevles's *The Physicists: The History of a Scientific Community in Modern America* (1977), which focuses on the physics community and is five hundred pages long. Cassidy's book is shorter and more broadly focused. At 170

pages and with five useful appendices, it is sure to be a basic introductory text.

Robert P. Crease
Stony Brook University
Stony Brook, New York

doi: 10.1093/jahist/jas288

Private Practices: Harry Stack Sullivan, the Science of Homosexuality, and American Liberalism. By Naoko Wake. (New Brunswick: Rutgers University Press, 2011. xvi, 263 pp. $55.00.)

In *Private Practices* Naoko Wake sets out to join the psychiatrist Harry Stack Sullivan's public life with his more private experiences as a homosexual man. Theorists of human sexuality were sometimes far more accepting of sexual variation in private than in public, and during an era when homosexuality preoccupied a generation of social scientists Wake believes that Sullivan's "life and work . . . offer a way into this troubled history of the making of the gap between public and private liberalism in the science of homosexuality" (p. 3).

Covering Sullivan's 1920s practice at Sheppard and Enoch Pratt Hospital in Baltimore, his 1930 move to a New York City clinic, and his participation in the wartime Selective Service System screening for military fitness, this study is at once an intellectual biography, an examination of Sullivan's changing ideas about homosexuality and mental health, and a broader study of midcentury sexuality. Sullivan is at the center, but the book pays extensive attention to fellow researchers, patients, friends, and influential social scientists of the era with whom he had close but fraught relationships. Wake argues that members of the group expanded American liberalism to include homosexuality, making it as central an identity category as gender and race.

Examining various levels of the "private"—including Sullivan's longtime live-in relationship, reports of his encouraging intimate relationships between patients and staff, and his own interest in some of his students—yields a complex portrait with sometimes-uneven results. In some chapters Wake's wide-ranging approach creates a complex and illuminating portrait; for example, chapters that link Sullivan's early work with homosexual patients to the changing terrain of same-sex relationships in the 1920s offer a persuasive portrait of how many patients' anxiety about changing sexual norms led Sullivan and members of his circle to view homosexuality as a paradigmatic symptom of sophisticated modernity. Similarly, a chapter on the rise and fall of the life history in social science offers a compelling analysis of how its use favored articulate and high-functioning patients who contributed their own subjectivity to theories of sexuality. Such analyses satisfyingly connect Sullivan's clinical practice, personal and social life, and developing theories, offering a new angle on the era. An examination of Sullivan in the 1940s, however, lays out his role in promoting psychiatry through wartime screening but is not as successful in relating intellectual and personal history to the broader field. Throughout, Wake's claim that Sullivan and members of his inner circle were developing "a unique form of private liberalism" (p. 41) is intriguing but ultimately unconvincing, whether because Sullivan's records were tantalizingly incomplete or because the meaning of "liberalism" varied so greatly over this period.

In addressing the gaps between private and public, and intent and effects, *Private Practices* takes up important issues and offers an analysis of Sullivan that will be useful not only to historians of psychiatry and the social sciences but also to philosophers of science, bioethicists, and anyone interested in twentieth-century gender and sexuality.

Miriam Reumann
University of Rhode Island
Kingston, Rhode Island

doi: 10.1093/jahist/jas278

A Quiet Victory for Latino Rights: FDR *and the Controversy over "Whiteness."* By Patrick D. Lukens. (Tucson: University of Arizona Press, 2012. xviii, 233 pp. $50.00.)

From the early days of the republic, U.S. immigration and nationality laws required that an immigrant be "white" to become a U.S. citizen. After the Civil War, the law was liberalized somewhat to also allow persons of African descent to become citizens. Immigrants who were neither black nor white—including immigrants from Asia—were not eligible to naturalize until 1952 when Congress eliminated the racial prerequisites for U.S. citizenship.

Given that persons of Mexican ancestry have long been treated as nonwhite in American social life, one might guess that immigrants from Mexico during the 1790–1952 period would have been classified as nonwhite and deemed ineligible for citizenship. U.S. immigration officers, however, generally did not invoke the whiteness requirement to bar Mexican immigrants from becoming citizens. The standard reason offered for that practice is that the Treaty of Guadalupe Hidalgo, which ended the U.S.-Mexican War in 1848, guaranteed the eligibility of Mexican citizens for U.S. citizenship. A federal court in Texas in the famous case *In re Rodriguez* (1897) reached precisely that conclusion (pp. 110–14).

A Quiet Victory for Latino Rights sheds much needed light on an obscure court case that could have limited Mexican immigrants' access to U.S. citizenship. The book's detailed historical analysis touches on an assortment of interesting topics, including immigration and nationality law, the emergence of the modern administrative state, interest-group politics, and the social construction of race.

In the depths of the Great Depression, a federal court in New York initially ruled that Timoteo Andrade, who, like many Mexican citizens was part Indian, was nonwhite and therefore could not naturalize. The book carefully documents the series of behind-the-scenes maneuvers that helped convince the court to reverse itself and allow Andrade to become a U.S. citizen (pp. 132–35).

A Quiet Victory for Latino Rights offers the first detailed account of the Andrade litigation, which included advocacy efforts of Latino activists, restrictionist commentators and politicians, and the U.S. and Mexican governments. While treading treacherous political waters, as many Americans sought to limit immigration from Mexico in hard economic times, the U.S. government quietly intervened because it was concerned about the foreign policy repercussions of deeming Mexican citizens to be nonwhite. Race was and is a contested and heated political issue in Mexico, just as it always has been in the United States. To have classified citizens of

Mexico as nonwhite would have been a serious affront to the Mexican government, which had endorsed as national policy the virtues of racial mixture (*mestizaje*) and applauded the emergence of *la raza cósmica* (the cosmic race).

Few scholars have considered the Andrade case in any depth. Ian Haney-López's classic book *White by Law: The Legal Construction of Race* (2006) reviews the published court decisions that address the whiteness requirement for U.S. citizenship. Even so, almost no scholarly work has looked at unpublished cases such as that of Andrade. Patrick D. Lukens's book thus does civil rights and race scholars a valuable service by raising awareness of this important decision and demonstrating the political nature of race through careful analysis of a historical event.

Kevin R. Johnson
University of California, Davis
Davis, California

doi: 10.1093/jahist/jas308

Warfare State: World War II Americans and the Age of Big Government. By James T. Sparrow. (New York: Oxford University Press, 2011. 336 pp. $34.95.)

At present, the United States is fighting an open-ended war overseas, the defense industry continues to thrive amid economic recession, and the state wields tremendous access to, and control over, the lives of citizens. Scholars such as Michael Sherry have sought to explain, in broad strokes, how American culture and politics and the U.S. economy became organized around the production of violence in the twentieth century. With *Warfare State,* James T. Sparrow provides specifics, narrowing the critical shift in civic culture to federal efforts to mobilize the citizenry during World War II.

The necessity of maintaining public morale during the war resulted in what Sparrow calls a "liberal imaginary" (p. 76) of public-private partnerships that solidified ideas such as freedom and the "American way," which were later deployed in the Cold War. Sparrow argues that government and corporate authorities constructed this partnership to ensure grassroots participation while obscuring their statist intent. According to him, the G.I./veteran is essential to understanding this new political culture. The idealization of the citizen-soldier in wartime propaganda entrenched the privilege of white males just as military service and wartime production were creating new opportunities for women and African Americans. But it was the citizen's duty to the soldier that legitimized state authority, as workers traced their contributions on the assembly line straight to the infantryman at the front, and taxpayers purchased bonds to ransom their sons from the grip of war.

Sparrow's book is an insightful blend of cultural deconstruction and abstract political analysis that examines the point at which state authority touches and intrudes on everyday life. His sources are tremendously rich and varied, and Sparrow shows a deft touch with popular culture, such as an inventive discussion of the 1938 *War of the Worlds* radio broadcast, which he uses to depict a society on edge in anticipation of war. Traditional sources such as tax records and government officials' correspondence are joined by vernacular expressions such as letters to the president, folk song recordings, bond drive radio marathons, and antistatist rumors. In whispers about Jewish draft evaders and Japanese American treachery, Sparrow finds evidence of challenges to the new statism, which later transformed into the virulent anticommunism that would flare up in the war's aftermath.

While Sparrow demonstrates great skill in a number of fields—economic, labor, social, and cultural history—his analysis occasionally comes up short. His search for agency in the machinations of the state at times takes an oddly conspiratorial tone, implying a degree of consciousness on the part of individuals in the Roosevelt administration that, in the rush to meet the demands of war, may not have existed. And his focus in a discussion of the zoot suit riots on the suits rather than the people wearing them subtly works to legitimize the rioters' claim that the "zoot suiters" were not real Americans. But these are minor quarrels with an ambitious book that is essential to understanding the world we live in today.

Meredith H. Lair
George Mason University
Fairfax, Virginia

doi: 10.1093/jahist/jas271

Helping Humanity: American Policy and Genocide Rescue. By Keith Pomakoy. (Lanham: Lexington, 2011. xii, 235 pp. $70.00.)

Using an array of primary sources, Keith Pomakoy presents case studies of American rescue or relief measures in response to genocide. From Spanish anti-insurgency measures in late nineteenth-century Cuba to cases of genocide and ethnic cleansing in the 1990s, the United States has never devised an easy way to halt genocide. Expanding upon Merle Curti's 1963 *American Philanthropy Abroad,* Pomakoy shows that private organizations often supplied effective assistance when government could not or would not.

If only he had stopped there. Pomakoy seems determined to rebut Samantha Power's Pulitzer Prize–winning study *"A Problem from Hell": America in the Age of Genocide* (2002), which depicts a pattern of indifference toward genocide without explaining it. To present the history carefully and to adjudicate the historiography fairly in each of these cases is a lot for one author.

Unlike Power, Pomakoy includes the Spanish-American War. He considers 1930s Stalinist policies in the Ukraine genocidal but argues that any kind of American intervention was militarily and politically impossible. In other cases, he claims that larger considerations prevailed: the "Somalia syndrome" (the result of highly publicized deaths of American soldiers in the East African nation in 1993) explains American hesitation in Rwanda and the former Yugoslavia. His most frequent tactic is to introduce philanthropic efforts as state-supported and realistic humanitarian involvement. Sometimes he presents new evidence and is convincing, as in the case of Near East Relief, an organization that gave sustenance to hundreds of thousands of Armenians during and after World War I. In general, he argues for an American moral impulse that bore results.

A long-standing historiographical discussion and debate about America and the Holocaust becomes here a contest between two extremes: David S. Wyman's *The Abandonment of the Jews* (1984), which has been influential, versus William D. Rubinstein's *The Myth of Rescue* (1997), which has not.

Favoring Rubinstein, Pomakoy tries to redress this imbalance, often equating a given scholar's disagreement with Wyman with support of Rubinstein. But it is one thing to argue that Wyman and his followers have oversold the possibilities of rescue during the Holocaust; it is another to proclaim rescue a myth.

In his survey of relevant literature Pomakoy discusses FDR *and the Holocaust* (1996), edited by Verne W. Newton, partly the transcript of a 1993 conference held at the Franklin D. Roosevelt Library and partly a collection of articles written by attendees of the conference. Bernard Wasserstein and I, who were present, are said by Pomakoy to question the value of "every rescue plan" (p. 140). But Wasserstein's classic study *Britain and the Jews of Europe, 1939–1945* (1979) was critical of British government policies. I wrote two articles for Newton's collection demonstrating that the U. S. government had missed some opportunities for rescue and relief. They are not discussed here. Citing several of my works to challenge Wyman, Pomakoy fails to mention my criticism of Rubinstein. One does not correct perceived exaggerations by leaning hard in the opposite direction. This book is too partisan.

Richard Breitman
American University
Washington, D.C.

doi: 10.1093/jahist/jas192

The Mauthausen Trial: American Military Justice in Germany. By Tomaz Jardim. (Cambridge: Harvard University Press, 2012. 276 pp. $29.95.)

When mention is made of American war crimes trials in Germany, most will think of the International Military Tribunal (IMT) at Nuremberg, which tried twenty-two Nazi party leaders in 1945 and 1946. As Tomaz Jardim shows, however, the Nuremberg trials tackled only a fraction of the 1,885 war crimes suspects in the U.S. occupation zone. Most of the American trials in Germany were held by the U.S. Army in military government courts at the site of the former concentration camp at Dachau. Between 1945 and 1947, these courts prosecuted 1,700 accused war criminals in 462 trials—a prodigious figure that marks the Dachau trials as the largest war crimes prosecution program in American history. Among the many crimes tried in these courts were atrocities committed in the concentration camp of Mauthausen near Linz, Austria.

In preparing the case against sixty-one former camp personnel at Mauthausen, the prosecutor William Denson drew on several precedents. Perhaps the most important—the Belsen trial from September through November 1945—was the first military proceeding to charge concentration camp staff with participating in a "common plan" to commit war crimes, thereby rendering each defendant vicariously liable. The Belsen trial later became the template for the U.S. Army prosecutions at Dachau, including the Mauthausen trial. Jardim lucidly distinguishes a common plan from criminal conspiracy: the former required no proof of an agreement between the defendants, only evidence that the defendants knew of the atrocities and contributed to them. Once the military court judges had accepted the existence of this plan, it became an established judicial fact in all subsequent trials of guards from Mauthausen's myriad subcamps.

Jardim deftly reconstructs the history of the case, exploring early military investigations, efforts to secure access to witnesses, and the conduct of the trial itself, which resulted in a 100 percent conviction rate and fifty-eight death sentences. Three defendants were spared the gallows, primarily, Jardim speculates, because of their youth and their service outside the camp fences.

One of Jardim's purposes is to deliver the Mauthausen trial from its undeserved historical obscurity. The trial demonstrates how knowledge of concentration camps developed immediately after the war and how survivor-witnesses contributed to the punishment of Nazi war criminals. These achievements, Jardim argues, must be balanced against the trial's shortcomings, which included, *inter alia,* abridged due process (the court deliberated for only an hour); an inadequate appellate process; and the trial's minimal resonance.

Some factual inaccuracies blemish Jardim's history: he misdates the Belsen trial, misrepresents defense motions at the 1945 Hadamar trial, mistakenly asserts that the IMT admitted prewar evidence of atrocities, and tends to conflate military commissions with military government courts. Further, his emphasis on the novelty of the common-plan charge is questionable. Nonetheless, these issues do not detract from the great value of Jardim's book, which, with sophisticated awareness of the virtues and failures of the U.S. Army's war crimes trial program, raises the important question of whether a flawed judicial process can nonetheless render justice for monstrous crimes.

Michael Scott Bryant
Bryant University
Smithfield, Rhode Island

doi: 10.1093/jahist/jas227

The Deaths of Others: The Fate of Civilians in America's Wars. By John Tirman. (New York: Oxford University Press, 2011. 408 pp. $29.95.)

John Tirman has written a compelling and impassioned plea for attention to a neglected and vital aspect of American history. He argues that Americans have ignored the human costs of their wars, and his book provides a grim tour of the devastation and suffering that the U.S. military has inflicted on civilians. Although the book reaches back to the era of North American settlement by whites, it focuses on America's three most destructive wars since 1945: the Korean War (1950–1953), the Vietnam War (1964–1975), and the Iraq War (1991–present)—each of which claimed the lives of between 1 million and 3 million people. Tirman supplements his analysis of these three wars with shorter assessments of strategic bombing in World War II, the Reagan Doctrine, and the Afghan War. He also provides a comparative treatment of the atrocities at No Gun Ri during the Korean War, My Lai during the Vietnam War, and Haditha during the Iraq War, and a critical analysis of the methodologies and importance of counting civilian casualties.

Tirman is struck by the callousness that Americans have repeatedly displayed toward the deaths of others. He believes the existence of such insensitivity is not in dispute, and so documenting it is not a major aim of the book. Instead, the author concentrates on providing an analytically wide-ranging explanation for

American callousness. The explanation combines racism, universal psychological impulses for distancing and disregarding tragedy, and the more particularly American myth of the frontier. Drawing on the work of Richard Slotkin, Tirman views the frontier myth as justifying and obscuring the suffering of civilians by constructing American wars as missions to tame a savage and threatening wilderness and as ordeals by which the nation could repeatedly regenerate itself through violence, energizing its sense of mission, identity, and moral purity.

Historians will find the narratives of American wars that Tirman provides familiar, including most of the material illustrating their human costs, since he draws heavily on the existing historical literature and, for the Iraq and Afghanistan conflicts, recent journalism. The book's sustained attempt to draw our attention to civilian suffering and urge the development of "a new epistemology of war" is refreshingly novel (p. 337). Beyond including a greater sensitivity to human costs, Tirman leaves open the question of what shape this new understanding would take.

Raising difficult questions is this book's true strength. Readers may wonder along with Tirman how American indifference compares with that of other nations. Likewise, if the bleak picture of American callousness that Tirman constructs has been determined by powerful and long-standing cultural, ideological, and psychological forces, how, if at all, could Americans change their attitudes and from where do contrary voices such as Tirman's come. There is also the fascinating and knotty question of what level of sensitivity to the suffering of war victims would allow a society to claim it was not indifferent to the deaths of others. Tirman has restarted an important discussion of the human costs of war. It is a conversation well worth continuing, and we can be grateful that Tirman has not provided all the answers.

Sahr Conway-Lanz
Yale University
New Haven, Connecticut

doi: 10.1093/jahist/jas228

Integrazione internazionale e sviluppo interno: Stati Uniti e Italia nei programmi di riarmo del blocco atlantico, 1945–1955 (International economic integration and home growth: The United States and Italy in the Western bloc rearmament programs, 1945–1955). By Simone Selva. (Rome: Carocci, 2009. 383 pp. Paper, €39.70.) In Italian.

Simone Selva's thorough study suggests that the rearmament that prompted the abrupt end of the 1947 European Recovery Program (more commonly known as the Marshall Plan) did not breach previous U.S. policy for Western European growth and eventually contributed to the economy of Italy. After 1950 military Keynesian economics would have allowed Italian industry—in particular Fiat and the state-owned Finmeccanica—to break industrial bottlenecks and speed the production of durable goods. To make his argument the author focuses on bilateral negotiations over North Atlantic Treaty Organization (NATO) aircraft, exploring in great detail the vagaries of military assistance programs—including the Mutual Defense Assistance Program, the lesser-known Medium Term Defense Plan of 1950, or the Mutual Security Act of 1951—for the production of components and then of whole fighter aircraft after the lifting of the restrictions imposed on Italy by the Paris Peace Conference in 1947. Selva argues that offshore dollar procurements improved the Italian balance of payments and eased trade liberalization. He goes quite far in explaining how Pentagon bilateralism, dressed as NATO multilateralism, sought a division of labor in Western Europe that assigned great autonomy to the United Kingdom and France and made Italy, the Netherlands, and others suppliers of spare parts and components.

Following a thesis advanced by Mario Del Pero, Selva is unconcerned about U.S. imperialism because he suggests that the Italian government could always play on U.S. worries about communism. To reconcile anticommunism and NATO coordination, the National Security Council and the Mutual Security Agency conceded to the Italian government on trade and aid more than would have been expected. On the other hand, Selva shows for the first time in detail that U.S. procurement of aircraft from Fiat was conditioned on the breach of the communist hold in the involved plant, which eventually occured at shop-steward elections in 1955. Selva uses top secret records to reveal the chain of negotiations that induced the Fiat general manager Vittorio Valletta to accept Ambassador Clare Booth Luce's requests and discriminate against CGIL members. Military procurements imposed security rules on some civil plants without any legal settlement, setting up a legal double standard that goes unexplored in the book.

This serious study deepens previous scholarship, such as that by Lorenzo Sebesta, Jeff Geiger, Luciano Segreto, Claudia Villani, and others. Selva has delved into an amazing number of American and Italian archives (including those of Fiat and the Italian Central Bank) as well as the papers of Dwight D. Eisenhower and Averell Harriman to give an account of the internal debate among U.S. agencies.

The book would have been stronger with better editing and a greater synthesis—even the expert reader can get lost in the details. Its major limitation is its attempt to solve large political issues through a bilateral diplomatic approach when such issues require a multilateral political and economic analysis. The absence of any quantitative assessment of the weight of U.S. military aid to Italy weakens Silva's thesis and calls for further study. Future research should consider whether military aid may have distorted previous recovery programs oriented toward export and whether rearmament polarized Italian society and paradoxically strenghtened the Italian Communist party against the wishes of the United States.

Carlo Spagnolo
University of Bari
Bari, Italy

doi: 10.1093/jahist/jas229

The Right Kind of Revolution: Modernization, Development, and U.S. Foreign Policy from the Cold War to the Present. By Michael E. Latham. (Ithaca: Cornell University Press, 2011. x, 246 pp. Cloth, $69.95. Paper, $22.95.)

Since the end of the Cold War there has been an enormous increase in scholarship by historians of U.S. foreign relations on American efforts to "modernize" or develop the poorest areas of the world after World War II. Michael E. Latham has been at the forefront of this

research. Indeed, his *Modernization as Ideology: American Social Science and "Nation Building" in the Kennedy Era* (2000) started the trend and is rightly considered a classic study not only of the Kennedy administration but also of modernization and of American liberalism packaged for the developing world.

In many ways *The Right Kind of Revolution* is a more ambitious work. Latham seeks to present the history of modernization as a theory from its roots in the Enlightenment to its post–Cold War resurrection as neoliberalism. He largely succeeds. This is an exceptionally well-written synthesis that will become a staple in college and graduate classrooms for years to come. Showing the interplay between theory and policy with a wide variety of case studies, not only of postcolonial leaders such as India's Jawaharlal Nehru and Egypt's Gamal Abdel Nasser but also of major developmental efforts such as population control and the green revolution, Latham explains how modernization became such a pervasive idea in the 1950s and 1960s. Modernization was a fairly malleable concept and its adherents, such as Nasser, Nehru, and Kwame Nkrumah of Ghana, were able to embrace, modify, and reformulate modernization theory for their own ends, often at odds with the United States.

Latham sees modernization as an overarching intellectual paradigm that asserted, largely based on a skewed understanding of U.S. history, that there was a single universal path from traditional to modern societies. Americans sought to coordinate development efforts in newly independent states as an "integrated process" to promote democracy and alleviate poverty (p. 19). U.S. policy makers embraced this paradigm for security reasons, arguing that modern nations would be less likely than traditional societies to start wars, embrace communism, or restrict private corporate investment. Modernization theory resonated with the American self-image of being an exceptional people with a mission to make the world safe for democracy. Like the "can do" and "fix it" mentality most Americans embraced, modernization posited that with the help of technocratic aids and expert advice even the most vexing problems could be overcome.

While this work is not an exhaustive study of modernization, the case studies it provides are one of its major strengths. Latham is able to show that modernization theory was "deployed across a wide range of geographic regions" over a sustained period, often with little regard for or understanding of local conditions and customs (p. 4). Apparently, although in retrospect predictably, local elites had little interest in creating democracy, giving up their privileges, or developing their societies. The result was a wave of *coups d'état* and the creation of dictatorial regimes throughout the developing world that proved difficult to eradicate. The failure of high-profile development programs such as the Alliance for Progress and of nation-building efforts in Vietnam discredited modernization in the 1970s and 1980s, but the theory rebounded (with often disastrous results) after the Cold War with the rise of neoconservatives and their embrace of neoliberalism and with the nation building that took place after September 11, 2001. Latham has provided an excellent book on an important topic. As long as the United States attempts to impose democracy on areas with little aptitude or experience and to use development assistance as a diplomatic tool for a variety of strategic and security interests, there will be a need for further study.

W. Michael Weis
Illinois Wesleyan University
Bloomington, Illinois

doi: 10.1093/jahist/jas207

Soldiers' Stories: Military Women in Cinema and Television since World War II. By Yvonne Tasker. (Durham: Duke University Press, 2011. xiv, 313 pp. Cloth, $89.95. Paper, $24.95.)

Yvonne Tasker is best known for her work on the representation of women in a range of film genres, particularly action. In her latest book, *Soldiers' Stories,* she turns her attention to the portrayal of military women in U.S. and British films and television from World War II to the present. Tasker carefully tracks variables that shape this figure, including genre, film versus television, time period, and nation, and concludes that the military woman remains an unstable figure regardless of context. A challenge to convention, yet contained within an essentially conservative institution, the military woman, Tasker argues,

remains a "contradiction in terms...either not really a soldier or not really a woman" (p. 278). Tasker charts the continuity of that contradiction over time thereby succeeding at the task she sets in the introduction: to "make the military woman a more visible figure within film and television history" (p. 3).

In part 1, Tasker covers the potentially disruptive presence of members of groups such as the Women's Army Auxiliary Corps and the Women's Royal Naval Service in World War II films. In part 2, she focuses on genre films, such as military musicals and comedies, and demonstrates how the female military character disrupts genre, often signaling, for instance, the introduction of a romance plot into the war film genre. Part 3 follows a shift to the genre of detection and suspense in films depicting the military woman, who typically represents a "problem" in such films to be investigated and often punished, not always in that order. Although the military woman is usually portrayed as threatening, Tasker notes subtle changes in representation over time. World War II films grapple with whether female military members are auxiliary or temporary, a concern reflected even in the military title Auxiliary Corps, while later war films concede women in the military as a given. Particularly in midcentury films, the presence of military women characters indicates a certain modernity, a forward-thinking mentality. Women run up against the limits of modernity in films of the later twentieth century, as the military woman is increasingly depicted as isolated and vulnerable to violence.

Tasker's bibliography demonstrates that despite the intense media attention regarding actual military women, particularly during the decade of the Iraq War, there have been few sustained studies of their fictional counterparts. Tasker builds upon work by Jeanine Basinger in *The World War II Combat Film: Anatomy of a Genre* (1986) and Cynthia Enloe in *Maneuvers: The International Politics of Militarizing Women's Lives* (2000), as well as drawing upon Linda Mizejewski's *Hardboiled and High Heeled: The Woman Detective in Popular Culture* (2004), particularly in the last third of *Soldiers' Stories,* which focuses on investigation and scandal surrounding the military woman.

Attentive to issues of race and class as well as gender, and sensitive to the range of volatile topics associated with the figure of the military woman, including violence, sexuality, and nationality, *Soldiers' Stories* conscientiously provides the military woman a well-deserved visibility in cinema and media studies.

Elaine Roth
Indiana University South Bend
South Bend, Indiana

doi: 10.1093/jahist/jas251

Hollywood Left and Right: How Movie Stars Shaped American Politics. By Steven J. Ross. (New York: Oxford University Press, 2011. xii, 500 pp. $29.95.)

Steven J. Ross challenges two pieces of conventional wisdom about Hollywood and American politics: that the film industry "has always been a bastion of the political left" and that liberals have had a greater impact on political life than have conservatives (p. 4). Ross maintains that "Hollywood has a longer history of conservatism than liberalism" and that despite liberals' strong support of causes, conservatives have been more successful in capturing power and have "done more to change the American government" (p. 4). Part of the reason for this success is that conservatives have offered a more effective story line. Liberals emphasized "hope of what the United States could be and guilt that we are not doing enough to achieve that vision," while Hollywood conservatives talked "about a nostalgic Golden Age of America that never was" and appealed to fear and patriotism (p. 412).

Ross provides portraits of ten people who reflect a major division in modern American politics. Five—Charlie Chaplin, Edward G. Robinson, Harry Belafonte, Jane Fonda, and Warren Beatty—are liberals who supported the New Deal and/or the Great Society programs. The other five—Louis B. Mayer, George Murphy, Ronald Reagan, Charlton Heston, and Arnold Schwarzenegger—are conservatives who generally opposed or (like Murphy, Reagan, and Schwarzenegger through elected office) worked to roll back many of these programs.

During the 1930s and 1940s Chaplin and Robinson risked their careers to support political causes. During that same time Mayer systematically began grooming his stars at Metro-Goldwyn-Mayer for membership in the Republican party. Long before he was elected to the U.S. Senate in 1964, Murphy was one of Mayer's early converts and had advised Dwight D. Eisenhower on how to use television to political advantage.

A strong feature of *Hollywood Left and Right* is Ross's focus on how new media have changed politics; images have proven especially powerful. During the 1960s opponents of Murphy and Reagan tried to discredit both men as mere movie stars, mistakenly thinking that the replay of their old films on television would weaken their chances of being elected. On the contrary, Ross says, those old films probably made both men seem more likeable. Media images were also particularly important in the careers of Fonda and Heston. A picture of Fonda sitting atop a North Vietnamese antiaircraft gun gave her critics ammunition to demonize her. Heston used his film image as Moses to enhance his appeal to conservatives on many issues, including gun control.

Schwarzenegger, elected to the California governorship in 2003, comes off as an opportunist but also as an innovator in using entertainment media. The former Mr. Universe became an international movie star, married into the Kennedy clan, and was eager to seize power. He realized that by appearing on television with John Stewart and Jay Leno he could reach nonvoters and take advantage of a platform from which to speak at length without being seriously challenged. But, Ross says, Schwarzenegger proved to be a more successful campaigner than a governor.

Ross, whose earlier work includes the important book *Working-Class Hollywood* (1998), has here produced a well-researched and fair-minded account of ten celebrities to show that they were not only famous but also engaged citizens who were influential in the politics of their day.

Stephen Vaughn
University of Wisconsin
Madison, Wisconsin

doi: 10.1093/jahist/jas194

Pop Song Piracy: Disobedient Music Distribution since 1929. By Barry Kernfeld. (Chicago: University of Chicago Press, 2011. xii, 273 pp. Cloth, $90.00. Paper, $29.00.)

A musician, musicologist, and librarian at Penn State University, Barry Kernfeld offers an engaging look at the ongoing battle for control of music in *Pop Song Piracy*. The book is a welcome addition to the growing literature on law, music, and technology, joining works by Joanna Demers, Adrian Johns, and Siva Vaidhyanathan. The study takes songs as its unit of analysis, an approach that allows the author to survey how music has been distributed through a variety of disparate channels, such as broadcasting and sheet music. The choice of terminology, however, can be misleading. For instance, the book suggests that the 1971 Sound Recording Amendment meant that "a song no longer had to be 'published.'. . . Now a song need only be 'fixed,' as, for example, on a disk or on a tape in order to be protected" by copyright, but the law did nothing to change the status of songs (p. 163). Rather, it conferred the first federal copyright for sound recordings themselves—as distinct from written compositions, which had been copyrightable since 1831. Legal details aside, this study offers a valuable perspective on the evolution of the music business.

Kernfeld presents the industry's history as an ongoing dialectic between monopolistic rights holders, such as broadcasters and record label companies, and their fiendishly clever opponents—the fans and entrepreneurs who devise new ways to produce and exchange music. The book describes a pattern of "prohibition, failed containment, and . . . ultimate assimilation into business as usual" in which industry incumbents attempt to suppress new modes of distribution but sooner or later yield to the public's desire to access music in novel ways (p. 218). This model provides a rubric for understanding how established players adapt to the exigencies of new markets and technology; it captures perfectly, for instance, the record industry's initial resistance to digital distribution and its eventual capitulation to Apple's online iTunes store in 2003. One danger of this approach lies in emphasizing technological change and consumer demand to the exclusion of other factors, such as

political or ideological struggle. For example, Kernfeld discusses a series of legal skirmishes over LP record and tape piracy but does not consider why sound recordings persisted so long without U.S. copyright protection.

Pop Song Piracy attributes the expansion of copyright in the late 1960s and early 1970s to the influence of technology—chiefly the surging popularity of magnetic tape as a bootleg medium in the 1960s—but does not take into account other cultural, political, or economic forces that might have contributed to the record industry's sudden success in winning long-sought protections. Notwithstanding these minor criticisms, this volume offers insight into the clashes that have shaped the music industry as we know it today, bringing to light important case studies of businesses and other institutions grappling with the threat of new methods of distribution. According to Kernfeld's model, current battles over intellectual property should eventually result in a compromise between the interests of artists, consumers, and business—but the outcome remains to be seen.

Alex Sayf Cummings
Georgia State University
Atlanta, Georgia

doi: 10.1093/jahist/jas214

What's Fair on the Air? Cold War Right-Wing Broadcasting and the Public Interest. By Heather Hendershot. (Chicago: University of Chicago Press, 2011. x, 260 pp. Cloth, $85.00. Paper, $27.50.)

In *What's Fair on the Air?* Heather Hendershot explores the colorful world of right-wing "extremist" broadcasting in the Cold War era. A broadly interdisciplinary work, the book focuses on the rise of political conservatism, the showdown between fundamentalism and evangelicalism, and debates over free speech and public interest. Hendershot follows the careers of four right-wing broadcasters: the secular anticommunists H. L. Hunt and Dan Smoot, and the politically engaged religious talkers Carl McIntire and Billy James Hargis. These men represented the far Right of American politics in the 1950s and 1960s, though, as Hendershot argues, their hard-line, even conspiratorial, anticommunism was not far from mainstream American sentiment in the 1950s.

Two central arguments run through the five chapters (each dedicated to a single broadcaster, with two for McIntire). First, these extremist broadcasters had to be purged from the movement to allow respectable conservatism to move forward. Second, contemporary right-wing broadcasters succeed in part because, unlike their predecessors, they present their ideas in more moderate language. The first is well documented in histories of conservatism, most notably in the case of the John Birch Society, which *National Review* read out of conservatism in 1965. *What's Fair on the Air?* explains why this purge was necessary: because these more extreme ideas had such powerful mouthpieces.

Hendershot admits that the second argument is more open to challenge, but she defends it convincingly in her discussion of right-wing broadcasting and civil rights. Southern politicians and commentators found that racist language and overt defenses of segregation and disfranchisement simply did not play outside the South once the civil rights movement began drawing national attention. Conservatives learned to moderate (at least rhetorically) or be marginalized.

But *What's Fair on the Air?* is not simply a history of shifting conservative messages. It is also a history of midcentury political broadcasting, and here Hendershot contributes her most profound insights. Approaching media as businesses beholden to a substantial regulatory regime, Hendershot demonstrates how business practices allowed right-wing broadcasters to thrive on small, nonnetworked radio stations and how regulations, particularly the Federal Communications Commission's Fairness Doctrine, contributed to their demise by the early 1970s.

The Fairness Doctrine argument is nuanced and insightful. Though the doctrine had little direct efficacy—only .1 percent of complaints resulted in Federal Communications Commission (FCC) action—its existence altered the practices of both station owners and right-wing broadcasters. Hendershot's extremists either altered their shows by introducing balance (inviting on, for instance, liberals to present their perspective, as H. L. Hunt did on his shows) or risked being booted from stations wary of running afoul of the FCC. This chilling effect contributed to the perception of a midcentury consensus in America, a point that could be better made with more attention to the doctrine's effect on the Left.

Hendershot concludes these broadcasters "were oddities who finally had to be left behind" for conservatism to flourish (p. 24). In showing how they functioned in the movement and defined the limits of acceptable speech, she makes a strong case why they should be left behind no longer.

Nicole Hemmer
University of Sydney
Sydney, Australia

doi: 10.1093/jahist/jas250

Countercultural Conservatives: American Evangelicalism from the Postwar Revival to the New Christian Right. By Axel R. Schäfer. (Madison: University of Wisconsin Press, 2011. xii, 225 pp. Paper, $29.95.)

In this book Axel R. Schäfer presents a closely reasoned three-part thesis that utilizes resource-mobilization theory and subcultural-identity theory. First, he argues that evangelicals are not simply traditionalists in morality and theology but are also modern and worldly. Second, he argues persuasively that evangelicals are not monolithically conservative culture warriors but comprise instead "a disparate movement whose political allegiances are tentative and negotiable" (p. 6). The third part of his thesis is the most provocative and helpful. "The New Christian Right," Schäfer argues, "was predicated less upon resentment against the cultural changes of the 1960s than upon the ability to merge the insurgent styles and rhetoric of the period with a forceful and unambiguous embrace of the dominant liberal capitalist order" (*ibid.*).

Historians of evangelicalism are well acquainted with nearly all the facts of the narrative, but Schäfer's interpretation of those facts is new and insightful. First, in the 1940s and 1950s a small cadre of neo-evangelical leaders brought conservative Protestantism back to the cultural mainstream. Second, in the 1960s and 1970s leaders in what is now called the evangelical Left attempted to mold a neo-evangelical progressive political activism centered on racial justice, concern for poverty, and a thoroughgoing critique of capitalism. Third, the "Jesus people" of the sixties and seventies co-opted central elements of the counterculture, finding personal fulfillment in Jesus rather than drugs, while opposing the dominant, materialistic, mainstream capitalist order. Fourth, the larger evangelical world moved away from doctrinal precision and toward therapeutic soft conversion, pietism, Pentecostalism, charismatic experimentalism, and other expressively individualistic forms of faith. In the final step of this process, conservative evangelicals marginalized the progressives of the evangelical Left in a series of intramural squabbles in evangelical organizations.

The Christian Right emerged from this history as a movement culturally engaged (neo-evangelical), expressively individualistic in a most modern way (Jesus people), but with a counter-cultural mentality (Jesus people and the evangelical Left). Whereas the Jesus people and the evangelical Left were hostile to a conservative, capitalist, bourgeois social order, countercultural conservatives embody a libertarian critique of an establishment that they view as overly statist— that is, a welfare state. The Christian Right engages in "countercultural capitalism" linked to the pietistic faith and traditional morality that have marked the broader evangelical movement (p. 154). The result, therefore, is that counter-cultural conservatives, far from representing a backlash, have rather co-opted modern America's expressive individualism in the form of evangelical pietistic conversion, while embodying the countercultural impulse of the 1960s in the Christian Right's opposition to the welfare state.

Schäfer's argument is judicious and complex without being dense or tedious. This book should be read along with Darren Dochuk's masterful, award-winning *From Bible Belt to Sunbelt: Plain-Folk Religion, Grassroots Politics, and the Rise of Evangelical Conservatism* (2011). Dochuk narrates in a much longer history what Schäfer argues using sociological theory. Both books contribute greatly to our understanding of the linkage between evangelicalism and conservative politics.

Barry Hankins
Baylor University
Waco, Texas

doi: 10.1093/jahist/jas265

American Protestantism in the Age of Psychology. By Stephanie Muravchik. (New York: Cambridge University Press, 2011. xii, 242 pp. $90.00.)

Stephanie Muravchik intends her book as a refutation of the critics of the psychotherapeutic ethos in American culture. Since the publication of Philip Rieff's classic *The Triumph of the Therapeutic* (1966), critics have claimed that the therapeutic undermines religion, ethics, and social solidarity, thus vitiating civil society and eroding the foundations of liberal democracy. Not so, says Muravchik, who presents detailed case studies to show how therapy aided the consolidation of pastoral calling and identity in the clinical pastoral training movement, the strengthening of self and community in Alcoholics Anonymous (AA), and even the enhancement of evangelism in the Salvation Army's Men's Social Service Centers (MSSCs), an outreach to the indigent.

Muravchik opens her study with a survey and critique of the literature on the therapeutic in American culture, a survey that readers will find interesting to the degree that they are attuned to and aligned in this debate among culture critics. Her argument, however, readily boils down to a distinction she finds in the work of Charles Taylor. There are two ways to attain authenticity in Western culture: an older way that seeks to realize true selfhood by way of models native to particular traditions or communities versus the more recent understanding that one's true self stands in contradistinction to all existing traditions and commitments. Muravchik's message is that this older way to the authentic self, thought to be fading by Taylor and others, has "retained (or regained) its viability among spiritual groups seeking to exploit the benefits of psychology in their outreach to the alienated" (p. 23).

Whatever one makes of Muravchik's arguments about the social criticism of the therapeutic ethos in American culture, the three stories of Protestantism and therapy she tells in the body of the book are well worth the cultural historian's attention. With fine-grained use of archival data and obscure in-house periodicals, she builds concise and clear accounts of how adopting therapeutic practices and values "democratized" and thus transformed the therapeutic ethos even as it aided the larger spiritual and community-building goals of these religious movements.

Perhaps, however, democratization is not quite the same thing as deprofessionalization, which seems to have been more the point for AA and for the MSSCs, which both tended to eschew the asymmetrical structure of the professional therapist seeing the client one-on-one. All three movements favored some form of peer-controlled group therapy as the center of their therapeutic regimen and their building of fellowship and religious community. Whether and to what degree this kind of therapy served the larger purposes of building civil society and undergirding liberal democracy will remain a matter of debate, but there is no disputing Muravchik's argument that in these three cases, at least, psychoreligious amalgams accomplished something quite other and better than the cultivation of irresponsible self-involvement decried by so many critics of the therapeutic.

A. Gregory Schneider
Pacific Union College
Angwin, California

doi: 10.1093/jahist/jas220

FDR, *Dewey, and the Election of 1944.* By David M. Jordan. (Bloomington: Indiana University Press, 2011. xiv, 386 pp. $29.95.)

David M. Jordan tells the story of the 1944 presidential election, and he tells it very well. In a clearly written, well-researched narrative he describes the various contenders for the Republican nomination, which eventually went to Thomas E. Dewey, the machinations over the choice of a vice-presidential candidate to share the ticket with Franklin D. Roosevelt, the successful efforts of a few well-placed Democratic loyalists to conceal the extent of the president's ill health, the campaigns mounted by the two major political parties, and the reasons for the Democrats' victory. In the end, Roosevelt was elected to a fourth term by a margin of 3.6 million votes, a far smaller margin of victory than in 1932 (7 million), 1936 (11 million), or 1940 (5 million)—smaller, in fact, than the victory margin of any candidate since 1916.

The book is based on wide-ranging research in secondary and primary sources. Jordan cites twenty-four manuscript collections (nine from the Franklin D. Roosevelt Library and six from the Harry S. Truman Library, as well as the papers of the Republican candidates Dewey and John W. Bricker) and more than seventy-five newspapers and magazines. For what proved to be the single most important decision of the campaign—Roosevelt's rejection of Henry A. Wallace and James F. Byrnes as running mates, and his selection, instead, of Harry S. Truman—the author sensibly draws on Brenda L. Heaster's essay "Who's on Second: The 1944 Democratic Vice Presidential Nomination," although her conclusion that "Roosevelt was devious to a fault" in how he handled the matter is not one that Jordan endorses (*Missouri Historical Review,* Jan. 1986, pp. 156–75, esp. 164).

The book should be most interesting to a general audience rather than to specialists in American political history. Nothing here breaks new ground in the study of wartime politics. Like others who have studied the election of 1944, Jordan concludes that the Democrats won chiefly because a sufficiently large number of voters did not want to "change horses in mid-stream" (p. 212). More precisely, the Republicans hardly made a dent in Roosevelt's support among urban voters. In New York, Illinois, Pennsylvania, Michigan, Missouri, Maryland, and New Jersey—seven states with enough combined electoral strength to have reversed the outcome—Roosevelt's plurality in the largest city in each of those states overcame a Republican majority in the rest of the state.

Jordan's work, though, offers further evidence that the true significance of the election lies in Republicans' recognition that their best—indeed their only—hope of regaining the White House was to accept the essentials of the welfare state created by the New Deal while simultaneously alleging, as Dewey did, that the Democratic party was being captured by the "forces of communism" (p. 294). That dual strategy, which the Republicans adopted in 1944 and again in 1948, would eventually pay rich dividends.

Richard Polenberg
Cornell University
Ithaca, New York

doi: 10.1093/jahist/jas190

The Roots of Modern Conservatism: Dewey, Taft, and the Battle for the Soul of the Republican Party. By Michael Bowen. (Chapel Hill: University of North Carolina Press, 2011. xii, 254 pp. $45.00.)

Michael Bowen contends that in studying conservatism's rise in the Republican party, scholars have missed something. They focus on the period just prior to 1964 and the rise of Goldwater conservatives as key to the Right's takeover; but Bowen argues that this period is actually connected to an earlier battle for the party's soul.

This struggle began as a personal one but broadened into an ideological battle. It started during the 1944 fight between the followers of Thomas Dewey, who favored a more liberal, pro–New Deal GOP, and those of Robert Taft, who supported a very conservative platform. The battle was both public and private, as the two sides competed for presidential nominations and for control of party machinery.

This is a story of the growth of conservative activists and ideas within the GOP. Yet it also concerns the moderate Dewey faction, helped immeasurably by the able politicking of liberal Republicans such as Herbert Brownell, holding off Taft and maintaining control of the party through 1960. Bowen argues that Deweyite moderation was not popular with the voters. Republicans took control of Congress in 1946, for example, using a conservative platform. In the 1948 election, evidence suggests that Dewey lost to Harry S. Truman because Dewey resisted making a conservative case to the electorate. Still, for years Dewey and Brownell were simply better at intraparty politics. For example, in 1952, despite their embarrassing defeat four years before, GOP moderates exercised enormous influence over the Republican presidential candidate nomination process. They prodded Dwight D. Eisenhower to run for the presidency, placed key members of the Dewey faction in his campaign, and steered the general's platform in a moderate direction.

Taft and his supporters were beaten again, but the senator was a pragmatic politician. When Eisenhower secured the nomination, Taft campaigned for him, and then in the early months of Ike's presidency worked very well with him. But Taft's sudden death in 1953 left conservative Republicans without a leader. Soon, led by old Dewey partisans, moderate Republicans worked to remove Taft conservatives from key party positions. But, as Bowen demonstrates, the resultant conservative frustration led not to the death of the Right but to its rebirth. By the end of the 1950s, strong conservative ideological views and a new crop of activists grew within the GOP. Soon William F. Buckley Jr. and *National Review* magazine became influential among young Republican activists such as F. Clifton White, who would lead the Draft Goldwater movement.

Bowen acknowledges that the Taftite old guard did not lead this conservative resurgence. But the connection between Taftites and the new Barry Goldwater generation was there. To conservatives, Eisenhower's middle-of-the-road policies and Richard M. Nixon's defeat in the 1960 election were both aided by the moderate, Dewey faction controlling the party since 1944. Thus the conservative triumph in 1964 was connected to party struggles dating back two decades. The rise of this new Right was a passing of the torch from the old guard to a new generation.

This book makes a necessary correction to our understanding of the history of conservatism and the Republican party, and it will be useful for scholars, graduate students, and upper-level undergraduates.

Kevin Smant
University of Texas at Arlington
Arlington, Texas

doi: 10.1093/jahist/jas242

Painting Dixie Red: When, Where, Why, and How the South Became Republican. Ed. by Glenn Feldman. (Gainesville: University Press of Florida, 2011. xii, 386 pp. $74.95.)

The entry of most of the American South firmly into the "red" column offers a case study for the classic continuity versus change debate within southern historiography. Is this another "solid South" or something new altogether? The editor of *Painting Dixie Red* makes an emphatic case for "the fundamental continuity of the region itself" (p. 3). The volume's contributors offer a more nuanced story, suggesting that the rise of the Republican South had many starting points.

Most of the stronger contributions are linked with existing or forthcoming monographs. Barclay Key's essay on Harding College probes the relationship of the Church of Christ to the Republican Right. Both Key and Daniel K. Williams cite postwar fundamentalists as early converts to the national GOP. In an analysis of Georgia politics since the 1950s, Tim Boyd evaluates "the discrepancy between the widespread predictions of an imminent Republican majority and the delay in the actual appearance of that majority" (p. 80). The Atlanta suburbs initially drove the Republican shift, but sometimes resisted it as the party reached out to backlash voters. John W. White explores a similar dynamic in South Carolina, where successful GOP candidates eventually recognized that "conservative whites . . . remained suspicious of rapid social change but were disinterested in fighting a losing battle over Jim Crow" (p. 166). As Michael Bowen demonstrates, the GOP's "southern strategy" dated back to immediate postwar efforts to expand the southern party beyond its "post-office Republican" base. This early outreach, Bowen argues, "had virtually nothing to do with race" (p. 235). Realignment was rarely a straightforward process: by the late 1960s southern Republicans had to adjust to an expanding black electorate, which was heavily Democratic. Leah M. Wright explores President Richard M. Nixon's efforts to quell this tide, noting that the southern strategist Harry S. Dent helped recruit African Americans for federal positions.

If the essays collectively suggest a polygenesis interpretation of southern republicanism, they leave several key matters unresolved. Historians driving the new sun belt history (whose suburban emphasis is often contrasted with the earlier backlash thesis) appear in the text and the notes. Missing, however, is much engagement with the spatial and ideological concept of the sun belt itself. A related problem is the role of the rest of the country. George Lewis demonstrates that elite Virginia segregationists pursued alliances with northern politicians. The precise status of the non-South needs more consideration, though. Southern Republicans sometimes benefited when race was an important consideration for the white electorate. The cause of national conservatism, however, succeeded in part by moving race off of center stage.

Many of the essayists are young historians who, as far as their scholarship is concerned, are not invested in the culture wars. All political history is at some level itself political—and this is especially true of southern political history. All too often, interpretation is treated like a zero-sum game; to stress economic influences is to downplay racial factors, and so on. The same goes for catalysts of the GOP shift, be they religious anticommunism, resistance to Democratic policies that threatened textile interests, or excessive fear of the Kennedy administration. Competing emphases on the electoral, party, policy, and ideological sides of political history further muddy the waters. The essayists do not transcend these historiographical dilemmas, but most of them avoid making political hay out of their subject matter—something that cannot be said of the volume's editor.

Glenn Feldman has collected several valuable surveys of recent scholarship on the modern South. As an editor, he is indulgent of countervailing perspectives. Unfortunately, Feldman's introductory and concluding essays are less a frame and more a vise. Put differently, they threaten death by a thousand outrages. Fortunately, the rest of the book can withstand Feldman's rhetorical excess. There is no New South, he argues, only a conservative South—conservative in every way, shape, form, and epoch. It is neither a surprising nor a courageous move to lament the state of southern (especially Deep South) politics. The majority of Feldman's readers most likely will share his sense of disappointment, if not necessarily his pessimism. In the end, righteous indignation is not really an interpretation; it is an attitude—one that the other contributors seem willing to save for the op-ed page or the blog post.

Steven P. Miller
Webster University
Saint Louis, Missouri

doi: 10.1093/jahist/jas280

Rule and Ruin: The Downfall of Moderation and the Destruction of the Republican Party, from Eisenhower to the Tea Party. By Geoffrey Kabaservice. (New York: Oxford University Press, 2012. xxii, 482 pp. $29.95.)

A few years ago, during a classroom discussion on the impact of the Watergate scandal on the American two-party political system, one of my brightest, most politically engaged students raised his hand and asked, with all sincerity, "What is a liberal Republican?" The question was indicative of both the current polarized political climate and the prevalence of conservatism as a historiographical topic over the last two decades. Geoffrey Kabaservice's *Rule and Ruin* provides much-needed balance to the literature through his well-researched, highly readable account of the decline of the once-dominant centrist wing of the GOP.

The decade of the 1950s was the heyday of moderate republicanism, thanks to Thomas Dewey's national, grassroots network of supporters and Dwight D. Eisenhower's popularity. By 1960, however, Dewey's organization had atrophied and conservatives were poised to retake control of the party following Richard M. Nixon's loss to John F. Kennedy. As this conflict unfolded during the early 1960s, Kabaservice makes clear that strategy was the most important difference between the two sides. While the Right captured the Young Republicans and built a base for Arizona senator Barry Goldwater's 1964 campaign at the lowest levels of the GOP, the moderates were waging a war of ideas. The Republican opinion journal *Advance* and the Northeast-based Ripon Society worked to influence elite opinion and develop policy solutions. Both openly prided themselves on their refusal to organize voters, but by 1970—the year Kabaservice labels the peak of moderate influence—their chance had passed. Through the rest of the decade, the emergence of social issues and a galvanized electorate would swamp the centrists and empower the conservatives.

Rule and Ruin is a top-down study of Republican presidential candidates, party officials, and auxiliary organizations. The Ripon Society is the glue that holds the story together. Relying on a mix of interviews and archival sources, Kabaservice painstakingly details the way many of Ripon's leadership cadre moved from candidate to candidate through the 1960s and early 1970s looking for the presidential contender who would best advance their cause. At various points Nelson Rockefeller's ego, George Romney's verbal gaffes, and Charles H. Percy's kindness dashed the hopes of the anxious activists. While Kabaservice is cognizant of down-ballot races and devotes a good deal of attention to individuals such as New York City mayor John Lindsay and Massachusetts congressman Bradford Morse, most of the action takes place at the presidential level.

Kabaservice approaches his subject with a dispassionate objectivity and provides an incredibly balanced account. Though it would be easy to criticize the Right for pushing the GOP down such a divisive and counterproductive path, Kabaservice holds his fire on most occasions. He concedes that the populist strategy aimed at the sun belt paid dividends for the Republicans, but he correctly argues that an ideologically driven party makes campaigning easy and governing difficult. Even though the years from 1972 through 2010 are dealt with in two synthetic chapters, Kabaservice has given us an indispensible book and one of the best accounts of the post-Goldwater Republican party to date.

Michael Bowen
Westminster College
New Wilmington, Pennsylvania

doi: 10.1093/jahist/jas223

The Republican Party and American Politics from Hoover to Reagan. By Robert Mason. (New York: Cambridge University Press, 2012. x, 310 pp. $80.00.)

While the history of conservatism, both within and outside the Republican party, has become a major subfield in contemporary American historiography, scholarship on the political parties has not kept pace. Lately, however, scholarly interest has grown in explaining how moderate or liberal Republicans countered the rise of conservatism within the GOP. Robert Mason provides an astute political history of the GOP, chronicling how the Republican party adjusted to its minority status electorally in an age dominated by New Deal liberalism. His focus on the period between Herbert Hoover's election in 1928 and the end of the Ronald Reagan era, when many Republicans thought party realignment had occurred, provides a satisfying historical trajectory.

Mason argues that

despite the South's electoral importance to the party by the end of the twentieth century . . . the solutions that Republicans developed usually involved policy, communication, and organization, rather than the breaking of the solid South as a key priority. (p. 7)

He relies heavily on records of directors of the Republican National Committee to show how the party contended with its minority status. During the Great Depression, the GOP continued to emphasize antistatist concerns, but hostility to the state proved unpopular with the American electorate. Forced to accommodate, Alf Landon in 1936, and later Wendell Willkie and Thomas Dewey, were convinced that the key to political victory lay in a "me-too" strategy. But this strategy also failed to lead to victory against New Deal liberalism.

One path to political power lay in embracing Cold War internationalism. Dwight D. Eisenhower played an important role in moving the party to a stronger commitment to the Cold War, and Mason shows how foreign policy played an important role in addressing the minority-status problem within the party, far more than the anticommunism embraced by Joseph McCarthy or other politicians. But splits within the party between conservatives such as Barry Goldwater and moderates such as Nelson Rockefeller complicated Eisenhower's efforts to be a party builder. Grassroots conservatism also contributed to problems for moderates' control of the party.

Such a complication—the rise of the Right within the GOP—is at the heart of any effort to delineate how the GOP solved its minority-status problem. Yet Mason wants to show how the party was often better off when it did not combat liberalism, an odd supposition given

the electoral history of moderate Republicans at the presidential level during the postwar era.

Mason's history is a well-researched assessment of intraparty battles within the Republican party as it dealt with the legacies of New Deal liberalism. The book is less satisfying in its documentation of the changes that occurred due to grassroots activists who contributed to moving the party to the right and, for the short term, solving its minority-status problem. The intersection of both party influence in the GOP and the wider grassroots conservative movement, documented by historians such as Donald Critchlow, is the main story of the Republican resurgence in recent decades.

Gregory L. Schneider
Emporia State University
Emporia, Kansas

doi: 10.1093/jahist/jas258

Red Pepper and Gorgeous George: Claude Pepper's Epic Defeat in the 1950 Democratic Primary. By James C. Clark. (Gainesville: University Press of Florida, 2011. xvi, 206 pp. $29.95.)

Red Pepper and Gorgeous George examines the 1950 Florida Democratic party primary that pitted the ultraliberal Claude Pepper against the antistatist George Smathers. As James C. Clark argues, this race established the template for Cold War campaigns that deployed anticommunism, appeals to white supremacy, and hostility to the New Deal that in the long run helped revivify the Republican Right. Pepper, described by Clark as "both the most enthusiastic and the last of the New Dealers," went down to a defeat when Smathers tied him to the Soviet Union, civil rights, and organized labor (p. 9).

Throughout the book, Clark recognizes that Pepper faced the southern Democratic dilemma: to retain office he had to oppose civil rights legislation, but that made it difficult to enter the national stage as a New Deal liberal. Despite his leftist allies, Pepper was no champion of civil rights. On key issues—the white primary, the poll tax, antilynching legislation, fair employment legislation—he hedged his bets in the language of states' rights, if not explicit white supremacy. Clark argues that Pepper sought instead to open a path "to higher office through international affairs," but that proved to be his Achilles' heel (p. 42). The farsighted internationalism that he preached in 1940 transmuted into Henry Wallace–style efforts to make peace with the Soviet Union in the postwar world. By the late 1940s, Clark observes, Pepper "was out of step with the American people, who increasingly believed that the United States was too soft in dealing with Russia" (p. 48). By contrast, Smathers, who began his career as a liberal Democrat (he won the backing of the Congress of Industrial Organizations in 1946) by 1950 "saw the threat that Russia posed, and said the United States had a major role to play to counterbalance Soviet aggression" (p. 103).

Given his extraordinary vulnerability, it is amazing that Pepper could even put up a fight. Over the years he had made powerful enemies, including the American Medical Association (he supported national health insurance), Florida's most influential financier (Edward Ball), and President Harry S. Truman, who deeply resented his opposition to the Cold War and his back-room opposition during the 1948 presidential primary. Both Ball and Truman threw their considerable financial and political weight behind "Gorgeous George."

Clark offers a breezy, readable political narrative, but one that ultimately lacks bite. The campaign takes up a scant fifty pages of an already short book. At times Clark's sympathy for Smathers and his dislike for Pepper—portrayed as self-absorbed and politically obtuse—show through. For example, Pepper's skepticism about the Truman Doctrine and his lack of enthusiasm for Truman in 1948 hardly put him outside the bounds of noncommunist liberal discourse at the time, though Clark often suggests that only the *Daily Worker* shared his views. While paying some attention to Smathers's attempts to link Pepper to civil rights, Clark emphasizes that "communism was the club he used against Pepper in every speech" (p. 117). Neither candidate could be considered a champion of black voters, but as Clark points out, "both . . . wanted the black vote, but without white voters finding out" (p. 134).

Smathers's victory helped usher in a new kind of sun belt politics that ultimately merged the remnants of the Dixiecrat South with an emergent business republicanism. By 1964 Florida senator Smathers opposed the Civil Rights Act because it threatened to "destroy this right of a man to control his own property" (p. 167).

Alex Lichtenstein
Indiana University
Bloomington, Indiana

doi: 10.1093/jahist/jas277

Eisenhower and the Cold War Economy. By William M. McClenahan Jr. and William H. Becker. (Baltimore: Johns Hopkins University Press, 2011. xviii, 304 pp. $55.00.)

This clearly written, accessible, and well-researched study is a welcome addition to the surprisingly small literature on the economic policies of the Eisenhower administration. It is the first major work in this field in two decades, since the first flurry of monographs based on newly available sources in the presidential archives appeared in the 1980s and early 1990s.

William M. McClenahan Jr. and William H. Becker's contribution to Dwight D. Eisenhower economics historiography lies less in challenging existing knowledge—they largely confirm revisionist orthodoxy on the subject—than in their wide-ranging approach to the administration's multifaceted program and the shaping influence of Cold War concerns. Whereas previous monographs focused on one area of Eisenhower administration economic policy, McClenahan and Becker's study assesses macroeconomic management in its first three chapters and analyzes microeconomic matters pertaining to agriculture, antitrust legislation, and foreign economic policy in subsequent chapters. In all these areas, the authors demonstrate that the president appreciated that the domestic and international dimensions of economic policy were inseparably intertwined during an era of intense global rivalry between the United States and the Soviet Union.

For economic policy specialists, the microeconomic chapters may be the more interesting section because they cover less familiar terrain. The authors regard Eisenhower as less successful in this area of his economic program because of the obstructive influence of powerful interest groups and their allies in Congress. This was particularly the case regarding the farm parity reform that the administration vainly labored to achieve. However, the administration's success in resuscitating and expanding overseas markets for agricultural products prompted changes in price-support programs in the 1960s and beyond, albeit not on the scale that Eisenhower had wanted. In their deft analysis of trade matters, the authors include a valuable assessment of how Eisenhower balanced Cold War concerns to reintegrate Japan into the international economy with domestic-producer anxiety about cheap imports—even accepting quantitative limits on Japanese trade in the late 1950s.

McClenahan and Becker laud Eisenhower's macroeconomic management for its prudence and for its attentiveness to its international consequences. While recognizing the differing structural contexts, they suggest that his reassuring concern for foreign dollar-holder sensibilities regarding deficits and inflation does not appear "quaint or irrelevant" from twenty-first-century perspectives (p. 109). Nevertheless, their admiration for Eisenhower entails skating over aspects of his program. Fiscal restraint may have had its benefits but it failed to address the slack in the economy, which kept unemployment relatively high in the late 1950s and caused double-dip recessions in 1958 and 1960. The 1960s new economics may have set the United States on the road to the great economic inflation of the 1970s, but it was an effort to address the shortcomings of Eisenhower's macroeconomic legacy. Moreover, nowhere does this study acknowledge the extent of poverty in the 1950s and its regional, racial, gendered, and generational concentration.

Whatever the book's omissions, however, its merits significantly outweigh them. McClenahan and Becker amply demonstrate that Eisenhower's economic policy continues to be an important and relevant field of historical study in the twenty-first century.

Iwan Morgan
University College London
London, England

doi: 10.1093/jahist/jas226

Defending White Democracy: The Making of a Segregationist Movement and the Remaking of

Racial Politics, 1936–1965. By Jason Morgan Ward. (Chapel Hill: University of North Carolina Press, 2011. xii, 252 pp. $34.95.)

More than a decade ago civil rights scholars began to make a case for a "long civil rights movement," beginning before the 1950s and rooted in the activism and political changes of the New Deal and World War II eras. If we imagine this movement originating in the 1930s and 1940s, we might then reasonably ask: What about the segregationists? How did they respond to this civil rights revolution? Jason Morgan Ward's *Defending White Democracy* addresses these questions and argues for a parallel "long segregationist movement" that formed two decades prior to the marches, boycotts, and court decisions of the 1950s.

In six chapters Ward charts the rise of a segregationist counterrevolution. This movement began in the 1930s with isolated criticisms of New Deal programs. The critical moments, however, came during World War II, with segregationists reacting to evidence and rumors of black protest and activism and an increasing federal presence in the South. By the 1950s, with mounting civil rights protests and the *Brown v. Board of Education* (1954) ruling against segregated schools, an already established segregationist movement was in transition. Many political elites were replacing an openly racist rhetoric of white supremacy with a toned-down language focused on segregation and on legal and constitutional defenses of Jim Crow. Ward suggests that these changes may have facilitated southern conservatives' entry into a national conservative movement in the post–civil rights era.

Ward narrates this segregationist movement largely through the words and deeds of familiar political elites in the South, including Eugene Talmadge, Herman Talmadge, and Richard Russell in Georgia; Theodore Bilbo and John Stennis in Mississippi; and James Byrnes and Strom Thurmond in South Carolina. At the center of these mobilizations existed an uneasy tension between the voices of moderation and economic modernization and the voices of radicalism and retrenchment. For example, this movement contained both Bilbo's calls for a violent response and Russell's efforts to seek compromise within the national Democratic party.

Defending White Democracy is a welcome addition to a growing body of work on segregationist responses to civil rights efforts and the rise of conservatism after the civil rights era. Especially impressive is Ward's discussion of the World War II era, in which he depicts a movement mutually constituted by political elites and their constituents. He illustrates, for example, the relationship between grassroots fears of black soldiers directing "white" traffic and the speeches against federal intervention coming from regional and national figures such as Jim Folsom and Eugene Talmadge. Unfortunately, these grassroots components fade into the background of the discussion of the 1950s. Thus for the crucial post-*Brown* period of "massive resistance"—presumably the climax of this mobilization—the reader is left to wonder about the role of local battles and the segregationist foot soldiers. Still, Ward's book is an important intervention. It provides a useful historical framework for rethinking how and when segregationists defended Jim Crow. As well, this study should lead other scholars to examine the additional economic, cultural, and social manifestations of this conterrevolution.

Stephen A. Berrey
University of Michigan
Ann Arbor, Michigan

doi: 10.1093/jahist/jas305

Georgia Democrats, the Civil Rights Movement, and the Shaping of the New South. By Tim S. R. Boyd. (Gainesville: University Press of Florida, 2012. xiv, 302 pp. $74.95.)

Tim S. R. Boyd is not the first to challenge the outdated and embattled white backlash thesis. But by shifting the focus from the South's insurgent Republicans to the region's indomitable Democrats and from sweeping regional narratives to state-level politics, Boyd shatters the myth of a linear and monolithic GOP takeover in the wake of the civil rights movement. Moreover, Boyd shows how prescient Georgia Democrats engineered their own political coup by wresting control of their party from old-guard segregationists. Not only did members of this new breed outlast the backlash politics of their intraparty rivals, Boyd contends, but they

also emerged as the "most significant" force in "determining the political landscape of the South in the post–Jim Crow era" (p. 4).

Georgia's recent political history defies generalization, and Boyd's masterful case study capitalizes on the state's distinctiveness while highlighting how events there illustrate important regional and national trends. Straddling the South's "deep" and "upper" subregions, Georgia dramatized the postwar showdown between black belt conservatives and metropolitan moderates. The leaders who emerged from these state-level power struggles—establishment politicians, white supremacist demagogues, and civil rights veterans alike—exerted enormous influence on the regional and national stages.

From its chronological framework to its cast of characters, Boyd's book does more than complicate the backlash story line. Rather, Boyd presents a useful "alternative narrative" that privileges long-term trends and intraparty struggles over political flash points and partisan opportunism (p. 7). By spending roughly a third of the book on political change before *Brown v. Board of Education* (1954), Boyd portrays a state Democratic party already divided between tradition-minded "regulars" and forward-looking "loyalists." The latter faction, though temporarily overwhelmed by a segregationist backlash, rode out a decade of racial reaction and eventually emerged as the leaders of a biracial Democratic coalition. Demographic trends and structural changes, particularly urbanization and the end of Georgia's county-unit electoral system, spelled doom for white supremacist "regular" rule.

From the end of the 1960s onward, Georgia politics pitted a transformed Democratic party against an ascendant GOP. Ironically, some of the same demographic factors that favored the "loyalist" Democrats fueled the rise of a rival Republican party that was "at its core an urban and suburban phenomenon" (p. 200). In this new era, New South Democrats employed a strategy of "progressive color blindness" to build a formidable statewide coalition, discredit conservative challengers, and reestablish influence within the national party. Boyd concludes his final chapter with the culmination of this two-pronged strategy—the victory of former Georgia governor Jimmy Carter in the 1976 presidential race.

Boyd's decision to end his story in the late 1970s, the thoughtful introductory and concluding commentary notwithstanding, begs questions about recent Republican dominance that scholars will continue to ponder. But by bridging the chronological chasm between the civil rights era and the rather brief history of state- and local-level Republican success in the South, Boyd has made a valuable contribution. Moreover, in an era when place-based scholarship seems to be falling out of favor, he reminds us of the limits of unmoored macro-narratives.

Jason Morgan Ward
Mississippi State University
Mississippi State, Mississippi

doi: 10.1093/jahist/jas293

Bridges of Reform: Interracial Civil Rights Activism in Twentieth-Century Los Angeles. By Shana Bernstein. (New York: Oxford University Press, 2011. xiv, 339 pp. Cloth, $99.00. Paper, $24.95.)

Shana Bernstein's *Bridges of Reform* is a welcome addition to the literatures on Los Angeles, comparative ethnic studies, and political activism. *Bridges of Reform* offers a carefully researched, in-depth analysis of interracial activism among African Americans, Mexican Americans, Jews, and to a much lesser extent, Asian Americans, from the 1930s through the Cold War. While many of the organizations and actors will be familiar to students of Los Angeles history, Bernstein provides a new lens through which to view the political landscape. Despite the title, the book centers on the Cold War, culminating in a case study of the Community Service Organization (cso). Bernstein's basic argument is that the conditions of the Cold War compelled many organizations to work together, and in this way, the era promoted interethnic relationships and solidarity.

Bernstein begins by sketching out Los Angeles's community activism in the 1930s, an era in which a dense and diverse activist infrastructure was developed that would be transformed by World War II. She discusses the Cold War and how civil rights activists responded to the new political climate. Bernstein details how organizations had to determine the goals around which to mobilize, with whom to ally, and who was a liability. Her focus narrows to organizations committed to surviving and working toward racial justice in an "acceptable" way. To survive, many organizations not only severed ties with activists considered too leftist but they also denounced them. Repudiating former comrades was called "pro–civil rights anticommunism" (p. 102).

Bernstein's comparisons of the Jewish, African American, and Mexican American organizational responses to the Cold War are especially illuminating. Bernstein argues that the Cold War compelled racial groups to cooperate—they needed each other like never before. She concludes that the cso became the most prominent organization working with and for Mexican Americans and that the differences between the cso and El Congreso de Pueblos que Hablan Español (Congress of Spanish-Speaking People), a Popular Front group, were relatively superficial. This claim is not entirely convincing, but it raises larger issues about what constitutes revolution versus reform.

The last chapter considers the significance of Los Angeles's Cold War activism to the national struggle for civil rights and includes discussions of *Mendez v. Westminster* (U.S. Court of Appeals, 1947) and the Warren court. This chapter is essential in broadening the appeal of the book to readers not interested specifically in Los Angeles.

Two of the book's strengths in particular stand out. First, Bernstein does an excellent job of placing Los Angeles activism in a global context. She explains Los Angeles's early international significance and traces how efforts in the city impacted various racial groups and their responses to changes of this era. Second, the focus on Jewish activism in Los Angeles alone is worth the price of the book. While Jewish participation in civil rights struggles is well documented, Bernstein illuminates how and why such organizational ties developed. For instance, she reveals early debates among Jews about whether to ally with African Americans and what such a move would mean for Jews' place in the racial hierarchy. Likewise, she analyzes the differing class position and racial status of Jews and how this affected their relationships with Mexican Americans. The story of interethnic activism is crucial to the study of civil rights, and *Bridges of Reform* is an excellent place to start.

Laura Pulido
University of Southern California
Los Angeles, California

doi: 10.1093/jahist/jas164

Mau Mau in Harlem? The U.S. and the Liberation of Kenya. By Gerald Horne. (New York: Palgrave Macmillan, 2009. x, 323 pp. $84.95.)

As a preeminent scholar of African American history and politics, Gerald Horne has tirelessly crafted an impressively prolific body of work. Without fail, his arguments are impassioned and his research is innovative in its subject matter, insurgent in its political commitments, imaginative in its political approach to sources, and almost always international in scope. By illuminating the historical and ideological forces that brought Kenya and the United States together, *Mau Mau in Harlem?* is another example of his laudable scholarly output.

Much like the Haitian Revolution a century earlier, legendary Mau Mau rebellion (1952–1960), Horne suggests, played a transformative role in reconstructing a more robust black racial identity alongside a radical political desire for national sovereignty. Within the scope of American popular culture, and for Americans across racial and political lines, though, the Kenyan insurgency was commonly deemed a vision of "bloody retribution for the centuries of slaving and colonialism that Europeans had visited upon Africans" (p. 3). According to Horne, the twentieth century witnessed the evolution of a long, complex relationship between the United States and Kenya based on the twin concerns of racial ideology, on the one hand, and national independence, on the other. In both regards, Horne suggests that long before Kenya had any immediate or meaningful geopolitical significance within U.S. foreign policy, the East African nation and its population inhabited a poignant place in the symbolic imagination of Americans for vastly different reasons. During the first half of the twentieth century, the author reveals, a wide array of white Americans ranging from church missionaries to U.S. presidents to Hollywood

movie stars envisioned East Africa as what Theodore Roosevelt fondly referred to as "a real white man's country," wherein concepts of white supremacy and Western imperialism could be exercised without moral recrimination or compunction (p. 17).

By midcentury, however, the racial and political dynamics associated with Kenya's role in the collective American imagination shifted drastically. In the wake of World War II, the emergence of black militancy and anti-imperialism among Kenyans such as Jomo Kenyatta and Tom Mboya not only aided in their decolonization efforts but also helped galvanize a pragmatic pan-African consciousness globally. As the author vividly illustrates, in the wake of the Kenyan rebellion against British colonial rule during the 1950s, the term *Mau Mau* became a metonym for the postcolonial struggle of African peoples for freedom justice and equality for African American civil rights activists such as W. E. B. Du Bois, Paul Robeson, Malcolm X, and Kwame Ture (Stokely Carmichael). Horne demonstrates how conservative elements of U.S. foreign policy toward Kenya during the Cold War, driven by the incessant need to moderate African political radicalism in maintenance of the racial and geopolitical status quo, unexpectedly and ironically contributed to the circumstances surrounding the birth of Barack Obama, the forty-fourth U.S. president. In the final analysis, Horne's book will be an indispensible resource on this subject for years to come.

Juan M. Floyd-Thomas
Vanderbilt University
Nashville, Tennessee

doi: 10.1093/jahist/jas183

Anticommunism and the African American Freedom Movement: "Another Side of the Story." Ed. by Robbie Lieberman and Clarence Lang. (New York: Palgrave Macmillan, 2009. xxi, 251 pp. Cloth, $95.00. Paper, $32.00.)

Robbie Lieberman and Clarence Lang's edited volume, *Anticommunism and the African American Freedom Movement,* is made up of six essays that challenge what has become popularly known as the Cold War civil rights thesis. Proponents of this thesis contend that the Cold War was a positive event for the civil rights movement because the U.S. government decided to support civil rights out of the fear that the Soviet Union would win the hearts and minds of the emerging nations in Africa and Asia due to America's racial practices. Lieberman and Lang instead argue that the Cold War destroyed many of the organizations and activists most able to articulate claims for genuine equality. They also take on supporters of the "long civil rights movement," acknowledging that the concept has advantages but accusing its proponents of downplaying the discontinuity model that created ruptures in the black freedom struggle.

One important argument in the book is that the Cold War separated the black freedom struggle from the campaign for global peace. Lieberman's essay, "'Another Side of the Story': African American Intellectuals Speak Out for Peace and Freedom during the Early Cold War Years," argues that with the exception of communists, civil rights leaders were muted when it came to U.S. Cold War policies. Despite outspoken individuals such as the journalist Eugene Gordon, Cold War repression resulted in the disappearance of "important expressions of opposition to colonialism, to U.S. support of European colonial powers and of the apartheid regime in South Africa, to the buildup of nuclear weapons" (p. 37). Women in or close to the Communist party receive a great deal of attention in this volume. Jacqueline Castledine's "Quieting the Chorus: Progressive Women's Race and Peace Politics in Postwar New York," describes how Ada B. Jackson, Annette Rubinstein, and other women on the left attempted to carve out a peace and civil rights agenda in the American Labor party. Even so, she also points out how a repressive government was eventually successful in silencing them. The activism of Esther Cooper Jackson, another woman on the left, is the subject of Erik S. McDuffie's essay. Instead of leading a black movement that "understood the African American freedom struggle in global terms," McDuffie argues that Jackson adopted a "black left feminism" that combined "Communist Party positions on race, gender, class, and black nationalism with black women radicals' lived experiences" (p. 82).

While those associated with the Communist party receive a great deal of attention in this volume, Rachel Peterson writes on the anticommunist Marxists who organized the newspaper *Correspondence* to target Stalinism and McCarthyism. Clarence Lang's essay on the demise of the National Negro Labor Council provides evidence of how the anticommunist assault challenges those who claim "unbroken" black radicalism in the long civil rights narrative (p. 164). Zaragosa Vargas's essay goes beyond the black-and-white paradigm of race relations by examining the long Mexican American civil rights struggle that had a strong communist influence.

A major contribution of this work is its reminder of the host of individuals and organizations that offered a more expansive view of peace and civil rights than what became the dominant narrow interest in voting rights and the desegregation of public accommodations.

Clarence Taylor
Baruch College
City University of New York
New York, New York

doi: 10.1093/jahist/jas212

Radicalism at the Crossroads: African American Women Activists in the Cold War. By Dayo F. Gore. (New York: New York University Press, 2011. xii, 231 pp. $39.00.)

Radicalism at the Crossroads provides many of the connecting links for a reconfiguration of African American history that accounts more substantially for a black Left. The 1940s and 1950s, which are often seen as a kind of waiting period before the 1960s explosions of activism, served as a major building period in which black women's activism flourished. Dayo F. Gore's work explores the international linkages, major figures, and organizational structures of women who

> shared a critique of U.S. capitalism as exploitative of workers and highlighted the role of white supremacy in buttressing a range of inequalities. Their analysis also carried with it a commitment to advancing women's equality and an internationalist vision of the black freedom struggle. (p. 3)

Radicalism at the Crossroads is divided into five chapters that detail the nature of black leftist feminist activism. The "crossroads" are those between "the fights for black liberation, women's equality, workers' rights and the U.S. left" (p. 5). At a time that identified women with domesticity, we learn that black leftist women

> traveled extensively for their activism. . . . Their mobility, coupled with their organizing experience and their internationalist politics, helped to solidify their contributions as leaders and strategists with national and transnational reach. (p. 10)

While some of these women were active in the Communist Party USA or in Popular Front or civil rights organizations, they consistently challenged limited articulations of class, race, and gender. They were a network of women who created new organizational structures and significantly impacted existing organizations.

One of the most valuable aspects of this work is its close examination of historical issues that have received only passing mention in other texts. One of these is the Rosa Lee Ingram case, which took place from 1948 to 1959 and is explored in chapter 3, "Reframing Civil Rights Activism during the Cold War." While the trial of the Scottsboro boys (1931) has become iconic of communist and civil rights activism in the 1930s, black leftist women saw the Rosa Lee Ingram case as representative of what is now defined as sexual harassment. Since Ingram fought back and was punished for doing so, activist women devoted considerable attention to bringing her justice through organizations such as Sojourners for Truth and Justice. Gore argues that in the process "they laid crucial groundwork for a range of civil rights, feminist, and black power politics that would emerge in later decades" (p. 78). One of the outcomes was the subsequent organizing work that led to the 1955 Montgomery bus boycott in which Rosa Parks figured prominently. For Gore, the result was that "black women's experiences began to be seen as integral to defining the struggle for black civil rights" (p. 99).

Another critical contribution of this work is its focus on the struggle to improve the conditions of black women workers, which has led to participation in contemporary unions. For Marvel Cooke, Victoria Garvin, Thelma Dale Perkins, Maude White Katz, Claudia Jones, and other black leftist women, this fight was a shared project. The creativity of the playwright Alice Childress or the actress Beah Richards and the issues they would stage in plays and performances reveal this political intent.

This highly readable book also includes wonderful photographs of beautiful, well-dressed women who did not see incongruity between elegant self-presentation and political activism and were friends and comrades of major activists such as Paul Robeson and Malcolm X. *Radicalism at the Crossroads* is necessary reading for all interested in black history and women's history, and is an invaluable contribution to the growing library of black leftist scholarship.

Carole Boyce Davies
Cornell University
Ithaca, New York

doi: 10.1093/jahist/jas209

Brown's Battleground: Students, Segregationists, and the Struggle for Justice in Prince Edward County, Virginia. By Jill Ogline Titus. (Chapel Hill: University of North Carolina Press, 2011. xvi, 279 pp. $34.95.)

The tragic history of the school crisis in Prince Edward County, Virginia, is well known and has been told most effectively by Richard Kluger in his magisterial *Simple Justice: The History of* Brown v. Board of Education *and Black America's Struggle for Equality* (1976), and by Amy E. Murrell in her outstanding essay "The 'Impossible' Prince Edward Case: The Endurance of Resistance in a Southside County, 1959–64" (Matthew D. Lassiter and Andrew D. Lewis, eds., *The Moderates' Dilemma: Massive Resistance to School Desegregation in Virginia,* 1998). In the excellent *Brown's Battleground,* Jill Ogline Titus looks beyond the contours of the familiar legal and political narrative to focus instead on the determined yet often futile and heartbreaking efforts of black parents and a handful of white supporters to overcome fierce resistance from white segregationists and ensure a modicum of justice for their children.

Titus faithfully covers the most familiar aspects of the story—a 1951 student strike that led to a landmark Supreme Court decision announced along with *Brown v. Board of Education* (1954), followed by the unconscionable decision of the county's whites in 1959 to close their entire public school system rather than allow token integration—but wisely devotes only a brief introduction and a single chapter to them. (The opening line of the introduction, "The fiddler came to Farmville in 1951, demanding payment for generations of neglect," perfectly sets the tone for the rest of the book [p. 1].)

Instead of revisiting old ground, Titus focuses her initial chapters on the efforts of African American leaders and staff members with the American Friends Service Committee, who worked assiduously to provide educational alternatives for the 1,700 black students in the county. The author also devotes important attention to the circumscribed sympathies of a handful of white moderates affiliated with Prince Edward County's two colleges. The main characters, however, remain the black parents and their children, who adopted a variety of strategies to fill the appalling void that threatened black children with a lifetime of illiteracy. A handful moved. Others sent their children to live with relatives in neighboring counties (one county caught on and expelled twenty Prince Edward children). The more fortunate found spots in schools as far away as Massachusetts, Iowa, and Michigan. Despite such efforts, some black children in Prince Edward County remained unschooled for five years.

The second half of Brown's Battleground makes an especially important contribution. Eschewing the usual focus on judges and political leaders, Titus argues persuasively that the arrival of the civil rights movement in 1963 had a more profound effect on the county than the court cases that led to the reopening of the public schools in 1964. Titus connects a direct-action campaign in the summer of 1963 to the establishment of the integrated, albeit temporary, Prince Edward Free School, which was supported by the Department of Justice and funded by national organizations such as the Ford Foundation and the Field Foundation. In a particularly revelatory chapter, Titus examines the intensity of white resistance after the reopening of the public schools in 1964. As the final chapters document, it was not until another student strike in 1969, the subsequent hiring of a new superintendent, and the slow return of white families to the public schools in the

early 1970s that white resistance finally began to ease.

J. Douglas Smith
Los Angeles, California

doi: 10.1093/jahist/jas286

Freedom Rights: New Perspectives on the Civil Rights Movement. Ed. by Danielle L. McGuire and John Dittmer. (Lexington: University Press of Kentucky, 2011. x, 392 pp. $40.00.)

Freedom Rights is dedicated to the historian Steven F. Lawson, professor emeritus at Rutgers University and the author of such seminal civil rights studies as *Black Ballots: Voting Rights in the South, 1944–1969* (1976) and *Running for Freedom: Civil Rights and Black Politics in America since 1941* (1991, now in its third edition). Lawson's essay "Freedom Then, Freedom Now: The Historiography of the Civil Rights Movement" (*American Historical Review,* April 1991, pp. 456–72), adroitly summed up the state of the field at the time and influenced, as the authors attest, a generation of scholars.

This essay collection demonstrates just how different, more complex, and more expansive civil rights historiography is twenty years later. From the initial Martin Luther King Jr.–centered, Montgomery-to-Memphis narrative, it now sprawls further in time, place, and themes than ever before. Yet Lawson's own contribution, "Long Origins of the Short Civil Rights Movement, 1954–1968," provides a timely note of caution about losing sight of what made the 1950s and 1960s such a unique episode within the larger struggle for African American freedom and equality. In so doing, Lawson launches against the current historiographical tide of the "long civil rights movement" that seeks to stress the continuities rather than the differences between the civil rights movement of the 1960s and earlier and later developments.

It is impossible to do justice in this short review to the breadth and depth of the scholarship in the twelve essays, but a brief survey indicates what readers can expect. Several essays look at the early decades of the civil rights movement: Justin T. Lorts examines the cultural activism of the National Association for the Advancement of Colored People in the 1940s in its campaigns against negative Hollywood stereotypes of African Americans in film and television; Abigail Sara Lewis looks at the Young Women's Christian Association's multiracial activism in the postwar era after it adopted a national policy of desegregation in 1946; and Sara Rzeszutek Haviland outlines the devastating impact of Cold War politics on the Floridian African American communist couple James Jackson and Esther Cooper Jackson in the 1950s.

The next two essays, by Krystal D. Frazier and Stacy Braukman, are set squarely within the more familiar time frame and events of movement activism in the 1950s and 1960s and both approach the subject clearly influenced by recent family and gender scholarship. Frazier contends that black family culture in the aftermath of Emmett Till's 1955 murder played an important role in nationalizing the African American freedom struggle because of the struggle's transregional northern and southern roots planted through twentieth-century migrations. Braukman studies the commingling of white anti–civil rights activism and sexual morality campaigns by Florida's Legislative Investigation Committee in the 1960s.

Danielle L. McGuire continues the gendered theme but in a different era in the North Carolina case of Joan Little, who in 1974 killed her white jailer after he allegedly sexually assaulted her. The subsequent Free Joan Little Campaign acted as a mobilization point for activist groups across a broad spectrum of interests. Jacqueline Castledine explores the contours of women's cultural activism against a backdrop of racial change from the 1950s to the 1980s through the careers of the black American women singers Nina Simone and Abbey Lincoln, and South Africans Dorothy Masuka and Miriam Makeba.

The remaining essays deal with aspects of the post–civil rights era: Emily Zuckerman argues that Clarence Thomas as head of the Equal Employment Opportunity Commission resisted to a greater extent than one might imagine President Ronald Reagan's attempts to dismantle the federal machinery of civil rights; Pippa Holloway shows that manipulation of the criminal justice system to disfranchise African Americans has a long historical legacy; and George Derek Musgrove and

Hasan Kwame Jeffries lament the changes in black political mobilization in Alabama, which in recent decades has led to several voter fraud investigations by whites that have served as tools of disfranchisement. Finally, Brian Ward interrogates the ambiguous symbolism of Barack Obama's presidency in relation to the civil rights movement's legacy.

Students, teachers, researchers, and a general audience will find this volume a lively, engaging, readable, and informative introduction to what civil rights scholarship looks like today and where it is headed in the future.

John A. Kirk
University of Arkansas at Little Rock
Little Rock, Arkansas

doi: 10.1093/jahist/jas317

Daily Demonstrators: The Civil Rights Movement in Mennonite Homes and Sanctuaries. By Tobin Miller Shearer. (Baltimore: Johns Hopkins University Press, 2010. xxiv, 360 pp. $65.00.)

Tobin Miller Shearer's main contribution to scholarship on religion and civil rights may not be the argument he makes in *Daily Demonstrators*—it may be the model of research and interpretation that he provides. Shearer situates his research in the homes and sanctuaries of members of the largest Mennonite denominations during the civil rights era: the General Conference Mennonite Church and the Old Mennonite Church. He shifts the focus of civil rights scholarship from "the street"—a public place of protest, political engagement, and, too frequently, violence—to the private sphere of individual religious believers, arguing that Mennonite activism was not always recognizable to those who understood demonstration to be only public but that it was nonetheless an important contribution to civil rights (p. vii). That argument, however, too frequently lacks precision or explicit grounding in the literature of civil rights history and overvalues the contributions of Mennonites without quantifying them. However, the shift of scene asks readers to consider how the themes of the civil rights movement—desegregation, equality, interracial relationships, and, eventually, black power—affected and were reflected in the personal relationships of everyday people. Those questions are valuable.

Mennonites, if not unique, are an intriguing subject, for they face competing impulses: a biblically grounded belief that all people were created with dignity by God (a belief that drove their early opposition to slavery) and a commitment to nonresistance and nonconformity. Fearing that engaging civil rights in the street could "lead to coercive, worldly ways" that did not align with traditional Mennonite values, midcentury Mennonites were able to live out their theology of racial justice in personal relationships (p. 68). But when Mennonites erred on the side of being too private, their commitment to social justice was questioned; but when they engaged civil rights in more public and politicized ways, they risked alienating traditionalists.

Shearer analyzes these relationships through typical archival sources such as church meeting notes and religious reporting but also innovatively incorporates personal interviews, photographs, and analyses of material culture such as head coverings. While the arguments that emerge from his visual and material analyses are, at times, tenuous, the incorporation of these sources is notable, and Shearer's analyses show sensitivity toward his subjects. Additionally, he intriguingly organizes his materials not by a strict chronology but in chapters that focus on different scenes within homes and sanctuaries—such as interracial friendships, interracial marriages, or the homes of rural white hosts of urban black children on Fresh Air Fund trips. Individual chapters serve as windows onto the private lives of Mennonites working out their faith commitment to civil rights in challenging broader contexts and contribute to the book's larger argument that such "daily demonstrators" were vital in moving civil rights forward. While *Daily Demonstrators* too often overvalues the work of these personal moments, Shearer's focus on the intimate aspects of activism is a scholarly direction to appreciate.

Rebecca Barrett-Fox
Bethel College
North Newton, Kansas

doi: 10.1093/jahist/jas224

After Freedom Summer: How Race Realigned Mississippi Politics, 1965–1986. By Chris Danielson. (Gainesville: University Press of Florida, 2011. xiv, 294 pp. $69.95.)

Frequently denounced by the Student Nonviolent Coordinating Committee as the most segregated state in the nation, Mississippi has provided rich pickings for historians of African American politics. Two of the most celebrated studies of the civil rights movement—John Dittmer's *Local People* (1994) and Charles M. Payne's *I've Got the Light of Freedom* (1995)—highlight the state's centrality to an understanding of the era, while other studies have drilled down to investigate particular organizations or counties. While most of these studies begin in the 1940s and end their narratives in the 1970s, Chris Danielson's evaluation of African American political action in Mississippi takes a slightly different approach, commencing in 1965 and ending in 1986, the moment that Mike Espy was elected Mississippi's first African American congressman since Reconstruction.

Danielson sees the five years after the passage of the 1965 Voting Rights Act as a period of great hope, when African Americans entered public office in numbers not seen since Reconstruction. This was most apparent at the local level since African American candidates proved less successful in statewide elections. While large campaigns brought publicity and, according to Danielson, "raised black consciousness," black candidates were hamstrung by the entrenched racial views of the state's white majority (p. 53). Charles Evers's 1971 gubernatorial campaign revealed a cruel irony that helps explain this dynamic. His use of television ads to boost his campaign only served to make him more visible to white voters, and the more visible he was, the more likely white voters were to mobilize against him. The failures of such campaigns highlight, for Danielson, the wisdom of the other major theme of post-1965 black politics in Mississippi. The struggle for representation was played out as much in the courts as at the ballot box, and Danielson charts the progress of numerous legal challenges to discriminatory practices such as gerrymandering. Thanks in part to the success of this approach, a new generation of African American politicians emerged in the 1980s. These younger politicians had few links to the civil rights movement, which rendered them more appealing to white voters, and they were able to mobilize a relatively powerful African American vote. Yet, as Danielson stresses, their appearance demonstrated exactly how institutionalized Mississippi's African American voters had become, since electoral success was now only possible through the two-party system. More troublingly, Espy's election might have symbolized a new era in Mississippi's politics, but like the earlier electoral successes, it "did little to remedy the problems of his impoverished black constituents" (p. 216).

Two additions would have improved this fine contribution to the literature: maps would have helped orient readers unfamiliar with Mississippi political geography and more attention to grassroots activism would have broadened the book's relatively narrow focus on electoral politics. Nevertheless, Danielson confirms the huge limitations of the two-party structure and the inescapability of race in the Deep South.

Joe Street
Northumbria University
Newcastle upon Tyne, England

doi: 10.1093/jahist/jas162

After the Dream: Black and White Southerners since 1965. By Timothy J. Minchin and John A. Salmond. (Lexington: University Press of Kentucky, 2011. x, 405 pp. $40.00.)

After the Dream offers a broad, synthetic overview of the forty-plus years since the zenith of the modern civil rights movement. Drawing on both recent historical scholarship and primary-source research, Timothy J. Minchin and John A. Salmond direct our attention to years that fall outside the conventional chronology of the movement—years in which black and white southerners navigated the new realities of race and civil rights.

The implementation of the 1964 Civil Rights Act and the 1965 Voting Rights Act frame the book. The far-reaching and long-lasting implications of these laws make them important touchstones for evaluating southern progress on civil rights in the realms of education, politics, economics, and public accommodations. Minchin and Salmond argue that the South's record in these areas is mixed, with gains in the early years often threatened

or rolled back as the decades progressed. They highlight the crucial, ongoing role that African Americans played in pushing for compliance with the federal laws, and they praise the National Association for the Advancement of Colored People (NAACP) for continually prodding federal officials to enforce the statutes. As they show, federal judges (through court rulings), congressional leaders (through the power of the purse), and presidential administrations (through agency appointments and the chief executive's use of the bully pulpit) had the power to speed racial reform in the region. But these federal officials could also impede progress by denying that racial discrimination remained relevant or by relegating civil rights issues to the back burner.

After the Dream shows that the South made the most progress in the realm of public accommodations. Despite lingering resistance from some white southerners, most welcomed—or at least came to accept—the integration of public facilities. Though to a lesser extent the same could be said of school integration and black political participation, the story in education was especially noteworthy. Southern schools became the most integrated in the nation after 1965 thanks to NAACP litigation, supportive federal courts, and the willingness of white parents to send their children to integrated schools. Although during the Ronald Reagan years the political climate became less supportive of efforts to address persistent educational disparities, debate focused on the level of racial integration and not the virtue of it.

Developments in the economic arena were less promising. African Americans struggled to avoid continued economic marginalization. While some—particularly middle-class blacks with access to good schools—found economic success, many other black southerners found it impossible to advance when faced with persistent discrimination in the workplace and inconsistent federal efforts to root out such differential treatment. The slow pace of black economic progress undermined the civil rights gains of the era and remains a cause of concern in the twenty-first century.

Minchin and Salmond have written a detailed study of a time period slowly coming into focus for historians of the South. Their mixed assessment of the region's progress on civil rights issues highlights the tenuousness of some of the gains. This gives their work a two-steps-forward, one-step-back tone; references to "mixed outcomes" and "hope and despair" suggest not just the complexity of developments but also their ambiguity (pp. 168, 130). Ultimately, Minchin and Salmond are optimists: the progress the South has made on civil rights since 1965 is real and enduring, and it can serve as the basis for confronting new challenges and old threats in the new century.

Gregg L. Michel
University of Texas at San Antonio
San Antonio, Texas

doi: 10.1093/jahist/jas200

Baltimore '68: Riots and Rebirth in an American City. Ed. by Jessica I. Elfenbein, Thomas L. Hollowak, and Elizabeth M. Nix. (Philadelphia: Temple University Press, 2011. xxii, 272 pp. Cloth, $74.50. Paper, $29.95.)

Baltimore '68 is a collection of ten essays and four expertly edited oral histories that provide useful insights into the local and national significance of the responses in Baltimore to the assassination of Martin Luther King Jr. Considered collectively, and in keeping with scholarship in recent urban history, the anthology reveals that looting and arson in Baltimore did not cause that city's urban decline.

Emily Lieb uses a case study of the deterioration of a middle-class black neighborhood to illustrate the devastating impact that federally funded highway projects had on communities along projected routes. Not rioters but municipal planners "turned a neighborhood of . . . homeowners into a slum," she argues (p. 64). Elizabeth M. Nix and Deborah R. Weiner's investigation of the economic vitality of three commercial districts demonstrates that many businesses survived the events of April 1968 and that their later decline resulted from multiple forces.

Though not the cause of urban decay, responses in Baltimore to King's assassination left an indelible mark on the city and the nation, several contributors assert. Maryland governor Spiro T. Agnew made national headlines when he publicly rebuked mainstream civil rights activists for not preventing the violence. The Republican governor also made clear his conviction that "'evil men and not evil conditions'" caused the crisis—a move that Alex Csicsek argues was in keeping with Agnew's political convictions (p. 73). The governor's provocative rejection of the liberal interpretation of events—that, as Langston Hughes had suggested decades earlier, a dream deferred by racism and injustice can indeed explode—won him the attention of the then–presidential candidate Richard M. Nixon. Peter B. Levy notes that Nixon's selection of Agnew as a running mate reflected the candidate's decision to woo white southern Democrats at the expense of African American voters—a strategy with long-term implications for national party politics and federal urban policy. Howell S. Baum argues that the violent reactions in Baltimore to King's assassination, in combination with Agnew's diatribe and its favorable reception among whites, undermined efforts to desegregate the city's public schools. Dismayed by whites' callousness, moderate African Americans lost faith in the effort. Simultaneously, surprised by the intensity of African American anger, Caucasians backed away from integration as well. The events of April 1968, these essays explain, revealed and widened what Barack Obama famously described as "the chasm of misunderstanding that exists between the races" ("A More Perfect Union," campaign speech, March 18, 2008, Philadelphia, Penn.).

Throughout the collection, contributors refer to the responses to King's assassination using a range of descriptors including *riots, disturbances,* and *uprisings.* Each term represents a position in the debate over the motivations of those who took to the streets. Unfortunately, *Baltimore '68* sheds no light on this issue; none of the essays focuses on African Americans who participated in the events—a striking absence especially in an anthology with origins in a public history project that involved the collection of over one hundred oral histories.

While the anthology includes few African American voices, progressive whites are the subject of four informative but largely uncritical essays. As a result, although *Baltimore '68* explains much about the consequences of April 1968, it leaves uninterrogated some of the most provocative issues that the uprisings evoke, including the political meanings participants gave their actions and the limits and promise of liberal reform.

Jane Berger
Moravian College
Bethlehem, Pennsylvania

doi: 10.1093/jahist/jas204

Body and Soul: The Black Panther Party and the Fight against Medical Discrimination. By Alondra Nelson. (Minneapolis: University of Minnesota Press, 2011. xviii, 289 pp. Cloth, $24.95.)

Alondra Nelson's text is the newest academic treatment of the Black Panther party (BPP), which existed from 1966 to 1982. New works on the BPP have furnished valuable insight into regional chapters, the role of women, and the party's community-organizing activity while downplaying the confrontational aspects of organization history. In keeping with this new scholarship, *Body and Soul* examines the BPP's free medical clinics.

The Black Panthers organized free breakfast programs, liberation schools, and free medical clinics to diffuse governmental pressure, and they provided services to their constituents to demonstrate the effectiveness of their political philosophy. The free medical clinics were the most professional of the party's community-service efforts and were well received. Nelson makes a valuable contribution by demonstrating that the party's medical outreach programs were a continuation of a tradition of self-reliance that began in the nineteenth century. Racial discrimination in American medicine resulted in fewer black doctors and nurses, in turn rendering blacks susceptible to "excess . . . mortality and morbidity" (p. 26). Poverty, poor sanitation, and overcrowded living conditions also subjected blacks to periodic epidemics. Chicago's Provident Hospital and Training School for nurses (founded in 1881) and the Tuskegee Institute Hospital and Nurse Training School (founded in 1892) were a response to these abysmal conditions. The Negro Organization Society of Virginia also urged blacks through the first decade of the twentieth century to emphasize "the matter of health . . .

cleanliness, [and] better sanitary conditions" (p. 29). Marcus Garvey continued this tradition by founding the Black Cross Nurses in 1920 as part of his Universal Negro Improvement Association.

Nelson connects the Black Panther party's medical work in the post–World War II era to Freedom Summer, when the Student Nonviolent Coordinating Committee (SNCC) and the Medical Committee for Human Rights (MCHR) organized medical outreach teams in response to the needs of underserved black communities in the Deep South. Many SNCC and MCHR volunteers were radicalized by their experience and were inspired to work toward change in health care.

Body and Soul argues that the Black Panthers began their community survival programs in 1969 to deflect intense police pressure and to serve as a demonstration of their political principles. In thirteen cities the BPP was able to establish free medical clinics, each named after Black Panthers who died in confrontations with the police: Bobby Hutton, Fred Hampton, Franklin Lynch, and Spurgeon "Jake" Winters. The clinics were staffed by a combination of BPP members, sympathetic medical volunteers, and community lay people. Supplies were donated and solicited from hospitals, doctors, and medical suppliers. Treatment was usually basic health care: "First aid and basic services, . . . testing for high blood pressure, lead poisoning, tuberculosis, and diabetes, . . . physical exams, . . . immunization against polio, measles, rubella, and diphtheria" (p. 106). Perhaps the most important clinic service was providing underserved communities with the benefits of preventive medicine while showing them the power of political organization. In fact, many former members continued in medicine even after the BPP ceased to exist. I hope *Body and Soul* will serve as the catalyst for continued analysis of other useful aspects of BPP history.

Paul Alkebulan
Virginia State University
Petersburg, Virginia

doi: 10.1093/jahist/jas221

Demanding Child Care: Women's Activism and the Politics of Welfare, 1940–1971. By Natalie

M. Fousekis. (Urbana: University of Illinois Press, 2011. xiv, 245 pp. $50.00.)

Natalie M. Fousekis recounts the history of a unique advocacy effort that preserved publicly funded child care in California after World War II yet made it available only to low-income people. This well-argued book is far more than a state-level case study. It includes thumbnail sketches of individual advocates, quotations from low-income women's letters to state officials, and astute analyses of state and national policies. Fousekis reveals unfamiliar dimensions of the "other women's movement" (prior to and separate from the "second wave") that Dorothy Sue Cobble has located primarily in trade unions. Fousekis locates it as well in coalitions of parents and child-care-center employees who argued for mothers' rights to work.

The main strength of the book is its engagement with a history that is still so unknown. In 1999 Sonya Michel published a single-volume history of child care, *Children's Interests/Mothers' Rights,* inspired in part by failed attempts to create a universal child-care system during the 1980s (in which I participated as staff of the U.S. House Select Committee on Children, Youth, and Families). A few scholars have followed Michel. But Fousekis's study is unique: she offers local views of nursery schools run by the Works Progress Administration (rarely noted in New Deal histories) and centers in areas of defense production under the Lanham Act during World War II (commonly thought to have been more widespread than they were). She details the virtually unknown attempts of wage-earning women to preserve their Lanham Act benefits, and she follows this history through the Cold War, the War on Poverty, and successive waves of welfare reform. Fousekis describes a robust movement on behalf of working mothers as breadwinners and parents, underlining the findings of Alice Kessler-Harris and others that women did not simply leave the labor force, willingly or unwillingly, after the war.

Fousekis's work has two weaknesses. First, it overstates the political naiveté of the advocates who worked to keep the wartime centers open. While she acknowledges participation of sectarian leftists in the child-care coalition and unions (or at least ladies' auxiliaries) in the Congress of Industrial Organizations, she

focuses on women who lacked political experience prior to their involvement with the child-care campaign. Second, Fousekis underplays the efforts of white child-care advocates to distinguish themselves from welfare recipients. The advocates were undoubtedly correct to assume that the link that was forged between child care and welfare-to-work policies under the 1962 and 1967 Social Security Act amendments would divert resources away from child care for poor working people who did not receive cash assistance. However, the advocates were also motivated by racism and biases on the basis of class or caste. Fousekis does not address the possible role of their arguments—which favored child care specifically as a means of avoiding welfare receipt—in heightening the marginalization of cash welfare programs and their recipients.

Felicia Kornbluh
University of Vermont
Burlington, Vermont

doi: 10.1093/jahist/jas311

Battling Pornography: The American Feminist Anti-pornography Movement, 1976–1986. By Carolyn Bronstein. (New York: Cambridge University Press, 2011. xiv, 360 pp. Cloth, $85.00. Paper, $25.99.)

In *Battling Pornography,* Carolyn Bronstein reorients our understanding of an important yet highly disputed phase of the modern women's movement. Bronstein takes an expansive view of the movement's history. She looks beneath the extremism of the early 1980s and points to the antipornography movement's mainstream "origins . . . in grassroots campaigns against sexually violent and sexist mainstream media content" of the mid-1970s (p. 3). Bronstein draws attention to two early organizations, Women against Violence against Women (WAVAW), and Women against Violence in Pornography and Media (WAVPM). While a more extreme third group, Women against Pornography (WAP), garnered much of the contemporary spotlight, Bronstein explores that faction's mainstream genesis.

Her study begins in the earliest days of the women's liberation movement, when many women were discovering that the sexual revolution had not, in fact, resulted in true heterosexual equity. Bronstein examines the early feminist action against the rise of pornography that accompanied the sexual liberalism of the late 1960s and early 1970s and concludes that this critique led to a focus on media portrayals of violence against women and ultimately to the formation of WAVAW in 1976, "the first national feminist organization to focus exclusively on the problem of sexual violence in the media" (p. 83). But unlike subsequent organizations, WAVAW did not emphasize "pornography per se" but rather violence in mainstream popular culture. Additionally, WAVAW "rejected government restriction" as a solution to the problem, a tactic that more radical antiporn activists would later employ (pp. 83–84).

In 1977 Women against Violence in Pornography and Media joined WAVAW. WAVPM was also established in response to mainstream depictions of misogynist violence, but, as the name suggests, WAVPM perceived pornography to be a crucial problem in American culture and thus expanded upon the precedent set by WAVAW. WAVPM also insisted that violent images motivated actual violence, a charge not embraced by WAVAW but one that came to dominate the antiporn movement in later years (pp. 129–30).

Women against Pornography, founded in 1979 by radical feminists such as Susan Brownmiller, grew out of WAVPM and became the leading antiporn organization. Bronstein portrays the organization's move to an exclusive focus on antipornography as a "monumental shift" (p. 19), one "calculated" by "media-savvy individuals" to generate significant national attention (pp. 203–4). This move not only "marginalized" WAVAW and WAVPM but also offered narrow and contentious definitions of acceptable sexuality (p. 236). Significantly, WAP also unwittingly aided the conservative backlash against sexual liberalism, weakening and creating a gulf in the women's movement in the early 1980s.

Despite where the movement ended up, Bronstein ably demonstrates that the roots of antiporn feminism were focused primarily on concerns of violence, not necessarily sex, in popular culture. This suggests paths not taken when one considers both the combativeness of the later movement and the continued ubiquity of violence against women in mainstream media in the twenty-first century.

Carrie Pitzulo
University of West Georgia
Carrollton, Georgia

doi: 10.1093/jahist/jas174

Those Girls: Single Women in Sixties and Seventies Popular Culture. By Katherine J. Lehman. (Lawrence: University Press of Kansas, 2011. viii, 312 pp. $29.95.)

Gender and popular culture is an especially well-mined field of cultural history; Katherine J. Lehman proposes to bring something new to the conversation by teasing out one aspect of the gendered culture: popular narratives about being single and female during an era of great social change. She explores the ways the culture talked about women living alone, negotiating their sexuality, and pursuing careers. She situates these experiences within larger trends: the sexual revolution, the singles subculture, rhetoric about workplace equality, sexual harassment and expanding job opportunities, the emergence of the single-woman market, and social concerns about sex and violence. Adding depth to her interpretation are new sources—not just the film and television features themselves but original scripts and memos that show how cultural producers struggled to stay within socially sanctioned boundaries. Lehman finds the classic dichotomy of the glass as half empty–glass as half full and a popular culture that reflected women's pursuit of sexual and gender equality and the pursuit of meaning in their own lives that was limited and shaped by more traditional norms and the realities of mass-market cultural forms.

Parts of this work really soar. Lehman is particularly adept at demonstrating just how quickly sitcom portrayals of working women reflected social changes. *That Girl,* which premiered in the fall of 1966, gave female viewers the vicarious experience of living single in New York City, always under the watchful eye of a vigilant father and chaste boyfriend. Although the lead character, played by Marlo Thomas, inspired many younger women, even Thomas's insistence that feminism find its way into the final script could not believably sustain the premise of the series by its 1971 demise. Similarly, Lehman compellingly describes how ideas about sexual liberation for women became juxtaposed against messages of concern—along with a certain amount of blaming the victim—first in television police dramas and then in films such as *Looking for Mr. Goodbar* (1977). Seeing the ways that film morphed from real-life story to novel to film effectively sets up the future backlash against women.

Unfortunately for Lehman, much of this story has been told before. She relies heavily on Susan Douglas's *Where the Girls Are: Growing Up Female with the Mass Media* (1995), Bonnie J. Dow's *Prime-Time Feminism: Television, Media Culture and the Women's Movement since 1970* (1996), and Elana Levine's *Wallowing in Sex: The New Sexual Culture of 1970s American Television* (2007), summarizing their arguments and adding a few of her own to the mix. Perhaps for this reason she signposts her own contributions with a less-than-subtle vigor, using phrases such as "I examine" (p. 68), "I analyze" (p. 116), and "I argue" (p. 159). Her summaries of others' arguments and her command of the broader backstory are clear, readable, and accurate; but she presents her own work sometimes more clumsily, and the book's many subsections emphasize detail over interpretation. Still, this is an early work of promise by someone who clearly has the gift for finding the social significance in what most Americans regarded as little more than mindless entertainment.

Judy Kutulas
St. Olaf College
Northfield, Minnesota

doi: 10.1093/jahist/jas216

Nixon's Court: His Challenge to Judicial Liberalism and Its Political Consequences. By Kevin J. McMahon. (Chicago: University of Chicago Press, 2011. xiv, 343 pp. $29.00.)

The standard view of Richard M. Nixon's staffing of the Burger court is that of "a counter-revolution that wasn't." *Nixon's Court* by Kevin J. McMahon effectively dispels this idea and replaces it with a well-researched, tightly written critique that demonstrates that Nixon cared about two issues—busing and crime—and that

he was effective in moving the Court to adopt positions close to his own. The Burger court moderated the Warren court's criminal-procedure decisions and basically brought northern busing to an end in *Milliken v. Bradley* (1974), where it held that suburbs could not be attached to inner-city school districts.

With the assistance of the South Carolina senator Strom Thurmond, Nixon actively courted southern delegates at the 1968 Republican Convention. The Supreme Court was topic number one in the conversations, especially since the new president would likely be replacing retiring chief justice Earl Warren. Nixon promised to appoint only strict constructionists to the Court. Then during the fall campaign Nixon (and George Wallace) ran against the Warren court, which Nixon portrayed as responsible for all of America's domestic ills.

Nixon had a loose view of who was a conservative strict constructionist: it was sufficient that the nominee held a position similar to Nixon's on busing (acceptable for southern de jure segregation but not northern de facto segregation) and crime; he did not care about other social issues. This indifference was reflected in who he considered and nominated to the Court. In less than two years Nixon filled four Court vacancies. In addition to the four successful nominees there were two who failed confirmation and two others whose nominations were scuttled by (accurate) claims that they were "legal mediocrities." Only one of the eight—William H. Rehnquist—was a conservative ideologue, owing his seat to liberal complaints about mediocrities.

McMahon shows that Nixon's pursuit of a "southern strategy" failed in the 1970 midterm congressional elections (despite his nomination of two southerners to the Court, the first from Thurmond's South Carolina) and that thereafter he focused on moving northern urban ethnics into the Republican party. Crime and the fear of busing, problems that Nixon successfully attributed to the federal courts, created strains within the liberal coalition, resulting in an electoral backlash that favored moderate conservatives such as Nixon. In a second major conclusion, *Nixon's Court* determines that "Reagan Democrats" is a misnomer; those voters were first Nixon Democrats in 1972.

McMahon sees Nixon as one of Stephen Skowronek's "preemptive" presidents, governing during an opposition political regime (Stephen Skowronek, *The Politics Presidents Make,* 1997). Nixon, however, was initially more successful than a typical preemptive president because he picked his issues of opposition so well that he created a win-win position. If the Court agreed with him, he could claim victory. If it disagreed and maintained its course, he could take advantage of electoral backlash. Busing and crime were his issues because they carried major electoral payoffs.

Nixon's Court is researched from multiple sources and is a valuable addition to regime politics. It vividly illuminates both the Nixon presidency and the Burger court.

L. A. Scot Powe Jr.
University of Texas
Austin, Texas

doi: 10.1093/jahist/jas177

Sexual Injustice: Supreme Court Decisions from Griswold to Roe. By Marc Stein. (Chapel Hill: University of North Carolina Press, 2010. xvi, 364 pp. $39.95.)

Surprise, surprise. Old white guys sitting on the Supreme Court were sexually conservative. They did not like homosexuals either. But why belabor the point? Justice Antonin Scalia never lets us forget it anyway. The more things change, the more they remain the same. Marc Stein's heart is in the right place; Supreme Court decisions were tepid at best, heterosexist in extreme, and reinforced a homophobic *zeitgeist.* That is an old story, however; a bitter truth nonetheless. Stein does a much better job, instead, when turning his attention to the tragic and unduly neglected case of *Boutilier v. Immigration and Naturalization Service* (1967). *Boutilier,* not *Bowers v. Hardwick* (1986), emerges as the first major defeat for gay rights in America. Stein's analysis is thorough, nuanced, and multifaceted.

Clive Michael Boutilier was a Canadian national who was first admitted to the United States in 1955 when he was twenty-one. When Boutilier applied for American citizenship, he acknowledged that he had been arrested on a sodomy charge in New York in October 1959. It was soon reduced to a simple assault and thereafter dismissed entirely. Being a good Canadian, however, Boutilier admitted the "dirty deed" anyway. It served as justification for deporting him. Homosexuality was presumed prima facie evidence of a "psychopathic personality," whatever that means. America could legally deport psychopathic personalities, however defined (undoubtedly a trope for being gay). This convoluted logic, and the ultimate insanity of its reach, are at the heart of this book and told with depth and feeling. Boutilier, incidentally, nearly died in a car accident while awaiting deportation. He spent thirty days in a coma and suffered significant brain damage but was deported nonetheless. This case is especially poignant to Stein, who is a gay American living in Canada as a professor at York University.

One other point to consider: Thomas Paine infamously intoned, "a long habit of not thinking a thing *wrong,* gives it a superficial appearance of being *right*" (*Common Sense,* 1776). Though Paine was applying this idea to liberty writ large, it is no less true of sexual rights in America. We have none; no reason to pretend otherwise. Cases such as *Griswold v. Connecticut* (1976), as depicted by Stein, are routinely overstated. I would add the following as well: they have nothing to do with sex. Being free from governmental intrusion is a zoning regulation, or perhaps even a "no trespassing sign." Sexual rights, instead, need to be safeguarded under the Ninth and Fourteenth Amendments. It should be self-evident that Americans have the right to choose to reproduce, or not to reproduce, including all manner of not reproducing. Until recognized as such, there is no reason to persist in the fiction that we have any sexual rights whatsoever. Similarly, there is no reason to scrutinize Supreme Court cases either, pretending that privacy means sex. Sex is sex; no one is empowered to tell you otherwise.

Paul R. Abramson
University of California, Los Angeles
Los Angeles, California

doi: 10.1093/jahist/jas296

The Morning After: A History of Emergency Contraception in the United States. By Heather

Munro Prescott. (New Brunswick: Rutgers University Press, 2011. xiv, 163 pp. Cloth, $69.00. Paper, $22.95.)

In December 2011 the Obama administration angered many women's health advocates by banning the over-the-counter sale of emergency contraceptives to women under the age of seventeen. Despite a scientific consensus that this drug, known as the "morning-after pill," was safe to take without a prescription, the contentious politics of reproduction muddied the waters. Heather Munro Prescott's timely book on emergency contraception offers insight into the scientific, historical, and political contexts of this and similar policy decisions.

Prescott works to place emergency contraception into an appropriate and broad context, asserting that its history needs to be considered as part of the history of reproductive politics, drug regulation, and contraceptive research. Prescott follows the history of emergency contraception from its appearance in the 1960s through the first decade of the twenty-first century. She begins her story with the reproductive scientists and population control groups who sought a way "to address the 'disease' of unwanted pregnancy," a "disease" they considered both social and individual (p. 4). The tension between the demographic and the individual usefulness of emergency contraception suffused its history for the next fifty years. The story is both familiar and frustrating: while scientists and politicians hoped that emergency contraception could be a significant population and poverty reducer, feminists debated about whether it was safe and reliable enough to contribute to women's reproductive autonomy and well-being.

The most intriguing chapters examine the shifting position of women's health advocates. Prescott argues that concerns over the safety of the birth control pill, the health consequences of drugs such as diethylstilbestrol, and the politics of abortion all shaped the feminist position on emergency contraception throughout the 1970s and 1980s. In the early years, feminists were more likely to express skepticism about the safety of emergency contraception and to direct their efforts toward federal regulation to protect women from what they

perceived to be the recklessness and indifference of the medical profession and the pharmaceutical industry. However, by the 1980s the issue of emergency contraception had bridged a gap among radical feminist organizations, moderate women's groups, and reproductive health professionals, all of whom sought an effective method of backup contraception as access to abortion was being attacked. In the 1990s, as part of a larger consumer movement to gain access to new medical treatments by accelerating the federal drug approval process, feminists reversed their earlier reticence. Instead of demanding protection from the Food and Drug Administration (FDA), they now charged that "the FDA was deliberately endangering the health and lives of women by suppressing knowledge about this important contraceptive technology" (p. 96).

From here Prescott moves on to cover the national media campaign launched by emergency contraception advocates in the 1990s and the effort to persuade pharmaceutical companies to manufacture and sell this product in the United States. Her last chapter brings us to the most recent controversy: the debate over making emergency contraception available over the counter, which began in earnest after the turn of the twenty-first century and continues today.

This is a complex story to tell in a slim volume, and yet it offers an enticing first attempt at both adding this chapter to the history of reproductive rights and broadening the scope of such research to include science and public policy.

Robyn L. Rosen
Marist College
Poughkeepsie, New York

doi: 10.1093/jahist/jas320

Trampling Out the Vintage: Cesar Chavez and the Two Souls of the United Farm Workers. By Frank Bardacke. (New York: Verso, 2011. viii, 836 pp. $54.95.)

Although there is yet no major and definitive biography of César Chávez, several studies of the farm workers movement and the rise of the United Farm Workers of America (UFW) during the 1960s and 1970s have recently been published. These new studies go beyond the glory years of the union when Chávez and key co-leaders such as Dolores Huerta accomplished what had never been done before: successfully organize farm workers in this country. Chávez showed that despite major opposition from growers and their political allies, including rival unions such as the International Brotherhood of Teamsters, it could be done (and from this grew his famous mantra "Si, se puede" [Yes, we can]). These newer studies examine the later 1970s and into the 1980s when the UFW lost membership due to attrition or internal differences, and when it also became more difficult to sustain new boycott initiatives that had helped achieve the earlier victories. These exposés reveal a different Chávez and a different UFW—a darker side composed of major strategic mistakes and a failure of leadership.

Frank Bardacke's book is part of this new historiography. His main thesis is that what success the UFW achieved even in the earlier periods had to do with the workers. While acknowledging Chávez's key leadership, Bardacke correctly believes that not enough attention has been given to the rank and file. An exhaustive study and the best single volume to date on the UFW, *Trampling Out the Vintage* examines the dual struggles of the union leadership and the rank and file but has a difficult time maintaining a balance between the two. The successes and failures of the union are inextricably connected—it is not one or the other. There are no good guys (the rank and file) and bad guys (the later Chávez). The farm workers movement has always been an uphill struggle and in that struggle many have made mistakes, including both the leadership and the workers (who, in some cases, too easily gave up on the union). What is needed is a balanced approach that conceptualizes the larger forces arrayed against the union. Bardacke does this but still overly criticizes Chávez's leadership.

Despite the recent revelations of the more problematic side of Chávez's leadership, his position in American history is significantly set. He did what had never been done before and therefore ranks as one of the great labor leaders in American history. The more problematic moments in his later history to me just humanize the man despite his aura in some circles as a secular saint. Although I can quibble with Bardacke's thesis, it represents a major scholarly achievement.

Mario T. García
University of California, Santa Barbara
Santa Barbara, California

doi: 10.1093/jahist/jas304

The Making of Chicana/o Studies: In the Trenches of Academe. By Rodolfo F. Acuña. (New Brunswick: Rutgers University Press, 2011. xxviii, 317 pp. Cloth, $75.00. Paper, $26.95.)

Written before and during efforts by Arizona lawmakers to do away with Chicano studies, Rodolfo F. Acuña's *The Making of Chicana/o Studies* is the first major history of Chicano studies written by a founder of the field. When Acuña arrived at San Fernando Valley State College (now California State University, Northridge) in 1969, only fifty Mexican American students were enrolled, but later that year he became the founding chair of the Chicano studies department, which eventually became the largest Chicana/o studies program in the country. Acuña is also the author of *Occupied America: A History of Chicanos* (1972), the most important Chicano history book. Acuña has had a "ringside seat" for the making of Chicana/o studies and continues to be dumbfounded by the "lack of literacy" about the field (pp. viii, vii). He offers a case study–based vignette approach to the topic, choosing issues with which he has familiarity. He makes excellent use of newspapers, Internet resources, and a myriad of other sources, and he provides an appendix of academic programs.

Acuña introduces pre-1965 efforts to study La Raza at the college level by highlighting the work of George I. Sánchez. He chronicles the 1960s rise of Chicana/o student organizations such as United Mexican American Students, Mexican American Youth Organization, and Chicano Student Movement of Aztlán (Movimiento Estudiantil Chicanos de Aztlán, or MEChA). Acuña also addresses the California state university system, including its unique attempts to improve Chicana/o education such as Operation Chicano Teacher. He argues that Chicana/o studies started to "get it right" by addressing sexism and homophobia (p. xi). Occasionally, efforts to build Chicana/o studies programs required extraordinary means, such as at the University of California, Los Angeles, where students organized a hunger strike to create the department.

Historians will not find an institutional history of Chicana/o studies across the country or an intellectual history of Chicana/o studies in *The Making of Chicana/o Studies,* and readers may still not understand why Chicana/o studies was necessary. Acuña shows that by using different strategies, activist students, professors, and writers were able to create Chicana/o departments, centers, and programs. He suggests that "mainstreaming" (the employment of Chicana/o scholars in already-existing departments) controls those scholars. Yet Acuña shows that sexism and homophobia have existed and even thrived in Chicana/o studies departments and programs. Acuña himself was disregarded by University of California, Santa Barbara Chicana/o academics.

Readers may want to know more about intellectual/theoretical influences on Chicana/o studies such as internal colonialism, Marxism, feminism of various persuasions, critical race theory, and cultural studies. Moreover, which creative writings, articles, books, journals, and newsletters have had a major impact? Acuña states that he believes pedagogy is more important than field content, but he does not discuss how Chicana/o studies has been taught. He correctly credits the scholar Gloria Anzaldúa's writing in the making of Chicana studies, but always the anti-individualist, Acuña does not discuss the impact of his *Occupied America.*

Future institutional approaches might focus on key departments, centers, and programs in regions across the nation. Moreover, the role of the National Association for Chicano and Chicana Studies might be included. Acuña reminds us that the "constant theme of the book is that students are the lifeline of the growth of Chicana/o Studies" (p. xi). Population growth and student activism suggest that Chicana/o studies will continue to grow even as Chicana/o studies transitions into Latina/o

studies. However, he reminds us that today "all Ethnic Studies programs . . . are under siege" (p. 209). Acuña has done a good job, considering that needed archives are stored away in the filing cabinets of each Chicana/o studies program across the country and that numerous oral histories are needed.

Cynthia E. Orozco
Eastern New Mexico University
Ruidoso, New Mexico

doi: 10.1093/jahist/jas253

A Plague of Prisons: The Epidemiology of Mass Incarceration in America. By Ernest Drucker. (New York: New Press, 2011. xiv, 226 pp. $26.95.)

Criminologists and physicians have long believed that crime control and the regulation of health go hand in hand, applying models from one field to the other. In this short, impassioned book the epidemiologist Ernest Drucker turns the traditional logic on its head. Rather than using public health models to contain the spread of crime, Drucker argues that prisons and American drug policy since the 1970s have become the real danger to the nation's well-being. To sensationalize crack epidemics or attendant crime waves is to miss the point, he suggests, because we have effective tools to manage drug addiction. Instead, the disease we must quarantine, the toxic agent we must control, is the prison itself.

Drucker suggests that what he calls inter-disciplinary social epidemiology can offer a new paradigm for assessing the impact of mass incarceration. Early chapters on the sinking of the *Titanic,* on London cholera outbreaks and public health responses, and on HIV/AIDS (human immunodeficiency virus/acquired immune deficiency syndrome) illustrate basic epidemiological method—mapping outbreaks, tracing vectors, identifying the demography of the afflicted—in the interest of preventing disease transmission.

The strongest chapters document the specific health consequences of incarceration in the wake of New York's highly punitive Rockefeller drug laws (named for Governor Nelson Rockefeller, who signed the acts into law in 1973). In memorable sections, Drucker adds empirical data to debates about the effects of mass incarceration through the public health concepts of "years of life lost" and "disability-adjusted life years," measurements that epidemiologists use to quantify the relative magnitude of disasters. Drucker counts the years that New Yorkers—disproportionately black, brown, and poor—have lost to drug sentences and the long-term, chronic disabilities that incarceration imposes. By these measurements, he argues, the Rockefeller drug laws are a public health calamity comparable to more recognizable disasters. The years of life lost to New York drug laws, for example, are three times greater than those lost in the September 11, 2001, World Trade Center attacks. By such measures, he writes, "our nation's drug laws count as a very significant catastrophe" (p. 74). Mass incarceration can be understood as akin to toxic exposure, with physical, psychological, and legal impediments that disrupt entire communities, across generations.

A Plague of Prisons identifies the Rockefeller drug laws as patient zero in the epidemic of punishment. There is much to be said for this argument, and many have, but it pays short shrift to other contextualizing factors in contemporary mass incarceration—deindustrialization, post–civil rights era white backlash—that others have identified. Moreover, as someone who has spent considerable time on earlier histories of punishment, I fear we lose much if we begin the story in the 1970s. Rather than chapters on the *Titanic* or cholera in London, discussion of earlier drug policies or shifts in medical conceptualizations of crime would have bolstered his analysis.

But Drucker is an epidemiologist, not a historian, and one gets the sense that he wrote for physicians and general readers. The final chapter proposes solutions to overincarceration and refers at one point to International Physicians for the Prevention of Nuclear War. Those doctors helped transform public understanding of nuclear weapons from sources of security to sources of risk. *A Plague of Prisons*'s promise of a paradigm shift may be overstated, but Drucker has nonetheless written an accessible, compelling book. If physicians join activists and engaged intellectuals, the social movement against hyperincarceration will gain

strength, and Drucker will have served as an important voice.

Ethan Blue
University of Western Australia
Crawley, Australia

doi: 10.1093/jahist/jas315

Madness Is Civilization: When the Diagnosis Was Social, 1948–1980. By Michael E. Staub. (Chicago: University of Chicago Press, 2011. xii, 252 pp. $40.00.)

I once read a book about the Civil War that detailed the battles beautifully, but when I had finished, I did not understand what the war had been about. I had the same feeling when I finished E. Michael Staub's *Madness Is Civilization*. The author does a praiseworthy job of detailing the antipsychiatry battles of the 1960s and 1970s, and as a factual history of that period in American psychiatry the book is good. Missing is a view of the forest through the trees.

The book focuses on three major antipsychiatry figures—Ronald Laing, Erving Goffman, and Thomas Szasz—but also looks at other antipsychiatry activists and, in a particularly strong chapter, at the women's movement that criticized psychiatry. The author correctly notes that Laing, Goffman, Szasz, and other antipsychiatrists are now "derided" or "summarily ignored" (p. 6).

The author fails to establish why anyone should be interested in the antipsychiatrists other than as historical footnotes. Laing, for example, claimed that schizophrenia was caused by faulty parenting. Staub neglects to add what Laing acknowledged in a 1982 interview: "I was looked to as one who had the answers but I never had them." His claim that schizophrenia was caused by faulty parenting ran aground when Laing's own daughter developed schizophrenia. His addiction to alcohol grew worse as he aged, and his 1994 biography by his son, Adrian, implies that Laing was a charlatan, not a thinker worthy of study.

Goffman's 1961 book *Asylums* argued that there was not much wrong with patients in psychiatric hospitals and that hospitalization itself was doing the damage. He suggested that the doors should be opened and the patients freed so they could live happily ever after. *Asylums* inspired Ken Kesey's *One Flew over the Cuckoo's Nest* (1962), which in retrospect was probably Goffman's main contribution. Some state administrators did as Goffman suggested and found that the released patients really did have brain diseases that, if untreated, turned them into psychotic homeless persons or left them incarcerated in jails. It is now clear that Goffman was dead wrong, so why should we study him?

Szasz is worth studying because he made important contributions to delimiting the role of psychiatrists and on the issue of personal responsibility for mental illness. However, Szasz is best known for his continuing insistence that schizophrenia is a myth, despite the now-overwhelming evidence that it is a brain disease.

Staub's greatest omission is the biological renaissance in psychiatric research. He claims, for example, that beginning in 1980 there was a psychiatric backlash against the antipsychiatrists, but he fails to note that this was precisely when the first computerized tomography (CT) scans and later magnetic resonance image (MRI) scans were published, proving that schizophrenia is, in fact, a brain disease. Thus the backlash had a biological basis.

There is certainly much to criticize about present-day psychiatry, including overdiagnosis, ignorance of the sickest patients, and psychiatrists acting as drug company shills. Exhuming the antipsychiatrists of the past does not add much.

E. Fuller Torrey
Stanley Medical Research Institute
Chevy Chase, Maryland

doi: 10.1093/jahist/jas215

The Transatlantic Collapse of Urban Renewal: Postwar Urbanism from New York to Berlin. By Christopher Klemek. (Chicago: University of Chicago Press, 2011. x, 315 pp. $40.00.)

Christopher Klemek offers an engaging intellectual and political history of the rise and fall of urban renewal in the Atlantic world. It is hard to disagree with the author's condemnation of the "policy debacle called urban renewal" (p. 2). One need not go far to see the deadening effects of large-scale modernist redevelopment projects.

That said, the book's title overstates its transatlantic reach. Berlin, London, and Toronto provide interesting points of comparison to New York City, establishing the transatlantic flow of ideas and planners, but the book's center of gravity is clearly the U.S. Northeast. Germany's early influence on U.S. urban planning is established. The British townscape movement is shown to be an alternative, albeit peripheral, to American thinking. Toronto makes an appearance because Jane Jacobs took refuge there. Its antifreeway movement is thus presented as little more than a sequel to New York City's. These international forays are intended to answer Klemek's central question: How distinctive was the U.S. experience? Not very, it seems.

Like the urbanists he critiques, Klemek fixes his attention on the built environment rather than on the inhabitants of these cities. We therefore learn very little about the economic crisis that devastated working-class families and neighborhood life. Corporations and market forces are peripheral to the story being told. Here, the villain is the state. This interpretation has become quite common in urban history scholarship, particularly in the United States, where the issue is framed as "urban change" rather than "economic change" or deindustrialization. The restructuring of the built environment therefore takes precedence over why these neighborhoods became disposable in the first place.

In many ways, the book pivots on the activism and writings of Jane Jacobs, the author of *The Death and Life of Great American Cities* (1961). Klemek lionizes Jacobs, papering over any contradictions in her thinking. (For an evocative alternative reading on Jacobs, see Sharon Zukin's *Naked City* [2010].) The Rockefeller Foundation's early financial support of Jacobs' research is never explained. How much of an outsider was she? I tend to agree with the geographer James Lemon, who criticized Jacobs's opposition to comprehensive urban planning and her faith in uncontrolled market forces (Lemon, *Liberal Dreams and Nature's Limits,* 1996). Klemek acknowledges Lemon's critique without actually engaging with it.

I am ambivalent about the politics of *The Transatlantic Collapse of Urban Renewal.* The problem with this kind of intellectual history is that it is very top down. Like Jacobs,

Klemek seems to side with the conservative backlash against the activist state. He agrees with those who argue against "the deeply held liberal assumptions that government action is a big part of the answer to urban problems" (p. 2). At no time does the author tie the decline of urban renewal to the ascendancy of neoconservativism in the United States. The rise and fall of the "urban renewal order" is surely part of wider ideological shifts, first to the left in the 1960s and to the right in the 1970s and 1980s.

Steven High
Concordia University
Montreal, Canada

doi: 10.1093/jahist/jas193

Allende's Chile and the Inter-American Cold War. By Tanya Harmer. (Chapel Hill: University of North Carolina Press, 2011. xviii, 375 pp. $45.00.)

The Cold War between the Soviet Union and the United States had hemispheric implications, shaping opportunities, challenges, and choices in Latin America and the Caribbean region. Yet the Cold War in the Americas involved more than a contest between Washington, D.C., and Moscow. Local and regional dynamics, Tanya Harmer explains, animated the inter-American Cold War. Her book, *Allende's Chile and the Inter-American Cold War,* is an outstanding addition to a growing literature on the North-South dimensions of a subject traditionally studied along East-West lines.

When the democratically elected Chilean president Salvador Allende sought to implement a socialist revolution—La Vía Chilena al Socialismo (the Chilean way to socialism)—in 1973, internal groups and foreign governments responded in complex and interesting ways. Harmer makes this complexity accessible and offers new information and insight into the role of key actors in the Americas and beyond.

The United States pursued a passive-aggressive approach as the U.S.-Chilean economic relationship frustrated leaders in both capitals. The Cuban revolutionary Fidel Castro, a close friend of Allende, thought Chile's peaceful revolution was unprepared to withstand a counterrevolution. The Brazilian military government steadfastly opposed socialism in South America. Internally, President Allende struggled to maintain a fragile coalition—and economic stability. In the end, the Chilean military, backed by Brazil rather than the United States, deposed Allende. He committed suicide during the fight for the presidential palace in 1973, the beginning of a long period of military rule in Chile.

Harmer's book is accessible, balanced, and compelling. It is based on impressive multiarchival international research that includes manuscript sources and oral history interviews in Brazil, Chile, Cuba, Poland, the United Kingdom, and the United States. Her international coverage of Chilean history, including the military coup, is engrossing. For these and other reasons, her book is already required reading for U.S. military personnel working in Chile. It should also become a standard for graduate and undergraduate students of the Cold War and twentieth-century inter-American history.

Allende's Chile and the Inter-American Cold War will certainly inspire additional work on the regional dynamics of the Soviet-American Cold War, resulting over time in a much more nuanced and reliable picture of the hemispheric aspects of this critical period. The net result of that work will likely show that the Western Hemisphere actually experienced—rather than an inter-American Cold War—a series of subregional conflicts, or "cold wars," defined by unique local dynamics and interacting throughout with the larger Soviet-American contest. As they describe and analyze those cold wars, writers will look to Harmer's book as a model for scholarship on the inter-American experience.

Bradley Lynn Coleman
U.S. Southern Command
Miami, Florida

doi: 10.1093/jahist/jas234

Human Rights Activism and the End of the Cold War: A Transnational History of the Helsinki Network. By Sarah B. Snyder. (New York: Cambridge University Press, 2011. x, 293 pp. $85.00.)

Despite an outpouring of literature on the topic, the end of the Cold War remains something of an enigma. Among the many theories advanced to explain the demise of the Soviet bloc, the role played by the 1975 Helsinki Final Act, which established the Conference on Security and Cooperation in Europe (CSCE), has often been acknowledged but seldom spelled out in any detail. Of particular interest is the act's so-called Basket VII, focusing on "human rights and fundamental freedoms, including the freedom of thought, conscience, religion or belief"—something that obviously went against the grain for Soviet leaders of the 1970s (p. 6). This book makes extensive use of primary documents not brought to light before and remedies that problem with considerable aplomb. It provides a compelling account of the emergence and role of the CSCE that helps further our understanding of the end of the Cold War and improve knowledge about the place of human rights in the evolution of Europe's (loosely defined) security institutions.

With impressive detail, Sarah B. Snyder examines how—quite contrary to the expectations of Soviet leaders at the time—the Helsinki Final Act came to play a significant role in shaping East-West relations. In particular, it shows how the rise of transnational advocacy networks stemming from the act—actively supported by the U.S. government—supported human rights advocacy inside the Soviet Union by using the standards agreed to at Helsinki as a basis for ongoing monitoring and advocacy, both of which placed pressure on the Soviet regime. Most notably, this network gave rise to the Moscow Helsinki Group, comprising activists supporting various agendas united under the banner of implementing Helsinki. What follows is a classic tale of what constructivist theorists of transnational networks and norms call "normative entrapment": having accepted the Helsinki principles on the grounds that they contained some "baskets" that suited Soviet interests and in the belief that the human rights basket could not be implemented, Moscow found itself unable to repress local activists who demanded that the human rights dimensions be implemented without undermining its prior commitments. The fact that the Moscow Helsinki Group was tightly connected to similar groups throughout Europe and North America only heightened this sense of entrapment. The

work of these groups opened space for dialogue on human rights inside the Soviet Union and helped create an understanding that with economic reform must come political reforms, a view taken up by Mikhail Gorbachev. The rest, as they say, is history.

Written with skill and meticulously researched, this important book brings new evidence to bear on the issue by precisely charting how the transnational advocacy networks that sprung up in the wake of the Helsinki Final Act changed political discourse in the Soviet Union.

Alex J. Bellamy
Griffith Asia Institute
Nathan, Australia

doi: 10.1093/jahist/jas289

The Invention of Ecocide: Agent Orange, Vietnam, and the Scientists Who Changed the Way We Think about the Environment. By David Zierler. (Athens: University of Georgia Press, 2011. xiv, 245 pp. Cloth, $59.95. Paper, $24.95.)

Between 1961 and 1971, U.S. military aircraft sprayed approximately 20 million gallons of various chemical herbicides on the Vietnamese countryside as part of Operation Ranch Hand, a joint U.S.–South Vietnam mission. Covering an area of about 5 million acres (a region roughly the size of Massachusetts), this program sought to defoliate the lush indigenous greenery and make the jungle transparent to U.S. and South Vietnamese military forces. In addition, chemicals were also deployed to destroy the ability of "enemy" forces to cultivate various food crops such as rice. The most infamous of these herbicides was Agent Orange, a mixture of equal parts 2,4-D (2,4-dichlorophenoxyacetic acid) and 2,4,5-T (2,4,5-trichlorophenoxyacetic acid)—substances that initiate plant death through uncontrolled growth among specific species of broad leaf plants. Agent Orange is the subject of David Zierler's book *The Invention of Ecocide* on chemical weapons use in Vietnam.

This is less an environmental or scientific history of Agent Orange and more a diplomatic and national security history of how the Kennedy, Johnson, Nixon, and Ford administrations formulated policies for introducing, and then ultimately outlawing, military herbicides based on both the downward spiral of the

Vietnam War and plans by the Nixon administration to finally push for verification of the Geneva Protocol, a treaty prohibiting the first use of chemical and biological weapons. The author argues that herbicide usage in Vietnam originated with President John F. Kennedy's policy of flexible response, where counterinsurgency (and technological proficiency) would contain global communism without need for nuclear weapons or large-scale troop deployments. "The president's strategy was simple: deny guerrillas their only tactical advantage with chemicals, not infantry" (p. 2). Any limits on the program ended with Kennedy's assassination as 15 million gallons of defoliating chemicals were dispatched between 1966 and 1969.

The author is interested in placing these chemicals into a larger historical debate on the legality of weapons of mass destruction over the course of the last century while simultaneously detailing the stories of individual scientists who either helped create these chemicals, or those who—such as the Yale University plant biologist Arthur W. Galston—also later worked to banish them. Galston, who coined the term *ecocide* (an environmental analog to genocide) at a War Crimes and the American Conscious conference in 1970, is one of a number of scientists who challenged both the government and the military about the toxicity of these chemicals and the potential catastrophic environmental and public health threat. One of the book's strengths is the social and political history of the scientists. Biologists such as Galston and Matthew Messelson of Harvard University, among others, saw themselves as opposed to the war in general and herbicide use in particular but nevertheless positioned themselves apart from other protesters in academe to facilitate reaching useful and lasting political ends from an arms control standpoint. While perhaps too brief, this book is nonetheless a useful addition to the fledgling environmental warfare literature and illustrates that much work remains to be done regarding the interplay between bodies and the land during times of war.

Gerard J. Fitzgerald
George Mason University
Fairfax, Virginia

doi: 10.1093/jahist/jas292

DDT and the American Century: Global Health, Environmental Politics, and the Pesticide That Changed the World. By David Kinkela. (Chapel Hill: University of North Carolina Press, 2011. xvi, 256 pp. $39.95.)

A growing body of scholarship has begun exploring twentieth-century American foreign and domestic Cold War policies and chemical pesticides, a major tool used in the modernization efforts that composed part of those policies. In *DDT and the American Century,* David Kinkela examines one chemical pesticide, DDT, and its uses both internationally and in the United States within the agricultural and public health arenas.

Developed in 1939, DDT earned its discoverer, Paul Müller, the 1948 Nobel Prize in Physiology and Medicine for the pesticide's public health benefits. DDT proved to be an effective killer of mosquitoes, the major carriers of malaria, and agricultural pests that lowered crop production. Kinkela begins with the use of DDT in World War II to decrease malarial infections among American troops. He then examines DDT's uses in eradicating mosquitoes in Italy and increasing agricultural production in Mexico in the postwar period. In one of Kinkela's strongest chapters, he revisits the challenge to DDT presented by Rachel Carson's *Silent Spring* (1962) over growing concerns that the pesticide remained and accumulated in the ecosystem, harming birds and other wildlife. He retells the 1972 Environmental Protection Agency's decision to ban DDT by including the paradox of the chemical's continued domestic manufacture for international export and use. The book ends with a consideration of the ongoing controversies surrounding the use of DDT.

Kinkela argues that the domestic and international stories of DDT "were intertwined" (p. 10). Examining the pesticide's uses in the United States and globally allows a reconsideration of not only U.S. environmental policy but also the nation's Cold War concerns. In this respect, Kinkela does an excellent job of writing a transnational history of an important chemical pesticide. DDT became a signifier of modernization, scientific progress, and the conflict between the First World and developing nations. One problem with the work, however, directly relates to its proclaimed focus on DDT. Much of Kinkela's excellent discussions on the links between U.S. foreign and domestic Cold War policy include much more than just the use of DDT, or sometimes they need further supporting examples. For example, the agronomist Norman Borlaug's work in developing new strains of high-yield wheat played just as important a role in the "green revolution"—attempts to increase global agricultural crop production—as did DDT. While Kinkela notes that the new wheat seed depended on significant chemical pesticide and fertilizer support, DDT was just one of the many chemicals used (p. 79). Instead of claiming primacy for DDT, Kinkela could have broadened his study to chemicals more generally. What about the use of herbicide chemicals as defoliants in the Vietnam conflict? Despite this slight misdirection, the book makes a valuable contribution to international environmental and public health history and offers a fresh means of assessing the significance and controversy *Silent Spring* provoked, issues that continue to the present day.

Amy Hay
University of Texas–Pan American
Edinburg, Texas

doi: 10.1093/jahist/jas267

Genentech: The Beginnings of Biotech. By Sally Smith Hughes. (Chicago: University of Chicago Press, 2011. xvi, 213 pp. $25.00.)

This book exemplifies a new crossover genre in history: business history puffery written by historians of science. What might have seemed an awkward miscegenation is now poised to become popular idiom, given the transformation in science since the 1980s into a commercial endeavor. Of course, business histories devoid of any whiff of failure, confusion over goals, underhanded ploys, and misguided executives already occupy a hallowed place in the annals of academic publishing; the incongruity comes when applying that template to Genentech, the firm that opened the floodgates to the biotech model of upstream biomedical research. It seems more than a little odd to avoid most of the thorny questions

in the period from the initial founding to floatation of the initial public offering in the interests of producing an "intimate and people-centered history" (p. xi); that is, a sort of *People* magazine version of events, where a parade of protagonists are briskly described as "risk-taking" or having a "winner-take-all personality," while both the technical science and the business questions of commercial considerations transforming the practice of science are sidestepped or waved away.

I will indicate a small subset of the issues that should ideally be addressed in a serious scholarly history of Genentech but are absent here. First and foremost, Genentech is interesting because it was the first manifestation of what later became the biotech business model, but it has also been an unusual outlier: of the thousands of similar startups, only Genentech and Amgen have a track record of making money over a substantial period of freestanding existence. I should think this is a phenomenon of paramount importance, requiring explanation in any history of the firm. Yet the author seems relatively uninterested in the business side of things (perhaps because the biotech model depends so crucially upon attracting venture capital without having any actual product to sell). The second way that Genentech (at least before becoming absorbed into Hoffman–La Roche) stands out among the vast phalanx of biotech firms is that its success derived from harnessing easily manipulated organisms to mass-produce proteins or enzymes already in human therapeutic use; when attention shifted to new drugs, the biotech model failed and these companies began attempting to milk research tools for revenue instead, hobbling the entire research enterprise.

There are other elisions in *Genentech*. Sally Smith Hughes repeatedly mentions the political controversies surrounding genetic recombination in the 1970s but treats it all as a frivolous sideshow best ignored; but there were (and still are) reasonable qualms about unrestrained trans-species modification; and in any event, one important source of Genentech's success was a demonstrated willingness to evade or otherwise circumvent attempts to regulate research and intellectual property restrictions. For instance, its choice to synthesize DNA (deoxyribonucleic acid) rather than isolate it from natural organisms was dictated as much by intellectual property considerations as by science. In one case, Hughes admits that Genentech freely used research inputs from other labs without acknowledgement, while restricting distribution of its own research tools. Success came as the result of many dubious gambits, but the upbeat genre has no room to take them to heart.

Philip Mirowski
University of Notre Dame
Notre Dame, Indiana

doi: 10.1093/jahist/jas298

The Temp Economy: From Kelly Girls to Permatemps in Postwar America. By Erin Hatton. (Philadelphia: Temple University Press, 2011. xviii, 212 pp. Cloth, $68.50. Paper, $26.95.)

By the year 2000 the temporary help industry in the United States employed some 3 million workers, and an amazing 90 percent of companies supplemented their full-time staffs with temporary employees (p. 1). Erin Hatton tells the intriguing story of how this once-despised industry moved to the forefront of the twenty-first-century economy. Even more important, Hatton makes a compelling argument that the temp industry played a large role in changing how corporate management views labor. Whereas the "human relations" asset model maintained (or at least pretended to claim) that valuing workers and improving their well-being were essential to continued profitability, today's "liability model" sees labor as an evil that detracts from profits and should be minimized or eliminated wherever possible. *The Temp Economy* is a masterfully written account of how human actors, operating within the confines of the structural changes in late twentieth-century capitalism, propelled the temp industry upward by redefining downward society's obligations to workers. The book also describes recent glimmers of opposition, and Hatton concludes with thoughtful prescriptions for reversing the degradation of work.

When the modern temp industry took off in post–World War II America, it had to overcome the negative image and legacy of the private employment industry as well as potential opposition from the then-powerful labor movement. It did this, Hatton argues, by creating the "Kelly Girl": a sophisticated white middle-class housewife who wanted the "fulfillment" and a little extra spending money that part-time employment could bring but who would not be in competition with unionized "breadwinners." That the propagation of this new cultural icon ignored not only the realities of life for working-class women who took temp jobs because they needed the money but also the many men who also worked as temps, attests to the remarkable success of the temp industry's strategy.

After gaining cultural legitimacy by the late 1960s, the industry reshaped its image again to capture a larger share of the labor market, including those "breadwinner" jobs it had studiously avoided earlier. Hatton demonstrates that during this transformation the industry also campaigned to redefine the meaning of labor. No longer were employees the central asset of a company; instead, in a kind of zero-sum game, they stole from the bottom line. Companies were urged to slim down to a nucleus of permanent employees necessary to perform the organization's core mission and take on temporary workers as needed to handle extraneous functions and peak loads. Manpower, Inc. rode this new model to its place as the nation's largest employer by the early 1990s, and the temp industry paradoxically found a permanent position for itself in the global economy.

Though Hatton tells her sharply focused tale well, historians will wish she had enriched her account by digging deeper into the many historical precedents of the temporary help industry. Nonetheless, *The Temp Economy* will be essential reading for anyone wanting to understand the process that led to the degraded job prospects of today's economy.

Daniel Sidorick
College of New Jersey
Ewing, New Jersey

doi: 10.1093/jahist/jas170

Collision Course: Ronald Reagan, the Air Traffic Controllers, and the Strike That Changed America. By Joseph A. McCartin. (New York:

Oxford University Press, 2011. x, 472 pp. $29.95.)

As Joseph A. McCartin reminds his readers in this wonderfully good book, even Franklin D. Roosevelt believed the prospect of federal workers enjoying the right to strike "unthinkable and intolerable" (p. 31). No president has since attempted to persuade Congress to grant such a right. The U.S. Code prohibits federal employees from striking: "An individual may not accept or hold a position in the Government of the United States . . . if he . . . participates in a strike, or asserts the right to strike, against the Government of the United States" (Title 5, part III, subpart F, chap. 73, subchapter 2, sec. 7311). That prohibition provides a framework within which the politics of general federal employment practices have developed. It thereby forms a backdrop for McCartin's account of how specialist civil servants came to be replaced in sufficient numbers to effect the obliteration of their union.

In this admirable account of President Ronald Reagan's destruction of the Professional Air Traffic Controllers Organization (PATCO) in 1981–1982, McCartin shows not merely where that destruction fits into a long narrative of the decline of organized labor in the United States but also how tensions between controllers and the Federal Aviation Administration (FAA) might have been resolved differently. Had PATCO members calculated accurately the president's resources and resolve, they might have emerged with something the union's leaders could have plausibly presented as a victory. At the very least, they would have avoided complete defeat.

Popular memory of PATCO's failure recalls that President Reagan refused to negotiate. McCartin shows that to be false. Secretary of Transportation Drew Lewis negotiated a new contract with PATCO that would have dramatically improved controllers' working conditions. Jesse Calhoon, a shrewd labor leader, thought it "the best civil service contract ever negotiated" (p. 269). Having prepared carefully to break the anticipated strike, the FAA regarded the contract offer similarly and thought it disastrous; Donald Devine, the director of the Office of Personnel Management (OPM) feared that such a settlement would encourage other federal unions to seek comparable deals. Fortunately for the FAA and the OPM, however, PATCO members rejected the deal, struck, and were replaced by military and other staff. The president fired the strikers and kept them out. Scarcely any of the strikers worked for the FAA again.

On the foundation of admirable scholarship, McCartin draws two broader inferences. The first is of a president whose professional reputation in domestic policy owed much to his success in projecting himself in the PATCO case as indefatigable, having a clear purpose and sense of power, and possessed of a sure confidence in himself, his country, and his values. The second is, as McCartin puts it, that PATCO's strike catalyzed "the multiple problems that beset American unions" because of its damaging psychological effects on workers (p. 361). PATCO's destruction was public politics in the raw, and one whose course and effects union and company negotiators in private and government sectors have had good cause to remember.

Nigel Bowles
University of Oxford
Oxford, England

doi: 10.1093/jahist/jas262

The Reagan Rhetoric: History and Memory in 1980s America. By Toby Glenn Bates. (DeKalb: Northern Illinois University Press, 2011. xii, 240 pp. Paper, $32.00.)

While social scientists have undertaken important studies of the use of rhetoric in politics, historians are just beginning to explore this topic. Toby Glenn Bates, an assistant professor at Mississippi State University, offers a well-written, balanced examination of Ronald Reagan's use of rhetoric throughout his presidency.

Drawing upon the work of the French sociologist Maurice Halbwachs and the French historian Pierre Nora, pioneering scholars on history and memory, Bates looks at how Reagan's rhetoric about states' rights, the Vietnam War, the Soviet Union, and the Iran-Contra scandal often "blurred the boundary between history and memory" (p. 7). The ambiguity in public attitudes toward these controversial issues, Bates argues, allowed Reagan to present a more palatable version of history, which was accepted by many Americans. Bates admits that it is difficult to "draw a direct line between cause and effect," and therefore asks readers "to make a leap of faith," based on "solid scholarship" (p. 11). He relies on polling and popular books, movies, television programs, and comics to establish a link between Reagan's rhetoric on specific issues and that rhetoric's reflection in popular culture.

Bates's discussion of Reagan's Neshoba County Fair speech in 1980 defending states' rights breaks new ground. The Reagan campaign was divided on whether Reagan should accept the Neshoba invitation as his first major speech after winning the GOP presidential nomination. Campaign strategists understood that since 1899 the Neshoba County Fair in Philadelphia, Mississippi, was a major venue for politicians seeking to reach the thousands of people who came to the fair from across the country. Winning the South was critical for the GOP in 1980, but Reagan strategists also understood that the killing of three civil rights workers in the county in 1964 created dangerous pitfalls for their candidate. Thus, they were dismayed when Reagan broke from his prepared script by promising to "restore to state and local governments the powers that belonged properly to them" (p. 21). Bates notes that this had been a Republican mantra for years and nearly echoed word for word Barry Goldwater's *Conscience of a Conservative* (1960). Reagan rebounded after the initial fallout from the speech, and, in the end, Jimmy Carter was labeled meanspirited after he accused Reagan of creating racial divisions. Neshoba later proved bad for other Democrats as well. When the Democratic nominee Michael Dukakis spoke there in 1988 he refused to mention the three murdered civil rights workers, an absence quickly picked up by the media.

Equally valuable are chapters focusing on the Cold War, the Vietnam War, and the Iran-Contra scandal. Bates maintains that the strength of Reagan's rhetoric rested in his consistency, regardless of the topic he was addressing. The picture that emerges is one of Reagan tapping into popular sentiment of American patriotism, but Bates also argues that this use of patriotic language enabled Reagan to escape

responsibility for an administration willing to skirt the law, at the very least, in supporting the counterrevolutionary Contras in Nicaragua.

This is a valuable book, full of new research. Political scholars will find less coherence in the discussions of how comic books, television programs such as *The A-Team* (1982–1984), and movies such as *Rambo* (1982) and *Platoon* (1986) are relevant to Reagan's rhetoric, but these chapters make for fun reading.

Donald T. Critchlow
Arizona State University
Tempe, Arizona

doi: 10.1093/jahist/jas294

The Neoliberal Deluge: Hurricane Katrina, Late Capitalism, and the Remaking of New Orleans. Ed. by Cedric Johnson. (Minneapolis: University of Minnesota Press, 2011. 416 pp. Cloth, $75.00. Paper, $25.00.)

Even before the floodwaters abated in New Orleans in late 2005, commentators began to question characterizations of Hurricane Katrina's devastation as a natural disaster. Many scholars have explored the ways the historic flood was also a human-made catastrophe, focusing variously on inadequate government planning for evacuating and sheltering residents, long-term policy decisions that left the Crescent City's levees vulnerable, and the social geography of inequality that placed some at greater risk than others. Cedric Johnson's edited volume, *The Neoliberal Deluge,* comprising twelve essays mostly by sociologists, political scientists, and communication scholars, makes a sustained case that the disaster of Katrina is rooted in something more pervasive and fundamental: global neoliberal restructuring.

Johnson and his contributors understand neoliberalism as an anti-Keynesian ideology in which a state divests itself of social spending in favor of privatized, market-driven solutions. The authors claim that this paradigm, which emerged full-blown in the United States during the Ronald Reagan presidency, is more critical to understanding modern American society than is neoconservatism because the latter often presupposes that socially conservative and fiscally libertarian agendas drove political change. Thus, while *The Neoliberal Deluge* is a new interpretation of the 2005 disaster, it is chiefly a case study of how neoliberal society creates and manages crises.

The essays focus on preparation, evacuation, sheltering, rescue, relief, cleanup, and reconstruction. They detail how neoliberal stakeholders such as hoteliers, home builders, and private security and reconstruction contractors were beneficiaries of so-called disaster capitalism and how celebrity philanthropists (notably Brad Pitt) and grassroots volunteers served as unwitting handmaidens of the neoliberal agenda by playing into the argument that private responses were most appropriate. The book contends that the federal government conceptualized crises as lying largely outside the realm of legitimate political control and managed the image of crisis through control of mainstream media. It also examines the responsibility of neoliberalism for troubling developments in public housing and education, neighborhood reconstruction, and comprehensive urban planning. Finally, the volume questions the extent to which progressive responses to neoliberalism could take root after Katrina, particularly in light of the brief window of time when news media stepped outside the normal constraints of disaster reportage.

Johnson's collection will interest historians of Hurricane Katrina with its close problematizing of post-storm responses, ranging from a philanthropic live-work compound for relocated storm survivors to the nation's most extensive charter school experiment. Some of the responses receive their first serious treatment in this volume. *The Neoliberal Deluge* is not without shortcomings, however, at least for an audience of historians. True to its title, it tends to force all aspects of post-Katrina responses into the mold of neoliberalism, which ignores the fact that nongovernmental actions were always part of the equation, even when New Deal liberalism was at high tide. Readers may detect an overreliance on textual analysis that assigns too much value to semantics, as well as a devaluation of long-term historical patterns. Recent historians of the new conservatism, moreover, may view this collection as one-dimensional when placed alongside a growing historiography that explores the

highly contingent nature of modern conservative power in the United States. Although the volume presents neoliberalism as an ineluctable, almost seismic force in recent history, historians may well counter that a range of social, cultural, economic, and political factors have constrained any wholesale shift to market-driven politics. Nonetheless, *The Neoliberal Deluge* is an original and important addition to the growing body of scholarly work on the human-made disaster that accompanied the natural disaster of Katrina.

J. Mark Souther
Cleveland State University
Cleveland, Ohio

doi: 10.1093/jahist/jas297

How Racism Takes Place. By George Lipsitz. (Philadelphia: Temple University Press, 2011. viii, 310 pp. Cloth, $76.50. Paper, $26.95.)

Emerging in the 1990s, whiteness studies examines racial hierarchy and privilege and provides some of the most significant research on race. George Lipsitz's *The Possessive Investment in Whiteness* (1998) is one of the key works in this area of study, and *How Racism Takes Place* builds on that work and his research on urban culture. This book strengthens Lipsitz's position as one of the major contributors to theoretical and historical works on race.

As Lipsitz notes, racial conditions have improved, as indicated by the election of Barack Obama in 2008, but his book describes a common misunderstanding of race based on these changes. Lipsitz writes that according to this view, "Black people have shown themselves to be simply unfit for freedom" because "in a time when civil rights laws clearly ban discrimination, the persistence of racial inequality demonstrates that Blacks have been unable to take advantage of the opportunities afforded them" (p. 1).

In powerful and compelling writing, Lipsitz examines the problems with this belief and provides insights into the broad context and multiple factors that shape the ways race continues to work in society. In particular, he shows "how social relations take on their full force and meaning when they are enacted physically in actual places" (p. 5). One of the major issues of place and neighborhood is how residential segregation is established and supported, and Lipsitz explains how racialized practices are deeply embedded in established practices and institutions. Lipsitz emphasizes that societal inequalities do not diminish with time; rather, they have a cumulative impact, and in the case of the accumulation of wealth, for example, are passed on from generation to generation.

Against this backdrop, Lipsitz builds case studies including one on the use of public subsidies to build a football stadium in St. Louis, which diverts funds from the public education system that serves primarily low-income African Americans. The television show *The Wire* (2002–2008), he points out, offers an insightful look at police officers and drug dealers in Baltimore but naturalizes segregated neighborhoods and income inequality by saying little about how these conditions were created.

Lipsitz uses the term "white spatial imaginary" for the assumptions and practices that generate and legitimate racial disparities in society. He uses the term "Black spatial imaginary" to capture the "creative and generative dynamics" of the African American experience rooted in place and space (p. 18). The white spatial imaginary disregards racism, portrays African Americans as failing to take advantage of opportunities, and fails to acknowledge the intellectual and cultural contributions that have emerged from the black spatial imaginary. Whites are harmed by this, Lipsitz argues, because ideas and practices that could contribute to a more democratic and just society are ignored. Lipsitz examines sites of intellectual and cultural production in the second half of his book, including the World Stage Performance Gallery in Los Angeles, the Project Row Houses in Houston, the Chicago of the playwright Lorraine Hansberry, New Orleans, and the Gospel Music Workshop of America.

Leland Saito
University of Southern California
Los Angeles, California

doi: 10.1093/jahist/jas161

Alabama Getaway: The Political Imaginary and the Heart of Dixie. By Allen Tullos. (Athens: University of Georgia Press, 2011. xiv, 364 pp. Cloth, $69.95. Paper, $24.95.)

As the title of this book suggests, Alabama's political culture has never been marked by excessive introspection or a penchant for enlightened self-criticism. Long known for Prussian-style alliances between big business and big agriculture, to say nothing of hollow demagoguery reinforced by poor education and evangelical religion, Alabama leads the nation in little beyond football fanaticism and low taxation of real property. The state's white electorate appears largely content with a status quo summed up in the 1990s by Republican governor Guy Hunt who proclaimed, "Alabama is doing just fine" (p. 128).

In refuting the latter idea Allen Tullos joins a very small band of critics such as Clarence Cason in the 1930s and Wayne Flynt a half century later who have attempted to expose the state's shortcomings not only to outsiders but more importantly to local residents. An Alabamian by birth, Tullos has spent most of his life in liberal enclaves far from his native grounds. He brings to his subject a blend of familiarity and critical distance one might expect from a narrative written in exile.

Alabama Getaway resists easy categorization. Part Menckenesque journalism, part history, part acerbic social commentary, it veers between the catch phrases of the interdisciplinary seminar (for example, "the fundamental sociality of haunting" [p. 65]) and more conventional political analysis drawn primarily from newspapers and other published sources. The book's stated subject, Alabama's "political imaginary," is defined rather vaguely as an outlook derived from "words and deeds of public figures of speech; through rumor, jokes, statistics, journalistic ascriptions, blog entries, art, and music," all of which contribute to "debilitating habits of judgment and feeling" that mar the state's reputation and impede change (p. 5). This theme emerges most clearly in a chapter entitled "The Sezyou State," detailing the propensity of Alabama residents to ignore unwelcome facts and reject outside criticism with an automatic reflex of denial.

Although focused on Alabama, Tullos presents a catalog of civic malfeasance that will be familiar to any student of the modern South. Major items in the bill of indictment include the prison and legal system, retrograde leadership by a dismal procession of third-rate governors (many destined for incarceration after leaving office), inadequate health and social services, and a tax structure weighing heavily upon those least able to pay—including black residents of the old plantation belt recently labeled "Alabama's Third World" (p. 198).

Tullos is at his best when examining the failure of Alabamians—including Condoleezza Rice—to deal honestly with their own history. The past that many Alabamians embrace, bereft of guilt over slavery and repositioning Robert E. Lee and Martin Luther King Jr. as spiritual soul mates, resembles nothing so much as a willed descent into historical amnesia. Upon completing the book, readers may find their thoughts turning to W. H. Auden's poetic lines: "We would rather be ruined than changed / We would rather die in our dread / Than climb the cross of the moment / And let our illusions die" (*The Age of Anxiety*, 1948).

Clarence L. Mohr
University of South Alabama
Mobile, Alabama

doi: 10.1093/jahist/jas178

Native Acts: Law, Recognition, and Cultural Authenticity. By Joanne Barker. (Durham: Duke University Press, 2011. x, 284 pp. Cloth, $84.95. Paper, $23.95.)

In *Native Acts* Joanne Barker makes a compelling argument that native peoples are only "seen" and recognized as "authentic" within legal structures, racialized discourses, and social constructs that reinforce and reify national narratives and existing U.S. power structures to maintain dependent colonial relations with aboriginal nations. Using thought-provoking case studies, the work illuminates how natives navigate those parameters and explores how notions of the authentic influence relations within and between American Indian communities and tribal status groups (federal, state, and unrecognized). Barker is among a small group of forward-looking scholars who are just now laying bare how concepts and assumptions about native cultural authenticity force presently recognized tribes to reproduce the very social inequalities and injustices (racism, sexism, homophobia, religious bigotry, and competitive capitalism) that are hallmarks of past and ongoing native oppression. Throughout this stimulating collection Barker calls on native peoples to challenge these discourses, imploring them to undertake a decolonization project that will finally free aboriginal peoples from the binaries that tie sovereign rights to untenable notions of aboriginal primordiality.

Organized around the themes of law, recognition, culture, and tradition, the first section of the book explores the concept of *tribe* and the Federal Acknowledgment Process (FAP) that Barker argues, in Foucauldian fashion, disciplines native nations to conform to national narratives and hegemonic structures (embedded in federal Indian law) that reinforce colonial and ahistorical notions about aboriginal social and political organization. A chapter on the bitter conflict between the Delaware tribe and the larger Cherokee nation of Oklahoma that envelops it explores how the FAP provides an ideological field on which the legal and cultural rights of Indian peoples are played out and contested. Barker's chapter on the "Indian Member" makes a compelling case that discourses linking legal legitimacy and culture to tribal citizenship and authenticity simply reinforce notions that the unenrolled, nonrecognized, and/or disenrolled are not authentic in terms of identity, cultural knowledge, ties to community, and race. A chapter on the casino-fueled disenrollment trend in California unpacks the implications of allowing tribes the absolute power to determine citizenship with little recourse to an appeals process on constitutional grounds (also explored in a chapter on the 1978 case *Santa Clara Pueblo v. Martinez*). Readers see how tribal decisions are girded by sometimes-heartfelt, sometimes-disingenuous discussion about tradition and culture when they commonly hinge on nonaboriginal concepts that privilege dominant notions of race, patriarchy, heterosexuality, and capitalistic greed. A fascinating chapter on the recent Cherokee and Navajo laws that mirror the federal Defense of Marriage Act of 1996 follows these themes in all their messy, modern complexity.

While Barker offers no easy answers and largely declines to explore the real economic and political ramifications of questioning existing discourses and criteria used to recognize peoples and nations, she does challenge established tribes to refrain from claiming a tribal sovereignty and a cultural tradition that simply reifies and reinforces problematic ideologies of authenticity—notions that uphold traditions of sexism, conservatism, homophobia, and capitalistic exploitation. This is an important study that challenges prevailing ideas about native traditions and cultures and what is authentically native. It invokes a timely call to scholars, tribal leaders, and policy makers to rethink and examine critically how we use terminology and notions that may reinforce social injustice and inequalities inherited from the past.

Mark Edwin Miller
Southern Utah University
Cedar City, Utah

doi: 10.1093/jahist/jas325

Web Site Reviews

Kelly Schrum
Contributing Editor

The *Journal of American History,* in collaboration with the Web site *History Matters: The U.S. Survey Course on the Web,* http://www.historymatters.gmu.edu, publishes regular reviews of Web sites. The reviews appear both in the printed journal and at *History Matters. History Matters* provides an annotated guide to more than one thousand Web sites for teaching U.S. history. The goal is to offer a gateway to the best sites and to summarize their strengths and weaknesses with particular attention to their utility for teachers.

The Web site reviews are edited by Kelly Schrum; please contact her at kschrum@gmu.edu if you would like to suggest a site for review or write a review. We also welcome comments on our review guidelines, available at http://www.journalofamericanhistory.org/submit/websitereviews .html.

Feeding America: The Historic American Cookbook Project, http://digital.lib.msu.edu/projects/ cookbooks/. Created and maintained by the Michigan State University Library. Reviewed Jan.–March 2012.

In recent years historians have discovered that cookbooks can be rich documents that offer clues not only about what people cooked but also about markets, nutritional ideologies, class and race relations, regional and ethnic cultural differences, immigration, technological change, social movements, ecology, politics, and religion. *Feeding America: The Historic American Cookbook Project* is an excellent Web site for those seeking to incorporate these sources into their scholarship and teaching. Sponsored by the Michigan State University Library, this site provides access to a select group of seventy-six cookbooks chosen for their significance in representing key themes of American history. The site's mix of important primary documents and interpretation makes it useful for students, food-history enthusiasts, and scholars.

The collection includes classics such as Amelia Simmons's *American Cookery* (1798), considered America's first cookbook, and also unusual volumes such as the butcher Thomas

Farrington De Voe's *Market Assistant* (1867), which provides an incredible glimpse into New York City's nineteenth-century markets. Cookbooks by African American authors, cookbooks created by charities, and several volumes representing ethnic and religious communities are also featured.

An introductory essay by the veteran culinary historian and curator of American Culinary History at the neighboring University of Michigan's William L. Clements Library, Jan Longone, offers helpful background for understanding the historic role of cookbooks in American society and provides specific suggestions for how the volumes might be used in research. In addition, for each cookbook, the site provides a short introductory essay on the book's author, what makes it distinctive, and its historical context. There are also biographic essays for many authors.

Visitors can browse the entire collection by title, author, time period, and theme (such as social issues or ethnic influences), or they can search by author, title, ingredients, and recipes. The digital archive includes page images and searchable full-text transcriptions, which means that in each volume, scholars can look for specific words, or even expressions, in a manner that is far more efficient than paging through archival materials.

Visitors will also find a helpful glossary that explains archaic food terms—such as *frumenty* (boiled wheat) and *codlin* (apples)—and a photo exhibit of historical kitchen implements from the Michigan State University Museum that shows what old-fashioned gadgets, such as piggins (dippers) and spiders (legged pans), look like.

For all its strengths, *Feeding America* now feels a bit outdated. Shortcomings include a video with poor resolution, conspicuous typographical errors, broken links to external sources, and a limited keyword search capacity across the entire site. When first published, the site offered pioneering access to rare archival volumes that were otherwise difficult to view; but with the explosion of digitized books over the past five years, one can now find many of the same books via *Internet Archive* or *Google Books* with an easier read-and-search interface and higher-resolution scanning.

Nevertheless, the well-curated mix of primary documents and pertinent, proximate background materials on *Feeding America* makes it an excellent site well worth visiting and revisiting.

Ann Vileisis
Port Orford, Oregon

doi: 10.1093/jahist/jas319

Digitizing Civil War Soldiers' Diaries and Letters. Reviewed Aug. 2011–Jan. 2012.

Diaries and letters written by Civil War soldiers and digitized recently by modern scholars and "volunteers" interested in the Civil War are scattered rather profusely around the World Wide Web. The availability of these personal documents, and particularly their searchability, give Civil War historians the chance to study soldier's viewpoints and military questions with unprecedented efficiency. Simply entering "Civil War soldiers' diaries and letters" in a search engine, however, yields results that are rather inefficient to use, mixing locations of digitized and nondigitized documents and listing random sites that offer no online sources. Locating and compiling digitized diary and letter sites should be a more

efficient process, and this essay provides a list of sites that do it well. While I do not provide a complete list of digital sites, I do describe those with the most to offer as of January 2012.

I will begin with the most ambitious and impressive project aimed at providing access to digitized personal documents, *The American Civil War: Letters and Diaries* (http://solomon .cwld.alexanderstreet.com). This Web site is part of Alexander Street Press's larger *American Civil War Online* enterprise, which is "the most comprehensive series of electronic collections available for research" on the Civil War. They provide personal documents from 2,009 authors, amounting to over 100,000 pages of rekeyed material (including 4,000 facsimile pages of previously unpublished manuscripts). This remarkable database is the largest collection of digitized personal Civil War documents in existence, and it is growing. Sources were chosen from standard Civil War bibliographies, and the texts are linked to E. B. Long's *The Civil War Day by Day: An Almanac, 1861– 1865* (1985). The site's unique "semantic indexing" system, using PhiloLogic software, makes it possible to answer questions such as "What did Confederate enlisted men write about in the months prior to Gettysburg?" and "How do letters by officers describe morale in the first three months of the war? After two years?" This is a commercial enterprise, therefore access to documents is available only via subscription by individuals or institutions. This is what the digital revolution is all about.

The volunteer enterprise *Civil War Voices: Soldier Studies* (http://www.soldierstudies.org) depends on devotion alone for its sustenance. This is a dynamic site that offers a substantial menu of Civil War materials—letters, diary entries, databases, announcements, relevant news items, and interactivity. The "Life of a Soldier" section provides scholarly essays by Chandra M. Manning, Aaron Sheehan-Dean, and Michael Barton. The site's organizers, the high school history teacher Chris Wehner and the Civil War enthusiast Devin Watson, have asked the public to upload transcripts of soldiers' diaries and letters, hoping users too will have "altruistic intentions." Hoping to collect transcripts even from archives and universities, Wehner and ·Watson say their "goal is to create a central location for the largest (future) collection of Civil War letters and all in a searchable database that is open to the public." At this time they list over 1,300 pieces of correspondence from soldiers and 377 "soldier profiles." The documents are primarily letters, but there are also diaries.

The Valley of the Shadow (http://valley.lib .virginia.edu/VoS/lettersp2.html), the most honored Civil War Web site, produced by the University of Virginia, has uploaded almost everything printed that Edward L. Ayers and his associates could find relevant to Franklin County, Pennsylvania, and Augusta County, Virginia. This includes antebellum, Civil War, and postbellum letters and diaries. The helpful abstracts provided by the editors indicate that, for Franklin County during the war years, there are personal documents written by thirty-six Union letter writers and seven diarists; for Augusta County, there are documents by eighty-six Confederate letter writers and eight diarists. In several cases there are only one or two letters, and it should be noted that often these documents were written by soldiers who were not residents of either county but who were simply passing through. Even so, that is one of the virtues of this truly impressive project—the inclusion of these external sources shows the strength of the editors' ambition.

Valley of the Shadow is a model for all of us. It represents the apex of digital history's public service and professional practice. Through collaboration with the Electronic Text Center at the University of Virginia, all the letters and diaries have been coded in eXtensible Markup Language (XML), rendering them thoroughly searchable. Keywords have also been tagged, making searching even more efficient. The site has very clear and helpful instructions, which makes it an excellent resource for students. The editors assure us that each transcription "has been proofread by two separate individuals. The final version of a letter and diary lists a transcriber, tagger, and reviser." (Linked to the *Valley of the Shadow* project and also sponsored by the University of Virginia are the *American Civil War Collections* at the university's Electronic Text Center [http://etext.virginia.edu/civilwar/].)

While not on a par with the more extensive sites, the University of Iowa's *Civil War*

Diaries and Letters Digital Collection: Civil Diaries Transcription Project (http://digital.lib .uiowa.edu/cwd/transcripts.html) is a unique offering. It provides opportunities for "crowdsourcing"—meaning that the general public is able to transcribe personal documents online. So far, over 8,000 pages of diaries and letters have been transcribed. The site shows completely transcribed diaries and letters and those with transcriptions in progress. Bar graphs show how much of each diary has been transcribed, and the work is reviewed by library staff members. Clearly, the significance of this site is that it demonstrates how volunteers or students can play an increasing role in digital history. Also available at the University of Iowa Libraries is the *Iowa Digital Libraries* site (http://digital.lib.uiowa .edu/cdm4/browse.php?CISOROOT=/cwd), featuring 205 items, which are scans of the manuscripts of individual letters and entire Civil War diaries.

Another unique resource comes from the *Indiana Magazine of History. Voices from the Past: Civil Soldiers' Letters and Diaries* (http://www .iub.edu/~imaghist/online_content/vcsfrmpst/ voices_cvlwr/index.html), which makes freely available fifty-nine of the magazine's previously published articles consisting of the text of Civil War diaries and letters. It would be very helpful if all scholarly journals and popular magazines published by state agencies would make their Civil War editorial work available in this way.

For the sake of economy, I will spend the rest of the essay providing a briefly annotated list of other sites that provide more than a few digitized Civil War diaries and letters and a list of sites that provide links to other relevant informational sites. Most of the documents have been transcribed and are searchable on these sites, while others have chosen to simply scan the original manuscripts.

Web sites sponsored by colleges, universities, and official agencies include:

Documenting the American South (http:// docsouth.unc.edu) is the home page of the extensive online collections sponsored by the library of the University of North Carolina at Chapel Hill. The pertinent section is "First Person Narratives of the American South," with searchable Civil War diaries and letters. It features 377 titles on its list, although, aside from diaries and letters, there may also be books, articles, transcriptions, or manuscripts.

Civil War Letters, Diaries, Manuscripts (http://www.vmi.edu/archives.aspx?id=3945) is a Virginia Military Institute's Web site, containing the full text of over three dozen Civil War diaries, letters, and other personal papers.

The *Civil War Era Collection* (http://www .gettysburg.edu/library/gettdigital/civil_war/civil war.htm) is the site of Gettysburg College, with a link to forty-two letters.

While Penn State University's *Civil War Collection* site (http://www.libraries.psu.edu/psul/digital/civilwar.html) has only two lengthy personal documents, it summarizes the digital resources available there and at other Web sites in the state, including *The People's Contest: A Civil War Era Digital Archiving Project* (http://peoplescontest.psu.edu/), sponsored by Penn State University's Richards Center. A handful of other Pennsylvanians' diaries and letters can be found at *Pennsylvania Volunteers of the Civil War* (http://www.pacivilwar.com/histories.html), a site for genealogists.

The *eHistory Archive* (http://ehistory.osu.edu/uscw/library/letters/index.cfm) at Ohio State University is home to twelve Civil War diaries, letter collections, and memoirs.

The *Digital Civil War Portal* (http://american-south.org/collections/) is a collection of varied digital primary source materials at Auburn University, Duke University, the University of Georgia, Tulane University, Louisiana State University, Emory University, and other institutions in the Association of Southeastern Research Libraries. It currently links to 9,226 items at twenty-seven libraries.

The *Vermont Historical Society* Web site (http://vermonthistory.org/index.php/library/research-resources-online/civil-war-transcripti ons.html) provides access to the scans and transcriptions of Civil War letters in the collections of the Vermont Historical Society and the libraries of the University of Vermont.

Wisconsin Goes to War: Our Civil War Experience (http://uwdc.library.wisc.edu/collections/WI/WIWar) offers various materials. Some personal documents are transcribed, some are scanned manuscripts, and much of the original material is located at the Wisconsin Historical

Society. The first phase of the collection comprises 630 pages and the organizers expect to have 2,600 pages by the conclusion of the project. There are forty-two diaries that will total nearly 2,000 handwritten pages.

American Civil War Digital Collections: Letters and Diaries (http://fletcher.lib.udel.edu/collections/cwc/index.html) is a small University of Delaware project.

American Civil War Manuscript Guides (http://spec.lib.vt.edu/civwar/) is maintained by the Special Collections section of the Virginia Technical Institute Library. Digitized personal documents can be found here, but each collection must be checked.

The "Civil War" section of the *Digital Library of Georgia* site (http://dlg.galileo.usg.edu/TimePeriods/CivilWar.html) contains a few transcriptions of soldiers' personal documents. *GeorgiaInfo: Civil War Letters and Diaries* (http://georgiainfo.galileo.usg.edu/cwletters.htm) also contains about twelve digital sources.

Web sites maintained by volunteers include:

The "Letters and Diaries" link of *The Civil War Home Page* (http://www.civil-war.net/searchlinks.asp?searchlinks=Letters%20and%20Diaries), does not hold documents but is a directory to fifty-six other sites containing Civil War personal documents—including soldiers' letters and diaries, women's journals, and family correspondence. This site sometimes has broken links.

The *Civil War Archive* (http://www.civilwararchive.com/LETTERS/letters.htm) contains soldiers' letters and diaries "that have not been edited by [the site organizer] in any way." Some of its 218 letters by thirty-nine men are available on the site and others are linked to external sites. The archive also contains seven diaries.

A Web site called simply *American Civil War* (http://www.factasy.com/civil_war/letters_and_diaries.shtml) says it will "remain free and open to the public" and asks users to upload letter or diary transcriptions. So far there are few contributions.

The digital world of online letters and diaries is evolving daily. The sesquicentennial of the Civil War appears to have stimulated the digitization of personal documents, and we can expect this development to continue, especially as online education in general expands. The possibilities for computerized content analysis are thoroughly improved by these emerging online digital archives. At this point it is only possible to estimate the approximate number of scans and transcriptions that may be online and the approximate number of men who wrote them. I would guess that we currently have access to the digitized letters and diaries of about 3,000 Civil War soldiers. That is an impressive—even amazing— beginning.

Michael Barton
Penn State Harrisburg
Middletown, Pennsylvania

doi: 10.1093/jahist/jas318

Prairie Settlement: Nebraska Photographs and Family Letters, 1862–1912, http://memory.loc.gov/ammem/award98/nbhihtml. Created by the Nebraska State Historical Society. Maintained by the Library of Congress. Reviewed Jan.–July 2011.

Scholars of the nineteenth-century American West have long known and appreciated the photographs of Solomon D. Butcher; his images of homesteaders on central Nebraska's plains make visible the hardships and aspirations of families such as those in Willa Cather's novels. Butcher published two books during his lifetime (*Pioneer History of Cusker County and Short Sketches of Early Days in Nebraska* [1901] and *Sod Houses, or, the Development of the Great American Plains: A Pictorial History of the Men and Means That Have Developed This Country* [1904]), but he amassed a much larger archive of images that was eventually acquired by the Nebraska State Historical Society. Those images—more than three thousand taken between 1886 and 1912—were annotated by Butcher and form the core of this archive.

Prairie Settlement integrates the digitized Butcher photographs with the extensive correspondence of the Oblinger family, whose patriarch, Uriah, left Indiana in the 1860s and settled in Nebraska in 1872. Over the course of 318 letters, Oblinger looks for land, marries, has children, loses his wife in childbirth, makes and loses a homestead claim, remarries, fathers additional children, and tries to support his six daughters through the vicissitudes of grasshoppers, economic depressions, ill health, and bad luck. The Oblinger correspondence—including letters from Uriah, his wives, offspring, and assorted in-laws—begins in 1862 and is concentrated in the remaining decades of the nineteenth century, with the last letter dated from 1911. Letters and envelopes from the Oblinger family papers have been digitized, transcribed, indexed, and combined with the Butcher photographs to "illustrate the story of settlement on the Great Plains."

Both collections are rich resources in their own right and can be mined for insights that extend beyond the rubric of "settlement." While Butcher's images concentrate on the now-iconic depictions of households (along with their animals and possessions) proudly arrayed in front of their sod homes, his photographs also show other less familiar subjects, including cowboys playing poker, the Nebraska Industrial Arts Building, and unusual landscape formations. On the Web site, Butcher's images—both swiftly loading thumbnails and larger reference photos—are fully cataloged and indexed by subject, though not as comprehensively as a material culture historian might hope. The Oblinger letters, at their best, reveal the daily challenges, celebrations, and concerns faced by those families whom Butcher depicts only at a single instant. The combination of the two collections in the *Prairie Settlement* site results from a 1990s Library of Congress initiative to support the digitization of nationally important primary resources from other institutions. Scholars and teachers can now benefit from the availability and searchability of Butcher's photographs and, with slightly more effort, can supplement them with salient quotations from the Oblinger saga.

This is, however, very much a first-generation digital project. Researchers accustomed to the functionality of more recent and sophisticated textual search tools will be chagrined to find that the Oblinger letters are indexed only to document level. Searching for "women suffrage," for example, will take the user only to a long letter rather than to the relevant

This photograph, "A. Fonda sod house, Ontario, Custer County, Nebraska," taken by Solomon D. Butcher in 1903, is one of more than three thousand Butcher images available on the Web site *Prairie Settlement: Nebraska Photographs and Family Letters, 1862–1912. Courtesy Nebraska State Historical Society,* NBHIPS *11971.*

passage within it. Looking for "furniture" in the Butcher photographs produces only one reference, although many other images contain household objects. The site could have benefitted from Nebraska maps to help users place the various locations mentioned in the letters and depicted in the photographs. In particular, the decision to honor the spacing and punctuation idiosyncrasies of the Oblinger letter writers (though silently correcting some spelling) means that these transcriptions can be daunting to read, particularly for students. While scholars will appreciate the careful editorial notes provided by the historical society staff members who digitized both collections, they may also lament the project's relatively crude navigational tools. Users of this archive will rely heavily on the site's "back" buttons to access material. Patience in the pursuit of information can be richly rewarded, however. Perusing the letter that referred to woman's suffrage yielded the

following, in a letter from Giles Thomas, dated September 24, 1882:

> Well yes—we had the pleasure of hearin Miss Susan B. Anthony deliver a discourse on woman Suf *{Begin deleted text}* a *{End deleted text}* rage on last day of fair There is quite an excitement in our State on the question of Woman Sufrage at the present time—the question will be brought before the people this fall to decide by vote whether woman shall have the privalage to cast their vote. So far as I am concerened I want my <u>wife</u> to have the same privalage I have in all <u>respects</u>.

Frustrations and pleasures await the patient user of *Prairie Settlement.*.

C. Elizabeth Raymond
University of Nevada, Reno
Reno, Nevada

doi: 10.1093/jahist/jas237

Editor's Annual Report, 2011–2012

Colleagues occasionally ask me what has been the biggest surprise in the almost seven years that I have served as editor of the *Journal of American History*. The honest answer is that there have been many surprises. If I had to pick one, it is that I did not expect that the book review section would be, year in and year out, the most sensitive part of the *Journal*. In retrospect, that this was such a surprise reveals both my naïveté about the complexities of journal editorship and the necessity of a superb staff to be in constant conversation with a new editor. (And any editor would be well advised to make such conversation an enduring habit.)

Issues with book reviews did not take long to surface. We receive more than three thousand books a year, we can review approximately six hundred, and we can list approximately 1,500. So when a colleagues asks why her or his book was listed but not reviewed—or worse, not mentioned at all—we must be satisfied that our criteria is clear, fair, and open to thoughtful revision. Discussions about particular books often lead to more expansive deliberations about if and when we should push the envelope. For example, should we review more popular history? Always guiding our conversation is the conviction that whatever we decide should best benefit the readership of the *JAH*.

There are other difficult issues. Book authors sometimes cannot understand why we selected a certain person to review their book. They assume we are aware, for example, that there is an unfortunate personal or professional history between them. Or we can be unaware that we chose a reviewer who is in the midst of larger battles in a particular subdiscipline that involve the book under examination. Our database of more than eleven thousand potential reviewers offers a wealth of information to help us make an appropriate match between reviewer and book, but it is impossible for us to be aware of the entanglements that might inappropriately influence a review. A favorite story of mine is that several years ago an angry author asked why we did not know that his book had been reviewed by a person with whom he had engaged in a vigorous disagreement at a conference hotel. "We did not know about it," I replied, "because keeping such track of all interactions between authors and reviewers would require a slightly larger staff!" In our invitation to potential reviewers, we do ask them to inform us if it would not be appropriate for them to take on a review. We are always heartened when colleagues are open with us about any possibly sensitive situations. It enriches the integrity of both the review process and resulting work.

Some of the most difficult issues arise, thankfully, only once in a great while. A reviewer will, for example, offer a piece of writing that is not a disciplined, critical assessment of a book but instead engages in personal attack or uses the occasion to fight larger battles in which the book under review becomes tangential. I always attempt to work with reviewers in what can be a quite charged environment, with the hope that a review appropriate for the *JAH* will emerge. Only once or twice in my tenure have I decided not to publish a review—a momentous decision in my view because we firmly believe in the independence of the reviewer's voice. These are, after all, "signed" reviews, so the reviewer owns what she or he wrote. Nevertheless, I do believe that on rare occasions it is my responsibility as editor to judge whether a particular review belongs in the pages of the *JAH,* and of course, it is my responsibility to offer reasons for a decision against publication.

We are delighted that Joel M. Sipress and David J. Voelker's March 2011 article, "The End of the History Survey Course: The Rise and Fall of the Coverage Model," received the 2012 Maryellen Weimer Scholarly Work on Teaching and Learning Award, sponsored by Magna Publications. This article was part of the "Textbooks and Teaching" section, edited by Scott E. Casper.

After several years of evaluating various policies regarding research misconduct in history journals, the OAH Executive Board unanimously passed procedures for addressing allegations of misconduct in OAH publications. Readers can examine the policy online at http://oah.org/about/papers/policies/.

Occasionally I am asked whether or not a manuscript written by a graduate student could be accepted for publication in the *JAH* (apart from the winner of the Louis Pelzer Memorial Award). My response to such queries has always been that we have a blind peer review process and a manuscript stands or falls on its merits rather than on the status of the author. Since I assumed responsibilities as editor, there have been only two manuscripts that have been offered a "conditional accept" after the first round of reader reports. One of these, accepted in 2011, was by a graduate student and appears in this issue. (I hope colleagues reading this will pass that interesting news on to your mentees.)

While every year brings changes in the staff of the OAH Publications Office, this past summer we bade farewell to a number of colleagues who have served the organization (and the *Journal* specifically) with distinction. Deneise Hueston, who for almost eleven years has worked as an administrative assistant, left to pursue other opportunities. Deneise was at the nerve center of the office, overseeing the book review and manuscript evaluation processes, keeping the schedule of special issues on track, and taking on so many other responsibilities. This past year, we were all saddened when Deneise lost her husband, and we

greatly admired her grace and courage during those difficult days. I—we—will miss her immensely. We are fortunate that Thomas Frick will continue his fine work in the front office. Also leaving is Carl Weinberg, who for four years has done a superb job as the editor of the *OAH Magazine of History.* Carl will remain at Indiana University, having accepted a position as a senior scholar in the College of Arts and Sciences and an adjunct professor in the School of Public and Environmental Affairs. Also leaving us to complete work on their dissertations are three exceptional graduate students: Eric Petenbrink, Sarah Rowley, and Angel Flores-Rodriguez. Last fall we welcomed Drew Clark, and in July 2012 Paula Tarankow also joined us—both as new editorial assistants.

Our contributing editors are crucial to the work of the *JAH,* and we are very thankful for having had the opportunity to work for more than five years with one of our contributing editors for exhibition reviews, Benjamin Filene, and our contributing editor for Web site reviews, Kelly Schrum. We welcome Jeff McClurken, who will assume responsibility for Web site reviews, and Kathleen Franz, who will serve as a co-contributing editor for exhibition reviews.

Each year four members of the editorial board complete their term and we welcome new colleagues to the board. This year Ann Fabian, Kristin Hoganson, Karen Leong, and Jonathan Schoenwald left the board; we thank them all for service that went above and beyond our expectations. We welcome to the board Benjamin Irvin, Melani McAlister, Matthew Mason, and Mae Ngai, and look forward to working with all of them over the next three years. We also thank John Belohlavek for the enthusiasm with which he embraced his work as a member of the Louis Pelzer Memorial Award Committee, and we welcome Susan Brewer to the committee.

We always enjoy hearing from our colleagues. Please feel free to contact us at jah@oah.org or, if you wish to contact me directly, at etl@indiana.edu or by telephone at 812-855-0335.

Many colleagues have offered their services in various ways to the *JAH.* They are crucial to the life of the *Journal.* Our deepest thanks to Philip Abbott, W. Andrew Achenbaum, Rodolfo F. Acuña, Leslie M. Alexander, Omar H. Ali, Paul Alkebulan, David Allyn, Edward Alwood, Michael A. Amundson, Kevin R. Anderson, Irvine H. Anderson, Frank Annunziata, Thomas H. Appleton, Stephen Aron, Chris Myers Asch, Susan Youngblood Ashmore, Thomas Augst, Bryan Bademan, David A. Badillo, Bruce E. Baker, Jean H. Baker, Davarian L. Baldwin, Michael B. Ballard, Helen M. Bannan, Charles Pete Banner-Haley, Edward E. Baptist, Elliott R. Barkan, L. Diane Barnes, William L. Barney, Dale Baum, John F. Bauman, Robert Bauman, Maurine H. Beasley, Michal R. Belknap, Louise Benjamin, James M. Bergquist, Edward D. Berkowitz, Iver Bernstein, Michael A. Bernstein, Amos J. Beyan, Jason C. Bivins, Brian C. Black, David Blanke, Mary H. Blewett, Ethan Blue, Daniel Bluestone, Stuart Blumin, David J. Bodenhamer, Howard Bodenhorn, John Bodnar, Michael D. Bowen, J. D. Bowers, Nigel Bowles, Anne M. Boylan, Richard Breitman, Jennifer Brier, Evan Brier, Mark Brilliant, Alessandro Brogi, Jeffrey P. Brown, Emmett H. Buell, Rachel Buff, Paul Buhle, Adrian Burgos, Richard Lyman Bushman, Robert Bussel, Jon Butler, Richard Butsch, Gerald R. Butters, James P. Byrd, Albert Camarillo, Ballard Campbell, Jacqueline Glass Campbell, Malcolm Campbell, Gregg Cantrell, Christopher Capozzola, Peter S. Carmichael, Richard Griswold del Castillo, Adrienne Caughfield, R. McGreggor Cawley, Derek Chang, Ernesto Chávez, Guy Chet, Catherine Ceniza Choy, Albert Churella, J. C. D. Clark, Claude A. Clegg, Christina Cogdell, Francis D. Cogliano, Daniel A. Cohen, Patricia Cline Cohen, Bradley Lynn Coleman, Michael C. Coleman, Sahr Conway-Lanz, Robert J. Cook, Nancy F. Cott, Thomas R. Cox, Robert H. Craig, Conrad C. Crane, Robert P. Crease, Joseph Crespino, Donald T. Critchlow, Matthew H. Crocker, Nick Cullather, Bruce Cumings, Carson Cunningham, K. A. Cuordileone, Kirk Curnutt, Michael Kent Curtis, Elizabeth Dale, Mariana L. R. Dantas, Richard O. Davies, Carole Boyce Davies, Gareth Davies, Donald G. Davis, Jack E. Davis, Sue Davis, Thomas J. Davis, Joseph G. Dawson, Kenneth De

Ville, Jennifer Delton, Michael Dennis, Andrew J. Diamond, Bruce J. Dierenfield, Hasia R. Diner, Brian R. Dirck, Thomas Doherty, Gregory Michael Dorr, Lisa Lindquist Dorr, Lynne Pierson Doti, W. Marvin Dulaney, Erica Armstrong Dunbar, Wayne K. Durrill, Eileen M. Eagan, Ronald Edsforth, Douglas R. Egerton, John Ehrman, Eldon J. Eisenach, George B. Ellenberg, Jeffrey A. Engel, John Ernest, Judith Ewell, Robert B. Fairbanks, Adam Fairclough, Patricia J. Fanning, David Farber, Marjorie N. Feld, Glenn Feldman, Michael Fellman, Karen Ferguson, Rosemary Feurer, Gayle V. Fischer, Maureen A. Flanagan, J. Brooks Flippen, Juan M. Floyd-Thomas, Richard Follett, Nancy Foner, Elizabeth Fones-Wolf, Miriam Forman-Brunell, Clyde R. Forsberg, Helen Bradley Foster, Thomas A. Foster, Kathleen Franz, James W. Fraser, Jeff Frederick, William W. Freehling, Susan K. Freeman, Barbara G. Friedman, Gunlög Fur, Vincent Gaddis, Beverly Frances Gage, William Galush, Margaret Garb, Mario T. García, Richard A. Garcia, Robert Genter, Louis S. Gerteis, James N. Giglio, Paul A. Gilje, Joyce S. Goldberg, Douglas Gomery, Sarah Barringer Gordon, Eliga H. Gould, Michael Johnston Grant, Susan-Mary Grant, Brian Gratton, Marilyn Greenwald, Patricia Grimshaw, Ariela Gross, Allen C. Guelzo, Joan R. Gundersen, Melanie Gustafson, Sandra Marie Gustafson, Paul C. Gutjahr, Andrew Gyory, Cindy Hahamovitch, Gwendolyn Midlo Hall, Stephen Gilroy Hall, David E. Hamilton, Barry Hankins, Anthony Harkins, Sidney L. Harring, John Mason Hart, Benjamin L. Hartley, Joseph M. Hawes, M. J. Heale, David S. Heidler, David Henry, Allison L. Hepler, Robert E. Herzstein, Earl J. Hess, Rodney Hessinger, Steven High, Robert C. Hilderbrand, Rebecca N. Hill, Hugh D. Hindman, David Hochfelder, Martha Hodes, Adam J. Hodges, Joan Hoff, Beatrix Hoffman, Wesley Hogan, E. Brooks Holifield, Michael W. Homel, Daniel Horowitz, Madeline Y. Hsu, Timothy S. Huebner, James L. Hunt, Karen M. Inouye, Kenneth R. Janken, Edward P. Johanningsmeier, Kevin R. Johnson, Kenneth S. Jolly, Howard Jones, Eric S. Juhnke, Benjamin James Justice, Theresa Kaminski, Craig A. Kaplowitz, Michael

B. Katz, Wendy Jean Katz, Jennifer D. Keene, Lisa Keller, Ari Kelman, Kathleen Kennedy, Kevin Kenny, Robert C. Kenzer, Cynthia A. Kierner, Daniel Kilbride, John Kirby, John A. Kirk, James E. Klein, Maury Klein, S. J. Kleinberg, Daniel Klinghard, Rebecca M. Kluchin, Anne Meis Knupfer, Felicia Ann Kornbluh, Joseph Kip Kosek, John D. Krugler, Douglas E. Kupel, Judy Kutulas, Louis M. Kyriakoudes, David E. Kyvig, Edward J. Larson, John Carol Lasser, Peter F. Lau, Robert G. Lee, Christopher P. Lehman, Daniel Levine, Elana Levine, Alex Lichtenstein, Nelson Lichtenstein, Michael Lienesch, Huping Ling, Ann M. Little, Larry M. Logue, Kelly Ann Long, Ronald Lora, Linda J. Lumsden, Jean Marie Lutes, Shane J. Maddock, William J. Mahar, Gloria L. Main, John Majewski, Nancy Weiss Malkiel, Kimberley Mangun, David Peterson del Mar, Margaret Marsh, Louis P. Masur, Cathy Matson, Tim Matthewson, Kevin Mattson, Randy D. McBee, Russell McClintock, Jeffrey W. McClurken, Mary McCune, Lawrence T. McDonnell, John T. McGrath, Danielle L. McGuire, Guian A. McKee, Gordon McKinney, Brian D. McKnight, James M. McPherson, Kim McQuaid, Jeffrey Melnick, Karen R. Merrill, Jimmy Wilkinson Meyer, Joanne Meyerowitz, Gregg L. Michel, Laura L. Mielke, Mark Edwin Miller, Randall M. Miller, Steven P. Miller, Worth Robert Miller, Steven Mintz, Philip Mirowski, Mary Niall Mitchell, Douglas Monroy, Chad Montrie, Anthony P. Mora, Iwan Morgan, Andrew J. F. Morris, Diane Batts Morrow, Kevin P. Murphy, Celia E. Naylor, Scott Reynolds Nelson, Harvey R. Neptune, Charles E. Neu, Joseph Nevins, Richard S. Newman, Mae Ngai, Christopher McKnight Nichols, David P. Nord, Robert J. Norrell, David J. Norton, Walter T. Nugent, Peter Onuf, Kenneth O'Reilly, Liesl Miller Orenic, Cynthia E. Orozco, Stephen R. Ortiz, Robert B. Outland, Eduardo Obregón Pagán, Phillip Papas, Damian Alan Pargas, Alison M. Parker, Katherine J. Parkin, Susan Scott Parrish, Elaine Frantz Parsons, Thomas R. Pegram, Richard H. Pells, Burton W. Peretti, Michael J. Pfeifer, L. Scott Philyaw, G. Kurt Piehler, Lynne Pierson Doti, Rebecca Jo Plant, Brenda Gayle Plummer, Richard Polenberg, William Scott Poole, Charles Postel, L. A. Scot Powe, Lawrence N. Powell, Walter F. Pratt, Jean Preer, Polly J. Price, Tyler Priest, Lisa Joy Pruitt, Laura Pulido, Stephen G. Rabe, George C. Rable, Gail Radford, Leigh Raiford, Edgar F. Raines, Jennifer Ratner-Rosenhagen, Kristofer Ray, John Louis Recchiuti, Kent Redding, Christopher Robert Reed, William J. Reese, W. Paul Reeve, Joseph P. Reidy, Akim D. Reinhardt, Matthias Reiss, Andrés Reséndez, Miriam Reumann, Chip Rhodes, Jennifer Ritterhouse, Randy Roberts, David M. Robinson, Greg Robinson, Naomi Rogers, Renee Romano, Robyn L. Rosen, David Rosner, Doug Rossinow, Joshua D. Rothman, Lori Rotskoff, Wendy Rouse, Kevin Conley Ruffner, Susan Sessions Rugh, Wanda Rushing, Peter M. Rutkoff, Robert W. Rydell, Jeffrey C. Sanders, Martha A. Sandweiss, Jonathan D. Sarna, Jennifer Scanlon, Axel R. Schäfer, Michael Schaller, David F. Schmitz, A. Gregory Schneider, Dorothee Schneider, Gregory L. Schneider, Ellen Schrecker, Kelly Schrum, Stephen A. Schuker, Leslie Schwalm, Thomas Alan Schwartz, Marlis Schweitzer, Loren Schweninger, Randolph Ferguson Scully, Micol Seigel, Robert M. Senkewicz, Jay Sexton, Timothy J. Shannon, Aaron Sheehan-Dean, Connie A. Shemo, Gordon Shepherd, Edward Shorter, Daniel Sidorick, Danielle Brune Sigler, Joel H. Silbey, Matthew Silver, Lyde Cullen Sizer, Nico Slate, Kevin Smant, Jason Scott Smith, John David Smith, Jon Smith, Sherry L. Smith, Susan L. Smith, Itai Nartzizenfield Sneh, Rickie Solinger, J. Mark Souther, Daniel Soyer, Randy J. Sparks, Paul J. Springer, Michael Stamm, Cathy Stanton, Lisa M. Steinman, Bonnie Stepenoff, John J. Stephan, Lester D. Stephens, Jason W. Stevens, James B. Stewart, Joseph A. Stout, David W. Stowe, Steven M. Stowe, Joe Street, David Stricklin, Mary E. Stuckey, Ned Stuckey-French, Yoneyuki Sugita, Eileen H. Tamura, Paul E. Teed, Richard F. Teichgraeber, Jesus de la Teja, Karen Kruse Thomas, Tracy A. Thomas, Dina Titus, Michael M. Topp, E. Fuller Torrey, Craig D. Townsend, Eckard Toy, Samuel Truett, John G. Turner, Steven W. Usselman, William E. Van Vugt, Barry A. Vann, Stephen Vaughn, Diane C. Vecchio, Kevern

J. Verney, J. Samuel Walker, Ronald W. Walker, Bryan Waterman, Clive Webb, Robert E. Weems, David F. Weiman, W. Michael Weis, Wyatt C. Wells, Beth S. Wenger, Thomas S. Wermuth, Laura M. Westhoff, Jeannie M. Whayne, Ashli White, T. Stephen Whitman, Vernon J. Williams, John Wills, Julie Winch, Michael P. Winship, Cary D. Wintz, David B. Wolcott, Raymond Wolters, Komozi Woodard, Christine Woyshner, John S. Wright, Ellen D. Wu, Judy Tzu-Chun Wu, Elliott Young, Natasha Zaretsky, Thomas W. Zeiler, Kyle F. Zelner, and Xiaojian Zhao.

Edward T. Linenthal
June 2012

doi: 10.1093/jahist/jas327

Letters to the Editor

To the Editor:

The fact that a reviewer may not agree with the arguments advanced by the book under review does not absolve that reviewer from the responsibility of describing the arguments the author *does* make. In his review of Manning Marable's *Malcolm X: A Life of Reinvention* (*JAH*, March 2012, pp. 1134–36), however, Komozi Woodard makes it plain that he thinks Marable ought to have written an entirely different book, and he spends most of his review discussing that hypothetical book rather than the one Marable actually wrote. Marable's interpretation of Malcolm X may have disappointed him, but Woodard ought at least to have summarized the key points of that interpretation. But Woodard's review tells us virtually nothing about Marable's book, and that is a great pity, especially in view of the many years of prodigious scholarship that went into *Malcolm X*.

Adam Fairclough
Leiden University
Leiden, Netherlands

To the Editor:

Malcolm X insisted that if black America was to be free, then self-transformation was the first step to liberation. Sadly, by neglecting the dynamics of racial oppression in the Jim Crow North, Manning Marable missed the fundamental force propelling the radicalization of Malcolm X. As Malcolm X traveled extensively, he made thoughtful comparisons, concluding that racial oppression and economic exploitation were not local problems in the ghettos of Harlem, Newark, Philadelphia, Boston, Detroit, Chicago, or Watts, but rather were systemic and international for oppressed peoples, parallel to those of colonial subjects in Africa, Asia, and Latin America. For Malcolm X, Cold War liberalism acted as the Novocain that not only kept black America from awakening and concentrating its fire on racial oppression in the funky streets of Harlem and Watts but also drugged it with theories of cultural poverty to keep African Americans asleep to their distinct genius and their powerful resources for self-emancipation and black renaissance.

The intellectual neglect of the ravages of racial oppression and economic exploitation, from the Jim Crow North to the Jim Crow West, took a heavy toll on civil rights history. For instance, scholars have missed the important freedom rides in the North aimed at segregated roadways between Boston and Washington, D.C. Wielding his poetic insight and brilliant oratory, Malcolm X and his political agitation were indispensable in the black awakening in the Jim Crow North. And the story of Malcolm's awakening is essential to grasping the radicalization of his thinking about black liberation. At the time black youth seized his message and organized the black student movement, black arts renaissance, and black power politics. For more on this subject, see the forthcoming article in the journal *Biography*, "Malcolm X: Black Women Radicals and Black Self-Determination," by Erik S. McDuffie and Komozi Woodard.

Komozi Woodard
Sarah Lawrence College
Bronxville, New York

doi: 10.1093/jahist/jas230

To the Editor:

Readers of the *Journal of American History* rightly expect its book reviewers to take the time to read carefully and thoroughly the works they have agreed to assess. Alas, such is not always the case.

John Darrell Sherwood, in his review of my book *Black Yanks in the Pacific: Race in the Making of American Military Empire after World War II* (*JAH*, Dec. 2011, pp. 873–74), devotes a substantial amount of his allotted space to allegations that I neglected to consult various sources. In particular, he asserts that my book "never references" *Black Soldier, White Army: The 24th Infantry Regiment in Korea* (1997) by William T. Bowers, William M. Hammond, and George L. MacGarrigle. I agree that failing to reference such a standard text would be inexplicable. And yet, if one consults the bibliography, lo and behold, that work is indeed listed (p. 193). It is also referenced multiple times in the notes (for example, at 163n75, 180n35, and 184n73). Sherwood further claims that I overlooked "many" of the military sources cited in *Black Soldier, White Army.* Yet the notes and bibliography both include such military sources as the Records of the Office of the Secretary of War; the Records of the Army Staff; the Records of the Supreme Commander for the Allied Powers; the Records of the Office of the Secretary of the Army; the Records of the Adjutant General's Office; the Records of General Headquarters, Far East Command; and so on.

Given Mr. Sherwood's evident failure to consult the book's notes, or even to scan its bibliography, how much of the book did he actually read? Regrettably for readers of the *JAH,* one can only conclude that he gave it the most cursory of glances, if that.

Michael Cullen Green
Washington, D.C.

To the Editor:

Michael Cullen Green is correct in pointing out that I missed seeing *Black Soldier, White Army: The 24th Infantry Regiment in Korea* in his bibliography. I searched under "Hammond" and not "Bowers." The initial research and writing for this book was a team effort, equally shared by William T. Bowers, William M. Hammond, and George L. MacGarrigle, but most of the rewriting and nearly all the publicity for the work was done by Dr. Hammond, so I have always considered him to be the primary author. That's no excuse for glossing over it in Dr. Green's bibliography. My apologies go out to the author.

This error of omission aside, the basic conclusions of my review still stand. *Black Yanks in the Pacific* presents some intriguing theories about black soldiers in Asia during the early Cold War, but I remain convinced that its cursory treatment of the subject does not fully support some of the conclusions put forth. While the book's bibliography lists some significant collections of military documents such as National Archives Record Group (RG) 338 and 407, it makes no reference to any of the materials on black soldiers in RG 159, Records of the Office of the Inspector General (Army); RG 206, Records of U.S. Occupation Headquarters, World War II (which contains significant material on the Ryukyu Islands from 1945 to 1972); or the original materials held by the U.S. Army Military History Institute such as its collection of 1,500-plus Korean War veterans surveys, including thirty-one from the Twenty-Fourth Infantry Regiment.

U.S. Army soldiers in Japan and Korea are the focus of *Black Yanks,* but some limited comparisons are made with black soldiers in Germany. More contextualization could have improved this work. How did the experiences of black soldiers in Asia compare with those in other regions, including the United States? How did they compare with black military personnel in other services? Dr. Green writes extremely well and has developed a provocative thesis. I hope he continues his work on African American members of the U.S. armed forces in the Cold War, and look forward to his future writings.

John Darrell Sherwood
Naval History and Heritage Command
Washington Navy Yard
Washington, D.C.

doi: 10.1093/jahist/jas231

To the Editor:

In his exhibition review about the Nixon Presidential Library and Museum in the December 2011 issue, Benjamin Hufbauer errs in his account of the transfer of the private library to the National Archives and Records Administration (NARA) (*JAH*, Dec. 2011, 790–96). We first tried to get the library into NARA in 1995–1996, not 2005, as Hufbauer writes. Also, this passage contains several incorrect or misleading assertions:

> [M]embers of the foundation thought they could still have a shrine to Nixon but have the government pay for it. They were wrong. In 2006 when NARA took over, the newly installed Archivist of the United States, Allen Weinstein, personally recruited Timothy Naftali to be the first director of the Nixon Library under federal management. Naftali and Weinstein agreed that the primary goal for the museum would be a detailed and historically accurate account of the Watergate events. (p. 791)

As the Nixon Library director and Richard Nixon's co-executor, I conducted the negotiations with NARA along with Kathy O'Connor, Nixon's last chief of staff. Before the handover, we agreed that the Watergate exhibit would be replaced. For the first federal director, I suggested one name to deputy archivist Sharon Fawcett: Tim Naftali, the Cold War historian and presidential tapes expert. Within days, she placed a call inviting him to be considered. Weinstein told me later that my idea had been brilliant and that the same notion "had occurred to me."

After Naftali was named, I suggested to Fawcett and Weinstein, and they agreed, that Naftali should redo the Watergate exhibit rather than our trying to design one that would be acceptable to the government. Before NARA had even taken possession of the museum, Naftali asked my permission to tear out the old exhibit, which I granted.

Hufbauer's account was apparently informed by the Bob Haldeman revanchists who took over Nixon's foundation in the fall of 2009 after Naftali invited John Dean to give a speech, who battled him relentlessly over the Watergate exhibit, but who had no involvement in the handover negotiations with NARA.

John H. Taylor
Yorba Linda, California

To the Editor:

I stand corrected. And I certainly regret the error and apologize for it.

To clarify briefly, financial considerations were in the background when the Nixon Foundation was working on transferring the Nixon Library to the National Archives. That process was certainly lengthy and complicated, and my review did not reflect that. Furthermore, although some members of the Nixon Foundation in 2005 may not have expected the extent of change represented by the new Watergate exhibit under management by the National Archives, others, like John Taylor, understood and accepted that the new exhibit would offer a quite different view of the scandal. The Nixon Foundation became virulently hostile to Director Timothy Naftali's work on the Watergate exhibit starting in 2009. At that time the membership and tenor of the Nixon Foundation changed quite significantly. As Rev. Taylor points out, my review inaccurately suggested that the views of the Nixon Foundation from 2009–2011 were similar to the views held by members in 2005, but they were not. I stand by the review's examination of both the new Watergate exhibit and the treatment that Dr. Naftali endured during his tenure at the Nixon Library

Benjamin Hufbauer
University of Louisville
Louisville, Kentucky

doi: 10.1093/jahist/jas232

To the Editor:

I was pleased to see the "celebrity animal," a Shorthorn cow, pictured at page 1035 of your March 2012 issue in "Meat in the Middle: Converging Borderlands in the U.S. Midwest, 1865–1900," by Kristin Hoganson.

Shorthorn cattle played a role in American history besides the many noted in Professor

Hoganson's informative article. Before the Civil War, Lewis Allen's herd of Shorthorns in Buffalo, New York, were his greatest pride. When his nephew, Grover Cleveland, stopped by on his way west, Mr. Allen invited him to ghostwrite a book about Shorthorn cattle. Uncle Lewis agreed to pay a small stipend besides free room and board—doubtless steak was on the menu—and introduced his nephew around town. Buffalo lawyers who had observed the ascent of an earlier Buffalo lawyer, Millard Fillmore, into the presidency signed on to boost Mr. Allen's literate and amiable nephew as an up-and-coming political prodigy who, after becoming a lawyer, could easily become mayor or sheriff (both of which offices Cleveland later held) and then the sky would be the limit. But it was the Shorthorns that first fueled Uncle Lewis's desire to publish and recruit his nephew, which in turn led to the connections and networking that made a second Buffalo lawyer into president of the United States.

Wayne Soini
Brookline, Massachusetts

Editorial note: Kristin Hoganson preferred not to respond.

doi: 10.1093/jahist/jas273

Announcements

Future annual meetings of the Organization of American Historians are as follows:

2013	San Francisco, California	April 11–14	Hilton San Francisco
2014	Atlanta, Georgia	April 10–13	Atlanta Hilton
2015	St. Louis, Missouri	April 16–19	Renaissance St. Louis Grand Hotel

For further information, write to: OAH Annual Meeting Information, 112 North Bryan Ave., Bloomington, Indiana 47408-4141, USA; or see the OAH Web site: http://www.oah.org/meetings/.

Call for Papers: Civil War

During the sesquicentennial of the Civil War, the *Journal of American History* would like to encourage the submission of articles that explore all aspects of the conflict.

JAH Podcast

The *Journal of American History* has launched a podcast section of our Web site (http://www.journalofamericanhistory.org/podcast/) where interviews with several *JAH* authors are available. Our most recent podcast features Brian C. Black, Karen R. Merrill, and Tyler Priest, the consulting editors of and participants in the June 2012 *JAH* special issue "Oil in American History." We will regularly be posting interviews with other *JAH* authors as well.

In the future we hope also to bring you podcasts of conversations with award-winning authors of books on American history. Anyone may listen to and download these high-quality audio files for free.

Civil War at 150 Podcast

Ed Linenthal, the editor of the *Journal of American History,* talks with Allen Guelzo, Henry R. Luce Professor of the Civil War Era and the director of Civil War Era Studies at Gettysburg College, comparing and contrasting the Civil War centennial with the ongoing sesquicentennial and the Lincoln bicentennial in 2009. You can listen to this December 2011 conversation for free at http://www.oah.org/programs/civilwar/podcast.

Article Submissions

All articles submitted to the *Journal of American History* must now include an abstract. The abstract must be on a separate page from the body of the article and may not be longer than 500 words.

Submit or Update Your Reviewer Data Sheet

The *Journal of American History* is always looking for qualified reviewers for books and articles. To make the best matches between reviewers and books or articles being reviewed, we need our reviewer information to be as complete and up-to-date as possible. It is crucial that prospective reviewers submit or update a *JAH* reviewer data sheet, which indicates areas of interest and publications and is available on our Web site at http://www.journalofamericanhistory.org/submit/datasheet/.

doi: 10.1093/jahist/jas321

Awards

The 2012 Maryellen Weimer Scholarly Work on Teaching and Learning Award was presented to Joel M. Sipress and David J. Voelker for their essay "The End of the History Survey Course: The Rise and Fall of the Coverage Model," which appeared in the March 2011 issue of the *JAH*.

The Louis Pelzer Memorial Award Committee invites candidates for graduate degrees to submit essays for the Louis Pelzer Memorial Award competition. Essays may deal with any period or topic in the history of the United States. The winning essay will be published in the *JAH*. In addition, the organization presents $500 to the winner. The deadline for entries for the 2013 competition is November 30, 2012.

For submission guidelines, see the OAH Web site: http://www.oah.org/awards/awards .pelzer.index.html. Manuscripts should be addressed to Pelzer Award Chair, *Journal of American History*, 1215 East Atwater Ave., Bloomington, Indiana 47401-3703, USA.

The Organization of American Historians gives the David Thelen Award biennially to the best article on American history that has been published in a language other than English. The winning article will be published in translation in the *JAH*. The deadline for entries published during 2011 and 2012 is May 1, 2013.

For submission guidelines, see the OAH Web site: http://www.oah.org/awards/awards.thelen .index.html. Please submit five copies of the entry, along with a one- or two-page essay in English explaining why the article is a significant and original contribution to our understanding of American history, to Thelen Award Chair, *Journal of American History*, 1215 East Atwater Ave., Bloomington, Indiana 47401-3703, USA.

Correction

In the June 2012 issue of the *Journal of American History*, the headnote on page 317 for the review of Tanya Sheehan's book, *Doctored: The Medicine of Photography in Nineteenth-Century America*, should indicate that the book's place of publication is University Park and its publisher is Penn State University Press.

Recent Scholarship

The "Recent Scholarship" section of the *Journal of American History* is available to the public free of charge online at http://www.journalofamericanhistory.org/rs/.

The *JAH* mission in providing "Recent Scholarship" is to foster interest in and awareness of new historical scholarship. Making "Recent Scholarship" available online to the public enables the *JAH* to fulfill that mission better by reaching a broad audience of both members and non-members. This online listing is analogous to the print version that appeared in past issues. Readers who prefer the traditional print format can still view each issue's "Recent Scholarship" section online at the *JAH* Web site and print it. The Web site also provides a permanent archive of each issue's "Recent Scholarship."

Recent Scholarship Online, a searchable, cumulative database of "Recent Scholarship" entries, continues to be available separately to individual members of the Organization of American Historians at http://www.oah.org/members/. The chart below compares the features of the free online "Recent Scholarship" and the members-only *Recent Scholarship Online.*

A Comparison of "Recent Scholarship" and *Recent Scholarship Online*

"Recent Scholarship"	*Recent Scholarship Online*
• Anyone with an Internet connection may access the listings.	• Only OAH members can access the database.
• Listings are grouped quarterly by issue.	• Listings are cumulative, beginning with the June 2000 issue of the *JAH.*
• Citations are listed only by their primary categories.	• Citations are assigned several categories and are searchable by multiple criteria.
• Anthologies are listed only by title; individual essays in them are not listed.	• Records include citations to essays in anthologies and to works reviewed in the *JAH.*
	• Users can sign up for monthly e-mail updates based on categories and keywords of interest.
	• Users can mark items to save in custom bibliographies.

If you need assistance, please contact our information technology manager by e-mail at jahtech@oah.org or by phone at 812-855-6039.

 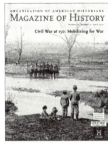 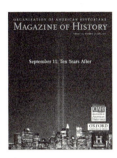 

Benefits of OAH Membership

The Organization of American Historians promotes excellence in the scholarship, teaching, and presentation of American history and encourages wide discussion of historical questions and equitable treatment of all practitioners of history.

Publications: Available in print and online: *The Journal of American History,* the *OAH Magazine of History,* and *OAH Outlook,* the membership newsletter of the organization.

JSTOR: Search, browse, download, and print past issues of the *Journal of American History* and *OAH Magazine of History* with a $15 subscription.

Recent Scholarship Online: RSO is a searchable database of the most current history-related citations. Quarterly e-mail updates of the latest scholarship are available, customized according to selected keywords and categories.

Annual Meeting: One of the best networking events in the profession and a multifaceted opportunity for historians to learn about current discourse, debate, and research in U.S. history. Members enjoy discounted registration rates and receive the *OAH Annual Meeting Program* in print and online.

OAH Career Center: Browse and search available jobs, and easily manage your job search with online tools found only at the OAH Career Center.

Professional Service Opportunities: OAH members are eligible for appointment to OAH committees, as OAH Distinguished Lecturers, as paid consultants to OAH/NPS collaborative projects, and/or presenters at OAH annual meetings.

Book Discounts: 25 percent off Oxford University Press publications.

Insurance Programs: The Trust for Insuring Educators offers discounted group insurance rates for professional liability, term life, automobile, disability, medical coverage, and more.

>>> For more information, visit
http://www.oah.org/membership

The OAH Career Center

Announcing a new online benefit for members

We are pleased to announce the opening of the OAH Career Center. Individuals wishing to make professional career connections may browse available jobs or use advanced search tools to target positions by keyword, location, and other criteria. Applicants can create a confidential portfolio containing contact information, cover letters, curriculum vitae, writing samples, and other documents that can be sent automatically to selected employers. The process is easy, safe, and convenient.

Is your department conducting a job search? Your department can quickly post available positions, manage job listings, search résumés, and communicate with applicants through the OAH Career Center.

Whether you are looking for a job or wish to find qualified candidates for your upcoming search, the OAH Career Center can help you every step of the way.

 Get started at http://careers.oah.org/

2013 OAH Awards and Prizes

Apply or nominate someone for 2013

The Organization of American Historians sponsors or cosponsors awards, prizes, fellowships, and grants given in recognition of scholarly and professional achievements in the field of American history.

>>> Deadlines are fast approaching. Visit http://**www.oah.org/awards** for details.

OAH

ORGANIZATION OF
American
Historians

www.oah.org ®

The Civil War Sesquicentennial

the Civil War at 150

Family members of a soldier are encamped with the troops in the fall of 1861. Courtesy of the Library of Congress.

Presenting the best current thinking on this complex era

Themes & Years

ORIGINS	2011
MOBILIZING FOR WAR	2012
TURNING POINTS	2013
TOTAL WAR	2014
LEGACIES	2015

ORGANIZATION OF
American Historians

www.oah.org

During the sesquicentennial commemoration of the Civil War, the Organization of American Historians is committed to bringing the best current thinking on this complex era to a wide audience.

For the next five years we will explore the war from its beginnings through its aftermath, keeping in mind the needs of history teachers and students, the challenges faced by public historians, and the curiosity of the general public.

We will consider several broad themes during the sesquicentennial years in our publications, at our conferences, in our Distinguished Lectureship Program, and through our online projects.

>>> Visit the OAH Civil War at 150 Web site at http://www.oah.org/programs/civilwar/

Upcoming OAH Annual Meetings

PLAN AHEAD

2013 — **SAN FRANCISCO, CA**
Thursday, April 11 to Sunday, April 14
HILTON SAN FRANCISCO

2014 — **ATLANTA, GA**
Thursday, April 10 to Sunday, April 13
HILTON ATLANTA

2015 — **ST. LOUIS, MO**
Thursday, April 16 to Sunday, April 19
RENAISSANCE ST. LOUIS GRAND
HOTEL and AMERICA'S CENTER

OAH
ORGANIZATION OF
American
Historians
www.oah.org

>>> **annualmeeting.oah.org**

EXCELLENCE IN EVIDENCE

Discover a wealth of knowledge

OXFORD JOURNALS ONLINE ARCHIVE

> uncover backfiles of content dating from 1849

> instant access to 146 years of research

> seamless access from Volume 1, Issue 1

> access by IP range, Athens or Shibboleth

> COUNTER-compliant usage statistics

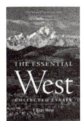
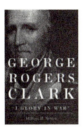

 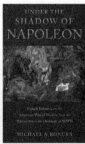   

The Cornell University ILR School,
in collaboration with LAWCHA,
is pleased to announce the winner
of the **2012 Philip Taft Labor History Award**
for the best book in American labor and working-class history
published in 2011:

Cindy Hahamovitch
No Man's Land:
Jamaican Guestworkers in America
and the Global History of Deportable Labor,
Princeton University Press

For information on nominations for the 2013 Prize,
due in by December 15, 2012, please visit the Taft Award website:
http://www.ilr.cornell.edu/taftaward/

Labor and Working Class History Association (LAWCHA)
announces the winner of the
2012 Herbert Gutman Prize
for Outstanding Dissertation in Labor and Working-class history in 2011:

Marjorie Elizabeth Wood
"Emancipating the Child Laborer:
Children, Freedom, and the Moral Boundaries of
the Market in the United States, 1853-1938"
(University of Chicago, Advisor: Thomas Holt)

For details on applying for the 2013 Gutman Prize, please consult
www.lawcha.org/grants.php.
The deadline is November 30, 2012.

BLIND OVER CUBA
The Photo Gap and the Missile Crisis
DAVID M. BARRETT AND MAX HOLLAND

Using recently declassified documents, secondary materials, and interviews with several key participants, Barrett and Holland challenge the popular perception of the Kennedy administration's handling of the Cuban Missile Crisis.

"Rarely has a book focused its attention with greater precision on the single most painful question about a great historical event than *Blind over Cuba* does in its careful study of the role of intelligence in the Cuban Missile Crisis of 1962 . . . a riveting book which will stand for many years to come as a classic account of slippery efforts to manipulate credit and blame. It is short, it is convincing, and there is nothing else like it."
—Thomas Powers, Pulitzer-Prize winning journalist and author, *The Man Who Kept the Secrets* and *The Killing of Crazy Horse*

240 pp. 4 b&w photos. 3 line art. Bib. Index.
$29.95 cloth

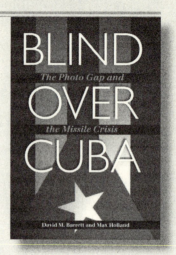

MILITARIZING THE BORDER
When Mexicans Became the Enemy
MIGUEL ANTONIO LEVARIO

Focusing on El Paso and its environs, *Militarizing the Border* examines the history of the relationship among law enforcement, military, civil, and political institutions, and local communities, while highlighting a binational focus that sheds light on other U.S.-Mexico border zones in the late nineteenth and early twentieth centuries.

". . . an important contribution to the continuing effort to excavate the past in order to provide a deeper understanding of the history of the people of Mexican origin in the United States, and more specifically, of the Tejano experience."—Alex M. Saragoza, Department of Comparative Ethnic Studies, University of California, Berkeley

256 pp. 8 b&w photos. 3 appendixes. Bib. Index.
$38.95 cloth

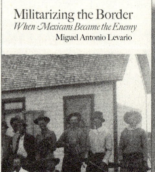

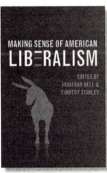

WAR ON THE WATERS

The Union and Confederate Navies, 1861–1865

JAMES M. MCPHERSON

"McPherson's many admirers in the Civil War community will be thrilled that he has turned his keen eye and eloquent pen to the naval war. In this new, concise history of the war at sea, McPherson not only tells an important story well, he shows how the Union Navy, with only five percent of Union military assets, had a disproportionate impact on the war."

—**Craig L. Symonds**, author of *Lincoln and His Admirals*

296 pages $35.00 cloth

Littlefield History of the Civil War Era

CREATING CONSUMERS

Home Economists in Twentieth-Century America

CAROLYN M. GOLDSTEIN

"Goldstein has done an excellent job of researching and reinterpreting the roles that home economists played in building the modern American consumer economy. Goldstein's home economists are complex historical actors. Nothing comparable is in print."

—**Nancy Tomes**, Stony Brook University

424 pages $49.95 cloth

HELP ME TO FIND MY PEOPLE

The African American Search for Family Lost in Slavery

HEATHER ANDREA WILLIAMS

"Williams speaks to scholars and to everyone interested in African American roots and family history as she delves into the short-run and long-run impact of family instability and disruption. A study of real importance."

—**Michael Tadman**, University of Liverpool

264 pages $30.00 cloth

HANOI'S WAR

An International History of the War for Peace in Vietnam

LIEN-HANG T. NGUYEN

"Nguyen has written the first truly authoritative account of the negotiations that led to the 1973 Paris Peace Accords. An extraordinary achievement, an indispensable contribution to the rapidly changing history of the conflicts in Vietnam."

—**George C. Herring**, author of *America's Longest War*

464 pages $34.95 cloth

A HARMONY OF THE SPIRITS

Translation and the Language of Community in Early Pennsylvania

PATRICK M. ERBEN

"In this masterful study, Erben recovers the world of those German Pietists and English Quakers who sought to transcend the chaos of a post-Babel world and craft a linguistically pure New World utopia. Along the way, he forces us to rethink the relationship between language, religion, and community in early America. A virtuoso performance."

—**John Smolenski**, University of California, Davis

352 pages $45.00 cloth

Published for the Omohundro Institute of Early American History and Culture, Williamsburg, Virginia

BONDS OF ALLIANCE

Indigenous and Atlantic Slaveries in New France

BRETT RUSHFORTH

"Brilliantly bringing together Native American and Atlantic History … offers a nuanced analysis of shifting forms, meanings, and experiences of slavery. A tremendous contribution to our understanding of the French Atlantic."

—**Laurent Dubois**, Duke University

424 pages $39.95 cloth

Published for the Omohundro Institute of Early American History and Culture, Williamsburg, Virginia

COLORS OF CONFINEMENT

Rare Kodachrome Photographs of Japanese American Incarceration in World War II

EDITED BY ERIC L. MULLER

With photographs by Bill Manbo

"Skillfully presents a multifaceted montage, integrating the insights of an historian, an expert on photography, and a former prisoner of Heart Mountain. Kodachrome images of Japanese American incarceration can offer a deeper understanding of the WRA camps, even as they raise troubling questions about memory, representation, and meaning."

—**Lane Ryo Hirabayashi**, University of California, Los Angeles

136 pages $35.00 cloth

Published in association with the Center for Documentary Studies at Duke University

 ⓔBOOK Most UNC Press books are also available as E-Books.

A REFORMING PEOPLE
*Puritanism and the Transformation of
Public Life in New England*

DAVID D. HALL

With a New Foreword by the Author

"Hall rescues the New England Puritans from
the dark myths of repression. . . . [He] reveals
our original revolutionaries in search of equity,
justice, and community."
—**Alan Taylor,** author of *The Civil War of 1812*

280 pages $24.95 paper

UNTIL THE LAST MAN COMES HOME
POWs, MIAs, and the Unending Vietnam War

MICHAEL J. ALLEN

448 pages $27.95 paper

EMPTY PLEASURES
*The Story of Artificial Sweeteners from
Saccharin to Splenda*

CAROLYN DE LA PEÑA

296 pages $24.95 paper

NO HIGHER LAW
*American Foreign Policy and the Western
Hemisphere since 1776*

BRIAN LOVEMAN

552 pages $29.95 paper

BUILDING A
HOUSEWIFE'S PARADISE
*Gender, Politics, and American Grocery Stores
in the Twentieth Century*

TRACEY DEUTSCH

352 pages $24.95 paper

FOR THE PEOPLE
*American Populist Movements from
the Revolution to the 1850s*

RONALD P. FORMISANO

328 pages $25.95 paper

ARMY AT HOME
*Women and the Civil War on the
Northern Home Front*

JUDITH GIESBERG

248 pages $24.95 paper

DAVID RUGGLES
*A Radical Black Abolitionist and the
Underground Railroad in New York City*

GRAHAM RUSSELL GAO HODGES

280 pages $23.00 paper

IN THE EYE OF ALL TRADE
*Bermuda, Bermudians, and the Maritime
Atlantic World, 1680-1783*

MICHAEL J. JARVIS

704 pages $35.00 paper
*Published for the Omohundro Institute of
Early American History and Culture,
Williamsburg, Virginia*

AN EXAMPLE FOR ALL THE LAND
*Emancipation and the Struggle over
Equality in Washington, D.C.*

KATE MASUR

376 pages $25.95 paper

NOT A GENTLEMAN'S WAR
*An Inside View of Junior Officers in the
Vietnam War*

RON MILAM

256 pages $24.95 paper

THE HOUSE ON DIAMOND HILL
A Cherokee Plantation Story

TIYA MILES

336 pages $24.95 paper

INTELLECTUAL LIFE AND THE
AMERICAN SOUTH, 1810-1860
An Abridged Edition of Conjectures of Order

MICHAEL O'BRIEN

Foreword by Daniel Walker Howe

400 pages $29.95 paper

FREDERICKSBURG!
FREDERICKSBURG!

GEORGE C. RABLE

688 pages $28.00 paper

THIS VIOLENT EMPIRE
The Birth of an American National Identity

Carroll Smith-Rosenberg

512 pages $27.95 paper
*Published for the Omohundro Institute of
Early American History and Culture,
Williamsburg, Virginia*

WE WERE ALL LIKE MIGRANT
WORKERS HERE
*Work, Community, and Memory on
California's Round Valley Reservation,
1850-1941*

WILLIAM J. BAUER JR.

304 pages $24.95 paper

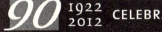

NEW FROM THE UNIVERSITY OF NEBRASKA PRESS

  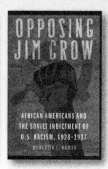 

The Approaching Fury
Voices of the Storm, 1820–1861
The Coming of the Civil War Told from
the Viewpoints of Thirteen Principal
Players in the Drama
STEPHEN B. OATES
A compilation of monologues of key
individuals in events leading up to the
American Civil War.
$24.95 paperback

The Whirlwind of War
Voices of the Storm, 1861–1865
The Epic Saga of the Civil War Told
from the Viewpoints of Eleven Principal
Players in the Drama
STEPHEN B. OATES
A unique study of the Civil War
recounting the great struggle through a
series of first-person monologues told in
the voices of prominent figures.
$28.95 paperback

Opposing Jim Crow
African Americans and the Soviet
Indictment of U.S. Racism, 1928–1937
MEREDITH L. ROMAN
A study of the Soviet policy of antiracism
from 1928-37.
$55.00 hardcover
JUSTICE AND SOCIAL INQUIRY SERIES

Shelby's Folly
Jack Dempsey, Doc Kearns, and the
Shakedown of a Montana Boomtown
JASON KELLY
Recounts the infamous heavyweight
boxing match held in Shelby in 1923,
emphasizing the social and economic
ramifications the match had on the small
Montana town and its residents.
$16.95 paperback

*For complete descriptions and to order, visit us online!

UNIVERSITY OF
NEBRASKA PRESS

WWW.NEBRASKAPRESS.UNL.EDU
800-848-6224 • publishers of Bison Books

KANSAS

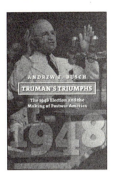 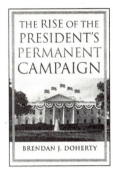 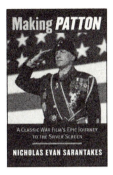 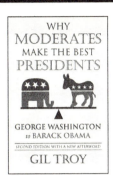

Truman's Triumphs
The 1948 Election and the Making of Postwar America

Andrew E. Busch

"The surest, shrewdest interpretation of the key election of 1948."—**David R. Mayhew**, author of *Partisan Balance: Why Political Parties Don't Kill the U.S. Constitutional System*

"Busch's rich and nicely paced narrative may be the best of the many books on this subject."—**Alonzo L. Hamby**, author of *Man of the People: A Life of Harry S. Truman*

American Presidential Elections
272 pages, 14 photographs, Cloth $37.50, Paper $19.95

The Rise of the President's Permanent Campaign

Brendan J. Doherty

"Doherty has taken on an important and much-discussed subject and executed his analysis with exemplary care and skill. . . . An extremely well-polished, well-crafted book."—**Michael Nelson**, editor of *The Presidency and the Political System*

216 pages, Cloth $34.95, Paper $19.95

Making *Patton*
A Classic War Film's Epic Journey to the Silver Screen

Nicholas Evan Sarantakes

"A wonderful story about how a Hollywood studio head, a determined producer, and a talented director—all World War II veterans who had fought against the Axis legions— joined forces with a charismatic lead actor (a former Marine) and a brilliant upstart scriptwriter to create a classic war film that became a 'Rorschach test' for society and media in America and abroad."—**Harry Yeide**, author of *Fighting Patton: George S. Patton, Jr., Through the Eyes of His Enemies*

280 pages, 21 photographs, Cloth $34.95

Why Moderates Make the Best Presidents
George Washington to Barack Obama
Second Edition with a new Afterword

Gil Troy

"Troy's mastery of his material and ability to condense it elegantly reflect both deep immersion in his subject and an ability to see forest through trees."—*History News Network*

360 pages, 20 photographs, Paper $19.95

 # University Press of Kansas
Phone 785-864-4155 · Fax 785-864-4586 · www.kansaspress.ku.edu

State of War
The Political Economy of American Warfare, 1945–2011
Paul A. C. Koistinen

"Makes a powerful case that American mobilization for war and defense has long gravely 'multiplied America's dysfunctions' so that even 'the military itself ends up being victimized.' What Eisenhower feared about the military-industrial complex has been, Koistinen shows, all too grimly realized."—**Michael Sherry**, author of *In the Shadow of War: The United States since the 1930s*

Modern War Studies
320 pages, Cloth $39.95

Theodore Roosevelt and the American Political Tradition
Jean M. Yarbrough

"Taking Roosevelt seriously as political thinker, Yarbrough's carefully argued and well-written book shows convincingly that the Rough Rider contributed significantly to a redefinition of the American social contract."—**Sidney M. Milkis**, author of *Theodore Roosevelt, the Progressive Party, and the Transformation of American Democracy*

American Political Thought
400 pages, Cloth $39.95

The Post-Presidency from Washington to Clinton
Burton I. Kaufman

"An erudite account of ex-presidents and the ex-presidency, chock full of fascinating facts, lively anecdotes, sparkling quotes and pithily stated judgments."—**John Whiteclay Chambers II**, author of *The Tyranny of Change: America in the Progressive Era, 1890–1920*

688 pages, 31 photographs, Cloth $45.00

The Failure of Popular Sovereignty
Slavery, Manifest Destiny, and the Radicalization of Southern Politics
Christopher Childers

"By analyzing the evolution of southerners' attitudes toward popular sovereignty from the 1770s to the Civil War, Childers has found much that is fresh and important to say about this venerable topic. A most welcome contribution indeed."—**Michael Holt**, author of *The Fate of Their Country*

American Political Thought
384 pages, 13 photos, 3 maps, Cloth $39.95

The Santa Fe Trail
Its History, Legends, and Lore
David Dary

"A grand, sprawling story, populated by characters whose voices emerge loud and clear from their journals and letters. . . . An unforgettable procession of dreamers and doers, losers and winners, villains and heroes (and heroines) in a well-told and carefully researched tale."—*New York Times Book Review*

384 pages, 108 photographs, 5 maps, Paper $19.95

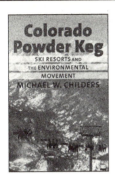

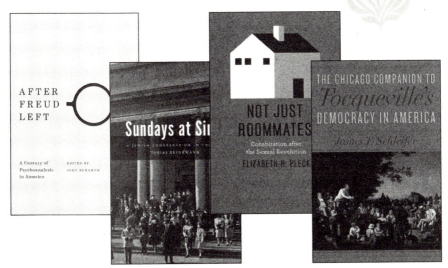

American History

FROM CHICAGO

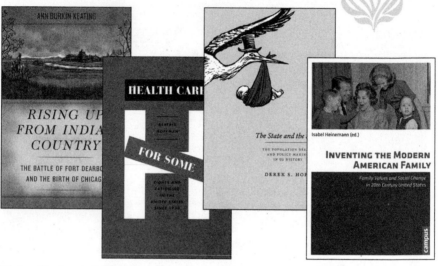

Rising Up from Indian Country
The Battle of Fort Dearborn
and the Birth of Chicago
Ann Durkin Keating
"How did Chicago stop being Indian Country and become American? Ann Durkin Keating has recast that struggle into a story far more complex than the conventional 'manifest destiny' tale. Well researched and written, this book is an eye-opening account."—Walter Nugent, University of Notre Dame
Cloth $30.00

Health Care for Some
Rights and Rationing in the
United States since 1930
Beatrix Hoffman
"Beatrix Hoffman offers a perspective very different from previous studies of health care. She also provides one of the most thorough histories—and compelling critiques—of the health insurance industry available."—Guian McKee, University of Virginia
Cloth $30.00

The State and the Stork
The Population Debate and
Policy Making in US History
Derek S. Hoff
"Derek S. Hoff has taken an important, complicated topic and traced it over the whole of American history. The research on display here is striking in its breadth and depth, Hoff's insights are penetrating, and his interpretation is original."
—Robert Collins, University of Missouri
Cloth $49.00

FROM CAMPUS VERLAG
Inventing the Modern
American Family
Family Values and Social Change
in 20th Century United States
Edited by Isabel Heinemann
This volume investigates the negotiations and transformations of family values and gender norms in the twentieth century as they relate to overarching processes of social change.
Paper $54.00

The University of Chicago Press • www.press.uchicago.edu